THE WHICH

SPA

*A panorama of mainland Spain,
plus Mallorca, Menorca, Ibiza and the
Canary Islands, all in one volume*

CW00430296

THE WHICH? GUIDE TO

SPAIN

*A panorama of mainland Spain,
plus Mallorca, Menorca, Ibiza and the
Canary Islands, all in one volume*

Published by Consumers' Association
and Hodder & Stoughton

This book was researched by the team of *Holiday Which?* magazine:
Editor: Anna Fielder
Authors: Ros Belford, Anne Harvey, Lindsay Hunt
Additional research: Rose Ashton, Stephen Clues, Lorna Dean, Marc
Dubin, Liz Piccin, Lucy Smith, Cara Williams

Which? Books are commissioned and researched by The Association for
Consumer Research and published by Consumers' Association,
2 Marylebone Road, London NW1 4DX, and Hodder & Stoughton,
47 Bedford Square, London WC1B 3DP

Typographic design by Paul Saunders. Cover design by Paul Saunders.
Cover artwork by Helena Greene. Maps by David Perrott Cartographics

Line illustrations by Bina Haria-Shah
Architectural drawings from *The Architecture of Europe* by Doreen Yarwood
(BT Batsford Ltd) Reproduced with permission
First published November 1991
Copyright © 1991 Consumers' Association Ltd

British Library Cataloguing in Publication Data
The Which? guide to Spain
  I. Consumers' Association
  914.60483
  ISBN 0340521937

Thanks for choosing this book . . .
If you find it useful, we'd like to hear from you. Even if it doesn't
live up to your expectations or do the job you were expecting, we'd
still like to know. Then we can take your comments into account
when preparing similar titles or, indeed, the next edition of the
book. Address your letter to the Publishing Manager at Consumers'
Association, FREEPOST,
2 Marylebone Road, London NW1 4DX.
We look forward to hearing from you.

Typeset by Wyvern Typesetting Limited, Bristol

Printed and bound in Great Britain by The Bath Press, Bath

CONTENTS

ABOUT THIS GUIDE

Holiday Which? magazine has been reporting on Spain for nearly twenty years; a report entitled 'Unknown Spain' was published in February 1976, long before this theme became fashionable with guidebook writers. We travelled again, all over Spain, for this new book. In the best consumer tradition, our aim is to give you an honest opinion on what it is like to be in Spain on a holiday in the 1990s, to give you good advice, solid recommendations and a very good read. To help us update for future editions, we would very much welcome your letters with comments on every aspect of the guide, and particularly on the hotels you have stayed in, whether they appear in the guide or not.

The guide is divided into regional chapters, and covers all the Spanish mainland and islands – the Balearics and the Canaries. Each chapter contains a boxed practical 'Planning your holiday' section and an easy to follow round-the-region gazetteer, aided by location maps of the main places described. There is also a thorough run-down of the resorts on the Costas, the Balearics and the Canaries. If you want to find a place quickly, the index at the back of the book will help, too. The book starts with general background features and ends with a comprehensive practical section with information on everything from money to health and getting around.

Hotel recommendations

Each chapter ends with a 'Where to stay' section which lists our recommended hotels – all inspected first-hand – in alphabetical order by town or village (by island and then place for the Canaries). Within the chapter, every place which has a recommended hotel is signalled with an (H) symbol – handy for advance route planning. You will also find a few hotels mentioned, with their telephone number, within the descriptions of the towns and villages. They are useful places to know about, clean and adequate, if you need a bed for the night – comments on these are particularly welcome.

All the hotels listed in the 'Where to stay' sections have bedrooms with bathrooms or showers and a restaurant or snack bar, unless we say otherwise. The price categories are based on the cost of a double or twin-bedded room in the highest summer season 1991, including VAT (IVA) but not any meals – a breakfast will cost less than £2 in a simple hotel, around £5 in a *parador*. At the time of going to press the rate of the Spanish peseta was 175 to the £.

£ Cheap – under 5,500 pesetas
££ Moderate – 5,501 to 10,000 pesetas
£££ Expensive – over 10,000 pesetas

Telephone numbers

All the telephone numbers listed in the guide have the full area code for calls within Spain. To ring from the UK, dial 010 34 and drop the first 9 from the area code – for example, the number (986) 35 51 33 becomes (010 34 86) 35 51 33.

Spanish and English names

Throughout the guide we have adopted the Spanish-language version names of regions, places and famous people; when places or names are particularly well known, we have used the anglicised version as an alternative to the Spanish – but the latter is given when the place or person is first mentioned. However, in regions such as Galicia, the Basque Country or Catalunya, where place names are both in *castellano* (Castilian, the official Spanish language) and in their own language, we use both versions when a place is mentioned for the first time, Castilian thereafter. This is because road signs display the Castilian version more prominently and the bulk of the tourist literature available in Britain still gives Castilian versions only.

Opening times of sights and churches

As a rule of thumb, sights in Spain open in the mornings (9 or 10am to around 1pm), close for a long siesta, and open again in the afternoon and early evening (3 or 4pm to 7 or 8pm). Closing days are most commonly Mondays or Tuesdays, and sometimes Sunday afternoons. Famous churches have the same opening times as other sights, but for smaller churches you will need to get a key from the caretaker (who usually lives nearby) or visit during services.

Always check opening times in advance, if you can: we often found them to be unreliable, with guidebooks and tourist office literature giving different times, and even the times written on the door not coinciding with reality. This caveat does not usually apply to the best known sights and museums – we list opening times for those at the back of this guide (see General information).

INTRODUCTION

Mass tourism to Spain goes back a long way. During the early Middle Ages, up to two million travellers a year made their pilgrimage to Santiago de Compostela from all over Europe. Hostels along the way served thousands of meals a day and the world's first-ever guidebook was written to help pilgrims find their route. The legacy of that first tourist boom was churches, monasteries and ancient towns. In the last 30 years, a new pilgrimage to Spain's sunny beaches has had rather less attractive results. The number of people visiting Spain escalated from half a million in 1960 to over 54 million in 1988 (the peak year) and the consequence in places has been overdevelopment and overcrowding, hideous architecture, polluted beaches, corrupt planning authorities, cheapskate buildings and the notorious lager lout.

Despite these blemishes, it is still possible to have a happy, good-value family holiday on the hot and sunny ribbon of beaches along Spain's heavily developed east coast, provided you choose your resort with care (see our guide on page 26). The north and west coasts facing the Atlantic are wilder and much less developed and are where the Spaniards themselves go to escape the crowds and the heat of the south.

After years of comparative neglect, Spain's beautiful hinterland is now becoming popular too. Since Franco's death in 1975, visiting Spain has been rather like watching a video on 'fast-forward' mode. Having emerged from a cocoon of isolation, poverty and arrested development, Spanish society is careering rapidly through processes of modernisation that took other European nations many decades. The transition is not always easy: growing prosperity and open government have brought their darker companions of crime, drug-dealing, unemployment and economic uncertainty – all unknown or fiercely suppressed in the old days. But it is the dynamism of the change that makes Spain such a fascinating country to visit.

There are Madrid and Barcelona, energetic, liberal and famous for their nightlife; there are the small towns with small-town life and strong community spirit; there are villages where life is still medieval, based on subsistence farming and fishing. On grand *plazas* the intricate stone frills of cathedral façades match the lace and frills worn by the women stepping through their doors and the embroidered gowns and jewelled crowns on the doll-like images of the Madonna inside.

If you do not want cities or noise or people, take to the paths of the Pyrenees or the Picos, or abandon the conventionally pretty scenery and explore the *meseta* – the vast central plain that sent Don Quixote's imagination on strange paths, and has its far horizons and hanging clouds echoed in El Greco's paintings.

To get the best out of Spain, you need to adopt a Spanish lifestyle and do as the Spaniards do: take your children everywhere (however late) and have long siestas, evening promenades, snacks in *tapas* bars

and meals late into the night. Do not forget to try the olives, the tortilla, the sherry from the cask, oranges fresh from the tree and dates fresh from the stalk, and proper deep-fried crisps; start the day with chocolate and *churros* and finish it with Rioja and *paella*.

Spain is still one of the easiest and cheapest countries to visit, for both package and independent holiday makers. If you want a fortnight of lager and chips in a big resort, you can of course opt for that. But don't forget that plenty of small specialist operators offer fly-drive, go-as-you-please deals to unusual locations. In inland Spain, increased efforts are being made to provide facilities for adventurous, self-sufficient travellers. More distinguished holiday accommodation is becoming available – smaller hotels in historic buildings, for example, or *gîte*-style self-catering units in converted farmhouses.

Book early if you are intending to visit in 1992, for, half a millennium after the Moors left and Christopher Columbus discovered the New World, Spain will hog the limelight of world attention. Barcelona will host the 1992 Olympic Games, Seville is holding a World Fair (Expo-92), and Madrid will be Europe's capital of culture. Millions have already been spent on improving services and renovating buildings; millions more will be spent on special events and exhibitions throughout the year.

Buen viaje!

HISTORY, ART AND PEOPLE

This section contains a brief outline of the main events of Spanish history, linking dates, places, art and architecture with the sights you can see today as you tour Spain, and with the central historical figures of each age.

Prehistoric Spain (Earliest times to 1000BC)

Paleolithic cave-dwellers and hunter-gatherers are believed to have lived in Northern Spain since about 25,000BC. From the eighth century BC, neolithic peoples arrived from North Africa, settling initially around Almería in southern Spain. The Greeks called them Iberians, from Iber, the Ebro river. Gradually they moved north and colonised the Castilian *meseta* in fortified villages, developing methods of agriculture and learning to work in metal. Around 900BC they were joined by Celts from beyond the Pyrenees, who spread all over the peninsula. Collectively these peoples are known as Celtiberians, although they formed distinct, tribal groupings.

Art and architecture
Cantabrian cave paintings, showing bison, wild boar, deer and other animals, and thought to date from about 15,000BC, are the first clear evidence of Spain's earliest inhabitants. The best examples were discovered at **Altamira** and **Puente Viesgo**. Visible remains from the Celtiberian period include the **Balearic talayots** (cones of stone covering a funeral chamber, and The Bulls of Guisando (bull or boar-shaped funerary stones called *verracos*).

Classical invaders (1000BC–AD406)

Phoenicians founded trading posts along the Mediterranean coast to exploit mineral resources (**Cadiz, Málaga**), followed by Greeks (**Ampurias, Denia**), and Carthagians (**Cartagena**) in the third century BC, who held sway until Rome's conclusive victory in 204BC. The Romans took total control of Iberia, and divided what they called *Hispania* into three parts: Lusitania (modern Portugal, Extremadura and Galicia); Baetica (Andalucía); Tarraconensis (central and eastern Spain). Gradually Christianity spread to Spain in Nero's reign (first century AD) and flourished despite many martyrdoms.

Art and architecture
The best Roman sites, mostly civil engineering – bridges, aqueducts, etc. – are at **Mérida, Segovia, Tarragona, Córdoba, Ampurias, Segobriga** (Cuenca) and **Itálica**, near Seville. These structures are exceptional examples of dry-stone construction, the aqueduct at Segovia, for example, surviving because of the precision of fit of its stone blocks, without the use of mortar.

People and places

The Carthaginian leaders **Hamilcar** and **Hannibal** spent most of their lives in Spain. Roman Emperors **Trajan, Hadrian** and **Marcus Aurelius** were all born in Spain, as were the Silver Latin writers **Lucan, Seneca** and **Martial**.

Vandals and Visigoths (AD406–711)

From the third century, Frankish and Germanic tribes swept over Spain. In the fifth century the Vandals invaded, leaving only a name for southern Spain (Vandalusia) and their lasting reputation as the principal hooligans of the Dark Ages. The warlike Visigoths, allied with and heavily influenced by Rome, re-established military authority in central Spain and set up their capital in **Toledo**.

Art and architecture

Most traces of the Visigothic period lie in a handful of early churches, notably **San Román** in Toledo, (which now houses a Visigothic museum), **Quintanilla de las Viñas** (Burgos), and **San Pedro de la Nave** (Zamora). These rough-stone churches are characterised by open horse-shoe arches, *bas-relief* friezes with geometrical or spiral patterns, and carved capitals. The best Visigothic jewellery, including chandelier-like votive crowns, can be seen in the Archaeological Museum of Madrid.

People and places

In 589AD, the Visigothic King **Reccared** embraced Christianity and became Spain's first Catholic monarch. The Visigoths' penchant for political plotting and factionalism proved their downfall. In 710 opponents of the newly acclaimed King **Roderick** sought help to overthrow him from Moorish forces in North Africa.

Moorish Spain (711–1492)

12,000 Berbers arrived in 710 from North Africa to defeat Roderick. But the Moors liked Spain so much that they stayed; by 714 most of the peninsula was under Muslim control. Even the intervention of Charlemagne, in 788, could not prevent the Moorish ascendancy. The Moorish invasion ushered in a remarkable period of Spanish history. In art and architecture, science and literature, and many decorative arts, the Arab world left a brilliant legacy. Several thousand words of Arabic origin are still used in modern Spanish. New crops of oranges, rice, cotton and sugar were planted with Moorish irrigation methods in the territories of Al-Andalus. The Moors, at least initially, were comparatively tolerant of other civilisations and over the centuries many cultural strands intertwined productively. Christians who were assimilated but continued to practise their religion were known as *mozarabes*. The Jews also fared well initially and occupied positions of authority; anti-semitism, when it came, was nearly always instigated by Christian factions.

In simple terms, the Islamic era falls into three dynasties. By 756 Abd al Rahman had set up an Emirate (later a Caliphate) in **Córdoba**, which became the power-house of Al-Andalus for several centuries. In its heyday Córdoba was the biggest and most important city west of Constantinople. After 1002, the glorious Caliphate disintegrated into quarrelsome petty kingdoms (*taifas*), and thus divided, it fell. A replacement horde of fanatical Berbers, the Almoravids, swept in after the fall of Toledo to the Christians in 1085, followed by yet another group, the Almohades, who set up the second Moorish dynasty, based in **Seville**. The Moors of this era were more fervent believers than their predecessors in Córdoba, and began a policy of driving *mozarabes* and Jews out of Andalucía, prompting further calls in Europe for Crusades against the heathen.

After many battles the tide gradually turned against the Muslims; by the decisive encounter at Las Navas de Tolosa in 1212, Moorish control of Spain was much weakened. In 1236 Córdoba fell to the Christians, followed by Valencia, Jaén and Seville. The Moors retreated to their final bastion, **Granada**. Here the Nasrid dynasty, under Christian protection, presided over the last and most amazing flowering of Moorish culture in Spain, which lasted over 200 years in a haze of jasmin-scented opulence.

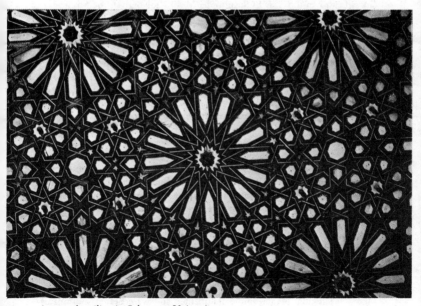

Artesonado ceiling in Salamanca University

15

Art and architecture

During the Córdoba Caliphate, the great **Mesquita** (mosque) was built in the classic horseshoe-arch and ornamental brickwork style that became the hallmark of so many Moorish buildings. Muslim doctrine forbids the depiction of human or animal forms, so the designs that inspired the craftsmen were foliage or geometric motifs and calligraphy. Seville's **Giralda** is an important building of the second dynasty. The Almohades developed the use of brilliantly decorated tiles so typical of Andalucía (*azulejos*), and the elaborate coffered wooden ceilings in the style known as *artesonado*. The last dynasty was the age of Granada's **Alhambra** and its extravagant decorative effects worked in stucco and mosaic, with stalactite and honeycomb ceilings. Pedro the Cruel's elaborate apartments in the **Alcázar** in Seville also date from this late Islamic period. Moorish military architecture can be seen in many surviving Andalucian fortifications: at Málaga, Granada, Almería, Ronda, Jaén and Seville.

People and places

The Caliph of Córdoba **Abd al-Rahman III** (792–852) was the greatest ruler of Al Andalus, presiding over a magnificent flourishing of Moorish culture. From Córdoba the dreaded warrior-Caliph **Al-Mansur** repeatedly raided Christian Spain and recaptured León, Barcelona and Pamplona, setting back the Reconquest by several decades. The bells of Santiago dangled as trophy lampshades in the great mosque of Córdoba. When the Catholic Monarchs finally regained the keys of Granada from the Moors in 1492, **Boabdil**, son of the last Nasrid Caliph, wept on the road into exile, at the spot just outside Granada known today as El Suspiro del Moro – the Sigh of the Moor.

Christian Spain and the Reconquest (711–1492)

One of the most successful propaganda coups of the Catholic side was the cult of Santiago (St James) de Compostela, all the more extraordinary for its complete lack of authenticity. After Santiago's starring role at the Battle of Clavijo on a white charger in 844, his credentials for supervising the Reconquest in his guise of *Matamoros* (Moorslayer) were assured. The Compostela shrine turned into an extravaganza spectacle for half the itinerant pilgrims, bandits and charlatans of the Christian world.

As in Moorish Spain, the history of the *Reconquista* is extremely complex. Kingdoms waxed and waned, plotted and intrigued, fighting sometimes in unison, sometimes against each other. El Cid switched sides from Moorish to Christian allegiance more than once. The level of intermingling between Christian and Moorish worlds was high and sometimes surprising. All the Castilian and Aragonese kings had Moorish blood in their veins, and many spoke Arabic. Some of the Moorish rulers 'went native' too, one marrying a Basque princess. In parts of Spain Moors and Christians co-existed quite happily for many years.

Over the centuries, the picture gradually polarised. Christian Spain joined forces and reconciled regional differences against the common foe. The Moors meanwhile became more fragmented and were beaten southwards towards their Andalucian headquarters. Piecemeal, Asturias blossomed into the Kingdom of León, the Basques enlarged their domains under the King-dom of Navarra, and the Pyrenean borderlands at the edge of Charlemagne's empire (modern Catalunya) took shape first as the independent County of Barcelona, then as an influential Mediterranean trading power united with Aragón.

Art and architecture

Many of the monuments you are likely to visit today date from this time (eighth-fifteenth centuries). Mostly they are religious buildings, or castles built to defend the reconquered lands. The Asturian pre-Romanesque style (eighth-ten centuries), best seen in **Santa María de Naranco** and **San Miguel de Lillo**, both near Oviedo, is simple and robust, based on the Latin rectangular plan, with plain rounded arches and frescoes. French influence filtered across the Pyrenees along the Way of St James, initially in the form of the Romanesque style (eleventh-thirteenth centuries): churches with tall square steeples, plain, barrel-vaulted interiors with rounded apses, and small, fortress-like windows. There are dozens of good examples concentrated all over northern and central Spain, particularly in Navarra, Catalunya, Palencia, Segovia, León and Galicia. Romanesque architecture in Spain reached its apogee in the huge cruciform cathedral of **Santiago de Compostela**. A second style evolved when Spain felt the influence of Gothic, again originating in France. Gothic is characterised by the use of pointed arches, vaults supported on ribs of stone, and flying buttresses as external structural supports compensating for the paring away of internal walls to allow large traceried windows. The great era of Gothic cathedral building (Burgos, León, Toledo) in Spain dates, as elsewhere in Europe, mainly from the thirteenth and fourteenth centuries.

Many Muslim craftsmen, once conquered, lived and worked alongside their new masters, adding Moorish architectural skill and artistry to the decorative arts of Christianity. They were known as *Mudejars* (from the Arabic word meaning 'vanquished'), and their influence on Spanish style was colossal. Jewish themes also found their way into the new buildings.

People and places

After the Moors arrived in Spain, the Visigothic leader **Pelayo** retreated to the Asturian mountains, and gathered round him a band of followers determined to keep the flame of Christian Spain alight. At **Covadonga** in 722, Pelayo won a clear victory against the Muslims. It was a small enough battle, scarcely enough to dent the Moors' morale when they had the whole of Spain at their feet. But for the Christians the victory of Covadonga was a decisive event from which the Reconquest charted its erratic course through the next seven and a half centuries.

Key figures in Castile's ascendancy during the *Reconquista* were **Fernán Gonzalez** (c930-970), Count of Burgos, who struggled for independence from León; **Sancho the Great** (970-1035) who united (temporarily) Castile and Navarra; **El Cid** and **Ferdinand III** ('The Saint', 1217-52) who finally joined Castile and León, and recaptured Córdoba and Seville from the Moors.

17

The Golden Age (1492–1700)

By the fifteenth century the two great power-blocks in Spain were the kingdoms of Aragón, controlling Catalunya, the Levant, and the Balearic Islands (even parts of Greece, Italy and France for a while); and Castile, now master of the rest of Spain apart from the last Moorish stronghold around Granada. The marriage of Ferdinand (Fernando) V of Aragón to his cousin Isabella (Isabel) I of Castile in 1469 bridged the final gap, and was tactically as significant as that English match made only a few years later, when Henry VII united the roses of York and Lancaster in astute matrimony. Their reign reached a glorious climax in 1492, when they took the keys of Granada from the Moors to unite Spain at last, and Christopher Columbus discovered the Americas. But the institution of the Inquisition in the same year (initially as an attempt to establish Spain's dynastic piety and thus its fitness to lead Catholic Europe) forever tarnished that *annus mirabilis*; Jews and Moors who refused conversion were expelled, tortured, burned, dispossessed or burned at the stake.

With the discovery of the New World, Spain's prestige and political significance in Europe soared. In the sixteenth century wealth began to pour in from the new colonies as Conquistador galleons laden with ingots of gold and silver sailed home. The search for the spices of the East Indies turned to an unexpected but fabulous gold rush in Mexico and Peru. Spain became a great power. Its new wealth funded the most extreme dynastic ambitions to control Europe. As a result Spain controlled huge areas including the Low

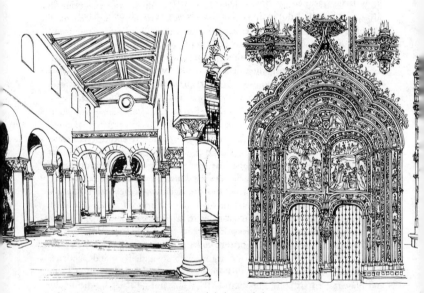

Left: *Mozarabic architecture: F. Miguel de la Escalada, near Léon*

Plateresque architecture: doorway, Salamanca new Cathedral

Countries, Flanders and the Netherlands, Naples and Sicily, the German states of the Holy Roman Empire, Austria, all Latin America except Brazil, and made a serious attempt to annex Portugal in 1581. Prosperity meant relative peace and stability at home too. The second half of the seventeenth century saw the beginnings of serious financial problems for Spain. The Peace of Westphalia of 1648, concluding the Thirty Years War, established the independence of the Netherlands hitherto ruled by Spain. This was a loss of great importance, especially as the nascent Dutch nation rapidly established itself as a major sea-power. Subsequent European wars culminating in the the War of the Spanish Succession further debilitated the Spanish. At the same time the decline in value of the silver and other materials from the New World and the parallel stagnation of the home economy, added further to Spain's predicament.

Art and architecture

The Isabeline Gothic of the Catholic Monarchs' reign, characterised by lacy and intricate carved façades in heraldic and fantastic designs, gradually merged into the filigree plateresque style (from *platero*, a silversmith), using Italianate ornaments with more attention to symmetry and balance. Some of the best examples of this style can be seen in **Valladolid**, **Aranda de Duero**, and **Salamanca**. Moves towards a less florid and more 'correct' Renaissance style took place from the late sixteenth century, culminating in the austere work of Juan de Herrera, architect of **El Escorial** (Felipe II's grandiose dynastic structure combining palace, monastery and royal mausoleum) and **Valladolid Cathedral**. Regular, rectangular shapes, steep, slate-roofed spires and corner towers are common features. One of the best examples of Herreran style is the Italianate palace of **Viso del Marqués** in La Mancha.

During this age too, artists emerged as individuals, a marked change from the anonymous brotherhood of Mudejar or Romanesque craftsmen. Sometimes mini-dynasties formed as fathers passed on their genius to their sons. **Simon** and **Johan of Cologne** were two of the great cathedral sculptors, **Juan** and **Enrique Egas**, architects of Toledo and Granada, **Diego** and **Gil de Siloé**, the brilliant Jewish sculptors from Antwerp associated with Burgos, and Granada, and the **Berruguetes of Palencia**, famed for their sinewy, naturalistic altar-pieces. The **Churriguera brothers** stamped their idiosyncratic and exuberant mark on Spain's baroque movement during the late seventeenth century, with barleysugar pillars, and riotous swirls of grapes, foliage, and rococo swags. The best examples can be seen in **Salamanca** (where the Churrigueras also designed the glorious Plaza Mayor), the *Transparente* in **Toledo Cathedral**, and the alabaster portal in **Valencia's Dos Aguas Palace**.

Among painters, the most important were **El Greco**, working in Toledo during Felipe II's reign, **Francisco Zurbarán** and **Bartolomé Murillo** of Extremadura, and **Diego Velázquez**, court painter to Felipe IV.

People and places

The marriage of the Catholic Monarchs, **Isabella** and **Ferdinand**, was a remarkable union of two intelligent and effective characters. Ferdinand was clever and subtle, masterly at statesmanship and military planning. Some say he was the model for Machiavelli's *Prince*. Isabella was courageous, energetic

19

and determined. A risk-taker, she backed one of the world's greatest ventures – Columbus's first voyage – by pawning her jewels. Her great failing was fanatical religiosity which developed into bigotry and intolerance as her reign progressed.

All was not plain sailing, however, when Isabella assumed the crown from her brother, Enrique IV. Supporters of Enrique's daughter **Juana la Beltraneja**, over whom the stigma of uncertain paternity perpetually hovered (Enrique was homosexual, and widely rumoured to be impotent), staged a revolt. The Catholic Monarchs quelled it with their habitual decisiveness at the Battle of Toro, in Zamora. Many other places in Castile have associations with the peripatetic Catholic Monarchs, who were always trudging about to visit different parts of their realm. Among prominent figures of their reign are the enigmatic **Cardinal Cisneros**, founder of Alcala University **Christopher Columbus**, discoverer of the New World (known as Cristobal Colón in Spanish), Amerigo Vespucci, Bernal Diaz and Hernán Cortés, the navigators and *conquistadores*; and the notorious but genuinely pious Dominican monk **Tomás de Torquemada**, the Grand Inquisitor, whose tortures and massacres of 'heretics' displayed the extremes of Catholic fanaticism. The last years of the Catholic Monarchs were clouded by the tragic early death of their beloved eldest son. Their daughter **Juana**, known as *La Loca* (the Mad), went demented when her Habsburg husband **Philip the Fair** died. The Spanish crown passed to her son **Carlos** (Charles I, later Charles V and Holy Roman Emperor), who established the Habsburg dynasty that lasted until the end of the seventeenth century. During his reign Spain's power gradually began to wane, weakened by internal dissent and constant foreign wars. His son **Felipe (Philip II)** was perhaps Spain's most complex monarch, a fascinating character of high intelligence, wide vision, and deep gloom. His reign saw great triumphs (the Battle of Lepanto, against the Turks, which gave Spain control of the Mediterranean) and equally great calamities (the Defeat of the Invincible Armada), which finally punctured Spain's claim to rule the waves.

After Felipe's reign and quasi-incestuous marriages, Spain's downward spiral gained momentum. A latent family madness began to emerge. Felipe III was a vapid, semi-imbecilic figure at the mercy of corrupt courtiers who squandered vast amounts of public money. Felipe IV, a little more effective, was hampered by the increasing power of the Church and the ambitious nobility. The final collapse of the Habsburgs came with the hopelessly insane Carlos II.

The Bourbons (1700–1931)

Apart from Carlos III (1759–1788), who practised 'enlightened despotism' most of the Bourbon monarchs who took over from the Habsburgs continued the same style of absolute monarchy. Wasting money on losing wars (the Wars of the Spanish Succession drained Spain's resources during this period), and grandiose palaces, the Bourbons bankrupted their Treasury. The Peninsular War, during which Spain was invaded by Napoleonic troops and eventually lost the navy at Trafalgar in 1805, showed more clearly than ever how far Spain's power and reputation had declined. The restoration of the

Bourbons in 1814 ushered in a new age of decadence, during which Spain's empire disappeared and the regions began to fragment into the separatist, anti-centralist factions (Basques, Catalans, etc.) which continued to dog successive governments to the present day. Between 1815–20, Spain suffered the serious loss of its Latin American empire and then the final loss of its remaining territories – Cuba, Puerto Rico and the Philippines – following unsuccessful campaigns in the last part of the century. The monarchy came into disrepute, particularly during the colourful and scandalous reign of his daughter, Isabel II. The Carlist Wars, contesting the rights of two branches of the royal family to the throne, began after the death of Fernando VII in 1833 and blighted the nineteenth century. By the twentieth disillusion with the monarchy was so great that in 1924 Alfonso XIII was forced to rule alongside Spain's first dictator, Miguel Primo de Rivera. A brief resurgence of hope for Spain's economic recovery followed, but the Depression of 1929 put paid to this, and in 1931 Alfonso (still nominally king) was forced to abdicate and flee the country. The Second Republic was declared.

Art and architecture

After the period of High Baroque, Spanish architecture, returned to the clarity of neoclassicism. The main façade of **Lugo cathedral**, built at the end of the eighteenth century, and the **Prado Museum** building in Madrid, are good examples. But later several artistic figures emerged to break existing moulds. **Francisco de Goya** is the supreme exponent of the anguish of the early nineteenth century. His portraits of the effete Carlos IV and his disloyal wife, the searing scenes of the Madrid Revolt (**Dos de Mayo**), and finally the despairing Black Paintings all show a nation in serious decline. Later, the brilliant Catalan architect **Antoni Gaudí** revolutionalised conventional ideas about buildings; his Modernist architecture uses curves, plant motifs and abstract mosaics to mimic natural forms. Gaudí's best work is in Barcelona, the most striking example being the unfinished cathedral of the **Sagrada Família**. In the early part of the twentieth century the 'Paris School' of cubists and surrealists was dominated by Spanish artists – **Pablo Picasso, Luis Buñuel, Salvador Dalí** and **Joan Miró**, and in the sphere of literature **Garcia Lorca** made an inestimable contribution.

People and places

Godoy, Charles IV's prime minister and his wife Maria Luisa's long-standing lover, was the chief architect of Spain's disastrous entry into the Peninsular War. His incompetent intrigues with Napoleon brought the ignominious occupation of Spain by French troops, the first since the Moors left, and his brother Joseph Bonaparte's enthronement as King of Spain.

Civil War and the rule of Franco (1931–1975)

A balanced view of this period of Spanish history is still hard to find: until recently, opinions still polarised into repugnance toward or adulation of one side or the other. Briefly, the government set up in 1931 was internally divided and weak. As well as a crippled economy, the result was growing political confusion and polarisation, with uneasy alliances between the communists and socialists on the left (the Republican Popular Front) and the Falangist youth party, conservatives and elements of the army on the right (the National Front). In February 1936 the Popular Front alliance won the election, but its government had virtually no authority and street fighting and assassinations were daily occurrences. In July 1936, military uprisings occurred across Spain, organised by the generals Francisco Franco and Emiliano Mola. The south and west fell to the Nationalists, but the north and east remained under the influence of the Popular Front. Over half a million Spaniards died in the ensuing Civil War, which became an international affair, with Fascist Italy and Germany actively helping the Nationalists and Russia lending sporadic support to the Popular Front. The Republic was finally through in 1939 and Franco declared himself Head of State. During his repressive reign in the '50s and '60s, opposition was stifled by the Army and a much-feared civil police force strongly supported by the Church and considerable numbers of landowners and industrialists. Dissent remained largely underground, except in the case of the terrorist movement ETA.

People and places

Many famous foreigners took part in the Spanish Civil War. Among them, Ernest Hemingway and George Orwell were war tourists, André Malraux led an air squadron and Willy Brandt was a newspaper reporter.

Modern Spain (1975 onwards)

In Franco's last days he appointed Alfonso XIII's grandson, Don Juan Carlos, as his heir, thus returning Spain to constitutional monarchy. Since his accession King Juan Carlos has avoided his forebears' disastrous lack of political acumen. In fact he has performed considerable feats of political leadership and personal courage, in particular at the time of Spain's greatest modern crisis in 1981, when a group of army officers led by Colonel Tejero held the Cortés (Spanish Parliament) hostage for several hours in an abortive coup. Today, there are still those in Spain willing to jettison the new democracy for a return to what they used to perceive as strong government, though their number is declining. After a period in which both conservatives and socialists have demonstrated the ability to govern efficiently as well as command the respect of the army, Spain's future looks more assured. In 1986 Spain joined the European Community, and is looking forward with optimism to celebrating the 500th anniversary of its unification in 1992.

THE ENVIRONMENT AND WILDLIFE

The Coto Donaña National Park in southern Spain is one of Europe's most precious wildlife habitats. Here the River Guadalquivir dawdles to the Atlantic through brackish mudflats, sand-dunes and lagoons where deer, wild boar, mongooses and lynx roam. Every winter thousands of birds visit and breed. Not long ago, hunters were allowed to blaze away with their twelve-bores at these creatures. Now a new threat looms. Plans are afoot to extend the nearby coastal resort of Matalascanas to provide 32,000 new hotel places. As water is drawn from this unique and fragile ecosystem, say ecologists, the *marismas* will die. 'So what', say the developers, setting fire to a bird sanctuary, 'Tourism is progress'.

Protective legislation for Spain's wild places began as long ago as 1916, when the first National Park was designated in Asturias (35 years earlier than any in Britain). Yet official attempts to preserve the environment for future generations have been pitifully inadequate. The pressures of the twentieth century, including Spain's rapid industrialisation programme, changes in farming methods and above all, the unprecedented tourist boom since the '50s, have had many unforeseen and disastrous effects on this rich environmental heritage. It is only now that Spain is reaping the whirlwind of its rapid and mostly ill-considered coastal development. Today's more adventurous traveller has higher expectations of holiday destinations, and the mess made of Spain's once-beautiful coastline has damaged its saleability. The tourist authorities are now trying to market a superior product: Spain's rural interior, and its remaining wildernesses. This policy may with luck result in an increased awareness of how precious and vulnerable the countryside is; or it could simply place intolerable pressure on it. The temptation to 'take the money and run' will undoubtedly weigh strongly with speculators who did well out of the Costas. Already the ski resorts of the Pyrenees, and popular walking areas like Las Alpujarras in the Sierra Nevada, have been subjected to crass building projects.

Huge agricultural grants from the EC have completely changed traditional patterns of land use. The biggest threats to wildlife are pollution from pesticides and industrial effluent, and the irreversible desiccation of wetlands caused by uncontrolled water extraction for irrigation, the damming of river systems, and the planting of thirsty non-native trees like eucalyptus. Besides Coto Donãna, other areas seriously affected by these problems are the vineyard country of La Mancha, and the fertile shellfish grounds of the Ebro Delta, now shrinking at a rate of ten metres a year and badly contaminated.

Spaniards are not noted for their concern for wildlife. Every year, thousands of birds of prey are slaughtered, in order that human raptors can better enjoy the pursuit of game. Countless millions of small birds are limed and netted as they migrate from Africa, ending up in *tapas* bars and French pâté. Spain still supports whaling, selling its catch to Japan.

Over a decade of democracy has produced disappointingly little in the way of controlled planning and *laissez-faire* attitudes still persist in many spheres of Spanish government. But now the economic advantages of protecting the environment are beginning to dawn on many sections of the community. Also, Spain's young, dynamic, and better-educated population is now much more aware of 'green' issues than the older generation to whom the countryside and wildlife seemed an apparently limitless natural resource, and conservation a luxury they could ill afford. Consumer and environmental pressure groups are being set up all the time. One is the Asociación para la Defensa de la Naturaleza (ADENA), a branch of the Worldwide Fund for Nature (WWF). Friends of the Earth and Greenpeace also have associate groups in Spain, and there is now a Green Party on the political scene. Spanish authorities, stung by criticism from outsiders, now say with some justification that if foreign tourists want to look at wildlife and scenery in Spain, they should share the cost of protecting it.

Spain has nine National Parks: three mountain zones in Northern Spain (**Covadonga**, **Ordesa** and **Aigües Tortes**); two wetland areas (**Coto Doñana** and **Las Tablas de Daimiel**); and four island habitats (the last are all in the **Canary Islands**). There are also about 20 'nature parks' with fewer restrictions. Only about four per cent of the land area has any protected status, and the acreage of national parkland is far outweighed by hunting reserves. All over Spain's countryside the *coto de caza* black-and-white signs are visible. The official authority in charge of Spain's protected land is ICONA, the Institute for Nature Conservation. For information about the National Parks, write to ICONA, Sección de Parques Nacionales, Gran Vía de San Francisco 35, 28071 Madrid.

BULLFIGHTING

'No one brought up on the works of Beatrix Potter can understand, much less appreciate, a bull-fight, and nothing can ever be done about it', according to H V Morton in *A Stranger In Spain*. It is no surprise then that after matador Frank Evans appeared on *Wogan* in April 1990, and demonstrated a perfect kill, using a sword in the air and an imaginary bull, the BBC was bombarded with calls of complaint. In fact, despite British sensitivity to animal welfare, as an uninitiated foreigner who does not understand the significance of the matador's moves and the pattern of events, you are far more likely to be bored than horrified by a bullfight. Often the show simply is not a good one, with matadors off form, bulls truculent and the action uninspired. According to experts, eighty per cent of bullfights are boring, and only about five per cent match up to expectations. It is rare for all components to come together and create a really superb fight. For those who think the whole affair barbaric, it is worth bearing in mind that you do not have to see a bullfight in order to confirm that you would not enjoy it.

If you do plan to go, the cheapest way is to buy a ticket from the ticket office at the bullring. Failing this, you can often buy tickets from your hotel reception, at booths around the city or, at a premium, from touts outside the bullring (check first before believing that the ticket office has none left). Some tour operators have stopped selling tickets to bullfights as a matter of principle. There are three main grades of seats: *sombra* (in the shade) are on the side where most of the action usually takes place and are the most expensive; *sol* (in the sun) are the cheapest, but you will be cramped and sweaty; *sol y sombra* (sun and shade) are somewhere in between. Get there early to stake out your patch on the concrete terrace.

Bullfights take place throughout Spain from March to October (in Andalucía the season is extended) and are generally held on Sundays. There are extra events on Thursdays in high season in Barcelona and Madrid. During annual festivals, including the April fair in Seville, the *Feast of San Isidro* in Madrid in May, the *Fiesta de San Fermín* in Pamplona in early July, the Valencia *fiesta* in July, and the Bilbao *fiesta* in August, there are fights every day. The fights (*corridas*) take place in the early evening, and you need stamina to keep up with the round-the-clock partying in between.

There are hundreds of bullrings (*plazas de toros*) in Spain, varying from village squares, where over-the-hill matadors and novices (*novilleros*) challenge under-sized bulls, to enormous arenas seating up to 50,000 where you can see performances by the very best bulls and matadors. There is no question that bullfighting in Spain remains popular despite protest groups' attempts to have it banned, some going as far as taking their case to the European Parliament. In the south at Tossa de Mar, the Mayor has banned bullfighting along with other sports which exploit animals. It is also banned in the Canary Islands, but these areas have no long tradition of bullfighting, so resistance to the ban, introduced in 1990, was limited. In some areas, notably Madrid, bullfighting is becoming more fashionable as 'yuppies' have discovered it is the place to be seen. Keen *aficionados* include King Juan Carlos.

Bullfighting in Spain began in the twelfth century, and for hundreds of years was something of a bloody scrum. Nelson attended a bullfeast in Cadiz in 1793, at a time when bull-dogs were let loose on the bull, monkeys were sometimes tied to a post in the centre of the arena as 'bait' to goad the bull, and horses were often gored as their riders attempted to stab pikes into the bull's shoulders. Despite his stomach for war, Nelson apparently felt sick at the sight of five disembowelled horses and two severely gored men, and later wrote to his wife complaining about the bloodthirsty spectators. In the eighteenth century Francisco Romero from Ronda in the south of Spain invented the *muleta* and the main part of the fight began to take place on foot, and more formalised rules began to be laid down. A modern bullfight, though of course still bloody, is a highly ritualised drama in three acts. Commentators today call themselves art critics, not sports correspondents.

The performance begins with a procession in which all the characters of the plot parade around the ring and bow to the President who is to judge the fights and reward those matadors who give a spectacular performance. After the parade the first bull is released into the ring. The most senior matador is matched against the first and fourth bulls, and the most junior against the third and sixth. So the most experienced matador now weighs up the first bull of the *corrida*. Assisted by *banderilleros* and *picadores* he makes a few passes with a large pink and yellow cape in order to test the bull's vision, get a feel for the way the bull charges, demonstrating his skill at various set movements as he does so. At the President's signal this scene is over and the first act begins.

Two *picadores*, who are mounted, are led into the ring and the bull encouraged to charge them. The idea is for the *picadores* to thrust a spear into the neck muscles of the bull as he attempts to attack. The horses' bellies are well protected with padding and they are blindfolded on one side so that they cannot see the bull charge. The *picadores* plant up to three pikes in the bull's neck at the matador's discretion; he will tell them to stop if he thinks the bull has lost enough strength after only one or two. With an injured neck, the bull is weaker and should keep his head low, which makes the matador's job easier and should enable him to kill the bull more swiftly. Again at the President's signal, the first act ends and the second begins.

This act involves a team of *banderilleros* planting three pairs of decorated darts into the hump on the bull's neck. Though the *banderilleros* are on foot, this is one of the least dangerous tasks for the men in the ring. The crowd love them to demonstrate dominance of the bull, and this time it is done by planting the darts and then walking coolly away.

Then comes the final act, the *faena*. If the bull has been a good one – aggressive with plenty of energy, charging without provocation and responding well to the cape – the matador will dedicate the bull to the audience and give a spectacular performance of graceful and increasingly dangerous passes. Using only a small red cloth (*muleta*) the matador attempts to master the bull before lining him up for the 'moment of truth', the kill. In order to kill the bull cleanly, the matador must drive his sword over the bull's horns and down between the shoulder blades into his heart. The bull must have his head down and his front legs together to ensure the task is carried out with only one blow. In fact this is rarely achieved, most bulls need several attempts before they finally die and are dragged out of the ring by a team of mules.

Judging him by his style (*pandar*), his mastery of the bull (*mandar*), his timing (*templar*), and the swiftness of the kill, the President awards the matador either one of the bull's ears, both ears, or both ears and the tail, and the matador makes a lap of honour. The crowd attempts to influence the President's decision by waving white handkerchiefs (do not forget to take yours), and throwing cushions, flowers, straw hats and anything else which comes to hand, into the ring. The plot then begins again with the second bull being released and the matador who is second in seniority taking up his position in the ring.

Bullfights are fairly formal events, which means you should not go along in shorts and t-shirt, but which does not mean inhibiting your reaction to what is going on before you. You can whistle, shout abuse and even throw things into the ring, as long as you do so at the right times. Knowing when to jeer and when to gasp with appreciation is important to the Spanish *aficionados* who follow their heroes from one venue to another during the season. But it can take a lot of experience to tell skilled moves from flash. Hemingway was something of a purist when it came to fancy tricks, like kissing the bull or pretending to call him on the telephone, which he thought humiliated the bull and thus demeaned the art as a whole. Some audiences love these tricks, if in doubt copy your neighbour's reaction. Remember, cheering on the bull, along with applauding if a matador gets injured, is considered barbaric behaviour by Spanish bullfighting enthusiasts.

THE GOOD RESORT GUIDE

Here is a run down on Spain's best resorts for a sun and sea holiday, whether you want a fun action-packed time or a quieter retreat in a relatively unspoilt part of the coast. We follow the mainland clockwise, starting with Galicia and ending with the resorts in the Balearics and Canaries.

Galicia
Baiona

Good for a quiet holiday in a picturesque resort little visited by foreigners
Baiona is a very special resort, an old golden granite fishing village on the west coast of Spain close to the Portuguese border. The weather is cooler (and rainier) than in the south, which makes the countryside greener and the season shorter. It is used mostly by Spanish families, who stay in small hotels in traditional houses along the sea-front, but there is also a *parador* built within the walls of an old fortress. The beaches in the town are very small, but there is an excellent beach, Playa de América, a few kilometres away, and you can take a ferry in summer to the beaches of the Ciés islands. You can also make day-trips to local fishing villages, to the historic towns of Pontevedra and Santiago de Compostela, or even down to Portugal. There is little in the way of nightlife – evenings are spent in seafront cafés and fish restaurants.

Basque Country
San Sebastían

A smart resort with a superb beach which appeals equally to trendy young things and Spanish families
A stylish and expensive resort with a tremendous beach in a shell-shaped bay, San Sebastían was developed at the turn of the century and you can still stay in its *belle-epoque* hotels. The town's restaurants are among the best in Spain and the lively old quarter is packed with *tapas* bars. San Sebastían is at its liveliest and ritziest during the jazz and film festivals which are held in July and September respectively.

Fuentarrabía (Hondarribia)

Good for a quiet, lazy holiday in a genuinely Spanish setting
A gorgeous whitewashed fishing village on the Bay of Biscay close to the French border. It has a good sandy beach, and accommodation in historic houses or intimate *pensiones*. There's a walled old quarter on a hill with lots of pretty cobbled streets to explore, and a lively main street parallel with the sea-front with pavement cafés and restaurants among the fruit and vegetable stalls.

Costa Brava, Catalunya
Cadaqués

Sophisticated fun for grown-ups in a superior, arty resort
Relative inaccessibility and a shortage of parking have allowed this town to retain a great deal of its original charm – steep cobbled streets, white arcaded houses, even the occasional fishing boat. The town basks in the reflected

27

glory of its connection with Salvador Dalí – many of the leading lights of the *avant-garde* visited him, bringing camp-followers in their wake, and establishing Cadaqués as a rather arty watering hole. It has tasteful, trendy shops, and a lively café society at night. The tiny beaches of dark slate are rather unappealing, and there is little here for children to do.

Calella de Palafrugell

A resort which has character, in the most scenic part of the central Costa Brava
This small resort sits between sheer, pine-studded cliffs in a beautiful setting. The low-rise buildings are traditional in style, and the narrow streets packed with smart boutiques. If the resort's small cove beaches get too crowded, walk over the coastal path to the neighbouring village of Llafranc, or, if you have a car, drive to the lovely cove beaches further north around Aigua Blava. There are lots of bars, cafés and restaurants to stroll between at night, although entertainment is low key.

Tossa de Mar

Traditional sun, sea and sand resort, with a dash of flair
Birthplace of the modern package holiday, and with its fair share of high-rise concrete, Tossa de Mar has somehow managed to remain an enjoyable family-oriented base. The local beaches, though small, are clean. The carefully restored twelfth-century walled town gives Tossa de Mar a distinct edge over its competitors in the interest stakes. The narrow streets of the old town are crammed with souvenir shops and bars, and prices are generally reasonable. Nightlife is restrained – nighthawks are advised to make for Lloret de Mar, 12 kilometres further south.

Costa Dorada (Daurada), Catalunya
Sitges

Smart resort with an interesting old town, and pleasant beaches
Less than an hour's drive from Barcelona, this is an attractive, bustling resort with a jumbled old town, pleasant promenade and a variety of good beaches. Most of the recent development is set back from the coast, so the integrity of the old quarter has been retained. There are three interesting museums, and some unusual shops. Good for families and young couples, Sitges is also very popular with gay travellers who have their own lively night scene.

Costa Blanca, Valencia
Benidorm

A cheerful British-dominated package resort; gets rowdy in summer, but is especially good for older people who want a sociable out-of-season holiday
Two good beaches, virtual year-round sunshine and scores of British

restaurants and bars make Benidorm a perennial favourite. It is a friendly and unpretentious place, and is at its pleasantest in low season – a time when many older British people choose to visit. The resort itself is rather ugly and accommodation is mostly in large concrete blocks built in the '60s and '70s. There is no shortage of bars, discos, cafés and restaurants – mostly serving British, Dutch or German-style food.

Jávea

A pleasant centre to dip into if you are staying in one of the nearby villas, and a good choice for a sedate low season holiday

A bustling (and rather traffic-congested) little town which lies in a dip between hills. It has a good sandy beach, a pleasant café-lined waterfront, and is a year-round resort popular with retired British people (many of whom live here permanently). There is a stylish *parador*, but most of the accommodation is in self- catering villas and apartments. The nicest of these lie scattered on the hillsides outside the town. If you do stay in one of these you will need a car to get to Jávea. The other beaches along this craggy section of coastline are minute – so it is well worth paying the extra to have a villa with a swimming-pool.

Costa de Almería, Andalucía

Mojácar

Still expanding family resort with long sand and shingle beaches, and an atmospheric old town on the hill above

The old Moorish town of Mojácar sprawls over a hill, above the rather utilitarian modern development that runs along the coast. Visitors can alternate sunbathing sessions with exploring the narrow streets of tightly packed white houses in the old-time town. Most of the accommodation is in good quality low-rise pueblo-style self-catering apartments, although there are a couple of high-rise hotels and a *parador*. A car is handy for visiting the more remote and wilder beaches to the south. There is little of the hectic nightlife you will find in the larger resorts.

Costa del Sol, Andalucía

Nerja

More than a vestige of genuine Spanish atmosphere despite the development of recent years

East of Málaga the Costa del Sol has so far escaped the worst of the architectural blight that runs rampant to the west. Nerja is the most pleasant of the eastern resorts, with a very pleasant promenade, the Balcón de Europe which runs along a clifftop at right-angles to the sea, as well as a couple of decent-sized beaches and several nearby coves. Most of the accommodation is in self-catering complexes, sometimes in hilly locations, and there are a number of smart privately owned British villas available for rent. If you stroll through the narrow side streets just behind the main central area at night, you will find Spanish grandmothers sitting outside their houses on dining chairs, deep in conversation with friends and utterly oblivious to tourists.

Torremolinos

Lively, friendly and unpretentious, a good bet for a cheap family holiday
Yes, really. Despite all the jokes, and the legendary and largely apocryphal antics of lager louts in Union-Jack shorts, it is perfectly possible to have a good – though not noticeably Spanish – time in Torremolinos. The long beaches are clean, there are loads of shops, competition keeps bar and restaurant prices low, and the sun shines reliably. Most of the accommodation is in ugly, sea-front towerblock hotels or apartments, but there is a pleasant old quarter with some good seafood restaurants behind Carihuela Beach. The nightlife is wild, and you have the chance to plan excursions to Granada, Córdoba, Gibraltar or even Seville.

Ibiza

Santa Eulalia

A good family resort spiked with the unmistakable Ibizan style
An amiable, relaxed and long-established Ibizan resort, though the beach is not great. It has an appealing mixture of people – ageing hippies, the beautiful set and lots of French and British families. There is a tree-lined avenue with pavement cafés and craft and trinket stalls but the resort is close enough to make a shopping, bar-crawling or clubbing trip to Ibiza Town feasible by bus or taxi. There are also regular ferries in summer to local beaches and the island of Formentera.

Menorca

Cala Santa Galdana

A relatively peaceful family resort
This is the best resort on Menorca, set on a gorgeous bay flanked by pine-wooded hills with a golden sandy beach. The season is fairly short, as Menorca is the most exposed (and windiest) of the Balearics. There are a couple of large hotels as well as small pensions, apartments and villas, and as night-time entertainment is largely based in the hotels, it is fairly peaceful. In summer there are ferries to some lovely undeveloped beaches.

Mallorca

Puerto de Pollensa

A rather classy resort in which you can combine days on the beach with exploring Majorca's mountain scenery

A package resort with quality hotels and restaurants sitting on a wide bay on the northern shore of Mallorca. The resort beach is skimpy and very close to the coast road, and even though it is improved in high season with lorry-loads of sand, it is much pleasanter to do your swimming and sunbathing on the pine-screened beach of Formentor, a few kilometres away. It is a good idea to hire a car, not only to reach the beach, but also because the resort is a good base for exploring the mountains, pretty villages and craggy coast of the Sierra de Tramuntana.

Tenerife
Puerto de la Cruz

Vestiges of fishing village character make this the most interesting of Tenerife's large resorts, which manages, most of the time, to be lively without being rowdy

Puerto is the oldest established, and still the most popular of Tenerife's resorts, though the weather is not as sunny as in the south. Located on the lush north coast amid the dense foliage of countless banana trees, it compensates for its lack of good sand with an imaginative and beautifully kept Lido on a rocky promontory. The old quarter boasts several picturesque squares full of trees and typical Canarian-style houses. The Paseo Maritimo walkway leading past San Telmo bay is a focal point for tourists. Some of its older traditional package hotels are now starting to look faded, lacking the space and facilities of more modern resorts. Redevelopment is scheduled for the run-down area by the castle.

Gran Canaria
San Agustín

The least frenetic section of the giant southern resorts, with a less aggressively uniform British or German feel than either of its neighbours

San Agustín is the older, residential section of Maspalomas, its slightly more exclusive air reinforced by one of Gran Canaria's best hotels (containing a casino and cabaret nightclub) and the smart Beach Club with its excellent restaurant on the rising land behind the shore. The hillier contours of the bay add scenic interest to the best beach below the Tamarindos Hotel, but there are other beaches of variable quality to either side, linked by tastefully land-scaped paths. If you are the sort of person who would not mind being approached to make up a bridge four, you may be happier in San Agustín than elsewhere.

Puerto de Mogán

A bright spark in Gran Canaria's dimmish tourist scene. Despite its stylishness, it is not expensive

An unusual departure from the classic Canarian style resort: a Scandinavian-financed 'marina village' of low-rise self-catering apartments and a hotel surrounding a luxury yacht harbour. The tourist complex, though built on the site of an existing community, is contrived, some might say twee. But the little 'houses' are genuinely imaginative, pretty and well kept, the atmosphere is peaceful, and the surrounding scenery offers good touring opportunities. Car hire is recommended.

Lanzarote
Playa Blanca

The best choice on Lanzarote for a peaceful, low-key beach holiday. Somewhat isolated from other centres: best to have your own transport

Much of the development in Playa Blanca is still very new, and services such as access roads and drainage have yet to catch up. As yet the resort has an unfinished, unplanned feel, but the quality of what is there seems high. Some complexes are quite a long way from the beaches, and the scenery inland is arid. Little nightlife or organised entertainment; life here begins and ends on the lovely white-sand beaches.

GOOD TOURING GUIDE

Even if you resolve to relax by the sea and do absolutely nothing for a couple of weeks, your horizons will probably extend beyond the deep end of the pool at some stage. A a half-day tour from the busiest Costa resort gives a glimpse of Spain's colossal scenic variety. Further afield, outside the dense population centres, Spain has vast areas of quiet countryside, much of it still virtually wild.

On scenic roads, look out for *miradors* (viewpoints) sometimes indicated by a camera pictogram. Here you will generally find a safe parking place off the road, sometimes a panoramic restaurant or bar from which to admire the view. Driving into unfamiliar Spanish towns and cities can be confusing and initially very off-putting: many are ringed by impenetrable-looking industrial estates or hideous modern suburbs. Promising signs for sightseeing zones include *ciudad monumentale* or *casco antiguo* (old quarter), *plaza mayor* (main square), *murallas* (walls), *iglesia/catedral* (church/cathedral), *castillo/alcázar* (castle). Failing all else, there is always the *oficina de turismo* (tourist office), where you can get a detailed map and some help. Many provincial tourist offices produce leaflets suggesting local touring routes through places of interest – always worth picking up while you are in town.

Below is a short selection of favourites in each region of Spain – if you are touring a region for the first time, do not miss these:

Galicia
- The pilgrimage city of Santiago de Compostela
- Rías Altas and Rías Bajas (coastal fjords and fishing villages)
- Baiona, Muros, Viveiro (granite seaside towns); Pontevedra (old quarter)
- The Sil Gorges

Cantabria and Asturias

- Picos de Europa (mountains – scenery and walking)
- Prehistoric painted caves throughout the region (including Altamira)
- Pre-Romanesque churches (especially in Oviedo)
- Santillana del Mar (medieval village)

Basque Country, Navarra and La Rioja

- San Sebastían (resort and old town)
- Pamplona (old town and famous fiesta)
- Fuentarrabía (fortress village)
- The pilgrim route to Santiago (Estella, Leyre; Sangüesa; Puente la Reina; San Millán)
- Haro and Laguardia (Rioja wine villages)

Aragón

- Pyrenees and Ordesa National Park (walking and wildlife)
- San Juan de la Peña, Monasterio de Piedra (monasteries)
- Mudejar Towers (in Teruel and Zaragoza)
- Sos del Rey Católico, Uncastillo (hill villages)

Catalunya

- Barcelona
- Costa Brava (scenery and beaches)
- Tarragona
- Gerona (cathedral and old quarter)
- Figueras (Dalí museum)
- Monasteries (Poblet; Montserrat)

Valencia and Murcia

- Morella (medieval town)
- Alicante (sweeping lively sea-front)
- Valencia (cathedral and old quarter)

Andalucía

- Seville; Córdoba; Granada (major historic centres)
- White Towns (Ronda, Arcos de la Frontera)
- Las Alpujarras; Sierra Nevada; Cazorla National Park; Coto Doñana National Park

Castilla-La Mancha

● Toledo (historic town)
● Cuenca (old town and scenery around)
● Sigüenza; Almagro; Alarcón; Belmonte (small historic towns)
● Don Quixote trail (windmills and vineyards)

Madrid and around

● Madrid
● El Escorial (royal palace and mausoleum)
● Aranjuez (royal palace and gardens)

Castilla y León

● Salamanca; Burgos; León; Avila (major historic centres)
● Valladolid (plateresque architecture; national sculpture museum)
● Sierra de Gredos; Sierra de Peña de Francia; Las Medulas; Laguna Negra de Urbión (touring routes)

Extremadura

● Trujillo, Cáceres (conquistador towns)
● Guadalupe (monastery)
● Merida (Roman remains)
● Las Hurdes; La Vera; La Jerte (touring routes)

Balearics

● Mallorca: Palma (historic capital); west coast scenery and villages; caves of Arta
● Ibiza: Ibiza Town (picturesque and trendy)

Canaries

● Tenerife (Santa Cruz – old quarter and port; Icod dragon tree; La Orotava and La Laguna; Mount Teide and Las Cañadas National Park)
● Lanzarote (Timanfaya National Park; La Geria; Jameos del Agua and Cueva de los Verdes; Yaiza, Haria, Teguise – white villages; Papagayo beaches)
● Gomera, La Palma, Hierro (mountain scenery)
● Gran Canaria (Cruz de Tejeda; west coast touring)

EATING IN SPAIN

There is a lot more to Spanish cooking than *gazpacho, tortilla* and *paella*. Regional variations of climate, terrain and seaboard produce a colossal range of foodstuffs, and there are now many good restaurants all over Spain. As in most countries, these need seeking out: interesting cooking is by no means universal. Many restaurants (especially in those areas most affected by mass tourism) still get away with serving a tedious range of steaks, chops and chips at inflated prices. Disappointed diners who patronise these places have only themselves to blame: by law, all Spanish restaurants must clearly display their menus (with prices) outside the premises. Restaurants, like hotels, are officially graded by the tourist authorities, though the number of 'forks' they possess (1–5) relates to service, décor and range of dishes rather than the quality of the cooking.

The smarter the surroundings, of course, the higher the prices. If you want to eat inexpensively, a *menu del día* or *menu turístico* (generally three courses, plus bread and a small carafe of wine) is certainly an economical, if not particularly interesting, way to eat, and helpings are nearly always generous. Bars in Spain nearly always serve food of some kind as well as drinks. *Bar, restaurante* or *cafetería* are obvious translations; other words meaning 'restaurant' include *comedor* (the dining section of a bar or hotel); *marisquería* (seafood restaurant); *asador* (specialising in roast meat dishes); *mesón* (inn); *economico* (a budget restaurant). Bars may also be called *bodegas, tabernas,* or *cervecerías*. 'Pubs' (especially 'English pubs') are flashily decorated, overpriced bars, generally best avoided. In the more basic eating places there is nearly always a TV blaring away in one corner, and if the football is on, a group of male Spaniards will be glued to it, dropping paper napkins, cigarette ends and olive pits casually to the floor around the counter (quite acceptable: the mess is swept up every so often).

The social aspect of eating is always important in Spain. It is very much a communal activity; friends, colleagues and families gather to enjoy it together with much conversation and laughter for hours at a time; and you will often find a group of Spaniards (from babe-in-arms to great-grand-mother) still eating Sunday lunch at 4pm. The hospitality involved in eating and drinking is all part of the generous Spanish character. You never see Spaniards arguing about how to split a restaurant or bar bill; rather, they will be stridently competing to pay it, telling everyone else to put their money away. It is not unusual for foreign visitors to be invited to join a party for a drink, or offered a brandy or liqueur 'on the house' by a restaurant at the end of the meal.

Spanish eating hours are a constant puzzle to foreigners. Spaniards eat late: lunch (*almuerzo*) rarely before 2pm; dinner (*cena*) sometimes not until 11pm. Concessions are made in tourist areas, but to enjoy Spanish food in local company; you need to adjust your timetable. Breakfast (*desayuno*), for a Spaniard, is rudimentary: a coffee, possibly a roll, croissant or cake, sometimes a *cognac*. *Paradores* and package hotels serve elaborate buffet breakfasts, which are good value if you can face stoking up early in the day. If you cannot, then head for a bar or café used by locals, and pay a fifth of the price. Coffee is *café con leche* (large milky coffee); *café solo* (small, strong black coffee) or *café cortado* (coffee with just a dash of milk). Lunch is usually the

35

main meal of the day for Spaniards, a long-drawn out affair. Hard-pressed tourists with limited sightseeing time may prefer a lunch-time *bocadillo* (large roll), a *sandwich tostada* (toasted sandwich), or a *plato combinado* (a one-course plateful of meat, vegetables, chips, salad or eggs, often easily identified by a picture). Or, of course, buy a picnic (before the shops shut for the siesta). *Tapas* (literally 'lids'), served in bars or *tascas*, are small snacks to keep you going before those late meals. They range from easily identifiable olives (*aceitunas*) or morsels of cheese (*queso*) – often served free with a drink – to plates of weird and wonderful things (hot or cold), better sampled before identification. Octopus salad, bull's tails, tripe and lamb's testicles require a certain adventurousness, but in rich sauces they can be delicious. Two or three *raciones* of *tapas* can make a satisfying meal (but not necessarily all that cheaply). Beware exotic seafood *tapas* or speciality cured hams (sometimes priced per 100 grams – precooked weight) which, though well worth trying, can clock up an alarming bill.

Spaniards do not sit politely waiting to be served. Ordering, particularly at a crowded bar, requires assertiveness. If you do not speak up people will assume you have not made up your mind. '*Oiga, por favor!*' will attract a waiter's attention. Persuading someone to bring you the bill can also be difficult ('*La cuenta, por favor*'). Try '*Tengo prisa*', if in a hurry. Tipping is customary, even where service is included (ten per cent in a restaurant is quite sufficient, or the last few coins in the saucer if you are at a bar). Where you sit also makes a difference to your bill: that sunny table on the terrace will almost certainly be more expensive than a place by the bar.

Vegetarianism is not widespread in Spain and it is often difficult to find interesting dishes without meat: *gazpacho*, *tortilla* and salads are the mainstay. Many apparently innocent dishes such as stuffed or Catalan-style vegetables may contain meat or fish, and soups are usually made with meat stocks. Ask '*¿Hay algo sin carne?*' for something meatless.

In tourist areas most restaurants provide translations in various languages, though these may be more amusing than illuminating. The startling description 'Eunuch stuffed with ham and slightly fried' on a Mallorcan menu turned out to be a chicken (capon) kiev! Practise your Spanish, and concentrate on the original menu.

Famous regional dishes are not necessarily confined to one area. In Madrid, for example, you can eat splendid fresh fish raced from the coasts every day in refrigerated planeloads. *Paradores* make a feature of preparing local specialities, and it is always worth reading their menus carefully. Most regions have some kind of local stew, given many different names. Vegetable hotpots include *menestra* and *pisto*; fish ones may be *suquet*, *zarzuela*, or *caldereta*; meat ones *olla*, *cocido*, *pote*, *escudella*, or *cazuela*. Wherever you are in Spain, there is no possible way of avoiding two essential ingredients: garlic, and olive oil.

Basque Country

Widely accepted as Spain's most sophisticated regional cuisine, Basque cooking (*a la vasca/a la vizcaina*) is hugely varied and complex. High-quality ingredients are available from its productive farmland and the well-stocked local fishing grounds, and the Basques themselves are intensely interested in food. Talented Basque chefs have pioneered Spain's recent conversion to *nueva cocina*. Fish dishes predominate, but rich, full-flavoured meat recipes are also popular. *Merluza* (hake) and *bacalao* (salt cod) are two fish very commonly seen on menus, spiced up with thick tomato and garlic or herby sauces (*salsa verde*). Others are *calamares en su tinta* (squid in its own ink) and *angulas al ajillo* (garlic elvers). The local fish stew of tuna and potatoes is a *marmitako*.

Cantabria, Asturias and Galicia

Again, the excellent Atlantic seafood (*mariscos*) forms a major part of the diet all along this northern coast. Many of these specialities can be eaten as *tapas*: *mejillones* (orange mussels farmed on *ría* rafts); *chiperones* (baby squid just an inch or two long); *ostras* (oysters, found especially in Vigo); *percebes* (goose barnacles, a great local delicacy, which look disturbingly like used condoms); *vieras* (Santiago's famous scallops – what we know as *coquilles St Jacques*); *pulpo* (octopus), *boquerones* (fresh anchovies in vinegar), *gambas* (shrimps) and *almejas* (clams) are just a few out of a vast range of fish. Fresh-grilled sardines sizzle on pavement or beach stalls. In Asturias, many dishes are cooked in the local cider (*sidra*), and a *fabada* is a local stew of white beans and sausage. The fierce goat's cheese, *cabrales*, is found around the Picos de Europa. Two Galician specialities are *empanadas* (flat savoury pies) and *caldo gallego*, a vegetable broth. Sweet dishes include *tarta de Santiago* (an almond cake), and *filloas* (pancakes).

Castile

The huge area spanned by the central Meseta reflects its role as the cereal- and grape-growing region of the peninsula, the *tierra de pan* and *tierra de vino*. Bread is added to the classic Castilian garlic soup, *sopa de ajo*, or fried into croutons in La Mancha (*migas*), and wine is drunk with meals as a matter of course. The most memorable dishes of Castile are the oven-roasted meats: *cochinillo asado* suckling pig); *lechazo* (milk lamb); and *cabrito* (kid). Pulses such as chickpeas and lentils flourish in the dry land, and add bulk to many stews and hotpots such as *cocido madrileño*, in which you may find anything from a piece of spicy sausage (*chorizo*) to a chicken's foot. Eggs are used extensively; whether poached gently in hot broths (*sopa castellana*), made into the classic Spanish potato omelette (*tortilla*), scrambled (*revuelto*), or used in sticky sweets such as *yemas de Santa Teresa*. Home-grown vegetables include slightly more exotic asparagus, aubergines and artichokes, and an unusual fruit, the quince, is made into a sort of jam called *membrillo*. Castile's famous cheese is *manchego*, found everywhere in La Mancha, and several places (notably Toledo) specialise in marzipan or other almond sweets. Game and liver are made into a mushy pate called *mortuerolo* around Cuenca. A speciality of Madrid is *churros*: dough extruded into snake-like chunks and deep-fried. This is a popular breakfast dish, often served with rich, thick chocolate. If you are counting calories, stick to watching the *churros* being made.

Extremadura

In some respects the food of this area is similar to Castile's, but it specialises in hams and sausages (*embutidos* and *salchichas*). The local pig, *Cerdo ibérico*, produces tasty and highly prized hams called *pata negra* (blackfoot), Its wilder cousin the boar, *jabalí*, is also hunted for meat. Many kinds of sausage are available here and all over Spain: *lomo, morcilla* (a type of black pudding). Excellent fruit (especially cherries) comes from the valleys of La Vera and the Jerte.

Andalucía

This huge southerly region is credited with the invention of two of Spain's best-known food specialities. It may now seem richly endowed with food of many kinds, but not so long ago most of its peasant population were reduced to near starvation, subsisting on a monotonous brew of tomatoes, onions, peppers and garlic. We now eat this delicate soup with pleasure, as *gazpacho*, but those who ate it for want of anything else must have been sick of the sight of it. An Andalucian variation of the classic dish is the addition of almonds. Almonds (*almendras*) are succulent and delicious here; one of the nicest ways to eat them is salted as *tapas* (the other famous Andalucian gastronomic idea) with a *copita* of crisp *Fino* sherry. Several of Spain's best speciality hams come from Andalucía too, including *jamón de Jabugo* and *jamón serrano* (air-cured and very expensive). Other specialities are fried foods, particularly stir-fried fish (*pascaito frito*), or sardines from the Atlantic coast west of Trafalgar. *Riñones al jerez* (kidneys in sherry) are another favourite dish, sometimes available as a filling *tapa*. Spaniards are not much into marmalade (the word *mermalada*) refers to any kind of jam, and orange jam isn't really the same as English marmalade. But you will see the ingredients growing in abundance here: groves of the famous bitter oranges glow all winter around Seville. Do not be tempted by them; they are horrible to eat straight off the tree. Moorish sweet pastries of almonds, walnuts and honey are better bets for pudding.

The Levante – Valencia and Murcia

Valencia is the land of *paella*, and all around the scene is more reminiscent of the Far East than of Europe, as the bright green rice shoots emerge through flooded paddy fields. A classic *paella* has to be made of the stubby-grained local rice, which is tricky to cook without becoming soggy. It always contains saffron from neighbouring La Mancha, but other ingredients are optional: fish, chicken or meat (rabbit is a favourite), and some say a true *paella* has a snail or two in it somewhere. Other less hackneyed rice dishes are *arroz negro* (black rice with squid) and *arroz a la banda* (a two-course fish and rice dish). *Horchata*, a cool, milky drink made of crushed tiger nuts, is an unusual speciality worth looking out for. *Sopa de dátiles* has nothing to do with the dates that grow around Elche, but is made with small black mussels. *Turrón* is just one of the local sweets – a kind of almond nougat often given as a present.

Catalunya

Another of Spain's most sophisticated regional cuisines, Catalan cooking is hugely varied and ambitious, again relying on a vast range of locally available ingredients: Mediterranean fish, mountain game and trout, fresh fruit and vegetables and excellent dairy produce for rich puddings. Two of its classic sauces are *alioli* (garlic mayonnaise) and *romesco* (made of sweet peppers, almonds and garlic). *Habas a la catalaña* and *espinacas a la catalaña* (broad beans and spinach, Catalan-style) are often seen as side-dishes in restaurants. *Suquet de peix* is the classic fish stew, and the startling combination of *llagosta i pollastre* (lobster with chicken and hazelnuts) is now a well-known speciality. An apparently simple concoction of crunchy bread spread with olive oil and chopped tomato (*pan con tomate*) makes a popular and surprisingly delicious breakfast. A local sausage of note is *butifarra*, both black and white varieties. For dessert, *crema catalaña* is the best of Spain's versions of *flan* (caramel custard).

Aragón and Navarra

Wherever you go in Spain, you are almost certain to come across *trucha a la navarra*, trout with ham, now a well-known favourite. Aragón is famous for game, so partridge (*perdiz*) is particularly good here, sometimes accented with chocolate. Another classic of Aragón is the *chilindrón* style of cooking, where red pepper sauces are served with meat and chicken dishes. Roncal cheese is a Pyrenean speciality.

Balearics and Canaries

The islands rely heavily on their local fish, though the Canaries have the edge with their location by the rich fishing grounds of Africa on their doorstep. Many fish you find in the Canaries are quite unknown in Britain: *cerne*, *vieja* and *sama* are all worth trying. Bananas, tomatoes, and *papas arrugadas* (wrinkled potatoes cooked in brine), are the other distinctive ingredients of Canarian cooking: spiced up with *mojo* (hot pepper sauce). The Balearics' contribution to the world of sauces is of course mayonnaise, from Mahón in Menorca. A special cake from Mallorca is the *ensaimada*, made of a light, lard-based pastry coiled into a snail-shape.

WINE IN SPAIN

Wine has been part of Spanish culture ever since the early civilising influences of the Phoenicians, and, later, Greeks, who introduced the practice of viniculture to the Mediterranean. Spain has more land under vines than any other wine-producing country in the world, but it is not as productive as many of its competitors in the rest of Europe. Low yields of wine per hectare of land under vines is attributed to low rainfall and antiquated agricultural techniques; the situation is not improved by government restrictions on irrigation.

Wine production is slowly being modernised with grants from the EEC, and the beginnings of quality control have been implemented with the creation of nominated regions known as *Denominaciones de Origén* (DO), like the French *Appellation Contrôlée* system. Each *denominación* is controlled by a *Consejo Regulador*, which is made up of local wine experts who draw up regulations based on their experience of local conditions. The regulation of the industry is in its infancy and up to one-third of the vineyards are not covered by a DO. Some of the more progressive vintners feel restricted by DO guidelines which can, say, forbid the use of foreign grape varieties such as the classic Cabernet Sauvignon; this can lead to a ridiculous situation where very high-quality wines are still classed as table wine.

Until recently, only a few Spanish wines were well known internationally and despite a long and proud tradition of wine-making, the bulk of Spanish wine generally does not have a good reputation. Often, as in La Mancha, the wine is made from dull, uninteresting grape varieties using methods that have not changed for years. Sherry is the main Spanish export to the international wine-drinking community, and Rioja, although a rising star several years ago, now has begun to fade. The situation is changing however, and the pace of change seems to be gathering momentum. A renewed interest in producing good-quality wines has been prompted by visionary vintners – such as the Torres family, Jean León and the Marqués de Griñon – and consumers with increasingly sophisticated tastes are demanding modern-style fresh white wines and red wines with more character.

The wine regions of Spain fall into four main geographical areas: the quality red, rosé and white wines to the north from Rioja to Catalunya, the light whites of Galicia and the idiosyncratic Vega Sicilia of Old Castille; the heavier, fruitier wines to the south (Andalucía); and the bulk wines in the centre and south-east (La Mancha, Murcia). Each region experiences very different types of climate which affect the type of wine produced. The warm climate influenced by the Mediterranean in the south does not vary greatly and so has little effect on wine production. To the north, the Atlantic has greater influence on weather patterns, drastically changing grape juice production, hence affecting the quality and quantity of wine produced in that year. Details of Spanish wines and their producers are outlined below.

Southern Spain: Andalucía

Jerez, Condado de Huelva, Málaga, Montilla y Moriles

Andalucía, in southern Spain, with its longer, hotter seasons produces fully ripe grapes, producing stronger, aromatic wines. Britons developed a taste for the fortified wines produced in Jerez in southern Spain at an early stage. In 1587 Sir Francis Drake returned from Cadiz after 'singeing the King of Spain's beard' (setting fire to the Spanish fleet while it was in harbour) with a booty of *sack*, which later became known as sherry, the anglicised version of Jerez. Sherry remained popular in Britain and in the eighteenth century, British merchants headed south to make their fortune in sherry. The Anglo-

Spanish link continues today, with names such as Harvey and Croft heading the main sherry houses in Andalucía.

Sherry is made from the *Palomino* grape variety, renowned for producing a bland juice which is the perfect building block for sherrymakers. The base wine is then aged, some of it under yeast (*flor*) before being fortified with brandy. Sherry does not have a vintage but is aged under a *solera* system. In this system, the wines from older years are kept fresh and fragrant by adding wines from later years. The younger wine acquires the personality of the older wine so that the wine drawn from the oldest barrel has the same qualities each year. Solera dates printed on the bottle, like *solera 1912* simply means that the solera for that wine was laid down in 1912.

The yeast-aged wines are known as *fino* or *manzanilla* and are the lightest of the fortified wines. Stronger, darker sherries are those called *oloroso*, meaning 'fragrant': these are very dry with a characteristic nutty, raisin and caramel flavours. *Amontillado* falls between the two, with an amber colour and dry nutty flavour. The greatest *oloroso soleras* contain a lot of very old wine (20 to 30 years of age) and are only drawn off in small quantities to improve blends, but the more commercial *fino soleras* brands are only kept for 4 to 5 years. *Fino* should be drunk as soon as possible, but *oloroso* can improve in the bottle for years. Sherries are often sweetened for the British market, but this is not how the Spaniards traditionally drink them. *Pedro Ximenez* is used as a sweetening agent for sherries, but occasionally it is released in its pure form as an incredibly sticky dessert wine. Cheaper alternatives to sherry from Jerez can be found in Montilla, slightly lower in alcohol than sherry and softer in taste. Moriles has even lighter wines than Montilla.

Wine production has been in decline in Málaga, but good exceptionally sweet wines can be found.

Recommended producers: Manzanilla; La Gitana (Hidalgo); Solear (barbadillo) Fino: Puerto Fino (Burdon); Dun Zoilo; San Patricio Amontillado, Gonzalez Byass, Hidalgo; Barbadillo Dry Oloroso; Osborne; Domecq Sweet Oloroso; Harveys; Gonzales Byass; Sholtz Hermanos.

The north-east

La Rioja

The Rioja area spreads some 80 miles along the River Ebro's banks in the high mountain valleys of northern Spain. Rioja's fame is built on its high-quality red wines, although it also produces good rosé and white wine. Rioja is often compared in quality to Bordeaux, although it is much cheaper in price. Wines are generally blended from the three Riojan regions: the higher-quality wines of the Rioja Alta centred on Haro, the lighter wines of Rioja Alavesa and the heavier, stronger wines of Rioja Baja. The *Tempranillo* grape variety (also known as *Cencibel*) is by far the most important for quality. In the cooler conditions of Rioja Alta and Alavesa it produces a light wine with a taste of strawberry or raspberry. *Garnacha tinta* is also a common grape variety, grown mostly in the hotter Rioja Baja region. It does not produce wine of very good quality and is often blended with lighter wines to give them body. A limited amount of *Graciano* is grown, known for its fragrant blackberryish fruit, and *Mazuelo* for its tannin and rough fruity taste. *Viura* is the dominant white grape variety which produces sharp-tasting, fresh white wine. There are two very different styles of winemaking in Rioja; companies like CVNE, renowned for producing more high-quality Rioja than any other bodega in the area, make wine in the traditional Bordelais way, ageing the wine in oak barrels to give overtones of vanilla flavour. Other high-tech producers, such as Bodegas Olarra, age few of their wines leaving them young and fruity. Check the classification of the wine on the label to get some idea of style of Rioja, but be warned that some Rioja has been disappointing in recent years.

Recommended producers: **Red Rioja** Campo Viejo; Contino; CVNE; Marqués de Cáceres; Marqués de Murrieta; Muga; La Rioja Alta; Riojanas. **White Rioja** CVNE; Marqués de Murrieta

Navarra and Aragón

Navarra is to the east of the main Rioja region and produces cheaper, less interesting versions of Rioja, with the poorer quality Garnacha Tinta being the main grape of the area. Improved winemaking facilities have resulted in better quality rosé wines.

Aragón also suffers from a preponderance of poor quality grape varieties, but the DO of Somontano is producing fresh reds from the local Moristel grape and deeper reds from Tempranillo and Cabernet Sauvignon.

Recommended producers: Chivite, Señorío de Sarria; Cooperativa Somontano de Sobrarbe, San Valero.

Catalunya

In the north east, just below the Pyrenees, the Penedés has become the most exciting area for innovative wine-making. A wide variety of styles of wine are produced, from ultra-modern fresh, fruity whites to sparkling Cava (*méthode champenoise* sparklers), to classic reds using quality grape varieties. Miguel Torres has pioneered many of the new methods and syles of wine, raising the profile of Penedés wine and competing effectively with Riojan and French counterparts. Another good name to look out for is Jean León. Outside the Penedés region, the Raimat winery in Lérida also produces quality reds, whites and sparkling wines. *Cava* is a sparkling white wine which will often be served if you ask for champagne in Spain, and although it does not have quite the same qualities as champagne, it is a good, cheap alternative. Increasingly the quality of Cava is improving and may one day compare favourably with champagne.

Recommended producers: **Cava**: Castellblanch, Codorníu, Cavas Hill, Loxarel, Mont-Marcal, Parxet, Raimat **Other DOs**: Cavas Hill (Penedés); Jean León (Penedés); De Muller (Priorato); Raimat (Costers del Segre); Cellers de Scala Dei (Priorato); Miguel Torres (Penedés).

The north-west

This area is in the northern centre of Spain, between La Mancha and the north coast of Spain.

Ribera del Duero

To the south-west of the Rioja region, *Vega Sicilia* is the most noted wine from this area, and one of Spain's most expensive. *Viña Pesquera* is also in demand, but less expensive.

Rueda

To the south west of Ribera del Duero, Rueda has French influences in wine-making, introducing fresh white wines to an area which used to make cheap sherry-style wines. Two top producers are Marqués de Riscal and Marqués de Griñon.

Toro

Closer to the Portuguese border than the other two regions, the best wines from this region are red and its top producer is Bodegas Farina. The wines must be made from at least 75 per cent *Tinto de Toro*, and the best wines are made purely from this grape variety, cheaper wines are blended with *Garnacha*. The better wines are soft fruity and easy to drink.

Recommended producers: **Ribero del Duero**: Alejandro Fernandez (Pesquera); Mauro; Pérez Pascuas (Vinas Pedrosa); Vega Sicilia **Rueda**: Marqués de Riscal; Marqués de Griñon **Toro**: Bodegas Fariña (Tinto Colegiata; Crianza Gran Colegiata).

Galicia

Delicate pale whites, slightly sparkling from Ribeiro, Rías Baixas and less appealing smoky reds and astringent whites from Valdeorras.

Central Spain

La Mancha in the monotonous, flat landscape of central Spain, is where the producers of bulk cheap wines rely on the dull *Airen* grape for strong white wine of little character, mixed with *Tempranillo* for ham-fisted red wines. *Airen* is noted for its incredible dullness and an almost unrivalled ability to produce alcohol, and so its main purpose is for blending with other cheap wines. The **Valdepeñas** region has a couple of producers who are reverting to oak-ageing, resulting in better quality reds, in particular *Reserva* and *Gran Reserva* from *Felix Solis* and *Senorio de Los Llanos*. Most other reds must be drunk as young as posible. **Valencia** has good sweet Muscat and dry rosé sold under the Valencia label but often produced in neighbouring Utiel-Requena, but the bulk of the production from regions in the south east has a high alcohol content and a flat earthy taste.

Recommended producers: Vinicola de Castilla (La Mancha, non-DO); Marqués de Griñon; Bodegas Los Llanos; Bodegas Felix Solis.

Balearics and Canaries

Neither of these groups of islands produce DO wines, and finding unadulterated local wine is difficult. In the Balearics, Mallorca is the biggest

Etiquette of wine labelling

If you are looking for a wine from a designated DO, the bottle will be labelled with the name and insignia of the DO region, and a bottling number issued by them to certify the wine. Other terminology to look out for includes:

Legal definitions

Vino de Mesa basic table wine
Vino de Tierra new super-category of table wine (c.f. *vins de pays*)
Denominación de Orígen demarcated region with certain quality requirements
Gran Reserva a wine made from a good vintage, aged for at least two years in an oak cask and three in a bottle.
Reserva a selected wine that has been aged for at least three years (two years for white wine) of which a minimum of one year must have been in the cask for reds, 6 months for whites and rosés.
Crianza or Con Crianza wines that have been aged for the minimum time in wood or bottle, according to local regulations, and therefore will have a mild oaky flavour. *Sin Crianza* or *Garantia de Orígen* wine has not been wood aged so it will be a light fruity red, crisp rosé or white
CVC wine is a blend of several vintages
Other details to look out for:
Bodega wine cellar or name of wine company
Clarete light red
Cosecha vintage
Dulce sweet
Embotellado por bottled by
Espumoso sparkling
Genoroso fortified
Vendimia vintage/harvest
Vina/vinedo vineyard
Vino Bianco white wine
Vino Rosado rosé wine
Vino Clarete light red wine
Vino Tinto red wine

Vintages

For white and rosé wines it is always better to go for the youngest vintages possible (unless an oak-aged Rioja, say). In reds, look for *Reserva* and *Gran Reserva* for more staying power, but drink simple red wines (*Garantía de Orígen*) as young as possible.

wine producer, concentrated around Binisalem in the centre, where the plantings are mainly of Manto Negro, giving dark strong wines. In the south, which is planted with the Fogoneu grape variety, fresh light wines with a fruity nose is common. José L. Ferrer is a well-known producer of good *Reserva* and *Gran Reserva* wines.

The Canaries have generally uninteresting wines, the wine from Tenerife to be drunk as cold as possible.

ACCOMMODATION IN SPAIN

Accommodation in Spain is inspected, classified, and price-regulated by the tourist authorities. Star ratings, clearly displayed on blue signs outside all classified establishments, are a guide only to minimum facilities provided, not to any aesthetic merit or attractiveness. The *Guía de Hoteles* is an annually produced list of all graded accommodation in Spain, though the regional lists available locally are more convenient to carry than this weighty tome.

At the top of the range, **hotels** (*hoteles*, signed **H**), range from 1 to 5 stars. The state-run chain of *paradores* (see below) are all classed as 3, 4, or 5-star hotels. Cheaper, and obviously simpler, are **boarding houses** (*hostales*, signed **Hs**), graded from 1 to 3 stars. (As a rough guide, a three-star *hostal* is about the same price and standard as a one-star *hotel*.) Hotel-residencias (**HR**), or *hostal-residencias* (**HsR**), are similar to *hoteles* and *hostales*, but have no restaurants and provide breakfast only, or no meals at all. *Hotel apartamentos* or *aparthoteles* (**HA**), rated from 1 to 4 keys, are apartment blocks with some hotel facilities found mostly in coastal resorts. Villas, bungalows and apartments in resorts can be rented locally if space is available (and you can sometimes drive a hard bargain if it is!), though most owners deal through tour operators and letting agencies.

Further down the range, *pensiones* (**P**), *fondas* (**F**), and *casas de huespedes* (**CH**), are all very simple types of guesthouse with correspondingly basic facilities. Other low-priced unclassified accommodation is sometimes available in popular holiday areas; ask at the tourist office for *casas particulares* (private houses), or look out for the signs *camas* (beds) or *habitaciones* (rooms). Here you will be staying and eating in Spanish homes, an excellent way of experiencing local life and customs. Recently, a scheme of *casas de labranza* (farmhouses) has been set up to cater for visitors wanting stay-put rural holidays: these range from old manor houses and small palaces, to farm buildings developed for tourism in scenic areas throughout Spain. Some are self-catering units (like French *gites*); in others you stay *en famille*. So far, the system is embryonic, and operates solely on direct booking, but the Spanish Tourist Office in London can provide you with lists of addresses to contact, or you can ask at local tourist offices in Spain. Most *casas de labranza* are in the north (Cantabria, Asturias and Galicia) and are very popular (i.e. likely to be booked up) with Spaniards and other European visitors in July and August.

If you get completely stuck without a place to stay, ask in a bar or shop; someone will usually be able to help you out. If you are approached by a tout (a common practice at bus and train stations), make sure you see the room (and agree on the price) before you take it. In university towns, you can often pick up student rooms very cheaply out of term-time. Monasteries (and occasionally convents too) sometimes accept overnight guests, usually single -sex and predominantly male, though accommodation is intended for people seeking to share the spiritual life rather than casual tourists: you must of course respect the rules of the Order while you are there.

Camping is permissible outside the hundreds of registered *campings* (campsites) as long as no fires, damage or nuisance are caused. You cannot camp within a kilometre of a village or town, or near sites of scenic or historic importance. The *Guía Oficial de Campings* gives a full list of campsites. If you are hiking in mountain areas, you can stay very cheaply in *refugios* (mountain huts) – take a sleeping bag. These are usually very basic shelters from the stormy blast, but some are surprisingly comfortable.

Despite the huge number and range of places to stay, accommodation is patchily dispersed. On the Mediterranean Costas, row upon row of concrete blocks stand forlornly waiting for tourists; in some Basque coastal villages, you may have a Hobson's Choice of one grim *fonda*. The Costa Brava is studded with campsites; elsewhere they are much less evident.

Hotel prices in Spain have risen sharply over the last few years, but they are still generally cheaper than the equivalent facilities would cost in Britain. Accommodation is nearly always priced per room, not per person, and since there are only a few single rooms, travelling alone can be quite expensive. Discounts for single occupancy are carefully specified by tourist authorities on the tariff, which by law must be prominently displayed in the reception area. When booking a room, check whether meals, or taxes are included (many hotels quote room-only rates without tax). In 1991, IVA (VAT) was levied at six per cent in mainland Spain and the Balearics (12 per cent in 5-star hotels); the Canaries have a sales tax (ITE) of four per cent. Bathrooms, balconies and sea views may also add to the price of a room. Usually three seasonal rates are listed on the tariff (*temporada alta, media* and *baja*). In the Canaries, and in ski resorts, winter is high season, not summer. Christmas, New Year and Holy Week are high-season periods too. Special *fiestas* such as San Fermín in Pamplona can cause tariffs to rocket, and tourist office price controls seem to go by the board. Some popular coastal hotels refuse single-night bookings in high season, and insist on half-board. A thin season means a buyer's market, however, and it is well worth asking nicely for a discount if a hotel is obviously not full.

When you arrive in a hotel, be ready to surrender your passport at reception. This will be returned to you when the necessary forms have been completed (don't forget it!). Just sign (*firmar*) the slip they hand to you; the hotel will do the rest. All hotels are required to have complaint forms (*hojas de reclamaciones*) available, on which disgruntled guests may inscribe comments for presentation to the Tourist Board, like a school report. In practice no one actually uses them; if you have a complaint the hotel will not resolve, tell the local tourist office.

One of the most annoying features of Spanish hotels is poor insulation. Spain is a notoriously noisy country, and modern construction methods often give the impression that hotel walls are made of cardboard. Even if a hotel is in a quiet location, and you have sensibly asked for *una habitación tranquilla* (a quiet room), your nights may still be disturbed when your neighbours crash in late slamming the doors, turn on all plumbing devices, and start snoring! If you are a light sleeper, take ear-plugs.

Paradores

A *parador* is an inn – literally, a stopping place. The term is now reserved almost exclusively for Spain's unique state-run chain of hotels. There are now 83 of these scattered in scenic spots and historic towns throughout Spain (plus three *hosterías* which are restaurants only), and they are enormously popular. The scheme was started in 1926 by the Marquis of Vega-Inclan, then Royal Tourist Commissioner. The first *parador* opened in 1928 on a site in the Gredos hills chosen by King Alfonso XIII. The idea of *paradores* was to establish and subsidise accommodation in areas where it would not be profitable for private enterprise to do so, wherever possible, converting existing buildings of historic interest.

So today you can stay in castles, monasteries, palaces, or pilgrim hostels that have played a part in Spain's colourful past. But not all *paradores* are in historic buildings. Some are purpose-built in traditional styles to match their surroundings; others are uncompromisingly modern in design. All *paradores*, however, are chosen for their attractive locations. There are few in large cities, and none in Madrid.

Despite the variations of architectural style, the internal design of *paradores* is very carefully controlled, and all have to meet high standards of cleanliness and facilities. In the past this 'quality control' has resulted in a certain predictability in *paradores*; furnishings in many are apparently dragged from some centralised lumber-room. Occasionally too, the dead hand of state-run enterprise has shown through, with undermotivated, off-hand staff revealing a 'jobsworth' attitude to their work. Recently the administration of the *paradores* has changed: a more business-like approach, and a steady programme of renovation, may sweep away a few bureaucratic cobwebs. In most *paradores*, you will find someone who speaks English.

Paradores vary enormously in size as well as in style: the smallest have only half a dozen bedrooms; the largest hundreds of rooms. Occupancy rates fluctuate a great deal: in many you will find rooms to spare at short notice, but if you have your heart set on a particularly popular location, it is wise to book as far ahead as you can. July and August are the busiest months on the mainland. Among the most popular *paradores* are Toledo, Segovia, Granada, Santillana del Mar and Carmona. Special events (congresses, *fiestas*, etc.) can put great pressure on certain *paradores*: Andalucian and Catalan *paradores* are likely to be especially busy during 1992 when Spain will be receiving huge numbers of visitors for the World Fair in Seville and the Olympic Games in Barcelona. In any case, it is always worth checking in advance whether a particular *parador* is actually open: at any one time, several may be closed for renovation.

Any *parador* in Spain will make a reservation in another *parador* for you; just ask at reception. You can also book from the UK, through Keytel International, 402 Edgware Road, London W2 1ED (Tel 071–402 8182/Fax 071–724 9503), who charge a £6 fee per booking (regardless of how complex your itinerary is). You can get a complete brochure of *paradores* and prices, from Keytel, or from the Spanish Tourist Office.

Food is an important feature of most *paradores*, and they are a good place to look out for regional cuisine. Standards are not consistent throughout the chain, however, and eating in *paradores* can work out quite expensive. Breakfast consists of an elaborate buffet where you can eat as much as you like (though most *paradores* take a dim view of guests snaffling a lunch-time picnic out of the breakfast room). The three *hosterías* (restaurant-only *paradores*) at Pedraza (Segovia), Alcalá de Henares (Madrid), and Cruz de Tejeda (Gran Canaria) serve particularly good food.

A touring holiday in Spain would not be complete without sampling at least one *parador*. If you stay and eat in *paradores* all the time, however, you will spend quite a lot of money. It is not the cheapest, or necessarily the most interesting way to see Spain, and an uninterrupted diet of *paradores* can become monotonous, even a little institutional. You will have more contact with local people if you vary your stays, making a careful selection of attractive *paradores*, but ignoring mediocre ones and choosing simpler accommodation. Some pleasant hotels offer much better value than nearby *paradores*, and we point these out in the *Where to stay* sections at the end of each chapter.

New *paradores* will soon be opened in Seville, Cangas de Onís (Asturias), and Cuenca.

Top twenty paradores

Below we list the *paradores* we consider the best of their type, considering location and setting, food and service, and architecture or décor. It is a difficult choice.

Castles: Sigüenza, Baiona, Villalba, Alarcón, Carmona
Palaces: Gomera, Ubeda
Convents/monasteries: Trujillo, Chinchón, Almagro, Granada
Regional style: Tuy, Arcos de la Frontera, Sos del Rey Católico
Modern: Toledo, Aiguablava, Vich, Seo de Urgel

Two *paradores* deserve a special mention. The pilgrim hostels on the Way of St James, the **Hostal de los Reyes Católicos** at Santiago de Compostela, and the **Hostal de San Marcos** at León, have both recently become members of the *parador* group, and are its only five-star hotels. Truly luxurious and of immense historic interest, they are inevitably expensive, but a night at either of them will be unforgettable. If you cannot afford to stay there, at least have a look at them while you are in town.

GALICIA

LUSH and hilly, with a coastline slashed with fjords and thrashed by the Atlantic, Galicia is rural, wooded with pines and eucalypti. The fjords are called *rías*, river estuaries which are glassy at high tide, scummy with mud and silt at low, and shelter fishing villages and sandy coves. Between the *rías*, exposed to the Atlantic, are expanses of white dunes and bleak rocky headlands. Along the north and north-west coast the sea of the Rías Altas (upper estuaries) is frequently whipped up by winds and storms; along the west, the Rías Bajas (lower estuaries) are deeper and calmer, with little islands lying just offshore.

Inland, the city of Santiago de Compostela is one of the loveliest in Spain. During the Middle Ages it was the focus of a most important pilgrimage, for it holds the remains of St James the Apostle (Santiago) in its tremendous cathedral. Pilgrims still come, along with visitors from all over the world.

In the rest of the interior, the land is sparsely populated, few of the towns or villages are interesting, and the mountains are not as exciting as the ranges elsewhere in Spain. The best landscapes are in the south of the region – the gorge formed by the River Sil and the lazily flowing River Miño on the border with Portugal.

Galicia is the wettest region in Spain, but the rain keeps the countryside green throughout the summer, nurturing moss, lichen and sprigs of wild flowers on churches and houses built of the local honey-coloured granite. In common with other parts of Northern Spain, many houses have *solanas* – glazed, white-painted balconies, often with intricately carved frames.

There are no big resorts, only low-key developments on some of the larger beaches, and small resorts in pretty seaside towns such as Baiona, Muros and Viveiro. The provincial capital of Pontevedra deserves a couple of days.

Many of the fishing villages look scruffy – Porto do Barqueiro and Corcubión are exceptions – but watching the daily routine of the fishing communities can be an engrossing pastime. Most quaysides have an ice-making factory, market and storage cabins where you can see fishermen mending nets in the afternoons. When the catch arrives, each boat crew sorts its fish and displays them in trays of ice. Fish company agents then crowd into the cold, clammy market hall for the auction, run by a local council official. The fish are weighed and packed into vans to be delivered all over Spain – though plenty find their way on to the menus of local restaurants.

Other fishy activities you will see are people prising goose barnacles (*percebes*) – they are considered a delicacy and are eaten raw – off rocks at low tide. The strange rafts moored in the *rías* are for cultivating mussels. They are anchored to the sea bed by cables: as there is nothing else for the mussels to cling to in the deep waters, they choose the cables.

The region has three large ports: La Coruña, with a crescent of *solana*-fronted houses sweeping along its water-front; Vigo, with a hard-edged nightscene, and Ferrol, a major naval base and birthplace of Franco.

Galicians consider their best beaches to be the Playa de la Lanzada, a short drive from Pontevedra, and the Playa América, outside Baiona. These can get very busy, especially in August and at summer weekends; you might prefer slightly less popular beaches such as the Playa de Mogor, across the *ría* from Pontevedra, the Playa de Area near Viveiro and the Playa de Xilloi over the water from Porto do Barqueiro.

Galicia and its people

Galicia is a fairly old-fashioned, undeveloped region, and many of its inhabitants still live in small villages, attempting to make a living from the sea and their tiny plots of land. The region is, and has been for centuries, one of the poorest in Spain, largely ignored by the rest of the country and receiving little attention or aid from central government. Ancient inheritance laws demanded that a family's land was divided equally between the children, resulting in minute plots – *mini-fundios* – crammed with potatoes, maize and turnips, and canopied with vines. Nowadays children usually agree that all the land should go to one of them, and in return each will be given a share of the produce, which is more often than not an annual supply of home-made wine, *vino país*.

Galicia has some industry, and as well as the traditional canning factories there are large industrial estates around the ports of La Coruña and Vigo. But industry cannot provide for everyone, and few fishermen survive solely on the income from the impoverished seas. Some supplement it with smug-gling, but more often they work abroad, in Switzerland, the USA, Britain or South America: there are said to be more Galicians in Buenos Aires than in Galicia, but nowadays few leave home permanently. Some go for five-month stints, others wait until they have enough money to build a house. The villages are full of houses built by the *emigrados* – classy *fin-de-siècle* villas and once-fashionable houses whose tiled

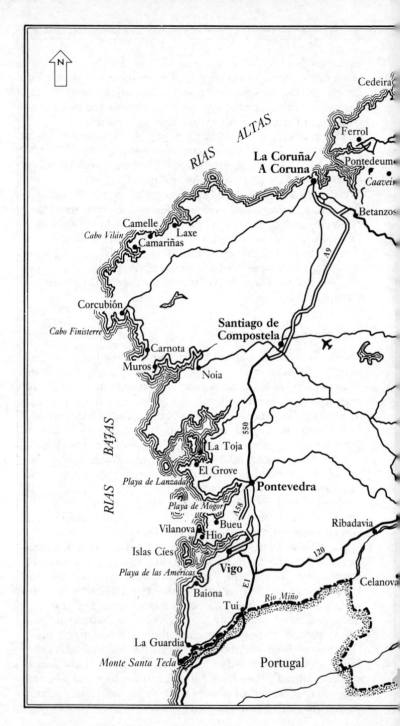

53

façades range from the watery yellows and blues of the '50s to the snazzy op art designs of the '60s. Don't be surprised, either, to see a cowboy lookalike in a stetson lording it in a bar, or women dressed country-and-western style at the weekly market.

Planning your holiday

You will get the best out of the region if you tour in a pottering sort of way, lazing by this or that beach, watching daily life in the fishing villages or visiting the handful of monasteries or churches whose solitary locations are more than half of their attraction. A few days in Santiago de Compostela are a must – the city is also good for a weekend break. Santiago itself can get very crowded with tourists from all over the world, but elsewhere the region is quiet: the majority of tourists are Spanish and Portuguese.

Galicia's rain and the Atlantic winds ensure that the region rarely gets unbearably hot, so it is a good choice for a mid-summer holiday. There will be rainy days even in July and August and days when it is too breezy to spend long hours on the beach – another good reason for touring.

July is a good time to go, too, if you want to see the celebrations of the Virgen del Carmen (patron of sailors and fishermen) on 16 July and head to Santiago for St James's day, 25 July. On 16 July there will be festivities of some sort in most of the fishing villages – often the fishing boats will be draped in streamers, chugging upstream to an ear-splitting accompaniment of fire-crackers. A statue of the Virgin will feature somewhere, but you are more likely to feel that you are in a battle zone. In Santiago there is a firework display on the night of 24 July, with the symbolic burning of a cardboard cut-out of the mosque at Córdoba, and there are more pyrotechnics at Mass on 25 July with the swinging of the giant incense burner. The day is a holiday throughout Galicia, and has been appropriated by Galician separatists, so there are likely to be street demonstrations.

Galicia is also a good choice if you want to explore a region on public transport, largely because the distinctive traditions of Galician village life mean waiting for buses is rarely dull. In addition, if you plan carefully, you can always end up within walking distance of a beach. There are buses to most fishing villages, though sometimes only one daily, and as there are no complete

The propensity to travel has been put down to the Galicians' Celtic blood (Celts from Central Europe swamped the region in the sixth century BC). It actually has more to do with economic realities. The real legacy of the Celts is to be seen in the bagpipe (*gaita*) which is also found in neighbouring

---

timetables you often have to rely on the driver for information about connections.

A RENFE (Spanish State Railways) train line runs from La Coruña to Vigo via Santiago; another line runs from just outside Tui, to Orense, Lugo and Ferrol – which you might want to use to get to Ribas de Sil; and there are about two trains daily running along the (mostly) coastal FEVE (privately owned narrow gauge railway) line from El Ferrol to Oviedo, usefully stopping at fishing villages such as O Barqueiro, Viveiro, Foz and Ribadeo.

If touring by car, you will find that few of the roads you will need to use are unsurfaced, though some, especially on the west coast, are slow. Many reasonably good roads are not marked on large-scale maps, so a reliable regional map, such as the Michelin *North West Spain*, 1:400 000, sheet 441, is essential. There are plenty of places to stay in Santiago and elsewhere in the region simple accommodation is not difficult to find. There are some pleasant *paradores*, and a number of attractive mid-price hotels in traditional granite houses – notably in Baiona.

A few tour operators offer packages with direct flights to Santiago, as well as fly-drive and *parador* touring holidays. For independent travellers there are daily scheduled flights from London Heathrow to Santiago. A once-weekly flight connects London Gatwick with the port of Vigo on the west coast.

If you decide to tour Galicia in your own car, via the Portsmouth-Santander ferry route, plan on spending a couple of days at least crossing Cantabria and Asturias, as there is plenty to see in these regions.

*Regional Tourist Board: Secretaria Xeral Para O Turismo, Plaza de Mazarelos 15, 15703 Santiago de Compostela, Tel (981) 56 41 00. Most of the information issued is in Spanish, but they have a useful guide giving a complete list of all types of accommodation in Galicia. Useful **tourist information offices** are in La Coruña (Dársena de la Marina), Santiago de Compostela (Rua del Villar 43), Ribadeo (Plaza de España), Pontevedra (General Mola 3) and Tui (Puente Tripes).

Asturias, and in the region's dolmens and Celtic settlements, none of which, save the fortified village on Monte Tecla, is likely to excite anyone but enthusiasts.

Though consciousness of the Celtic ancestry may lie at the root of Galician nationalism, the current movement is more often inspired by dissatisfaction with central government. There are patriotic graffiti everywhere and hardly a street or road sign the spelling of which has not been messily changed from *castellano* (Spain's official language) to *gallego*. *Gallego* is a living language, not a dialect, spoken by about 85 per cent of the region's population, despite being banned by Franco (himself a Galician). It sounds rather like a cross between *castellano* and Portuguese. Unlike *catalán*, which is spoken by Catalans of all classes, *gallego* is the language of the worker and peasant.

Nationalism is also expressed by a rather romantic return to traditional values. *Hórreos*, granaries built on stilts to protect the contents from damp and rats, and the local granite rock, have both become symbols of Galician independence. Those who can afford it now build houses of granite using traditional methods, and some even build a miniature *hórreo* in their garden. More startling, perhaps, is the anti-eucalyptus lobby. Central government has covered Galicia with the trees, because they grow quickly and provide a swift return on investment. Unfortunately they also consume vast quantities of water, and multiply madly, drying out the soil and smothering the indigenous pines – which are also set to become a symbol of Galician nationalism.

SANTIAGO DE COMPOSTELA (H)

Home to the remains of St James the Apostle, and focus of one of the most important medieval pilgrimages, Santiago de Compostela today attracts as many tourists as pilgrims. It is one of the most beautiful and distinctive cities in Spain, with streets paved and churches and palaces built of a golden–grey, mineral–flecked granite. Apart from the cathedral, a museum and a couple of churches, most of what you will want to see is outdoors. You could easily spend hours taking in the exuberance of the cathedral's various façades, and at least half a day sitting in cafés, or wandering narrow, partially arcaded pedestrianised streets and browsing in the market and quirky shops. The tourist-pilgrim industry flourishes in the form of shops selling St James bottle-openers, St James cigarette-lighters, and plastic monks. But they also sell, as they have for centuries, scallop shells, gourds and jet votive offerings. The knowledge that the commercialism is nothing new somehow makes it all easier to accept.

Santiago is saved from being simply picturesque and touristy by its university. Feminist, anarchist and socialist graffiti are scrawled across many a wall, students swot among the tourists in cafés, and street stalls sell hippy jewellery and hookah pipes. Every night buskers fill the streets with the sounds of Vivaldi, jazz and folk music. The players of the latter are grouped into bands of medievally dressed strolling minstrels known as *tunas*, who entertain tourists with foot-tapping tunes on bagpipes, accordions, guitars and tambourines.

At the same time Santiago gets on with ordinary life, if in a rather old-fashioned way. There are haberdashers, gents' out-fitters, milliners and little dark grocery shops, and you will still see women carrying shopping bags on their heads, queuing to have knives sharpened by the grinder at a daily market where tiny stalls selling pulses, cheeses and cooked meats are tucked between the hanging carcasses of pigs.

Surrounding the old quarter is a modern town built on a grid plan, which you only need pass through as you arrive and depart. Getting your bearings in old Santiago is no problem. The cathedral is surrounded by four *plazas*, and leading south are three roughly parallel streets, Calle de Franco, and Ruas del Villar and Nueva, linked at intervals by alleyways.

Eating out and accommodation

There are lots of bars and restaurants on Calle de Franco, though you might prefer the less frenzied ambience of Suso, Rua del Villar 65, and the vintage décor of Derby, Calle Huerfanes 26. Santiago's most famous restaurant (and one of its cheapest) is El Asesino, an unmarked establishment opposite the university on Plaza de la Universidad. Other good options are Victoria, just off Calle de Franco at Calle Bautizados 5, which is known for its seafood, and the more upmarket Don Gaiferos, Rua Nueva 23, which offers Galician specialities as well as international fare. Be warned, though, that people dine very late, and even at 10.30pm you could find yourself alone in a restaurant.

The old town is full of simple *hostales* and rooms in houses and except on and around 25 July you should not have too many problems finding somewhere to sleep as long as you are not too fussy. If you can afford it, it is worth splashing out to stay in the Hostal de los Reyes Católicos (see Where to stay, p. 90). There are some rather characterless three-star hotels in the modern town, used by tour operators, such as the large Hotel Gelmirez, Hórreo 92, Tel (981) 56 11 00, conveniently sited just outside the old quarter.

Exploring the town

Plaza del Obradoiro, a vast pedestrianised quadrangle, is a splendid introduction to Santiago. Vendors demonstrate flying plastic pigeons, old ladies feed real pigeons, becloaked musicians hawk Galician folk cassettes and tourists look awestruck at the cathedral's main façade. A vivacious baroque pyramid of scrolls, volutes and statues of St James, flanked by two florid bell-towers, it was added to the original Romanesque cathedral in 1750. Adjoining is the **Palacio de Gelmirez**, Romanesque home of Santiago's first archbishop, Diego Gelmirez, who was responsible for rebuilding the cathedral, constructing the city's water system, and 'discovering' a ninth-century document which demanded that a bushel of corn be donated annually to St James from every acre of land reconquered from the Moors. The palace is not particularly interesting, just a series of dank, empty vaulted rooms echoing to the cry of birds, with views up to the soaring bell-tower next door.

Standing at a right-angle to the cathedral, the **Hostal de los Reyes Católicos** was founded by Isabella and Fernando in the early sixteenth century as a hospice for sick and poor pilgrims, and largely funded by the profitable seizure of Granada from the Moors in 1492. On its plateresque portal an extravaganza of masks, foliage and urns provides a sumptuous setting for statues of saints (along with Adam and Eve modestly concealing their genitals). It is now a luxurious *parador* – if you cannot afford to stay, ask about guided tours.

Heading clockwise around the cathedral, you reach **Plaza de la Azabachería** (Square of the jet-makers), where pilgrims used to buy jet souvenirs before entering the cathedral. Today most shops sell the usual ecclesiastical kitsch, though a couple of shops on Calle Azabachería still specialise in jet statuettes and votive offerings.

The monks of the **Monasterio de San Martín Pinero** above the *plaza* used to give new clothes to ragged pilgrims following the example of their patron saint, who is credited with cutting his cloak in half to clothe a beggar – the statue of him on the pediment shows him doing precisely this. The monastery is currently undergoing restoration, but when it reopens it should be worth going inside to see a reputedly excessive altarpiece by the architect of the Obradoiro façade.

Continuing around the cathedral you reach the **Plaza de la Quintana**, a stage-like space on two levels linked by steps. Students sit on the steps, studying or watching the children below roller-skating and hula-hooping to a whining soundtrack of Galician bagpipe music from a record shop. Above the square is the cathedral's **Puerta Santa**, which is opened only in Holy Years. Flanking it are 24 apostles, removed from a Romanesque choir carved by Maestro Mateo, architect of the Puerta de la Gloria.

Round the corner from Plaza de la Quintana, **Plaza de las Platerías** is the last and most intimate of the four cathedral squares, overlooked by the intricately carved Romanesque door, the Puerta de las Platerías, named after the silversmiths who once worked in the square – their descendants still sell jewellery, crucifixes and religious souvenirs in the arcade shops. The door's carvings are well worth a close look, for they include such bizarre and questionable images as a winged, hunchback monkey and a woman giving birth to a skull.

The main sights

● **The cathedral** In the cathedral, Santiago's tourists and pilgrims meet head on. Pilgrims attending Mass do so to an audience of gawping, chattering holiday-makers, who, as the host is blessed, have been known to hurtle down the nave and squat, paparazzi-style, in front of the altar, dazzling the scarlet-clad ecclesiastics with camera flashes.

The cathedral is entered through the magnificent **Pórtico de la Gloria**, the twelfth-century west front, which now lies behind the Obradoiro façade. Do not be perturbed if the first thing you see is a queue of people waiting to knock their heads against the central column – the sculptor, Maestro Mateo, carved himself crouching at its base, and there is a long-standing superstition that if you bump your head against Mateo's, some of his talent will rub off on you. Mateo was something of a medieval trail-blazer, decorating the three arches with relaxed and realistic characters instead of the usual stiff, chunky figures.

The central arch is dominated by a huge figure of Christ, flanked by the four Apostles and eight angels bearing the instruments of the Passion – the lashes with which Christ was whipped, the cross, the sponge, the lance and nails, the crown of thorns, and the bowl in which Pilate washed his hands. Tightly packed above the heads of the angels are 40 figures

THE SANTIAGO PILGRIMAGE

In the Middle Ages the shrine of St James at Santiago de Compostela was almost as popular a destination as the Spanish costas today. Between half a million and two million pilgrims from all over Europe visited it each year, some seduced by the promise of receiving a signed document, or indulgence, thereby halving their time in purgatory, others seeking adventure, marriage, business or, like the poet Villon, opportunities for crime. The first-ever guidebook was written in the twelfth century by a monk, Aymery Picaud, to help the pilgrims on their way; it detailed the most interesting routes, the best places to stay and the customs of various countries. There were many ways to Santiago through France and northern Spain, jointly known as the Camino de Santiago; the most popular went through Pamplona, Burgos and León. Nowadays many of the former pilgrims' paths have become modern roads, with blue roadside panels marked by a scallop shell describing the various stages and sights of the *Camino*. There are useful little lay-bys in which you can park your car and read these.

People of all classes were attracted to Santiago. English peasants had to get permission to go from their feudal lords – usually granted only on the understanding that they returned before the harvest – and were often helped financially by their neighbours. Once on the road, they actually needed little money, for the route was punctuated with monasteries and hospices which provided free food and shelter, although anyone who could afford it was expected to make a donation. Nor did the pilgrims carry much with them. Traditional dress was a *sclavine* or long tunic, sandals, a broad-brimmed felt hat, a *scip* or wallet, a gourd to carry water and a long staff. Equally important was the scallop shell, the symbol of St James, which could also serve as a begging bowl (and as modern pilgrims have discovered, a plate, cup and shaving dish).

The cult of St James
There is absolutely no reason to believe that St James ever visited Spain, let alone that his corpse ended up in Galicia. It is claimed

representing those saved by Christ's death, and sitting around the arch playing musical instruments sit the 24 Elders of the Apocalypse. Directly below Christ, St James acts as intercessor, standing on a column carved with Christ's family tree, the tree of Jesse. In its roots are five shiny indentations, formed by millions of pilgrims pressing their fingers on the

---

that he came to Spain to spread the gospel some time between the Crucifixion and his martyrdom in Jerusalem in AD44. According to legend, two of his disciples removed his corpse to Jaffa, and a boat without sails or crew miraculously appeared and carried them across to the port of Padrón, 20 kilometres south of Santiago, in seven days. The body was buried, and forgotten until the year 813 when the grave was pointed out to Theodimir, the Bishop of Padrón (or to a hermit or a band of shepherds), by a star.

The rediscovery could not have been more timely. During the previous century the whole of Spain, apart from the northern kingdom of Asturias, had been overrun by Moors, who, fighting in the name of Muhammad, introduced the idea of a Holy War to the West. The Christians had their own champion, and it was not long before the saint proved his fitness for the job by personally slaying 60,000 Moors at the Battle of Clavijo (now in La Rioja). The Bible's preaching fisherman thus earned himself the surname Matamoros, or Moor-slayer, and came to be depicted on churches as a knightly scourge of the Arabs.

A church was built on the site of the discovery of the grave, and as word of the saint's military exploits filtered across Europe, the pilgrims began to arrive. There were enough kings and aristocrats among the pilgrims to make it a lucrative business for the Church.

The pilgrimage came to an abrupt end in 1589 when Francis Drake attacked La Coruña, and the Bishop of Compostela hid the remains of the saint in Santiago cathedral. In fact they were so well hidden that they were not found until 1879 by a workman. The question of authenticity was swiftly settled – there was a nick in the saint's skull and a sliver of his bone in Rome turned out to be a perfect match for it – and the relics were immediately blessed by the Pope. The pilgrimage flourished again, and even today pilgrims come from all over the world, especially in Holy Years, when the saint's feast day, 25 July, falls on a Sunday. Indulgences are granted and Santiago once more is visited by two million pilgrims. The best reminders of the medieval *Camino* are in Estella, Sanguesa and Puente la Reina (Navarra, page 159); Suso (La Rioja, page 163); León and Astorga (Castile-León, page 468).

column, a ritual that persists today. Supporting the pillars of the central arch are four Prophets and four Apostles, who still bear traces of paint, and include a smiling Daniel and John. The scenes above the two outer arches represent the Jews waiting for the Messiah, and the Last Judgement, where children are devoured by monsters and the sinners include a glutton munching an *empanada* (a typical Galician pie) and a drunkard glugging wine from a skin.

The plainness of the interior draws your eyes straight to the **high altar**, a sumptuous frenzy of gilt and silver surmounted by a Moor-slaying St James on horseback. In front of the altar is a Heath Robinsonish rope-and-pulley system from which, on special occasions, the world's largest censer, or *botafumeiro*, is swung in a great arc above the heads of the congregation, the wind whistling through its vents as it trails sparks and blue clouds of incense. The origin of this ecclesiastical circus is unclear, but it is thought that it was introduced either to outdo Rome or to fumigate the cathedral in the days when pilgrims slept inside. In six hundred years of use there have been only four accidents, most dramatically in 1499 when the censer broke free and flew out of the Platerías door. No one was hurt.

For true pilgrims, the serious climax to their journey is a visit to the thirteenth-century painted statue of St James enthroned behind the altar. Worshippers climb the stairs, embrace the statue, kiss his jewel-studded gown, and make a donation to the guard, for which they are given a printed prayer. Most tourists who take part in the ritual emerge looking distinctly uneasy. St James's bones are kept below the statue in a crypt which is sometimes used by pilgrim groups for services.

Disappointingly, given the status of the cathedral, its treasury and museums are poor and badly labelled. Access to the cloister, tapestry museum, archaeological museum, library and crypt of the portico is by ticket only. However, it is worth the low price to stand in the sober cloister for a view up to the towers, see the *botafumeiro* in the library, and to walk through the tapestry museum to a balustrade along the Obradoiro façade. The ticket also allows you to visit the vaulted crypt which Mateo built below the Pórtico de la Gloria.

● **Santo Domingo: Museo do Pobo Gallego** A well-displayed collection of Galician crafts housed in an old convent with a remarkable triple spiral staircase. The exhibits are only labelled and explained in *gallego* so the English-language guide on sale at the ticket desk is indispensable. If you have spent any time in Galicia's fishing villages, you will want to see the section devoted to the sea, with restored fishing boats, hempen fishing nets and faded photographs of old boats. The section on popular architecture details the different types of Galician houses. Elsewhere there are displays of crafts ranging from lace-making and basketry to those of *zogueiros* or clog-makers, *carboeiros* or charcoal-burners, and *cantorleiros*, who travelled from village to village repairing earthenware with wire.

● **Santa María del Sar** In a dusty yard on the edge of town, where children play football and the old lady caretaker spends her days sewing at the door of the cloisters, stands the quirky Romanesque church of Santa María del Sar. The reason for its immense arched buttresses becomes clear when you go inside to see the dramatic slant of the walls and columns, caused by the vaults pushing down too heavily. The interior is so damp that moss grows on the columns, above a painted statue of St James with a bruised leg. In the partially restored cloisters a TV aerial protrudes above the tiny, richly carved capitals.

THE RIAS ALTAS

Ribadeo (H)

This modest fishing port on the west bank of the Ría de Ribadeo has the charm of decay. On houses eroded by time and weather, ochre-washed plaster has crumbled to reveal multi-hued stone; paint has faded to a ghostly stain, balconies have rusted and slate roofs are carpeted with lichen and weeds.

From the gardens of Plaza de España, dominated by the burnished copper domes of a flamboyant folly, narrow streets descend steeply to the waterfront. You can have lunch here, on the raised terrace of the Mesón Andarica, watching small craft gliding silently up the *ría* under the concrete spans of the road bridge. On most days you will also see fishermen disentangling slithery fish from reams of net, and passengers gingerly stepping on to the tiny open boat that plies across the water to the villages of Castropol and Figueras.

A short drive or walk along the estuary takes you to the

castle of **San Domain**, its rubbly ruins rising on a rocky spit. The castle is currently being restored, but if the workmen are there they will let you in and you can stand on a turret and look down at golden seaweed swaying in the limpid turquoise water between sharp tongues of striated rock. The serrated coastline continues north to the lighthouse, below which is a tiny, sheltered rocky cove – ideal if you have children who want to splash about.

There are half a dozen basic *hostales* in Ribadeo and a pleasant, peaceful *parador*. You might, however, consider staying in the opulent hotel Palacete de Peñalba, across the *ría* in Figueras (see Asturias, Where to stay, page 128).

The good beaches near Ribadeo are at Tapia de Casariego across the border in Asturias, and an exciting, unnamed beach reached along a rough road from the village of Rinlo, to the west. White sand is backed by jagged rocks, and boulders lie offshore at crazy diagonals forming a small splashy bay.

San Martín de Mondoñedo

In a sleepy hamlet two and a half kilometres inland from Foz (not somewhere you will want to dawdle), the massively buttressed eleventh-century church of San Martín de Mondoñedo is worth a visit. An eroded crucifix outside shows the Crucifixion in four stages – you can just make out Christ on the cross, a *pietà* group, and a headscarved Mary. Inside are ghostly frescoed images of the Magi and shepherds, and some imaginatively sculpted capitals – notably one with Adam and Eve giving themselves the heads of beasts (representing their post-Fall animality) and another with Lazarus rising from the dead at a jolly feast. If you speak Spanish, it is worth asking the *padre* to show you around.

Viveiro (H) and Playa de Area (H)

Glimpses of flaking ochre *plazas* and irregular perspectives of wrought-iron balconies and jutting *solanas* lure you through Viveiro's narrow streets. Jazz riffs, pop beats and video-game bleeps get louder as you approach a restaurant, bar or amusement hall, then fade to a small-town quiet of chirping canaries and clattering cutlery. Children play and pigeons scratch around a Romanesque church, a grand mansion houses a small shopping centre (its escutcheon standing proudly above a display of flimsy lingerie) and the splendid Gothic apse of San Francisco backs on to a dusty sports-pitch.

Viveiro stands on its *ría*, a tangle of narrow streets on the hill behind the glassed-in balconies on the waterfront. The coast road runs straight through, so if you elect to drink at one of the three pavement cafés for a view across the water, you will have to shout to make yourself heard above the rattling lorries and zipping cars. And if you want to take a good look at the elaborate coat of arms on the Carlos V gateway which gives access to the old town, be prepared to risk standing in the middle of the road.

The port is just outside the town, at **Celeiro**. It is backed by tuna and sardine canneries, with the standard quayside arrangement of fishermen's huts, a market and an ice factory, as well as a gutsy little bar. If it is the first sizeable fishing port on your tour, you might want to watch the catch arriving, fish being auctioned, or fishermen mending the nets on a dead afternoon.

The best nearby beach, on the Ría de Viveiro, is at **Playa de Area**; its pale-gold sand is backed by grassy dunes and sheltered by two promontories. The water is usually calm, there is a tiny islet offshore, and the river forms a small natural pool. There is a small campsite, a handful of villas and two good hotels, so it is a good place to stay if you want a couple of lazy days by the beach punctuated by trips into Viveiro.

Porto do Barqueiro (H) and around

West of Viveiro is the Ría do Barqueiro. Tucked into its wiggly eastern shore are two good beaches, and on the western bank is Galicia's loveliest fishing village, Porto do Barqueiro (O Barqueiro).

Playa Aerealonga is a fairly long crescent of fine white sand, backed by a row of smart little chalets, and has no facilities. Though it lies virtually at the head of the *ría*, its bay is sometimes stirred by Atlantic winds. The smaller crescent of **Playa de Xilloi**, beyond the straggly village of Vicedo, is less exposed, being sheltered by two rocky pine- and eucalyptus-crowned headlands and backed by low dunes sprinkled with wild flowers. It has a large restaurant-bar, and is popular with unofficial campers.

In **Porto do Barqueiro** whitewashed houses, with fish-scale slate roofs, are stacked above a small harbour; fishing nets and lobster pots are piled up along the quayside by a single petrol pump; and tiny fishing boats bob on the wind-ruffled water. It is a great place in which to do nothing except wander the tight tangle of streets and steps and sit outside one of the waterfront cafés watching the villagers. If you need shops or a bank, there is a small new quarter above the old village, and if you want to stay overnight – or even base yourself here, there is one *pensión*.

From Porto do Barqueiro you can drive to the most northerly point in Spain – a lighthouse on the tip of the bleak **Estaca de Bares** peninsula. The wind has tortured blackened gorse into deformed bonsai; the gleaming, white helicopter blades of a wind-power station spin among bracken and heather; the village of Vila de Bares is surrounded by stunted crops; and pro-American graffiti are scribbled on a boulder outside the wire fence of a US military base. If you want to stop for lunch or a drink, there is a fish restaurant in **Porto de Bares** on the coast below Vila.

Ortigueira and Cabo Ortegal

Ortigueira stands on the Ría de Santa Marta, a dullish sort of village with a massive waterfront disco. It used to be the annual venue for an international festival of Celtic music, which was banned in 1989 when two people where killed in a fight. There is no particular reason to stop here, but there are two good beaches just outside the village: the **Playa de Ortigueira** is large, flat and sandy and the **Playa de Cabalar** is soft and backed by pines, with a large outdoor bar.

Opposite Ortigueira, the Sierra de la Capelada slips into the Atlantic, forming the west flank of the *ría* and the hazardous reef-fringed **Cabo Ortegal**. If you value the tyres and undercarriage of your car, do not approach this headland along the western shore of the *ría* (the road which heaves over the mountain is no more than a rubble track). Instead, take the C-646 to Cedeira, and from there drive along the mountain's forested flank.

Wild horses roam freely on upland meadows here – they are rounded up for branding, cowboy-style, into *curros*, or corrals, on the last Sunday in June. The corrals are beyond the Mirador Penedo Edroso (it is on a marked side road, from which there are great views), but you would be lucky to see a wild horse there.

Considerably more interesting at most times of the year is the bizarre village of **San Andrés de Teixido**, where a homespun tourist industry surrounds the cult of the obscure saint. The village is reached down a steeply snaking road and on San Andrés' feast day, 8 September, the (extremely) faithful mortify their flesh by shuffling down here on their knees. It is a tiny place where chickens scratch around make-shift stalls from which the locals sell home-made biscuits and souvenirs. Most intriguing are the strings of gaudily painted bread dough formed into the shape of a hand, a ship, a sardine, a flower and a crucifix, which are supposed to represent aspects of the saint's life. At the foot of the main, manure-encrusted cobbled street stands a peculiar building with crazy-paved walls. It contains a glittering altar, slot machine candles, and a motley array of wax arms, heads, feet, cows and kids. According to local legend (Galicia abounds with bizarre stories like this), all this activity is due to an ancient superstition that everyone must make the pilgrimage to San Andrés de Teixido at least once or else they will be reincarnated as an insect. Consequently, insects are treated with the utmost respect by pilgrims en route to this village, lest they be erstwhile humans.

The coast to Pontedeume (H)

A number of beaches with dunes nestle in the indented coast below Cedeira. The largest is at **Valdoviño**, a vast – and very popular – golden beach. The strong breakers do not make for lazy swimming. The eastern end, with a couple of restaurants, a campsite and a large car park, can get crowded, but the western end is quieter. Beyond Valdoviño the road cuts across the coastal hills to Ferrol. The large fishing village of Pontedeume, 17 kilometres beyond, is a far nicer place to linger. Though there is a lot of traffic passing through, it is a relaxed place, with a pretty waterfront of red-roofed houses with glazed balconies.

Time in the village is best spent watching the activity in the harbour, or joining off-duty fishermen in one of the water-front cafés. It is also worth checking out the temporary exhibitions in the medieval granite Torre de Andrade by the water's edge.

The **Playa de la Magdalena** lies across the *ría* from the village, a crescent of soft white sand in a sheltered bay backed by plane trees, with a couple of beach bars and a good, family-run hotel.

Like the Torre de Andrade, the **Castillo Andrade**, about five kilometres inland, was built by and named after the region's medieval rulers. The road winds up through pines and eucalypti to the lichen-mottled castle keep, rising austerely from the bracken and brambles. There is a path right the way up the walls, and there are good views on clear days. It is also a good place for a picnic – especially when you have the place to yourself and the only sounds are of bees, crickets and birds.

Even lovelier is the drive to the **Monasterio de Caaveiro**, along the limpid, tree-fringed River Eume. The road crosses the river and ends in a car park, from which a broad, leaf-vaulted track climbs up to the ruined twelfth-century church. High above the river and encircled by lush hills, the graffiti-covered shells of monastic buildings, a Romanesque apse and escutcheon-bearing tower stand among wild flowers, brambles and the remains of campfires. Some of the outbuildings are currently undergoing restoration, and are intended to house a café.

Betanzos

Standing among vine-clad hills, Betanzos was a port until the estuary silted up. It now provides a picturesque arena for the everyday events of Spanish provincial life. In the main square, amid the roar of traffic and surrounded by the chaos of glass, granite and whitewash, a farmer sells strings of garlic from the back of his battered lorry, watched by townspeople dressed for church sitting in pavement cafés; and old ladies nibble sesame biscuits and *churros* beneath a fountain of a green Diana.

Three medieval churches add focus to a wander in the old town. Calle Portal heads straight up from the *plaza* to the fifteenth-century **Santiago**, with St James in his Moor-slaying guise brandishing an axe and club on its granite façade. Back down the street, turn left at the Banco Pastor and along the main shopping street to **Santa María de Azogue**. On its lop-sided façade musicians form an arch above an Adoration, beasts wrestle on column capitals, and in niches on either side of the door an angel calmly informs a rigid Mary that she is about to become the Mother of God. Inside is a cheerfully painted St George killing a gruesomely fanged dragon. Directly below Santa María stands the fourteenth-century church of **San Francisco** where you can amuse yourself by seeing how many wild boar and bears you can spot. These were the heraldic beasts of the church's founder, Fernán Perez de Andrade, Lord of Betanzos and Pontedeume, and he had them carved all over the church. There's is a crucifix-holding boar on the roof, a bear and boar hunt carved on the walls of the high altar and on Andrade's tomb. The tomb itself is supported on the backs of two almost life-size beasts.

You will find neither boar nor bear on the menu of Betanzos' restaurants, but you can eat pretty well at Casanova on the main square, as long as you avoid the undercooked *tortilla*. There are only a couple of one-star hotels here, of which Los Angeles, Tel (981) 77 15 11, just off the main square, has simple but adequate rooms with bathrooms.

La Coruña (A Coruña, Corunna) (H)

On the fringes of Galicia's wealthiest city sheep graze alongside industrial estates, and tumbledown hovels squat below the walls of an oil refinery. In the city itself state-of-the-art tower blocks soar above flats, and an avenue entirely lined with glazed balconies overlooks oil cylinders, cranes and corroded cargo ships. The same contrasts are evident on the streets. Respectable citizens retire to the main square to sip aperitifs, demi-mondish youths sulk outside backstreet bars, and along the waterfront parents hurry their children past a fisherman spitting in the gutter.

La Coruña is known in British history books as Corunna, the town from which the Armada fleet of 130 ships and 29,000 men set sail in 1588, and limped back with a third of its ships destroyed and over half its men dead. A year later, Francis Drake was sent to attack the Spanish and Portuguese coasts – they fired on La Coruña, but the town was saved when a woman, María Pita, gave the alarm. She rapidly became a Galician hero, and the town's main square is named after her.

The city is a good place for an overnight stop, its veneer of elegance and buzz of life comes as a refreshing change if you have been touring small fishing villages. It is unlikely to hold you for any longer, however, as the local beaches are poor and it is not conveniently located for day-trips. As La Coruña is built upon a narrow isthmus it has two waterfronts. The western one holds the two long, rough sand beaches; the eastern, with the port and main avenue, is the focus of activity.

Strolling along Avenida de la Marina to the hilly streets and Romanesque churches of the old town is a good way to spend an evening. Start with a wander through the Jardines de Méndez Núñez, where willows, palms and magnolias form a voluptuous canopy. Stretching beyond are nineteenth-century houses with several upper storeys of *solanas*, now incorporating a motley array of banks, bars and cafés.

Running parallel to Avenida de la Marina, Calle Real, gaudily decked with flashing neon signs, is the main shopping street. Behind the sea-front hides Plaza María Pita, where the granite arcades and the flamboyantly pompous *ayuntamiento* form a civilised stage for pavement cafés; from here side streets take you across to the lovely Plaza General Azgarraga, shaded by plane trees. Close by stands the Romanesque church of Santiago, with St James on horseback above its portal. Up the hill is the more elaborate Santa María del Campo; Italianate, with its low-pitched façade and blind arcades, it has a smiling Adoration of the Magi carved above the door.

You will find many cheerful restaurants along the sea-front, or you could dress up and eat carefully prepared food among the muted voices and Muzak of exclusive Coral, Calle Estrella 2 Tel (981) 22 10 82. There are three or so impersonal business-style large hotels and plenty of simple little *hostales* in and around the old town.

The main sights

● **Torre de Hercules** A three-kilometre drive (or bus ride) to the tip of the isthmus will take you to reputedly the oldest lighthouse still in use in the world: it is Roman, dating from the second century AD, and encased in a baroque tower.

● **Castillo de San Antón** A sixteenth-century fortress, jutting into the sea at the head of the harbour, which now houses an archaeological museum. The courtyard holds some intriguing statues – notably a medieval pig bearing a crucifix – and half an arch of angel musicians, including one playing a *gaita*, a Galician bagpipe. Inside, highlights are the *cuadrafaz* – a stone carved with four faces, displayed on a rotating plinth – and a glorious collection of ancient jewellery. There are wonderful views from the parapets and tower.

Laxe (H) to Camariñas

Most of the fishing villages immediately west of La Coruña are predominantly modern, functional places. **Laxe**, however, on the south bank of the Ría de Corme y Laxe, is slowly developing into a resort, and has a long, sheltered beach. The promenade has been paved and planted with baby palm trees, and some houses in the old quarter are undergoing renovation – but it currently has only one hotel.

If you arrive in the late afternoon, you should head straight for its neat little harbour. On the quayside, overlooked by the sturdy apse of a Romanesque church, are tidy piles of nets with detergent containers and blocks of polystyrene as makeshift floats. Men and women sit outside the row of fishing huts, mending nets with flying fingers, and fishwives dump slithery octopus on to trays of crushed ice ready for auction.

The village is worth a wander: sandwiched between blocks of low-rise flats, a tangle of stone and whitewashed houses leads up to the church, its walls randomly scattered with images of Christ and Mary. Inside are statues of a long-haired virgin in a shiny gold-braid trimmed dress, St James accompanied by a greyhound with a bread roll clamped in its jaws, and an ancient St Agnes. A primitive frieze carved on the altar wall depicts Christ rising from his sepulchre and a descent to hell.

West of Laxe the coast road undulates through pines down to the bay of Traba, with an exposed, duny beach at the head of a broad flat valley. As you continue down to Ponte do Porto, look out for women sitting on the roadside making lace: age-withered fingers move tens of little wooden bobbins with the agility of a virtuoso pianist.

You will probably find a couple of lace-makers at **Camelle**, an unassuming fishing village at the head of a long, narrow inlet. Here you could also visit the resident German hippy. His beard descends to the navel of his emaciated torso, his eyes are spacey, and his voice has been reduced to a whisper. He spends his days retouching the circles he has painted on the harbour pier, and adding to the freakish rock sculptures he has created around his shack: sea-rounded rocks have been cemented into a fantasy of whirling towers and bobbly chains. To see them you will have to agree to sketch your impressions on the page of a tiny notebook, appending it with your name, date of birth, nationality and profession.

If you want to see why this stretch of the Galician coast is known as the Costa de Morte, or Coast of Death, a treacherous, pot-holed track, without passing places and rid-dled with blind curves, takes a cliff-hugging route from Arou, just above Camelle, to the lighthouse of **Cabo Vilán**, near Camariñas. You will be rewarded with views of an untamed, indented coast, where breakers crash on to remote beaches – but the track is dangerous, and it is best to take the inland road to Camariñas, drive past the village to the light-house, park your car, and walk.

With its dishevelled '60s and '70s houses standing on the

shore of a broad estuary, **Camariñas** is a workaday fishing village. Old ladies with sun-scorched faces rub backs aching from hours of lace-making, and politely inform an American tourist haggling over the price of a handkerchief that it has taken three days to make it.

Indeed, a few hours spent here is sufficient to dispel any romantic notions about life in a fishing village. Like the rest of the Galician coast, Camariñas is suffering from an over-fished sea. We witnessed, in the early morning, the sight of a young fisherman rowing up to his wife at the harbour wall with barely enough fish to fill a carrier bag, let alone the trolley she had brought to push them along to market.

One of Galicia's loveliest beaches lies across the water from Camariñas. The **Playa Lago** is not signposted, but lies three kilometres from Molinos; its fine white sand, backed by pines, undulates gently down to the sheltered waters. Do not confuse it with the first, shadeless, beach you pass. At Lago there is a campsite under the pines, and a basic *hospedaje* above a café.

Corcubión and the End of the World

An enormous calcium carbide factory is hardly an auspicious introduction to the Ría de Corcubión, but **Corcubión** itself, a couple of kilometres down the road, is considerably more appealing. Granite houses with glazed balconies, and handsome, flaking mansions give the village an air of faded elegance, though it can sometimes feel rather lifeless. It is also a timber port, with neat towers of wooden planks stacked on its quayside waiting to be shipped to Morocco, Britain and the USA.

About sixteen kilometres from Corcubión, the **Cabo Finisterre** headland is the westernmost point in Spain, and was long believed to be the end of the world – hence its name. The drive is atmospheric in the mist, when the trees and bracken are drained of colour. But in sunny weather even the final stretch to the lighthouse, along the corniche road, is no more evocative than any of Galicia's numerous capes.

Ancient myths have been replaced by contemporary legends about a Panamanian cargo ship, *Casón*, wrecked off the cape in 1988. If you chat to locals, you will be told about the evacuation of 50,000 people, how all the animals died, and that the ship was carrying radioactive material (or contraband, or radio equipment for Iraq… or Iran…). In the drab village of **Finisterre**, three kilometres inland from the cape, the wreck is remembered almost fondly for the extra tourist revenue it brought in, and the local photography shop still sells postcards of the rescue operation.

There are a number of beaches between Corcubión and Finisterre, of which the most sheltered is **Queijo**, directly outside the village.

THE WEST COAST – RIAS BAJAS

Corcubión to Muros (H)

The Rías Bajas are approached from Corcubión through a bleak landscape of boulders and pines, tiny fields and the occasional remote hamlet backed by wild stony hills. The beaches are exposed, and the four kilometres of windswept dunes at **Carnota** are a melancholic climax. The village's 44-legged *hórreo* provides a lighter note. It is Galicia's longest, and, locals say, was built so that the village priest had room to store the tithes of produce amassed from his parishioners. But there is nowhere worth stopping until you reach Muros.

Ranged on a hill that curves around its bay, **Muros** is a pretty fishing town, slowly developing into a resort. The main *plaza*, overlooking the *ría*, has been smartly repaved in granite and given a new bandstand and fountain; an artificial beach has been created; and pubs, *hamburgueserias* and a disco have opened. But Muros lads play cards outside MacBurgers, old men chain-smoke in designer bars, and in the local shops lobster pots, sheath knives and waterproofs are sold alongside barbecues, flip-flops and beach mats. Wandering along the backstreets you come across dogs scratching themselves in the shadows and women making lace or peeling vegetables. At the harbour you can watch the fish being laid out in the cool, damp market for the evening auction and locals queuing up to buy slimy octopus or barnacle-encrusted mussels on the stalls outside.

Muros is a pleasant place to stay, though it is not particularly well located for touring. There are upretentious fish restaurants just to the west of town and about five kilometres beyond is the **Playa de San Francisco**. A crescent of fine sand backed by a shaded park, it can get busy with Spanish families staying in its low-rise holiday apartments.

Heading east round the estuary from Muros you will pass through **Noia**, an unkempt old town. The market by the waterside is good fun here, selling home-made cheeses, fresh milk in old brandy bottles and *pan de maís*, a heavy corn-meal bread which tastes something like pumpernickel.

Pontevedra (H)

Pontevedra stands on the estuary of the River Lérez; it is a provincial capital in which anonymous suburbs enclose a mazy granite centre where perspectives of wrought-iron balconies, frilly *solanas* and toffee-hued shutters draw you past sawdust-strewn bars, ancient cobblers' shops, and dim arcades. It is liveliest on market days when old women stagger home carrying their purchases on their heads, and local villagers sell produce from their *minifundios* on street corners. In the early evening parents chat and children play on Plaza La Herrería or the Xardines de Colón, and at night throbbing Heavy Metal music and revving motorbikes reverberate along the narrow cobbled streets.

Though you might want to take a look at some of Pontevedra's churches, or drop in on the ad-hoc collection of archaeological remains, paintings and folk art in the provincial museum, the main appeal of the place is wandering the old town and watching the street life. It is also a convenient base for exploring the beaches and remote fishing villages of the Península de Morrazo, which form the south bank of the Ría de Pontevedra, and for visiting Combarro and A Toxa on the Península de Salnes. There are pleasant hotels and bars where you can make a lunch of *empanadas* or seafood – notably *percebes* (goose barnacles) served from wicker baskets and eaten with a pin in an unnamed bar on Plaza Armesto – and the excellent, unpretentious Restaurante O Merlo, Calle Santa María 4, which serves typical dishes such as *chiperones* (deep-fried baby squid), *caldo gallego* and *tarta almendra*. You can eat downstairs with local families, by a bar bedecked with hundreds of keyrings, or upstairs in the restaurant.

A walk round town

The old town lies between the river and traffic-choked Calle Michelana. At the foot of Calle Michelana is Plaza Peregrina, dominated by the shell-shaped baroque Peregrina chapel. Across the road Plaza de la Ferrería, overlooked by the Gothic church of San Francisco, forms a civilised arena for Pontevedran family life, with pavement cafés from which parents fondly watch their roller-skating children menace the pigeons.

Calle Figueroa leads into the old town, passing little bars and the Zapatería Martínez, with a window display of clogs and wooden-soled boots. The street emerges on Pontevedra's most photogenic (but usually deserted) square, Plaza de Leña, with a granite crucifix and colonnaded houses. Two mansions hold the **Museo Provincial**, with a collection which includes seeds and nuts from Celtic settlements and folksy earthen-ware. There is also a good collection of jet votive offerings from Santiago, and a variety of paintings. Considerable space is devoted to Méndez Núñez, a local admiral who led expedi-tions to the Indies, and an entire gallery is dedicated to the works of local artist Castelao – among his numerous seascapes and landscapes are some vivid Latin American dancers and musicians.

Next to Plaza de Leña, arcaded and tree-shadowed Plaza Armesto is the old town's liveliest square. It adjoins Calle Padre Sarmiento, which with its continuation, Calle Isabel II, forms the old town's main thoroughfare. From it, streets lead downhill to the granite market building, where the voices of vendors echo over stalls of mercury-silver anchovies, flaccid yellow-skinned chickens and hand-made cheeses.

Up Calle Isabel II, you reach Pontevedra's most impressive church, Santa María Mayor, its elaborate façade overlooking a busy main road. The façade is designed like an altar, with reliefs of the Crucifixion and Dormition and Assumption of the Virgin carved into its creeper-sprouting granite. Columns twist and piped-icing rib-vaults intertwine in the pungently musty, damp interior, and a Madonna in frills looks pertur-bed at the mess her dying son is making of her dress.

Península de Salnes

Though there are some long, sandy beaches along the north shore of the Ría de Pontevedra, they are less sheltered than those on the south bank. An interesting place to stop for a wander and lunch is **Combarro**. Below the modern roadside development is a small harbour, and if you clamber up the steps carved into a granite rock at its far end you reach a row of waterfront *hórreos*. Most are still used to store crops and food, and to shelter lines of washing and stacks of wood, but a few enterprising villagers have set up little tables outside them selling souvenirs and black market cigarettes. Alongside one is a tiny outdoor restaurant which serves delicious salads, home-cured sausage and ham, home-made *empanadas* and freshly caught fish, with alarmingly large cups of *vino país* brewed in the family's cellar.

Further along the peninsula is the **Playa de la Lanzada**, made up of eight kilometres of dunes. It is reckoned to be Galicia's best beach and coach parties pour in on summer weekends. It is, however, directly exposed to the Atlantic and unless you are a confident swimmer or love windsurfing you will probably be better off just splashing about and sunbathing. There are pedaloes to hire, a handful of beach bars and a few hotels on the scruffy plain behind.

La Toja (A Toxa) and El Grove (O Grove)

El Grove is a shabby resort strung along the coast on the end of the peninsula opposite the islet of La Toja, with seafood restaurants, cheap *hostales* and tacky souvenir shops along its newly paved promenade. A road bridge crosses over to **La Toja**, where exclusive holiday apartments with floridly exotic gardens line the approach to a luxury hotel and casino complex.

Until the end of the last century La Toja was a barren, uninhabited island. Then, legend goes, a couple of peasants from El Grove left their old donkey to die there, returned a year later to give him a decent burial, and discovered that he was full of energy but caked in mud. The mud was analysed, found to be radioactive, and a spa established, which rapidly became voguish with members of the smart set seeking eternal youth. A factory was also set up, which still produces soaps and cosmetics containing the supposedly youth-enhancing black mud.

But despite the ritzy hotels and apartments, La Toja's glamorous days are over: the spa building is abandoned, and the hotel and casino are frequently filled with business people on conferences. It is, however, an oddly haunting place, and worth a quick visit, particularly out of season.

The Peninsula de Morrazo

The huge, and often stinking, paper factory, *La Cellulosa*, is not a pleasant introduction to the southern shore of the Ría de Pontevedra, and nor is the industrial port of **Marín** somewhere to linger. Outside Marín things rapidly improve, with a series of small, sheltered sandy coves. Local children head down to **Playa Portocelo** after school, and the **Playa de Mogor** is a cheerful place where the local radio station belts out music from the vine-canopied terrace of the beach bar. A crescent of soft, sugary sand curves between a heap of rocks and a protective headland, making the swimming good, even when the wind is up. There are pedaloes for hire and the bar serves local wines and fresh fish.

If you look closely at the granite rocks, you can see that they are carved. They are the work of an old shoemaker who spent his last years praising God and Franco by chiselling religious and fascist symbols and slogans into rocks all over the area. This caused something of a stir in the late '70s, when a professor pronounced them prehistoric; eventually it turned out that there were indeed some megalithic carvings among the shoemaker's contributions, and a television documentary was made. If you want a quieter beach, head down to **Bueu**. Just before you reach the village are the long, white undulating sands of the **Praia de Agrelo e Portomaior**, more exposed than Mogor, but the swimming is still good. The beaches in Bueu itself are less appealing, and the village, with a salty, semi-abandoned waterfront has little to hold you.

South of Bueu you enter a hilly landscape where pines and eucalyptus scent the air and fishing villages are scattered among *minifundios*. On the peninsula's wobbly triangular tip the grey village of **Hio** holds Galicia's most elaborately carved scene at Calvary, depicting men on ladders removing Christ from the cross. Tucked into the indented coastline are lovely sandy beaches. The sheltered **Playa Donón**, reached along a rough road from a wild rocky promontory can get quite busy, as there is a popular campsite behind it, but few people other than locals go to the beach at **Vilanova**, four kilometres from Hio. Part of the attraction here is watching the life of a remote fishing village: clothes being washed in the concrete wash-house, men watering the tiny plots of their *minifundios*, and fishermen drinking in the bar before heading out for the night's catch. The sea on this stretch of coast gets deep rapidly, and waves can be quite strong, so take care.

Unless you are camping, there are few places to stay on the Morazzo peninsula, so it is best seen in day-trips from Pontevedra.

Vigo

Spain's most important fishing port sprawls for five kilometres along the coast of the Ría de Vigo, its high-rise blocks forming a disorderly concrete skyline against green hills. It was here that Laurie Lee landed for the walk across

Spain that is wonderfully described in his book *As I Walked Out One Midsummer Morning*, and from here many a Galician emigrant has left Spain for a new life in South America. It is a big, noisy, vigorous city, where congested avenues trap the heat, and a dingy old fishing quarter of overflowing dustbins and ultraviolet-lit bars plays host to a tough nightscene.

Palm trees, nineteenth-century apartments and a yacht club built in the form of a cruise ship give the waterfront a veneer of elegance, and unless Vigo exerts a sudden fascination for you, this is all you need to see. From the Estación Maritima next to the yacht club, regular ferries ply the water to the villages of Cangas, Moaña, the Playa de Nerga and the Islas Cíes.

There is, however, a certain gutsy appeal to the dilapidated fishing quarter, tucked behind the waterfront. On Rua Pescadería fishwives sell oysters on granite tables and on Calle López Puigcerver (also known as Calle Real) there are basic bars littered with cigarette-ends and sunflower seeds. As for eating, slum it if you dare, and eat fish in one of the sailors' dives on Calle López Puigcerver, or go for sardines and octopus straight from the brazier at Cafetería Alfonso on the waterfront by the fish market. Alternatively retreat to the civilised El Mosquito on Plaza Villaviciencio, below the fishing quarter's ugly cathedral.

If you have time to spare in Vigo, head for the fish market, or drive up to the **Castro**, where there are great views of the town from the park and restaurant within the old castle walls. When the weather is very hot, avoid heading down to the Playa de Samil, south of the town, unless you want to lie shoulder to shoulder with the rest of Vigo. Though the sands are vast, so many people go that sunbathers overspill on to the paved promenade, and it is virtually impossible to swim without colliding into someone.

The Islas Cíes

From mid-June to the end of September ferries regularly cross to the Islas Cíes from Vigo's Estación Maritima, carrying crates of chickens, vegetables and sacks of bread, along with the campers and day-trippers. You can also get there from the resort of Baiona, south of Vigo. Of the three small islands, one is an out-of-bounds bird sanctuary and the other two are linked by a tremendous white sand bar. The swimming is good and sheltered – though the sea-bed around the island shelves pretty quickly – and as few people stir from the island campsite (just across the sand bar from the ferry pier) until mid-day, there is a good chance of having only seagulls for company if you go in the morning. Alternatively, walk in the opposite direction along a broad track through the trees. Signposts point you to the beautiful **Praia de Figueiras**, its talcum-powder sands set against a backdrop of dunes and trees. Once again, few people go down in the morning, though you will see why if you plunge into the deep, icily bracing waters. There are walks up to the lighthouse, and places to eat and drink by the ferry pier and campsite.

Baiona (H)

For over eighty years Baiona has been trying to attract tourists – there was even a cynical plan to transform it into a place of pilgrimage by faking a miracle. It is now Galicia's best resort, and has nothing in common with the packaged concrete of the southern costas. In the old centre the pale gold of Galician granite twinkles in the sun, contrasting with the white of fancy *solanas* and elaborate wrought-iron balconies. Most of the visitors are Spanish, though the *parador*, secluded on a pine-cloaked promontory, attracts discerning foreigners. Other hotels are small, family-run and mostly housed in traditional buildings. There are gleaming Italian-style cafés on the pretty waterfront and traditional *tapas* bars in the old town; small fishing craft bob among the yachts in the harbour, and the beaches are packed with picnicking families. The best beaches are just outside the town, and you can also take a ferry across to the good beaches on the Islas Cíes. The tourist office is in the Town Hall in the old town and has maps, leaflets, details of ferry and bus times, and information on local events. Baiona is ranged around a gently curving bay within a small fjord. The town's beaches, tucked beneath a promontory encircled by the turreted walls of the castle-*parador*, are small and get very crowded in high season. You can walk right round the promontory on a tiny path which winds through a tangle of sea-grasses, cow parsley, brambles and ivy. Between the main beaches low rocky spits with tiny patches of sand are just large enough for a quiet sunbathe and splash.

From the promontory there are views over the *ría* to the long beaches of América and Ladreira, and out across the sea to the Islas Cíes. About seven kilometres from Baiona, the fine golden sands of the **Playa de América** are backed by holiday villas, and sweep between two wooded headlands.

The sandy sea bed initially shelves gently, but a few strokes take you into deep water. América is one of Galicia's most popular beaches – so try to avoid it on weekends in July and August. Directly outside Baiona, the **Playa de Ladreira** is almost equally busy, and rather less attractive, backed for half its length by modern apartments and building sites and for the other half by the coastal road.

In Baiona itself, you can wander the old town, walk through the grounds of the *parador*, or head up through woodland to the giant granite statue of the **Virgen de la Roca**, built in the '30s with money from ex-pat Galicians in Cuba. It was here, twenty years earlier, that an enterprising town councillor decided to engineer his miracle. He planned to bury an old statue and sprinkle the earth with salt to attract the local cattle and sheep, knowing that eventually someone would demand an investigation, the statue would be unearthed, and a miracle proclaimed. However, his fellow councillors were too scrupulous and the plan came to nothing. Today people come to picnic under the trees, and on feast days, when the door in the virgin's gown is opened, climb up inside her and stand on the boat she holds in her right hand. Even without climbing to the top, there are lovely views from her rocky pedestal over to the *parador* and down through the pines to the sea frothing against the rocky shoreline.

South to La Guardia

South of Baiona the road heads along a rugged coast of foam-licked rocky crags, where wild grasses shake and maize bows in the sweeping winds. You pass wayside restaurants and *hostales*, bleak villages and the weather-beaten ruins of a baroque monastery outside Oia. Further inland, wild horses roam the hills, and on Sundays in May and June are chased and lassoed, Wild West-style, by men on horseback, then herded into wooden corrals to be counted and branded, before being released again. The events are accompanied by much boozing and picnicking. Few tourists go as the *curros* are not advertised. Ask for details in Baiona's tourist office, or in village bars.

Just above the mouth of the River Miño, which forms the border with Portugal, stands **La Guardia** (A Garda), a tacky, but intriguing, fishing village. It has been largely settled by emigrants returned from Puerto Rico. You can tell when a family came back by the style in which their house is built. There are flaking turn-of-the-century villas, '60s houses with tiled op art façades, and even a pink and green post-modern apartment block. You can eat in one of the extremely cheap sea-front fish restaurants, notably the Xeito, beyond the harbour, where diners sit outside under a striped awning and watch the sun set over the sea.

Monte Santa Tecla

The main reason for coming to La Guardia, however, is to drive or walk up the wooded Monte Santa Tecla to the superbly preserved Celtic *citanía*, a fortified hill settlement. Huddled within protective walls about two-thirds of the way up are the foundations of scores of circular stone huts, which are thought to have been occupied from the Bronze Age, and abandoned around 200 BC, when the Romans took control of the area. A couple have been rebuilt and topped with thatched roofs, and finds from the site are housed in a museum at the top of the hill. The road continues up here, or you can walk along a path punctuated with the stations of the cross. There are extensive views across the Miño and down the Portuguese coast from the settlement and from mountain-top mirador, spiked with radio antennae. A simple hotel, Pazo Santa Tecla, open in summer only, has a terrace overhanging the mountainside.

INLAND ROUTES

Along the Miño: Tui (H)

Drained by a hydro-electric station upstream, the River Miño is barely a hundred metres wide in its final reaches. For much of the drive from La Guardia to Tui (Tuy), the river is barely visible behind bank-side villages and plots of vines and maize. If you are heading down to Portugal, you can cross by car ferry at Goián, or carry on to the iron road bridge designed by Eiffel (of Paris tower fame) at Tui.

Stacked above the river and crowned by a fortified cathedral, **Tui** is Galicia's main frontier town. The outskirts are modern, but the old town is, at least initially, enticing, with silent streets winding up to the cathedral past granite houses with lacy white *solanas*. If you seek tranquillity, consider staying in the *parador*, gorgeously sited above the river outside the town.

Many people head into Portugal to visit the walled town of **Valença do Minho** just across the border. It is pretty enough, but wholly dedicated to tourism. Most of its houses hold shops and their walls are concealed behind gaudily coloured bath towels, sold by the kilo.

Tui's cathedral

The cathedral is an austere Romanesque-Gothic structure fortified against invasion by the Portuguese, with strategic views over the Miño from its sentry paths. The west portal's carvings temper the severity with an ingeniously carved Jerusalem, the towers and walls of which appear to be suspended in mid-air. Inside, bridges across the nave brace the cathedral against earthquakes, and the light picks out the foliage, figures, grotesque masks and angels carved on the elaborate organ. In the vaulted cloisters serpents writhe on capitals and the sun glares on an overgrown garden of roses, geraniums and daisies. Dazzled, you plunge into the darkness of an unlit tower and feel your way up the steps with hands and feet to a sentry path along the turreted parapets.

Ribadavia

From Tui the minor PO-400 road follows the Miño through its valley, carpeted with maize plots and vineyards. The river is loveliest between Sela and Ribadavia – narrow, shaded by trees, and with Portuguese and Spanish children swimming from the rocks on either bank. After the hydro-electric dam at Frieira the river becomes broad, green and glassy.

Set among undulating vineyards above the river, **Ribadavia** is the centre of the Ribeira wine-producing region. You can sample some of the wines – and the sharp, white sherry-like *pazo* – in a stone-vaulted cellar-bar on the main arcaded square.

The old honey-granite centre is worth a wander. Spilling below a creeper-dripping castle is a steep maze of arcaded and balconied, collapsing half-timbered buildings, trendy cafés and Romanesque churches. The town is currently undergoing a thorough face-lift, perhaps with a view to setting itself up as a tourist attraction, but at present it has the claustrophobic feel of a small provincial town in which strangers are a rarity.

From Ribadavia the main N-120 takes you to **Ourense** (Orense), the provincial capital, home town of the singer Julio Iglesias, the fashion designer Adolfo Dominguez and

Fidel Castro's ancestors. Ourense is hideous, its grimy old granite centre hemmed in by faceless modern blocks, and as the traffic is unrelenting, it is advisable to stick to the major roads and head straight out. A drive along the Sil Gorge (Las Gargantas del Sil), to the north-east is a must, but first you might want to make a diversion to the south and see the monastery at Celanova and the castle town of Verín, near the border with Portugal.

Celanova and Verín (H)

First impressions of **Celanova** are of a small, modern town of no character. However, above the main road, hidden behind a screen of plane trees, is a fascinating monastery, its florid baroque façade overlooking an appealing square with a fountain and three pavement cafés. The monastery was originally founded by the Galician Saint Rosendo, bishop of San Martín de Mondoñedo (see p.86) in 936. Celanova was on the pilgrim route to Santiago de Compostela from Portugal, so over the years it developed into the impressive complex you see today.

The Mozarabic chapel of San Miguel in the monastery garden is all that remains of the original foundation, a diminutive structure with horseshoe arches and a ceramic tiled pavement. To see this and the rest of the monastery, you apply for a guide at the *Centro de Servicios Sociales* situated in the extraordinarily lovely vaulted baroque cloister. You will be taken to the second, neo-classical cloister and shown around the seventeenth-century church. The highlights here are the exotically carved cupola, a series of translucent, delicately painted alabaster scenes from the life of Christ on the high altar, and the (very) late-Gothic choir-stalls, high up in a gallery, where the misericords include a *gaita* player, a sheep-shearer, Sagittarius, and a merman.

From Celanova it is an easy journey south-east to the castle town of **Verín**, near the Portuguese border. The old town in the valley has many dignified mansions bristling with coats of arms in its narrow streets. On the hilltop (where there is an attractive *parador*), is the twelfth-century castle of Monterrey, with a keep, snail-shell tower and arched courtyard. The doorway of the tiny church next door is carved with a primitive Christ in Majesty, accompanied by strange childlike animal figures with all four legs in a line. From Verín you can easily detour to the Portuguese border, to explore the green, hilly vineyards around Chaves and Braganza.

Las Gargantas del Sil

The drive along the Sil Gorges is inland Galicia's most memorable. The River Sil, a tributary of the Miño, flows through a gorge of magnificently cascading rock, periodically tempered by lush woods and tiny terraced plots of maize and vines. To get there from Ourense, take the N-120 along the Miño to Os Peares from which a road winds up above the Sil to **San Esteban de Ribas de Sil**, a former monastery superbly sited on a spur above the gorge. The complex includes a dull Romanesque church and three rather lovelier cloisters. An imaginative restoration project has provided the first three-storied cloister with a bar (complete with fruit machine and tremendous views). In the second cloister steps climb up to the gallery for another superb view of the gorge.

You can head straight back down to the main road, but a better choice would be to continue above the gorge, across upland heathery moors, through sleepy villages and forests, for views of the green river snaking between rocky bulks and painstakingly terraced mountainsides. The roads are narrow, but adequate, and so rarely used that local drivers stop for a mid-road chat. Beyond **A Teixido** the road descends and crosses the river to the vast cultivated plain around the town of **Monforte de Lemos**.

Monforte de Lemos is a pleasant enough place to stop for lunch, its tower and church-crowned hill rising from a modern quarter which dribbles across the sun-baked plain. There are extensive views from the platform below the sturdy tower and rubble-walled church, and you can eat just down the hill on an open terrace at La Fortaleza restaurant. If the church is open pop inside to see some saints in niches and a hippy-like Christ in an almost psychedelic embroidered purple velvet gown. If you need a bed for the night the Puente Romano, Plaza Dr Goyanes 6, Tel (982) 40 35 51, has small, modern rooms (with bathroom) above a noisy riverside bar.

Lugo

The drive from Monforte to Lugo is largely unexciting, passing through a gentle landscape of hayfields and coppices. The local stone here is slate, used to roof farms, and to create walls which look like rows of gravestones. But the most distinctive slate creation is to be found in Lugo itself.

Lugo is a very ordinary town enclosed by an extraordinary circuit of Roman slate walls. Under the Romans Lugo was, as it is today, a provincial capital at a major road junction. In later centuries Santiago pilgrims would make a substantial detour just to visit the town. It is no longer worth going out of your way to see Lugo, but if you are passing by on your way to Santiago or Portugal you may as well stop for an hour.

You have to climb through drab, traffic-congested outskirts to reach the walls. They are up to 15 metres high, over six metres thick, and defended by 85 towers, and you can still only get into the old town through one of the ten gates. Though they have been restored many times, the orderly, mortarless stacks of thin slates sprouting clumps of greenery remain a feat of engineering, and you can still walk around them along the sentry path.

Within the walls, leafy squares provide a necessary escape from streets choked by cars, dreary modern buildings, a seedy market area and dilapidated old quarter. Shopping streets are full of respectable families.

Villalba (H) and Mondoñedo

Lugo is only a couple of hours' drive from the north coast, but it is worth staying overnight in **Villalba**, where there is a tiny *parador* in a converted octagonal tower. Villalba itself is less appealing, with a few scruffy granite and whitewashed houses among '60s and '70s apartments. Make sure you drop in for a coffee at the grocery-café on the main road by the bus stop, marked *Alimentación Confitería Pastelería*. You drink at the counter among fresh cheeses, *tartas de Mondoñedo*, piles of milk cartons, Saint Christopher statuettes, souvenir *hórreos* and clogs. If you order a decaffinated coffee, you will be given a jar to make your own.

Less than an hour's drive from Villalba, is **Mondoñedo**. Cradled in a story-book valley, the bitter smoke from its wood factory mingles with the smell of manure, and at times the streets are so quiet that you can hear scissors clipping in the old-fashioned barber's shop. The reason to visit Mondoñedo is the main *plaza*, sloping from a row of arcaded houses embellished with frilly moulding, to the warm, golden façade of the cathedral.

In the eighteenth century the cathedral's rather plain façade was flanked with knobbly, domed and balustraded towers. Inside is a fresco, *The Massacre of the Innocents*, full of black women with bared breasts and tears splashing on their cheeks. On the vaults images of John the Baptist's head on a

85

platter and a skeleton in a grave gradually swim into focus through the soupy light. You may even hear the eighteenth-century organ being played. If the organist is only practising scales it still sounds wonderfully spooky, with wobbling, cracking notes and hissing pipes.

As for the rest of the town, there are streets of whitewashed houses, in which the textures and hues of scuffed and cracked façades, a cobbler's shop with a nice line in platform wellies, and bakeries selling the glacé fruit-studded *tarta de Mondoñedo* are as absorbing as details of coats of arms or *solanas*. Mondoñedo's socialising happens in the three bars on the square in front of the smartly *solana*-fronted Casa Consistatorial, and in the time it takes to drink a beer in each, you get to see all the local mavericks.

The eleventh-century San Martín de Mondoñedo is not here, but in a little hamlet further north, just inland from Foz.

WHERE TO STAY

BAIONA

Las Tres Carabelas   £
Ventura Misa 61
36300 Pontevedra   *Tel (986) 35 51 33; Fax (986) 36 55 67*

A family-run B&B hotel, tucked behind the waterfront, in a restored inn, where the neighbours drop in for a chat in the all-purpose reception area. Rooms have dark wood furniture, brown carpets and small bathrooms, and those facing the street can be a bit noisy.

Open: all year; **Rooms**: 10 **Credit/charge cards**: Amex, Diners, Eurocard, Visa

---

Hotel Pinzon   £
Elduayen 21
36300 Pontevedra   *Tel (986) 35 60 46*

A whitewashed and granite building with ornate wrought-iron balconies on the waterfront; it has simple, spotless rooms above a sparkling Italian-style café-bar. Rooms vary – some are furnished with Formica, others with wood. Expect some street noise from rooms facing the sea-front.

Open: all year **Rooms**: 18 **Credit/charge cards**: Amex, Diners, Eurocard, Visa

Hotel Caís £
Alferez Barreiro 3
36300 Pontevedra *Tel (986) 35 56 43*

Flounced curtains and valences compensate for lino floors in a small
waterfront hotel with white wrought-iron balconies.

Open: all year **Rooms**: 12 **Credit/Charge cards**: None

Parador Nacional Conde de Gondemar £££
Monterreal
36300 Pontevedra *Tel (986) 35 50 00; Fax (986) 35 50 76*

Built in the style of a Galician mansion, with open galleries and
pointed crenellations, the *parador* stands on a landscaped headland
within the three-kilometre circuit of walls that once belonged to
Baiona's fortress. A heavy candelabra dangles from the granite
vaults of the reception area, suits of armour stand on the stairway
and tapestries hang from the walls. The café-bar opens on to a patio
with a fountain, the lounge has a terrace with sea-views and the
restaurant specialises in seafood. Bedrooms have wooden floors and
are furnished with heavy antique-style furniture. The bathrooms are
paved with white marble.

Open: all year **Rooms**: 124 **Facilities**: beach, swimming-pool,
playground, parking, sauna, tennis **Credit/charge cards**: Amex,
Diners, Eurocard, Visa

LA CORUNA

Hospedaje Monterosso £
Travesia Zapatería 3
15000 La Coruña *Tel (981) 20 97 97*

This is picturesquely located in the old town close to Plaza General
Azgarraga and the church of Santa Maria. Simple, spotless rooms
with satiny valanced coverlets on the beds.

Open: all year **Rooms**: 13 (5 with own bath) **Credit/charge cards**:
None

LAXE

Hostal Beiramar £
Cesario Pondal 59
15117 Laxe *Tel (981) 72 81 09*

Smart, pretty furnishings are to be found in this *hostal*, on the sea-
front above a pub-disco-restaurant.

Open: all year **Rooms**: 14 (8 with own bath) **Credit/charge cards**: Diners

MUROS

La Muradana	££
Avenida de la Marina Española,	
107 15250 Muros	Tel (981) 82 68 85

La Muradana offers simple but clean good-quality rooms above a waterfront bar.

Open: all year **Rooms**: 16 **Credit/charge cards**: Visa

PLAYA DE AREA

Hotel Louzao	££
Playa de Area	
27850 Viveiro	Tel (982) 55 06 42

A recently built hotel of local slate with a black, white and grey designer interior. Rooms are smart, and tasteful and slickly co-ordinated. Some have balconies with views to the sea over a garden with swings as well as benches and tables.

Open: all year **Rooms**: 26 **Credit/charge cards**: Amex, Diners, Eurocard, Visa

Hotel Ego	££
Playa de Area	
27850 Viveiro	Tel (982) 56 09 87

The hotel is a five-minute walk up the hill from the beach, just off the main road. Dark glass windows overlook a terrace set with black chairs and steel tables, and rooms have cork floors, rough cream walls and co-ordinating furnishings.

Open: all year; **Rooms**: 30 **Credit/charge cards**: Amex, Eurocard, Visa

PONTEDEUME

Hostal Iberia	£
Playa de la Magdalena Cabanas	
15600 Pontedeume	Tel (982) 43 07 49

A clean and simple hotel with light, airy rooms. Ideal for families as it is right behind the beach.

Open: July-Oct; **Rooms**: 40 **Credit/charge cards**: None

PONTEVEDRA

Parador Nacional Casa de Barón	£££
Plaza de Maceda	
36002 Pontevedra	*Tel (986) 85 58 00; Fax (986) 85 21 95*

Comfortable rooms with antique-style furniture and ample bathrooms in a sixteenth-century mansion on a square in the old part of town. The rug-strewn floor and heavy stone staircase in the entrance hall suggest a manor-house, but terrace drinkers are in full view of passers-by, audible telephone conversations suggest bedroom walls are not authentically thick; unimaginatively arranged furniture gives the public rooms a rather unlived-in feel.

Open: all year **Rooms**: 47 **Credit/charge cards**: Amex, Diners, Eurocard, Visa

Hotel Ruas	££
Sarmiento 37	
36002 Pontevedra	*Tel (986) 84 64 11*

This newly opened hotel is in a pale granite mansion in the old town. Rooms have wooden floors, white walls and good-quality furniture, and the tiled bathrooms have marble wash-stands. There is an Italian-style bar on the ground floor with marble tables and black chairs.

Open: all year **Rooms**: 22 **Credit/charge cards**: Amex, Diners, Eurocard, Visa

PORTO DO BARQUEIRO

La Marina	£
15337 La Coruña	*Tel (981) 41 40 98*

If you want somewhere to stay overnight in this pretty fishing village, one of the limited options are these clean and simple rooms above a quayside restaurant.

Open: all year **Rooms**: 4 (shared bath) **Credit/charge cards**: None

RIBADEO

Parador de Ribadeo £££
Amador Fernández s/n
27700 Ribadeo *Tel (982) 11 08 25; Fax (982) 11 03 46*

A modern *parador* built in traditional style and designed to take advantage of the views across the estuary to Castropol and Figueras. Black and white tiles in the reception area and on landings lead into cool white corridors full of plants. Rooms have parquet floors, whitewashed walls and most have large balconies with garden furniture. The lounge, is strewn with tapestry-style rugs and has islands of leather suites; the bar has a terrace, and the restaurant a salami-marble floor and heavy candelabra.

Open: all year **Rooms**: 47 **Credit/charge cards**: Amex, Diners, Eurocard, Visa

SANTIAGO DE COMPOSTELA

Hostal de los Reyes Católicos £££
Plaza Obradoiro 1
15705 Santiago de Compostela *Tel (981) 58 22 00; Fax (981) 56 30 94*

Expensive by Spanish standards, but cheaper than an equivalent hotel in Britain, you might consider it worth the money to sleep in such a beautiful, historic building. The *hostal* is designed on a cross-plan around four colonnaded courtyards. There are two lounges, one with a scattering of antiques and a symmetrical arrangement of chairs and sofas overlooked by polychrome saints and portraits of long-haired men in doublet and hose, the other with a stone-flagged floor and long wooden table. Along the corridors large copper utensils are chained to the walls, and rooms are soberly furnished with sturdy repro-antique furniture. The food in the basement-vaulted cellar restaurant is good, though not exceptional for the price.

Open: all year **Rooms**: 157 **Credit/charge cards**: Amex, Diners, Eurocard, Visa

---

Bar Mundial 82 £
Conga 82
15700 Santiago de Compostela *Tel (981) 58 68 79*

The proprietors have just refurbished three small, spotless rooms with a shared bathroom in another house just off Plaza Cervantes. If they have no room the owners know virtually everyone in Santiago, so may be able to help you out.

Open: all year **Rooms**: 3, no own bath **Credit/charge cards**: None

Forest Cafetería   £
Don Abril Ares
15700 Santiago de Compostela

There is no phone, so you have to apply in person. Gleamingly clean
rooms, some of which have glazed balconies, above a café behind
Plaza San Martín. The bathroom is communal.

Open: all year **Rooms**: 10, no own bath **Credit/charge cards**:
None

Hostal Mapoula   £
Entremuralles 10
15702 Santiago de Compostela   *Tel (981) 58 01 24*

Small rooms with private showers and wash-basin but no toilet; the
accommodation is well cared for by the family owners. The Café
Derby is just across the road, so you can go there for breakfast.

Open: all year **Rooms**: 10 (no restaurant) **Credit/charge cards**:
None

TUI/TUY

Parador Nacional de San Telmo   ££
Avenida Portugal
36700 Tui   *Tel (986) 60 03 09; Fax (986) 60 21 63*

The hotel is perched above the Miño outside the town, and there are
views from the garden across to Portugal and over to Tui. The
parador itself is a modern reproduction of a typical nobleman's house.
The bar has a veined red marble floor, and opens on to a terrace. The
restaurant is simply decorated with whitewash and toffee-coloured
varnished wood. Rooms are traditional in style but comfortable.
Book in advance if you want to stay in July or August.

Open: all year **Rooms**: 22 **Facilities**: tennis, swimming-pool
Credit/charge cards: Amex, Diners, Eurocard, Visa

VERIN

Parador de Monterrey   ££
32600 Orense   *Tel (988) 41 00 75; Fax (988) 41 20 17*

On the hill by the castle, this quiet modern *parador* takes advantage
of the views over the Monterrey valley of vineyards. Comfortably
furnished in local style, with rugs on wooden floors and a suit of
armour in the entrance hall, the *parador* has friendly staff and a good
restaurant.

Open: all year; (restaurant closed Tues in winter) **Rooms**: 22 **Facilities**: swimming-pool **Credit/charge cards**: None

VILLALBA

Parador Condes de Villalba   **£££**
Valeriano Valdesuso
27800 Villalba   *Tel (982) 51 00 11; Fax (982) 51 00 90*

This *parador* is a converted octagonal medieval tower. You cross the dry moat by a drawbridge, and walk through the portcullis into a parquet-floored reception/lounge area hung with medieval-style banners. Rooms are large, with windows cut into the immense walls. The basement restaurant has a granite-flagged floor, granite columns and arches, and a modern beamed roof.

Open: all year **Rooms**: 6 **Credit/charge cards**: Amex, Diners, Eurocard, Visa

VIVEIRO

Tebar   **££**
Nicolas Cora Montenegro 70
27850 Viveiro   *Tel (982) 56 01 00; Fax (982) 55 04 08*

A dull, functional ten-storey block above the old town, whose rooms are surprisingly characterful, with wooden floors, white walls and grey-stained furniture. There is no restaurant.

Open: all year **Rooms**: 27 **Credit/charge cards**: Amex, Diners, Eurocard, Visa

Hostal Vila   **£**
Nicholas Cora Montenegro 57
27850 Viveiro   *Tel (982) 56 13 31*

Well-maintained, clean and simple rooms, just along from the Tebar (see above).

Open: all year **Rooms**: 12 **Credit/charge cards**: None

CANTABRIA AND ASTURIAS

WEDGED between the Atlantic Ocean and the mountains of the Cordillera Cantábrica, **Cantabria** is a tiny, green, hilly, rainy region credited with having more cows per square kilometre than anywhere else in Europe. The landscape is pleasant, though rarely spectacular, and the main attractions are prehistoric caves, rustic Romanesque churches and the photogenic villages of Santillana del Mar and Bárcena Mayor. It is not a region in which to spend an entire holiday, but does provide a gentle introduction to Northern Spain.

Cantabria used to be part of Castile, and resorts like Comillas and Santander were popular with the Castilian aristocracy and royalty. Since 1983, when it became an independent region, there has been the incentive to make the hinterland as well as coastline attractive to tourists, and almost everywhere you go you will see roads being improved and Romanesque churches being restored. Nevertheless much of the interior is little visited, and life is hardly affected by the twentieth century. On narrow country lanes spattered with manure you will be held up by flocks of goats and grass carts, and you will meet old men out for a walk in their slippers.

It is Cantabria's resorts which attract the crowds, though few of them really deserve it. If you arrive by ferry from Plymouth, you may need to stay over in Santander, though Santillana del Mar is only 24 kilometres away, and close to the famous (but virtually inaccessible) Altamira caves. As for the rest of the region, only Castro-Urdiales and San Vicente de la Barquera stand out along the coast, while inland, the mountain villages of Bárcena Mayor and Carmona are exquisite.

Asturias is far more distinctive, with its people who are fiercely proud of their region, their dialects and their cider; you will be told time and time again that Asturias is the true Spain. The claim is largely valid – the Kingdom of Asturias was the only part of Spain not to be colonised by the Moors, and the Reconquest started with bands of Christian resistance fighters formed in its mountains. Covadonga, the place where Asturias' first king, Pelayo, and a band of warriors vanquished the only Moorish contingent ever to attempt to annexe the region, is now an extremely popular nationalist-religious shrine. Pelayo founded the Asturian monarchy in the year 718 and in 810 his descendants made Oviedo – today's regional capital – their seat. During the ninth and tenth centuries kings peppered the region with churches – notably in Oviedo and the Valdedíos – whose architectural style foreshadows Romanesque. Today Asturias is still a principality, and the heir to the Spanish throne is the Prince of Asturias.

In 1934 Asturian miners took up arms against the Republic, an insurrection which was quashed only by shipping in troops from Morocco, among them the young officer Francisco Franco. Asturias still has its mines which fuel one of the most densely concentrated industrial areas on the Iberian peninsula. Nowadays the steel and coal industries are beset by the recession and rising unemployment and if you drive through Gijón and Avilés you will see the kind of pollutant-belching manufacturing plants more usually associated with Eastern Europe.

But the rest of Asturias is largely untouched by industry, and if you plan your routes carefully, it is easily avoided. The Asturian shoreline is known as the Costa Verde, the Green Coast, though the 25 kilometres between Gijón and Avilés would more aptly be dubbed the Costa Negra – the Black Coast. Much of it is fringed by undulating meadows, with the odd exception of a village like Llanes, and beaches at La Vega and La Isla, the stretch east of Gijón is not particularly attractive. Things improve rapidly west of Avilés, with the pretty fishing villages of Cudillero and Luarca and an isolated pine- and eucalyptus-edged beach known locally as the Playa de Winston y Chesterfield because it is used by cigarette smugglers.

The mountains of the Cordillera Cantábrica reach their climax in the anarchic pinnacles of the **Picos de Europa** which straddle both Cantabria and Asturias (and part of the neighbouring Castile-León, too). You will probably want to spend most of your time here either touring or walking. Though not the highest mountains in Spain, they are argu-ably the most spectacular. Limestone spears jab the sky and the three massifs are severed by deep rocky gorges. The tour-ist infrastructure is relatively low-key; only a handful of villa-ges have hotels and *hostales*, and apart from one *parador* (at Fuente Dé) and a country house hotel (in Cosgaya), these tend to be simple. If you can do without luxury, there are simple places to stay in Espinama, Posada de Valdeón and Oseja de Sajambre, all of which are good bases for walks.

The Asturian mountains do not stop with the Picos. The Cordillera Cantábrica rumples through the region into Galicia. Driving in the mountains, you will come across remote, weather-lashed villages, notably those along the

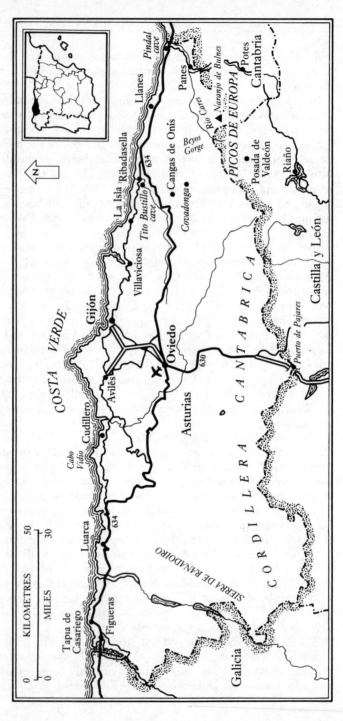

96

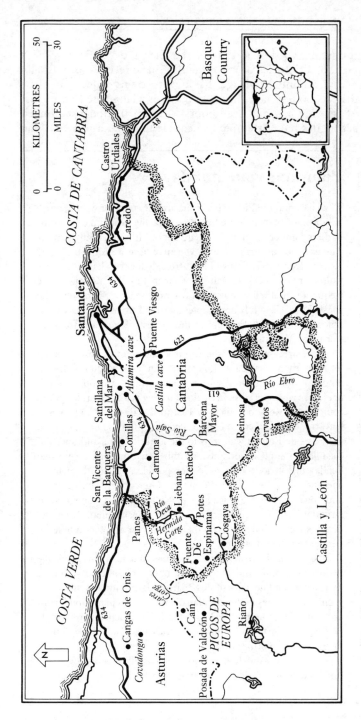

97

mountain road that crosses the Sierra de Rañadoiro into Galicia. Centuries of inaccessibility have resulted in virtually every mountain village having its own dialect. Because dialects do not have the same status as a language (unlike that of their Galician neighbours) certain nationalist-minded academics have attempted to cobble together a pan–Asturian

Planning your holiday

The coast and the Picos de Europa are very popular with Spanish holidaymakers (who come here to escape the heat and the crowds in their southern regions), and are packed from mid-July to mid-August – in the main centres you may have a problem finding somewhere to stay. You will be extremely lucky to have a holiday without rain, whenever you go; even in July the mountains are frequently swathed in mist, and morning sea-fogs hang over the coast. June, early July and September tend to be the pleasantest times to visit, with September the hottest. There are frequent storms in May and June.

There are few places where you would want to base yourself for more than a few days, though you can book beach holidays in hotels or villas on the Asturian coast through a couple of tour operators who specialise in Spain. Touring is a good option – you could travel west to Galicia or east to the Basque Country and Navarra, or – a splendid choice – combine touring or walking in the Picos de Europa with trips to the historic sights and towns of Castilla y León. To organise all this you can book a fly-drive holiday to Bilbao, Santiago de Compostela or Madrid (or fly to one and come back from the other). Alternatively you can take your own car on the Plymouth to Santander ferry operated by Brittany Ferries. This is not necessarily cheaper than flying and hiring a car: it all depends on the time of year and the number of people travelling together.

The few main roads across Asturias and Cantabria link the main towns and tend to get very busy with industrial traffic. There is a good network of slow, narrow and winding roads, often scenic, sometimes potholed, unmade or under repair. Good maps are essential – numbers 441 and 442 in the Michelin large-scale (1:400,000) *España* series cover Asturias and Cantabria and most of the rest of Northern Spain.

Travelling on public transport is a possibility, though you will not be able to reach everywhere worth seeing, and can expect

language, which is universally ridiculed. More accessible totems of Asturian nationalism are *fabada*, a hearty stew of white beans, pork and sausages; *hórreos*, the granaries on stilts which you also find in Galicia, and cider *(sidra)* which is poured from on high to give it a fizz.

long waits between buses or trains. ALSA has the most detailed network of all the different bus companies operating in Asturias. There are no comprehensive timetables; in large bus stations you usually have to look at the lists of destinations displayed in each company's booth and copy them down – or question the driver. The most useful bus services are those running from Santander east and west along the coast and, if you are a walker, those around the Picos (see also Walking in the Picos, page 124).

The privately-owned FEVE railway runs between Bilbao, Santander and El Ferrol in Galicia; its trains have recently been refurbished and you can even book an Orient Express-style luxury tour. But for everyday travel its trains are slow and frustratingly infrequent, so stick to the buses. RENFE, the state railway, links Santander and Oviedo with other regions of Spain, including Madrid.

In the Picos de Europa you can book jeep excursions which take you into the mountains on rough dirt tracks – the main centres are Potes, Fuente Dé and Espinama. Tourist offices or bars in Espinama or Fuente Dé have details, but trips are very expensive and only really practical if you can get a group together to share the cost.

Virtually every little village in this region has a taxi and drivers can make very good guides if you have a smattering of Spanish. You will be charged by the kilometre with an additional waiting fee – an expensive alternative to hiring a car, but good value if you want to be delivered and picked up at the start and end of a walk for example.

● **Regional Tourist Boards**: Dirección Regional de Turismo, Plaza Porticada 1, 39001 Santander, Tel (942) 21 24 25 (for Cantabria). Directora Regional de Turismo, Plaza de España s/n, 33007 Oviedo, Tel (985) 24 25 27. The Asturian board in particular publishes good booklets in English on art and architecture of the region and the Santiago pilgrimage route. Useful **tourist offices** include those in Santander (Plaza Porticada), Santillana del Mar, Oviedo and, around the Picos mountains, at Potes, Cangas de Onís, Panes and Covadonga.

SANTANDER

Concrete towers forming a gap-toothed skyline, endless ranks of cranes and warehouses, and a sea-front of tatty apartment blocks are hardly likely to endear Santander to you. But first impressions are deceiving. To the west, separated from the modern town by an isthmus, is El Sardinero, an enclave of *belle époque* grand hotels and fantasy villas which recalls Santander's heyday as the playground of Spanish royals and the beau-mondish set. The Plymouth-Santander ferry provides the town with a steady stream of trade from the British, but at most times of the year you will probably feel that one night here is enough. It does, however, have a flourishing classical music and ballet scene with concerts held in the atmospheric surroundings of the arcaded Plaza Porticado, around the cathedral and in the candy-striped Teatro de Festivales.

The majority of Santander's visitors are middle class Spaniards – genteel elderly ladies, dignified men who spend their days behind newspapers, and smartly dressed families. Days are spent window shopping, promenading along the sea-front, lingering in pavement cafés, and, when the weather is good, heading to one of the four good sandy beaches. Contrasting with all this are scenes of locals haggling over prices in the market, down-and-outs sleeping under the arcades of the cathedral, and a surprisingly vigorous nightlife, focusing on the *bodegas* on Daoiz y Velarde and Calle Hernán Cortes, which get so crowded that people spill out into the street. You will also find plenty of good places to eat here.

El Sardinero, west of the town centre and beyond the La Magdalena isthmus, is the site of a palace on the lines of Osborne House, which the city built for King Alfonso XIII's English wife, Victoria Eugenia, as she was attracted by the familiarity of Santander's bracing (and often damp) climate. The palace is now home to a summer university.

There is a certain forlornness about El Sardinero as it tries to adapt itself to the late-twentieth-century holiday market. The ritzy casino now offers bingo; dark-suited businessmen and pale-skinned Englishmen emerge from the glitzy lobby of a luxury hotel, and some undistinguished '70s apartments and restaurants have joined the old élitist boltholes. The two good sandy beaches, however, compensate somewhat for the odd atmosphere.

Ferries from Plymouth dock about halfway along the sea-front, a couple of minutes' walk from Plaza Porticado. If you need a room for the night it is best to drive straight out to the quieter hotels of El Sardinero, rather than trying to negotiate the busy streets of the town. The hotels Roma, Tel (942) 27 27 00, and cheaper Paris, Tel (942) 27 23 50, on Avenida de los Hoteles are in beautiful *belle époque* buildings in El Sardinero, but their interiors are undistinguished. Both are easy to find.

The main sights

● **The cathedral** An awkward, and much-restored Gothic stack which was partially destroyed, along with much of the old town, when a vessel with a cargo of armaments exploded on the quayside in 1941. Passing the debris of the down-and-outs' miniature cardboard city, you enter the cathedral's early Gothic crypt, which now forms the separate church of **Santissimo Cristo**. Low Gothic vaults rest on stubby columns, and glass let into the floor would reveal the foundations of a Roman building below, if they were illuminated.

● **Museo Municipal de Bellas Artes** A collection of Goya's powerful etchings (and the occasional outstanding temporary exhibition) make an otherwise dull gallery of mostly contemporary Spanish works well worth a visit. The Goyas are on the top floor. *Los Desastres de la Guerra*, 52 images of the brutality of war, includes the distressing *Para eso habeis nacido* ('For this you were born') in which a man vomits over a heap of dead bodies. The *Los Caprichos* series unflinchingly details the actions of a corrupt, rapacious society. There is also one painting by Goya, a portrait of Fernando VII, unflatteringly depicted as a belligerent oaf, with a monster of a dog painted in a nightmarishly impressionistic style, sprawled at his feet.

● **Museo Provincial de Prehistoria y Arqueología** A largely unremarkable collection of local prehistoric, Roman, Celtic, and medieval finds, labelled only in Spanish. Bones engraved with animal silhouettes from the province's pre-historic caves will intrigue enthusiasts, as no one knows what they were used for, but most people will be more interested in the photographs of cave drawings.

● **Museo Maritimo** With ghoulish delights like a pickled placenta, shark's skull and whale foetus, this is not a museum

101

for the squeamish. But children seem to love it, and there are less nauseating displays of fish, shellfish, molluscs and sea-plants, as well as the skeleton of a whale. The museum is near the port.

THE COAST EAST OF SANTANDER

There is a superb ten-kilometre crescent of sand at Laredo fifty kilometres east of Santander, which is unfortunately backed by a dull, clinical resort. If you want to spend a day on the beach you would be better off going to **Islares**, where there is a tremendous sweep of golden sand in a hilly bay backed by jagged limestone cliffs. The best stretch is below the restaurant (El Langostino) and a small caravan site. **Oriñón**, slightly closer to Laredo, is a similar beach, flanked by limestone hills covered with scrub.

Close to the border with the Basque Country, **Castro Urdiales** is a great place to stop for lunch. The outskirts are modern and semi-industrialised, but turn-of-the-century houses with *solanas* line the waterfront, and the small fishing harbour is headed by a sturdily buttressed cathedral and a lighthouse encircled by castle walls. Behind the waterfront is a mazy old quarter where neighbours on balconies chat across the narrow streets to one another, and men hop from one dark bar or *tasca* to another. Steps lead up from here to the cathedral, a sprawling Gothic structure with cracked windows and eroded carvings.

Back down on the harbour, on a little square opposite the mock-castle *ayuntamiento* are a few fish restaurants, notably the Mesón Marineros, which spreads its bar with an irresistible array of fresh, imaginative fish and seafood *tapas* – glistening prawns, *mejillones* (vibrant orange mussels) and slices of toast and french bread with scrumptious sea-food toppings.

There is little accommodation in Castro – the best bet is El Cordobes (Calle Ardigales 11, Tel (942) 86 00 89) in a neat stone building behind the waterfront. Failing that, ask about rooms at the Pizzería Pérgola on the sea-front, or take a room in one of the bland hotels on **Brazomar Beach** (Playa de Brazomar), a kilometre or so to the east of town. The beach with soft, golden sand in an enclosed bay, is adequate, but it gets packed with day-trippers from Bilbao and Santander.

SANTILLANA DEL MAR (H)

A postcard of Santillana del Mar makes an unlikely appearance in Jean-Paul Sartre's *Nausea*, in which the village is dubbed the most beautiful in Spain. Mellow escutcheon-bearing mansions, stone houses with timber-framed galleries, and a disarmingly lovely Romanesque church certainly make Santillana photogenic. Despite the coach parties, hotels, restaurants and souvenir shops, it is still a working dairy village. Tractors with loads of grass drive along cobbled streets splashed with manure; washing dries on balconies above the obligatory pots of geraniums, and at the back of the village the ground floors of houses are still used as byres. In addition to its own considerable charms, Santillana is just two kilometres from the Altamira Caves (see page 104), and gets very crowded in summer. It is none the less still a pleasing place to stay, and is considerably less busy in the evening once the coach parties have left.

Santillana is accustomed to visitors: throughout the Middle Ages the relics of Santa Juliana, housed in what is now the Colegiata church, attracted pilgrims. Santa Juliana was something of an early feminist, defying the wishes of her father and the devil and refusing to marry. In the fifteenth century, nobles began to build themselves the mansions that make Santillana what it is today. The coats of arms, however, are by no means limited to the grander mansions – many a farmer has seen fit to stick his family crest on the façade of his house.

The village is split in two. The older part, consisting of two parallel streets, lies on one side of the main road, and the newer, but nevertheless pretty half stands around a large green beyond the Regina Coeli convent. The hotels in the older half are converted mansions, but if you want something cheaper, head to the houses around the village green where there are a couple of *hostales* and several village houses letting high-quality rooms.

The main sights

● **Colegiata de Santa Juliana** Santa Juliana's relics are housed in the golden Romanesque Colegiata. In the cloister honeysuckle clambers through a curtain of Virginia creeper, its scent mingling with the sour smell of horse dung, and your eyes move from carvings of monsters, snakes and centaurs on capitals to a line of washing drying on the balcony of the house next door. In the church there are more skilfully carved capitals – notably a mask with its tongue sticking out and some pelicans pecking their breasts – and the Renaissance retable includes a scene of Santa Juliana, as she ignores the pleas of the devil and her father, and refuses to marry one of

PREHISTORIC CAVES

The limestone of the Cantabrian Cordillera is riddled with caves. Some contain stalagmites and stalactites and about 30 show signs of prehistoric habitation in the form of primitive wall-paintings. The paintings are between 10,000 and 25,000 years old, and are almost exclusively of animals. Unfortunately, very few caves can now be visited as a protection against damage to the paintings, and you would be extremely lucky to see the most important and beautiful of them all, Altamira (there is a replica of it beneath the courtyard of Madrid's Archaeological Museum). If you cannot see Altamira, Castillo is the next best one to choose – it is easy to see, but make sure you turn up early in high season. Pindal and Covalanas are well worth visiting as much for their setting as for their artwork.

Altamira The caves of Altamira, two kilometres inland from San-tillana del Mar, were discovered in 1879 and for generations visitors flocked to see the paintings; so much so that the murals began to deteriorate in the moisture of the breath of their visitors'. To see them now you have to book at least six months in advance by writing to the *Centro de Investigación y Museo de Altamira*, 39330 Santillana del Mar, Cantabria. Only around 25 people are allowed in daily. Quite often, however, appointments are not kept, so if you are keen to see the paintings, it is worth turning up early in the morning to see if a place has fallen vacant. Altamira has become something of a place of pilgrimage, with many people going just for the experience of being there and to visit the museum and a couple of unpainted caves near it.

The highlight of a visit is the Painted Hall, whose ceiling is covered with fifteen bison, three wild boar, three deer, two horses and a wolf, all were painted in red and brown wash. Their outlines were defined with thickly applied black paint and engraving, and many look incredibly realistic, with the contours of the rock giving their bodies natural curves.

Cueva del Castillo If you cannot see Altamira, the Puente Viesgo caves are an enjoyable substitute. Discovered in 1903, the caves lie

her suitors. Her defiance of the devil is represented in symbolic form elsewhere: on her sarcophagus and in a side chapel where she is shown standing on the devil with his long ropey tail held firmly in her hand.

● **Museo Diocesano** A collection of Cantabrian ecclesiana

south of the dull town of Torrelavega, and are hollowed out of a grey limestone crag above a pretty village of whitewashed houses with pantile roofs. There are a number of caves, but at present only Castillo is open to the public. The prehistoric community lived in the outermost cave, creating a sanctuary of the vast inner caverns which were covered with painted bison and stencilled negative handprints adding to the mysterious beauty of stalagmites and stalactites. When at first you look at a drawing it seems very simple – a couple of dark lines on the surface of the rock – but the guide uses a torch to trace its outlines, and suddenly the skill of the prehistoric artist becomes clear, as you see how the natural contours of the rock were exploited to create a realistic animal. As for the negative handprints, no one can be sure of their significance, but the theory that they were a sort of signature is seductive.

Cuevas de Covalanas (To visit apply at the *ayuntamiento* in Ramales de la Victoria). The caves stand three kilometres outside the town, hollowed out of a soaring limestone cliff. There is a steep climb up to the entrance, but the reward is the sight of red paintings of does and cattle intriguingly outlined by dots – one theory is that this was to save paint.

Cueva del Pindal This is the most dramatically sited of Cantabria's caves, a recess in the rugged cliff-walls of a narrow jagged inlet. Inside there are palaeolithic engravings and drawings of animals, as well as stalactites. It is worth a visit even when the cave is closed, for you can walk along a narrow cliff path where butterflies dart among bracken and holly bushes, the sound of crickets underpins the roar of crashing breakers, and sunlight flickers on the swelling turquoise sea.

Tito Bustillo These caves are just outside Ribadesella, and have good stalactites, as well as wall-paintings which include a beautiful black horse's head.

Cueva del Buxu (Only 25 people admitted daily.) These caves are a half-mile trek off the Cangas de Onís to Panes road. They have engravings of horses and stags, two hinds, an ibex and a fallow deer, and a painted ibex head – all quite tiny and difficult to spot. For enthusiasts only.

lovingly restored by nuns, housed in the beautiful Regina Coeli convent. The objects are displayed to show the development of certain religous images.

● **The Zoo** If you failed to see the prehistoric bison painted on the walls of the Altamira cave, make do with a pair of real ones here. The zoo is prettily landscaped, and has an appealing variety of birds and animals, including, sadly, some miserable-looking wild cats in cramped cages. The zoo is outside the town on the road to the Altamira caves.

TOURING INLAND CANTABRIA

The gentle foothills of the Cordillera Cantábrica are scattered with dairy farms, small villages of stone houses, and Romanesque churches. Higher up, deep grassy valleys crested with rocky outcrops lie between the mountains of the Cordillera. The scenery is nowhere near as dramatic as the Picos de Europa further west, but you can spend a pleasant day following the purple-painted road signs to the diminutive churches (most of which are currently undergoing restoration) and taking remote mountain roads through switchback passes.

The area to the east of Puente Viesgo along the S–580 from El Soto is good for this kind of scenery. When you have seen all you want, you can press on through Villacarriedo, with its splendid baroque palace built by an Italian architect for a Castilian noble, and over the La Braguia pass into the remote valley of the River Pas dotted with shepherds' huts. You could then head back north along the Miera valley (S–572), or via the dramatic Alisas Pass (S–531), known as the 'viewpoint of Cantabria' for its panoramic views.

Alternatively, if you are interested in cave paintings, you could drive west to Ramales de la Victoria, to visit the nearby Cuevas de Covalanas.

The Ebro basin

From Puente Viesgo the N–623 heads south to the Ebro reservoir (Embalse de Ebro) a vast glassy expanse of water on the southern flanks of the Cordillera Cantábrica, filled by the River Ebro, which is circled with ancient churches. The most memorable of them is just above the lake at **Retortillo**, its walls in many shades of gold standing alongside the foundations of a Roman villa. To see the inside – there are two unusual capitals depicting warriors against a background of acanthus leaves – apply to Ramón González at the house at the centre of the village.

The nearest town to the Embalse, **Reinosa**, is surrounded by dire industrial suburbs, and is best known in Spain for a headline-hitting case of police brutality in 1987. Its proximity to the mountains secures it a certain amount of tourist trade, but even its old core of stone mansions is unlikely to tempt you to stay. It is well worth making a short diversion south to **Cervatos**, a sleepy hamlet of cobbled streets and whitewashed houses just off the busy N–611, to see a splendid Romanesque church with unexpectedly erotic carvings on the capitals of its apse.

Bárcena Mayor

West of Reinosa the C–628 passes through Fontibre, from which you can walk up to the source of the Ebro, Spain's longest river. Beyond Fontibre, the C–625 heaves over the mountains to the Saja valley. A tortuously winding road, it demands careful driving at any time, but becomes nightmarish when the mists descend, drastically reducing visbility. Eventually it drops into the broad valley, from where a beautiful mountain route to the Picos de Europa begins just beyond Renedo (see page 117).

Before you head for the Picos, however, it is rewarding to make a diversion to **Bárcena Mayor** – perhaps even staying here, as it is an astonishingly lovely village into which the Cantabrian authorities are currently pumping cash in the hope of creating another Santillana. It lies off the main road, to the east of the Reserva Nacional de Saja, a protected mountainous area stretching east to the Picos mountains, whose beech, oak and birch forests are home to roe deer, stags and wild boar. The narrow lane to Bárcena is being widened considerably to cope with the anticipated explosion of tourist traffic, and the village itself is heralded by an immense car park. A few years ago Bárcena was largely abandoned and in ruins, but most of the mellow, honey-coloured stone houses with wooden galleries have been restored, and the streets have been smartly paved and lit by pretty wrought-iron lamps. Though in danger of becoming bijou, it is at present home to a small farming community and a handful of back-to-nature craftsmen and intellectuals. The recently restored stone trough is used to wash cars as well as water animals. The main inn,

Venta la Franca, Tel (942) 70 60 67, plays classical music and sells hand-crafted *rabeles* (lute-violins), tambourines and rocking horses, along with rakes and baskets. The village is also visited for its mountain cuisine – try it at the Venta, or the Mésón Rio Argoza, Tel (942) 70 60 33. Both these have rooms to rent.

WEST OF SANTANDER

The first stop of note west of Santander is **Comillas**. The town, with its mansions and cobbled streets, retains an air of refinement and contained the summer residence of Alfonso XII. On his heels came members of the Madrid and Barcelona aristocracy, among them Alfonso's industrialist friend, the first Marquis of Comillas, who commissioned the architect Gaudí (see page 226) to build a folly in the garden of his mansion. Sadly Comillas' pursuit of elegance has not been taken as far as the sea-front, where a messy modern resort dribbles along the edge of the soft sandy beach.

Give the resort a miss and while away a couple of hours exploring the town and dining, if you can afford to, at the prestigious restaurant in Gaudí's folly, El Capricho. As playful as its name suggests, El Capricho is an eclectic extravaganza of sinuous wrought iron, cheerful sunflower ceramics and capitals carved with birds, and there is a bronze of Gaudí sitting cross-legged on a stone bench in the garden. Up a slope from the folly-restaurant is the Marquis' palace, a Moorish-Gothic fantasy designed by one of Gaudí's contemporaries, Juan Martorell. There are ornate mansions in various states of repair throughout the town, and, round the sloping main square, well-maintained houses with glassed-in balconies, a Bishop's Palace studded with colourful coats of arms, and the Gothic cathedral combine to make a pleasant arena in which to enjoy a lazy drink.

There are a number of popular beaches to the west of Comillas, notably **Labrana**, long, white and duny, with a big car park and campsite. **San Vicente de la Barquera** (H) a few kilometres further along the coast, is approached by an arched bridge across its estuary and is Cantabria's most relaxed resort. The pavement cafés and seafood restaurants under the arcades of the main street are full of animated Spanish families, and above them old people stare from balconies hung with washing or caged canaries. The waterfront is lined with cheerful pizzerias and bars, the small harbour is overlooked by flaky, ochre-washed houses and a tiny ice-making factory. If you want to escape to somewhere quieter, the old walled town, dominated by a church and grim castle has sleepy, off-stage feel. A stepped street from the square leads past the backs of houses through a gateway into the old town. You can either head straight up to the church, past pastel-washed stone mansions, or follow a soggy path through a tangle of musk-scented undergrowth to a sentry path along the walls; this will also take you up to the church. The thirteenth-century Our Lady of the Angels (Nostra Señora de los Angeles) sits on a broad terrace with views over the estuary and inland, towards the Picos. Only the north and south portals survive from the Romanesque period – the rest of the church is Gothic.

The fact that traffic on the main coastal road speeds right through the centre of San Vicente seems to bother no one, but the town beach, a long, clean sandy strip on the far side of the estuary, is rather exposed, and swimming here is not always safe.

THE ASTURIAN COAST TO GIJON (H)

The verdant, hilly coastline between San Vicente and Gijón holds a series of indented bays with sandy beaches, mostly used by Spanish campers and day-tripping locals. There are no resorts as such – development consists usually of a couple of bars, a car park and maybe a campsite. The N-634 runs parallel to the coast, with side roads leading off to the beaches and campsites.

Lovelier than any of the beaches, however, is the rocky stretch of coast by the **Cuevas del Pindal** where you can walk along the clifftops. The first village worth stopping at is **Llanes**, a lobster port with pavement cafés and a *sidrería* (cider bar) on a scruffily picturesque quayside. Within the village tall crumbly houses stand around a little square, the vanilla and cream neo-baroque town hall looks ridiculously ornate, and on the fringes there are a number of elaborate houses built by returned emigrants. A ruined castle overlooks a neat beach in a horseshoe cove, and there is a fine promenade following the medieval walls along the clifftop. If you wish to stay here, there are a number of adequate hotels, of which the historic Don Paco (Posada Herrera 1, Tel (985) 40 01 50) is the most distinctive.

Continuing west, you pass a number of beaches, none of

which is special. Nor is it worth stopping for long in **Ribadasella**, an ordinary fishing town split by a gaping river estuary, with a messy old quarter lurking behind a screen of modern buildings. The **Tito Bustillo** caves (see page 105) are close by. The **Playa de Vega** is also very near; approached by a road that passes through the narrowest of rocky gorges and then through a whitewashed and red-roofed village, it is a long and rather exposed duny beach, with a plain of maize-fields behind it. The breakers can be quite high, but it is quieter than La Isla beyond.

Villaviciosa and two churches

In 1517, Charles I, grandson of Isabella and Ferdinand spent his first night in Spain unintentionally at Villaviciosa. He had been crowned two years earlier in Brussels, but had been brought up in France, never visited Spain, and spoke no Spanish whatsoever. His first taste of the country did not augur well. His fleet and his entourage of 200 ladies and gentlemen in waiting were supposed to arrive at Santander, but ended up at Tazones, on the tip of the Ría de Villaviciosa, by mistake – much to the excitement of the villagers, who immediately arranged a *corrida* in his honour. Charles, accustomed to the sophistication of the French court, was not impressed.

Villaviciosa today is likely to elicit the same reaction – though the Romanesque church of *Santa María de Villaviciosa* is worth a look. It stands at the head of a pretty street of stone and whitewashed houses, has some animated carvings on its portal capitals, with a Virgin and (now headless) child suspended above.

There is a more memorable church nine kilometres inland, in the fertile Valdedíos valley two kilometres off the road to Oviedo. Ninth century **San Salvador** stands next to a ruined Cistercian church, and shows Mozarabic influence in its horseshoe arches and strapwork capitals.

From Villaviciosa you could continue along the coast, though the stretch between Gijón and Cudillero to the west is heavily industrialised. A better option would be to head inland to Oviedo (see page 113), and rejoin the coast at Cudillero, most pleasantly along the winding valley of the River Nalón, where the best Asturian cider apples are grown.

Gijón (H)

A gutsy port whose inhabitants play hard, long and fast, Gijón is not only an industrial centre, but also a magnet for tourists, as an alarming number of people flock to its two-kilometre-long beach. A resolute socialist stronghold, Gijón suffered severely in the Civil War and had to be virtually rebuilt. In the centre, traffic-jams block streets of concrete towers, and in what remains of the war-damaged old quarter, cider-flushed revellers swarm from one bar to another. Waiting at traffic lights, you will have plenty of time to read the local graffitti, whether it is deriding the army, sneering at the EC or expressing support for Nicaragua, and see such other sights as an Internacional sex shop advert on the football stadium and a bar named Spitting.

Entering the town from the east, lines of villas on avenues of lollipop trees give way to characterless housing estates. A further leap down the social scale brings you to the sea-front where a grimy high-rise crescent (housing the social security office as well as pavement cafés) overlooks the beach.

If you do find yourself in Gijón, there are a handful of museums and monuments which you might visit. The most engaging are the small but well-preserved **Roman baths** in the old quarter, and the **Museo de La Gaita** devoted to the world history of the bagpipe and sited in the new Pueblo de Asturias on the right bank of the River Piles.

THE COAST ROAD TO GALICIA

Cudillero (H) and Cabo Vidio

An uncompromisingly industrial landscape exerts grim fascination on the twenty-five-kilometre drive between Gijón and Avilés. Entering **Cudillero** past bland roadside houses and a bleak concrete port, your first instinct is to get away as quickly as possible. However, beyond the modern port is a tiny fishing harbour picturesquely backed by a stack of red-roofed houses tumbling down a cliff. There are pavement cafés and fish restaurants around the harbour, and a maze of steep, stepped streets to explore. Hotels can be found in the hamlets around, including a recommendable one nearby.

Most of the beaches close to Cudillero are rocky or shingly – though this does not deter the crowds from **Playa de la Concha de Artedo**. They cushion themselves with towels to lie on the large pebbles, or simply sun-bathe on the wall of the café. The **Playa de Holero** reached along a track through a forest is a secluded, curving sweep of shingle in a bay backed by cliffs and woods, but as it is not signposted you will need to ask for directions. Easier to find is the popular **Playa de San Pedro**, two kilometres outside the village of Soto de Luiña. Running between two cliffy headlands, it is a narrow strip of soft golden sand rising to angular pebbles. There is a shadeless campsite full of Spanish families, and when the sea is choppy, as it frequently is, children can play in the sandy, reedy river.

If you are thrilled by dizzying drops, head out to the light-house on **Cabo Vidio**. On a clear day there are great views up and down the coast, but more memorable is the narrow clifftop path in front of the lighthouse – from which a wall of striated rock plunges into the waters. There is a more unusual attraction at nearby **Puerto de Portiello** – a crab and lobster farm where you balance along slithery walkways above tanks of angry crustaceans.

Luarca (H) to Figueras (H)

There are some pretty stretches along the coast road to Luarca, with glimpses of the sea through mixed forests along with expanses of rolling fields. Embraced by green cliffs and bisected by a narrow, silty river, **Luarca** is one of Asturias' more attractive fishing villages. Six-storey apartment blocks mingle unobtrusively with tall old buildings, and in the sheltered harbour colourful fishing boats are anchored in neat rows overlooked by elegant houses and huddled fishermen's cottages. Civilised and relaxed, it attracts a steady stream of visitors, and is one of the few places on the Asturian coast where you are likely to bump into your compatriots. Luarca's two beaches are of hard-packed sand, (sometimes sprinkled with coal dust) backed by slate cliffs, and each has an old-fashioned row of changing cabins. Early in the morning, the sun filtering through mist, turns into silhouettes the pension-ers collecting barnacles by the shore. There is a helpful tourist office in the riverside *ayuntamiento*. Bars along the river, of which Salinas with its traditonal and colourful tiled interior is the prettiest, sell cider in large unlabelled green bottles . Most of the restaurants are by the harbour. La Darseña is cheap, popular, noisy, serves great fish (try the grilled *bonito*) and has a menu in English.

The N-634 heads west from Luarca, running between the coast and the foothills of the Sierra de Rañadoiro, through a wealthy agricultural area with farmhouses dispersed among large fields. It joins the coast again at **Navia**, where heavy lorries hurtle down to the harbour along a main street lined with *fin-de-siècle* houses and modern blocks. **Tapia de Casariego**, 25 kilometres further on, is a resort of villas, most of which are private, and has a good beach of dark gold sand in a long, cliff-flanked inlet. There is an appealing little harbour, with pavement cafés on the quayside, and a centre saved from blandness by a grand town hall and palm-shaded square.

Figueras, on the shore of the Ría de Ribadeo (which forms the border with Galicia), is a nicer place to stay than Tapia, a small fishing village and port with a mixture of scruffy cottages and modern houses. A privately-owned ramshackle palace overlooks the port – its occupants live in faded splendour among a chaos of ancient heirlooms, and if they are at home will show you a labyrinth of dusty beamed halls, and an overgrown garden of toppled statuary.

OVIEDO AND ITS CHURCHES

Though the capital of the Principality, Oviedo had its heyday in the ninth century, as the power-centre of the peninsula's only Christian kingdom. This period bequeathed to what is now a characterless industrial city some of Asturias' best pre-Romanesque churches: if you are not interested in these, there is little point in visiting. Oviedo does have an old town, but its streets are too grimy to be picturesque, and the café life too fragmented to animate them. A ten-minute walk takes you from the bustling and noisy Plaza y Mercado del Fontan (the market square), through the boring conventionality of Plaza Mayor, to Plaza de Trascorrales, a haven for the rich Oviedans. Here ladies sit in cafés wafting the hot air with expensive fans, while their men occasionally lurch sideways to pour cider from on high. The balconies above are crammed with geraniums and TV aerials.

Plaza de Alfonso II, dominated by the asymmetrical and eroded façade of the cathedral, has a certain charm. The Valdecarzana Palace, built of the distinctive peachy-gold Oviedan stone, displays a boisterous coat of arms on which a long-haired thug clubs an indignant lion, while pollution has rendered anorexic the armorial figures on the fifteenth-century Casa de la Rúa.

If you cannot afford to eat in the restaurants on Plaza Trascorrales, try a remarkable fast food restaurant: Cabo Penas, Melchiades Alvares 24. Hams and strings of garlic and dried peppers hang from metal beams, and you can either eat in the front bar, or on high chairs in a restaurant full of families echoing with voices and the rumble of the air-conditioning fan. The menu is imaginative, ranging from onions stuffed with tuna to chicory with a Roquefort dip, and food is served swiftly and without ceremony.

The sights of Oviedo can easily be seen on a day-trip from the coast, but if you need to stay the night, try the homely and central Hostal Porlier (Plaza de Porlier 3, Tel (985) 22 47 20).

The main sights

● **The Cathedral** A flamboyant Gothic structure with a lacily pierced spire, Oviedo's cathedral was built between the fourteenth and sixteenth centuries, though there has been a church on the site since the days of Alfonso II. Inside, the altarpiece is the most eyecatching feature, a glinting dolls' house crammed with 3-D scenes from Christ's life. (Twenty-five pesetas in a slot will illuminate all the detail). The early Asturian Kings are buried in the Panteón del Rey Casto – the Chaste King's (i.e. Alfonso II) Pantheon – though as a well-meaning baroque face-lift obliterated the inscriptions, no one is really sure which grave is whose.

You have to pay to see Alfonso II's early ninth-century church, the **Cámera Santa** or the Holy Chamber, built to house relics rescued from Toledo when it fell to the Moors. Although much restored – most recently after Civil War damage – it has wonderful details, like the pairs of chatting apostles supporting the vaults. In the apse are the Toledo relics, notably a silver-plated coffer and a jewelled Maltese cross. These also had to be restored after being stolen and smashed by vandals in 1977.

The ticket also admits you to the **Museo de la Iglesia**, opened in 1990. Ecclesiastical sculptures and architectural fragments, processional crosses and paintings are all well-displayed, but the real treasure is a fourteenth-century ivory diptych, exquisitely carved with minute details such as the dog bouncing at Christ's ankles as he rides into Jerusalem, and Judas pinching the last fish at the Last Supper. You leave the cathedral through the sooty Gothic cloisters.

● **Museo Arqueológico** Housed in a Renaissance convent, whose plateresque apricot-painted cloister, with its trickling fountain and garden of fuchsias and roses, is as enticing as the exhibits. Ignore the cases and cases of prehistoric flints, and head straight for the rooms where exhibits trace the development of church design from pre-Romanesque to Gothic using photographs of churches and pieces of architecture and sculpture. Equally appealing is the folk art collection, with kitchen utensils, drinking horns, bagpipes, tambours and a freakish accordion-violin hybrid.

● **Santullano** An ancient church with intriguing frescoes, which unfortunately now stands right next to a dual carriageway. Built between the years 792 and 842, it is Spain's oldest surviving pre-Romanesque church, and no one quite knows why it should have been covered with frescoes imitating the walls of a Roman villa, with elaborate *trompe-l'oeil* windows, curtains and eaves.

● **Santa María del Naranco** and **San Miguel de Lillo** Wonderfully located on the slopes of Monte Naranco, beyond Oviedo's most desirable suburbs, Santa María del Naranco is considered to be Asturias' best pre-Romanesque church. It was built around 850 as a summer palace for Ramiro I, but converted into a church some fifty years afterwards. San Miguel, 200 metres up the hill, was the palace chapel.

The opening hours are unreliable, and the guide divides her time between the two churches, so be prepared to hang around. Once she arrives you will have to endure a stone-by-stone description of both churches, in Spanish. Santa María is a rectangular structure of warm golden stone, with arcaded galleries at either end, columns carved to resemble rope, and medallions seemingly suspended from stone ribbons. Flat, grooved buttresses take the strain of the interior's innovative arched vaults, which are supported inside by rope-carved columns and there are good carvings on the Byzantine-style capitals.

San Miguel, probably built by the architect of Santa María, is an unusually tall cross-plan church with a flaking plaster interior, chewed capitals, and a gallery reached by a narrow staircase. The best features are the intricate rope-motif windows, and the reliefs of acrobats and lion-tamers on the door jambs.

115

THE INLAND ROUTE TO GALICIA

From Oviedo you can take a wild, mountainous, and frequently unmetalled route into Galicia. It begins innocuously enough, with the N-634 whipping you through a succession of ordinary towns like Grado, and villages which make their living from forestry. **Salas** is worth a brief stop to visit a fortified palace which now houses a café, hotel and helpful tourist office. A member of the tourist office staff will take you up to the palace's tower for views of gentle hills and scattered hamlets.

Turn off on to the C-630 at La Espina, and head up through Tineo, an ugly place with pretty views, and on to the mountainous route across the **Sierra de Rañadoiro**. Beyond Pola de Allande a spectacular but alarmingly pitted pass road climbs through spartan landscape of limestone screes, heather, bracken and the occasional scrawny tree. From the Puerto del Palo you get your first glimpse of Galicia, and then carry on across smooth barren hills and conifer-planted lower slopes, passing abandoned cars and isolated villages, to the skeletal hydro-electric installations on the River Navia. As you enter Galicia, the harsh vegetation continues but villages of granite houses with fish-scale slate roofs and *hórreos* punctuate the route to Lugo.

THE PICOS DE EUROPA

The southern outcrop of Cantabrian mountains known as the Picos de Europa measures only about 45 kilometres across at its broadest point. That is the same as Britain's Lake District, though the Picos are nearly three times as high. Like the Lake District, the region is packed with an extraordinary variety of scenery for its size. This miniature mountain range contains enough of Spain's grandest limestone landscapes to keep the most demanding walker or rock-climber happy. If your mountaineering ambitions do not reach such heights, there is still plenty to enjoy. The crests are snow-capped for several months of the year, towering above fertile orchards and meadows full of alpine flowers in spring. Tourers are mostly confined to the edges of the region, following river valleys cut by spectacular swooping gorges. Docile, bell-clanking cows frequently slow your progress along country roads. The rough tracks through the central massifs are negotiable only by rugged four-wheel drive vehicles.

The region is roughly triangular in shape, bounded by the roads connecting Cangas de Onís, Panes and Riaño. Much of the land within this area, and surrounding it on the southern side, is given over either national parkland or nature reserves. To the north, the coast is only a few miles away. The region's administration is complicated: the Picos fall into three different regions, so Asturias, Cantabria, and Castilla y León all have a share in its management (not always seeing eye to eye). Asturias' green lobby woke up sooner to the threats facing the environment than those elsewhere in Spain, and has fiercely opposed unsuitable development.

Apart from one or two minor churches, and the famous shrine of Covadonga, there are few man-made 'sights' or wet-weather diversions and few towns and villages are especially pretty or individual. What the Picos offer is outdoor pursuits, making the most of the magnificent scenery. If you are exceptionally unlucky with the weather you may find yourself reduced to quaffing sour Asturian cider in dark bars.

The approach route from Cantabria

The swiftest route into the Picos is from the Asturian coast, but the inland approach from Cantabria is more spectacular. Take the winding C-6314 from Cabuerniga, just beyond Renedo in the Saja Valley which leads across to the Hermida Gorge.

A succession of narrow passes link fertile valleys barricaded by mountains on whose slopes grassy meadows give way to uplands of bracken and heather splashed with yellow broom and silver oak-scrub. In the villages which cluster in the valleys, old men in berets and slippers sit outside bars, measuring their days with cigarettes, younger men fork the nearby hayfields, and women take a brief pause from chores to examine the racks of cheap frocks in the mobile clothes shop. One of the loveliest villages is **Carmona** (H), where geraniums drip from wooden balconies, and the only sounds are of bees humming in hives. If you want a restful night in this sleepy village there is one gorgeous hotel.

The most exciting part of the route is at **Linares**, its limestone cottages dwarfed by towering limestone peaks, streaked black, cream, grey and ochre. The mountain road joins the N-621 at La Hermida, a dull village at the head of the Hermida gorge.

Panes (H), the Hermida Gorge and Liébana

Panes is one of the crossroads towns where you could start your tour of the Picos. The town is useful for filling up with petrol, buying picnic food (there is lots of good cider and cheese) and changing money. There is also an extremely helpful tourist office. Panes is not an attractive place to stay – far better to make a ten-kilometre diversion east to the hamlet of Besnes-Allés, and stay in a tranquil country hotel.

South of Panes, things get rapidly more exciting as you enter the **Hermida Gorge** (Desfiladero de la Hermida), where the road swings wildly alongside the River Deva between spurs and spikes of splintered crags. Beyond the village of La Hermida, the gorge broadens out at Liébana, a verdant valley of riverside meadows, vineyards and orchards. There are many places where you could stop for a picnic – try any meadow marked with a 'no camping' sign.

Secluded among vines and fruit trees off the road is the tenth-century Mozarabic church of **Santa María de Liébana**, built of mauvish-gold limestone, with a bell tower, horseshoe arches and a pantiled porch. The key is at the Garcia house in the village of Liébana, a short walk along a dirt track – be prepared to jog on your way back to keep up with the tiny old lady caretaker. Inside, capitals are carved in a Visigothic style with acanthus leaves and weird owl heads, and a vase of artificial flowers stands before an altarpiece on which a mean-faced Madonna with improbably sized breasts, the Virgin de la Buena Leche (Virgin of the Good Milk) feeds a Woodentop Christ. Most intriguing, however, is a Celtic tombstone carved with a pinwheel sun, still bearing an abstract human figure painted in blood and ashes. For centuries the slab lay face down in front of the altar and was used as a step, and it was only a few years ago that the stone was turned over and the Celtic symbols discovered.

Potes

Potes, bisected by a river, is the main tourist centre of the Picos, and is a useful place to buy food and maps, change money, and get information from the tourist office, which is on the market place. For facts about jeep trips, horseriding and other activities go to the sports and excursions centre at Calle del Obispo 9 (where Fnglish is spoken). Unless reliant on public transport, you probably will not want to stay in Potes. It is, however, worth a quick look around. Beyond the modern periphery the fifteenth-century Torre Infantada (now a mountain-guides' base) overlooks the congested main road, and on the market square (the market is held on Monday mornings) a trim neo-classical church dwarfs a second, tumbledown church which now holds a tile warehouse. You may also want to take a short stroll through an enclave of old whitewashed houses on the west bank of the river.

A side-trip: Santa María de Piasca

In the Middle Ages it was fairly normal practice for monks and nuns to live in the same mountain monasteries. **Santa María de Piasca**, some six kilometres south-east of Potes, was one such foundation. Perched on a hillside above the River Bullón, it is a twelfth-century church surrounded by ramshackle monastery buildings, a farmyard and a wood-smoky hamlet. Outside, at eye-level, its capitals are carved with snakes, bearded musicians, an armoured knight and a fatuous-looking monk. The church is kept locked, but word is likely to get round the hamlet that strangers have arrived to see the church, and the leathery old caretaker will appear with the key, and point out everything from the Mozarabic windows to a bird's nest.

To the source of the River Deva

Views of scrunched, serrated peaks accompany you on the dead-end route west from Potes, on a newly surfaced river-side road through the wooded Deva Valley. In the hills above the road is the monastery of **Santo Toribio de Liébana**, a Gothic rebuilding of a seventh-century foundation where, around the year 786, the monk Beatus de Liébana wrote his *Commentary on the Apocalypse* later copies of which were some of the Middle Ages' most remarkable manuscripts. There are only reproductions of these on show in the cloisters, but they are well worth a close look, with their abstract decoration and stylised figures. Visitors come in droves here to see yet another fragment of the True Cross, kept in an ornate baroque chapel. Far more engaging is the Mirador de San Toribio above, from where there are magnificent views of the Andara massif.

Back on the main road you pass the La Isla campsite, (where you can book a pony trek for a day or half a day), and the village of **Cosgaya** (H). Sheep graze in the neat gardens of villas, a stream babbles by the roadside, and a tight maze of stone and timber houses huddles above, making it a pretty and convenient place to stay.

Espinama, beyond, is a more down-to-earth village, split by a stream, with muddy stone streets tumbling down between rundown houses, barns and woodstacks leading to the villagers' allotments. It stands at the beginning of the jeep track to Sotres – though this is not one of the Picos' most spectacular routes – and you can book jeep excursions at the Mésón Maximo on the main road. If you want to stay and get a taste of Picos village life, there are some very simple *fondas* – try the more secluded Puente Deva Tel (942) 73 01 19.

Fuente Dé (H)

A *parador* resembling a comprehensive school and the cables of the *teleférico* dampen the impact of this 800-metre-high curving limestone wall which soars above the meadow at the source of the River Deva. Only masochists climb it – saner mortals ascend by cable car braving stomach-churning lurches. The ride is extremely popular, and even on a dull day you may have to wait over an hour. You are given a numbered ticket and then have to wait until your number is called over a loud-speaker. Once at the top you can walk four kilometres (or take a jeep-ride) to the Refugio de Aliva, a comfortable mountain refuge with a café-restaurant and sun terrace which is a good base for walkers.

Apart from the *parador* and cable car station, Fuente Dé itself has just a campsite and restaurant, El Rebeco, Tel (942) 73 09 65, where you can book jeep excursions. In high season you will need to do this a couple of days in advance.

Potes to Posada de Valdeón

Going back to Potes, the N-621 skirts the eastern massif, running through a deeply incised river gorge and up through scrub-covered hills past high meadows where the hay is scythed by hand and lies in fields to dry out before being stacked. The Mirador Puerta Gloria (the Gate of Glory viewpoint) perched above the steep valley, with views over a series of peaks, is a favourite with hang-gliders, who pose to impress their groupies, then skim down to the valley bottom far below.

The road descends to a miniature gorge draped with wild roses and clumps of broom, and riverside meadows blazed with daisies and poppies. At Portilla de la Reina, a tiny grim village hemmed in by boulders, take the northern fork up to the **Puerto de Pandetrave**. From here there is a sensational view of the Caben de Romona peak, often to be seen rising like a child-drawn castle above the clouds.

Beyond Santa Marina de Valdeón, a village of crouched houses and haystores on stilts, you squeeze along a lane, so narrow that the banks of wild flowers brush the sides of the car, to **Posada de Valdeón**. A gateway to the southern end of the Cares Gorge (see opposite), it is a pleasant but rapidly expanding walking base which inappropriately large coach tours have discovered. You can stock up on provisions at an ugly but useful supermarket, and there is a friendly information centre with maps and wildlife charts. In the heart of the village is the Picos de Europa bar, a lively and amiable place where giant *bocadillos* (sandwiches) satisfy the most ravenous walker. It gets very busy, so place your order in assertive Spanish style. There are several places to stay in Posada. The best bets are the geranium-bedecked Fonda Begoña, Tel (987) 74 05 16, next to the Picos de Europa bar, or the Casa Abascal, Tel (987) 74 05 07, a well-kept white building on the edge of the village.

Walking the Cares Gorge

You can see most of the Picos gorges the easy way from your car window, but the Cares Gorge is inaccessible by road. To see it you have to get on your feet and it is well worth it. The River Cares cuts north from its source at the Panderruedas Pass, separating the central Urrieles massif from the westerly Cornión massif and the Covadonga National Park. For twelve kilometres it flows through a tremendous gorge, passing through a spectacular verdant cleft at its southern end to a bleak, dry landscape of shattered rock at its northerly end. The path is mostly good, rarely steep, and almost anyone of reasonable fitness should manage it without difficulty in two or three hours. Wear sensible shoes; the sharp stones can be very hard on thin trainers, and there is some loose scree. If you are short of time or energy, begin at the southern (more spectacular) end, at Caín, and double back when you have had enough. If you want to walk the whole length of the gorge, you can arrange for a jeep taxi to bring you back to your starting point from either end. This is expensive for one or two passengers; ask the tourist office to book you with a group.

From Posada de Valdeón, a narrow poorly surfaced lane

121

leads the ten kilometres or so to the tiny hamlet of Caín, where the gorge proper begins. It is a lovely journey past the Mirador del Tombo, where a monumental ibex perches on a slim pinnacle of rock, surveying a panorama of fierce jagged crests. The River Cares tumbles over boulders far below. The tough ones who walk this stretch can feel infinitely superior to the car-borne weaklings who embarrass themselves by getting stuck in single-track traffic jams. But to save your energy it is quite possible to drive (the smaller your wheelbase the better), or take a jeep taxi to Caín. Courteous National Park rangers with short-wave radios guide you through the most congested sections, and help you park in Caín. It is hard not to feel sorry for the inhabitants of this tiny, once-isolated mountain community, now swamped with tourists' vehicles. Anywhere else, cars would be banned or charged for parking. But one suspects Caín's population may find watching tourists try to extricate themselves from tricky parking places more fun than the daily round with the milk churns. And after all, there is always a place for a bar or three in Spain! So far though, only one place has rooms to let.

From the village a path leads through riverside fields where goats play, and soon you find yourself on a metre-wide track zigzagging across footbridges and through damp rock tunnels. A fine August weekend turns this well-known route into something of a motorway, but there is plenty of room to pass. This southern section of the gorge is very beautiful, trees clinging to precipitous crags, birds, butterflies and flowers decorating the orange- and grey-striped rocks, and the constant sound of water. After about an hour you find yourself walking beside a colossal sheer drop (children and vertigo sufferers beware). There are some good spots on sun-baked rocks above the path to enjoy a picnic.

Soon afterwards the path enters a more austere landscape, stretching far ahead along brown and grey ledges like a Roman road, up hill and down dale. In clear conditions you should get a glimpse of the most famous Pico of all, the awesome Naranjo de Bulnes to the south-east, gleaming orange at sunset. A side-path leads off to the bleak mountain settlements of Bulnes and Sotres, near the highest part of the central massif. At the northern end of the gorge you reach Puente de Poncebos, where there are only a couple of graceless *hostales* with bars. The roadsides turn into an unlovely car-park in high season, but you can dabble your hot weary feet in the Cares from some obligingly placed boulders. Northwards it is an easy drive of five kilometres to Arenas de

Cabrales, now elevated by its location to resort status. Here there are banks, petrol, cider-bars (*sidrerías*) and many shops selling souvenirs and local produce. The speciality is Cabrales, a ferociously acidic blue cheese of sheep's milk (usually detectable from afar by its stench). During the last week of August a popular fiesta of cheese-testing takes place amid feasting and fun. Places to stay include the pink-painted three-star Picos de Europa (good rear views), Tel (985) 335 54, and the Naranjo de Bulnes, Tel (985) 84 51 19, a plain but friendly *hostal* along the main road to Cangas de Onís.

Posada de Valdeón to the Beyos Gorge

If you are not going to walk the gorge, continue to the **Puerto de Panderruedas**. There are great views on a clear day, but it is an even more evocative spot when the valley is occluded, and the violent jags of limestone thrust up from a lake of clouds. Mists also frequently shroud the forest-clad slopes beyond, diluted to wisps wafted on the air currents as you descend to the corniche road which winds down to the valley of the River Sella and **Oseja de Sajambre**. A no-frills roadside village close to the head of a popular trail across the western massif, Oseja has some simple places to stay (try the Casa de Huespedes, Tel (987) 74 03 46). The main bar is in the grocery store, where you drink outside under a plastic canopy, or inside with the village's men, among tins of food, toothbrushes and three-heeled clogs.

Continuing along the main road, you enter the **Beyos Gorge** (Desfiladero de los Beyos). Towering slabs, pillars of vertical strata, concavities and vaults testify to the ancient strength of the River Sella, which now flows, narrow and docile, beneath a canopy of trees.

Cangas de Onís (H) and Covadonga

Prestigiously known in tourist brochures as the first capital of Christian Spain, Cangas de Onís was the home of the early Asturian kings. Today it is a dull, modern town, distinguished only by the sour smell of cheese from the many shops selling Cabrales cheese, and a twelfth-century bridge, swathed in creepers, spanning the Sella. There is also one of Spain's earliest Christian sites – the Capilla Santa Cruz, founded in the eighth century above a Celtic dolmen, but rebuilt after the Civil War. Just outside Cangas is the El Buxu cave which has some tiny palaeolithic drawings. Far more

WALKING IN THE PICOS DE EUROPA

The Picos de Europa are the largest limestone massif in Europe and the second most visited Spanish alpine area. They are divided into three subgroups, the Eastern, Central and Western massifs, separated by deep gorges which also mark the perimeter of the mountains. The central and western groups are the most spectacular: here you can go on easy day-long hikes or enjoy high rock climbing.

The Picos do not offer the most straightforward walking, however; as a maritime range, they are prone to violent storms and fogs, so you must stay on the trails or marked routes at all times. The rock is riddled with sinkholes and caves, has little vegetation and retains water poorly, with few springs above 2,000m. During clear weather the sun reflects mercilessly off bare crags and moonscape basins, which, added to the stiff altitude changes and tricky terrain, make walking even more difficult; you will need to carry at least two litres of water with you, topping up whenever possible. There are nearly a dozen mountain refuges, but they occur at odd intervals and are often full in season (May to early October). Camping is complicated by the lack of water and level, soft ground.

You might prefer to use the villages which ring the high summits as bases, though they are relatively low – none over 1,100m – and falling as they do in three provinces, access by public transport is complicated. With careful planning, though, you can devise satisfying traverses spending your nights in unspoiled villages.

You will need at least three maps: two large-scale ones for the western and central groups, and a single, smaller-scale sheet showing the relative locations of the trailhead hamlets and the mountains. The best maps at the moment, available in the towns around the Picos or from specialist dealers in the UK, are the 1:50,000 *Plano de los Tres Macizos* (published by GH Editores); the 1:25,000 *Macizo Central* (Miguel Andrados), and the *Mapa del Macizo del Cornión* an alias of the Western massif (J R Lueje).

Two popular gateways to the central zone are the villages of Sotres and Espinama, both with shops, accommodation and restaurants. Espinama has a bus service from Cantabria, though Sotres does not, and, for the lightly laden, can be reached by a magnificent, if steep, ancient cliffside trail up from Urdón (on the Espinama-bound bus route) through the hamlet of Tresviso – an eight-hour undertaking. From Sotres, the favourite destination is the new Delgado Ubeda refuge at Vega Urriello meadow, at the base of the 2,519-metre sugarloaf Naranjo de Bulnes, official logo of the Picos. An ill-advised new jeep track has disrupted the first couple of hours of the climb, but beyond the small shelter of Terenosa, a newly graded trail completes six hours' walking.

From Espinama, buses take you to the base of the overcrowded *teleférico* at Fuente Dé, a meadow at the base of a sheer rock-face. There is a tortuously steep and difficult three-hour trail up if you do not want to wait for the car, but assuming you ride up, there is still a half-day's trekking across first the Horcajos Rojos saddle and then a lunar landscape to the Delgado Ubeda hut.

Easier is the stiff, three-and-a-half-hour ascent (or descent) between Delgado Ubeda and the roadless hamlet of Bulnes, reached in turn from either Sotres or the north end of the Cares gorge (see below). Starting from Bulnes with just a daypack, the trip up to Vega Urriello and back is a popular day out.

The gorge of the Cares river separates the Western and Central massifs, and the walk along it is the most popular excursion in the Picos. Committed trekkers can reach its south end from the top of the Fuente Dé cable car by a moderate march west to a campsite at Vega de Liordes, followed by the descent of the scenic Asotín ravine to Cordinanes; otherwise you start at the hamlet of Caín (see page 121). Cangas de Onís offers access to the Western massif, with seasonal bus service all the way up to the lakes of Enol and Ercina past the shrine at Covadonga. From these an easy, well-marked trail strikes east to the refuge and meadows at Ario, three hours away and a good day-trip destination – and start of the steep, three-to-four-hour treks leading down into the Cares Gorge via the Culiembro or Trea ravines. For further progress into the western group you will have to return to the lakes and take another easy, grassy trail for two-and-a-half hours to a new refuge at Vega Redonda. A favourite short (two hours plus) excursion from here is the stroll west to the Mirador de Ordiales, with views over the Dobra river valley. Moving south along the base of the high peaks, however, is moderately difficult – the trail ends after two hours, and you have three more hours cross-country through karst to the camping meadows by the ruined Vega Huerta hut.

A good path resumes here, leading south, then west to the two villages of Soto and Oseja de Sajambre, with all facilities including bus links with Cangas de Onís. If you are keen on rambling through gentle foothills, Soto de Sajambre marks the south end of the Senda del Arcediano (the Archdeacon's Path), a medieval route based on a Roman road. It is a full day, gently downhill through idyllic scenery north to Amieva, a village just off the road to Cangas de Onís.

significant than Cangas in Spanish eyes is **Covadonga**, 11 kilometres from Cangas. It was here in the early eighth century that Pelayo, a Christian tribal chief who claimed descent from the Visigothic kings, with a small band of warriors ambushed and resoundingly beat a Muslim army. According to legend there were three hundred Christians against 150,000 Moors, which is pretty unlikely, but it is a fact that after the victory the Moors left Asturias alone, and that Spain's first Christian kingdom, the Kingdom of Asturias, was founded – whose kings would go on to lead the Reconquest.

Today souvenir stands, bars, and families engrossed in elaborate picnics line the approach to the village, and the authorities have felt obliged to admonish the 'pilgrims' with signs saying 'Remember this is a sanctuary'. Some do take the pilgrimage seriously – old ladies with carrier bags of garden flowers to lay before the Virgin, and middle-aged women without transport hitching lifts up the hill – but most people comfortably combine attending Mass in the pink and white basilica and paying their respects to the Virgin of Covadonga, with having a good day out.

More unusual than the basilica – a nineteenth-century neo-Romanesque extravaganza – is the **Santa Cueva**, which Pelayo is said to have made his headquarters. Perched above a waterfall and pool (into which everyone throws a peseta or two) it houses the tombs of Pelayo and his wife, and the image of the Virgin of Covadonga, credited with interceding on Pelayo's behalf, but represented as a sweet little doll in a stiffly embroidered gown. You leave through a tunnel, flickering in the light of scores of votive candles, and emerge outside the basilica. Before leaving, do not omit to call at one of the souvenir shops for a Virgin of Covadonga doll, plate or key-ring.

WHERE TO STAY

CANGAS DE ONIS

Hotel Peñalba   £
La Riera-Covadonga
33550 Cangas de Onís   *Tel (985) 84 92 31*

A useful stop-over by a rushing stream and an *hórreo*, on the road leading up to Covadonga, which is busy during the day but quiet at night. Newly renovated in peachy stucco, the interior is kitted out in contrived rustic style (artificial beams etc.). Bedrooms are a fair size and prettily furnished, with good shower-rooms. A good place to try a traditional Asturian *fabada*.

Open: all year **Rooms**: 8 **Credit/charge cards**: none

CARMONA

Venta de Carmona
Barrio del Palacio   ££
39554 Carmona   *Tel (942) 72 80 57*

A tastefully converted seventeenth-century signorial mansion, whose public rooms are a museum of medievalish and folksy memorabilia. There is a good restaurant, a beamed lounge with a stove (and used) fireplace and rustic-style rooms upstairs. The hotel is understandably extremely popular, so book well in advance.

Open: all year **Rooms**: 9 **Credit/charge cards**: Visa

COSGAYA

Hotel del Oso   ££
39539 Cosgaya-Potes   *Tel (942) 73 04 18*

On the road from Potes to the cable-car at Fuente Dé, this is a solid stone house with wooden upper-storey balconies and a garden with pool on one side. Inside, beamed public rooms have polished floors and rugs, copper pots, plants, fireplaces, hunting memorabilia and cosy darkwood furniture. Bedrooms are in similar rustic-mountain style and comfortable.

Open: all year except 7 Jan to 15 Feb **Rooms**: 36 **Facilities**: swimming-pool **Credit/charge cards**: Diners, Eurocard, Visa

CUDILLERO

La Lupa   £
San Juan de la Piñera
33159 Cudillero   *Tel (985) 59 00 63*

The hotel is 1.5 kilometres outside Cudillero in the hamlet of San Juan de la Piñera. The spotless rooms are tastefully equipped with Habitat-style furniture.

Open: all year **Rooms**: 17 **Credit/charge cards**: Visa

FIGUERAS

Palacete Peñalba ££
El Cotarelo
33794 Figueras *Tel (985) 62 31 50*

The building is a fantasia of curvaceous cream façades, with delicate floral moulding, designed by one of Gaudi's followers. Inside, creepers drip and a chandelier cascades in the circular hall, lit by a stained glass roof, the bar has exquisite tiles and the restaurant is gorgeously elegant. You should book well in advance.

Open: all year **Rooms**: 12 **Credit/charge cards**: Amex, Visa

FUENTE DE

Parador del Río Deva ££
39588 Espinama *Tel (942) 73 00 01*

A comfortable, if disagreeably institutional *parador*, with regularly placed prints and an octagonal-patterned carpet along its endless corridors. In the lounges, rigid layout and synthetic upholstery undermines attempts at a rustic ambience, but rooms are spacious and flooded with light through the floor-to-ceiling windows.

Open: all year **Rooms**: 78 **Credit/charge cards**: Amex, Diners, Eurocard, Visa

GIJON

Parador El Molino Viejo £££
Parque Isabel la Católica
33204 Gijón *Tel (985) 37 05 11*

The *parador* is housed in a converted mill, with the old millstream still running through its grounds. It overlooks the one peaceful place in Gijón, the Isabel la Católica park, and you can watch black swans gliding on the glassy green pool from the bar and some bedroom windows. A cool airy reception hall and marble-paved corridors lead to pristine rooms with wooden floors, textured white walls, matching wooden furniture, and large bathrooms.

Open: all year **Rooms**: 40 **Credit/charge cards**: Amex, Diners, Eurocard, Visa

LUARCA

Hotel Baltico ££
Paseo del Muelle 1
33700 Luarca *Tel (985) 64 09 91*

The hotel is in a good position overlooking the village harbour, and the rooms have polished wooden floors and white-washed walls.

Open: all year **Rooms**: 13 **Credit/charge cards**: Amex, Visa

PANES

La Tahona	**££**
33578 Besnes	*Tel (985) 41 42 49*

Rustically furnished rooms in a beautiful converted barn by a secluded babbling stream. There is a good, traditional restaurant and a terrace alongside the stream. The hotel is about ten kilometres east of Panes, off the C-6312 to Cangas de Onís and is signposted.

Open: all year **Rooms**: 19 **Credit/charge cards**: Visa

SANTILLANA DEL MAR

Parador Gil Blas	**£££**
Plaza Ramón Pelayo 8	
39330 Santillana del Mar	*Tel (942) 81 80 00*

Comfortable accommodation in a restored manor house on the main square. Corridors paved with pebbles and slabs of stone, stone and white-washed walls, and a scattering of antiquish furniture compensate for the occasional institutional give-away, like rigidly arranged sofas, plastic garden furniture and a glossy modern bar-front.

Open: all year **Rooms**: 56 **Credit/charge cards**: Amex, Diners, Eurocard, Visa

Los Infantes	**£££**
Avenida L'Dorat 1	
39330 Santillana del Mar	*Tel (942) 81 81 00*

Simple and comfortable rooms in a subtle extension built on to the façade of an eighteenth-century mansion. Bedrooms are comfortable and public rooms are furnished with period antiques, and so full of atmosphere that you might find yourself staying in for the experience of writing a letter at an eighteenth-century desk.

Open: all year **Rooms**: 30 **Credit/charge card**: Amex, Diners, Eurocard, Visa

Posada Santa Juliana	**££**
Carrera 19	
39330 Santillana del Mar	*Tel (942) 84 01 06*

Thoughtfully and recently decorated rooms in a medieval inn on one of Santillana's two main streets. Walls are white-washed, floors boarded with honey-coloured wood, and furnishings are in co-ordinating pastels. There is no restaurant, but plenty of places to eat nearby.

Open: all year **Rooms**: 10 **Credit/charge cards**: Diners, Eurocard, Visa

SAN VICENTE DE LA BARQUERA

Luzón   £
Avenida Miramar 1
39540 San Vicente de la Barquera   *Tel (942) 71 00 50*

A family-run hotel in a restored mansion set back from the N-632 next to the main tree-canopied *plaza*. The reception hall's furnishings co-ordinate with the marble floor and paintwork, and bills are run-up on an ornate silver cash register. The lounge is furnished with comfy leather chairs, and grandfather and gilded baroque clocks. The breakfast room is light, airy and decorated in pink and white. Rooms are simple and immaculate, with wooden floors and pastel bedspreads.

Open: all year **Rooms**: 34 **Credit/charge cards**: none

THE BASQUE COUNTRY, NAVARRA AND LA RIOJA

STRETCHING from the Bay of Biscay to the orderly vineyards of La Rioja, and rippled by the foothills of the Pyrenees, the area of northern Spain covered in this chapter is scenically varied, though none of its landscape is particularly spectacular. The region does, however, offer great pleasures to those seriously interested in drink and food, for the famous Rioja wines complement the best cuisine in Spain. The Basques are both inveterate eaters (they invented the little snacks, the *tapas*) and excellent chefs: San Sebastián alone has over thirty gastronomic clubs (men only!) where the members take turns to cook elaborate meals.

The Basque Country (Euskadi/País Vasco) is the most industrialised region on the Spanish peninsula, though only the areas around its three big cities are affected – Bilbao, San Sebastián and Vitoria. The most attractive part of the Basque Country is its coast: San Sebastián is the main resort, its superb beach and vestiges of high-society *élan* ensuring that it is virtually always crowded and that prices remain high. Fuenterrabía, on the border with France, has fewer pretensions, but is a fishing village with great charisma, a good beach and excellent accommodation. There are many other sandy beaches along the coast, but the shelter and shallow waters of the Ría de Gernika (Guernica estuary) are particularly safe and suitable for children.

The better scenery of La Rioja is along the luxuriant Iregua and bleak Leza valleys; the rest of the region consists of dull expanses of barely undulating vineyards, wheat and potato fields. Only a few of the wineries (*bodegas*) have organised tours, but most are willing to show you around if you are interested; many have some English-speaking staff, and you can usually taste their product before buying at the cheaper *bodega* prices. Most restaurants of the region have extensive wine lists, and you can get a catalogue of vintages, and often useful advice, from any good wine shop. The viticultural centres of Haro and Laguardia are pleasant to spend some time in, and both have *bodegas* which are open to the public.

The pilgrim route to Santiago (see page 159) runs through La Rioja, but there is little worth making a special trip for. An exception is the diminutive shrine of Suso, one of the two at San Millán de la Cogolla, which were visited for centuries before the Santiago pilgrimage started.

The pilgrimage has left more interesting monuments in Navarra. The churches of Santa María la Real in Sangüesa, Santa María de Eunate near Puente de la Reina and Santo

Sepulcro at Torres de Río are all memorable, and you can stay at the monasteries of Leyre and La Oliva, where the Gregorian chant is still sung at certain services. The pilgrimage town of Estella is a very enjoyable overnight stop, too: the whole place has a party on Saturday nights, celebrating weddings with wine, food and fireworks.

The Navarrese Pyrenees are lower and gentler than those in Aragón and Catalunya, but the valleys of Roncal and Salazar have considerable bucolic charm. In the last foothills before the Aragonese plain lie the Toy-townish castle village of Olite and the fortified one of Ujué.

All the large cities of this region have old cores in which narrow streets squeeze between tall, balconied houses scrawled with Basque nationalist graffiti. Bilbao's historic centre has been thoroughly restored and endowed with smart shops, but in Pamplona, Vitoria and Logroño gentrification is slower, and they are still peppered with antiquated groceries, art nouveau pharmacies and salt-cod stores. One feature they all have in common is the concentration of basic bars, where men stand ankle deep in fag ends and scrunched-up napkins, with eyes glued to TV sports bulletins. Pamplona, Bilbao and Vitoria have excellent museums (one in each) and make convenient and enjoyable overnight stops for shopping, bar-hopping and eating well. Logroño, however, is a bland place with little to recommend it except its wine connections.

The Basque people

The Basques are a race of less than a million people who have lived since ancient times around the western end of the Pyrenees. They call their land Euskadi and it covers the three Basque Country provinces of Vizcaya, Guipúzcoa and Alava, part of Navarra and south-western France. The origins of the Basques are unknown and it has been impossible to link their mysterious language, with an intimidating array of Xs, Ks and Ts to any other, though the region's role as mountain shelter and refuge dates back to prehistoric times (the many cave paintings found throughout the mountains of northern Iberia are witness to that).

Much of the population now lives and works in and around the big cities, but traditionally the Basques are a hill people, living between the mountains and the sea; some of their old customs and traditional sports, such as tossing the caber or lifting great boulders, still survive. Much more common, and now popular throughout Spain, is the national game of pelota

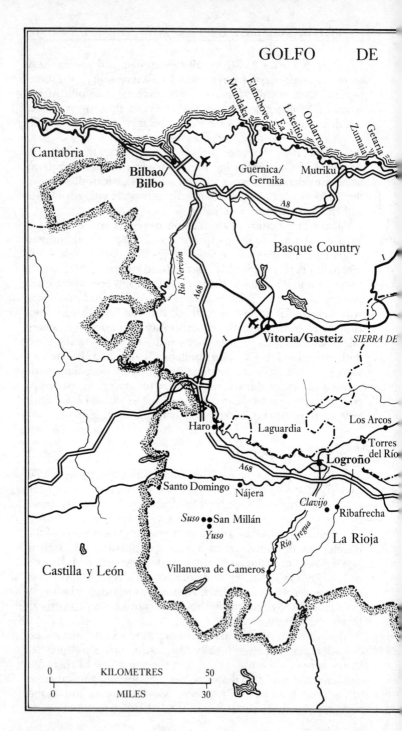

GOLFO   DE

Cantabria

Mundaka

Elanchove

Ea

Lekeitio

Ondarroa

Zumaia

Getaria

Bilbao/
Bilbo

Guernica/
Gernika

Mutriku

A8

Basque Country

Río Nervión

A68

Vitoria/Gasteiz   *SIERRA DE*

Haro

Laguardia

Los Arcos

Torres
del Río

Logroño

A68

Santo Domingo

Nájera

Clavijo

Ribafrecha

Suso ● ● San Millán

Yuso

Río Iregua

La Rioja

Castilla y León

Villanueva de Cameros

| 0 | KILOMETRES | 50 |
| 0 | MILES | 30 |

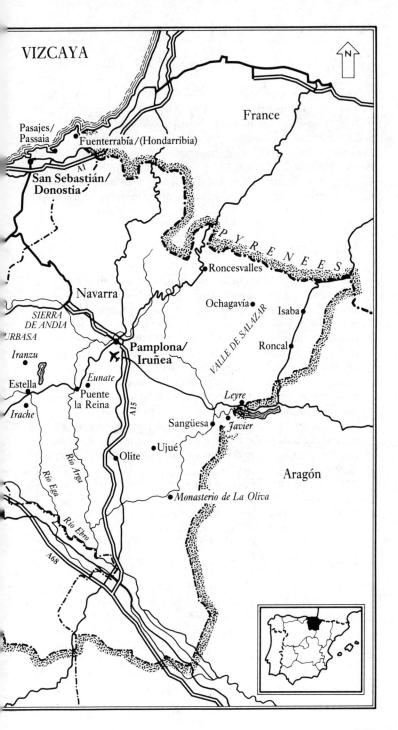

VIZCAYA

N

Pasajes/
Passaia

Fuenterrabía/(Hondarribia)

France

A1

San Sebastián/
Donostia

PYRENEES

Roncesvalles

Navarra

Ochagavía

Isaba

SIERRA
DE ANDIA

URBASA

Iranzu

Pamplona/
Iruñea

VALLE DE SALAZAR

Roncal

Estella

Eunate

Puente
la Reina

A15

Leyre

Irache

Sangüesa

Javier

Río Arga

Ujué

Olite

Aragón

Río Ega

Monasterio de La Oliva

Río Ebro

A68

135

(*jai-alaí*), played in a walled court with stick, ball and wicker baskets.

The Basques were conquered neither by the Romans, nor by the Moorish invaders, and they are proud of that. Since the earliest times, the main characteristics of Basque society have been religious puritanism, agricultural self–sufficiency and a fierce sense of political independence. Throughout the Middle Ages, the Basque Country remained part of the Kingdom of Castile, and acquired for itself a distinctive and advanced form of democracy; assemblies of representatives of all men

Planning your holiday

The quickest way to get to this area of north-east Spain is by air to Bilbao, which is connected by direct scheduled flights to London Heathrow. There are also internal flights from Madrid and Barcelona to Pamplona. Many Britons visit the Basque Country in their own cars via France or via the Plymouth-Santander ferry route. Organised packages, such as fly-drive holidays, touring with accommodation in *paradores* or longer stays on the coast are available through specialist tour operators. If you are touring by car, the best of the region can be seen in less than a week, but combining it with some of Castilla y León's great cities to the south, the Pyrenees to the east or parts of Aragón and Catalunya would make a very satisfactory touring holiday. You could also arrange a fly-drive holiday to Bilbao, with the return flight from Barcelona.

The region has a good and fast road network connecting the main towns, though Bilbao is one of Spain's more confusing cities for motorists. If using public transport, the bus network between main centres works well, and with patience you can get to most villages. There are also good rail links between Bilbao and Logroño, Vitoria and Pamplona, and Pamplona and Zaragoza (in Aragón) via Olite. The most useful road map is the Michelin *Northern Spain*, 1:400,000, sheet 442.

The town of Vitoria makes a useful overnight stop if you're heading for the wine villages of La Rioja or the Navarrese pilgrim route. Pamplona is a feasible base for exploring southern Navarra and the Pyrenees, but it is far better to tour, staying in the *paradores* at Olite and Sos del Rey Católico (in Aragón), see page 209), and the monastery at Leyre. Along the coast there are good hotels at San Sebastián and Fuenterabía, but most accommoda-

aged over 21 would meet every two years under an oak tree (the Tree of Guernica – see page 147) in the ancient town of Guernica and would elect an executive to rule their affairs. In time, the name of Guernica came to acquire an emotional – and ultimately tragic – significance for the Basque people.

From the early nineteenth century Basque politics have remained far to the right, monarchist and very critical of the liberal, republican central government. To these deeply Catholic people the decadence of Madrid – its provocative music, scandalous fashions and habit of mixing the seating of

---

tion is pretty basic and there is little choice. Many Pyrenean hotels are in lovely older-style houses, but you may end up without a bathroom if you do not book in advance.

Like the rest of northern Spain, the Basque Country and Navarra are rainy regions, but the summers are pleasantly hot. La Rioja is a much drier region, and in high summer the southern lowlands (La Rioja Baja) can be unbearably hot. July is a good time to visit, if you like festivals: the riotous San Fermín Pamplona is unforgettable (6–14 July) and during the third week of the month there is international jazz in Vitoria. San Sebastián also holds a jazz festival in July and an international film festival in September. You must book accommodation well in advance for all these events, and for the Pamplona *fiesta*, as much as a year ahead.

The most memorable time to visit La Rioja is during the grape harvest in October. However, unlike some of the famous wine-producing areas of France, the wineries of La Rioja are not generally set up for casual visitors. If you would like to see more than the ones open to the public in Haro and Laguardia, write to ARBOR at Gran Vía 43, 26002 Logroño, Tel (941) 22 53 04. They have ten quality wineries in their group and can help with arranging a visit.

● **Regional Tourist Board**: Viceconsejero de Turismo, Duque de Wellington 2, 01011 Vitoria, Tel (945) 24 60 00 (for the Basque Country); Director General de Commercio y Turismo, Carlos III 36, 31002 Pamplona, Tel (948) 24 65 08 (for Navarra); Director General de Turismo, Villamediana 17, 26003 Logroño, Tel (941) 29 12 00 (for La Rioja). Useful **tourist information offices** can be found in Bilbao (Alameda Mazarredo), San Sebastián (Reina Regente) and Pamplona (Duque de Ahumada 3).

men and women in church – seemed almost like heresy. But only in the later years of the last century did the economic development of the region bring the Basques to the centre-stage of Spain's history. Bilbao had become a great industrial town and port, largely due to the export of local iron ore. A prosperous urban middle class grew up in the city, whose wealth is still reflected in the fine buildings, meeting clubs and banking halls of modern Bilbao. To these serious and sober men, autonomy from central control seemed the only way to develop the country's backward, rural and reactionary society. So began the demands of Basque nationalism which were to haunt successive Spanish governments – republican, fascist and democratic alike – to the present day.

By 1932 the beleaguered republican government in Madrid had been forced to concede the essential demand for auto-nomy and, in a plebiscite, the Basques accepted the offer. But a group of right-wing army officers centred around Franco did not forget or forgive such 'treason'. Five years later Franco took his terrible revenge by inviting Hitler's Germany to carpet-bomb the ancient capital of Guernica; this was a test of international reaction to the German entry into the Spanish Civil War and a 'model punishment' for the Basque people, whose terror is so graphically commemorated in Picasso's painting, *Guernica*, now on display in its own museum in Madrid (see page 411)

The Franco era after the war was characterised in the Basque Country, as elsewhere in Spain, by repression: murder of prominent citizens, prohibition of the Basque language, and laws and alteration of Basque place names to obliterate the country's culture from memory. In these dark days ETA was set up: *Euskadi Ta Akatasuma* (Euskadi and Freedom), an underground 'resistance movement', often sup-ported by the local priests.

Present-day politics may be less easy to define. After the accession of King Juan Carlos in 1975, and the promulgation of a new democratic constitution in 1978, the government in Madrid began to pass successive measures of local autonomy, cautiously at first, but more ambitiously under the socialist government of Felipe Gonzalez in the '80s. So the Basque language is now flourishing, the country has its own police force, recognisable by their red berets, runs its own justice system and collects its own taxes. Bilbao, after the recession of the last decade, when many of its iron, steel and shipbuild-ing works went bankrupt, is undergoing a visible revival. But tensions still remain: you will see graffiti supporting ETA and its political wing Herri Batasuna everywhere you go and intermittent acts of terrorism hit the international headlines – some are aimed at the foreign mass tourism areas of the Spanish Costas.

BILBAO (BILBO) (H)

Home to the brains, money and imagination that have made the Basque Country one of the most powerful industrial regions in Spain, Bilbao is a dynamic city in the throes of regeneration. The old quarter, the Casco Viejo, severely damaged by a flood in 1983, has been stunningly revamped as a consumer heaven; among the corporate glass and concrete of the city centre, grand nineteenth-century town houses and municipal buildings are being restored; a metro system is being built to fine designs by Norman Foster; and work has started on the redevelopment of the dockside.

The city stands on the Nervión estuary and stretching for several kilometres inland along the turgid waters of the river are decayed slums and factories, gantries, pulleys and cranes, lugubrious tugs and cargo ships, all grime-and rust-caked in a throat-rasping smog of sulphur, tar and steam. In 1981 the city council launched a multi-million peseta scheme to clean up the Nervión – at the time some 385 factories were dumping their chemical waste into it. The hope is that by the mid 1990s, the river will be safe to swim in, but as it is still a nasty shade of yellow and reeks of sulphur, this seems rather optimistic.

Though Bilbao is not a city to stay more than one night in on a holiday, you can spend an undemanding evening window-shopping and *tasca*-hopping in the Casco Viejo. There are prestigious restaurants if you can afford to splurge, or you can make an extremely pleasant inexpensive meal of *tapas*. And anyone interested in art should make time to see a quality collection of ancient paintings (and a handful of good contemporary works) in the Museo de Bellas Artes.

The centre of the city is split by the Nervión, with the old quarter on the right bank and the commercial centre and modern district on the left. If you drive in late in the evening from the airport, 11 kilometres to the north-east at Sondika, you will end up on the right bank and, to avoid tackling the city's one-way system, it is easiest to select a hotel on Campo Volantin or in the Casco Viejo – though the latter is pedestrianised and you will have to park some way away.

Most of the large hotels are in the modern area, best approached across the Arenal bridge (Puente de Arenal), which leads on to the main axis of wide roads – Calle Navarra, Calle López de Haro and Gran Vía de Don Diego. On leaving the city, main motorway routes are fairly well signposted, but other roads are more difficult to find and you can easily end up lost in industrial suburbia along the narrow valley. If using public transport, it is best to ask for advice and timetables at the tourist information office in the Alameda de Mazarredo (where it joins Calle Ercilla).

As well as the recommended hotels, you could try a number of modest *hostales* in the Casco Viejo, of which the Gurea, Bidebarrieta 14, Tel (94) 416 32 99, is one of the nicest and most convenient.

Exploring and eating out

Two of the city's most exuberant buildings, the *ayuntamiento* (town hall) and the recently restored Teatro de Arriaga, lie by the river just outside the **Casco Viejo**. Both are splendidly floodlit at night. You can enter the old quarter across the road from the theatre – Calle del Correo and Calle Sombrerería will take you to the central square, Plaza Nueva, a neo-classical stage which is currently undergoing major restoration. Life happens in the bars beneath its severe arcades, the best of which is Victor Montes, an upmarket *tapas* bar and delicatessen. The menu includes prettily presented salads, a fine *revuelto de espinacos con langostinos* (scrambled egg with spinach and prawns), caviare and smoked salmon, and a great variety of drinks. If you want to eat cheaply elsewhere in the Casco Viejo you should choose carefully – most of the basic restaurants serve greasy food and rock-bottom bottles of wine. La Tortilla, by the town hall, is better value and has an imaginative selection of omelettes.

On Plaza de Santiago, the outdoor tables of the Café Askari near the grimy Gothic cathedral are good for a drink while watching people; the place is civilised and popular with local women. The cathedral itself is not worth a visit.

The smartest shops in the old quarter are on Calles Bidebarrieta, Correo, de la Torre and Banco de España, though you may still stumble on oddities, such as the medical supply shop on Bidebarrieta with its unabashed display of bedpans.

The **modern town** is worth visiting to drink in Bilbao's best café and, if you can afford it, eat in one of the city's top restaurants. The Café Iruña is a mock–Moorish extravaganza of inlaid wood and scalloped arches, on Cólon de Larre-tegui by a garden square and the Palace of Justice. At midday it serves a good value fixed menu lunch and is full of office workers; in the evenings a band plays honky-tonk music and trendy youths spill on to the pavement.

The current stars among Bilbao's restaurants are Goizeko Kabi, de Estraunza 4, Tel (94) 441 50 04, and Gorrotxa, Alameda Urquijo 30, Tel (94) 443 49 37. If you cannot afford these, Rogelio, Carretera de Basurto a Castrejana 7, Tel (94) 431 30 21, is more reasonable, and serves thoughtfully cooked, well presented local dishes.

Museo de Bellas Artes

The Fine Arts Museum can be found in the Doña Casilda Iturriza park, in a nineteenth-century building with a modern extension. It has enough fine works to keep you absorbed, but not so many that you will be overwhelmed or exhausted. Room 6 houses the El Greco paintings – two gaunt and ascetic *San Franciscos* and a *Repentent Magdalen* with beautiful liquid eyes. Room 7 holds several works by Zurbarán: his figures (even the hands) have an almost sculptural quality, and one can almost hear the rustling of St Catherine of Alexandria's red robe. In the same room Ribera's *Martyrdom of St Sebastian* plumps for sensationalism – look at the hand of the woman holding down the flesh of the Saint's thigh in order to lever the arrow out.

In room 8 there is a Velázquez portrait of Felipe IV, whose simian mouth and flabby chin will be familiar if you have visited the Prado in Madrid; room 10 has some striking Flemish works – notably Quentin Metsys' *The Moneychangers*, with evil eyes and lips and an obscenely glittering pile of money; in Ambrosius Benson's *Pietà*, the Magdalen looks at Christ's wound as if she wants to kiss it, and Mary is on the verge of tears. Room 13 has some Italian works, including a virtuoso piece by Julio Romano and a *Judith and Holofernes* by Guido Reni, depicting Judith as virile swaggerer. Wind up your tour of the old masters with Goya's daring *Queen María Luisa* in room 16, portrayed as a greedy and untrustworthy harridan.

The Basque Art section contains folksy scenes and landscapes. In the Contemporary Art section highlights are Francis Bacon's contorted, *Lying Figure in a Mirror*, sculptures by Eduardo Chillida, notably the beautifully subtle *Torso*, and

Andrés Nagel's disturbing plaster and fibreglass sculptures, which include a horrifying *Suicide* in which a figure tumbles from a window, leaving behind him one eye to witness the death.

SAN SEBASTIAN (DONOSTIA) (H)

Mention San Sebastián to certain Spaniards, and a faraway look comes into their eyes: 'it's special...it's magical'. To an extent it is: golden sands sweep round a beautiful scallop-shaped bay, closed in by wooded promontories; the promenade is fringed by tamarisks and punctuated by frilly pavilions; and it has restaurants whose names are spoken in awed whispers, and hotels which appear to have been plucked from the pages of a high society journal.

In the 1880s the Spanish royal family began to take their holidays in the town, and commissioned an English architect to build a mock (and rather suburban-looking) Tudor palace. San Sebastián rapidly became fashionable, but its heyday is over. The once glamorous casino is now the town hall, and today's gamblers prefer bingo to blackjack; the paint is flaking on the fancy pavilions, the spiral steps that lead down to the sands are rusty, and many of the *belle époque* villas have been abandoned. In the town's old quarter, the façades are just as graffiti-scrawled and the bars just as deep in fag ends as in any other sizable Spanish town.

But San Sebastián is a perfectly pleasant place for a seaside holiday. The beaches are superb, you can take boat trips to the offshore islet of Santa Clara, breakfast on decadent pastries in pretty *pastelerías*, and spend lively evenings in the old town. The resort is expensive though, and accommodation – which ranges from lavish to family hotels – is virtually impossible to find on spec, even outside the holiday season, because the hotels are regularly filled with conference delegates.

Most of the roads near the beaches and in the old town have controlled parking, but there are convenient underground car parks in the Plaza Easo and Plaza Cervantes. Trains to Bilbao depart from the station on Plaza Easo (the FEVE line), those to France and Madrid from the station on the right bank of the River Urumea (the state RENFE line). Both stations are reasonably near the centre.

Exploring the town

San Sebastián has a predominantly modern centre of wide avenues built on a grid between the river Urumea and the sea. Tree-lined **Alameda del Boulevard**, with a splendid art nouveau bandstand sandwiched between lanes of traffic, runs from the Zurriola bridge to the sea, and forms the border between the old and new quarters. The pavement cafés at the western end, close to the *ayuntamiento*, are good places to sit and watch people. Close by, the sea-front **Alderdi Eder Park**, planted with flower beds and over two hundred tamarisks, is a favourite spot with picnicking tourists and local people alike. Beyond the gardens the esplanade sweeps around the bay above the splendid golden sands of its two beaches, the **Playa de la Concha** and **Playa de Ondarreta**, split by a diminutive headland on which the royal palace and gardens stand (the latter are open to the public). The beaches, especially la Concha, get impossibly crowded in July and August: at high tide you may find there is barely room to lie down.

Evenings are best spent in the **old quarter**, a pocket of nineteenth-century streets lying between Alameda del Boulevard and the foot of Monte Urgull, where you will find plenty of *tapas* bars, restaurants and shops selling anything from religious statues to harpoons. The quarter has two churches: **San Vicente** is the older, a severe sixteenth-century structure, while **Santa María**'s outrageously ornate baroque façade is rather more in keeping with its exuberant neighbourhood. Below Santa María is San Sebastián's small fishing harbour. You can catch a boat to the Isla de Santa Clara here in summer (a nice place for picnics), and there are simple fish restaurants under the arcades of the tiled and colour-washed fishermen's cottages.

The resort's two museums, Santo Telmo and the Aquarium and Naval Museum, are not particularly good and the fifteen-minute walk up the pine-wooded **Monte Urgull** is worth it more for the views of the town, bay and coast than the scant remains of the castle (watch out for your bags and cameras here). **Monte Igueldo**, on the west side of the bay, provides more views with less effort, as you can drive up or take a funicular in summer. There is an amusement park at the top, and, at the bottom of Plaza Peine del Viento, three weather-rusted sculptures of bent iron bars by the San Sebastián sculptor (and hotelier) Eduardo Chillida. Aptly named Combs of the Wind, you will find them elemental, ugly or fun to clamber on.

143

Eating out

San Sebastián's classiest restaurants are so well thought of that people reserve weeks in advance. The places to splash out on a meal are Arzak, Alto de Miracruz 21, Tel (943) 27 84 65 on the east bank of the river and Akelarre, Pases del Orcolaga, Tel (943) 21 20 52, on the road to Monte Igueldo. A slightly cheaper alternative in the old quarter is Kokotxa, Calle del Campanario 11, Tel (943) 42 01 73.

If you prefer your cuisine *haute*, Panier Fleuri, Paseo de Salamanca 1, Tel (943) 42 42 05, on the river bank by the Zurriola bridge, is at once relaxed and civilised, though not all its dishes are successful. For fish, you could either eat cheaply and simply at the harbour, or try: Salduba, Calle de la Pescadería 6, Tel (943) 42 56 27, just off Plaza de la Constitución; Casa Urbano, Calle del 31 de Agosto 17, Tel (943) 42 04 34; and the more modestly priced Bretxa, Calle del General Echague 15, Tel (943) 42 05 49. Many of the *tapas* bars also serve full meals, usually from a limited menu.

Finally, there are some good *pastelerías* for breakfast pastries or afternoon cakes. A particularly decadent selection is in La Dulce Allianza, on Calle de Urbieta, and in Argitan, at the east end of the Alameda del Boulevard by the Zurriola bridge, where you have river views to go with your croissants.

EAST OF SAN SEBASTIAN

Pasai San Juan (Pasai Donibane) is a picturesque old fishing village where geraniums cascade and washing flutters on wrought-iron balconies. It is one of three villages, jointly known as Pasajes (Pasaia), around a sheltered deep-water harbour, and looks over the water to the ugly docks and modern apartments of the ports Pasai Antxo and Pasai San Pedro. San Juan consists of one long narrow street crossed by arches; tiny alleys run off down between houses to the water. The street opens out into the waterside Plaza Santiago, with a couple of bars and a bandstand jauntily decorated with stave and notes. The fish restaurants Casa Camara or Txulotxo on the main street are good places to eat.

From Pasai San Juan take a wonderfully scenic road over the pine and gorse-clad **Monte Jaizkibel**, with extensive views up and down the coast. This brings you to the village of **Fuenterrabía** (H) (Hondarrabia), a gorgeous fishing village with a creamy sand beach in a sheltered bay, and a noble old quarter built on a hill. In the lower village whitewashed houses are trimmed with brightly painted wood and decked with geraniums; on the main street baskets of bread and crates of fruit and vegetables stand outside the shops; and old men in berets stroll along the quayside of the harbour, full of tiny fishing boats painted in primary colours.

The old quarter is still ringed by ramparts and crowned by a stern castle, dating from the days when Fuenterrabía was perpetually in danger of being attacked by the French, just across the water. Within the ramparts, steep streets climb past balconied houses with elaborately carved eaves to the castle, founded in the tenth century, and rebuilt by Charles V, which was until recently a *parador*. Sadly this has closed down because its structure is thought to be unsafe, but there are some other nice places to stay in the village.

WEST OF SAN SEBASTIAN

The fishing village of **Guetaria** (H) (Getaria), is splendidly approached along a corniche road from the dull resort of Zarautz. Its narrow cobbled streets are suffused at lunchtime with the smells of fish cooking on grills outside restaurants. Guetaria is famous for *txakoli*, a green and slightly sparkling Basque wine, cider and *chipirones en su tinta* – squid cooked in its own ink – all of which can be sampled in the harbour-side restaurants. To reach them, walk down the hilly main street and through an arcade underneath the octagonal-towered church of El Salvador. Arcaded brick houses with their half-timbering painted blue line a quayside stacked with fish trays; a smart concrete pier, popular with sunbathers and daydreamers, protects the harbour, as does the El Ratón islet, shaped like (and named after) a mouse. If you want to swim, there are decent sandy beaches to either side of the village.

The corniche road continues beyond Guetaria, snaking between shale mountains and shelving foam-licked rocks. Tourism and light industry have taken over from fishing in the village of **Zumaia**, but unless you want to go surfing on its grey sand beach it has little to hold you. Near the entrance to town is the Villa Zuloaga, once the home of Basque artist Ignacio Zuloaga, and now a museum. His vibrant colours, and rather superficial portrayals of gipsies, bullfights and brigands have not stood the test of time.

Beyond Zumaia the road heads inland, passing isolated farms and grassy hillsides so steep that you wonder how the cows succeed in remaining upright. It rejoins the coast at the drab, messy resort of Deba, and continues between magnificently striated cliffs and the pine-fringed shore to **Mutriku**. The village's outskirts are choked with apartments, but its location on a steep-sided inlet is striking, and an old quarter of tall whitewashed stone houses remains above the harbour. Mutriku still has a sizeable fishing fleet, but there is far more to see a few kilometres beyond at Ondarroa.

In **Ondarroa**, on the banks of the river Artibay, are a heftily buttressed church dripping with creepers, and invigorating old streets full of traffic and bustling bars. Along the sea-front the rituals of the evening *paseo* are staged on a scruffy little *plaza* and bar-lined promenade. But the main attraction is the harbour. In the evenings you will see people preparing the large boats, in which twenty men will spend as long as two months at sea; three generations of women sit on legless seats repairing nets and old men bait their hooks with offal as they prepare to fish in the harbour water irridescent with petrol. If you get up early enough in the morning, you should be able to watch the catch arrive and be auctioned – ask any of the locals for the times.

Ondarroa has only one hotel, the Vega, Avenida de Antigua 8, Tel (94) 683 00 02, which has twenty-three rooms above a restaurant on the sea-front close to the harbour. If it is full, drive on along the coast to **Lekeitio**, a lively, if rather untidy village. Here, a deep inlet protected by a pine-clad islet forms a natural harbour, unfortunately marred by bland apartment blocks. When we visited it, the waterfront was a mess, as the main square was being dug up and re-plumbed, but once it is finished, the complex buttressed church and row of houses with green and brown painted *solanas* may come into their own. But it is not a bad place to spend a night – especially if you eat at Kresala on the waterfront, a civilised restaurant serving a wonderful house salad with chunks of grilled salmon. Or you can have a set cheap meal on wooden benches at the nearby Kai Abiya. Next morning you can work off your meal with a swim from the sheltered sandy beach next to the harbour. If you need a bed for the night the Beitia, Avenida Pascual Abaroa 25, Tel (94) 684 01 11 has clean basic rooms and serves great breakfasts.

Further along the coast, **Ea** is a handsome place, its red-roofed, whitewashed houses with flower-decked balconies ranged along a stream which runs into a deep, narrow inlet. Ea can get quite busy in summer, but out of season you will see more ducks bobbing on the stream than people. **Elanchove**, beyond, is rather more substantial, piled up on a hillside above its port, but the main attractions around here are the rosy-golden beaches of **Laga** and **Laida** which fringe the sheltered waters of the Ría de Gernika (Guernica).

Santimamiñe Cave and Guernica

Inland from the estuary of Guernica (Gernika), reached through pine forests and fields strewn with pumpkins, is the Santimamiñe Cave. The setting, on a pine-clad hill just below a rustic hermitage, is attraction enough, and it is worth bringing food so you can join the Spaniards picnicking at the tables and grilling *chorizos* on the barbecue. The cave is thought to have been inhabited for over 30,000 years, and the walls are decorated with charcoal drawings of horses, bears, stags and goats. Only 30 people are allowed in at a time, so aim to arrive about half an hour before each visit.

Were it not for its name, you would drive straight through **Guernica**, but Picasso's disturbing black and white painting, depicting the horror of 26 April 1937 when the Nazis bombed the town, killing over 2,000 people in three hours, has ensured that it will never be forgotten. It was the first-ever mass bombing raid on a town, and the event shocked the world (see the Basque people, page 137). Today the rebuilt Guernica is a very ordinary place, but the **Casa de Juntas**, the Vizcayan parliament building, is open to the public and in its grounds, sheltered by a rotunda temple, you can see the hollowed trunk of the immense oak, the Tree of Guernica, under which the the meetings of the ancient Basque parliament took place. A nineteenth-century offspring of this oak grows nearby. Inside the Casa de Juntas, the parliament chamber can be visited and, rather more interesting, the aptly named Stained Glass Window Hall. Its ceiling, created in 1985, is a romantic celebration of the Basque Country's culture and economy, featuring dependable fishermen, farmers and miners, Romanesque churches and factory chimneys.

From Guernica the C-6315 follows the west bank of the *ría* back to the coast. There are some good beaches here, and although the sheltered water is too shallow at low tide to swim, it is ideal for young children. One of the nicest beaches is the **Playa de San Antonio**, just after the village of Pedernales. The beach is not marked from the main road – follow the sign to the Asador Zaldua. The golden sands are backed by pines (with picnic tables) and there is a tiny islet offshore which you can paddle to at low tide.

The nearest accommodation is at **Mundaka**, near the mouth of the estuary. It is backed by apartment blocks, but older houses with *solanas*, a park overlooking a small harbour of little fishing boats, and a sandy beach in a sheltered bay make it a pleasant place to stay. It is also popular, especially at weekends, so phone ahead if you want a room in one of its two small hotels, the Atalaya, Tel (94) 687 68 88, in a pretty white house just above the harbour or El Puerto, Tel (94) 687 67 25, in a fisherman's cottage on the harbour front.

VITORIA (GASTEIZ) (H)

At first sight Vitoria, spread on a dull plain, is not enticing, but it improves on acquaintance. In the old quarter, shops selling horsemeat and slabs of salt-cod stand shoulder to shoulder with contemporary art galleries and antique shops, and whole streets are transformed on Saturday nights into one big, noisy, student party. More sedate pleasures include an elegantly refurbished shopping district of broad pedestrianised streets, a good museum housed in an ancient mansion and plenty of pavement cafés. The town is a fine place to spend a night, and convenient if you are heading from Bilbao to Pamplona or Estella. It is the capital of the Alava province, the administrative centre of the Basque countries and the seat of a dynamic university, if its streetlife is anything to go by.

Finding your way around the old quarter is easy, as the narrow streets lie webbed over a hill in parallel lines, linked by little alleys. By day this is a traditional workers neighbourhood where men drink or play cards in bars and women do the shopping, and by night it is taken over by the students. On **Calle Correría** a row of medieval brick and timber houses have been restored; at the northern end, one of them, El Portalón, houses a well-known restaurant in a fifteenth-century shop, another is the Tulipán de Oro bar where you toast your own *chorizo* on a pottery grill in the shape of a pig; yet another, across the road contains the rather poor collection of the Archaeological Museum. Nearby is the rambling Gothic structure of the Santa María cathedral, hemmed in by houses.

In 1813 the Duke of Wellington won a battle against Napoleon's army near Vitoria – a victory which proved to be decisive, as the French then retreated to France. The event is remembered by a melodramatic monument on the town's main square, **Plaza de la Virgen Blanca**, which is sloping and wedge-shaped, and overlooked by the arcades and bell-tower of the fourteenth-century San Miguel church. The square is a pleasant place to sit and drink – there is a pavement café at the foot of the square – and it forms the link between the old quarter and the elegant shopping streets. Pedestrianised **Calle de Dato** is the prettiest of these, and leads directly down to the railway station, where you can cut under a rail bridge to a leafy quarter of florid *fin de siècle* villas and the Museo de Bellas Artes (Fine Arts Museum).

Finding accommodation in Vitoria is no problem, except during the international jazz festival in the third week of July. Among some commonplace business hotels there are a couple of small but above average *hostales*, one near the bus station at the foot of the old quarter to the east, the other on Calle de Dato – see our recommendations at the end of the chapter.

The main sights

● **Santa María Cathedral** The interior of the fourteenth-century cathedral at the north side of the old quarter is serene – except when the out-of-tune bell clanks the hours. The white columns rise to simple cross-over vaults, and the stained glass is enhanced by the purity of the stone. The artwork, however, is rather less subtle: the capital of the third column of the south aisle is carved, unusually, with a bull fight, though binoculars would be useful to see it properly, and the second chapel off the south aisle contains a painting of St Bartholomew being flayed, which should be avoided by the squeamish.

● **Museo de Bellas Artes** The eclectic collection of this museum is housed in a lovely mansion with modern sculpture among the topiary in the grounds. There are also some beautifully restored Flemish triptychs and three works by Ribera, including a stark *Crucifixion*.

The contemporary section is strong, and includes a ceramic mural by Miró, an *Imaginary Portrait of Philip II* by Antonio Saura, and a light-hearted Picasso, *Mosquetaire à la Pye*.

The Heraclio Fournier factory in Vitoria is Spain's main producer of playing cards, and the factory's historic collection is displayed in the museum. There are fifteenth-century designs, a set of miniature nineteenth-century cards for children, and the tarot collection which includes cards designed by Dalí, and a pornographic Dutch pack. Best, though, is the satirical pack of cards dating from 1973, with caricatures of famous people ranging from Princess Anne and Jackie Onassis to Idi Amin and Colonel Gadaffi.

149

PAMPLONA (IRUNEA) (H)

To Spaniards Pamplona means one thing: the festival of San Fermín, a July week of riotous excess focussing on the daily *encierro*, or running of the bulls through the town on their way to be slaughtered in the ring. Unfortunately not only bulls are killed. For hundreds of men, San Fermín is an opportunity to demonstrate their masculinity by charging with the bulls through the streets, and some poor fool gets seriously maimed, if not killed every year. Injury figures are further swollen by another time-honoured San Fermín ritual – revellers leaping off buildings, in the deluded belief that the crowd below will catch them.

The whole town goes completely mad, intoxicated in equal measure by the thrills-and-spills atmosphere and prodigious quantities of alcohol. There are fireworks every night in the citadel, local bands playing on the main square, parades, street dancing, and a spiralling petty crime rate. If you decide to go, take your oldest clothes (you are bound to get drenched in drink), bear in mind that hotel prices double, and book your room at least six months in advance (though you will not get much sleep). Finally, unless you have incredible stamina, you will probably find a couple of days at San Fermín more than enough.

Even at other times of the year, Pamplona is far from dull. It has been the capital of Navarra since the days when the region was a medieval kingdom, remaining totally uncowed by a past in which it was sacked by virtually everyone from the Romans to Napoleon's French army. Today it is still more dynamic than many other provincial capitals. Its university blesses it with liberal numbers of trendy boys and girls, suitable shops to dress them and throbbing bars. If this is not your scene, there are more civilised cafés full of people quietly chatting, reading newspapers or scribbling on foolscap. Along narrow streets with façades scrawled with graffiti, there are old-fashioned grocers and fishmongers among the smart boutiques and leather stores; look out for the gorgeous art nouveau pharmacy on Calle Mercaderes. The cathedral and Museo de Navarra deserve visits, but there is not much else in the way of 'sights' – time is most pleasantly spent wandering the old town, dawdling in cafés and strolling in the parks: the best are Taconera and the landscaped grounds of the adjacent Ciudadela, a pentagonal sixteenth-century fortress built on the orders of Philip II to defend the Pyrenean foothills.

Pamplona has a typical selection of city hotels – from glossy, but bland business hotels, through mediocre mid-priced establishments to basic *hostales*. As the town's train station is way outside town, it is better to arrive by bus. The bus station is on Calle Conde Oliveto, a five- to ten-minute walk from Plaza del Castillo. The city centre is easily explored on foot, so there is no need to use public transport. If driving, it is best to leave your car in one of the car parks conveniently situated between the Ciudadela and the old town.

Exploring and eating out

Old Pamplona sits within a loop of the River Arga, with the modern grid-plan town tacked on and spreading south to the smaller River Sadar. The old quarter forms a rough rectangle around **Plaza del Castillo**, a large arcaded square of elaborate nineteenth-century buildings and pavement cafés. The newsagent here sells English papers, and the Cafe Iruñea is a good place to read them, a *fin-de-siècle* creation of etched glass, mirrors and ornate columns. Adjoining is a marble-and-gilt galleried cafeteria and an equally opulent *tapas* bar, where a pair of oriental women lamp-bearers light the way to the palatial lavatories. On certain evenings you will not be allowed into the main café unless you are playing bingo – a longstanding Basque and Navarrese tradition, as testified by the ancient boards on the walls, alongside the modern digital display unit. The café's home-fried crisps are a revelation if you have only eaten the packeted variety.

Ernest Hemingway made the town and its *fiesta* famous in his novel *The Sun Also Rises*. His favourite watering hole was the *Txoci* bar on the main square, where he was ticked off by a young American journalist for wasting his time 'sitting in a bar seeking adulation making wise cracks with your sycophants and signing autographs'. It is a small, plain bar, and today's Pamplona holds far livelier places, more conducive to wasting time.

Round the corner from the cathedral, which is close to the old ramparts and the only surviving sixteenth-century gate, the **Portal de Zumalacárregui**, the Mesón del Caballo Blanco is an ancient inn with a turreted tower, where you drink at wooden benches to an accompaniment of Bob

151

Marley or Bob Dylan. There are also lots of bars along **Calle San Nicolás**, which leads east from Plaza del Castillo. Casa Otano, at number 5, is one of the most appealing, serving an array of *tapas* in a beamed old room, and more substantial meals in the restaurant above (it also lets out rooms – see Where to stay).

Pamplona is well off for good restaurants, but the Europa, on Calle Espoz y Mina 11, just off Plaza del Castillo, is a superb family-run restaurant, serving *nouvelle cuisine* at its best. Its extensive wine list includes the wonderful Navarrese merlot-based Magana, a soft, clean fusion of vanilla and blackcurrant.

The main sights

● **Cathedral** The neo-classical façade, an unendearing eighteenth-century addition, gives access to a warm, incense-redolent Gothic interior, with light filtering through stained glass to splash colour on the walls. In the centre of the nave is the tomb of Carlos III, founder of the cathedral, and his wife Eleanor, their alabaster faces skilfully carved to suggest the skulls beneath their skin. The highlight of the cathedral, however, is the cloister where a stone crochet of trefoils, quatrefoils and pinnacles is supported on columns which appear to be no broader than the edge of a knife – an illusion achieved through using tall, thin, but deeply scalloped columns. Almost as lovely is the aptly named Puerta Preciosa, delicately carved with scenes from the life of the Virgin.

The cathedral's refectory and kitchen hold the **Museo Diocesano** where you can trace the stylistic development of polychrome statues of the Virgin and Child: in the earliest Christ is represented as a crowned mannequin, while in the later ones he is more realistically depicted as a toddler or baby. The kitchen is a tremendous structure with five chimneys – the central one is 24 metres high – and beyond is a collection of reliquaries and, for some reason, four sets of silver oil and vinegar jugs.

● **Museo de Navarra** Re-opened in 1990 after a long refit, the museum is stylishly laid out in a converted sixteenth-century hospital at the north end of town. The collection ranges from Iron Age daggers to local artist Gustavo de Maetzu's portraits of glamorous women. The most interesting exhibits, however, are in the Roman, Romanesque, Gothic and Renaissance sections.

The Roman collection includes subtly coloured mosaics, notably a fragment of a *Triumph of Bacchus* featuring a stripey tiger; glass urns used to hold funerary ashes, gravestones carved with flowers, birds and bunches of grapes; and a display of domestic bric-à-brac which includes needles and teaspoons.

The pre-Romanesque figures from the late tenth century may look like stick men, but the capitals rescued from the cloister of Pamplona's first Romanesque cathedral are carved with marvellously animated scenes – fine examples of the new sophistication and skills which developed along the Santiago pilgrim route. Equally fascinating is the fusion of Christian and Muslim art in the *Arqueta*, an eleventh-century chest from Cordóba, carved with western animals and people in an abstract geometric setting.

Upstairs are some memorable frescoes detached from local churches and monasteries. Styles range from the ease and confidence of line in the frescoes from Gallipienzo to the nightmarish monochrome Old Testament scenes from the Palace of Oriz.

The undoubted highlight of the Baroque Collection is Goya's *Portrait of the Marqués de San Adrian*, vain, arrogant and with top hat at the ready.

The San Fermín festival

The *fiesta*, as Hemingway put it, explodes at noon on July 6, with the firing of a rocket outside the baroque *ayuntamiento*. The crowds yell 'Viva San Fermín!', put on red neckerchiefs, and set about processing, singing, dancing and drinking, setting out as they mean to carry on. The bullfighting begins next day, and to see the *encierro*, which starts at 8am, you will need to get to the wooden barriers set up along the route for about 6am. The route runs from the corral near Plaza Santo Domingo, and along Calle Mercaderes and Estafada to the bullring – the best views are from the *plaza*. After this, bullocks (with their horns padded) are let loose among the crowds in the bullring. If you want to watch, start queuing for a ticket at around 6.30am. Bullfights happen nightly at 6.30pm, and entrance is expensive, even if you avoid the rip-off touts. The action can get rough for spectators in the cheaper *sol* (ground) seats, and if you have not served an apprenticeship on Britain's football terraces, you would be wiser paying the extra for a seat in the shade. The festivities are wound up with a candlelit procession on July 14.

SOUTHERN NAVARRA

South of Pamplona the motorway, railway and main N-121 road follow the Río Cidacos valley to the unremarkable town of Tafalla, beyond which the last two branch towards **Olite**. This, at first sight, appears to consist solely of its castle: a romantic confection of towers and witch-hat turrets. Once through the splendid castle gate, however, you discover that within its walls is a thoroughly revamped medieval village of narrow streets and cobbled squares, where even the butcher's has a smart new calligraphed sign. Olite, the past home of Navarrese kings, has now been set up as a major tourist attraction and as such gets impossibly crowded in high season. If you want to stay in its *parador*, housed in a wing of the castle, you should book ahead, Tel (948) 74 00 00.

There are guided tours around the prettified rooms of the castle, but Olite's best building is the delicately decaying church of Santa María la Real, the old royal chapel. Outside it has a frail and now roofless Gothic atrium, and carved around the portal are clusters of oak leaves and mostly headless saints. The church of San Pedro is also worth a look; its steeple resembles a hand grenade, and carved on its façade are two eagles, one protecting a sleeping lamb, representing the eagle of gentleness; the other, with talons sunk into a dead lamb, representing the eagle of violence.

The **La Oliva Monastery**, is reached across a plain of cereal fields, vineyards and almond and olive groves. A simple Cistercian church forms a fitting focus for the community of monks who work the fields, make wine and honey and still sing the Gregorian chant at mass. The façade of the church is pierced by two low alabaster windows and decorated with a frieze of grotesques – look out for the toothy grinning dog. Nothing disturbs the purity of line of the interior, where daylight filters through the alabaster panes to reveal cross-vaulting which climaxes in an umbrella-vaulted apse.

Ten kilometres north-east of Olite, the village of **San Martín de Unx** appears from a distance as a patch of silver in a fold of the hills, and close up it is no disappointment. Squeezing up between old stone houses, you emerge below a Gothic church, worth a visit for its Romanesque crypt. The key is at the house at the bottom of the ramp that winds up to the church. The crypt is exquisite, with simple leaf form capitals, and traces of coloured patterns on the walls which suggest that it was once cheerfully, if amateurishly, painted.

About nine kilometres beyond San Martín, approached along a cornice road up a hill planted with almonds and scattered with bee-hives, is **Ujué**. The village is wrapped around a fortified church completely surrounded by a vaulted sentry walk giving strategic views of the surrounding countryside. Carvings by the first door include a woman riding a lion, and a washerwoman who appears to be asking an angel if she can scrub his halo. Do not miss the rusty safe by the side door, used for important documents and valu-ables. As a security measure it had three different locks; a key was given to each of three trusted men, who could open it only together. Local almonds coated with local honey are on sale in a small shop by the car park.

THE NAVARRESE PYRENEES

Lush pastures, pine plantations, forests of oak and beech, and trim mountain villages make for a pleasantly bucolic landscape. Sheep farming traditionally provided most of this area's employment and you can still encounter shepherds clad in goatskin capes, but forestry is now taking over and lorries piled high with logs clog the narrow mountain lanes. The valleys are loveliest in late autumn, when the forests are a blaze of yellow, coral and orange, but be prepared for sudden mists on the heights, even when the valleys are clear and sunny. You could explore the Navarrese Pyrenees in a day trip from Pamplona, but it is worth taking your time and breaking your journey with an unforgettable night at the Monasterio de Leyre on the Pyrenean fringes.

Roncesvalles

The western branch of the Santiago pilgrimage route from France enters Spain at the head of the Roncesvalles, but despite the fame bequeathed to it by the pilgrimage, the *Song of Roland*, and more recently Ernest Hemingway's *The Sun Also Rises*, Roncesvalles is the least appealing of Navarra's Pyrenean valleys. **Burguete**, where Hemingway stayed, is a neat roadside village where houses have cheerfully painted half-timbering, and has a number of *hostales* with creaky pine floors. If you want to stay here try the Burguete, Tel (942) 76 00 05, or Hostal Loizu, Tel (942) 76 00 08 both of which are on the main road.

The monastery of **Roncesvalles** a little further up the valley, was founded in 1132 by a Bishop of Pamplona, disturbed by the numbers of pilgrims who were eaten by wolves or died of exposure. Until the eighteenth century, travellers could spend three nights free in the monastery's hospice, have hot baths and hot meals, a hair cut and their shoes repaired. In the thirteenth century the monastery was serving 30,000 meals a year.

Today Roncesvalles' two restaurants are frequented by coach parties and logging lorry drivers, and school children picnic by the walls of the ossuary. The monastery is a melancholy place, its corrugated zinc roofs rattling alarmingly in the wind as you walk through the sturdy Gothic cloisters, rebuilt in the seventeenth century after being hit by an avalanche. In the Chapterhouse (Sala Capitular) is the recumbent effigy of king Sancho VII, measuring over seven feet (reputedly his real height!) and stained glass windows show his victory in 1212 over the Sultan Miramamolín El Verde at the battle of Navas de Tolosa, which crushed the Moorish Almohad dynasty. On the walls are fragments of the chains used to lock the Sultan in his tent, elements subsequently incorporated into Navarra's coat of arms.

In the church, bare stone walls contrast with colourful stained glass and a glittery Virgin of the Sorrows shedding a single diamond tear. There are more treasures in the museum, including an emerald which is supposed to have fallen from Sultan Miramamolín's turban during the Navas de Tolosa battle and a fourteenth-century chequered reliquary known as Charlemagne's Chessboard.

Beyond the monastery, the Puerto Ibañeta, at 1,057 metres, is better known in literature as the Roncesvalles Pass. According to the twelfth-century French epic poem *Song of Roland*, the Christian knight, Roland, and his small band of followers were massacred here after a brave fight against hoards of Saracens. In fact, the poem was written some four hundred years after the event, and the reality is rather different. Charlemagne's Frankish army had destroyed the ramparts at Pamplona, and the Navarrese retaliated by ambushing his rearguard at Roncesvalles. If you are heading for France, the valley snakes on through woods, crags and pastures to the village of Valcarlos, and beyond to the border at Arnéguy.

The road to Aragón

From Pamplona, the N-240 sweeps you past softly contoured cereal fields to the Puerto Loiti Pass, with views of the distant

Pyrenees beyond a plain patchworked with red fallow and beige wheat fields. A diversion north-east past the village of **Lumbier** takes you up to a *mirador* perched above the plunging ochre and silver walls of the **Foz (Hoz) de Arbayún**, and beyond to **Aranqüite** for views which, on a clear day, encompass the monasteries of Leyre and Javier. Returning to Lumbier, a narrow lane signposted Foz (Hoz) de Lumbier leads through a tunnel into a gorge walled by scooped and sheer sheets of rock. A rubble road, which was once a railway track, runs right through the gorge.

The eastern branch of the Pilgrim Way to Santiago from France passed through Aragón, entering Navarra near the monastery at Leyre (see below) and then onto **Sangüesa**. Just south of the main road, this is a sleepy agricultural village whose fortified churches and palaces speak of its former glory. The Vallensantoro Palace is a splendid baroque structure with grotesque masks glowering down from its eaves. Until the tenth century the inhabitants, frightened of attacks by the Moors, lived on a mound above the river, but in the eleventh century the kings of the Reconquest persuaded them to settle by the river and defend the bridge. In the following century Alfonso I of Aragón further swelled the population by building a castle (which no longer exists) and attracting freemen from all over Europe to the town.

The star attraction of the village is the church of **Santa María la Real**, whose twelfth- and thirteenth-century south portal, facing the main road, is carved with fascinating scenes. The door is flanked by statue columns – one of which shows a slumped Judas Iscariot just off the gallows – and in the tympanum, the damned smile as they slip into the fanged mouth of hell. Finally an entire arch is carved with figures representing various trades, though sadly these are difficult to make out.

Seven kilometres beyond Sangüesa, the castle of Javier was the birthplace of St Francis Xavier, patron of Navarra and, along with Ignatius Loyola, founder of the Jesuit Order. The turreted castle with its adjoining baroque church, is prettily positioned at the head of a lovely valley, but unless you are an enthusiast, a guided tour in Spanish, given by a monk with an antiquated microphone and speaker slung over his shoulder through a series of much-restored rooms, is not particularly thrilling. You will have more fun joining the Spaniards indulging in large Sunday lunches at the Hostal Javier, or in an elaborate picnic in the tourist park.

Monasterio de Leyre (H)

The Romanesque monastery of Leyre lies about ten kilometres from Javier, high up in the Pyrenean foothills, on a mountain swathed in evergreen oak, crested by a craggy limestone escarpment and overlooking the Yesa reservoir. The oldest part of the monastery is the eleventh-century crypt, but hermits are known to have lived in caves in the mountains long before that. Even today, despite the monastery being a tourist attraction, complete with hotel, restaurant and shop, the place retains an ineffable, spiritual quality.

The primitive crypt with its uneven arches, stumpy columns and hefty capitals – all at different heights – has an eerie solemnity, especially when the coin-operated lights go out; with the help of an English-language leaflet, you can spend a happy quarter of an hour identifying the carvings on the church's marvellous west portal.

Every night at 9.15pm the monks attend the compline service during which they sing the Gregorian chant. It is worth coming to the church earlier, to sit in the candlelight, breathe in the incense-thickened air, and listen to the sound of the bell reverberating dully in the ancient stone. Then the lights are switched on, the monks file in and fill the church with the clumsy echoes of footsteps. The organist takes his place, the air hesitantly rustles into the pipes, and then the chant is intoned, sombre and unadorned, its modal intervals at first sounding strange, but with time becoming familiar. Towards the end, all the lights except those illuminating statue of the Virgin and Child in the apse are switched off, reducing the monks to silhouettes.

Valle del Roncal

The Valle del Roncal, easternmost of Navarra's Pyrenees valleys, follows the course of the River Esca, and emerges just over the Aragonese border, at the end of the Yesa reservoir. You will pass through limestone gorges and good-looking villages: Sigüés with its pepperpot chimneys and Burgui whose whitewashed houses with stone quoins will become familiar as you explore the valleys, but the first place worth a stop is Roncal itself.

Split by the River Esca, **Roncal's** wooden galleries and lashings of geraniums give it the air of a Swiss mountain village. You should visit the bakery (*panadería*), up the narrow street by the Caja de Ahorros, which will sell you a few slices of local cheese – mild, but with a pleasant kick, and so highly thought of that it has a *denominación de origen* control like wine – along with a hunk of fresh crusty bread. Incidentally, if you become intrigued by signs to the house and mausoleum of one Julian Gayarre, he was a nineteenth-century tenor born in the village.

Continuing up the valley, you reach Isaba which, though picturesque, is considerably more touristy and has rather less of a community feel than Roncal. There is a fair amount of accommodation here, ranging from the institutional Hotel Isaba, Carretera de Roncal, Tel (948) 89 30 00, which has fifty clinical but spotlessly clean rooms, to small simple *pensiones*. The nicest are the Pensión Txabalkua, Tel (948) 89 30 83, signposted from the main street and tucked away in the mazy heart of the village, and the Fonda Tapia, Tel (948) 89 30 13, which has fourteen pine-furnished rooms and is situated on the main road.

From Isaba a road climbs through a beech and pine forest into the adjacent **Valle de Salazar**, and down to the village of **Ochagavía** (H), an immediately alluring village with a spruce terrace of traditional houses lining its neat, almost canal-like river. If you want a quiet base, this is a good choice for an overnight stay.

Just south of Ochagavía there is a road of sorts over to Roncesvalles, but this eventually dwindles to a rubbly track, not easily navigable unless you have a jeep.

PILGRIM WAY FROM PAMPLONA

Heading south-west from Pamplona, the N-111 traces the old pilgrim route across a ridged and rumpled plain where the pale earth is polka-dotted with vines, grooved with rows of wheat, feathered with peach trees and speckled with clumps of grass. About 24 kilometres from Pamplona, the twelfth-century church of **Santa María de Eunate** was the last stop for pilgrims travelling from France through the Somport Pass and Aragón before they joined the Navarrese route (which went via Roncesvalles and Pamplona) at Puente la Reina. The irregular octagonal Templar church, isolated among cereal fields, is one of Navarra's most singular. Pilgrims could spend an uncomfortable night on the herringbone pavement outside, sheltered by an arcade, though the discovery of a considerable number of human bones here suggests that the church's main function was as a funerary chapel. It is a haunting place, the octagonal form inspired by the Holy Sepulchre in Jerusalem, and the interior mystically lit by light soft-filtered through alabaster windows.

A short way to the east, Puente la Reina, owes its existence to the Santiago pilgrimage and its name to the elegant eleventh-century bridge spanning the River Arga. The old pilgrim way ran through the heart of town, along what is now the Rúa Mayor, entering below a vaulted passageway linking the **Iglesia del Crucifijo** with the town's hospice. The church is entered through a porch carved with scallop shells and the interior is lit by alabaster windows, and has one Romanesque and one Gothic aisle. The latter was added in the fourteenth century to house a carved wooden Christ nailed to a Y-shaped cross, which is thought to have been brought to the church by a German pilgrim.

On a rather different note, you can arrange to visit the Señorío de Sarria winery just to the north of the town (phone (948) 26 75 62 in advance) famous for its dry rosé wines, or sample local wine and food in the rustic-style setting of the Mesón de Peregrino along the road to Pamplona.

Estella (H)

Estella is one of the most vibrant and charismatic towns on the pilgrim route. Go if you can on a Saturday, when there are usually weddings (frequently two or three), and the whole town celebrates. In the early evening the two restaurants on the arcaded main square host the parties; wine-flushed wedding guests with glad-rags in disarray lurch into the balconies; rival bands compete in their efforts to split the eardrums of the nuns, grandparents, parents and children sitting in the cafés below; and any gipsies in town for the harvest seize the opportunity to make a few extra pesetas by dancing in the street. The festivities go on all night, until, at around 5am, having kept the whole town awake with raucous singing and firecrackers, the revellers collapse. If you are really lucky, Sunday will turn out to be a religious festival, and you will be serenaded at 6am by the local choir singing hymns in the street.

The town itself is also best seen in the evening, when the street lights mask the decay of many of the buildings and create flattering perspectives of the wrought-iron balconies. The oldest part of Estella is south of the River Ega, a quarter settled in the eleventh century by Frankish and Jewish merchants attracted by freedom from taxes – an incentive established to persuade people to come and live in the Christian borderlands. In the twelfth century it became seat of the Kings of Navarra, and was said to have been so thoroughly 'Frenchified' that everyone spoke Provençal. The Kings made their home close to the Ega, in the twelfth-century **Palacio de los Reyes de Navarra**, one of Spain's oldest civic buildings and now home to various municipal offices, including the tourist office. The best view of the mighty Romanesque palace is from the steps leading up to Estella's most beautiful church, **San Pedro de la Rúa**, whose main doorway, with its zigzags and keyhole scallops, looks as though it should lead into a mosque. It is most likely to be open during or immediately after the evening service; the most notable feature of the interior is a graceful column of intertwined serpents in the central of the three Romanesque apses. Two walks of the Romanesque cloister were destroyed in 1512 when Ferdinand of Aragón's army blew up the nearby castle. The surviving original galleries have capitals carved with animals and plants and scenes from the lives of Christ and Sts Lawrence, Andrew and Peter.

Calle de la Rúa takes you past some of the old merchants' mansions, and up to the little houses of the Jewish ghetto, built in the thirteenth century below a twelfth-century church which was once a synagogue and is now on the verge of collapse. The Christians lived on the other side of the river, access to which is across a modern hump-backed bridge at the foot of the Jewish quarter. Elaborate coats of arms and flaking frescoes testify to the quarter's former prosperity, but it is now somewhat unkempt, and there is little to see until the restoration of the main church, San Miguel, which has a reputedly magnificent north portal, is completed.

The rest of the evening is best spent in one of the pavement cafés on the main square, or in the lively young bars along nearby Calle Mayor. It is also worth looking into the Bodega del Vino on the riverbank by the main road bridge for a very cheap tumbler of wine. The *bodega* is frequented mostly by local men, who in turn drink and blow grotesque tunes on a strange-looking reed pipe until their wives come to drag them out. It is an ancient, dust-caked cavern, lit by a naked bulb, and furnished with strings of garlic, copper kettles, immense decorative mushrooms, and a red-eyed skull in black gown bearing the message 'Te espera' (I'm waiting for you).

Estella's most exclusive restaurant, the Navarra, housed in an old palace in its own garden, becomes anything but exclusive on wedding nights. The alternative is Rochas where, in October, it is worth asking for *pochas*, even if they are not on the menu: white beans, here cooked in a tomato and pepper sauce, a speciality Navarra shares with La Rioja.

Around Estella: the Sierras de Urbasa and Andia

Not least of Estella's attractions is its position at the foot of the Sierras de Urbasa and Andia, and you can do a lovely circular drive into the mountains. Head first for the **Puerto de Urbasa** (the Urbasa Pass), along a lane lined with tangled hedgerows which climbs up above the poplar-fringed River Uredella. The pass gives a panoramic view of the valley with clusters of pantile-roofed villages, and beyond, you emerge on to a high meadow equally popular with sheep, horses, picnickers and acorn-seeking pigs. A drive through a luscious forest precedes a hairpin descent to the dull flat Araquil valley. Turn east on the main road towards Pamplona and south again at the turn marked Lizarraga, which takes you up into the Sierra de Andia, to a *mirador* with vertiginous views of the valley and distant sierras from a high platform below a crucifix. After crossing the scantily vegetated uplands, you descend to the village of Iranzu, from which a back-lane winds through a gorge of poplars and ilex to the **Monasterio de Iranzu**. The much-restored Cistercian monastery is less appealing than its backdrop of scrub-furred rocky hills, though, as entrance is free, it is worth popping inside to see what remains of the delicate tracery in the Gothic cloister and the kitchen with its tapering chimney. Above all, though, it makes a nice place for a picnic – if you stock up on *chorizo* there are braziers to grill them on – and in autumn you can collect walnuts from the surrounding trees.

The road to La Rioja

Just east of Estella, the Cistercian monastery of Irache is dull, and the wine museum owned by the Castillo de Irache winery, producers of some of Navarre's best rosé wines, scarcely more interesting. The main reason to visit this is to stock up on wine.

About 20 kilometres beyond, Los Arcos is an extremely ordinary roadside village, worth a visit for the extraordinary interior of its **Asunción** church. To get inside you will probably need to apply to the nuns who live just below the church's main entrance, on Calle Bagera Nunsat (in the house with the plaque to one Andrés Huberto on its façade). One of the nuns will show you round the feverish baroque interior, guiding you from one sumptuous gilt altar to another with a whispered commentary in French and affectionately patting the polychrome feet of her favourite saints.

Torres del Río, seven kilometres down the road from Los Arcos, is an immediately likeable village of well-maintained stone houses with overhanging eaves. The **Santo Sepulcro** church is an octagonal Romanesque structure which is thought to have been a funerary chapel. The interior is simple, decorated only with a chequerboard band, miniature castles, and some once-painted grotesque masks, but the place emanates a serenity which remains with you long after you have left.

Logrono (H)

The capital of La Rioja is prosperous but insipid. Smart modern and post-modern apartment blocks testify to its recent expansion, and anonymous hotels and expensive restaurants service its many business visitors. In the old quarter, refurbished houses highlight the decrepitude of their unrestored neighbours; and in the modern town the stylish topiary and fountains of the main Paseo del Espolón surround a monument to the four virtues of prudence, abnegation, patriotism and victory.

Logroño is well known for two things: coffee caramels and a notorious horse. The caramels are available all over the town but are factory-produced and very ordinary. The horse forms part of a baroque Moor-slaying tableau above the main (north) portal of the church of Santiago el Real: a banner waving, sabre-brandishing St James, in flowing gown and plumed hat, charges through a group of screaming Moors on a steed displaying outrageously oversized genitalia. The battle recorded in this statuary allegedly occurred about 15 kilometres south of the city, at **Clavijo**, a shabby village huddled below the half-ruined walls of a tenth-century castle. Only a rusty crucifix indicates the site's significance. Legend tells that in 844 the Christian King Ramiro I refused to pay the annual tribute of a hundred virgins to the Moors, and gathered his army to confront the enemy on the plain below his castle. The battle lasted all day and the Christians were on the verge of defeat, when St James appeared with a band of angels and massacred 70,000 Moors. Both the battle and the appearance of St James are probably the invention of Reconquest propagandists seeking a patron saint for their

163

movement and funds and arms from the rest of Christian Europe.

Clavijo and stone horses apart, the main reason to break a journey through Logroño is to eat a good meal, though it might take you some time to find a place to park. The town's most famous restaurant is La Merced on Calle Marqués de San Nicolás 109 (the street that leads off into the old quarter just south of the Piedra Bridge), where you eat in the lavish surroundings of an ancient mansion. This is extremely expensive, but the same owners run the more modest Mesón Lorenzo, across the road in a vaulted brick cellar, where you can lunch on Riojan specialities such as *patatas con chorizo* (chorizo sausage with potatoes), *setas a la plancha* (grilled mushrooms), or a particularly fine *menestra de verduras* (green vegetables soup).

Nájera and Santo Domingo de la Calzada

The N-120 largely follows the old pilgrim route across the Riojan plain's vineyards, cereal, and potato fields. Neither the towns nor the landscape are particularly endearing, and unless you are keen to follow the pilgrim route, you are better off heading for the more distinctive scenery of the southern lowlands, Rioja Baja (see page 168).

Pilgrims would halt at **Nájera**, a faded town by a willow-fringed river. The eleventh-century monastery of **Santa María la Real** has a fine cloister, pilgrimage scenes carved on its choir-stalls, and the tombs of various Navarrese, León and Castile royals in its pantheon.

The history of **Santo Domingo de la Calzada** (H), a dull town surrounded by potato warehouses, is even more closely linked to the Santiago pilgrimage. It is named after a medieval saint who, in the early eleventh century, having applied unsuccessfully to join two local monasteries, built himself a small hermitage by the River Oja. Seeing the problems pilgrims had crossing the river, Santo Domingo decided to build a bridge, improve the road, and establish a *hostal* and hospice for the pilgrims. The saint's full title means Santo Domingo of the Road and he is now the patron of public works. In the town the saint's miracles are catalogued in the mostly Gothic cathedral: by paintings on the wall of the choir, carvings on the saint's elaborate tomb and, most bizarre, by a white cock and hen in a cage (they were involved in one of the Saint's deeds of reviving a pilgrim who has been hanged unjustly). The birds are changed twice a month, and the cage is high up on the wall to prevent renegade pilgrims plucking out feathers as souvenirs. The most notable feature in the rest of the cathedral is the warren of corridors and spiral staircases tunnelled into walls, dating from the time when the building formed an integral part of the town's defences.

The town itself, despite a handful of eroded sandstone hospices and mansions, has little of interest. You could eat at the Mesón El Peregrino, Calle Zumalacárregui 18, which has a restaurant and outdoor terrace as well as a beamed *tapas* bar, but what is widely reckoned to be La Rioja's finest restaurant is only 14 kilometres away, in the summer apartment resort of **Ezcaray** (H). The Echaurren restaurant, Tel (941) 35 41 44, serves carefully thought-out and well presented *nouvelle cuisine*, and its menu is changed daily. (The restaurant also has good bedrooms.)

San Millán de la Cogolla: Suso and Yuso

Centuries before the establishment of the pilgrimage to Santiago, local pilgrims were paying homage to a shepherd hermit and miracle worker, San Millán de la Cogolla. A drive through a rather spartan landscape brings you up to the village and the two monasteries inspired by his cult: Yuso, in the valley, and Suso, built on to the caves in the hillside where San Millán lived.

Of the two, **Suso** is by far the more interesting, an intimate, homespun muddle of Visigothic, Mozarabic and Romanesque elements. It is silent, except perhaps for birdsong and the distant chugging of a tractor, infused by the smell of woodsmoke, and you stand on an age-polished pavement of swirls and herringbones, and look down into a lush terraced valley. Inside there are two aisles, Visigothic capitals carved with rosettes and animal heads, a Mozarabic cupola and faint traces of geometric Mozarabic frescoes. An alabaster effigy of San Millán lies on a Romanesque tomb surrounded by praying disciples, and a glass screen reveals the bones and skulls of dead pilgrims. The caretaker will take you, without a torch, into the dusty red caves where San Millán lived in the fifth century, an experience not to be recommended unless you are agile, dressed in old clothes, and able to cope with total darkness and musty air.

The monastery of **Yuso** was built in the sixteenth century, and was intended to be the El Escorial of La Rioja, but in reality it is a dreary mixture of Renaissance, neo-classical and baroque architecture, with little of genuine artistic worth.

The monastery is currently undergoing restoration, and there are plans to open a hotel in the old monks' quarters, which is due to open at the end of 1991.

RIOJA WINE COUNTRY

The best of Rioja's wine comes from the Rioja Alta (Upper Rioja) and Rioja Alavesa zones, both to the north of the River Ebro. Villages crowned by churches cling to small humpy hills, and fields of fudge-coloured soil striped with rows of stubby vines lazily undulate towards the scrunched escarpments and pinnacles of the Sierra de Cantabria mountains. The vines barely reach knee height, as the use of wires is forbidden by the Riojan authorities – the claim that it is for aesthetic reasons is less likely than the fact that it keeps production low, and prices high. Harvesting the grapes is consequently an unenviable task, and much of the back-breaking work is undertaken by gypsies.

Haro (H)

Haro is the so-called wine capital of Rioja Alta, and home to some of the area's best wineries. On a hill above the River Ebro, it has a pretty centre of sandstone houses adorned with escutcheons and white *solanas*, and squares and streets where life is lived at a leisurely pace. A hotel in a converted Augustinian monastery and a couple of good restaurants make the town a comfortable base for those who are particularly interested in wine.

The wineries are in the valley, ranged along the aptly named Avenida Costa del Vino. One of the best to visit is **CVNE** (Compañía Vinicola del Norte de España) which is open to the public mornings and afternoons (closed Sundays). The guided tour passes through rooms where the wine is aged in oak barrels which are plugged, in time-honoured fashion with sacking, and into a cellar encrusted with stalactites of fungus and cobwebs where bottles are stored. The modern part of the complex has the most to see, especially during the October harvest. Grapes cascade from lorries into gleaming containers, in which they are churned to a paste by a giant mincer, and swung across a gantry to be poured into immense vats. Equally fun to watch is the bottling process, when the bottles are cleaned, filled and corked by machine, but have to be packed tediously by hand.

Evenings are best spent in one of the cafés on the main square, with its wrought-iron bandstand and florid baroque *ayuntamiento*. The church of Santo Tomás, just above the main square, has some violent Crucifixion scenes on its portal and, if you want to buy wine or just get good advice, the shop at nearby Calle Santo Tomás 13, easily found by its sign *Todos los Vinos de Rioja* (All the Wines of the Rioja), has a knowledgeable and helpful owner.

Haro is liveliest during the Semana del Vino (June 24–29) which reaches its climax on the morning of the 29th with a wine battle. This takes place near a hermitage some six kilometres north-west of the town, and involves chucking around 50,000 litres of young wine. To ensure that no one escapes without getting drenched, a wine-spraying helicopter hovers above. At midday, with everyone pickled within and soaked without, the festivities move down to the town.

At other times of the year, Haro's pleasures are rather more sedate. Beethoven II, Santo Tomás 3, Tel (941) 31 11 81, serves good local food, and retains the feel of a family-run restaurant, though you dine to the accompaniment of Muzak rather than Beethoven quartets. Their *revuelto* – eggs scrambled with garlic stalks, wild mushrooms, prawns and asparagus – is particularly good. The other good restaurant, Terete, Lucrecia Arana 17, (941) 31 00 23, specialises in *cordero asado*, and like the Beethoven has a strong wine list. At lunchtime, you can get good, unpretentious food at Kika, up the street from Beethoven.

Laguardia (H)

The wine centre of the Rioja Alavesa, 25 kilometres east of Haro in the Basque Country, Laguardia is the other place well worth visiting in this area: a well-maintained walled hilltop village which makes for a pleasant lunch stop.

Strings of red peppers and lines of washing dry on the wrought-iron balconies of sandstone houses with hefty overhanging eaves. At midday there is nothing to be heard along its narrow, traffic-free streets except kitchen clatters and radio jingles. Weighty doors open on to cool stone-flagged halls, which lead down into cellars where the inhabitants once made their own wine; nowadays most people work for the big wine companies, or band together into co-operatives. The village has two churches: the modern porch of the Santa María de los Reyes protects an exuberant and colourful late Gothic portal and the blocky, fortified church of San Juan, which has a band

167

of musicians carved around one of its windows, including a violinist and a bagpiper.

The **Palacio winery**, just outside the village, is open to the public, and like CVNE in Haro combines state-of-the-art processes with traditional ageing methods. Palacio and other local wines can be quaffed with a generously portioned lunch at the Marixa restaurant in the village, where the menu includes most of the Riojan culinary specialities; there are also ten bedrooms with own bathrooms above the restaurant, Tel (941) 10 01 65, useful if the recommended hotel is fully booked.

La Rioja Baja

Little visited by foreign tourists, the lowland Rioja is a region of orchards, vines and olives, bare hills, rocky gorges and open moorland. The prettiest landscape can be found along the valleys of the Río Iregua and Río Leza, dotted with pan-tile-roofed knots of crumbling houses.

The N-111 from Logroño follows the River Iregua through a fertile valley of one-street villages, orderly orchards, vegetable plots and vineyards. The landscape gets more dramatic at Islallana, huddled below a series of crags which resemble giant loaves of bread. After this the valley narrows to a deeply wooded rocky gorge, where strata of rock jab through the trees. **Villanueva de Cameros** is worth a stop, a sleepy hamlet of stone sited above a poplar-fringed river. The primary school shares its premises with a bar, and there is one *hostal* with a small restaurant on the main road. This, the Hostal Los Nogales, Tel (941) 46 22 08, has eight spotless rooms (but none has its own bathroom).

From Villanueva the road continues above the river, which is currently in the process of being diverted to form a reservoir. Beyond the collapsing village of San Andrés, a left turn signposted Ribafrecha (LO-611) takes you into the Río Leza valley, and through some of La Rioja's best scenery. Cows, sheep and horses graze on open moorland of stubbly grass and stubby shrubs below hillsides cloaked with oak and fir. From the 1,391-metre-high pass, the Collado de Sancho Leza, there are views of bleaker hills.

Throughout the valley you will pass villages of pink-and-gold-tinged stone houses with half-timbered upper storeys; sleepy places smelling of woodsmoke and manure, where horses and donkeys are still a much-used form of transport. Beyond Soto de Cameros, the river snakes through a narrow gorge flanked by striated rocks before the valley flattens and broadens out around the village of Ribafrecha.

WHERE TO STAY

BILBAO

Conde Duque   £££
Campo de Volatín 22
48007 Bilbao   *Tel (94) 445 60 00*

A bland but reasonably comfortable businessman's hotel, on the right bank of the Nervión. It is easy to get to from the airport and parking is not too difficult. By Bilbao standards, the rooms are good value.

Open: all year **Rooms:** 67 **Credit/charge cards:** Amex, Diners, Eurocard, Visa

---

Indautxu   £££
Plaza Bombero Etxaniz
48010 Bilbao   *Tel (94) 421 11 98*

A recently opened hotel housed in an erstwhile maternity hospital, with a dazzling mirror-glass extension. Rooms are attractively furnished in shades of blue, and there is an outdoor terrace.

Open: all year **Rooms:** 145 **Credit/charge cards:** Amex, Diners, Eurocard, Visa

---

EZCARAY

Echaurren   £££
Héroes de Alcazar 2
26280 La Rioja   *Tel (941) 35 40 47*

Tasteful, simple wooden-floored and white-walled rooms above an excellent restaurant.

Open: all year except Nov **Rooms:** 26 **Credit/charge cards:** Amex, Diners, Eurocard, Visa

---

ESTELLA

Cristina   £
Baja Navarra 1
31200 Navarra   *Tel (948) 55 07 72*

A recently refurbished *hostal* on the corner of the main square. The bedrooms are spotless with white walls, pretty bedspreads and compact tiled bathrooms, and some have shutters and balconies.

Open: all year **Rooms:** 15 **Credit/charge cards:** none

FUENTERRABIA

Pampinot	£££
Calle Mayor 3	
20280 Fuenterrabía	*Tel (943) 64 06 00*

A sixteenth-century mansion just below the castle, which retains the cultured intimacy of a private home. In the stone-flagged hall a Corinthian capital supports a table, a gilded altarpiece frames coats of arms and the horned skulls of mountain goats hang on the wall. In the small bar the wall is decorated with a collection of plates and a tapestry hangs in the cork-floored lounge. The bedrooms are all different, but you will probably have a chandelier and Persian rugs, and may have a frescoed wardrobe or carved screen.

Open: all year, except Feb **Rooms:** 8 **Credit/charge cards:** Amex, Diners, Eurocard, Visa

San Nicolás	££
Plaza de Armas 6	
20280 Fuenterrabía	*Tel (943) 64 42 78*

A tasteful family-run hotel whose owners speak excellent English. Bedroom floors are tiled with terracotta, and have whitewashed walls, pretty furnishings and pristine bathrooms.

Open: all year **Rooms:** 14 **Credit/charge cards:** Amex, Diners, Eurocard, Visa

Hostal Txoko Goxoa	£
Murallas 19	
20280 Fuenterrabía	*Tel (943) 64 46 58*

A small *pensión* overlooking the ramparts. None of the clean and simple bedrooms has *ensuite* bathrooms, but there are five bathrooms down the corridor.

Open: all year **Rooms:** 6 **Credit/charge cards:** Eurocard, Visa

GUETARIA

San Prudencio £
20808 Getaria *Tel (943) 83 24 11*

Views over lush hills to the sea and a well-thought-of restaurant compensate for rather basic rooms without own bathroom. The hotel is signposted from the coast road about a kilometre to the west of the village.

Open: Mar–Oct; **Rooms:** 10 (none with own bath) **Credit/ charge cards:** Visa

HARO

Los Agustinos £££
San Agustín 2
26200 Haro *Tel (941) 31 13 08*

A stylishly converted sandstone monastery, with an arcaded court-yard, relaxing bar with quarry tiles and chintzy chairs, and comfort-able rooms. These have whitewashed walls, balustrade-headed beds, and gleaming tiled bathrooms.

Open: all year **Rooms:** 62 **Credit/charge cards:** Amex, Diners, Eurocard, Visa

LAGUARDIA

Pachico Martinez £
Sancho Abarco 20
01300 Alava *Tel (941) 10 00 09*

Simple rooms with whitewashed walls and wooden floors in a long traditional sandstone building with varnished *solanas* and iron balconies just outside the town walls. Eight of the bedrooms have their own terrace with extensive views of the surrounding vineyards, and there is also a communal terrace for other guests.

Open: all year **Rooms:** 24 **Credit/charge cards:** Eurocard, Visa

LEYRE (MONASTERIO DE)

Hospedería Monasterio de Leyre ££
31410 Navarra *Tel (948) 88 41 00*

Though accommodation in the monastery is simple, the rooms are by no means cell-like. Walls are whitewashed, and doors, wardrobes and shutters are of pannelled wood. It is a wonderfully evocative place to stay and the only sounds are the wind and the bells summoning the monks to church. The restaurant has a limited daily menu, with simple local dishes.

Open: Mar–Oct **Rooms:** 30 **Credit/charge cards:** Amex, Diners, Eurocard, Visa

LOGRONO

Hostal París £
Avenida de La Rioja 8
26001 Logroño *Tel (941) 22 87 50*

Pleasantly located on the Paseo del Espolón, this upmarket *hostal* has bedrooms with tiled floors and antique-style furniture. Sixteen of them have balconies overlooking the square. The owner also runs a 'pub' next door, which has a wide range of whiskys.

Open: all year except 22 Dec-7 Jan **Rooms:** 36 **Credit/charge cards:** none

OCHAGAVIA

Hostal Orialde £
Urrutia 6
31680 Navarra *Tel (948) 89 00 27*

A traditional stone and whitewashed house on the riverside. The reception hall is paved with stone flags and pebbles, and has a rough-hewn bench, and carved chest and doors. Rooms are of mellow pine with woven bedspreads.

Open: Apr-Oct **Rooms:** 12 (3 with own bath) **Credit/charge cards:** none

PAMPLONA

Europa ££
Espoz y Mina 11
31001 Pamplona *Tel (948) 22 18 00*

A family-run hotel just off Plaza del Castillo which has recently been dazzlingly refurbished to bring it up to the standard of its very good restaurant. Corridors are of Travertine marble, and rooms are stylishly decorated in subtle shades of grey and coral, with marble bathrooms.

Open: all year **Rooms:** 25 **Credit/charge cards:** Amex, Diners, Visa

Yoldi   **££**
Avenida San Ignacio 11
31002 Pamplona   *Tel (948) 22 48 00*

Dull rooms in a hotel frequented by bullfighters during San Fermín, who may give it the atmosphere it otherwise lacks. It is, however, perfectly adequate and conveniently located about five minutes' walk from Plaza del Castillo.

Open: all year **Rooms:** 48 **Credit/charge cards:** Diners, Eurocard, Visa

---

La Perla   **££**
Plaza del Castillo 1
31001 Pamplona   *Tel (948) 22 77 06*

If faded *fin-de-siècle* elegance appeals, this is the place to stay. Rooms vary in standard, and not all have own bathrooms, but if you are lucky you could sleep in a frescoed bed, sit on chipped antique chairs, preen yourself in a gilt-framed mirror, and make calls on a bakelite phone. Even the simpler rooms have character, and the lounge is typically Pamplonan, with two stuffed bulls heads on the wall.

Open: all year **Rooms:** 67 (25 with own bath) **Credit/charge cards:** Amex, Diners, Eurocard, Visa

---

Casa Otano   **£**
Calle San Nicolás 5
31001 Pamplona   *Tel (948) 22 70 36*

Clean, simple rooms with wooden floorboards and white walls above a *tapas* bar and restaurant just off Plaza del Castillo.

Open: all year **Rooms:** 30 (6 with own bath) **Credit/charge cards:** Amex, Diners, Eurocard, Visa

---

SAN SEBASTIAN

María Cristina   **£££**
Paseo República Argentina 4
20004 San Sebastián   *Tel (943) 42 49 00*

An exclusive *belle époque* hotel, lavishly renovated two years ago, standing between the river Urumea and a manicured *plaza*. In the palatial reception hall mock marble columns, soft furnishings and the luxurious carpets are in shades of coral, cream and gold and the

173

restaurant is a similarly styled feast for the eyes. Rooms are immense and sumptuous.

Open: all year **Rooms:** 139 **Credit/charge cards:** Amex, Diners, Visa

---

De Londres y de Inglaterra   £££
Calle Zubieta 2
20007 San Sebastián   *Tel (943) 42 69 89*

A more modest turn-of-the-century hotel on the sea front, close to the Aldredi Eder Park, and a short walk from the old town. Public areas have seen better days, but the rooms have been redecorated, and have marble bathrooms and co-ordinating furnishings.

Open: all year **Rooms:** 142 **Credit/charge cards:** Amex, Diners, Eurocard, Visa

---

Europa   £££
San Martín 52
20007 San Sebastián   *Tel (943) 47 08 80*

Opened in March 1990 in a refurbished turn-of-the-century hotel, the Europa is on a busy road a short walk from the beach. Rooms are comfortable, decorated and furnished in soft pastels.

Open: all year **Rooms:** 60 **Credit/charge cards:** Eurocard, Visa

---

Niza   ££
Zubieta 56
20007 San Sebastián   *Tel (943) 42 66 63*

This is owned by the Basque sculptor Eduardo Chillida, so posters and prints of his work, a painting by his son, a portrait of his mother and father, and a reception hall of stylish modern and notable antique furniture make it a very special hotel. The old cage lift takes you up to the bedrooms which are clean, fresh, and recently decorated in blue and white. Some have balconies with sea views.

Open: all year **Rooms:** 41 **Credit/charge cards:** Amex, Diners, Eurocard, Visa

---

Parma   ££
General Jáuregui 11
20003 San Sebastián   *Tel (943) 42 88 93*

Clean, plain rooms in a dull modern hotel by the river close to the old quarter. The main reason for recommending this establishment is that it is conveniently located and likely to have rooms available when other hotels are full.

Open: all year **Rooms:** 21 **Credit/charge cards:** none

SANTO DOMINGO DE LA CALZADA

El Corregidor £££
Zumalacárregui 14
26250 Santo Domingo de la Calzada   *Tel (941) 34 21 28*

A new hotel with gleaming marble public areas, and a characterless café and restaurant. The bedrooms have satiny bedcovers, floor-to-ceiling mirrors and large bathrooms.

Open: all year **Rooms:** 32 **Credit/charge cards:** Amex, Diners, Eurocard, Visa

VITORIA

Savoy £
Prudencio María de Varestegui 4
01004 Vitoria   *Tel (945) 25 00 56*

The hotel is just round the corner from the bus station, at the foot of the old town. It has simple spotless rooms with whitewashed walls and flowery pastel bedspreads, though not all have bathrooms.

Open: all year **Rooms:** 30 **Credit/charge cards:** Amex, Visa

Dato 28 £
01005 Vitoria   *Tel (945) 23 23 20*

A quirky hotel on Vitoria's most elegant shopping street. Painted wooden animals and two angel musicians adorn the stairway, a budgie chirps above the reception desk and plastic parrots hang from the balconies, yet you could find yourself sharing a room with a modern sculpture of two naked men. The best bedroom has a *solana*. However, there is no café and no restaurant.

Open: all year **Rooms:** 14 **Credit/charge cards:** Diners, Eurocard, Visa

ARAGON

ARAGON is a region of extremes, a land of sun-bleached desert and snow-veined peaks, lush valleys and inhospitable uplands, vast cereal plains and glassy reservoirs. The regional capital, Zaragoza, is a slick, fast-paced business city, but elsewhere in the region there are villages where cows wander in the streets, houses are heated by wood fires and mail arrives on the daily bus.

The countryside is severely underpopulated: abandoned and semi-abandoned villages are evidence of the massive exodus from the land to the towns. In the province of Teruel the death rate exceeds the birth rate; in Huesca there is an average of six inhabitants per square mile; and in the '60s many men who wished to remain working on the land had to advertise in the poorer regions for wives because the local women were interested in marrying only the more affluent factory workers.

In the early Middle Ages the border of the Moorish territories ran straight across this region. The Pyrenean valleys in the north remained under Christian rule, which expanded southwards little by little. By 1134 the Christians had conquered Zaragoza, which they made capital of Aragón. In 1154 the marriage of an Aragonese princess, Petronila, and the Count of Barcelona united Aragón and Catalunya. The Kingdom of Aragón took over Valencia, the Balearic Islands, Naples, Sicily and Sardinia, and by the mid-fifteenth century it was a formidable Mediterranean power. Another dynastic marriage, between Ferdinand of Aragón and Isabella of Castile (the Catholic Monarchs) in 1476 marked the beginning of modern centralised Spain, and of Aragón's decline. Aragonese institutions were axed and the Inquisition expelled all Muslims: Moriscos, who remained in Aragón after the Reconquest, converted to Christianity, and who accounted for over 16 per cent of the population.

Although some intriguing early Christian buildings remain in the Pyrenees, notably the Monasterio San Juan de la Peña and the Castillo de Loarre, it was the Morisco craftsmen who made the most significant contribution to Aragonese architecture. They developed a style which became known as Mudejar, the best examples of which are the church towers of intricate geometric brickwork studded with glazed ceramic tiles in Teruel, Tarazona and Zaragoza.

But the most striking aspect of Aragón is its landscape. The region is completely surrounded by mountains – an acute contrast with the endless cereal plains and arid Los Monegros

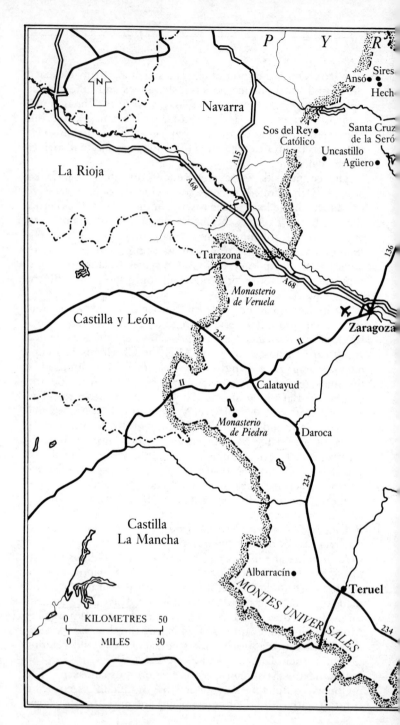

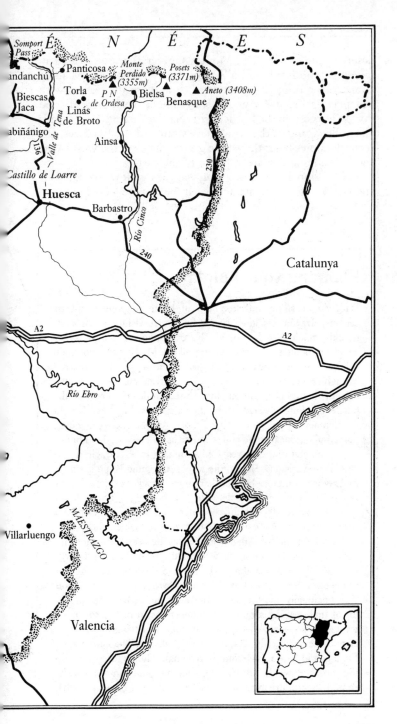

desert in the centre. The Montes Universales are covered in pine plantations where bulls roam freely before being hauled along to the ring; El Maestrazgo, straddling the border with Valencia, is a sparsely populated range of bleak plateaux and savage gorges; on the border with Navarra are neat, tight hills and valleys; and in the Aragonese stretch of the Pyrenees, the scenery ranges from the gentle green valleys of the west to the sheer cirques and soaring peaks of the east.

The regional capital, Zaragoza, has a few worthwhile sights, but it is not attractive. It cannot be avoided com-

Planning your holiday

With no coastline and hemmed in by more popular tourist regions, Aragón is seldom visited by foreign visitors and consequently much less developed; the exception are the Pyrenees which are popular with skiers and walkers. Many of the mountain villages have been heavily developed in the '70s and are marred by ugly concrete hotels and apartments characteristic of that period; in summer, without the white mantle of snow and the bustle of colourfully clad skiers, the villages look soulless. Recent development, though, has been more sympathetic, with hotels being built in local stone and wood or using converted old buildings – notably the 500-year-old seminary in Albarracín and a cinema in Tarazona. But on the whole, accommodation is simple in Aragón, with more budget than upper-bracket choices. Eating out is less exciting here than in neighbouring Navarra or the Basque Country, though the red and raisiny local wine, Cariñena, makes up in alcohol content what it lacks in refinement.

The highlights of Aragón can easily be seen in a motoring holiday of ten days or so, or you could combine parts of it with Navarra, Rioja or Catalunya. It is not easy to see this area on public transport: buses link the main towns, but rarely run more than once daily into the mountains and you are likely to spend a lot of time waiting around for connections in places you never wanted to see anyway. Virtually all the main roads meet in the capital, Zaragoza, with fast motorway links to Bilbao and Costas Dorada and Brava (including Barcelona). The picturesque touring routes, however, are narrow, winding mountain roads which require careful driving and can be far more time-consuming than

pletely, as all main roads pass through it. The towns of Teruel and Huesca merit a couple of hours' sightseeing, too. The main target to the west of Zaragoza is the Monasterio de Piedra, set in one of Spain's loveliest parks; in the foothills of the Montes Universales, Albarracín is a good-looking peach-washed town. The hill village of Sos del Rey Católico, on the border with Navarra, is also picturesque – though it makes more sense to use it as a base for exploring the sights of eastern Navarra than Aragón.

you expect. For touring, use a good map such as the Michelin *Cataluña/Catalunya-Aragón-Baleares*, 1:400,000, sheet 443. The good bases are the town of Albarracín or the *parador* just outside Teruel in the south; Tarazona and Sos del Rey Católico (and its *parador*) in the west; and the stone villages of Hecho, Ansó and Linás de Broto or the Monte Perdido *parador* in the Pyrenees.

For walkers, bird-watchers or botanists the Pyrenees are excellent, and you could base yourself either on the Aragonese or Catalan side or cover both in one long holiday – for more details, see Walking in the Pyrenees, page 202.

The most practical way to get to Aragón from Britain is by arranging a fly-drive holiday to Barcelona or Bilbao, both some 300 kilometres away. The car ferry terminal at Santander is within a long day's drive. Other internal, longer-distance, transport connections include air, rail or coach to Madrid; Zaragoza is connected by rail or coach to Barcelona, Bilbao or Valencia.

Aragón's summers can be unbearably hot, its winters long and freezing. Spring and autumn are the best times to visit, though in the Pyrenees the weather is notoriously fickle, even in high summer.

● **Regional Tourist Board**: Dirección General de Turismo, Edificio Pignatelli, Paseo María Agustín 36, 50071 Zaragoza, Tel (976) 22 43 00. Particularly useful information includes a guide to all the tourist services and accommodation in the region and a leaflet listing *Casas de turismo rural* – rooms available in old houses, in some of the small, remote villages of the region. Useful **tourist information offices** can be found in Zaragoza (three, including Don Jaime 4), Ainsa, Huesca, Albarracín, Teruel and Tarazona.

ZARAGOZA (H)

A dour brick city on the sluggish River Ebro, Zaragoza is the capital of Aragón, and home to more than half the province's inhabitants. It is one of Spain's fastest growing cities, and in the last twenty years over 100,000 people have come to seek work in its factories. The exodus from the land has created a city in which the contrasts between wealth and poverty are visibly acute: there are residential quarters, a Parisian-style boulevard with exclusive shops, and a gaudily domed basilica that is reputed to be the wealthiest church in Spain. But inside this church tramps shelter, and across the *plaza*, semi-demolished houses rot and ecclesiastical kitsch glitters in a dank, mouldy arcade; close by, in slums, immigrants from Africa and southern Spain huddle in winter around braziers listening to reggae and flamenco.

Zaragoza's origin is ancient, and its name, a corruption of Caesaraugusta, dates from its days as a Roman colony. It was later occupied by the Muslims for four centuries, who left behind them the Aljafería, the finest Moorish palace outside Andalucía. The city fell to the Christians in the early twelfth century, but the Muslim community remained, and its masons worked on many of the new churches, building the Mudejar towers of elaborate brickwork. The square tower of the Santa María Magdalena church, on Calle Mayor, is the most ornate, decorated with glazed tiles.

A handful of palaces and a glorious commercial exchange, La Lonja (open only for temporary exhibitions), testify to Zaragoza's prosperity during the Renaissance. Unfortunately however, much of the old city was destroyed in 1809 by Napoleonic troops during the Peninsular War (or the War of Independence): in the second of two long sieges the French took the city house by house and left behind a pile of smoking ruins and 54,000 dead. Today the surviving old buildings rise up abruptly at the end of a dark, grubby street, in the midst of a sorrowful red-light area or beside a dual carriageway.

Though Zaragoza is far from picturesque, it attracts hundreds of thousands of people each year. They come to pay homage to the Virgen del Pilar, a diminutive statue of the Virgin perched on top of a jasper pillar inside the basilica. Her image is all over the city and is most often found stamped on souvenir ashtrays, fans and cruet sets. The story goes that St James was passing through Zaragoza in AD 40 when he saw the Virgin descend from heaven on a pillar. The fact that St

James never visited Spain, let alone Zaragoza, has not hindered the growth of the cult, nor deterred Catholics from all over the world from showering the Virgin with jewelled gowns, crowns, necklaces and bracelets. The Virgen del Pilar's basilica is only second in importance to the one in Santiago, and her feast day, 12 October, is a national holiday, celebrated in Zaragoza with processions, bullfights, fireworks and traditional dancing.

Exploring the town

Visiting Zaragoza needs careful planning, as the best areas and sights in the city are scattered. The tourist information office on Calle Don Jaime 4 (one of three such offices in the city) is a good starting point. As well as the Aljafería palace, out of the centre to the east, there are some good museums, though not least of Zaragoza's attractions is the **Primo de Rivera park**, to the south. It holds Zaragoza's art nouveau masterpiece: a delicate wrought-iron bandstand crowned with a pineapple dome. You could spend a pleasant afternoon here, among the pine woods and formal water garden, watching old Zaragozans gather for the daily game of cards and children mesmerised by a local maverick who simultaneously smokes cigarettes and sucks lollipops.

Art nouveau became popular in Zaragoza at the beginning of the century, with the development of industry and rise of an urban bourgeoisie. New residential quarters were built, notably along the Parisian-style boulevard, **Paseo de Sagasta**. A handful of art nouveau town houses remain here, the loveliest of which is the Casa Juncosa at number 11, with its elegant wrought-iron flowers and foliage. The Paseo also has the city's most exclusive shops. Other good shopping streets nearby are Calle San Ignacio de Loyola and Calle General Sueiro.

The rest of Zaragoza is not very appealing. The vast **Plaza de Nuestra Señora del Pilar**, which links the city's two cathedrals, was recently excavated in order to create 3,000 underground parking places. It is due for completion in the summer of 1992, but until then you can expect to see the basilica's turquoise, yellow and white tiled domes bobbing like hot-air balloons above what resembles a bomb site. La Seo cathedral has been concealed behind scaffolding for the last few years (and is due to reopen in 1993).

Directly south of the Plaza Pilar is the old quarter, **El Tubo**, bordered by slums to the west and the shopping Calle

Don Jaime to the east. Lottery ticket-sellers, cigarette vendors and garish plastic signs give it a tawdry feel. You may, however, want to visit the two museums housed in restored Renaissance mansions in this area of the town. The Camón Aznar, just off Calle Don Jaime, has a virtually complete set of Goya's prints, and the Pablo Gargallo museum is devoted to the striking sculptures of the above-mentioned Aragonese sculptor, a contemporary of Picasso. It is approached through a small, but sinister red-light quarter from Calle César Augusto.

The third museum worth visiting, Museo de Bellas Artes is in the new quarter of the city, divided from the old by the busy Calle Coso.

Eating out and accommodation

There are lots of bars on Calle Mayor (just south of La Seo cathedral), most serving *tapas*, and a few of them cheap lunches. The bars and restaurants of El Tubo, concentrated along Calle Libertad, Calle Cuatro de Agosto and Calle de los Martires, tend to be tacky places, though Casa Lac at the top of Calle de los Martires is an exception: a cosy nineteenth-century bar with a restaurant above. Another pleasant and convenient café in the centre is El Espejo on Calle Santiago near Plaza Pilar. It is popular with students and locals and often displays contemporary works of art.

A better choice of bars for *tapas* and drinks can be found in Calle San Miguel, which runs between Avenida de la Independencia and the church of San Miguel. There are a number of alternatives here, ranging from Akelarre with a designer interior hidden behind rough stone walls, to the Pilsen which serves good *tapas*, including a tasty *tortilla* stuffed with salad. There are a couple of more exclusive places to drink on Calle Costa, also off Avenida de la Independencia – the cocktail bar of the Gran Hotel, and the subdued Gregory's Bar. It is frequented by businessmen, but is a peaceful place in which to sit and read the papers for an hour or so. The streets between the Paseo de Sagasta and the Paseo de la Constitución have some stylish but reasonably priced places to eat and drink: try the pristine pine-clad self-service Cafetería Rincón on Calle General Sueiro (open from 1–4pm) or the nearby La Marmita with its reasonably priced daily menus and contemporary art displayed on the walls.

The simplest thing to do at dinnertime is to head down to Calle Santa Teresa de Jesús, just north of the Primo de Rivera park. Aldaba at number 26, Tel (976) 56 48 09, is run with great care by the Basque chef and his wife. The food is special, yet unpretentious, and you should leave room for one of the sweets – the home-made apple pie is unforgettable.

The main sights

● **Basilica de Nuestra Señora del Pilar** The eighteenth-century basilica stands on the banks of the murky river, its jauntily tiled domes contrasting with the dull brickwork. Inside the cathedral, the chandeliers are rarely switched on, and the soupy gloom blurs the details of the alabaster retable (sculpted by Damián Forment) on the high altar, and reduces the statues perched on the rims of the frescoed cupolas to ghosts. The Lady Chapel, in contrast, is drenched in light. It forms a luxuriously glinting marble and gilt palace for the little statue of the Virgin, who stands on her pillar, haloed with jewels and clad in a sumptuous robe. After praying, people walk round to the back of the chapel, to kiss or pat an exposed patch of the column. Part of the Virgin's wardrobe is on display in the Museo Pilarista; worth a brief visit to see sequin, gold and gem-caked robes and opulent jewellery glittering behind heavily guarded doors. You can also take a lift up one of the towers, then climb a dank, graffiti-scrawled stairway for a view of the Zaragozan sprawl.

● **La Seo** Of the two cathedrals in Zaragoza, this is the more important and the older. It has been undergoing restoration for many years and is not due to reopen until 1993. La Seo (short for San Salvador) was built on the site of a mosque in the twelfth century, shortly after the Moors had been overthrown. It has since been rebuilt numerous times, and the result is a hotchpotch of architectural styles. The basic structure is Gothic, the apse is Romanesque, the tower is baroque, and the outer wall of the Parroquieta Chapel is the work of Mudejar craftsmen and has a multi-coloured Moorish cupola; the gallery houses a collection of French and Flemish tapestries. The interior is no less eclectic, featuring a plateresque chancel closure (*trascoro*), some ornate Churrigueresque side-chapels, and a Gothic alabaster retable, carved in part by a German, that contains some markedly Teutonic figures.

● **Museo Camón Aznar** Camon Aznar was a Zaragozan art historian and Goya expert who died in 1979. He also amassed a considerable art collection, now on show in this restored Renaissance palace. There are minor works by Velázquez, Zurbarán and El Greco, a typically flushed and fleshy knight by Frans Hals and a hallucinatory scene of pipe-smoking, card-playing beasts by David Teniers. But the greatest impact is made by a virtually complete set of Goya's etchings, comprising a bleak and devastating vision of humanity, typified perhaps by *A Caza de Dientes*, part of the *Los Caprichos* series, in which a woman retches into a hand-kerchief as she extracts the teeth from a corpse rotting on a gibbet.

● **Museo Pablo Gargallo** Pablo Gargallo (1881–1934) was an Aragonese sculptor who made an important contribution to twentieth-century sculpture by developing the traditional techniques of Spanish metalcraft. Works include a haunted Great Prophet (*Gran Profeta*), a comical series of fauns (decked with monocles, beards, earrings and pipes), and the chic and sexy Kiki de Montparnasse. There is also an intriguing dis-play of the sketches and cardboard cut-outs Gargallo used when planning his sculptures.

● **Aljafería** An exotic, slightly sinister atmosphere hangs over the Aljafería palace, one-time seat of the Aragonese Inquisition, and fictional prison of the captive Manrico in Verdi's *Il Trovatore*. Now standing by the multi-laned road to Bilbao and overlooked by apartment blocks, the formidable moated fortress was built for the Muslim dynasty that ruled Zaragoza in the tenth and eleventh centuries. In the fifteenth century the Catholic Monarchs built a palace on the first floor.

The first thing you see is a courtyard where walls of lacy tracery overlook a sunken garden and what appears to be a pool of blood. On closer examination you will see that much of the carving round the pool is painted crimson. Just off the courtyard is an exquisite miniature mosque, and upstairs the elaborately coffered rooms of the Catholic Monarchs open off a gallery punctuated with liquorice-twist columns.

● **Museo de Bellas Artes** A collection devoted to Aragonese archaeology and art, housed in a mock-brick building with a pseudo-Renaissance courtyard. In the archaeology section a model of Roman Zaragoza gives the impression of a small, rather bleak town occupied mostly by veteran soldiers. Finds from this era include coins stamped with the profiles of

Augustus, Tiberius and Caligula, the bust of a deified Augustus from Tarazona, and mosaics that include panels from a calendar and Orpheus enchanting animals with his lyre. But the museum is best known for its collection of Aragonese Gothic paintings, vividly painted religious works which pay minute attention to detail, whether it be a flower, a gown or a saint's whiskered wart. There are also a few works by Goya, notably a pair of portraits of the affable but eccentric Carlos IV and his scheming wife, María Luisa, gripping her fan as if she were a schoolteacher with a cane.

● **Museo Etnológico** Works of local crafts and folk art pleasingly displayed in a replica of a Pyrenean farmhouse in the Primo de Rivera park. There are traditional costumes, ceramics and furniture from different parts of the region.

TARAZONA (H)

A labyrinth of steep alleys and stepped streets, stacked high above the River Queiles, Tarazona is a town with a scruffy, lived-in feel. Washing sags and strings of peppers dangle from wrought-iron balconies; plastered walls are cracked or have flaked to reveal multi-hued brick and warped beams, and in the morning the streets bustle with children scampering to school, old men shuffling to the cafés, and women chatting on their way to the shops.

Tarazona's position, close to the borders with Navarra, La Rioja and Castile, rendered it an important frontier town from the twelfth century when the Christians seized it from the Moors, and, until the fifteenth century, it was the residence of the Kings of Aragón. The splendid cathedral, a handful of Mudejar towers and the Bishop's Palace, once the royal Alcázar (Moorish palace) remain from its days of glory and are worth a visit, though it is the ambience of the town as a whole which is the most memorable.

The **cathedral** stands across the river from the old town. It is closed for restoration (and not due to reopen for another nine years). The Mudejar belfry and cupola are still visible.

A brief walk along the river brings you to Tarazona's unusual eighteenth-century bullring, a shabby octagonal structure now converted into 32 flats. Back on the other bank of the river, a flight of steps climbs to the old upper town and the **Bishop's Palace**, a muddle of Gothic, Mudejar, Renaissance and baroque architecture, supported on soaring arches

187

and surrounded by a tangle of tiny streets, squares and passageways.

The **Magdalena church**, above the palace, has the town's finest Mudejar tower, patterned with diamonds, blind arches and zig-zags. Directly behind the palace is the distinctive stepped and cobbled **Rua Alta**, crossed by a brick *cobertizo* (an archway with a room or rooms on top), and overlooked by run-down houses known as *casas colgadas*, or hanging houses, because of their overhanging upper storeys. On parallel **Calle de la Judería**, a cul-de-sac at the heart of the old Jewish quarter, three hanging houses have been smartly restored. At the foot of the Calle de la Judería is the main square, splendidly dominated by the sixteenth-century *ayuntamiento*, or Casa Consistatorial. This is Tarazona's most flamboyant building. The open loggia is a copy of the cloister gallery at the nearby Monasterio de Veruela (see below) and the frieze under it shows Carlos (Charles) V and entourage processing into Bologna for a meeting with the Pope. Underneath are three bizarre figures – Hercules, who is supposed to have rebuilt the town after some long-forgotten siege, and two mythical giants Pierres, who plagued the Tarazonan countryside by stealing animals, and Caco, who burgled houses. The town is not well off for restaurants, but you could eat either at the Turiasso hotel or the El Galeón restaurant. On Calle Visconti, which leads into the old town from the river, is one of Tarazona's best *tapas* bars, the Visconti. The tourist office next to the cathedral has a good supply of maps and leaflets.

Monasterio de Veruela

Fifteen kilometres south of Tarazona, beyond the wild, undulating hills and a plain terraced with vines, olives and almond trees, is the Cistercian monastery of Veruela. Founded in the mid-twelfth century by French monks, it is protected by a sixteenth-century wall spiked with turrets and punctuated with bulky towers. It is one of the oldest Cistercian foundations in Spain, but is somewhat lacking in atmosphere as the rooms around the cloister have been converted into exhibition halls. The Gothic cloister inset with translucent panes of alabaster, and with the heads of men carved along the gallery, is the highlight. The church at first seems rather plain – and eerie, as there are usually birds flapping around – but walk to the west end of the nave for an exquisite perspective of the vaults. Most of the exhibitions are of contemporary Aragonese art, and there is an annual season of classical concerts between June and September. The tourist office at Tarazona will have the most up-to-date details.

CALATAYUD AND AROUND

On a *plain* of orchards, olive groves, wheat and barley fields, the only striking feature is the abruptness with which the soil changes from a fudge colour to a gaudy crimson. The first place of any interest is the town of **Calatayud**, where the walls of the Moorish castle disintegrate on a white-veined clay hill, and Mudejar towers poke up from a tangle of scuffed and tilting façades skirted by apartment buildings. The town was founded by the Moors in the eighth century and though it is an unremarkable, sluggishly-paced place today, it is worth wandering through to look at the intricate brickwork of the towers (notably San Andrés and Santa María) and then driving up the rubble track to the castle.

Fused to a cliff, scented with wild herbs, strewn with rabbit droppings and soggy picnic litter, the castle instils a melancholic mood which is intensified by views of bleak hills and the dishevelled town. The castle is unsupervised, so you are free to scramble into its towers, and teeter along the sentry walls, though you should take great care as the walls have completely collapsed in places.

Monasterio de Piedra (H) and Daroca

South of Calatayud the Monasterio de Piedra stands in a luxuriant enclave of trees, lakes, waterfalls and grottoes amid the dry Aragonese hills. Below a canopy formed by a deciduous forest, water cascades over hills, veins grassy banks, or lies still in lakes: they are called the Lake of the Mirror, the Bath of Diana or the Spring of Health. Sadly the Cistercian monastery is dilapidated and the ornate altar in the cloister is dusty and covered in graffiti, its images of saints mutilated. The images are said to have been vandalised during the disentailment of the Church in 1835, a move by the liberal government to pay off the national debt and finance the Carlist war. A wing of the monastery has been coverted into a hotel and there are restaurants and cafés around the car park.

From the monastery a road heads east across a high plateau where quartz veins the soft, red rock like fat in a cut of beef. Stark villages are heralded by rubbish dumps where discarded cookers rust on piles of refuse. Eventually the road twists in hairpins down a mountainside planted with vines and almond trees into a valley of poplars.

Entered through a white toytown gate, **Daroca** is a compact town, lost within a three-kilometre circuit of walls. It was a prosperous crafts centre in the Middle Ages, and still retains houses of that era with carved eaves and a couple of Romanesque churches with Mudejar towers. The most interesting of these churches is the **Colegiata de Santa María**, undergoing restoration. According to legend, in 1239 the town was attacked by the Moors, just as Mass was being celebrated. The consecrated bread was hidden between two altar cloths, and when it was removed, left the cloths stained with blood. Teruel and Calatayud also claimed the miraculous cloths, and to settle the matter it was decided to place them on the back of a mule, set it free, and see where it ended up. It headed for Daroca, and though it died just outside the city gates, the cloths have been in the town ever since. The church of Santa María was built to hold them, and once it re-opens you should be able to see them in the Holy Relics chapel.

If you find yourself in need of a bed for the night, Hotel Daroca on the main street (Calle Mayor) is adequate.

SOUTH TO TERUEL (H)

From Daroca the N-234 heads south to Teruel along the Jiloca valley. Narrow at first, and planted with almonds, vines, maize and poplars, it broadens out to a vast plain beyond the shabby town of Calamocha. *Jamón de Teruel* is sold in many of the roadside farms. The *jamón* is an acquired taste, a cured ham which is a bit like prosciutto, but darker, more pungent, and often served in thick, chewy slices.

Teruel is better known in Spain for the tragic lovers who died here of despair in the thirteenth century, and is traditionally visited by newly-wed couples. An undistinguished provincial capital ringed by red-brick apartments and jam, ham and sausage factories, it might seem an unlikely place to spend a honeymoon. But beyond the industrial areas and housing estates is a small historic centre. At night, when its magnificent Mudejar towers and the cathedral are illuminated and the soft light from wrought-iron lamps lends a decayed magic to the flaking façades, it does have a certain romance.

The town was an important Moorish centre, and its towers are the work of Muslim masons who remained after the town had been reconquered by the Christians in 1171. There are four intricately worked brick towers, studded with shining ceramics, which stand like minarets, detached from their churches. The most elaborate are San Salvador and San Martín, the former standing on an arch across Calle San Salvador, the latter, just behind the cathedral.

The romance, however, is only a veneer, and once you have seen the towers, cathedral and tomb of the doomed lovers, the mood is broken by tired housewives waiting at bus stops and bored adolescents slouching in shadowy alleys. The best hotel and also the best place to eat is the *parador* on the outskirts of town. None of the sights is more than five minutes' walk from the central square, the wedge-shaped Plaza del Torico. If you arrive by train, you have a splendid approach to the old centre from the station, up a flamboyant mock-Mudejar staircase.

The main sights

● **The cathedral** With its green and blue tiled tower and wedding-cake cupola enchantingly lit at night, the cathedral is exposed in the daylight as a shabby, rambling building. It is more fun to visit it in the dark. Grope your way down the north aisle to the coin-operated light-box, drop four 100 peseta coins in the slot, and watch the lights flash on to reveal a colourfully painted coffered (*artesonado*) ceiling and splendid bunches of spiky tulips on the ironwork grille of the choir. You should then run swiftly up the steps by the choir, to a gallery from which the extraordinary detail of the ceiling can be examined at close quarters. The work of thirteenth-century Mudejar craftsmen, the illustrated panels include a cat and some decidedly unholy women among the saints. Four hundred pesetas gives just twelve minutes of light, so do not get stranded on the gallery.

● **The Lovers' Tomb** Isabel de Segura and Diego de Marcilla are Spain's Romeo and Juliet, young lovers forbidden to marry by the girl's father. Isabel's father favoured a richer suitor for his daughter, but agreed to give Diego five years in which to better himself. Diego duly went off to war, won fame and fortune, and returned on the appointed day – only to discover that Isabel had already been married to his rival. Diego rushed to Isabel's house and begged her to kiss

191

him. She refused, he died of grief, and the next day at his funeral she died of guilt. Their mummified bodies were discovered in a tomb in the sixteenth century, along with a document detailing the tragic events. *Los Amantes de Teruel* have since been the subjects of various plays, most famously by Tiraso de Molina, and of an irreverent nursery rhyme.

The lovers' remains now lie in a mausoleum adjoining the church of San Pedro, just off Plaza del Torico. If it is closed call at the first-floor flat in the house (marked No. 3), next door to the mausoleum's scabby yellow entrance. The caretaker flaps along in her slippers, unlocks the great door, and sweeps back a heavy green velvet curtain to reveal the tomb. Sculpted of delicately veined alabaster, the lovers' efigies lie side by side on sarcophagi, their hands just touching, and below, you can see their mummies eerily lit by wrought-iron lamps. The sculptures are recent, and undeniably sentimental – but do not be surprised to find yourself moved.

The road to Albarracín (H)

Heading north-west from Teruel, along the N-254 and minor TE-901 road, you soon leave the tawny plain behind for swiftly undulating hills and a poplar-filled valley. Eventually the road runs alongside a striated cliff in which holes are visible at intervals – part of a Roman channel system, constructed to conduct water from the hills to the plain.

Steeply tiered above the river, **Albarracín** is a tightly knit medieval village where timber-framed houses with coral-tinted walls and weathered, rough-hewn beams lean across narrow streets, virtually robbing them of light. Protected by a ring of walls which stretches way beyond the village, it is a marvellously atmospheric place to wander, with some parts carefully restored and others quietly decaying. There are just enough bars and restaurants, and two good-quality *hostales* as well as a number of *fondas* and a hotel (overpriced), so you might well decide to stay.

The ramshackle cathedral is worth a brief visit, less for the interior (the one notable feature of which is an action-packed wooden retable recounting the life of St Peter) than for the museum. In a small room hung with sixteenth-century Brussels tapestries is a modern safe which the guard unlocks to reveal ancient enamelled crucifixes, a small portable altar attributed to the Florentine sculptor Cellini and other rare treasures.

Driving up into the Montes Universales, just to the west of

the village, is worth it if you like pine forests. In winter the forests are populated with bulls awaiting death in the ring, who roam freely among pine trunks smothered in lichen. In summer the forests are full of camping school children. The few villages are centres for forestry and carpentry; in the bars with nicotine-stained strip-lights and sawdust-strewn floors, you can expect to be scrutinised by the locals.

The Maestrazgo

Progress is slow through the inhospitable mountains of the Maestrazgo, a wild, scantly populated range straddling the Valencian border. Only the occasional field has been ploughed on the stony, barren hillsides. Understandably, many people have left the area, but some stay on and make a living from curing *jamón de Teruel* or working on the pine plantations. Most people live in small villages of peeling whitewashed or rubblestone houses that are more often than not heralded by a cabbage plot and rubbish dump. Others soldier on in isolated farmhouses, frequently semi-ruined places, where the only signs of habitation are a few neat fields. Not surprisingly, there are few places to stay up here, so plan your day carefully and take the tortuous mountain roads into account.

The most direct approach to the Maestrazgo from Teruel is along the TE-800 via Cedrillas, a workaday village where the schoolmaster lives in a mock-Greek temple. If you are not pressed for time, the road north from Mora de Rubielos (the TE-802) is more dramatic. Both roads meet at Allepuz, beyond which is a pock-marked, scrunched and splintered gorge.

The loveliest stretch, however, lies a slow 28 kilometres further on, along the TE-804 which runs north from the Puerto de Cuarto Pelado, through a gorge where sharp blades of rock stab through slopes of juniper, rise to a vicious dragon-like spine beyond the village of **Villarluengo** (H), then climax in the **Organos de Montoro**, the anarchic pinnacles of which look like a meeting of members of the Ku Klux Klan. The road emerges from the mountains after the village of Ejulve and a main road runs east to Alcañiz through a fertile valley of almonds, vines and olives, strung with poor-looking villages. **Alcañiz**'s castle (now a *parador*) and church sit on a hill above an unappetising stretch of tractor repair shops, brick works and motels. Traffic zips up the steep, narrow streets past grimy old houses and a couple of neglected mansions to the main square, where a florid baroque church, Italianate town hall and Gothic exchange building form an improbably grand stage for small-town routines.

LAS CINCO VILLAS

Stretching from the Zaragozan plain to the hilly border with Navarra, the north-west corner of Aragón is known as Las Cinco Villas, or the Five Towns. It is named after its five main villages, elevated to the status of town by Philip V for support in the War of the Succession. Sos del Rey Católico and Uncastillo are up in the hills and more attractive than Tauste, Ejea and Sádaba on the plain. The region is most pleasantly approached from Sangüesa (off the N-240 Pamplona–Jaca road, see page 157) over the border in Navarra, though if you are heading up across the plain from Zaragoza, Tauste's Mudejar tower and Sádaba's grim castle merit a look.

The Pyrenean foothills form a neat landscape of cosy valleys with miniature fields surrounded by gentle hills covered with heather, broom and evergreen oak, or tidily planted with pines. The forests support large numbers of boar and on winter weekends gun-shots disturb the silence.

Wrapped around a hill below a massive church and the scant remains of a castle, **Sos del Rey Católico** (H) is understandably the most popular of the five villages. It is also a convenient base for exploring parts of Navarra. Steep cobbled streets smelling of woodsmoke meander among prosperous mansions and houses with wooden galleries, many of them recently restored. The Palacio de Sada is the supposed birthplace of Ferdinand of Aragón, the Catholic Monarch or *Rey Católico*. It is also undergoing restoration and may eventually house a museum, but for the moment, other than the crypt of the church, which has traces of frescoes on its walls, there are no real 'sights' in the village. It is the atmosphere of the place which is to be savoured, something best done by staying overnight in the pleasant *parador*.

Uncastillo, a very slow 22 kilometres south-east from Sos, is a refreshingly unpretentious place, notable for its Romanesque church with an incongruous fairy-tale tower. The portal is also elaborate, carved with beautifully detailed figures. The village has narrow streets that wind up past arched doorways and overhanging eaves to a simple church and sturdy castle. If you speak Spanish, you could take a guided tour of the village (Wednesday to Sunday only) by applying at the Casa Consistatorial on your way to the castle.

HEADING FOR THE PYRENEES

East of Uncastillo the road follows the contours of the Sierra de Santo Domingo's stream-grooved flanks along tight valleys, through sleepy stone villages, and over wooded hillsides. You might catch sight of wild boar foraging for acorns, though you are more likely to see lots of horses, most of them sorry-looking animals, destined for the meat factory.

From the main road at Ayerbe, the Pyrenees are less than half an hour's drive, but there are some fine sights in the foothills, all reached via side roads off the main N-240 travelling north. The **Castillo de Loarre** is the nearest, an eleventh-century fortress built on a rocky knoll above a plain patterned with ponds, trim fields and olive and almond groves. The road to it winds up the hill to a dense pine forest, above which the turreted keep and square towers soar amid pinnacles of rock. It was built in 1071 on the orders of Sancho Ramirez, King of Aragón, as a defence against the Moors, but a couple of decades later became a monastery. A Romanesque crypt with an ingenious beehive roof is linked by a narrow flight of steps to a church with alabaster windows, bare rock jutting through a wall, and 84 imaginatively carved capitals. Up on the defences, you can walk along the sentry path. The iron rungs clamped to the walls of the towers look unsafe for clambering up.

To the north of Ayerbe, rising like immense pink tombstones above the village of Riglos, are a series of severely eroded crags known as **Los Mallos**. There are more Mallos, and a tiny Romanesque church just to the west near the village of Agüero. The church, **Santiago**, stands among pines on a hummock just before you reach the village, and is approached along a rubble track. The church is most remarkable for the carvings around its miniature door. The work of the mason also responsible for the carving at San Juan de la Peña (see below), it is notable for the detail of hair and costume, and for a capital showing an erotically dancing Salome.

Just beyond Los Mallos, the River Gállego runs into the Embalse de la Peña, a serene reservoir. To the north rises the Sierra de la Peña, a 1,142 metre-high mountain barrier crossed by two roads – one for the Valle de Hecho, the other for Jaca and the Monasterio de San Juan de la Peña.

San Juan de la Peña and Santa Cruz

High above the village of Santa Cruz, splendidly located on the forested slopes of the Sierra de la Peña is San Juan, the most unusual and significant monastery in Aragón. A tiny tuna-pink building embedded in a rock-face, it is at first sight neither impressive nor beautiful. But walk through the dim hall chilled by a mountain stream, or stand before the stone slab altar in an apse roughly hacked from the rock, and you cannot fail but be impressed by the tenacity of the monks who built it, and of those who lived in the cold damp rooms.

The monastery was founded in the ninth century and rebuilt in the eleventh. In its early days it housed the Holy Grail, the Roman chalice (now in Valencia Cathedral) from which Christ was supposed to have drunk at the Last Supper. Substantial royal donations to the monastery proved to be a sound investment. San Juan de la Peña became a potent symbol of Christian resistance to the Moors, so much so, that it was selected by local monarchs and aristocrats as their pantheon.

The partly underground council chamber leads to the lower church, a primitive place with two altars carved into the roughly painted rock. Outside, the monuments to the nobility stand in a courtyard virtually roofed by an overhanging rock, and beyond, in the upper church, stone altars are placed in clumsily chiselled apses, an odd contrast with the over-ornate baroque royal pantheon. The highlights, however, are the figures sculpted on the capitals of the crag-sheltered cloister, who appear to accept with an astonishing serenity the bizarre situations in which they find themselves: Adam discovering his nudity, the wedding guests at Cana and even a poor fellow having his head axed.

The monks abandoned the dank monastery in the seventeenth century, after it had been gutted by fire, and moved into what is now a neglected baroque complex further up the mountain. It is worth walking up through the woods for a panorama of the Pyrenees. A viewing table helps you identify the visible peaks.

There are a couple of other churches worth stopping for in Santa Cruz: San Caprasio, a sweet little eleventh-century hermitage, and the sturdier Santa Cruz, a Romanesque convent church which was once showered with gifts by royal princesses from many Iberian kingdoms.

THE ARAGONESE PYRENEES

The three highest Pyrenean peaks, all of them well over 3,000 metres, rise in Aragón. There are plenty of opportunities for walkers, but fewer medieval villages and churches to explore than on the Catalan side. Touring by car is pleasant enough, but obviously the sheer magnitude, beauty, and even grimness of the mountains have far more impact when you are on foot. Less experienced walkers should head for the Parque Nacional de Ordesa, where the walks are signposted and are relatively straightforward (see page 200) and the scenery magnificent. More ambitious walkers might like to undertake a three-week trek of the most interesting of the Catalan and Aragonese peaks. (See Walking in the Pyrenees, page 202).

Most of the roads through the Pyrenees are along the several north-to-south valleys, with few mountain passes linking them – so much of the driving is at a low level where the scenery is not as stunning. Particularly beautiful routes include the HU-610 (off the Valle de Tena road) up the Garganta del Escalar to Panticosa, the N-260, a rare mountain pass road linking the Tena and Ordesa valleys, and the road along the River Cinca to the Monte Perdido *parador*, itself a wonderfully restful place to stay. Three of the valleys, Somport, Tena and Cinca, are linked by tunnels or passes with France and can get very busy.

The westernmost valleys, Hecho and Ansó, are lush, relatively gentle, and have simple, but pleasant places to stay. Ansó village is particularly convenient, as it lies between pass roads to the Valle del Roncal in Navarra, as well as the Hecho valley. Consequently it is a feasible base for exploring the foothills of both regions.

Jaca (H)

The main centre in the Aragonese Pyrenees is Jaca, once a stopping point for the Santiago pilgrims walking through the Puerto de Somport from France. Today it is a largely modern town of holiday apartments, hotels and winter sports shops. It is also home to a sizeable garrison, and has a military training centre, so do not be surprised to come across columns of sad-looking troops jogging along the road. Jaca is a sensible base if you are using public transport, but if walking, or touring by car, a hotel in one of the mountain villages is a far pleasanter option.

Strategically sited at the foot of the Somport Pass into France, Jaca has been a military town since Roman times, and later became a base for Christians in their struggles against the Moors. It made its reputation in the eighth century when its women helped repel a Moorish attack – an event now commemorated by a procession and dancing on the first Friday in May. In 1035 the town was made capital of the first kingdom of Aragón.

The only notable relic from these days is the cathedral, a sombre, grimy and very early Romanesque building. Its decorative sculpture influenced the architecture of many churches along the pilgrim route. The capital carvings of David and Musicians and the Sacrifice of Isaac in the south porch are reputedly the best, although they are difficult to see. The interior has been much altered and is of little interest, but a fine museum is laid out in the cloisters and adjoining rooms, where column capitals are displayed at eye level. The disarmingly naïve Romanesque and Gothic frescoes taken from local Pyrenean churches are enhanced by good lighting.

Jaca has plenty of restaurants, the majority of which close outside the walking and winter sports seasons. The most famous is the traditional La Cocina Aragonesa, on Calle Cervantes 5, but a slightly more reasonable option is the Casa Labon on Calle Baradilla, in the old centre, just below the cathedral. Behind the unprepossessing bar is a restaurant which serves imaginative dishes, such as hake stuffed with salmon, along with local meat courses and *entremeses* (starters). Unfortunately the service is not tip-top.

Valle del Hecho and Valle de Ansó

The valleys of Hecho and Ansó, with their green meadows, forests and fast running trout rivers have more in common with the bucolic valleys of Navarra than the grand mountain landscapes of eastern Aragón. Not long ago the people of Hecho and Ansó were among the most remote in Spain. They spoke in dialect, wore traditional costume and were virtually self-sufficient. But, doubtless in order to stem the exodus from country to city, the Aragonese authorities decided to encourage tourism in the area. Today, old stone houses have been restored, small hotels and folk museums have opened, roads are being improved, and Hecho has become the unlikely host of an international symposium on modern art and sculpture. If you come in July and August, you will be greeted by the bizarre sight of contemporary sculpture scattered over the surrounding hills.

Nowadays the villages become crowded in summer, but though tourism has brought much needed income into the area, farming is still the main occupation. Mud-caked cows wander through the streets and communities remain tight-knit. Recently, villagers overturned plans to make the lower Hecho valley into a reservoir and to run a gas pipe through the Ansó valley.

The Hoz de Biniés, a cool, shadowy gorge, gives access to the Ansó valley. The road then snakes between thickly wooded slopes to the village of **Ansó**. It is a tidy village of mountain houses, and, in high season, old men in slippers lean outside the bar wryly observing tourists. The church of San Pedro, crammed with dusty altars and crookedly hung paintings, holds a small museum. The priest (who lives in the house opposite) will open it for you. Local costumes, a replica of a shepherd's kitchen, a loom, jewellery, furniture and agricultural implements help build a picture of traditional life. There are a few bars, a restaurant and three simple places to stay – try the Posada Magoría, next to the Fonda Estanes on the main road, Tel (974) 37 00 49.

Just south of Ansó a road crosses over to Hecho, the main village in the next valley. Overlooked by a grey rocky mountain, it is a smartly restored village of grey stone and whitewashed houses, with steeply pitched roofs, pepperpot chimneys and neat stacks of wood by front doors. There are hotels, restaurants, a bar and a disco, as well as the obligatory folk museum. If you want a quieter base it might be worth staying in Siresa, further up the valley. This earthy, stone village with sagging roofs has an early Romanesque church, a *fonda* and a hotel (Castillo d'Archer) in a traditional-style mansion.

The Somport Pass: Aragón's ski resorts

There is no reason to venture up the valley of the Somport Pass unless it is to go skiing in winter. Development continues apace in villages already smothered by holiday apartments and chalets; the only pretty buildings are owned by the heavily present *Guardia Civil*. In summer the long-established resorts look miserable and bedraggled. Nowhere more so than **Canfranc**, a once thriving resort, which has been slowly decaying since the railway line that linked it with France was dismantled (you can however still get to Canfranc by train from Jaca). Today the main resort is the twin-centred **Astun-Candanchu** close to the French border. Candanchu is the older half, with dated hotels surrounded by modern apart-ment blocks, a shopping arcade, disco and supermarket; Astun, eight kilometres away up a tributary valley, is newer and a better place to stay. If you go as far as Candanchu, you might as well head up to the border post, where you can nip over the mound behind the guard's hut to the café in no-man's land.

The Eastern Valleys

Each of the valleys that groove the eastern side of the Ara-gonese Pyrenees is worth exploring. If you approach from Jaca, you can skirt industrial Sabiñánigo and head straight into the **Valle de Tena**. Initially broad and planted with wheat, the valley narrows beyond the village of Biescas, then broadens out again at the immense hydro-electric reservoir of Búbal. There is a ski resort, El Formigal, higher up the main valley, but the highlight is the **Garganta del Escalar**, or Escalar Gorge. The road was closed for major repair at the time of writing. It passes through a narrow gorge to **Panti-cosa**, a spa resort backed by the barren slopes of a mountain named Inferno, famed for its sulphurous, radioactive waters. The route is said to be particularly exciting at snow-melt, when the swollen waterfalls spray on to the road.

Unless heading for France, you need to return to Biescas, where the old core of whitewashed houses is gradually being surrounded by holiday apartments. From here, a lovely mountain road leads to the Parque Nacional de Ordesa. Beyond the village of Yésero, the road hairpins up a ledged mountain to **Linás de Broto** (H), a stone-built village in a green valley. It is an attractive base for visiting the Ordesa park, as long as you do not mind staying in fairly simple accommodation.

The Parque Nacional de Ordesa

Ordesa is one of Spain's great national parks, a magnificent flat-bottomed canyon where striated cliffs form ramparts above forested slopes, and the River Arazas rushes along the lush valley floor. The park should be avoided in July and August, when upwards of 4,000 people visit daily, and you are likely to spend much of your time in a traffic jam. In an average year, snow makes the park inaccessible between

October and May, but the mild weather of recent years means that you will probably be able to drive up without problems in November and have the place to yourself. In fact, the park is particularly lovely in late autumn, when the peaks are capped with snow, and the vibrant gold and yellow leaves in the valley contrast with the green slopes of conifers. The spring snow-melt is also splendid, with water spilling down the canyon sides, swelling the many waterfalls. The reason for the park's popularity is that the stupendous scenery is easily accessible. There is an information kiosk at the car park (open in season only) and walks are well signposted. A pair of strong walking shoes should be adequate.

Most visitors stay at **Torla**, a woodsmokey, cobbled greystone village a few kilometres outside the park. Grim concrete holiday apartments surround the village, as well as a handful of hotels, of which the family-run Vinamala, on Calle Fatas 5, is the best. There is no chance of finding anywhere to stay here in late July or August, but at other times of the year Torla is a good base from which to visit the park.

Ainsa (H)

Experienced walkers can trek from the Ordesa park canyon to Monte Perdido, the third highest Pyrenean peak (11,007 ft or 3,555 m), also within the park boundary. Drivers have to take a very long circuitous valley route via the town of **Ainsa**. This is no hardship, as there is a good hotel in the lower modern town, and some appealing restaurants on the beautiful medieval square in the walled and gated upper town. The old town sits on a rocky bluff above the meeting point of the Cinca and Ara rivers. It is most pleasantly approached on foot: up a flight of steps and along a road which leads to one of the solid stone gates. Plaza Mayor has a Romanesque church at one end, a castle (undergoing restoration) at the other, and terraces of arcaded stone houses in-between. Some of the houses are now bars and restaurants. Casa Albas is a simple eating-place with rough stone walls and beams and the Bodega del Sobrade an upmarket restaurant in a similarly ancient setting, at the far end of the square. Alternatively, head for the more reasonably priced Bodegón Mallacón, where the food (particularly the quail – *codorniz* – casseroled with onion) is delicious, the house Rioja quaffable, and gilt medieval-style chairs (with coats of arms and velvet cushions) and hand-painted tiled tables compensate for the plain room.

WALKING IN THE PYRENEES

Although the Pyrenees straddle most of the Franco-Spanish border, the peaks above 2,000 metres, beloved of climbers and ramblers, fit into a rectangle approximately 200 by 30 kilometres at the centre of the range. Catalunya and Aragón share the highest ridges, with more forests on the Catalan side – and also more medieval villages to explore. In both regions botanists and bird-watchers will be amply rewarded; and everywhere above the treeline you can see chamois – wild antelopes.

The Pyrenees are good for all kinds of walking – from roped glacier traverses to strolls along grassy lanes. The route summarised below falls somewhere in-between, much of it along the marked GR-11 long distance trail. The entire hike would take over three weeks, but it is made up of self-contained sections of one-to three-day trips (each paragraph is one such section). There are numerous mountain refuges or huts, and most stages finish at one of them (but you can also pick up the trail or use as a base for day-trips several Pyrenean-valley villages). If you intend to walk for more than a day, you would be wise to carry a tent, as the refuges are popular and often fill up by early afternoon in season – from July to September.

As far as equipment is concerned, you should be cautious and overpack. The weather in the Pyrenees is notoriously fickle: tropical heat with biting flies gives way to blinding mists or pelting, cold rain – all on the same morning of a summer's day. But you will not need extra water bottles; drinking water is nearly always not far away. Decent large-scale maps, 1:25,000 to 1:40,000, are published by *Editorial Alpina* (numbers 203 to 211 cover most of the area described below), and are widely available, either in Spain – sometimes even in villages at the start of the trails – or from good travel bookshops in the UK.

From Catalunya to Aragón: across the Pyrenees

Start in the Catalan foothill town of Pobla de Segur, which has bus connections with the villages higher up. From the village of Llavorsi you will have to take a taxi (or hitch) up the Vall Ferrera or Vall de Cardos, where the Vall Ferrera refuge and the village of Tavascan are the bases for good circular walks. These can be taken from the GR-11 trail, through lake-spangled cirques at the Andorran and French borders. A short day round-walk through the Sotllo and Baborte valleys, above Vall Ferrera, is the easier of the two. To complete a round tour out of Tavascan you will have to spend a night at the refuge by the shore of Certascan lake before crossing the pass of the same name and returning to Tavascan.

The best jump-off point for the Parc Nacional d'Aigües Tortes is Capdella, a bus ride away from Pobla. You enter the mountains quickly in the easy half-day walk up to the Colomina refuge, and could spend the rest of the day touring the surrounding lakes (some are spoiled by dams). Further progress is harder. There are four passes into the park: if you are not carrying a tent, aim for the J M Blanc hut, beyond the Saburo saddle. The difficult Peguera Pass leads to the heart of the park and another hut, Ernesto Mallafre (this one can also be reached by road from the village of Espot). From the hut, leave the park heading northwest along the GR-11 over the easiest col in Catalunya, dropping by numerous unspoiled tarns to the Colomers dam and hut.

From the Colomers refuge you can return to the villages of Vall d'Aran to the north, or continue west past more lakes. A faint trail takes you across the moderately difficult Colomers pass in five-plus hours to the fancy Ventosa i Calvell refuge. Alternatively there is a less strenuous six-hour passage via the cols of Caldes and Collcrestada to the Restanca reservoir and a rustic hut. The route to Ventosa i Calvell is more versatile, as you can end your trek in Boi to the south and see its Romanesque churches, or strike north to Restanca by a short but scenic path linking the two alternate routes.

At Restanca you have the final chance to descend to the Vall d'Aran or continue along the GR-11. The relatively luxurious Boca Sud refuge, four hours from Restanca, overlooks the road tunnel into the Vall d'Aran; across the road lies the classic, challenging day-long route up the Mulleres valley and pass to the border with Aragón, where it drops into the Esera river valley. The more southerly traverse into Aragón via the Salenques valley and pass is easier but not as interesting.

The River Esera flows down the 3,408 metre-high Aneto mountain, highest in the Pyrenees. In its upper valley is the refuge of Renclusa (not that conveniently placed). Better camping is to be found at Aiguallut meadows, near the river's source. Walks up from here to the border ridges with France and back toward Catalunya are popular, but the slog down to the town of Benasque is long and dull, the only highlight en route being the full-day detour to the giant lake of Cregüena, tucked into the west flank of Aneto.

Benasque is an enjoyable place to sleep and stock up while you decide how to walk around Posets, second highest Pyrenean peak. The easiest route follows the Estos river, just above Benasque, to the new Estos refuge, a half-day up the valley. A more rewarding, if moderately difficult, alternative is the two-day traverse from Eriste, just below Benasque but you will need a tent.

Another easy-to-moderate, though long walking day takes you around the west flank of Posets to the delightful Viados refuge, part of a farming hamlet. If you need to stop walking, or do not fancy the next sector, you might get a lift south on the dirt track to the three Gistain villages, and from there another over to Bielsa. The most direct link from Viados to Bielsa is a low-altitude, all-day tramp, easy but scenically humdrum.

Beyond Bielsa you will need a taxi ride (or hitch) up the steep-sided, glacial Pineta valley (the Monte Perdido *parador* is here). All trails scaling its walls are difficult and some should only be attempted by experts. The GR-11 climbs up to the Anisclo saddle but becomes dangerous or tedious thereafter. If your main interest is in the Parque Nacional de Ordesa, it is easier to approach from the west – though this may involve descending from Bielsa or Gistain to Ainsa, from where there is a bus to Torla.

The national park, one of Spain's first, is unbearably crowded in season; the best hope of solitude is to follow the highest of several trails which run the length of the spectacular Ordesa canyon, the

The upper Cinco Valley and Monte Perdido (H)

Dwarfed by the massive rocky cirque of Monte Perdido is one of the quietest country *paradores* in Spain. The route there from Ainsa is initially dull, and as it follows one of the main routes into France as far as Bielsa, it can get very busy. However, there are views of snow-capped peaks for much of the year, and beyond the Laspuña reservoir is the Desfiladero de las Devotas, a tight, zig-zagging gorge hemmed in by jabbing strata and rocks. **Bielsa** is a whitewashed and stone village which is in danger of being smothered by apartment blocks and hotels, most of which have been built since the construction of the tunnel into France. It is however, a useful place to stop, as it has a bank, supermarket, and some reason-ably-priced accommodation. From Bielsa the road twists for 14 kilometres to Monte Perdido, an amphitheatre of rock streaked by waterfalls, which rears up at the head of a lush valley.

Faja de Pelay route on the south flank. This ends at the popular refuge of Goriz. Return to the mouth of the Ordesa valley by the Cotatuero trail along the north side.

Beyond Ordesa the GR-11 follows up the Ara river to a restored medieval hospice at Bujaruelo, a junction for numerous trails. There is a lapse in the *Editorial Alpina* series of maps here, so you will need to buy SGE (Spanish Ordnance Survey) sheets 30–8 and 29–8. The GR-11 heads west up the Otal valley to the Tendenera pass and then down to the resort village of Panticosa in the Tena valley – an easy but dull crossing. More scenic, if harder, are several alternative routes taking off from further up the Ara valley, including the highest traverse directly to the spa of Panticosa; in all cases allow for a long day out of Bujaruelo.

The spa, eight kilometres above the village, makes a good base for day walks up into the border cirques, crowded with lakes reminiscent of those in Catalunya (including the dams). There is a more untouched group of tarns to either side of the Infierno and Piedrafita passes, but getting over these is tough and you will need full hiking equipment. If you make it, you will spend the night at or near the unmanned, primitive Respumoso shelter. But this is more commonly reached as another day's walk along the impressive Aguas Limpias gorge leading up from Sallent de Gallego, where a two-and-a-half day traverse from Panticosa ends.

The lower Cinco Valley and Huesca

Beyond Ainsa the road follows the River Cinca. The series of green, dammed lakes which lie between fir-clad mountain slopes and eroded grey hillsides forms a serene and majestic landscape, unlike any other in Aragón. Such is the location for a sanctuary, **Torreciudad**, belonging to Opus Dei, an influential and sinister Catholic sect whose members take a vow of poverty and regularly mortify their flesh. It was founded in 1928 by an Aragonese priest, Escriva de Balaguer, who was particularly fond of a twelfth-century shrine to the Virgin at Torreciudad. After the priest's death in 1969, Opus Dei had the sanctuary erected on this site and it can be visited.

Barbastro, further south, is an ugly town which you can drive straight through, unless you want to see the wonderful alabaster retable by the Renaissance sculptor, Damián Forment, in the sixteenth-century cathedral.

But Damián Forment's real masterpiece is just an hour's

drive away in the cathedral of the grey and grimy provincial capital of **Huesca**. Forment's altarpiece, a collection of early Aragonese paintings in the museum, and a gruesome painting in the town hall, make for a varied sightseeing itinerary.

The cathedral is a late Gothic structure with severely eroded figures and a wooden gallery on its façade. Inside, nothing distracts you from Forment's alabaster altarpiece of chatting Apostles and scenes from the Passion and Crucifixion. To see it properly you will need to illuminate it by dropping 100 pesetas in the slot-machine, which gives plenty of time to take in the detail, as well as switching on a Spanish commentary and some appropriately atmospheric music.

Across the square from the cathedral is the Renaissance *ayuntamiento* which holds a very different work of art. In the twelfth century King Ramiro II summoned some insurgent nobles to his palace to watch the casting of a bell which he said would be heard throughout Aragón. But, as the nobles entered, they were beheaded instead, an event unflinchingly captured in a gory nineteenth-century painting which you can see by asking at the *oficina* (office) in the town hall.

The old palace room where the massacre took place was incorporated into the unusual octagonal building of the seventeenth-century university. It now houses the **Museo Provincial**. As well as the notorious room, which looks exactly as it does in the painting, you can see a fine collection of early Aragonese paintings, including a depiction of the Crucifixion by Bernardo de Aras, in which the various moods of the onlookers are skilfully captured in their eyes.

For a coffee or snack, the Café Apollo on Plaza de Navarra (by the bus station) is hard to beat, as it serves a wide range of sweet and savoury-stuffed croissants along with a more usual selection of *tapas*.

WHERE TO STAY

AINSA

Hotel de Dos Ríos	£
Avenida Central 2	
22330 Huesca	*Tel (974) 50 00 43*

Conveniently located in the modern lower town about ten minutes walk from the upper town, this new hotel is beautifully decorated.

Downstairs are a pristine *tapas* bar and a café, each with mouth-watering displays of nibbles and cakes. Rooms have polished wooden fittings and sparkling bathrooms.

Open: all year **Rooms** 22 **Credit/charge cards**: Eurocard, Visa

ALBARRACIN

Hotel Arabia   ££
Bernardo Zapater 2
44100 Teruel   *Tel (974) 71 02 12*

The rooms and apartments in this recently converted 500-year-old seminary have quarry-tiled floors studded with ceramic coats of arms, whitewashed walls, beamed ceilings, pine furniture and new bathrooms. There is a cafeteria for breakfast, but no restaurant.

Open: all year **Rooms**: 11 (10 apartments) **Credit/charge cards**: Visa

JACA

Pradas   £
Obispo 12
22700 Huesca   *Tel (974) 36 11 50*

This is conveniently located in the old part of town near the cathedral. The recently refurbished rooms with orange carpets, candlewick bedspreads, and flowery wallpaper may not be to everyone's taste, but they are clean and comfortable. There is a café on the ground floor.

Open: all year **Rooms**: 39 **Credit/charge cards**: Amex, Diners, Eurocard, Visa

LINAS DE BROTO

Hotel Cazcarro   £
Carretera Biescas
22378 Linas de Broto   *Tel (974) 48 61 09*

The head of a boar shot by the owner has pride of place in the entrance hall of this small family-run hotel and restaurant. Bedrooms are plain but clean. The restaurant serves local fare but is open from July to September only.

Open: all year **Rooms**: 14 **Credit/charge cards**: none

MONASTERIO DE PIEDRA

Hotel Monasterio de Piedra ££
50210 Nuévales *Tel (976) 84 90 11*

Given that it is housed in a converted monastery in one of the most beautiful places in Aragon, this hotel is disappointing. The vaulted hall with alabaster windows and the long, serene corridors are impressive, but rooms have shabby wallpaper, dated furniture and functional furnishings. On the other hand, all rooms have balconies overlooking the park, and it is a very peaceful place to stay. All rooms have a phone.

Open: all year **Rooms**: 61 **Facilities**: swimming-pool, tennis **Credit/charge cards**: Amex, Diners, Eurocard, Visa

MONTE PERDIDO

Parador Nacional Monte Perdido £££
Valle de Pineta
22350 Bielsa *Tel (974) 50 10 11; Fax (974) 50 10 11*

Splendidly sited at the foot of the wild rocky Monte Perdido cirque, this is a modern stone building in traditional style, with a pitched roof and terrace. The lobby is stone flagged and the wooden walls are hung with animal skins and stuffed animals. The rooms have polished wooden floors, goatskin rugs and brown soft furnishings. The restaurant is cosy and in rustic style, with a warm golden wooden floor and terrace, and the lounge has an old-fashioned chimney-piece, stone walls and leather seats.

Open: all year **Rooms**: 24 **Credit/charge cards**: Amex, Diners, Eurocard, Visa

SOS DEL REY CATOLICO

Parador Nacional Fernando de Aragon ££
50680 Sos del Rey Católico *Tel (948) 88 80 11; Fax (948) 88 81 00*

Imaginatively decorated rooms in a modern *parador* built in traditional Aragonese style with a wooden gallery, capped chimneys and a tower. Rooms are spacious with pale, glazed earthenware tiles, bright woven bedspreads and white walls. The dining-room has stone arches and a beamed ceiling, and opening off the bar is a terrace. The restaurant has a good, interesting menu though Muzak ranging from 'Mack the Knife' to 'Yellow Brick Road' rather spoils the medieval atmosphere.

Open: all year **Rooms**: 66 **Credit/charge cards**: Amex, Diners, Eurocard, Visa

TARAZONA

Hotel Turiaso ££
Calle Virgen del Rio 3
50500 Tarazona *Tel (976) 64 31 96; Fax (976) 64 06 44*

A new, comfortable hotel in a stylishly converted pink and white cinema by the river. There is a gleaming cafeteria downstairs, and a restaurant upstairs. The rooms, reached along curving corridors, have varnished cork floors, smart modern furniture, flowery bedspreads and small, but well-designed bathrooms.

Open: all year **Rooms**: 17 **Credit/charge cards**: Amex, Diners, Eurocard, Visa

TERUEL

Parador Nacional de Teruel £££
44000 Teruel
(N-234 to Daroca) *Tel (974) 60 18 00; Fax (974) 60 86 12*

Built in the style of an Aragonese country house, this primrose-washed villa is a relaxing place to stay – despite the fact that it is just off a main road. Rooms are simple, with polished floor-boards and whitewashed walls, and all have mini bars and hair-dryers. The restaurant is very good, serving many regional dishes. It attracts locals as well as residents.

Open: all year **Rooms**: 60 **Credit/charge cards**: Amex, Diners, Eurocard, Visa

VILLARLUENGO

Hostal de La Trucha ££
Las Fabricas
44559 Teruel *Tel (974) 77 30 08; Fax (974) 60 53 63*

A traditional cream-washed building by a trout stream (and trout farm), seven kilometres beyond the village. There is a beamed bar with open wood fire, a restaurant whose walls are hung with ceramics and guns, and a riverside terrace. The rooms are adequate, but could do with redecoration.

Open: all year **Rooms**: 54 **Facilities**: swimming-pool, tennis, children's playground, fishing **Credit/charge cards**: Amex, Diners, Eurocard, Visa

ZARAGOZA

Hotel Sauce ££
Espoz y Mina 33
50003 Zaragoza   *Tel (976) 39 01 00; Fax (976) 39 85 97*

This hotel just off Plaza del Pilar is likely to be many people's first choice. It is in a pretty whitewashed house, and the bedrooms are stylish, with unusual soft furnishings and paintings by contemporary local artists. The café is furnished with black, chrome and marble, and the basement TV lounge has a quarry-tiled floor strewn with rugs, squashy leather sofas, and prints by Matisse and Modigliani.

Open: all year **Rooms**: 20 **Credit/charge cards**: Eurocard, Visa

Hotel Via Romana ££
Don Jaime I 54
50001 Zaragoza   *Tel (976) 39 82 15; Fax (976) 29 05 11*

A recently built hotel close to Plaza del Pilar. Rooms are comfortable, though quite plain.

Open: all year **Rooms**: 78 **Credit/charge cards**: Amex, Diners, Eurocard, Visa

Hotel París ££
Pedro María Ric 14
50001 Zaragoza   *Tel (976) 23 65 37; Fax (976) 22 53 97*

Located in the upmarket shopping area near Paseo de Sagasta, so it is ideal if you are not interested in sightseeing. Rooms are comfortable and fairly recently refurbished, though a little plain, and bathrooms have hair-dryers. There is a gleaming cafeteria, but the dining-room is dull.

Open: all year **Rooms**: 62 **Credit/charge cards**: Amex, Diners, Eurocard, Visa

CATALUNYA

A SMALL triangle of land bounded by the Pyrenees to the north, the Mediterranean to the East, and the neighbouring communities of Aragón and Valencia to the west, Catalunya is geographically and ideologically on the Iberian fringe, but its contribution as an economic powerhouse has been central to Spain's attempt at an economic miracle.

For about 150 kilometres from the French border, the wild and rugged coastline of the Costa Brava skirts the ocean, with Mediterranean pines cleaving to precipitous rocks. Towards the great port of Barcelona it becomes less dramatic, finally flattening out into the paddy fields of the Ebro delta. In the north the Pyrenees soar over a fine landscape of meadows, forests, rivers and lakes, dotted with ski resorts and Romanesque churches.

In Catalunya, all roads lead to **Barcelona**. This is where you will find the best of the work of the Modernist architect Antoni Gaudí (1852–1926) whose surreal art nouveau confections such as Parc Güell, and the awesome but unfinished church of La Sagrada Familia symbolise the exuberant non-conformity of the city.

The Catalan interior is sparsely populated and less visited than the coast, but should not be overlooked. **Gerona**, (Girona) has a memorable medieval quarter and a vast Gothic cathedral, and there are other important ecclesiastical sights at Poblet, Ripoll, Vich (Vic), Montserrat, Lérida (Lleida) and Seo de Urgel (La Seu d'Urgell), close to the border with the principality of Andorra. Most inland villages are dreary and forgettable, the occasional exceptions, such as fortified Montblanc or Valls, being truly noteworthy. Wine buffs can explore the Penedès region, including Vilafranca del Panedès (Vilafranca de Penedès), the base of Spain's best-known winemakers, the Torres family, and the various *cava* cellars of companies such as Frexeinet and Cordoniú.

The **Costa Brava** is the finest stretch of coastline by far, though its two biggest resorts, Lloret de Mar and Playa de Aro (Platja d'Aro), are overdeveloped and best avoided. Aim instead for the smaller attractive villages such as Calella de Palafrugell, Tamariú or Cadaqués, or even the surprisingly agreeable Tossa de Mar, where the modern package holiday was born. The **Costa del Maresme**, running from Malgrat de Mar to Barcelona, is a succession of charmless resorts. Beyond Barcelona the historic town of Sitges is the **Costa Dorada's** (Costa Daurada) premier resort. You will find good beaches almost everywhere.

Art lovers can have a jamboree in Catalunya, as they follow an aesthetic trail from the Romanesque devotional art of the Pyrenees, to the whimsical, surreal and the neo-blasphemous at Salvador Dalí's theatre-museum in **Figueras** (Figueres). But the richest pickings are in Barcelona, with its fine Picasso museum, as well as the Miró Foundation, and the stunning works of Gaudí.

Catalunya and its people

'Catalunya non es España' – Catalunya is not Spain. You'll see this affirmation of faith daubed on walls and bridges throughout the region, but particularly in the north. For Catalunya *is* different, with a distinct language, a history, culture and outlook. Throughout this chapter, the *castellano* spelling appears the first time a place is mentioned, with the *catalán* version shown in brackets and used thereafter.

Catalunya is a thrusting, dynamic region which is conspicuously prosperous compared with other parts of Spain, and its large middle class forms the backbone of the nationalist movement. Language and culture are pivotal to the Catalan's sense of identity, and these concerns will make themselves felt during your visit. On the *autopistas*, road signs display place names in both *castellano* and in *catalán*, but off the beaten track, *catalán* rules. Street names, too, have been Catalanised (the usage adopted for this chapter) and this, together with the re-naming of streets which formerly honoured now discredited Falangist generals and their supporters, can occasionally lead to confusion.

The Carthaginians dropped by in the third century BC, but it was the Romans (who colonised more successfully here than elsewhere in Spain) who recognised the potential of Catalunya's geographical position and began to develop the port that was to be the key to Barcelona's future prosperity. Their successors in occupation, the Moors, were evicted several centuries before their expulsion from the rest of Spain and by 874 the conquering hero, *Vilfredo el Peloso* (Wilfred the Hairy, or Shaggy depending on your translator) had established himself as the first of the powerful, independent Counts of Catalunya. He created a flourishing principality which became famous for its seafaring, mercantile and commercial skills.

A golden age followed from the twelfth to the fourteenth centuries, and Catalunya forged an alliance with Aragón

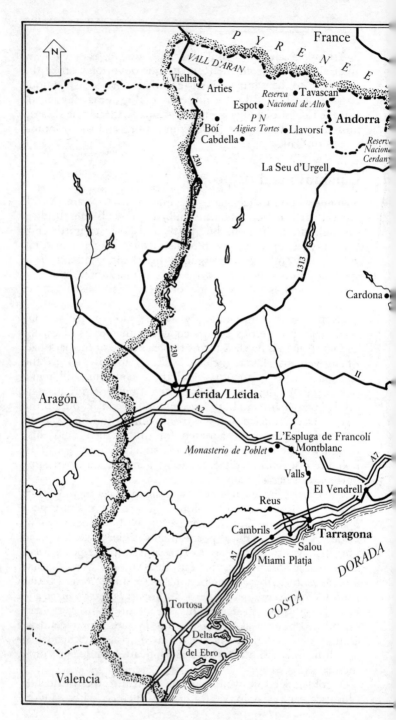

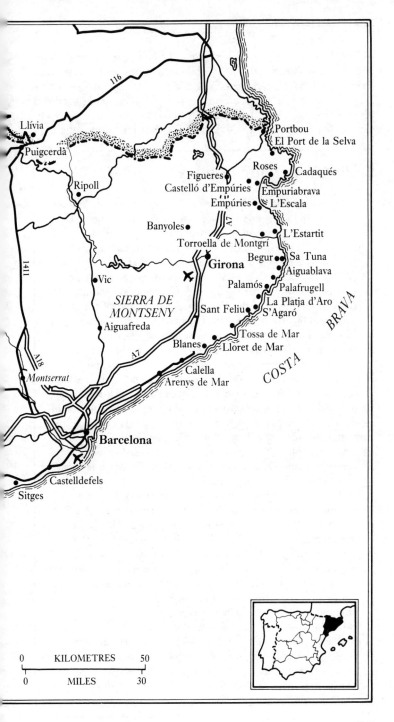

COSTA BRAVA

SIERRA DE MONTSENY

215

whereby it retained its own language, law and customs. The region prospered, and a Catalan–Aragonese empire was created extending over much of the Mediterranean basin and beyond, as far as Greece. But imperial adventuring strained the resources of the state, causing a banking collapse in 1381 which started Barcelona's decline. Although Columbus was

Planning your holiday

As ever, the golden rule is not to try to do too much. You *can* rattle around Catalunya in a fortnight, but you will not get the chance to relax or form more than a passing acquaintance with any of its areas. However you decide to structure your time, give yourself at least four days in Barcelona, if you are a first-time visitor. You can combine this with a resort-based holiday on the Costas, or slowly drift from one resort to the next. Alternatively, contrast the bustle of the city with the splendour of the alpine scenery of the Pyrenees. On the coast you will find large numbers of north Europeans, from Scandinavians to the Irish. Inland – except at the *paradores* – visitors are likely to be Spanish.

June or September are good times to visit – by July and August – you will find many seaside hotels block-booked by package operators, and in August many of Barcelona's best restaurants put up their shutters for the month as their owners flee the heat of the city. Be prepared for rain even in the summer, though it is wettest between March and May. Catalunya's tourist season is short. Except in the cities and ski-resorts many hotels close between October and Easter, or even May. These Costas aren't warm enough to sustain a winter sun trade.

Barcelona is particularly pleasant to visit in spring and early autumn. Its main fiestas are San Antonio, with parades and fireworks in January; religious processions around Holy Week and the feast of Corpus Christi; Sant Jordi (St George) on 23 April, and the June fiesta in the Poble Espanyol at Montjuïc. In September a lot of pomp and circumstance marks Catalunya's national day on the 11th, and the feast of the Virgen de la Merced has free concerts, fireworks, death-defying human towers and a group of papier-mâché giants on the march.

Catalunya doesn't have any world-ranking festivals to match Seville's *Semana Santa* or Pamplona's San Fermín bull-run, although the week-long festival of Nuestra Señora de la Merced is held in Barcelona in September. The streets of Sitges are transformed into carpets of flowers at the feast of Corpus Christi

welcomed in triumph when he landed on his return from the Americas in 1492 (and a huge monument to him presides over the port area at the foot of the Ramblas), the effect of his discovery was to shift economic advantage and opportunity from the Mediterranean to the Atlantic port of Cádiz and inland Seville, as new trade routes developed. Catalunya was

in June. The best place to see the human towers known as *castelles* built by men called *xiquetes* is in the village of Valls, near Tarragona, in September.

This is a region to explore by car. The roads (including the N-11 toll road to the French border) are for the most part good, and where they are not, there is usually some evidence of Euro-funded improvement under way. A reliable regional map like the Michelin *North-East Spain*, 1:400 000, sheet 443, is essential.

There are decent bus services along the coast and to Girona, but further inland, service is patchy. From Barcelona, railway lines strike out for France, Madrid, Valencia and several Andalucian cities. A local RENFE railway runs along the Costa del Maresme from Malgrat de Mar to Barcelona, often severing beaches from the resorts they serve, and on the Costa Dorada to Tarragona and beyond.

There are plenty of hotels and *pensiones* in Barcelona, and thousands of package hotels and apartment blocks on the Costas. Inland, while there are some little gems, small hotels of character and quality are rather thin on the ground, but you can still find some real bargains.

About twenty operators offer weekend or short breaks to Barcelona, and dozens sell sunshine packages to the Costas, using charter flights to Girona or Reus airports from Gatwick or several UK provincial airports. This year the only ski-resort in the Catalan Pyrenees to be served by a UK package operator is the ritzy and expensive resort of Baqueira-Beret, near Vielha. In the valley below the resort are the *paradores* of Vall d'Aran and Arties.

● **Regional Tourist Board**: Gran Via de les Corts Catalanes, 658 Barcelona (301 7443) has a large collection of English-language information about the region. You will find **tourist information offices** – 98 in all – in most places, but we found particularly helpful offices in the cities of Girona (Ciutadans 12) and Tarragona (Fortuny 4), and in the resorts of Tossa de Mar and Cambrils de Mar.

absorbed in the unified Spanish state as it became, temporarily, the world's greatest power.

Spain's earliest industrial development was centred on Catalunya and the Basque Country, and as Barcelona's population grew (quadrupling between 1850 and 1900) due to widespread immigration from other parts of Spain, socialist and separatist ideas took root, leading to conflict with Madrid. Industrialisation saw a revival in the city's fortunes as the textile, iron and steel industries grew and prospered, and a literary revival promoted the Catalan language, which became a vehicle for nationalist sentiment and aspiration.

An autonomous Catalan republic was declared following the plebiscite called after the fall of the dictator Primo de Rivera in 1931, and throughout the Civil War years (1936-39), Barcelona was a bastion of the left. As Franco's troops kept Madrid under heavy attack, the Spanish Republican government transferred its capital to Barcelona in October 1937. The city held out until January 1939. Franco exacted terrible revenge on Catalunya – political murders were commonplace, its autonomous status was rescinded, and use of *catalán* banned.

Only after Franco's death in 1975 were the Catalans able successfully to reassert their claims to home rule, and secure equal status for their language. Since 1981 Catalunya has been an autonomous territory within Spain, although nationalists continue to seek greater independence from Madrid.

BARCELONA (H)

The city offers pleasing architectural contrasts. The medieval city walls were demolished in 1858 and a smart New Town (the Eixample), designed by Idelfons Cerda, was laid out on a regular grid pattern with wide streets, which contrasts starkly with the narrow, twisting lanes of the Barri Gòtic, the old Gothic quarter. Such mathematical precision could be stifling, but studded throughout the chessboard matrix of the New Town are stunningly flamboyant works by the Modernist architect Gaudí, a riot of colour and undulating organic forms which animate the whole area.

The city

Barri Gòtic

The narrow medieval alleys of the **Barri Gòtic** are the place to find the great medieval cathedral, shabby palaces, idiosyncratic museums and lively *cava* bars where you can nibble at fishy *tapas* and quaff very acceptable fizz at a fraction of the price of the French stuff. Outside in the cathedral square, Peruvian musicians play guitars and pan-pipes, and during Advent the site is transformed into a colourful Christmas market with dozens of stalls selling tinsel, tree decorations, bunches of mistletoe tied with ribbon in the Catalan colours, and appallingly kitsch nativity cribs. Come on a Sunday morning, or on a Saturday between 5pm and 6pm and watch the locals form a closed circle, and dance the *sardana* to curiously infectious oompah-style music.

The Ramblas

Stretching up from the seedy port to the grand Plaça de Catalunya, **the Ramblas** is a succession of wide, shop-lined streets where horn-tooting cars pass by on either side of a central pedestrianised boulevard. A lot of rather dreary souvenir shops line the central boulevard on both sides, and the port end has a liberal sprinkling of sex shops. At this end you are likely to find market traders offering leather goods and colourfully embroidered waistcoats; nearby, regiments of stout Barcelonan matrons sit on kitchen chairs, their tarots laid out on card tables before them, ready to disclose what the future holds (in *catalán*, Spanish or French).

Further up, towards the Plaça de Catalunya, there are lots of news-stands selling foreign newspapers, maps, tee-shirts, postcards, guide books – and whole libraries of soft-core porn magazines. As you progress along the street, past stalls decked out with hanging baskets of flowers and plants, and chirruping caged birds, shoe-shine boys appear, ready to spring into action. Crowds gathered round a little table effectively conceal a sleight-of-hand merchant, bidding the gullible to 'Find the Lady'. Political activists offer books, badges and tee-shirts; the less organised invite you to choose a scarf from a rainbow assortment spread out on a sheet on the ground. At night, prostitutes wait ready to accost you (whether you're accompanied or not); and in the early hours outrageous transvestites parade past you, pouting.

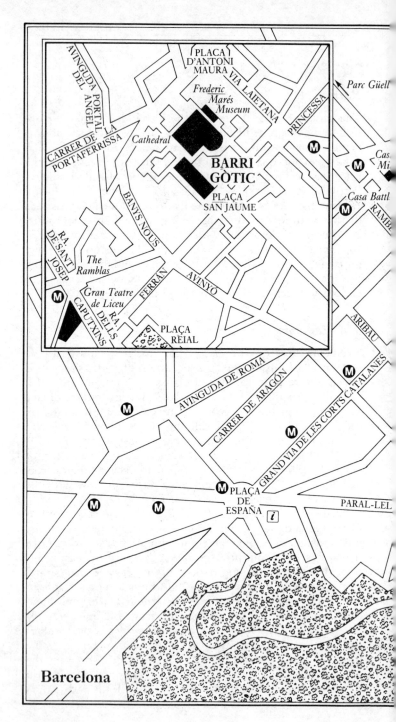

Barcelona

220

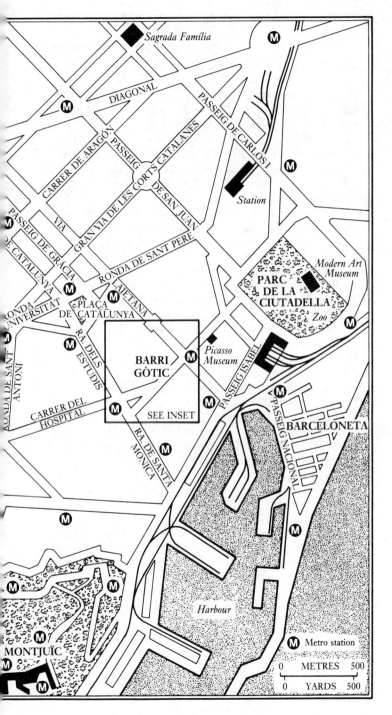

221

Barcelona practicalities

● **Getting there** British Airways and Iberia operate daily flights between Heathrow and Barcelona. Costs vary considerably according to season. If you are staying over a Saturday night, look out for PEX and SUPERPEX fares. BA's are generally more competitive, but, although this is not a major charter destination, have your travel agent check up on charter fares – you may decide that the extra flexibility of a daily scheduled service justifies paying a little more.

About 15 tour operators offer breaks in Barcelona. Tour operators offer a good quality and price-range of hotels, situated mostly (though not entirely) in the Eixample, and generally in refurbished, three-or four-star hotels. As a general rule of thumb packages tend to cost less than independent travel in the summer. During the winter it is cheaper to make your own arrangements.

● **Arrival and departure** El Prat airport is a hub of Spain's transport system, and is large and well equipped by Spanish standards. A fine new terminal building opened in April 1991 to cope with the anticipated Olympic traffic.

● **Getting around** The underground (Metro) is the fastest and cheapest way to make your way around the city. There is a flat fare but a 10-journey 'T2' ticket is a bargain, and also allows you to use the train to Tibidabo and the funicular railway to Montjuïc. For a little more you can get a 'T1', which is also valid on buses. Trains run from 5am to 11pm (6am to 1am Saturdays, Sundays and the night before public holidays). Five lines cover most of the city and connect with the funicular.

A word of warning – do not carry large sums of money around with you when exploring the Barri Gòtic and the Ramblas, especially at night – thieves and muggers are always on the look out for soft targets.

● **Sightseeing tours** There are two tour companies – Julia Tours at Ronda Universidad 5 (just behind the Plaça de Catalunya) and Pullmantur at Gran Via de los Corts Catalanes 635. The city tour has two components – the Cathedral, Barri Gòtic and Montjuïc in the morning, and an arts tour with the Picasso museum and the works of the architect Gaudí in the afternoon.

Alternatively (and much more cheaply), bus no. 100 tours the city in 90 minutes and you can hop on and off as you please. It leaves from the Plaça de Catalunya every 45 minutes during the day between June and September.

There are popular excursions to the heavily commercialised but wonderfully located monastery at Montserrat – home of the Black Madonna, the most potent symbol of Catalan nationalism, and to the resorts of the Costa Brava. Sarfa buses leave for the coast from Plaça Antoni Lopez, near the post office at the foot of Via Laietana.

● **Booking accommodation** Downtown, hotels are clustered around the Ramblas (the smarter ones up towards Plaça de Catalunya – it is advisable to forgo the view and stay in a quieter back room) and the Barri Gòtic, where you will find the majority of *pensiones* and cheaper hotels, which are almost universally unenticing. In the Eixample, which is slightly less convenient, the hotels are largely spread along or around the Passeig de Grácia and the Diagonal; some are purpose-built multi-storey blocks, but most are converted townhouses.

Most city buses can be caught at the Plaça de Catalunya, but if you're unfamiliar with the layout of the city, it's probably better to stick to the Metro. The main station for long-distance buses is at the Estacio de Nord on Avinguda Vilanova, three blocks north of the Parc de la Ciutadella (nearest Metro station Arc de Triumf). **Taxis** are black with yellow stripes, plentiful, cheap and metered. Most journeys to tourist sites from the Plaça de Catalunya cost less than £4. Small tips are welcomed, but not demanded as of right. Taxis available for hire display a green light, or a sign reading *'lliure'* in the windscreen.

It is not necessary to have a car to get the best out of this city; the vibrant atmosphere is better absorbed on foot, and public transport is good. Parking is difficult, especially in the Barri Gòtic and in the Eixample, the New Town, with its wide streets and boulevards. Tow-away zones are enforced around the Avinguda Diagonal. If you are planning to explore the Costa Brava, car hire might be worth considering.

Trains to the city centre (about 13 kilometres) are very cheap, run every 30 minutes (20 minutes during the summer), and the journey takes around 20 minutes – about the same time as the taxi journey which costs around £10.

● **Information** Local tourist offices are called *Oficinas de Información Turistica*. The main office is at Gran Via de les Corts Catalanes, Tel 658 (301 7443). The airport office is open Mondays to Saturdays 9.30am to 8pm; it is also open on Sundays 9am to 3pm. A special office will be opening at Montjuïc to deal with enquiries relating to the Olympic Games.

Do not forget the side streets. Down at the port end there are tiny antique shops, full of interesting clutter, and off to the right the Boquería market is full of locals buying bread, shellfish, various meats and skinned rabbits, as well as exotic fruit such as rambutans and numerous varieties of giant plate-shaped mushrooms.

The Eixample

Beyond the Plaça de Catalunya, an elegant recreational square, the straight, wide streets of the nineteenth-century New Town, **the Eixample**, open out. Some of the hotels here are refurbished *belle époque* piles, on one of the streets around the Passeig de Gràcia – the acme of Eixample addresses, with its imposing marble-halled bank headquarters, chic boutiques and designer jewellery shops. You will find most of the city's favourite night spots in the Eixample in the streets off the appropriately named Diagonal and Carrer d'Aribau.

Montjuïc

The hill of Montjuïc, crowned by a castle, rises over 600 feet above the harbour, and is the setting for a large park which houses a number of museums and an old-fashioned fun-fair. It is also the site of the main Olympic stadium. To get to Montjuïc, take the Metro to Plaça d'Espanya and walk up Avinguda de la Reina Maria Cristina, or take the funicular railway from Paral-lel Metro station. This interconnects with a cable car which will take you from the amusement park to the castle, home of the Military Museum. The famous illuminated fountain that fronts the magnificent façade of the Palau Nacional is currently boarded up, suspended by the city fathers following a long period of drought. When in operation it is illuminated to musical accompaniment on Thursday, Saturday and Sunday nights from 9pm (weekends only in winter).

The **Museum of Catalan Art** is Montjuïc's premier museum, a stunning collection centred on Romanesque works from the eleventh and twelfth centuries, and Catalan religious paintings. Dozens of frescoes, transplanted from small churches in the Catalan Pyrenees, show wide-eyed figures framed in brilliant colours.

The **Miró Foundation** is a fine, white clean-lined building endowed by the artist himself, with an extensive collection of his works including paintings, drawings, bulbous sculptures and three-dimensional tapestries in brilliant reds, yellows and blues.

The **Archaeological Museum** houses a number of items from prehistoric and Graeco-Roman times excavated locally, including many of the finds from Empúries including a Venus and a torso of Aphrodite. A Greek-style amphitheatre, designed for the 1929 exhibition, hosts classical plays during the summer months. An **Ethnological Museum** displays a number of early man-made artefacts from diverse cultures, with visiting exhibitions supplementing unusual collections from Japan, Guatemala, the Philippines and New Guinea.

The **Poble Espanyol** is a collection of reproduction vernacular buildings from all over Spain, assembled in one location on an enormous site for the 1929 International Exhibition, and maintained as a permanent attraction.

The eighteenth-century Castell de Montjuïc, a notorious Civil War prison, now houses a **Military Museum**, reached by cable car from the fun-fair, with one of the biggest collections of model soldiers you're ever likely to see.

The sights

The cathedral

Called La Seu by locals, this superb Gothic church is strangely deceptive, its most striking apparently medieval features – the ornate façade on the Plaça del Rei and the soaring spire – being nineteenth-century additions, built in accordance with the original plans and financed by a wealthy industrialist. Outside the ornate doors, sightless beggars stand with outstretched palms, muttering supplication at all who enter. Inside, a remarkable carved choir-stall screen, enlivened by the coats of arms of the Knights of the Golden Fleece who assembled here in 1519 interrupts the nave.

Frederic Marès Museum You will find this wonderfully eccentric museum just around the corner from the cathedral in the heart of the Barri Gòtic. There's an incredibly extensive and somewhat awe-inspiring collection of religious artefacts – particularly sculptures of the crucifixion and of the Madonna Marès, sculptor, was also an inveterate collector of secular items, and his eclectic assembly of items in the upstairs **Museu Sentimental** includes all sorts of ephemera such as cigarette cards, tarot cards, matchboxes, unusual clay pipes, as well as dolls, walking sticks and penny-farthings.

Picasso Museum This is not the best collection of the

modern master's works but it is the best in Spain (although the epic *Guernica* is in Madrid). Barcelona was his adopted city, and the thirteenth-century Aguilar palace has been magnificently restored to house this collection, exceptionally rich in early figurative works, and recently bolstered by gifts from Jacqueline Picasso. The galleries are laid out in chronological order, meticulously labelled in *catalán* and Spanish, and rough notebooks are often displayed alongside the finished work, giving an insight into the creative process. The best-known works displayed are the *Meninas* sequence, studies on a theme of Velázquez, and studies from the famous

Gaudí

Antoni Gaudí was born at Reus near Tarragona in 1852. The son of a coppersmith, his extravagant genius was first seen in flamboyant railings, gates and other ironworks. His early domestic architecture shows the free-flowing lines, undulating surfaces, and identification of stone as an organic substance that was to characterise his work. His buildings are the most exciting sights in the New Town, and of these the most stunning is the unfinished (after more than 100 years) **Temple Expiatori de la Sagrada Familia**, an almost surreal building, responsibility for which Gaudí assumed from a more conventional colleague in 1884, and which obsessed him until his death in a tram accident in 1926. Its four spires topped by coloured ceramic caps soar over 100 metres high above the city like giant, skewered cigars, and its porches have stalactite-like canopies which somehow make the tortured stone look like dripping wax. To visit the site is to find yourself in a building site for, haphazardly funded, work has been going on since 1952 in accordance with Gaudí's final, rather sketchy plans. The commitment to completing the building is controversial, as some argue that as an intuitive designer, Gaudí – had he lived – would have modified his conception as work progressed, constantly incorporating new ideas. To adhere rigidly to pre-determined plans is antithetical to his perception of architecture. Others simply believe that the finest tribute to a great Catalan nationalist would have been to leave the building unfinished. An opposing faction believes that Gaudí knew that the building could not be completed in his lifetime, and would have wished his successors to complete it, to the glorification of God. Either way it would be tragic not to see it. You can take an elevator up one of the spires and see the extraordi-

Harlequin sequence. **Museu Marítim** opposite the port at the foot of the Ramblas is Europe's only surviving medieval ship-yard, the Drassanes – now the maritime museum. You will find a fascinating collection of mariners' artefacts, as well as a colourful reproduction of the *Real*, a sixteenth-century galley. In the harbour opposite the museum is an exact replica of Christopher Columbus' ship the *Santa María*.

Modern Art Museum Most of the works on display date from the late nineteenth and early twentieth centuries. The big names of modern Catalan art, Dalí and Miró, are barely represented, but there is some wonderful furniture by Gaspar

---

nary detail of the work. There is a small museum, with an interesting audio-visual on his work.

It is a building you will either love or hate. In *Homage to Catalonia* George Orwell pronounced it to be 'one of the most hideous buildings in the world' and found its spires to be 'exactly the shape of hock bottles'. Others find it a superbly uplifting building, and a great testament to human spirit and vision.

There are two examples of Gaudí's domestic architecture on the Passeig de Gràcia. The contours of the *Casa Mila* – an apartment block on the Passeig de Gràcia – whose strangely undulating forms seem to flow around a corner, is said to be inspired by Montserrat, the saw-toothed mountain that is almost sacred in Catalan folklore and religious life. Because of its resemblance to an eroded rock face its nickname is *La Pedrera*, the rock quarry. On the roof you'll find weird chimneys forming a sculpture garden of *espantabruixas* – witch-scarers! **Casa Batlló**, four blocks down towards the Plaça de Catalunya on the other side of the road, has a colourful ceramic façade, and strangely mask-like balconies. Its insurance company owners placed it on the market in 1991 with a £55 million price-tag. At **Parc Güell** a similarly startling ginger-bread house guards what was intended originally to be a smart housing development. Only the gate-house, and Gaudí's own house (which now houses a small museum) were completed, but the concept is a theme park ahead of its time. There is a definite Hansel and Gretel feel to it, with a strange hall of columns like a sinister grotto, a giant decorative lizard, enormous mosaic benches and weird steps which flow like lava. **Palau Güell**, now a theatre museum, is just off the seedy southern end of the Ramblas. It is a sombre, wood-panelled palace, whose rooms seem to flow from one to the other in a stream of glass doors and inner windows.

Homar, and a strange indoor sculpture park of 1927 by Josep Guinovart.

Zoo If you are tired of museums and galleries, take a walk through the Parc de la Ciutadella until you come to the zoo. Only the big cats are caged, and there is a fine collection of primates, and a detailed family tree that shows the success of the zoo's breeding-in-captivity programme. There is a dolphinarium with performance times widely posted, but the real star of the show is the enormously photogenic Snowflake, the only albino gorilla in captivity.

Shopping

Shopping is fun in Barcelona. Wander down Avinguda del Portal de l'Angel from Plaça de Catalunya and see the constant stream of customers for the religious statuary shop; admire the brightly coloured handcarved wooden mobiles, ideal for the nursery, sold at little stalls in the narrow cobbled streets behind the cathedral in the heart of the Barri Gòtic, or choose a keyring (from a selection of 5,000) in an eccentric little shop called El Mond del Claver at Carrer de l'Hospital 33, just off the Ramblas.

Market stalls at the bottom of the Ramblas and around the cathedral (on Thursdays) have a wide choice of heavy, calf-length brocade skirts, and colourful embroidered waistcoats. The maze-like streets of the Barri, especially Carrer Banys Nous, have dozens of little antique shops.

A flea market, called El Encants at Carrer Dos de Maig, all day Monday, Wednesday, Friday and Saturday is a treat. On Sunday mornings coin and stamp stalls set up shop in the Plaça Reial; books and comics can be found between Carrer Manso and Carrer Urgell, just off the Paral-lel at the same time. There is a wonderful selection of Catalan foods with colourful displays of unusual fruit, vegetables and sausages at the Mercat de Sant Josep, just off the Ramblas.

Ceramics make good souvenirs, as do bottles of local *cava*. You can browse among beautiful fans at La Cubana at Carrer de la Boquería 26, or flip through modern art prints in the shops near the Picasso museum on Carrer de Montcada.

Eating out and drinking

Barcelonans, while not exactly early risers, are less torpid than their fellow countrymen. So you will see see lots of locals eating *einsimadas* (turnovers) on the hoof, especially on the Ramblas at lunchtime. Wander the backstreets and you will encounter queues at *sandvitxerías* and patisseries while many restaurants are virtually deserted. Look out for the **Forn d'Aviný** at the corner of Carrers Avinyó and Ample. Tourists with a bit more time can plonk themselves down and have a filling *menu del día* at a fairly anonymous place for around £4. If you want a snack, but prefer more stylish surroundings have a drink and a sandwich in the splendid green and white *belle époque* **Café de l'Opera**, with its classical echoes, opposite the Liceu, the opera house on the Ramblas. Other good places for light meals on the Ramblas include the fast-food **Viena**, and the terrace of the **Café Zurich**, at the Plaça de Catalunya end. In the Eixample, the cool, design-conscious **La Jijonenca** at Rambla de Catalunya 35 is a stylish ice-cream parlour, with geometric black and white fittings, Dalí prints and a good-value *menu del día* which makes it a popular choice with apparently incongruous elderly patrons. The **Cerverzería d'Or** on Carrer del Consell de Cent is another good choice.

A good place to experiment with *tapas* is the satisfyingly ethnic, unnamed bar opposite La Pizza Nostra in Carrer de Montcada, near the Picasso Museum.

Cavas is Spanish sparkling wine made in accordance with the *méthode champenoise* (the second fermentation takes place in the bottle). It is inexpensive, and often of excellent quality. It is the ideal accompaniment to *tapas*.

When it comes to more substantial fare, menus are heavily weighted towards fish, and there is a host of seafood restaurants around the Passeig Nacional near the port in the Barceloneta area. The rough and ready **Restaurante Paris**, Carrer Maquinista 29, is good value. Just off the Ramblas, try the *paella* (or the snails) at **Los Caracoles**, at Escudellers 14, the distinctive restaurant where chickens, dripping fat, rotate on a spit over a grate set in the outside wall. It is just off the seedy section of the Ramblas. Also in the Barri Gòtic **La Bona Cuina**, Carrer de Paradis 4, is expensive and touristy, but has excellent meat and fish.

Around the Picasso Museum, try the *tortilla catalana* at the unpretentious **Nou Celler** at Princesa 161 and Barri de Ferro 3. Near the port, the more expensive **Restaurante 7 Portes** on Passeig de Isabel is popular with locals and tourists, particularly on Sunday nights when much of the opposition is closed. The food is competent – but not outstanding – and the menus are in *catalán* (there's a translation on display outside); oysters and *cava* are specialities.

For a splurge take yourself to **La Punalada**, Passeig de Gràcia 104. It is expensive, particularly the starters, but the salads are big enough for two, the chicken cooked to perfection, the *butifarra* (sausage) and mushrooms are delightful, and the service is extremely solicitous. Also in the Eixample, **Ca La Marión**, Carrer d'Amigo 53, offers excellent Spanish *nouvelle cuisine* at reasonable prices.

Nightlife and entertainment

Check the weekly *Guía del ocio* or the (less useful) newspaper *La Vanguardia* for listings covering cinema, theatre, opera, dance, music and so on and ideas on bars and restaurants.

Music, dance and plays are staged at the Greek theatre on Montjuïc and at the Parc de la Ciutadella during the summer. The **Gran Teatre de Liceu** on the Ramblas, an opulent orgy of gilt and velvet, is one of the world's leading opera houses, with a formidable reputation for its Wagnerian productions. You will find jazz in several bars, particularly at weekends. A bit off the tourist trail, try the bar at Carrer de la Fussina 6, in Barceloneta, around midnight.

Much of the city's heavy-duty nightlife is centred in the Eixample, in the streets around Aribau and the Diagonal, where there are a number of smart cocktail bars.

If you want to join the smart set and go clubbing till dawn try **Up and Down,** Carrer Numancia 179, or **Otto Zutz** at Carrer Lincoln 13.

MONTSERRAT

The most heavily touted excursion from Barcelona (and the Costa Brava) takes coachloads of tourists up the spectacular sandstone, saw-toothed rockface to the monastery and hermitages of **Montserrat**, 40 kilometres north-west of the city. Tour guides feed their clientele a stream of legends; the famous image of the Virgin, discovered in a mountain cave amid celestial music and ecstatic visions in 880, had reputedly been hidden there by St Peter around AD 50 (this legend, in turn, inspired Wagner's *Parsifal*). Many miracles are attributed to the Virgin's intervention. Modern research, however, rather spoils a good yarn, since it now seems unlikely that the Romanesque Virgin pre-dates the eleventh century.

The figure of the Madonna, set high above the altar and

blackened by centuries of candle-smoke, is the centrepiece of the nineteenth-century basilica, which replaced the sixteenth-century foundation destroyed by Napoleon's troops. The famous Escolania boys' choir sings daily at 1pm.

The cult of the Madonna is an important focus of Catalan nationalism, but if you are seeking spiritual uplift, you are likely to be disappointed. There is a huge commercial operation at work, with busy coachparks, cafeterias full of sticky cakes, and gift shops with shelves groaning with replica Madonnas, other quasi-religious memorabilia, and assorted Montserrat confectionery and liqueurs.

But the views and the mountain walks to the hermitages, plus the spectacular approach with views of the Llobregat valley, are enjoyable. Get the best views by coming on the funicular railway and cable car. Drivers approaching from the north get an unforgettable first sight of the sierra at **Manresa**. The *Ferrocarriles Catalanes* leaves from below the Plaça de Espanya and connects with the cable car. The exposed position of the tracks to the various hermitages leaves them liable to storm damage, which can disrupt the service. The monastery's art collection – the Montserrat Museum – is divided into two sections. The first features much classic religious art by heavyweights such as El Greco, Zurbarán and Caravaggio. The other, housing a collection of modern art, is more enjoyable. There are a couple of very early Picassos as well as the simple but engaging *Sardana of peace*, several works by Santiago Rusiñol and a host of Spanish impressionists.

Alternatively, head north and then west on the C-1410 and use your visit as a reason to indulge yourself by visiting the splendid *parador* in a converted medieval castle above the River Cardener at **Cardona** (H). This *parador* has a very high reputation for its food. Next to the *parador* stands a handsome eleventh-century Romanesque church, Sant Vincenç. The town is known as the capital of salt, and the presence of a nearby mountain of pure salt was first documented by the Roman geographer Strabonus. You can learn everything there is to know about salt at the Museu de Sal at Pompeu Fabra 4. Cardona also makes a good base for nipping across to the area around Lleida to visit **Solsona** with its ruined castle and streets dotted with medieval houses.

SOUTH TO SITGES (H)

Heading south from Barcelona the road winds and undulates, following the indents and topography of the coastline. Fifteen minutes after El Prat airport you catch glimpses of wide open belts of sandy beach at **Castelldefells**, beyond which the road soars higher, overlooking rocky inlets and cliffs studded with Mediterranean pines. **Sitges** is an attractive mixture of modern resort, interesting old town and artists' colony. It is a 40-minute drive from Barcelona, so you will not have the place to yourself; but, if you avoid July and August and weekends when the day-trippers pour in, it makes a good seaside base. It is lively, but more sophisticated than most, and is popular with gay travellers. Of its several golden sand beaches, La Rivera and Platja Balmins are separated by a headland on which a cluster of venerable buildings of various tints are stacked, linked by narrow cobbled streets that are fun to explore. The Museu Cau Ferrat in Carrer Fonollar contains an eclectic collection of local artefacts displayed in the former studio of the nineteenth-century romantic artist/writer Santiago Rusiñol. You will find examples of his work as well as that of El Greco and Utrillo, and lots of local tiles and pottery. In the upstairs gallery there is some fine stained glass, and lots of religious artefacts. Unfortunately, labelling is in *catalán* only. The next door Museu Maricel del Mar houses a collection of mainly Gothic religious art. For a return to the secular there is the Museu Romántico Can Llopis on Carrer Sant Gaudenci, a lavish eighteenth-century mansion, which houses a number of collections.

In June the feast of Corpus Christi is marked by a floral carpet competition which transforms the grey cobbles into bright organic mosaics. There are lots of shops, including some classy art stores and several confectioners and patisseries. Eat at one of the sea-front restaurants on the smart Passeig de la Ribera – opt for the seafood specialities on the terrace of La Fragata or El Velero. On the Passeig Vilanova the emphasis shifts to grilled meat at La Masia, a rustic-style farmhouse serving traditional Catalan dishes.

Around Sitges

Some distance from the town there are long expanses of sand at **Cunit** and **Calafell**. Lacking the chic of Sitges, these beaches are agreeably uncrowded, although the stripling resorts that serve them are somewhat characterless. A few kilometres inland **El Vendrell** has retained one of the gates of its medieval walls, and like Sitges it celebrates Corpus Christi with floral carpets. Visitors interested in modern classical music will enjoy the museum dedicated to the cellist Pau Casals, and might be able to attend a concert in the adjoining auditorium.

North-east of El Vendrell, just off the A-7 *autopista*, wine buffs find their holy grail at **Villafranca del Panedès** (Vilafranca de Penedès). Fans of modern architecture will be similarly rewarded as the town is a showpiece of modernist architecture, the growers having commissioned extravagant buildings from leading turn-of-the century architects. The best-known Penedès wines come from the Torres vineyards, and there are guided tours and tastings at the *bodega* (Tel 3 890 0100). Affordable labels that are worth looking out for include the whites *Gran Vina Sol* and *Vina Esmeralda*, and the reds *Gran Coronas* and *Sangre de Toro*. The excellent Museu de Vi, housed in the fourteenth-century Gothic palace of the Kings of Aragón at Plaça Jaume 1, explains the history of wine-making in the region.

Twelve kilometres further north, at **Sant Sadurni d'Anoia** on the Carretera 243, you will find the centre of the *cava* industry. Catalunya's sparkling wines, made in accordance with the *méthode champenoise* are deservedly famous. The Cordoníu winery is notable both for the size of its underground cellars, reached by special train, and for the splendid estate buildings designed by Josep Puig i Cadafalch, architect of the Casa Amettler which adjoins Gaudís Casa Batlló on Barcelona's Passeig de Gràcia.

TARRAGONA (H)

As Catalunya's second port, Tarragona is a more hectic place than the ancient remains north of the city – the triumphal *Arco de Bara* and the three-storey *Torre de Scipio* – might suggest. Parking is tricky; chances are you will need to settle for one of the multi-storey or underground car parks signposted throughout the centre.

The city sits on a limestone cliff which subsides into the sea. The massive rough-hewn blocks of cyclopean rock forming the base of the imposing ramparts enclosing the highest part of the town point to it being founded by people from the eastern Mediterranean in the sixth century BC. An Iberian settlement was founded, but the city fell to the Romans commanded by Publius Scipio in 218 BC. Its stunning ocean views and fine climate were very much to Roman taste, emperors such as Augustus and Hadrian adopting it as a favoured resort. They proceeded to develop it as a major overseas stronghold called Tarraco, destined to become the capital of the important province of Hispania Citerior, subsequently known as *Tarraconensis*. During the Punic Wars it served as a depot for the most important fleet of the Mediterranean. What remains tells us a lot about the Roman way of life (and death), with a splendid aqueduct and amphitheatre among the structures that survived the waves of Franks, Visigoths and Moors who succeeded the Roman legions in occupation.

Exploring the city

There are two parts to the city – the old walled Roman and medieval quarter; and below that a modern city laid out on a grid pattern, with some ritzy shopping streets. Perhaps the best place to begin is at the **Museu Arqueologic** (the National Archaeological Museum) on Plaça del Rei, part of which is housed in the austere building that was once the palace of Augustus. The highlight is the polychrome representation of Medusa, with snakes like a frame of spaghetti and a suitably intimidating and penetrating stare. The adjacent **Museu d'Historia de Tarragona** (museum of the history of the city) occupies the building known as the Palace of the Aragonese Kings, rumoured to be the birthplace of Pontius Pilate, and built over the Roman vaults of the Praetorium, which you can explore. On display here are more Roman, plus Visigothic and medieval finds. It is worth visiting for the third-century marble Sarcophogus of Hippolytus, rescued from the sea in 1948 – a series of photographs show the salvage operation.

The medieval quarter of town is a few blocks from the museums. At its heart is the **Catedral de Santa Técla**, the biggest in Catalunya, and named after the city's patron saint, a convert of St Paul who was repeatedly rescued from persecutors by divine intervention. Work began in 1194, and continued into the fifteenth century, making it transitional Romanesque/Gothic in style. The church is entered through its large and unusual cloister, which resembles those of the Cistercian abbeys at Poblet and Vallbona, and has carved capitals illustrating biblical themes and fables such as 'The burial of the cat by rats'. The cathedral museum has a fine collection of Flemish tapestries. On the main façade a large, elaborate and indisputably Gothic portal (two hundred years in the carving) is flanked by Romanesque doors. The interior of the apse is filled by a fifteenth-century *retablo* depicting scenes from the life of a double-chinned St Técla, carved out of alabaster and marble and painted in bright tones. The steep streets around the cathedral are worthwhile, with lots of little antique shops in Carrer de la Nau, and a thicket of colourful, sweet-smelling florists in Carrer Mayor.

Just north of the cathedral you can enter the **Passeig Arqueologic**, a pleasant half-mile walk through gardens at the foot of the massive city walls whose layers span pre-Roman times to the legacy of English builders during the War of the Spanish Succession in the opening year of the eighteenth century. The walk brings you past the original city gates and a number of statues, including one of the Emperor Augustus. If you make your way back down towards the sea, you will come to the **amphitheatre**, built into the natural slope of the hillside. The shape and tiered rows are clearly visible, and some investigative and restoration work is currently under way. In AD 259 the local bishop and two other Christians were martyred by fire in the arena on the orders of the Emperor Valerian. A Visigothic basilica was built in the sixth century to commemorate this, and a Romanesque church was subsequently built on the ruins. Because of its importance as a provincial capital, Tarraco had not one forum but two, the provincial forum near the cathedral, and a local one in the present new town, where elegant columns and arches hint at the splendour of the temples and law courts which once occupied the site. Further west, the **Necropolis Paleocristiana** off Avinguda Ramón y Cajal (same ticket and opening hours as the Archaeological Museum) was the burial ground of Tarragona's early Christians, as well as its still pagan Romans. Graves dating from the third to the sixth centuries were uncovered during the construction of a tobacco factory in 1926. A museum was erected on the site of the original discovery, and works of Visigothic sculpture, tombs and mosaics are displayed there, including a very fine polychrome fourth-century mosaic.

THE COSTA DORADA (COSTA DAURADA)

From Tarragona you can either proceed south along the coast to the Ebro Delta or head inland towards Lleida (Lérida). If doing the latter the first resort you come to after Tarragona's industrial sprawl is **La Pineda**, a long ribbon of characterless beach sandwiched between the city's oil refineries and **Salou**, the largest resort on the Costa Daurada. It hit the headlines in 1989 following an outbreak of typhoid which decimated its tourist trade. Vast sums have been devoted to sorting out the sewage-pipe problems, and although Salou is a typical '70s concrete resort, it is much less awful than many of the genre. For a start it has a long, decent, roughly L-shaped beach of golden sand, Platja Levante, in the town centre, plus some attractive out-of-town cliff and pine-backed coves at Cala Cranes and Platja dels Llenguadets. The high-rise hotels that now scar the pine-fringed headland are far from pretty, but the long, tiled, palm-lined promenade is genuinely attractive. Prices in the many bars and cafés reflect the fact that the resort has yet to recover from the damage its reputation has suffered. With a fun-fair, gently shelving sands and lots of family-oriented attractions such as a safari park and water-parks nearby, this would be a good bet for families looking for a traditional beach-based budget holiday. The neighbouring resort of **Cambrils** is the place to eat in these parts. Although building work continues apace, particularly on the southern fringe of town, at the centre of the resort is a genuinely picturesque but busy little port, where tiny fishing boats, rigged up with lights for night-fishing, are moored. Fish and seafood are often served with the local 'romesco' sauce, a combination of almonds, pine-nuts, dried sweet peppers and tomatoes. Among the surprising number of restaurants are Eugenie, Consolat de Mar 80, with a particularly attractive terrace and garden, Casa Gatell, Paseo Miramar 26, overlooking the port, and Mas Gallau on the N-340 Barcelona road. From Cambrils things go downhill rapidly, with a string of campsites leading to the dreary resort of **Miami Platja**. Before the Ebro Delta, the only spot worth exploring is the precipitous fishing village of **L'Ametlla de Mar**, where a nightly fish auction is held. Some pretty bays lie north of the villages, with open bibs of coarse sand surrounded by pine groves.

THE EBRO DELTA

For centuries, silt has been disgorged at the mouth of the River Ebro, causing the formation of a large delta with long beaches of fine sands. Here the vineyards, and hazel and almond groves of the rest of the region give way to rice paddies, irrigated by the canals dug in the last century, when the first serious attempts were made to tackle the endemic malaria that dogged the land. As one of Western Europe's most important wetlands, the delta has been designated a Natural Park. Visitors can see some spectacular birdlife, especially in October and November after the rice has been harvested.

The beaches at Platja del Trabucadeor and Platja Marquesa are good for getting away from it all. There are campsites at various points on the delta, and hotels at Sant Carles de Ràpita and Amposta. Inland, **Tortosa** (H), the area's main city and one-time seat of the Aragón parliament, is still partly surrounded by medieval fortifications. The recently restored **Castillo de la Zuda**, which dominates a grassy hill, was a stronghold of the Knights Templar during the twelfth century and gives splendid views of the river and Sierra de Cardo. The building, with sympathetic modern extension, now houses a *parador*. The cathedral, begun in 1347 but worked on until the eighteenth century, and hemmed in by other buildings, is worth seeing.

Tortosa is also notable for the fierce Battle of the Ebro, which raged for four months from July 1938, the last major Republican offensive of the Civil War. Many thousands were killed – estimates vary from 35,000 to 150,000 dead.

TARRAGONA TO LÉRIDA (LLEIDA)

The journey from Tarragona along the N-240 is an enjoyable one, with historic old towns to explore along the way. It is worth taking a little detour off to the east on to a minor road to **La Secuita**, where Gaudí's collaborator Jujol (who designed the ceramics for Casa Batlló on Barcelona's Passeig de Gràcia, see page 224) designed a spiky little Modernist church – *Vistabella* – which looks a little like the nose-cone of a rocket. **Valls** is famous as the home of the most daring *castellers* (human towers of up to six storeys), and a statue celebrates their skill. You can see them in action on 24 June; in early August at the *Firagost* when local farmers give thanks for their produce; and on the first Sunday after 21 October, at the Fira de Santa Ursula. There's a single-aisled sixteenth-century Gothic church here, Sant Joan Baptista, whose chapel of *Nuestra Señora del Rosario* has depictions of scenes from the naval Battle of Lepanto executed in *azulejo* tiles. Between Valls and Montblanc from February to May roadside restaurants advertise *cocotada* – gatherings at which large shallots are barbecued over an open fire until blackened, and then eaten, often with lamb. The walled medieval town of **Montblanc** (H) is fascinating, but the best place to stay in these parts is at the **Hotel Coll de Lilla**, in a saddle of the hills above the little hamlet of Lilla, between Valls and Montblanc. The N-240 bypasses the town, so once inside the walls it is like a secret domain of narrow streets with balconies strewn with washing and cheerful pots of geraniums. The wall, with its two gates and 28 towers completely encircles the the hill, which accordingly became known as the 'white hill', giving the town its name.

A plan pinned to the main gate of the fourteenth-century walls maps out the sights, and it is a pleasant place to spend two or three hours wandering up and down the stairways that connect the different tiers of the town, taking in the old-fashioned shops as well as the Romanesque and Gothic architecture. The plain fourteenth-century **Santa María la Mayor** has a plateresque façade of apostles and saints added for show in 1688. By contrast, the interior is darkly Gothic. The Catalan-Aragonese *cort* (parliament) used to meet in the nearby Romanesque church of San Miquel. The **Museu de la Conça de Barbera** takes you through the history of the area from prehistoric times, and a small museum of secular and religious art, collected by Frederic Marès, is housed in in the Church of San Marcal. Back on the N-240 a side road near the village of **L'Espluga de Francoli** (H) will take you to the excellent monastery of Poblet. Beyond Poblet, a minor road to the south-west leads to the walled village of **Prades**, with a fine spherical fountain. The castle at **Siurana de Prades** was the Moors' last stronghold in Catalunya. In the village of **La Conreria d'Escala Dei** you will find the ruins of the Priory of Santa María, from which the area of El Priorat takes its name. This was Spain's first Carthusian monastery, and the monks cultivated the vineyards that produce the infamously potent 24 per cent proof Priorat wine. At **Falset** the area's capital (on the N-420, west of Tarragona) there's a Modernist-style *bodega* by César Martinell, a contemporary of Gaudí.

LERIDA (LLEIDA)

Lleida is the capital of the eponymous landlocked province that stretches from the border with Aragón to the lofty snow-capped peaks of the Catalan Pyrenees which sprawl into Girona. The city is a much-battered place in the middle of a vast plain, watered by the River Segre. The Iberians who founded it as *Illtirda* waged guerilla warfare on the Romans (themselves engaged in internecine conflict) and Carthaginian invaders, setting a tradition that has seen the city host many bruising battles. The Moors, utilising their expertise in irrigation, laid the basis of the present-day fruit farming that underpins the local economy.

The principal sight is La Seu Vella (the old cathedral) which, like the adjacent Moorish castle La Zuda, is visible above the sprawl of the city from the main road. The corner stone was laid in 1203, but construction lasted over a century, and the style is transitional Romanesque/Gothic. The exterior is rather plain, although the fifteenth-century octagonal belfry and the main portal (the doorway of the apostles) are memorable. Inside, the cathedral bears the scars of its various misadventures with the military, from the War of the Spanish Succession when it was commandeered as a barracks, to the Peninsular War and the Civil War. Amazingly, some fine (though badly damaged Romanesque) paintings have survived, notably in the Chapel of Sant Tomás. But the highlight of the cathedral is undoubtedly the magnificent thirteenth-century Gothic cloister, with delicate tracery making each of its 12 arches quite different.

THE CATALAN PYRENEES

From Lleida the N-230, signposted **Vielha** or **Vall d'Aran**, will take you into the heart of the Catalan Pyrenees, a spine of mountains that runs across the roof of the province, finally falling into the sea at **Cape Creus** near Cadaqués north of Girona. The contrast with the Catalunya of Lloret de Mar could hardly be more complete; instead of golden sand backed by brutal high-rise concrete architecture you will find soaring grey-green peaks dotted with snow, quiet valleys and still meadows, and a legacy of sensational Romanesque churches.

For the most part the N-230 is an excellent, though often

winding, road. The landscape is alternately open with wide, green panoramas, and claustrophobic as walls of rock crowd in on either side. The route takes you temporarily out of Catalunya and into Aragón as the road skirts the River Noguera Ribagorçana. Even in May you will see cars with skis strapped to their roof-racks, heading towards **Vielha** (H). Below the family-oriented Parador Vall d'Aran there is a bustling resort of alpine appearance with chalet-style sloping roofs, shops crammed with fluorescent-toned ski gear and lots of restaurants and pizzerias. Seven kilometres east at **Arties** (H) there is another *parador* (Don Gaspar de Portolá), although the village itself has little to recommend it, except the restored church of Sant Juan. The best skiing in the Catalan Pyrenees is to be found at **Baqueira**, an exclusive modern development which attracts a well-heeled crowd. It lies on the northern side of the mountains near Vielha and has more reliable snow, and more challenging skiing than its competitors.

Admirers of the Romanesque will find churches to enjoy at Salardú, the capital of the upper Arántales, which also has good views over the valley, at the twelfth- and thirteenth-century Basilica of Santa Eulalia at **Unya**, at **Bagergue** and at **Gessa** and **Trédos**.

Aigües Tortes National Park

The main magnet for hikers is the **Aigües Tortes National Park**, a vast, harsh but beautiful landscape of rock-strewn hills and snow-capped peaks. Chamois and wild boar roam around a terrain planted with Scotch pine and fir trees, while jagged peaks soar to 3,000 metres and beyond. The name means 'tortuous waters', derived from the twisting paths of its rivers, torrents and waterfalls as they flow between its two hundred lakes, including the lovely San Mauricio. Eagles and other birds of prey soar overhead, and flora in the alpine meadows includes Pyrenean broom, anemones and oxslips. There are hotels at **Espot**, and in **Caldes de Boí** in the Vall de Boí west of the park. The exteriors of a number of Roman-esque churches, including **Sant Joan de Boí** and **Sant Maria de Taüll** with its leaning tower, have recently been restored. The highlight is the six-storey bell tower of **Sant Climent de Taüll**.

The drive from Vielha over the Bonaigua pass to La Seu d'Urgell is a challenging one for the driver if the road is affected by snow and fog, as it can be even in May. The C-

147 winds up and down as the topography demands, with crazy bends and sheer drops in places. At **Sort** those heading towards La Seu d'Urgell and the Principality of **Andorra** fork off on the N-260, a new road that quickly shoots upwards, leaving the lights of Sort twinkling far below.

La Seu d'Urgell

La Seu d'Urgell (H) is a good base in the heart of the fertile valley of the River Segre, backed by the Sierra de Cadí and the mountains of Andorra. The town has its share of narrow cobbled streets and arcaded shopfronts, but the only real sight is the **Cathedral of Santa María** built between the eleventh and twelfth centuries as a replacement for the original eighth-century church. It was designed under Italian influence with three aisles and a large transept with five apses. The façade culminates in a lovely campanile. The inside is dark and rather forbidding but there are fine thirteenth-century cloisters. Best of all (and one of Catalunya's most under-rated sights) is the diocesan museum – a modern, thoughtful display of ancient religious art, including a number of statues of the Madonna and child, and 26 mural paintings, 19 of which are from the twelfth and thirteenth centuries. The greatest treasure is the tenth-century *Beatus*, a commentary on the Apocalypse named after an eighth-century abbot of the monastery of San Martín in Liebana who originated the practice of copying these texts in this way.

The area around La Seu d'Urgell is famous for cheeses, and you can pick up the local sausages and pâté at the Tuesday and Friday market. At Castellcuitat, the restaurant at the Hotel El Castell is one of the best in the area with delicious dishes such as 'rucksacks of lamb' (spiced parcels of tender meat) and a fine line in speciality teas.

From La Seu d'Urgell the N-260 continues to follow the path of the River Segre towards the frontier town of Puig-cerdà, past fields of horses and cattle. As you first approach, **Puigcerdà** presents a screen of houses seemingly built across the path of the road. It is curiously schizophrenic – Alpine style houses in Mediterranean pastel colours. They took a hammering from bombers during the Civil War, and a war memorial stands on the site of the church (of which only the bell tower survives) in Plaça de Santa María.

THE PYRENEAN FOOTHILLS

From **Puigcerdà** the N-152 heads south towards Girona. At times the descent seems relentless, as the narrow road twists and turns, snaking through villages like **Toses**, 2,000 metres up, and roadsigns point to isolated communities off improbably precipitous roads. The snow-capped mountain scenery is grand, and the drive on a fairly quiet road enjoyable. From **Ribes de Freser** the highway follows the path of the River Freser, gradually winding its way down to the old town of **Ripoll**. The former **Benedictine Monastery of Santa María** was founded in 888 by Wilfred the Hairy, and rose to prominence as a distinguished centre of learning with one of the most important libraries in Christendom. The eleventh-century Abbot Oliva (also the Bishop of Vic) developed it as a bridgehead of understanding between Christian and Arab civilisations, attracting scholars such as Brother Gerbert who later became Pope Sylvester II. Catalan notables including Wilfred and Raymond Berenguer III are buried here, but the major focus of modern interest is the great twelfth-century portal to the original church, one of the most important works of Catalan Romanesque. Its impressive carvings depict important biblical stories and allegories in seven concentric bands. Among the stories told by what is effectively a great stone graphic novel, are Jonah and the Whale, and the Parting of the Red Sea. There are also fine cloisters to admire.

It is worth seeking out the little municipal museum in Plaça Abot Oliva, the monastery square, with its wonderfully eclectic collection ranging from Civil War memorabilia (including Franco's declaration of the town's capture) and a display of gas masks, to a skull and crossbones-shaped pipe carved by a local shepherd.

If you return to Ripoll, the N-152 continues south into Barcelona province and the town of **Vich** (H) (Vic). There has been a village on this site since the Ausentani Iberians made it their capital before the Roman occupation – you can visit a restored Roman temple dating from the second century.

The best-known sight is the neo-classical cathedral, built in the late eighteenth century, but incorporating the crypt and elegant bell-tower of the original eleventh-century Romanesque church built by Archbishop Oliva. The most striking feature, however, is much more recent; in 1930 the artist Josep María Sert began work on huge frescoes in sepia and grey. Those seen today are the third cycle he painted. The first set was scrapped as unsatisfactory, and the second sequence was destroyed when the church was fired in 1936. A fine fifteenth-century Gothic high altar *retablo* by Pere Oller survived the Civil War conflagration. The next-door Museu Episcopal has a collection of Romanesque and medieval art bettered only by Barcelona's. There is a fine fresco of the Last Supper from La Seu d'Urgell, and a stylized wooden Descent from the Cross.

Vic is famous for the salami-like *salchichón* and other sausages including *butifarra*, *llonganisses* and *fuetes*, found in aromatic side-street shops. The important market is held in the attractive arcaded Plaça del Mercadal on Tuesdays and Saturdays. The fine *parador* is in fact situated in a quiet spot 14 kilometres from the town centre, but is clearly signposted.

There is a last chance for some serious walking in peaceful surroundings before the hurly-burly of Barcelona in the Natural Park centred around the densely forested **Sierra de Montseny**, plus a couple of scenic drives for more sedentary types. The first takes you from **Tona** – where you leave the N-152 to enter the park – to **Sant Celoni**, via pine and beech woods and a detour to the pretty village of **Viladrau**. The second climbs from Sant Celoni via a series of hairpin bends and a corniche to reveal views of the coastal plain near **Lake Santa Fe**.

GERONA (GIRONA)

Both the *autopista* A-7 and the N-11 run south to the relatively unexplored city of **Girona**. Millions of foreign tourists pile off charter flights at the city's airport, but few come to wander around the old town, located at the confluence of the Onyar and Ter rivers.

As the provincial capital it has a long and distinguished history. It was founded by Iberians the remains of whose walls can still be seen. The Romans named it *Gerunda* and established it as an important stopping point on the Via Augusta, and its strategic importance owing to its proximity to the Pyrenees assisted its growth. It was often the scene of protracted battles, and became known as 'the city of a thousand sieges'. The most celebrated was in 1809 when the inhabitants withstood 35,000 of Napoleon's French troops for seven months, until they were starved into submission. Little remains of the impressive medieval defensive walls.

There are several *hostales* around the railway station and near the archaeological museum. A smattering of restaurants offering reasonably priced tasty food are found in the streets around the cathedral. In the new town Cal Ros, Cort Real 9 is the best place for Catalan specialities. Using the *autopista* – the fast toll road – from Barcelona you can reach Girona in about 90 minutes.

Exploring the city

As you drive into Girona the townscape is dominated by the golden Romanesque bell-tower of the cathedral. Leave the car in one of the parking areas on the west bank of the river and walk across one of the pedestrian bridges, stopping to admire the tall multi-hued row of old houses that rise sheer from the river, with the cathedral in its elevated position soaring above them in a faded Italian scene of medieval life.

Once in the old quarter you are engulfed in a labyrinth of steep, narrow streets, not least in the atmospheric and sensitively restored Jewish quarter, the *Call*, one of the best-preserved *juderías* in Europe. Parallel to the river bank you will find the Rambla de la Libertat, the main street of the *ciudad antigua* with pavement cafés, arcaded walls and shops. In the sloping side-streets leading to the cathedral you will chance upon antique shops, dusty cobblers and dark recess-like shops selling wicker-ware. If you cross the river by the Pont d'en Jimez near the new town's Plaça Independencia, you will arrive at the north end of the old town and the church of **Sant Felix**, a Gothic pile built on Romanesque foundations.

Save your puff for the steep walk up the majestic sweep of ninety seventeenth-century steps that leads to the splendid **Cathedral of Santa María**, with its baroque doorway. Work began in 1312 and continued until the end of the sixteenth century, after which ornamenatation continued piecemeal. Despite the baroque façade, the cathedral is essentially Gothic, although the eleventh-century cloister is Romanesque and, like the Charlemagne tower, is a remnant of the original church. Once inside, your jaw will drop as you are confronted by the widest Gothic nave in the world – 22 metres across – and some fine fourteenth-century stained glass. Good views over the city can be had from the bell-tower. Underneath a silver canopy in the chancel there is a gilt fourteenth-century altarpiece retracing the life of Christ. The cathedral also has an unusually interesting treasury, the **Museu Capitular de la**

Catedral, which includes a fine Romanesque Madonna and a late-Gothic cross inlaid with pearl and enamel – ask to borrow the English-language notes to guide your way around the galleries. There is also a rare Commentary on the Apocalypse by Beatus, dated 975, and the supreme treasure, a magnificent tapestry from around 1100 depicting the Creation in various scenes with allegories radiating from a central Christ in Majesty.

North of Girona

If you do not want to head back to the coast from Girona, and hanker after some peace and quiet, head for **Banyoles** on the C-150, whose pretty lake will host the Olympic rowing events in 1992. On the west side of the lake you could visit a fine Romanesque chapel at **Porqueres**. Fourteen kilometres further north is **Besalú** – a fine medieval town on the River Fluviá, with a trio of Romanesque churches, including the three-aisled **Sant Pere** which was once part of a Benedictine monastery founded in 977. The restored twelfth-century fortified bridge spans the river at an unusual angle and leads to the old Jewish quarter, which preserves the only *mikwah* or ritual bath still found in Spain, and originally part of a synagogue. The route to **Olot** passes an area of lunar landscape, pitted by volcanic craters. The largest crater is at **Santa Margarita**, north-west of the town, where the nearby beech woods make an attractive spot for a picnic. Olot is notable for its number of Fine Art schools and workshops which specialise in religious imagery. From here the road to **Sant Joan de les Abadesses** is picturesque and leads ultimately to **Ripoll** (see page 242).

FIGUERAS (FIGUERES)

Figueres is best known these days as the birthplace of Salvador Dalí – and site of the **Teatre-Museu Dalí** where he is buried. The museum is well signposted, but you are unlikely to miss it – a terracotta structure topped by giant eggs, and studded with loaves of bread, symbolic of life. Golden figures stand on pedestals separating the eggs. There is a lot more to the museum than a collection of paintings, and the Mae West Room and the plant-filled Cadillac are justly famous. After the Prado this is Spain's most-visited museum, and gets busy in peak season. Following your visit, browse through the Dalí and other modern art prints and memor-abilia at Distribuciones d'Arte Surrealiste, a shop across the plaça.

The small city centre has some fine Modernist buildings, and taken with the Dalí museum, there is enough of interest to fill a day enjoyably. Figueres has held an important place in Catalan history from the time of the expulsion of the Moors to the Civil War, when Republican leaders met in the dungeon of the seventeenth-century castle which was their last bastion in Catalunya after the fall of Barcelona.

There is a wide range of restaurants in the narrow lanes around the Dalí museum, and some lovely pavement cafés on the central Rambla. The most famous place to eat in town is at Hotel Durán, Casavca 5, which features good regional dishes with modern flair. Out of town on the N-11 the restaurant of the Hotel Ampurdán is famous for its lamb with anchovies and home-made sorbets. The best place to stay however, is five kilometres out of town on the road to Olot; Hotel-Restaurant Mas Pau (H) has stylish but expensive bedrooms and excellent food served in rustic surroundings.

THE COSTA BRAVA

The modern package holiday was born on the Costa Brava more than thirty years ago.

The Costa Brava proper runs from the French border at Portbou to Blanes in the south – Girona province's coastal strip. The rugged cliffs that won the area the appellation 'wild coast' in the first place are found in the north, and this remains a remarkably unspoilt area of hidden coves, pine-clad rocks and excellent golden beaches – all the Costa Brava's beaches pass the European Community's pollution tests.

From Portbou to Cadaques

The border town of **Portbou** is most notable for its railway yards and for the number of liquor shops. It is unlikely that you'll want to spend much time here, but there is a pretty natural harbour and a stony beach where you can while away an hour or two. The seafood restaurants along the quay are your best bet for something to eat.

The narrow, winding road – hard work for the driver – by-passes the sleepy low-lying village of **Colera**, and moves on to the more developed fishing town of **Llansa** (Llança) with a traffic-free promenade, a few restaurants and bars near the harbour where a flotilla of tiny motor boats lie moored, and a short sandy beach. There are a couple of seafront hotels here if you want to stay here overnight to visit the monastery of **Sant Pere de Rodes**, which involves a 15-kilometre drive, followed by a 15-minute walk uphill. The ruins of this eleventh-century Romanesque foundation are at their most atmospheric when shrouded in the mist which swirls around you as you trek up to the elevated site. The three-aisled church, with its barrel-vaulted nave is the best preserved section. Animal heads ornament the capitals, although the best examples have been carted off to the **Museu Marès** in Barcelona (see page 225). The bell-tower, pillaged in the eighteenth century, has fine arcades, but overall the setting is more impressive than the ruins themselves, with views that sweep from Cerbère in France to **Cabo de Creus**.

An inland road winds over the hills to **Cadaqués**, where steep cobbled alleyways of whitewashed pantiled houses look out over a bay full of brightly-painted fishing boats tied at their moorings. The village is in a fairly inaccessible spot, and its position on a promontory, and the narrowness of its streets, have helped to isolate it from the worst excesses of tourist development. The tiny beaches of red-blue slate and shingle are not for sun-worshippers, and this is an upmarket resort targeted at arty adults rather than families. There's a lively café society at night with jazz to listen to, and there's a chance to take part in the *sardana* at 10pm on a Sunday night. In the old days the superstars of the *avant garde* – Picasso, Buñuel and their entourage – came to visit Salvador Dalí's house at nearby **Port Lligat**. Local hostelries proudly display evidence of their patronage. Agreeable as the ambience is, it comes with a hefty price tag, with trendy boutiques and expensive craft shops rubbing shoulders with snazzy but pricey pizzerias. The best options for eating are La Galiota, Narciso Montumol 9 which specialises in seafood, and Don Quijote, Caridad Serinána 6. None of the town's hotels reflect the sophisticated style of the resort. For a lively, activity-based holiday there's a Club Mediterranée complex at Port Lligat.

The sights in Cadaqués are aimed at art lovers. The **Perrott-Moore Museum**, Vigilant 1 displays a collection assembled by Dalí's former secretary, and is a taster for the Figueres museum. You can admire several early sketches by the old wizard, and read fan mail from the rich and famous. In keeping with the surreal subtext there is a vintage car with effigies of Dalí, Picasso, Buñuel, and Llorca. A small municipal **Museu d'Art** at Carrer Narcis Monturiol 15 (near La Galiota) has local paintings plus a sprinkling by big names such as Toulouse-Lautrec. The rather plain parish church has a fine baroque altarpiece by Pau Costa.

Roses to L'Estartit

From Cadaqués the scenic GE-614 bisects the Cabo de Creus peninsula and a short detour leads to **Rosas** (Roses) the largest resort on the northern Costa Brava. Although it has a fine situation, this is now an ugly over-developed resort but a new man-made beach improves the attractions of the town centre. There is another small beach beside the busy harbour, but the main swathe of fine, clean sand has been colonised by the characterless *urbanizaciones* of Salatà and Santa Margarida.

If you want a base with some local character, choose the reasonably priced hotel-restaurant Allioli, 8 kilometres from Roses on the C-260 near **Castelló d'Empúries** (H). This old inland town has a fine thirteenth-century Gothic church, **Santa María**, with a Romanesque bell-tower and ornate alabaster *retablo* carved with scenes of the Passion.

South of Roses lies the curious villa-based resort of **Ampuriabrava** (Empúria-Brava). The nearby **Aiguamolls de l'Empordá Natural Park** is a huge area of parkland run as a nature reserve. The flat wetlands support a host of flora and fauna, and good birdwatching can be had here as there are lots of hides. The road runs inland until a spur brings you to the ruins of **Empúries**, two kilometres north of the resort of **La Escala** (L'Escala). Here layers of Spain's ancient history lie one above another. The Phoenicians founded a colony on **Sant Martí d'Empúries** (then an island) in 575BC, and this became the Greek city of *Emporion* ('trading station'). The original Greek city occupies the site closest to the shore. During the third century BC the Romans under Scipio captured the port and established an important settlement, ten times the size of its Greek predecessor, which is by far the more interesting to explore today. Inland of the Greek colony on an elevated site you'll find the foundations of houses and an amphitheatre as well as stunning mosaics in black and white. A small museum has been established, although many of the original finds have been transferred to Barcelona's Archaeological Museum (see page 225), and replaced with reproductions. It is worth investing in the English-language guidebook to steer your way around the site, especially the

Greek area which, without additional information, is otherwise rather dull. The decaying walled town of Sant Martí d'Empúries is an atmospheric little place, with a couple of bars to recuperate in after exploring the ruins in the full glare of the sun. A small, clean, very Spanish *fonda* offers acceptable accommodation. Be warned that bathing off the shore here can be dangerous, especially if the weather changes suddenly. The resort of **L'Escala** is a rather exposed place at the southern end of the Gulf of Roses. There is one acceptable package-style hotel on the promenade, the Nieves-Mar, Passeig Maritim 8 (Tel 77 03 00).

The next resort is **L'Estartit**, a fairly large, yet quiet place that concentrates on the budget family-oriented self-catering market. The tiny off-shore islands, the **Islas Medes**, are a magnet for underwater enthusiasts, who come to check out the abundant marine life.

Five kilometres inland on the GE-641, **Torroella de Montgri** provides a marked contrast. It was an important port until the Middle Ages, but centuries of silting have left it stranded inland. It is rewarding to explore its rambling rows of medieval buildings, good shops, and a couple of *pastelerías* with tempting sticky cakes. The town's well-presented Natural History museum is more enjoyable if you ask for the explanatory notes in English at the door. Above the town the squat thirteenth-century fortress crowns a bare hill.

Medieval diversions

There is a cluster of memorable sights to visit a little way inland before you return to the coast. **Pals**, nine kilometres south of Torroella de Montgri on the GE-650, is a small hilltown with a restored fourteenth-century quarter which houses a number of ceramic and other craft shops. There are fine coastal views from the **Torre de les Hores** (Tower of the Hours). Its beach, five kilometres away – the Platja de Pals – has a discreet nudist section. The GE-652 and C-255 take you to **La Bisbal**, a famous ceramic centre, which retains a medieval huddle around its **Plaça Mayor**. Bargain-hunters will find opportunities to buy the traditional black or glazed green, yellow or red pottery in one of the studios in Carre 6 de Octobre. If you follow the C-255 Palamós road out of La Bisbal and turn left at **Vulpellac**, you will reach the fourteenth-century town of **Peratallada** whose ruined castle, fortified church and noble houses have an air of timeworn desolation. Some of the narrow streets, like Roman streets, are carved into the natural rock. The castle can be visited only with a guide. There are a couple of good restaurants, La Riera, Plaça les Voltes 9, and Can Nou, Den Bas 12. Four kilometres north-west at **Ullastret** you can visit the oldest known Iberian settlement – founded in the seventh century BC – with the remains of the town wall and foundations of houses clearly visible among attractive gardens.

If you retrace your steps to Pals you can follow the GE-650 to **Begur**, a little market town crowned by a seventeenth-century fortress, which was used by the military until 1810. Climb up to the castle for fine views over the coast. In narrow, dusty backstreets lurk town houses with fading frescoes, and old men in berets – like figures from Hemingway – watching the world go by. A crescent of sand sweeps the coast east of Begur, and is best enjoyed in the small coves from Sa Riera to Aiguablava, which are known for the intense blueness of their waters. The more southern resorts: Tamariu, Llafranc and Calella de Palafrugell can only be reached via the inland towns of Begur and Palafrugell.

Aiguablava to Calella de Palafrugell

The small coves, **Sa Riera**, **Aiguafreda**, **Sa Tuna**, **Fornells** and **Aiguablava** have tiny beaches, often littered with little boats. Thick pine forests spring from honey-coloured rock which soars above the inviting bays of clear, blue water. Sa Tuna is particularly attractive, its roads lined with bougainvillea. Pink and cream-coloured houses spread over the hillside like a dismembered Battenburg cake. **Aiguablava** (H) has an architecturally undistinguished though superbly situated *parador*, and a wonderfully friendly up-market hotel.

The next run of small but slightly more conventional resorts are reached via the old market town of **Palafrugell**. A twisting stretch of pine-guarded road leads to the lovely small cove beach backed by a couple of clean but basic hotels at **Tamariu** (H). A small strip of fairly fine sand cowers below the green-gilt rocky headlands, and old men play pétanque while windsurfers and excursion boats sweep into the bay. There are a few cafés and bars and a pervasive air of relaxed charm. The hotels serve reasonable food.

Llafranc to the south has a crescent-shaped bay, a marina of smart boats and a beach that gets very busy. **Calella de Palafrugell** (H) is the archetypal fishing village at its most clichéd – rough cliffs, small cove beaches, arcaded, whitewashed houses and narrow, twisting cobbled streets –

irresistible. There are no ugly multi-storey buildings, and a couple of decent package hotels overlook the bay. The best bets for eating are Rems, Pintor Serra 5 and Can Pep, Lladó 22.

Follow the signs to the **Cabo Roig Botanic Gardens** for a colourful display of flowers and plants from all over the world, and good views of the headland and Calella .

From Palamós to Sant Feliu de Guixols

Between Calella and **Palamós** there's a good beach at *La Fosca* where trees tumble right down to the golden sands between rocky promontories. Palamós is a bustling little town where fishing boats bob in and out of the bay and the long crescent of sand gets busy especially on Sunday mornings. From the harbour you can gape at the awful concrete sprawl that seems, from here, to over-run everything.

Palamós displays a splutter of whitewashed, pantiled low-rise buildings (a couple of skyscrapers stick out like sore thumbs) with the bell-tower of the fourteenth-century Gothic church of Santa María which occupies an elevated *plaça* visible above them. The wooded surrounding hillsides are intensely developed. From here the coast road runs unannounced into **San Antoni de Calonge**, a sleepy sort of place where you will not find many Britons. The watersports facilities are good. Some very professional-looking windsurfers glide over the waters, sweeping past small, masted catamarans, as queues wait to try out a pulley-system of water-skiing.

Further south is **Playa de Aro** (Platja d'Aro)(H), the second biggest resort on the coast. A wall of ugly '60s high-rise hotels and apartment blocks in washed-out hues of khaki and orange slump directly on to one end of a long stretch of clean but desolate beach. Below the skyscrapers stretches a bleak concrete walkway of beach gear shops frying in the full glare of the sun. Behind this, the main road slashes through a parade of over-priced boutiques. This is a dismal place. Our recommended hotel – the Park Hotel Sant Jorge – is two kilometres out of town overlooking a small cove beach and shares nothing with this place but a postal address.

Beyond Platja d'Aro, the pine-backed, rocky shoreline of **Sa Concha** beach offers welcome pockets of shade and spurs of rugged red rock that reach into shimmering blue waters. It is a popular but unspoilt spot to while away an afternoon. You can walk along the seawall from here to the wonderful

Hostal de la Gavina – the Costa Brava's premier hotel – in the pleasant resort of **S'Agaró** (H), the brainchild of José Ensesa who created an up-market housing development centred on the hotel and the good beach of **Sant Pol**. There is a reasonably priced family-run hotel, the Caleta Park at the southern end.

The next town **Sant Feliu de Guixols** lies almost encircled by hills and still feels like a real town with a modernist Casino. The narrow beach of golden sand is backed by canopied bars selling point-at-the-picture *platos combinados*. The broad promenade lined with plane trees is an agreeable stroll to the port area. A lively fruit and vegetable market takes place in the main square, and an excellent seafood restaurant Eldorado Petit at Rambla Vidal, 23.

A corniche road skirting the sheer cliff-tops and dropping into pine-shaded patches runs from San Feliu to Tossa de Mar.

Tossa de Mar

Tossa de Mar is undoubtedly the best of the bigger resorts. Its long curving bay shaped like an inverted question mark is skirted by a trail of gritty but popular Blue Flag beaches, bounded at each end by shafts of grey-brown rock. It gets very crowded. Beyond the promenade where a statue of Minerva incongruously shares the billing with Jonathan Livingstone Seagull, there is another beach, **Mar Menuda**. Snorkellers surface in a flash of mask and flippers, and you can rent sub-aqua gear or pedaloes. Avoid the glass-bottomed boat trips unless you have a peculiar interest in rusty drinks cans.

It is the walled twelfth-century old town, the **Vila Vella** perched defiantly on the southern headland, that is the big draw, its heavily restored medievalism a soothing antidote to Lloret's brutal architecture. In the Municipal Museum you can see mosaics excavated from the nearby Roman house, and a painting by Chagall.

Outside the walls there is a tangle of steep, whitewashed, narrow streets where bars and restaurants jostle shoulder to shoulder for your custom in a cheery strollable quarter, intimidating for cars, which houses some of the older hotels. There are a couple of outstanding places to eat Es Moli Tarull, 5 in an elevated section of the old town near the Hotel Neptuno (the most stylish of the package hotels) gives you the chance to try that old Catalan favourite *pan con tomate* –

coarse bread rubbed with tomato and garlic in an agreeable patio-style setting. In the Vila Vella try Castell Vell, Plaça Roig i Soler 2. In the evenings mock-predatory males prowl the seafront bars, searching for young female company. This is an attractive resort, but the nightlife is decidedly low-key.

Lloret de Mar (H)

Lloret de Mar is by far the biggest resort on the Costa Brava. It is ugly, noisy and vulgar.

Many of the hotels are set a long way back from the over-crowded, coarse-sanded (but clean) main beach. The busy main road scythes through the ranks of grim, ageing concrete towers like a bowl through skittles. The main artery from the front to the inland hotels is a solid screen of functional high-rise blocks, with wall-to-wall burger bars and ground-floor amusement arcades.

Even so, all is not lost. Take to the sea to escape the banality and let the water-bus take you to one of the better, quieter beaches nearby – **Santa Cristina**, **Fanals** and **Canyelles**.

Our recommended hotel, the Santa Marta is six kilometres out of town at Santa Cristina beach on the road to **Blanes** (H). This is an unglitzy, pleasantly understated resort. Despite its marina, it is not a glossy place and has lots of budget accommodation, including apartments and several campsites. We found some reasonable hotels tucked between the supermarkets and tacky souvenir shops near S'Abanell beach. The best place to eat seafood specialities is at Can Flores II, Explanada del puerto 3.

The main sight is the **Marimutra Botanical Gardens** which cover a fine hillside position with more than three thousand Mediterranean plants and flowers.

The Costa del Maresme

Beyond Blanes you enter the Costa del Maresme, and the beaches become wider, though they are often severed from the resorts they serve by a railway line, meaning that access to the sea is by dull graffitti-ridden subways. There is little of the magnificently wild, rugged scenery that makes the northern and central Costa Brava so special. The first resort **Malgrat de Mar** has *Marineland*, a small water-based theme park where you can watch performing dolphins and (sometimes) death-defying high-divers. It is a ten-minute drive from

Blanes and a much-touted excursion along the coast. The following tranche of resorts – **Santa Susanna**, **Pineda de Mar** and the fairly large, lively but awful **Calella de la Costa** have little to recommend them. **Arenys de Mar** has a fishing harbour, a clean beach, and a lace museum. It is the only resort on this Costa where you might want to spend some time.

WHERE TO STAY

AGARO (S')

Hostal de la Gavina £££
Plaza de la Rosaleda
17248 S'Agaró   *Tel (972) 32 11 00; Fax (972) 32 15 73*

The Costa Brava's plushest hotel, set amid secluded gardens in a smashing position above an attractive stretch of coastline. The interior design is as tasteful as you would expect, with a fine array of antiques. A very pleasant path runs along the seawall to Sa Concha beach. Food in the pleasant restaurants is French-influenced. Expensive.

Open: all year **Rooms**: 74 **Facilities**: swimming-pool, tennis
Credit/charge cards: Amex, Diners, Eurocard, Visa

Hotel Caleta Park £££
Playa de Sant Pol
17248 S'Agaró   *Tel (972) 32 00 12; Fax (972) 32 40 96*

A friendly but smart family-run hotel in a good position overlooking Sant Pol beach. British visitors are not numerous, but are well looked after by a helpful and efficient staff.

Open: Easter–Oct **Rooms**: 105 **Facilities**: swimming-pool
Credit/charge cards: Access, Amex, Diners, Eurocard, Visa

AIGUABLAVA

Hotel Aigua Blava £££
Playa de Fornells
17255 Aiguablava   *Tel (972) 62 20 58; Fax (972) 62 21 12*

A slightly wacky hotel with wonderfully friendly staff and a very special ambience. As well as the main hotel building, guests are accommodated in a number of comfortable annexes set in delightful landscaped gardens. Eager and attentive waiters serve constant entertainment as well as very good food. There are excellent views.

Open: 22 Mar–21 Oct **Rooms**: 90 **Facilities**: swimming-pool, tennis **Credit/charge cards**: Access, Amex, Eurocard, Visa

---

Parador de Aigua Blava   £££
Aiguablava
17255 Begur   *Tel (972) 62 21 62; Fax (972) 62 21 66*

An undistinguished modern building in a stunning, elevated cliffside position above wooded peninsula. Spacious, public rooms are decorated in contemporary style. It offers comfortable bedrooms, and top-of-the-range examples come with sunken baths and exercise equipment. Most have splendid views. Good, regional food is served in popular restaurant.

Open: all year **Rooms**: 85 **Facilities**: swimming-pool
Credit/charge cards: Amex, Diners, Eurocard, Visa

ARTIES

Parador Don Gaspar de Portolá   ££
Carratera de Baqueira
25599 Arties   *Tel (973) 64 08 01; Fax (973) 64 10 01*

A modern low-rise building in vaguely alpine ski-lodge style. Large open-plan public areas have feature fireplaces and chunky contemporary furniture. Bedrooms are rather simple yet comfortable and quietly stylish with traditional woven-style bedspreads. Splendid mountain views are a bonus.

Open: all year **Rooms**: 40 **Credit/charge cards**: Amex, Diners, Eurocard, Visa

---

BARCELONA

Astoria   £££
Carrer Paris 203
08036 Barcelona   *Tel (93) 209 83 11; Fax (93) 202 30 08*

This is in a fairly quiet and convenient position next to a cinema in the heart of the Eixample. It has an airy, neo-classical style with a white marbled and pillared reception. Dark leather armchairs and sofas add to the smooth feel of the lounge. The bedrooms are light with pine furnishings and good bathrooms with twin basins.

Open: all year **Rooms**: 114 **Credit/charge cards**: Amex, Diners, Eurocard, Visa

Colón £££
Avenida de la Catedral 7
08002 Barcelona   *Tel (93) 301 14 04; Fax (93) 317 29 15*

In the heart of the Barri Gòtic and overlooking the thirteenth-century cathedral, the hotel was built in 1951, but blends well with its venerable surroundings. The panelled reception is warm and busy; an ante-room and bar off it are relaxed and tasteful. Bedrooms are carpeted and comfortable. Ask for a terrace overlooking the cathedral.

Open: all year **Rooms**: 155 **Credit/charge cards**: Access, Amex, Diners, Eurocard, Visa

Condes de Barcelona £££
Passeig de Gràcia 75
08008 Barcelona   *Tel (93) 487 37 37; Fax (93) 216 08 35*

Your chance to stay inside a Gaudí building, the Casa Battló. Tiles and wrought-iron railings adorn the façade. Off the reception is a bizarre gallery surrounded by columns and arches ascending five floors to a large skylight. The hotel is elegant and modern, and the bedrooms attractive and inviting. The 'Condal' bedrooms are particularly spacious.

Open: all year **Rooms**: 100 **Facilities**: swimming-pool
Credit/charge cards: Amex, Diners, Eurocard, Visa

Gran Via £££
Gran Via de les Cortes Catalanes 642
08007 Barcelona   *Tel (93) 318 19 00; Fax (93) 318 99 97*

This is a small nineteenth-century palace converted into the most original and cosy hotel in the city centre, near Plaça de Catalunya. The unassuming and rather grubby exterior is deceptive. There are pillars and arches in reception and the formal drawing-room propels you back to the last century. Bedroom furniture is rather more modern, if somewhat basic, although mini-bars are standard. Bathrooms are old-fashioned. Breakfast is the only meal available.

Open: all year **Rooms**: 48 **Credit/charge cards**: Amex, Diners, Eurocard, Visa

Oriente £££
Ramblas 45–47
08002 Barcelona   *Tel (93) 302 25 58; Fax (93) 412 38 19*

An ex-Capuchin convent, the Oriente is a romantic place that has seen better days. The large lounge, with pillars like Victorian lamp-posts, is eccentric; stranger still is the octagonal restaurant above it, with dainty chandeliers and an art deco skylight. Bedrooms are light and clean with decent bathrooms. For a quieter night, ask for one not facing the Ramblas.

Open: all year **Rooms**: 141 **Credit/charge cards**: Amex, Diners, Eurocard, Visa

---

Ramada Renaissance   £££
Ramblas 111
08002 Barcelona   *Tel (93) 318 62 00; Fax (93) 301 77 76*

An extremely expensive, recently opened hotel which attracts visiting stars like Michael Jackson. Spotless throughout, the peach-coloured exterior has been refaced and is adorned with wrought-iron lamps. Inside, there is lots of marble, gleaming glass and deep comfortable armchairs. The bedrooms are attractive and a good size.

Open: all year **Rooms**: 207 **Credit/charge cards**: Amex, Diners, Eurocard, Visa

---

Ritz   £££
Gran Via de les Cortes Catalanas 668
08010 Barcelona   *Tel (93) 318 52 00; Fax (93) 318 01 48*

Barcelona's premier hotel, opened in 1919, retains all the glamour of a bygone age. A large oval drawing-room with mirrored walls, a marble floor and numerous sofas and armchairs occupies the centre of the building. The oval restaurant is dominated by elegant pillars and crystal chandeliers. The rooms are large and comfortable, although some are a bit plain.

Open: all year **Rooms**: 158 **Credit/charge cards**: Amex, Diners, Eurocard, Visa

---

Rivoli Ramblas   £££
Rambla dels Estudis 128
08002 Barcelona   *Tel (93) 302 66 43; Fax (93) 317 50 53*

A refurbished art deco building on a smart section of the Ramblas, opposite stalls of caged birds. The stylish reception has modern columns painted with classical scenes. A white marble staircase leads to a pine-floored restaurant and a bar overlooking the ground floor. Bedrooms are attractive and well-equipped. There is also a fitness centre, and a terrace to relax on.

Open: all year **Rooms**: 87 **Credit/charge cards**: Amex, Diners, Eurocard, Visa

BLANES

Park Hotel Blanes £££
Playa de Sabanell
17300 Blanes   Tel (972) 33 02 50; Fax (972) 33 71 03

A relaxed family-oriented hotel set amid a secluded garden of pines, across the busy road from the long, sandy Sabanell beach. Bedrooms are simple but comfortable.

Open: May to Oct **Rooms**: 127 **Facilities**: swimming-pool, tennis
Credit/charge cards: Amex, Diners, Eurocard, Visa

Hotel Stella Maris £
Villa de Madrid 18
17300 Blanes   Tel (972) 33 00 92; Fax (972) 33 57 03

A modest but well-kept older-style package hotel with modern extension. A small restaurant serves tasty unpretentious food.

Open: 15 Mar to Oct **Rooms**: 90 **Facilities**: swimming-pool
Credit/charge cards: Amex, Diners, Eurocard, Visa

CALELLA DE PALAFRUGELL

Hotel Sant Roc ££
Pl Atlántic 2
17210 Calella de Palafrugell   Tel (972) 30 05 00; Fax (972) 61 40 68

A traditional, family-run hotel in a good position high on Calella's cliffs. A package tour operator's regular award-winner, the owners nevertheless succeed in making their guests feel like individuals, and décor is more characterful than stylish. Bedrooms are clean with traditional Catalan-style furnishings. Food is tasty but unexceptional. Please note that there is no swimming-pool.

Open: 27 Apr to 15 Oct **Rooms**: 42 **Credit/charge cards**: Amex, Diners, Eurocard, Visa

CARDONA

Parador Nacional Duques de Cardona £££
Castillo de Cardona s/n
08261 Cardona   Tel (93) 869 12 75; Fax (93) 869 16 36

A very fine *parador* situated inside an impressive medieval castle perched on top of a bare hill, and so visible for miles inducing a real sense of anticipation. You are unlikely to be disappointed. Well-chosen furnishings are in keeping with the period spirit, though rooms are clean and comfortable. Excellent regional food is served.

Open: all year **Rooms**: 59 **Credit/charge cards**: Access, Amex, Diners, Eurocard, Visa

CASTELLO D'EMPURIES

Hotel Allioli   ££
Carretera Figueres-Rosas-urb Castellonou
17486 Castelló d'Empúries   *Tel (972) 25 03 00*

The position beside the Danone yoghurt factory is unpromising, but this old Catalan farmhouse has considerable charm. Huge hams hang over the simple, rustic bar. Bedrooms are very simple, but clean, with rough walls, woven bedspreads and television – an unexpected bonus at this price. The restaurant is at the heart of the enterprise – generous portions of sizzling tasty local specialities, including thrushes. It offers friendly, efficient service and is very good value.

Open: 15 Jan–15 Dec **Rooms**: 39 **Credit/charge cards**: Amex, Diners, Eurocard, Visa

ESPLUGA (L') DE FRANCOLI

Hostal del Senglar   ££
Pl Montserrat Canals 1
43440 L'Espulga de Francoli   Tel (977) 87 01 21; Fax (977) 87 10 12

Attractive gardens somewhat obscure this family-run hotel, though you are unlikely to miss its huge, rather lurid yellow sign. This is a good base for visiting the monastery of Poblet; indeed the bedrooms, while clean, are small and rather cell-like. The whitewashed, arcaded restaurant is sweet and serves tasty good-value food. Other public areas are rather institutional. The local cinema and library are next door.

Open: all year **Rooms**: 44 **Facilities**: swimming-pool, tennis
Credit/charge cards: Diners, Eurocard, Visa

FIGUERES

Hotel Mas Pau   £££
Carratera de Olot
17442 Figueres   *Tel (972) 54 61 54; Fax (972) 50 13 77*

An excellent restaurant in quiet location set back from the main road. The seven bedrooms located in a separate annexe are stylish – indeed rather glitzy – large and very comfortable. The rustic-style restaurant has lots of character, and is particularly famous for its prawns. In the morning a very grand continental breakfast is brought to you in your room.

259

Open: 3 Mar–7 Jan **Rooms**: 7 **Facilities**: swimming-pool
Credit/charge cards: Access, Amex, Diners, Eurocard, Visa

LILLA-MONTBLANC

Hotel Coll de Lilla   £££
Carratera N240, km29
43414 Lilla-Montblanc   Tel (977) 86 09 07

This is a very friendly hotel in a saddle in the hills near the interesting
walled town of Montblanc. It is surprisingly quiet at night despite
being on the main Tarragona-Lleida road. Bedrooms are good-
sized, very comfortable and tastefully decorated. Welcome extras
include mini-bars, television and clock/radio-alarms. Both dining-
rooms are simple but elegant, and serve decent food.

Open: all year **Rooms**: 25 **Credit/charge cards**: Amex, Diners,
Eurocard, Visa

LLORET DE MAR

Hotel Santa Marta   £££
Playa de Santa Cristina s/n
17310 Lloret de Mar   Tel (972) 36 49 04; Fax (972) 36 92 80

An excellent up-market hotel in a stunning location, with direct
access to the splendid Santa Cristina beach. Tasteful public rooms
are decorated in local style. Decent-sized comfortable bedrooms
have either coastal views, or overlook the pine forest in the extensive
and very attractive grounds. The hotel is situated three kilometres
from Lloret and is reached by a winding road off the main Blanes
highway. Seafood specialties are served in the highly regarded
restaurant, breakfast on the elegant terrace.

Open: 21 Jan–15 Dec **Rooms**: 78 **Facilities**: swimming-pool, tennis
Credit/charge cards: Access, Amex, Diners, Eurocard, Visa

PLATJA D'ARO

Park Hotel San Jorge   £££
Condado de San Jorge
17250 Platja d'Aro   Tel (972) 65 23 11; Fax (972) 65 25 76

This is a superior hotel in mock-baronial style in lovely elevated
position overlooking a cove beach some way from the resort. Public
rooms are tastefully and somewhat formally decorated in local style.
Bedrooms are a decent size, clean, comfortable and well maintained.

Open: Apr–Sept **Rooms**: 104 **Facilities**: swimming-pool, tennis
Credit/charge cards: Amex, Diners, Eurocard, Visa

SEU D'URGELL (LA)

Parador de la Seu d'Urgell   £££
Santo Domingo 6
25700 La Seu d'Urgell   *Tel (973) 35 20 00; Fax (973) 35 23 09*

An attractive modern *parador* in the heart of the Pyrenees,
incorporating the cloister of a fourteenth-century Romanesque
church. Décor is contemporary, bright and airy with bags of style.
The lovely, patio-styled high-ceilinged lounge which contains the
cloister is a triumph of sensitive modern design, with a veritable
jungle of plants. Bedrooms are boldly modern. Cuisine is Catalan.
The indoor swimming-pool is spectacular. Most emphatically one of
the most successful of the modern *paradores*, and justifiably popular.

Open: all year **Rooms**: 79 **Facilities**: swimming-pool
Credit/charge cards: Access, Amex, Diners, Eurocard, Visa

Hotel El Castell   £££
Castellciutat
25710 La Seu d'Urgell   *Tel (973) 35 07 04; Fax (973) 35 15 74*

Just off the Lleida highway in an elevated position, a luxurious,
stylish hotel in a splendid position ringed by mountains. Public
rooms are elegant and attractive. The restaurant is justifiably famous
with local specialities such as ruck-sacks of lamb, and – bliss for tea
drinkers – a wide range of leaf teas. The wine list is very impressive.
Bedrooms are a decent size and attractively furnished in opulent
style, with television and radio. You get a ritzy bathroom and lots of
thoughtful extras.

Open: 16 Feb–14 Jan **Rooms**: 40 **Facilities**: swimming-pool
Credit/charge cards: Access, Amex, Diners, Eurocard, Visa

SITGES

Hotel Romantic   ££
Sant Isidre 33
08870 Sitges   *Tel (93) 894 06 43; Fax (93) 894 81 67*

Restored nineteenth-century buildings with loads of atmosphere
about five minutes' walk from one of the resort beaches. There is no
chance of a siesta – the area is noisy by day, but quietens down after a
late dinner. There are pretty *azulejo*-style tiles and loads of knick-
knacks throughout the public rooms, and a Latin-American style
cocktail bar. Breakfast is served in the palmed-patio garden, or in a
small breakfast room. No other meals are served. Bedrooms are
rather basic with antique or old furniture, and small functional *en
suite* facilities. The mattresses are rather too thin.

Open: Apr–15 Oct **Rooms**: 60 **Credit/charge cards**: Eurocard, Visa

TAMARIU

Hotel Tamariu   ££
Passeig del Mar 3
17212 Tamariu   *Tel (972) 30 01 08*

A small, simple hotel right on the beach in one of the loveliest coves of the coast. It offers enjoyable, unpretentious food and clean, simple bedrooms.

Open: 15 May–Sept **Rooms**: 54 **Credit/charge cards**: Access, Eurocard, Visa

TARRAGONA

Hotel Imperial Tarraco   £££
Balcon de Mediterraneo
Paseo Palmeras
43003 Tarragona   *Tel (977) 23 30 40; Fax (977) 21 65 66*

A large, modern business-style hotel in an excellent position above the beach and Roman amphitheatre, which is handy for exploring both the antiquarian sights and the medieval town. The food is rather ordinary, but bedrooms are comfortable and many have splendid views.

Open: all year **Rooms**: 170 **Facilities**: swimming-pool, tennis
Credit/charge cards: Amex, Diners, Eurocard, Visa

TORTOSA

Parador Castillo de la Zuda   £££
Tortosa 43500   *Tel (977) 44 44 50; Fax (977) 44 44 58*

This is a splendid restoration of a medieval castle in a grand position high above the River Ebro. Public rooms are decorated in traditional *parador* style, with a hunting-lodge theme in the restaurant. The bar and lounge are rather gloomy. Bedrooms are a reasonable size, comfortable and decorated in local style. This *parador* is rather badly let down by its staff, many of whom are sullen and inefficient, so it is recommended with reservations, as there is no suitable alternative in this little-visited town.

Open: all year **Rooms**: 82 **Facilities**: swimming-pool
Credit/charge cards: Amex, Diners, Eurocard, Visa

VIC

Parador de Vic	**££**
08500 Vic	*Tel (93) 888 72 11; Fax (93) 888 73 11*

A wonderful setting overlooking a reservoir fourteen kilometres from the centre of Vic is an attraction of this *parador*. The modern building is a decent mime of a traditional Catalan farmhouse, with a gallery-style entrance area and stained-glass ceiling. Public rooms are rather plain. Bedrooms are comfortable with attractive carved headboards. It is worth asking for a room overlooking the water. The cooking is competent but unexceptional.

Open: all year **Rooms**: 36 **Facilities**: swimming-pool
Credit/charge cards: Access, Amex, Diners, Eurocard, Visa

VIELHA

Parador del Val d'Aran	**£££**
25530 Vielha	*Tel (973) 64 01 00; Fax (973) 64 11 00*

A skiers' *parador* located above the resort of Vielha, not far from the lengthy tunnel cut through the mountain. The modern, grey building is rather unprepossessing,but its unusual circular lounge has picture windows giving fabulous views. Public rooms are modern and the general ambience is more family-oriented than in most *paradores*. Bedrooms are comfortably furnished in an unremarkable modern style. Staff are friendly and helpful. Food is regional, and the menu often features trout.

Open: all year **Rooms**: 135 **Facilities**: swimming-pool
Credit/charge cards: Amex, Diners, Eurocard, Visa

THE GOOD RESORT GUIDE

Cadaqués, Costa Brava
Verdict: Sophisticated fun for grown-ups in a superior, arty resort.

The road to Cadaqués climbs over the pass through the almond and olive groves of the Sierra Alseda. Relative inaccessibility and a shortage of parking have allowed the town to retain a great deal of its genuine charm – steep, cobbled streets, white arcaded houses, even the occasional fishing boat. The town basks in the reflected glory of its connection with Salvador Dalí, who for many years lived at nearby Port Lligat. Mellow jazz wafts from seafront bars, and there's a lively café society at night. The tiny beaches of dark slate are

263

rather unappealing, and there's little here for children to do. Hire a car to mount expeditions to the Dalí Museum at Figueres, the ruins of Empúries, and interesting inland towns like Castelló d'Empúries.

Calella de Palafrugell, Costa Brava
Verdict: A pretty village with character in the most scenic part of the central Costa Brava.

This small resort sits between sheer, pine-studded cliffs in a gorgeous setting. The gleaming, white buildings are low-rise and traditional in style, and the narrow streets packed with smart boutiques. If the resort's small cove beaches get too crowded walk over the coastal path to the neighbouring village of Llafranc, or jump in the car to one of the lovely cove beaches further north around Aiguablava. There are lots of bars, cafés and restaurants to stroll between at night, although entertainment is low-key. There are wonderful views and quiet corners in the nearby Cabo Roig Botanic Gardens.

Tossa de Mar, Costa Brava
Verdict: Traditional sun, sea and sand resort, with a dash of flair.

Tossa de Mar is an enjoyable family-oriented base. The local beaches, though small are clean, and the carefully restored twelfth-century walled town, the *Vila Vella* gives it a distinct edge over its competitors in the interest stakes. Prices are generally reasonable. Its proximity to larger resorts makes it very popular with day-trippers. Nightlife is restrained.

Sitges, Costa Daurada
Verdict: Smart resort with an interesting old town, and pleasant beaches.

Less than an hour's drive from Barcelona, this is an attractive, bustling resort with a jumbled old town, pleasant promenade and a variety of good beaches. Most of the recent development is set back from the coast, so the integrity of the old quarter has been retained. There are three interesting museums, and some unusual shops.

Mojacar, Costa de Almeria
Verdict: Still-expanding family resort with long sand and shingle beaches, and an atmospheric old town on the hill above.

The old Moorish town of Mojacar sprawls over a rugged hill, about two kilometres above the rather utilitarian modern development that runs along the coastal strip. Visitors can alternate sunbathing sessions on the long rough sand and shingle beach, with exploring the winding narrow streets of tightly packed white houses in the old-time town. Most of the accommodation is in good-quality low-rise pueblo-style self-catering apartments, although there are a couple of high-rise hotels and a *parador*. A car is handy for visiting the more remote and wilder beaches to the south. There's little of the hectic nightlife you'll find in larger resorts.

Nerja, Costa del Sol
Verdict: More than a vestige of genuine Spanish atmosphere despite the development of recent years.

East of Málaga the Costa del Sol has escaped the worst of the architectural blight that runs rampant to the west. Nerja is the most pleasant of the eastern resorts, with a very pleasant promenade, the Balcón de Europa which runs along a cliff-top at right-angles to the sea, as well as a couple of decent-sized beaches and several nearby coves. Most of the accom-modation is in self-catering complexes, sometimes in hilly locations, and there are a number of smart privately owned British villas available for rent.

Torremolinos, Costa del Sol
Verdict: Lively, friendly and unpretentious, a good bet for a cheap family holiday.

The long beaches are clean, there are plenty of shops, low bar and restaurant prices, and the sun shines reliably. Most of the accommodation is in ugly, seafront tower-block hotels or apartments, but there's a pleasant old quarter with some good seafood restaurants behind Carihuela beach, and the chance to plan excursions to Granada, Córdoba, Gibraltar or even Seville.

VALENCIA AND MURCIA

THE coastal regions of Valencia and Murcia are together known as the Levante (the East), a name which conjures up oriental visions – bazaars, sticky sweets, opium dens and heavy perfumes. The Arabs did live here, for 500 years, and Phoenicians, Carthaginians and Romans passed through before them. Present-day Iberian Levante does not, however, live up to the expectations of its name. There is plenty of hot sunshine, gooey nougat and date palms, sweet drinks made of almonds, and mile upon mile of orange and lemon groves. But the shops by the sea sell day-glo plastic bags, straw donkeys and cheap imitations of famous perfumes – the only opium you will find. The resorts are home from home British, with no shortage of pubs and places serving fish and chips.

A land of arid plains, stony soil, scrub-strewn mountains and barren hillocks, the Levante is also one of the most agriculturally productive areas in Spain. This is largely thanks to the Moors, who designed a complex irrigation system and created a vast and fertile coastal plain around the city of Valencia which is known as the *huerta*, or garden, and is the producer of most of Spain's oranges. Artichokes, tomatoes, almonds, dates, vines and olives grow on the drier land, while La Albufera, just south of Valencia city, is one of the largest rice paddies in Europe. Levante food is lovely: the *paella* originates from Valencia and there are other, even more imaginative rice dishes, as well as a profusion of fresh oranges and dates.

Most of the 500 kilometres of coastline are flat and the beaches featureless. The **Costa Blanca** stretches from the town of Denia right down to the border with Andalucía. It is one of the Costas which is riddled with the overdevelopment and environmental problems that have given holidaying in Spain a bad name in recent years. The areas just north of Benidorm and south of Alicante are the worst, and large complexes of tiny white villas continue to spring up everywhere. Despite all this, the Northern English camaraderie in the resorts can be infectious and the opportunities for having a good time (in bars and discos, that is) are plentiful. It is more pleasant out of high season, when older holidaymakers and young families take over the resorts. Benidorm is the most popular, a jovial '60s period piece with two good beaches.

The **Costa del Azahar**, the region's other stretch of coast, sweeps round the wide bay of Valencia and is marshy, flat,

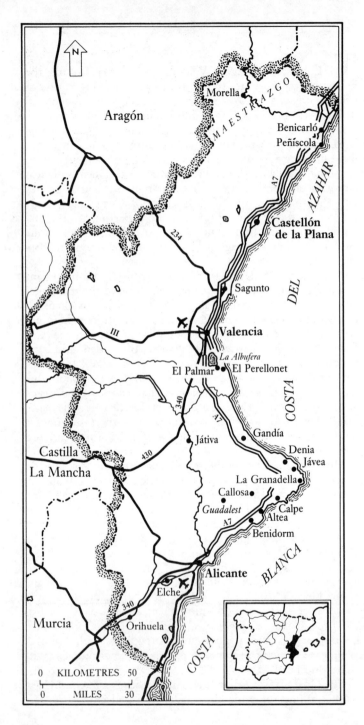

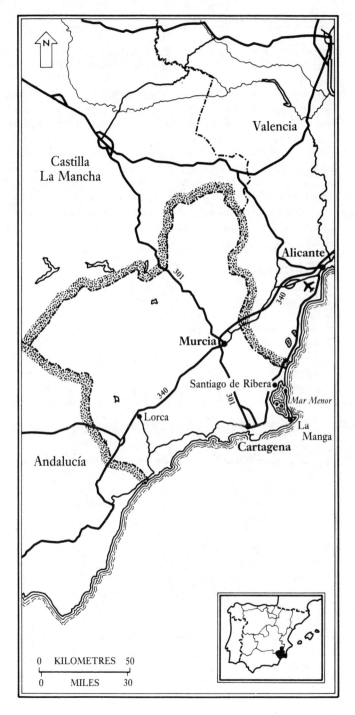

Valencia

Castilla
La Mancha

Alicante

301

340

Murcia

Santiago de Ribera

Mar Menor

340

301

Lorca

La
Manga

Cartagena

Andalucía

intensively farmed (the citrus groves for which the region is famous are here), industrialised in parts and backed by fast busy roads.

It is the peninsula which separates the Costa del Azahar from the Costa Blanca, where a series of sierras ripple down into the sea, that is the most attractive part of the coast. Here is the town of Altea, a whitewashed stack of houses on a hillside; Denia, crowned with a turreted castle, and Jávea, a bustling town and ex-pat resort, are also worth visiting. The mountains behind are neatly terraced and planted with almonds, which blossom in February.

Unfortunately the interior of the region is less appealing,

Planning your holiday

The main reason why the Costa Blanca is so popular with the British is that it offers hundreds of cheap sun-and-sea holidays. It also offers good weather all year round: hot and dry in summer, warm and sunny in winter. Lots of tour operators organise packages to this area, from self-catering in simple apartments to full-board in three- or four-star hotels. Few package hotels are in any way outstanding, though many offer good facilities and there are plenty of watersports on the beaches. There is no point in organising your own sun-and-sea holiday here. Most hotels, in any case, are block-booked by tour operators in high season.

Many cheap charter flights land at Alicante and Valencia from airports all over Britain. These two cities are useful springboards for holidays combining touring with a couple of days by the sea, and fly-drive packages are available to both. Direct scheduled flights also link Alicante and Valencia with Britain; with Iberia airlines you have the further advantage of being able to fly to one city and back from another (including those in other regions) which makes route planning even easier. From Valencia, you could drive north and spend a couple of seaside days at Peñíscola, or in the *parador* at nearby Benicarló, then on into the Maestrazgo mountains via Morella, before heading for Aragón. An equally good option is to head for La Mancha – Cuenca is about 220 kilometres away. Alicante itself makes for a short pleasant stop (or stay at San Juan, if sunbathing and swimming are your priority) and from here you could continue into southern La Mancha or Andalucía.

Public transport links between major towns are good. The rail-

and driving through it is dispiriting: lethargic villages where apartment blocks huddle around dilapidated fortresses and hem in flaky old centres, or grime-caked industrial towns. Only Morella, high up in the bleak Maestrazgo mountains close to the border with Aragón, merits a detour.

The three cities are more promising. Valencia and Murcia have good cathedrals and Alicante has a sea-front which is fun to promenade along. Good shops, *tapas* bars and restaurants can be found in all these towns. Alicante also has a strong museum of twentieth-century art, and Valencia holds Spain's National Ceramics Museum.

---

way from Barcelona runs down to Andalucía, through Valencia, Alicante and Murcia, but you can also make the journey by bus. Driving round the city of Valencia is a nightmare and some of the hairpin roads of the Sierra de Aitana are rather alarming. The main coast road (N-332) gets very congested, but the E-15/A-7 motorway which follows the coast from France to Alicante via Barcelona is underused and worth the price of a toll. South of Alicante the inland E-15/A-7 and the coastal N-332 are both fairly swift. The best map for detailed touring is the Michelin 1:400,000, *Central and Eastern Spain* sheet, 445.

The region also has good transport connections with the Balearic Islands: from Valencia by air or ferry to Mallorca and Ibiza; from Denia by ferry to Ibiza, and from Alicante by air to Mallorca and Ibiza.

Valencia is famous for its Moros y Cristianos celebrations, dramatic re-enactments of the battles between the Moors and Christians. These are held throughout the year in lots of different towns, but the best is at Alcoy (23 April). The region is also known for its *fallas*, when carnival floats and giant effigies are taken through the streets before being burned. The most elaborate is the Fallas de San José in Valencia (12–19 March) but there is also a good one in Alicante (21–24 June). The most outstanding are the Holy Week celebrations in Lorca, near the border with Andalucía, when colourful ancient personalities and gods parade through the streets.

Tourist Boards: Director General de Turismo, Isabel la Católica 85, 46004, Valencia, Tel (96) 386 77 83/5/6. Director General de Turismo, Isidoro de la Cierva 10, 30001, Murcia, Tel (968) 36 20 00. There are useful **tourist information offices** in Valencia, Benidorm, Morella, Alicante and in Murcia.

VALENCIA (H)

Valencia is the third largest city in Spain, and its centre is clenched by a nightmarish system of multi-laned, badly sign-posted roads, on which the local drivers play dodgem cars. The centre is a curious and haphazard patchwork: grandiose churches and civic buildings face large squares and back on to decayed quarters of litter-strewn cobbled streets; trendy students sit in cafés watching children and stray dogs play in the dust; and in an instant you can step from a broad sunny avenue into a shady backstreet where caged birds hang from rusty balconies.

The city is bisected by the River Turia, long-since dried up, its bed half-heartedly landscaped into a park. The old centre, and most of what you will want to see, lies on the south bank, but the Museo de Bellas Artes and the concert hall, the Palau de Música, are on the north bank. So too is the university and its nightlife.

Valencia used to be known as Valencia del Cid, for El Cid seized it from the Moors in 1094 and ruled it until his death in 1099 (see page 478). The city was finally reconquered from the Arabs in 1238 by the Aragonese and Catalans under Jaime I, who made it the capital of the kingdom of Valencia. The Moors stayed behind, however, working as farmers on the land which they had irrigated, and as craftsmen in silks and ceramics, for which the region became famous. They were expelled in the seventeenth century and Valencia declined rapidly, only regaining momentum two hundred years later. By the end of the nineteenth century it was confident enough to tear down the city walls and build exuberant commercial buildings and town houses.

Valencia is an extremely businesslike and not particularly relaxing city, but you can enjoy some good sightseeing and evening entertainment here, combined with shopping, eating and drinking.

Routes to the centre are well signposted as you drive into the city, but spotting directions south out of Valencia is a different matter. If all else fails, head out to the airport (at Manises, six kilometres to the east) and turn round – the routes are reasonably well marked from here. Parking in the central streets is almost impossible, but there are several public car parks, including underground ones dotted conveniently around.

For those using public transport, the main railway station is right in the centre and the bus station a fifteen-minute walk, or bus ride, to the north-east.

Exploring the city

The best place to start a tour of the city is **Plaza de Ayuntamiento**, a large, heavily congested triangle headed by a grand fountain, lined with flower stalls and overlooked by opulent houses and the ornate, copper-domed *ayuntamiento*. The tourist office is in this town hall. Unfortunately none of the pavement cafés is particularly pleasant here, and it is better to have a drink in the arts cinema café, the Filmoteca, at number 17.

Calle de San Vicente Mártir leads out of the square up towards Plaza de la Reina and the cathedral. Off to the west, **Plaza Redonda** is a decaying square, or rather circle, with old-fashioned market stalls selling haberdashery, clothes and bric-à-brac. To the east, Calle Abadia de San Martín takes you to the Museo Nacional de Cerámica (closed for restoration), housed in the **Palacio de Dos Aguas**, an eighteenth-century palace with a beautifully carved alabaster doorway supported by two bald, sleeping giants. Across the road, on **Plaza Patriarca**, is the Colegio and Museo del Patriarca.

Plaza de la Reina has neat flowerbeds, a pavement café, a chocolate and *churros* wagon, and quirky shops, including one selling fans, mantillas and shawls. There are also tourists, beggars, lottery ticket sellers and lots of Valencians rushing to work or waiting at bus-stops. At the north end of the square is the cathedral, its curvy, diminutive baroque façade dwarfed by the massive octagonal Miguelete tower. The best place to drink is at the foot of the *plaza*'s second tower, Santa Catalina, which is crowned with corkscrew columns. The Horchatería Santa Catalina has been serving *horchata* for two hundred years, a very sweet, thick milk-shakey drink made from almonds.

The best of the cathedral's entrances is the north Apostles' Door, whose rose window curiously incorporates a Star of David, and eroded saints stand among the delicate Gothic tracery. Every Thursday at noon an ancient ritual takes place here: eight black-dressed members of the water tribunal meet to judge disputes over the irrigation system of the region's *huertas*. Nothing has ever been written down and there is no right of appeal. The Apostles' Door is at the corner of Valencia's prettiest square, **Plaza de la Virgen**, where a couple of pavement cafés are well positioned for people-watching. Pigeons perch on the colossal limbs of a reclining ancient god surrounded by water-pouring nymphs, and frill the cornice of the pale green-washed church of Nuestra Señora de los Desamparados. This holds Valencia's most venerated statue, a painted image of Our Lady of the Abandoned, dressed in a lavishly jewelled and embroidered gown, and crowned with a sumptuous tiara and halo. The Abandoned, so the story goes, were a group of fourteenth-century pilgrims who vanished from a locked, windowless room, leaving the statue of the Virgin behind. During Holy Week the air in the church is thick with smoke and the Virgin glitters in the flickering light of hundreds of burning candles.

You can only go on a tour of the Gothic Palacio de la Generalidad, headquarters of the medieval tax collectors, if you are part of a group, or apply for permission in advance, Tel (963) 32 02 06, so you will probably have to make do with a quick look at the entrance hall, which has a gory sculpture of scenes from Dante's *Inferno*. Two magnificent *artesonado* ceilings are the most remarkable feature inside.

A short walk south in Plaza del Mercado is another relic of fifteenth-century Valencia, the **Lonja**, or silk exchange, which is now used for a coin and stamp market on weekday mornings, and for classical concerts on some Sundays. It is well worth going in, to see the main hall's delicate spiralling columns and piped-icing vault ribs. In the Salón del Consulado upstairs, there is a gorgeous fifteenth-century gilded coffered ceiling rescued from the old city hall which was destroyed by fire. Opposite the Lonja is an equally delicate market building, this time made of iron and glass, and the stalls are piled with fresh and dried fruit, nuts and pulses, quails' eggs and snails, sheets of dried cod and folds of pork fat.

The Museo de Bellas Artes is on the other bank of the river, a walk along backstreets north from the cathedral, crossing the river by the Puente de Serranos, a bridge guarded by the Torres de Serranos, a smartly turreted and double-towered gate – rare survivor of the medieval city walls.

From Plaza de Ayuntamiento it is about 15 minutes' walk (or a bus ride) to Valencia's smartest shopping area, best approached along Calle de Colón, which gets increasingly upmarket at its eastern end. The classiest shops are on the side streets of Calle de Sorní, Calle de Jorge Juan and Calle Isabel la Católica, the minimalist displays of designer clothes stylishly contrasting with the opulence of the art nouveau town houses. For more down-to-earth shopping you could head to the mall by the central bus station, north-east from the centre of town across the river. There is also a hippyish and ethnic crafts market on Plaza Alfonso el Magnánimo, just off Calle Colón.

Finally, even if you are not travelling by train, it is worth having a look at the central turn-of-the-century railway station, exuberantly decorated with ceramic oranges and foliage.

Eating out, accommodation and entertainment

Places for eating and drinking are plentiful throughout the city, but those in the big central squares are to be avoided. To the north-west of the centre the area around Plaza del Carmen is good for cheap eats. To the south-east, just off Plaza Cánovas del Castillo, along Calle Conde de Altea, there is a variety of reasonably priced places to eat, ranging from the traditional Spanish El Plat, through Japanese and Chinese restaurants, to the Pizzería Stromboli.

If you can afford it, try Ma Cuina, Gran Via Germanías 49, where the food is sophisticated and extremely expensive, but unforgettable. A more modestly priced, but creative restaurant is the stylish La Sota, Calle Cabelleros 10, off Plaza de la Virgen.

One of the best bars in the centre is the Cerveceria de Madrid in Calle Abadia de San Martín, an affable bohemian place. They specialise in Agua de Valencia, a cocktail of vodka, champagne and orange juice served in jugs and drunk from champagne glasses.

The liveliest area for nightlife is around the university along Paseo Blasco de Ibañez. If this is not to your taste, check out concerts at the Palau de la Música (posters around the city advertise them and a list of events is obtainable from the tourist office) which looks like a state-of-the-art conservatory, but has gorgeous acoustics.

Two or three of Valencia's hotels are in beautiful turn-of-the-century buildings, but the majority of the city's hotels are either impersonal modern business hotels or cheap *hostales* which tend to be basic.

The main sights

● **Cathedral** Light streams through translucent alabaster panes in the delicate tracery of the octagonal lantern tower, gently illuminating the newly exposed brickwork of the

Gothic vaults. They were recently stripped of their neo-classical plaster, but unfortunately money ran out before the side chapels could be renovated, so at present the cathedral looks rather odd. The high altar is fascinating, for it was painted by the Renaissance artists Fernando de Llanos and Yáñez de la Almedina who trained in Italy, and in this work introduced the style of Leonardo da Vinci to Spain. Leonardo's influence is particularly clear in the *Resurrection* and *Adoration* panels. Round the back of the altar is a rather less appealing sight, the flat, wizened, brown arm of San Vicente Mártir, with rings on his long, shrivelled fingers.

Valencia cathedral is best known for housing the so-called Holy Grail, a small chalice of delicately veined agate and gold, from which Christ allegedly drank at the Last Supper. The cup was brought to Spain during the fourth century and was kept in the monastery of San Juan de la Peña in Aragón (see page 196). It later became the property of the Crown of Aragón, which presented it to the cathedral in the fifteenth century and it now stands in the Chapel of the Holy Grail, an austere Gothic room smelling of incense and lit by rays of sunlight stabbing through the windows. To see the chalice, and the museum, you need to buy a ticket in the souvenir shop which sells replicas of the chalice. The ticket also enables you to see a gory painting by Goya showing San Francisco Borja performing an exorcism. If you have plenty of energy, you can climb the Miguelete tower, for great views of the city and its surroundings.

● **Colegio de Patriarca** (The Patriarch Collegiate Church) The church of this sixteenth-century seminary is particularly worth a visit on Fridays at around 10am. The interior, with its blue, yellow and white tiled frieze and vividly frescoed walls is attractive enough, but the main reason to come is to experience the service. The microphone catches the wheezing of the priest, an acolyte swings an incense censer, and at the climax the painting by Ribalta of the *Last Supper* on the altar suddenly descends, to reveal a purple curtain. This is then swept back to show a statue of a crucified Christ on a gold background.

The Colegio also has a small, but good museum approached through an Italianate Renaissance cloister. The collection of fifteenth- to seventeenth-century paintings includes a wonderfully expressive and gentle *Adoration of the Kings* by the Valencian Renaissance artist Juan de Juanes and a strangely elongated *Adoration of the Shepherds* by El Greco.

● **Museo de Bellas Artes** The strongest sections of this fine arts gallery are the Valencian Gothic and Renaissance displays. The former, vividly painted on carved and gilded wood, includes panels from a *Virgin de la Leche* (Virgin of the Milk) by Juan de Sivera, with Christ being breastfed on a donkey, and a fantastically expressive *Scenes of the Passion* by Reixach, which shows the different moods of Christ in the days before his crucifixion – crying while he is whipped, but dignified on the cross. The Italian-trained Renaissance artist Fernando de Llanos is represented by a feminine *St Michael*, but the most memorable Renaissance work is a chilling triptych *Los Improperios* (the Mocking of Christ), by Hieronymus Bosch. Other works by famous artists include a sharply shadowed *St Sebastian* by José Ribera, a softly lit *St Augustin Washing the Feet of Christ* by Murillo, and a couple of portraits by Goya – a tenderly painted one of Joaquina Candado, his housekeeper, and a refined study of Bayeu, Goya's old teacher and brother-in-law.

● **Museo Nacional de Cerámica** (National Ceramics Museum) Around five thousand ceramics, dating from Iberian times to the twentieth century are displayed here. The museum was closed for restoration at the time of going to press, but should be well worth a visit when it reopens.

MORELLA (H)

Morella is the one town in Valencia which is worth going out of your way to visit, and is located in the heart of the Maestrazgo mountain range. It is fortified and medieval, wrapped around a sharp pinnacle of rock. The drive away from the coast along the N–232 is magnificent though time-consuming, climbing through olive and almond groves into wild mountains where smooth, naked crests emerge from slopes furred with broom and heather. Suddenly Morella comes into view, looking from a distance as unreal as a stylised town in a medieval painting. The illusion intensifies, as for a long time you appear to get no closer. On arrival, the road curls round the town past golden limestone walls and houses painted white, peach and buttermilk.

It is advisable to park outside the town gates then walk along the narrow arcaded streets up to the Basilica of Santa María la Mayor and the castle. The church is fourteenth-century Gothic, and its best external feature is a portal carved with apostles whose moods, ranging from amusement to disapproval, are conveyed as much by the disposition of their bodies as by their faces. Inside, there is a unique raised choir, reached by a staircase winding round one of the aisle columns and sculpted with biblical figures.

A short walk uphill from the church brings you to the Monastery of San Francisco, which gives access to the castle. In the late thirteenth century the local people asked the Franciscan order to establish a friary amongst them. The town undertook to build the monastery and provide money to buy food, wine and clothing, in return for the monks' preaching and listening to confessions. At first things went well, but by the fifteenth century the monks had become misbehaving drunkards and the angry locals asked the Franciscan authorities to replace them with a more sober crowd. The church is currently undergoing restoration, but you can visit the delicate Gothic cloisters, and then follow a steeply spiralling path around the rampart walls to the castle. This is in ruins, but there are beautiful views of Morella's rooftops and the surrounding countryside.

Morella is a lovely place to wander, with some good shops, bars and restaurants along the main street, and lots of little alleyways to explore. Life still happens on the streets, and even in winter you see women knitting under the dark arcades, and men chatting and smoking on street corners. If you want to stay overnight, there are a couple of good hotels.

THE COSTA DEL AZAHAR

Costa del Azahar means 'coast of orange blossom' but the reality is far from romantic. The orange groves for which Valencia is famous stretch for miles and miles along a dull, flat coastal plain and the beaches are just long ribbons of sand, interrupted by the large towns of Castellón and Valencia.

There is an extremely pleasant *parador* with a good restaurant at **Benicarló** (H), but the resort itself is dreary, with an industrial estate and red-brick apartments rearing up from fields of artichokes and orange groves. **Peñíscola**, a couple of kilometres south, is considerably better, with a picturesque old town built on a rugged crag and capped by a castle, above a small fishing port. The old town is lovely, particularly at night when the castle is floodlit, but in high season the tortuous, narrow streets are packed, and elbowing your way past souvenir stands is not very enjoyable. The beach is fairly long, but shadeless and backed by a busy road. Peñíscola cannot be recommended for a long stay, but it is a pleasant enough stop-over in low season, especially if you stay in one of the few hotels in the old town. Try the Hostal del Duc, Tel (964) 48 07 68, housed in a seventeenth-century mansion on Calle Fuladosa, which is open from April to September. If it is closed, the simple Hostal Vell, Tel (964) 48 92 28, on Calle San Roque is open throughout the year.

The castle founded by the Knights Templar in the fourteenth century has been heavily restored. The last of the breakaway Avignon Anti-Popes, Papa Luna, lived here for six years after he had been removed from his office.

To escape the crowded streets, walk down to the fishing port, where at 5pm the daily auction is held. Squid on trays squirm in their own black ink, and fish are loaded into vans headed for the region's restaurants.

When travelling towards Valencia, it is better to use the motorway as it is far less congested than the main coastal road. South beyond Castellón de la Plana, a very industrialised provincial capital, are the **Grutas de San José**, a network of caves bored by an underground river. They are explored by boat. Their weirdly eroded rocks and strange concretions are gorgeously illuminated, but the caves are heavily commercialised, with tacky souvenir shops, restaurants and cafés. If there has been a heavy rainfall the caves are likely to be closed due to flooding, so it is wise to phone ahead and check, Tel (964) 66 32 98.

A few kilometres further south, **Sagunto** is a drab market town bisected by the N-340. It was once a port allied to Rome, and in 218BC was attacked by Hannibal the Carthaginian. Abandoned by Rome and with no chance of holding off the invaders, the inhabitants decided to commit mass suicide rather than surrender. They built an immense fire, then the women, children, sick and elderly threw themselves into it, while the men went on an equally suicidal mission against the Carthaginians.

Sagunto's history is more memorable than what remains of the old settlement. The harbour has silted over and Sagunto now lies inland, looking out to a distant steel-works. A maze of houses climbs the hill above the high street to the scant remains of a Roman theatre below a ramshackle fortress. Iberians, Phoenicians, Romans, Carthaginians, Visigoths, Arabs and Spaniards all occupied the hilltop, and today wild flowers and weeds choke a confusing palimpsest of ruins.

South of Valencia

Not far south of Valencia, the lagoon of La Albufera is famous for its eels, wild duck shoots and sunsets. On the edge of its reedy waters is **El Palmar**, a village of flimsy '60s houses and of whitewashed cottages with steeply pitched roofs thatched with reeds or rice straw. Shrouded in early morning mist it is a grim place, but it is fairly pleasant in the evenings, when people come to eat paella or *all i pebre*, eels fried with garlic and peppers. You could easily go there for the evening from Valencia.

Continuing along the coast road from El Palmar, **El Pere-llonet** is a modern fishing village where mid-morning you can watch the fishermen disentangling eels from their nets. Further south is Cullera, with a charmless highrise resort and busy plain town between its lighthouse and very ruined castle.

Gandía is worth a brief stop; it is a bustling, but ordinary, town which was the seat of a Duchy given to the Borgias by Ferdinand the Catholic in 1485. Their name (Borja in Spanish) rose to fame in 1492 when the Duke Rodrigo, Arch-bishop of Valencia and father of Cesare and Lucrezia, became, through bribery, Pope Alexander VI. Notoriously lascivious, ambitious and corrupt, he continued to extend his family while acting as God's representative, and became one of the most despised Popes in history. Gandía prefers to remember a more reputable member of the family, Francisco (1510–1572). Born in the Borgia Palace, he became a Jesuit on the death of his wife, and was responsible for sending missionaries to Spain's American colonies. He was canonised in 1671. The palace stands in the heart of the old town and is now a Jesuit college, and clerics take you on a guided tour. You see the alcove where Francisco was born, with a tapestry depicting the birth on the wall, and are led through grand rooms decorated with gilded eagles, coffered ceilings and glazed tile floors.

Inland, some 40 kilometres from Gandía is the old town of **Játiva**. It lies among fields of lettuces and onions surrounded by hills, and retains a small core of simple whitewashed houses full of the sounds of kitchen clatters and chirping birds. It is only mildly interesting as the birthplace of Pope Alexander VI (the corrupt Rodrigo Borgia), and of the artist José Ribera. There are a couple of works by the latter in its museum.

THE COSTA BLANCA

Between Denia and Altea the coast is hilly and fairly attractive, with craggy capes jutting into the sea, but apart from the charismatic town of Alicante, the rest of the Costa Blanca is monotonous and crowded with mostly ugly resorts.

A small port crowned by a castle, **Denia** is flanked by self-catering developments. Those to the west are sandwiched between the coast road and a shingle beach, and hemmed in by restaurants catering for the Dutch, French, German and English holidaymakers. Those to the west are more attractive; villas are scattered on a pine-covered hill above a rocky shore.

Denia itself has neat rows of cottages behind the harbour or rising on the hill between the castle and the old town walls. There are pleasant bars and restaurants overlooking the harbour, but the one sandy beach is unpleasantly close to the main road. Pines, date palms and flowers grow within the burnt-gold thirteenth-century castle walls which are patrolled by scores of cats. The museum here has an eclectic collection ranging from an Egyptian candelabrum to a third-century BC perfume vial in the shape of the god Mercury.

The next resort, **Jávea** (H), lies in a dip below the pine-covered San Antonio headland, its lively core surrounded by villa-sprinkled slopes. There is a good beach of golden sand overlooked by the exotic garden of a *parador* and cafés where retired British expatriates chat over a drink.

The indented coast immediately south of Jávea shelters a number of small white shingle beaches, and the clifftops and hinterland are scattered with villa developments. As the beaches are skimpy and pebbly you should book a villa with a pool, or hire a car. At **La Granadella** the villas are well-spaced on slopes covered with pines, broom and lavender which rise above a tiny white pebble beach, a row of fishermen's cottages and two café-restaurants. Most of the other villa-complexes, particularly around Moraira, are unpleasantly cramped, but there is a small comfortable family hotel just below Costa Nova, about seven kilometres from Jávea.

Calpe to Benidorm

Calpe is dominated by the scrunched sillhouette of the Peñón de Ifach, a volcanic rock linked to the mainland by a cause-

281

way. It could have been a remarkably lovely resort, but unfortunately development has been unrestrained and unplanned. The causeway leading to the Peñón is untidily studded with high-rise blocks, the hillsides are packed with look-alike villas and the beaches on either side of the Peñón get very busy and noisy. There is an odd mix of people in Calpe – middle-aged Germans singing hearty drinking songs at lunchtime, retired British couples walking their dogs, and parties of youngsters on a day-trip from Benidorm subjecting everyone on the beach to a loud tape of pop songs. The best part of the resort is down by the harbour, where there are fish restaurants and cafés.

The village of **Altea**, to the south, is piled on a hill below an immense blue-domed basilica. Streets cobbled with pebbles climb steeply between houses cascading with flowers, many of which hold small restaurants and cafés. Altea gets packed with coach parties in season, but it is still worth a visit. There is an artificial beach, backed by the road and overlooked by dull apartments.

Almost as soon as you leave Altea, **Benidorm** looms up like a mini-Manhattan. This is the land of kitsch and Yorkshire pudding, where souvenir shops sell teddy-bear charms, middle-aged couples wear matching track suits, and where you can drink Tizer, eat roast beef sandwiches and watch Sky TV in a bar plastered with posters of the Beatles and John Bull. Depending on taste, you either love or hate it, but it does well what it sets out to do and the atmosphere is extremely friendly.

The amount of high-rise architecture makes Benidorm look more like a city than a resort. However, the avenues between the blocks are broad and lined with palm trees, and effervesce with holiday fun. What is more, some buildings are so bizarre that you grow to love them: the tower with hemispherical windows which could be a relic from a '60s sci-fi film, and the church with a crucifix-bearing office block for a steeple. There is also a tiny old quarter, the survivor from the erstwhile small fishing and smuggling port, now packed with cheery 'British' bars.

The main beach is Playa de Levante, a broad and gently shelving sweep of soft yellow sand, backed by hotels. The second beach, Playa de Poniente, is narrower, backed by a palm-lined promenade, and is less built up as hills rise up behind it.

Though the British dominate the resort, it is also popular with Germans, Scandinavians and the Dutch, so when you have had enough of Sunday dinners and sausages, beans and mash, you can try herrings on toast, *Bockwurst* and *frikadella*.

Benidorm has a long season – many pensioners spend the whole of the winter there – but is probably best avoided in high summer, when its infectious camaraderie is destroyed by the pitiful antics of drunken louts.

Excursions from Benidorm

The mountains inland from Benidorm are well worth exploring, though the sights themselves are mostly manufactured. There are two safari parks (at Aitana and Vergel), an almond nougat factory in the brutally ugly town of Jijona, and several absurd (and absurdly expensive) museums at Guadalest (see below). There are also some pretty waterfalls at Algar, and a couple of caves: the Cuevas de Calaveras are disappointing, those at Canalobre slightly better.

The real attraction, however, is the landscape, and if you want to enjoy it without being marched around the 'sights' on an organised excursion, you will need to hire a car, and have a steely-nerved driver. The road from Benidorm to the dull town of Callosa is quite tame, with villa developments and restaurants standing among almond and citrus groves below bare speckled hills. From here a mountain road east leads up to **Guadalest**, a prettified medieval village topped by the scant remains of a castle and ingeniously clamped to a spur of rock. Here you can visit an Ethnographical Museum with a collection of reproduction rustic furniture, or one of the two fiercely competitive museums of silly miniatures, such as one of a carved couple making love on the back of a beetle. There are also lots of places to eat egg and chips, and shops selling ceramics, lace, Toledo metalwork, leather goods, bags of nuts and slabs of *turrón* – a gooey almond nougat.

Returning to Callosa, the C-3318 north leads into a landscape where corrugated grey-gold crags top neatly terraced slopes planted with olives, almonds, citrus trees and chestnuts. Beyond the village of Tárbena the landscape is increasingly wild, with cracked and crumbled boulders protruding from carpets of gorse. Then the road teeters along the brink of a punch-bowl-shaped valley to the village of Parcent. The Planet restaurant here is a friendly, Dutch-run place, where you can have full meals or snacks of warm crusty *boccadillos* and chips.

ALICANTE (H)

It comes as a surprise to those who think of Alicante as a cheap charter flight destination for Costa holidays to discover a relaxed and civilised seaside town. With its sweeping promenade, pedestrianised shopping streets and pavement cafés, it is a perfect place for aimless strolling and lingering over drinks while watching life pass by. There is not much in the way of sightseeing, and the town beach is not particularly attractive, so there is no need to spend more than a couple of days here, but it makes a good start or finish to a holiday.

The Romans called Alicante City of Light, the reason for which is obvious as soon as you step out of the airport. Alicante skies are pellucid, the sunsets translucent, and everything looks astonishingly crisp.

A rugged sandstone crag, out of which grows a castle, rears above Alicante's tower-blocks, while the masts of yachts and struts of cranes spike views out to sea. The most striking part of Alicante is its water-front, the Explanada de España, where pizzerias, cafés and ice-cream parlours edge a palm-shaded esplanade eye-catchingly tiled with wave patterns of dusky pink, cream and charcoal grey. Hippies sell costume jewellery, Indian scarves, and copies of famous perfumes; Africans (Alicante has a large Algerian community) sell fake Gucci watches; old men and women sit reading with dogs tied to their chair-legs; children on roller-skates race a slalom course marked by Coke cans; and chirpy teenagers beg in perfect English. Fortune-tellers, puppeteers and portrait artists tout for trade, and in the pavement cafés scantily clad tourists sit alongside locals dressed in tweeds and bow-tied blouses.

Leading away from the sea-front are pedestrianised shopping streets; one, Calle Castaños, is packed with fashionable shoe shops. Running parallel with the esplanade is Calle Mayor, a narrow and pretty street with some good places for snacks. At the end of it, the weather-stained sandstone front of the *ayuntamiento* heralds a rather different Alicante. The area around the blank-façaded cathedral is rather down-at-heel; flimsy apartments and houses with rusty iron balconies stand among the rubble of demolished buildings. Above the town hall, climbing the hill below the castle, is the old Santa Cruz quarter, a patchwork of decaying houses holding punkish bars and newly whitewashed cottages with geraniums growing in cans painted red, blue and green. Electricity cables are draped along house fronts and slung across the narrow streets, peeling façades are scrawled with Spanish and Arabic graffiti, and the only sounds come from caged birds and radios. This area should be avoided at night.

Alicante's beach, the Playa del Postiguet, is crowded in season and fairly dirty, but there is a lovely long sandy beach, backed by a palm-planted promenade, at **San Juan**, six kilometres to the north, accessible by bus C1 or C2 from Plaza del Mar. There are ferries, frequent in season, from Alicante to the little off-shore island of Tabarca, which also has good beaches.

Alicante's airport, twelve kilometres inland, is linked to the city by bus. There are good public transport connections with the rest of Spain as well as around the region, and the train and coach stations are conveniently near the centre of town.

Eating out and accommodation

The Peret pavement café, on the corner of Plaza Puerta del Mar, is the best place to sit and watch people, and also serves a good lemon *granizado* (iced juice). Youngsters will be relieved to see branches of McDonalds and Burger King with pretty terraces, and the Boutique de Jamón has a reasonable range of cold meat- and cheese-based *tapas* and snacks. You have to order at the bar, but can eat at tables outside. (There is a larger branch on Calle Arzobispo Loaces 15, near the bus station, which serves everything from stuffed aubergines and salads to caviare and kebabs.)

On Calle Villegas Nou Manolín is one of Alicante's most seductive restaurants. It has an upmarket *tapas* bar whose glistening spread of snacks attracts well-heeled locals, and the restaurant above offers superb and varied rice dishes, cooked to order and served straight from a sizzling iron pan.

On Calle Mayor the Bremen is a delicatessen-cum-café, and the Hamburguesería Gracia has a surprisingly varied range of *tapas* as well as burgers. It is also a good place for sticky hot chocolate and *churros*. In the same street is a wonderful bar, Los Garrafos, inside which beams are hung with oil lamps, drinking horns and bottles, and walls are covered with photographs of bull-fighters (including the legendary Manolete). Just off Calle Mayor is the Rincón Gallego, a small neighbourly restaurant specialising in Gali-cian seafood and pies (*empanadas*).

There are some restaurants on the square behind the *ayun-tamiento* and a couple of earthier places in the streets nearby –

try Bruno's on Calle Miguel Soler, which serves cheap pasta, pizzas and couscous.

A few large, anonymous-looking hotels are on the town's sea-front while lots of small and often basic *hostales* can be found in the quarter around the cathedral.

The main sights

● **Museo de Arte Siglo 20** (Museum of Twentieth-Century Art) Perhaps the last thing you would expect in Alicante would be a collection of twentieth-century works of art which includes works by Miró, Tapies, Chagall, Dalí and Francis Bacon. But they are all represented here, along with less well-known names. The ground floor holds mostly sculpture, notably *Kiki de Montparnasse*, by Pablo Gargallo, and some cutaway woodchip cubes by Eduardo Chillida. There is also a Miró, whose slightly warped canvas, and raw splashes and blobs will come as a welcome change if you have only seen silky smooth reproductions. Tapies is represented by a small work, *Pintura*, on which brushstrokes are superbly energetic.

If you have children with you, take them up to the op art section on the first floor, where they can dazzle themselves dizzy with mobiles and mirrors, and watch their reflections fragmented by a confection of shiny cubes by Victor Vaserely.

On the top floor you will find all the famous names, mostly serigraphs and lithographs. One of the best is Saura's *Cocktail Party*, a colourful abstract chaos brilliantly suggesting eyes, breasts, glitz and glamour. Also worth a long look are Francis Bacon's disturbingly distorted *Boxer*, drawings by Picasso and Giacometti, and a print of a bunch of flowers by Chagall.

● **Castillo de Santa Bárbara** The rugged crag which dominates Alicante is scattered with the austere remnants of a castle. It was probably founded by the Carthaginians, but most of what you see today dates from the sixteenth century. You can drive up, or get there by lift from the beach-side at Playa del Postiguet. The ruins are rather dull, but there are extensive views over the city and down the coast, and a collection of the prize-winning (and tasteless) effigies from the Hogueras de San Juan, Alicante's *fallas* festival.

The coast south of Alicante

Driving down the coast road south of Alicante and into Murcia is very dispiriting and it is not worth stopping until the **Mar Menor**, an inland sea formed by a long sand bar, which is extremely popular with sailors and watersports enthusiasts. **Santiago de Ribera** has smart fish restaurants and cafés along its palm-lined promenade, and a large marina. The beach is of greyish sand. There is a military airport nearby, and a prestigious air force pilot-training school in town, so men with regulation haircuts mingle with the yachting set.

La Manga Club is an upmarket resort development which lies inland among low arid hills at the foot of the Mar Menor. There are restaurants, a hotel, villas with pools, two golf courses, tennis courts, and facilities for watersports, fishing trips and horse riding. It hosts major sporting events ranging from the Spanish round of the Davis Cup to the Henry Cooper Classic (which attracts amateur golfers such as Jasper Carrott and Rachel Heyhoe-Flint). La Manga itself is an unendearing high-rise resort built along the sand bar.

In the far south of the Costa Blanca is the port and naval base of **Cartagena**. Although Cartagena is ancient – it gets its name from the Carthaginians who founded it in 223BC – there is little of historic interest, as the town was badly damaged in the Civil War. Today it is a town of broad avenues lined with tower-blocks and narrow streets of houses with rusty balconies, faded blinds and grimy windows. The naval presence is unmissable, with barracks all over town guarded by cadets who whistle at passing girls.

The most striking part of Cartagena is the splendid shell-shaped bay, where grey warships lie at anchor overlooked by hills crowned with military antennae. The submarine was invented by a Cartagenan lieutenant, Isaac Peral, in 1888, and the first model is displayed on the sea-front. Just behind the turn-of-the-century town hall on the water-front, there are some nice pavement cafés on Plaza del Rey, notably El Pico which has tasty *tapas* and four kinds of *tortilla*.

Elche (H)

If you fly to Alicante and do not feel up to driving in the city, you could spend your first night in the small town of Elche. It is a straightforward twenty-minute drive from the airport, and though the town itself is uninteresting, it lies on the edge of Europe's largest palm grove. Keep your eyes sharp for signs to the Huerta del Cura, which take you through a labyrinth of dusty backstreets to a vivid oasis where bunches of almost translucent amber-coloured dates drip from majestic palms. These form a canopy over the grounds of the secluded Huerta del Cura Hotel and the exotic flora of the Huerta del Cura Park next door, which has as its centrepiece the Imperial Palm, 150 years old and branched like a candelabrum.

The palms were introduced by the Phoenicians, and are the only ones on mainland Europe to produce dates. Shops outside the park sell dates on palm branches or by the sticky kilo, along with piles of just-collapsed figs and raisins, and the hotel specialises in puddings made with dates. Elche also provides Spain with blanched palm fronds for Palm Sunday celebrations.

South from Elche to Murcia

South of Elche olives, almonds, citrus trees and fields of artichokes grow in stony soil which ranges in colour from cumin to fawn. Hillsides are speckled with scrub, the riverbeds are usually dry, and the houses often seem little more than hovels.

Orihuela is not a bad place to stop for a drink, though there is no access to the palm grove on its fringes and it is difficult to believe that the now-decaying town was, until the fourteenth century, the capital of Visigothic and Moorish Murcia.

Much of Orihuela was destroyed by an earthquake in 1829, but a couple of memorable buildings survive. Just off the main road from Elche, the solemn sandstone Colegio de Santo Domingo housed a university from the sixteenth to the eighteenth centuries, but is now a school. Children's voices mingle with birdsong and school-dinner smells waft from the kitchens. You are allowed to visit the two cloisters, one studded with brilliantly expressive stone faces, the other more sombre. You might also be able to enter the colourfully frescoed church and tiled refectory.

In the town centre the cloisters of the cathedral open directly on to the street, and have pretty portals surrounded by keyhole scallops and eroded saints. The interior has unusual spiral columns and vault-ribs. A painting by Velázquez, *The Temptation of St Thomas Aquinas*, hangs in the tiny museum.

MURCIA (H)

Ringed by red-brick apartments, and backed by bare hills, Murcia is hardly the most enticing of capitals. But it retains an elegant, if small, old centre, and the River Segura, which cuts the town in half, is edged by a park. The town makes for a very pleasant overnight stop.

Head straight to Plaza Santo Domingo, which has a couple of pavement cafés, including a Burger King housed in a palace with two hairy club-wielding ruffians carved on its façade. From here the pedestrianised Calle Trapería, leading down to the cathedral, is lively in the evenings, full of gipsies, beggars, buskers and smartly dressed Murcians. There are pavement cafés, and florid buildings, notably the late-nineteenth-century casino, whose façade sprouts shaggy lions' heads, scrolls, rosettes, flowers and caryatids. This was never a gambling den, but a smart club where the local bigwigs would meet and is now used for art exhibitions and classical concerts. You can usually get inside to see an entrance hall decorated like a Moorish temple, with plasterwork forming an intricate lattice over red, blue and gold walls; an elegant neo-classical gallery adorned with grey and white marble and Grecian-style statues, and a glittery stuccoed hall lit by a dazzling chandelier. Women should also make sure they visit the sumptuous toilets, with garish angels frescoed on its ceiling.

The **cathedral** rears up at the end of the street, a magnificent building with an elaborate four-tiered tower rising above a theatrical baroque façade. The interior is mostly Gothic and rather plain, but there are a couple of elaborate chapels – notably the Capilla de los Velez, an exotic Moorish-Gothic confection with complicated star-vaulting.

The tower is fun to climb (tickets are for sale in the museum), up an increasingly steep spiral ramp lit at intervals by sunlight darting through the windows. The museum displays painted wood statues by the eighteenth-century Murcian sculptor Francisco Salzillo: unashamedly melodramatic works, designed to tug at the heart-strings of the simple peasant. There an upside-down saint being flayed; St Michael killing a dragon, weighing souls and sending the devil into the fanged mouth of hell; and a wrinkled and intensely penitent St Jerónimo. Salzillo created around 1,800 works, some of which are still paraded through the streets on Good Friday. If you want to see more of Salzillo, there is a whole museum devoted to his works, the **Museo de Salzillo** on Calle Antonio García Alix, to the west of the city.

The nicest place to eat in Murcia is the Rincón de Pepe on Plaza Apóstoles, near the cathedral. It has an upmarket *tapas* bar, and the restaurant serves good rice dishes, traditional ragouts, and unusual salads.

The road to Andalucía

South of Murcia oranges, almonds, tomatoes, vines and olives grow on an irrigated plain barricaded from the coast by the long ridges of the Sierras de Carraces and Almenara. At first sight the town of **Lorca**, with its grubby apartments and neglected buildings, appears no different from any other Murcian town, but huddled on the hillside behind the ugly streets is an old quarter of sandstone houses with gnawed coats of arms, chewed mouldings and white *solanas*. It is a good place to wander for an hour or so, but there is a shortage of good cafés and restaurants.

You enter the town along Calle López Gisbert, where the tourist office is housed in a seventeenth-century palace (Casa de los Guevara) decorated with twisted columns and baby angel musicians. It has free maps and leaflets about the town. The side streets to the east lead up to Calle Corredera, the pedestrianised artery of the old town, with ground-floor modern shops looking incongruous under elaborate house fronts. From here streets climb up to Plaza de España, dominated by the refined façade of the Iglesia Colegial San Patricio, which, despite its multitude of cherubs, bishops, pilasters, columns, pediments, shells and scrolls, looks remarkably uncluttered. The square itself is lit by wrought-iron lamps, but looks at its best in Holy Week, when medieval-style tents are erected for a craft market. This is the time when the locals dress up as Marc Antony, Julius Caesar, Cleopatra, Nero, Solomon and the Queen of Sheba, and act out the triumph of Christianity over paganism. Those masked and gowned in purple represent the penitent, and religious statues draped in opulent embroideries are drawn on carriages. The effect is gorgeously operatic, and the whole event is thrilling.

WHERE TO STAY

ALICANTE

Hotel Cristal £££
López Torregrosa 11
03002 Alicante *Tel (965) 14 36 59*

Behind a dated façade of aluminium, glass and green paint is a dazzlingly refurbished hotel. Contemporary works of art are displayed in the reception area and the rooms are decorated in shades of mint and pistachio, with cream marble bathrooms. All rooms have TV and hair-dryers. There is also a pretty restaurant.

Open: all year **Rooms**: 53 **Credit/charge cards**: Amex, Diners, Eurocard, Visa

---

Pension Les Monges £
Calle Monjas 2
03002 Alicante *Tel (965) 21 50 46*

An eccentric hotel run by an exuberantly friendly family, just behind the *ayuntamiento* which rambles over a storey of a 1917 house. The walls of its corridors and TV-room are decorated with everything from a nineteenth-century tapestry to (so the owner claims) an original Dalí. Every room is different, some modern and some antique in feel, and one even has gold taps. Guests are allowed to use the family fridge.

Open: all year **Rooms**: 6 **Credit/charge cards**: none

Hostal Rialto £
Castaños 30
03001 Alicante *Tel (965) 20 64 33*

This has rooms with white walls and teak-effect formica bedheads and furniture, and is sited on a pleasant pedestrianised shopping street about five minutes' walk from the sea-front. It does not serve breakfast.

Open: all year **Rooms**: 32 **Credit/charge cards**: Diners, Eurocard, Visa, Access

BENICARLO

Parador Costa del Azahar £££
Avenida del Papa Luna 5
12580 Benicarló *Tel (964) 47 01 00*

A restful seaside hotel which turns its back on ugly Benicarló. The modern, low-rise whitewashed building looks over a lawn planted with palms and shrubs to the sea. The rooms are spacious, with terracotta-tiled floors, white walls and pale furnishings, and have terraces, satellite TV and minibar. There is an outdoor pool, but as the town beach is poor, and that at nearby Peñíscola is only adequate, this hotel is best treated as an overnight stop. Public rooms are open plan, and lead on to a terrace. The restaurant specialises in steaks and seafood.

Open: all year **Rooms**: 108 **Facilities**: swimming-pool, tennis **Credit/charge cards**: Amex, Diners, Eurocard, Visa

ELCHE

Huertó del Cura £££
Federico García Sanchiz 14
03203 Elche *Tel (965) 45 80 40*

The hotel lies in exotic grounds on the fringes of Elche's palm grove, and is an easy drive from Alicante airport. Accommodation is in uninspired and rather drearily furnished cabins, but the gardens compensate. The hotel is just a couple of minutes' walk from the Huerta del Cura Park. The restaurant serves some particularly good vegetable dishes – try the aubergine and cheese soufflé, or locally grown artichokes and asparagus.

Open: all year **Rooms**: 70 **Facilities**: swimming-pool, tennis, sauna **Credit/charge cards**: Amex, Diners, Eurocard, Visa

nr JAVEA

Hotel Bahía Vista £££
Portichol 76
03730 Jávea *Tel (965) 77 04 61*

A small, homely English-run hotel about seven kilometres from Jávea. The rooms are fairly plain, but there are lovely sea views and pretty grounds, with an arrowhead-shaped swimming-pool and a terrace with barbecue. It is a good choice for a family holiday, especially if you have young children as there are lots of familiar English dishes on the menu

Open: all year **Rooms**: 17 **Facilities**: swimming-pool, bowling green **Credit/charge cards**: Amex, Diners, Eurocard, Visa

MORELLA

Hostal Elías £
Colomer 7
12300 Castellón *Tel (964) 16 00 92*

An amiable family-run *hostal* close to the centre of old Morella. The rooms have terracotta-tiled floors, cream artex walls, traditional-style furniture and bright woven bedspreads. All have balconies. It does not serve breakfast.

Open: all year **Rooms**: 17 (3 without bathroom) **Credit/charge cards**: none

---

Cardenal Ram   ££
Costera Suñer 2
12300 Castellón   *Tel (964) 16 00 00*

A mighty sixteenth-century mansion on the main street, with thick stone walls and carved eaves. The reception lobby sets the tone, with a stone-flagged floor, and the heavily beamed bar/dining-room has a polished wood floor, whitewashed walls, and a tremendous view over the town's rooftops to the hills. Rooms were not seen as they were being redecorated.

Open: all year **Rooms**: 19 **Credit/charge cards**: Amex, Diners, Eurocard, Visa

MURCIA

Arco de San Juan   £££
Ceballos 10
30003 Murcia   *Tel (968) 21 04 55*

The grey and vanilla neo-classical façade of an eighteenth-century palace forms the front wall of this stylish contemporary hotel in the historic centre of Murcia. The colour schemes in the rooms vary, but all are imaginative and comfortable, with satellite TV.

Open: all year **Rooms**: 115 **Credit/charge cards**: Amex, Eurocard, Visa

VALENCIA

Hostal Venezia   £
Plaza de Ayuntamiento
46000 Valencia   *Tel (96) 352 42 67*

The newly decorated rooms, with cream walls, basket-work furniture and smart bathrooms are excellent value for money. The hotel is on the second floor of a fancy turn-of-the-century town house on Valencia's main square, half-way between the railway station and the cathedral.

Open: all year **Rooms**: 50 **Credit/charge cards**: Visa

Hotel Inglés   £££
Marqués de Dos Aguas 6
46002 Valencia   *Tel (96) 351 64 26*

A mid-sized hotel in an elegant mansion in the old centre of
Valencia. The bedrooms are rather plain, though kitted out with
vaguely art deco furniture, but there is a lovely restaurant with
brocaded walls, candelabra and tapestries.

Open: all year **Rooms**: 62 **Credit/charge cards**: Amex, Diners,
Eurocard, Visa

ANDALUCIA

Andalucía. There is a whisper of music in the name that identifies Spain's most southern region, a vast tranche of land sweeping from the Sierras bordering Castile in the north to the long ribbons of sand that skirt both the Atlantic and the Mediterranean. Phoenician traders, Roman legions and the Visigothic tribe, the Vandals, all left their mark on this land, but it was the Moors, a Berber people from North Africa, who bequeathed the most enduring legacy, best seen today in the great cities of **Seville**, **Córdoba**, and at its zenith in **Granada**'s Alhambra. The stock images of Spain distributed throughout the world in a flurry of tourist posters – dark-eyed *flamenco* dancers, bullfighting and majestic prancing white horses – are primarily Andalucian.

For most visitors, Andalucía means a fortnight on one of the costas, basking on the beaches of **Torremolinos** or **Roquetas de Mar**, with perhaps an excursion to Granada or Seville to inject a bit of native colour to the well-tried formula. Others head inland to explore the *pueblos blancos*, while some arrive to ski in the Sierra Nevada or to walk or ride in the Alpujarras.

Most of Andalucía's 700 kilometres of coastline is flat, and the beaches, though sandy, are often rather featureless, even if backed by a spine of mountains. The **Costa de Almería** stretches from the border with Murcia to Punta Negra where the coastline metamorphoses into the famous **Costa del Sol**, Spain's 'sun coast'. The best-known resorts – Torremolinos, Fuengirola and Marbella – all lie west of Málaga airport. The gritty greyish sand in these resorts is less inviting than on the Costas Blanca or Brava, or Andalucía's own Atlantic coast, the **Costa de la Luz**. Beyond **Tarifa**, the Iberian peninsula's most southern point, the beaches become wider, more golden and less developed, with a rash of small resorts running up to the Portuguese border.

Torremolinos is by far the largest, ugliest and brashest resort, though its no-nonsense, good-time mentality and its unassuming informality are, in their way, endearing. Marbella is the 'quality' resort of the coast, with expensive shops, a charming old town, and a well-honed capacity to tease cash out of pockets. **Nerja**, east of Málaga, is on a more human scale, with a lot of self-catering accommodation, good beaches, and a fine promenade, the Balcón de Europa.

Inland, the three great Moorish cities compete with the great outdoors for your attention. The Sierras around **Grazalema** and **Cazorla** are bracing places to walk and the

Coto Doñana National Park near **Huelva** is one of Europe's finest wild spaces. **Cádiz** has a good art museum, and the curiously unexplored towns of **Baeza** and **Ubeda** are splendid centres of Spanish Renaissance architecture.

MALAGA

Andalucía's second city is a combination of utilitarian modern structures and ramshackle housing fast succumbing to the bulldozer. However, several natural advantages, including a fine position resting between mountains and the sea and an agreeable climate, have made it a target for a succession of invaders throughout history – Iberians, Phoenicians, Carthaginians, Romans and Visigoths all found it to their taste, and it subsequently became an important Moorish centre. Eventually recaptured by the Christians in 1487, it paid a heavy price for prolonged resistance. Its fortunes declined when trading impetus shifted from the Mediterranean to the Atlantic port of Cádiz and inland Seville after the discovery of America.

Nevertheless, during the nineteenth century Málaga found new favour as a winter watering hole. The British, in particular, loved to promenade along its fine, elegant flower-bedecked boulevard. The city received a hammering during the Civil War, but even before then the gloss had gone. Málaga is worth a day of your time, but it pays to be vigilant with your belongings. The River Guadalmedina runs north from the sea and forms an east-west curtain through the centre of the city. Everything of tourist interest, with the exception of the RENFE station, lies in the eastern half.

Routes to the west of the city, along the main Cádiz highway – the N-340 – are well signposted, though visitors heading for the major resorts from the airport need never venture into the city, since the airport lies between Málaga and Torremolinos. As you head east, however, the signposts fizzle out, and you might find yourself in narrow backstreets.

The promenade and park are attractive spots to linger. At its western end, Calle Alameda and Calle Marín García are ideal places to go in search of good, fishy *tapas*. The shabby, dimly lit **Casa Antigua Guardia** (Alameda 16, at its junction with Calle Comisa) is satisfyingly ethnic, with a bank of barrels. This is an atmospheric spot to try Málaga's infamously sweet dessert wines. When it comes to food, fried fish is the best bet and good places to try it include **Antonio**

299

Planning your holiday

For most British visitors Málaga, the transport hub of the Costa del Sol, provides the gateway to Andalucía. Lots of tour operators offer relatively low-cost packages to its resorts, from self-catering deals in simple apartment blocks to half-board arrangements in three- or four-star hotels. If you simply want a family beach holiday in a major resort, you are probably best advised to plump for a package; it is likely to work out cheaper than making your own arrangements, and many hotels are block-booked by tour operators throughout the summer months.

The sunshine record is encouraging. You can expect hot and dry weather in the summer, and warm, sunny days in winter. All but masochists should avoid inland areas (particularly around Seville) in July and August, when the average daily maximum temperature is 36 degrees.

A number of operators also visit the resorts of the Costa de Almería, of which **Mojacar** is by far the most attractive. As yet, only Spanish specialist operators offer packages on the Costa de la Luz, sometimes using flights to Gibraltar, or to Jerez airport.

There are cheap charter flights to Málaga from most British airports, and to Almería from Gatwick, Birmingham, East Midlands, Manchester and Glasgow. From Málaga airport you can drive to Granada in under two hours and to Seville in less than three. Both British Airways and Iberia have daily scheduled flights from London to Málaga. Iberia also offer scheduled flights to Almería, Seville and Jerez.

Public transport links between major towns and cities are good, with rail links between the Andalucian cities, and on to Madrid and Barcelona. Trains run along the coast from Málaga to Fuengirola. If you prefer luxury rail travel where the glamour of the journey is an integral part of the trip, the *Al Andaluz* Express trundles in *belle époque* elegance between Málaga, Jerez, Seville, Córdoba, and Granada. You can get details on the 1992 programme from the UK agents, Excalibur Holidays of Distinction, Tel (0202) 751844.

For the most part, roads are good, though those inland are often tortuous, and they can be daunting in the Sierra Nevada.

Martín, Paseo Maritimo 4, (Tel 952 22 21 13) and several ramshackle bars and cafés on the sea-front at **Pedregalego** or in **El Palo**, the old fishermens' quarter.

The main coastal highway – the N-340 – still deserves a word of warning: a high incidence of accidents makes it one of Europe's most dangerous roads, with British visitors accounting for a high proportion of the fatalities. Driving in Seville is confusing mainly because of the one-way system and on-street parking is all but impossible. In any event, security demands that you entrust your car to a supervised underground car park for the duration of your stay. The toll roads from Huelva and Cadiz to Seville are under-used and speedy. The best map for touring is Michelin *Andalucía – Costa del Sol*, 1:400 000 sheet 446.

Many towns stage colourful carnivals in February and March. Seville's Holy Week rituals – *Semana Santa* – are world famous. Hotel prices shoot through the roof at this time and all available accommodation is booked in advance. Hot on its heels comes the April Fair, the *Feria*. A merry carnival atmosphere develops with lots of stalls and daily bullfights. Bull runs (with the animals' horns tipped with wooden balls) are held in Arcos and Vejer on Easter Sunday. **Jerez**, an important equestrian centre and home of the famous riding-school, hosts a Horse Fair in April or May. Córdoba's Festival of the Patios, when competitive owners bedeck their *patios cordobeses* with glorious splashes of flowers, takes place during the first ten days in May. Andalucía's most important pilgrimage, *Romerío del Rocío* takes place at **El Rocío**, within the Doñana National Park 15 kilometres from Almonte on Whit Sunday. Granada's festival of Nuesta Señora de las Angustías on the last Sunday in September is a colourful day of pomp, music and religious processions.

One consequence of the governmental largesse prompted by Seville's 1992 jamboree is that scores of monuments throughout the region have been *en restauración* for a couple of years, and are closed to visitors while unimaginable amounts of pesetas are spent on sprucing them up. We hope that by the time you come to use this book the scaffolding will be down, and some of Europe's most worthwhile sights will be once again open to visitors.

Tourist Offices: Avenida de la Constitución 21, 41004, Seville, Tel (957) 22 14 04. Torrijos 10, 14003, Córdoba, Tel (957) 47 12 35. Plaza de Mariana Pineda 10, 18009, Granada, Tel (958) 22 66 88.

The Main Sights

The **Cathedral of the Assumption**, begun in 1528 next to a parish-imposed church on the site of a mosque, has an ornate baroque façade which was completed in 1783. The locals call it *La Manquita*, 'the One-handed one', since its second, southern tower was never completed. Fluted columns support flat arches as late-Gothic nudges the baroque, reflecting the 250-year construction period. The most notable feature is the seventeenth-century choir-stall, showing scenes from the lives of forty saints, carved by the important sculptor Pedro de Mena.

East of the cathedral, the **Alcazaba** was begun as a Moorish fortress in the ninth century. Its interior, a treasury of classic Moorish design, has recently been restored after years of neglect. Attractive flower gardens have been laid out around it. The Archaeological Museum, situated within its walls, displays local finds from prehistoric, Roman and more recent times. At the foot of the Alcazaba to the north, the remains of a Roman amphitheatre are being excavated.

The **Castillo de Gibralfaro** commands an adjacent hilltop behind the Alcazaba, and is connected to it by a long double wall. You can wander around ramparts and towers that have seen action in conflicts from the Reconquest to the Civil War. The Parador de Gibralfaro shares the site. (This is likely to close for refurbishment during 1992). The **Museo de Bellas Artes** (Fine Arts Museum) on Calle de San Augustín is signposted from the north side of the cathedral, and is situated in a fine sixteenth-century palace that belonged to the Counts of Buenavista. The collection is eclectic and runs the gamut from Roman mosaics to works by Murillo and Zurbarán. There are also some juvenilia by the most famous Malagueño of modern times – Picasso was born here in 1881. A plaque marks the house at Plaza de La Merced 15.

North of Málaga

Antequera (H), 57 kilometres north of Málaga on the N-331, can claim the distinction of having been called *Antikaria* – the ancient city – by the Romans. On two sites just outside the town there are prehistoric dolmens, **the Cuevas de Viera** and **Menga**, which are regarded as being among the most important in Spain.

The town has a number of Mudéjar and baroque churches, including San Sebastian which has an octagonal belfry, and Santa María whose Renaissance western façade takes the form of a Roman triumphal arch. There is also a small museum with a number of prehistoric and Roman finds. The comfortable, modern *parador* makes a good base.

El Torcal is a National Park 15 kilometres to the south of Antequera on the C-3310. Exposure to the elements has sculpted a number of limestone rocks into strange shapes.

THE COSTA DEL SOL

The 300 kilometres of the Costa del Sol, from Punta Negra to Tarifa, encompass some of the most congested areas of tourist development in Europe. For much of its length, the coastline has a backdrop of mountains to protect it from winds and ensure the agreeable climate that has made this costa a year-round holiday playground. Its beaches are long and character-less, and consist of coarse, brown-grey sand. Some are polluted, and there are few of the pine-strewn cliffs and scenic coves that make parts of the Costa Brava so attractive. The long beaches are ideal for organised watersports and activities, from water-skiing to pedaloes, as well as some fairly hectic nightlife.

The sheer volume of accommodation which has sprung up means that there are lots of reasonably priced hotels. Moving upmarket, there are several golf courses around Marbella, and a clutch of luxury hotels where a different sort of package – over £2,000 for a 14-day break in high season – is on offer.

WEST OF MALAGA

Torremolinos (H)

Torremolinos is much maligned, a big, brash, lively resort with enough energy to activate the most torpid sunworshipper. Much of the resort now looks scruffy at the edges, and a bit past its sell-by date.

Tourism is its *raison d'être*, and Torremolinos has no pretensions to being anything other than a large pleasure park. The main highway runs some way inland and above the coast, and it is usually possible to park on Bajondillo beach's Paseo Marítimo. Beach facilities are excellent, though the sand is grey and gritty. Watersports on offer include water-skiing and windsurfing, and there is an Aquapark.

The two main beaches, El Bajondillo and La Carihuela, lie below the town, and are divided by a headland, La Roca, crowned by an old castle. The steps which lead from the beach to the town are transformed at night into a bazaar, where you can buy table-linen, costume jewellery or ornaments, and caricature artists set up their easels, ready to catch your likeness in five minutes. Most of the towerblock hotels and high-rise apartments lie east of La Roca, although there are several big package hotels on the streets that lead down to Carihuela beach. Development here is on a more human scale, with lots of two-storey buildings in narrow, whitewashed streets, though this area, too, has its share of dusty unfinished specimens with 'For Sale' signs all over them. The sea-front here has been pedestrianised and good fish restaurants have sprung up, particularly around Calle Carmen and Calle Mar. Good places to eat include La Jabega, Calle Mar 17, Casa Prudencio, Calle Carmen 43 and in the same street at number 35, El Roqueo. The restaurant of the Parador del Golf (near the airport and signposted off the N-340) is also worth considering.

The main shopping street, Calle San Miguel, is jammed with shops selling clothes, jewellery (especially Mallorquín pearls), perfume and Lladro figures, as well as *salons de thé*.

You would be hard pushed to spot where Torremolinos becomes **Benalmádena Costa** (H), the next resort along the coast. It is notable for its sporting harbour and a stylish marina for small and medium-sized boats. The championship-level Torrequebrada golf course attracts sun-seeking golfers on specialist packages to the smarter, quieter hotels which can be found here. The beaches are man-made and of very variable quality.

FROM FUENGIROLA TO MARBELLA

The N-340 by-passes **Fuengirola**, another large high-rise resort, with sprawling *urbanizaciónes* at either end. Although similar in many ways to Torremolinos, Fuengirola is rather more staid and family-oriented. The western end, behind the coarse brown-grey sand of Santa Amalia beach, is rather drab and dated. A central marina divides it from the more attractive eastern beach, Los Boliches, where the sand becomes finer and more inviting. Dogs, litter and camping are prohibited, and there are lots of watersports on offer and cycles available for hire. An attractive, tiled mosaic studded with balding palm trees runs behind, backed by lots of eating places with names like 'The Great British Breakfast Bar' and 'Scoffers'. The town has retained a genuinely Spanish district, Santa Fé de los Boliches. Otherwise, away from the sea you should find unflashy bars serving decent *tapas*. Try the Bar La Paz Garrido on the Avenida de Mijas or the area around Callejón Moncayo.

Mijas (H)

From Fuengirola a steep winding road spirals six kilometres up to **Mijas**, the most visited of the *pueblos blancos*, a favourite target of the Costa coachparties. It is a spruce, impossibly well-manicured place, backed by green-draped mountains, its centre given over to a crescent of bars, cafés, restaurants and tourist shops. Despite the total surrender to the most blatant commercialism this is a pleasant place to visit, with wonderful views of the coast, particularly from the outcrop beside the shrine of the Virgen de la Peña. Steep narrow streets lead to the small **bullring**, allegedly square, but most definitely with rounded edges.

The Plaza de la Constitución is a good spot from which to watch village life, and you can try Basque food at the Miro Blanco, Tel (952) 48 57 00. The Hotel Mijas is a stylish setting for a self-indulgent afternoon tea. You will also find good food at Valparaíso, four kilometres south on the Fuengirola road, Tel (952) 48 59 96. If money is no object you will enjoy the totally sybaritic Hotel Byblos Andaluz (one of Spain's few five-star Gran Luxe hotels) between Fuengirola and Mijas at Urbanización Mijas Golf, Tel (952) 47 30 50.

MARBELLA (H)

While Torremolinos and Fuengirola can be summarised as cheap and cheerful, Marbella can lay claim to neither epithet. Beyond Fuengirola, the emphasis shifts from towerblocks to hacienda-style villas and apartments, aimed for sale to Northern Europeans. 'East Marbella' starts 12 kilometres from the town (in what is actually west Calahonda). In fact the name is used indiscriminately to cover everything from the fringes of Fuengirola to San Pedro de Alcantara – about 38 kilometres. The out-of-town beaches are better than those in the town centre.

The really luxurious hotels, such as Los Monteros (to the east) and the Marbella club (to the west), sit in extensive grounds, screened from the road, as do the ritzy villas of celebrities and oil sheiks.

Coming into Marbella town rather than its more exotic

fringes means that accommodation costs become more realistic, although here too, packages to the smartest hotels cost well over £1,000 in high season. The town is disappointingly ordinary and unattractive, with cranes announcing the imminence of still further development, and many hotels sited uncomfortably close to the main road. The town-centre beaches are man-made, backed by a busy promenade, and can get very busy in high season.

So why all the hype? What Marbella has that its rivals lack is a small, well-preserved old town of whitewashed houses and cobbled streets, situated just behind the main drag of the Málaga-Cádiz highway. The central square of orange trees and topiaried hedges – the Patio de Los Naranjos – is attractive, particularly by night, when *al fresco* diners and last-minute shoppers combine to create a definite buzz. Acceptable places to eat here include Mena, Los Naranjos, and the Crepería Marbella.

Further inland, agreeable fare, especially fish, is served on the *patio andaluz* of La Fonda, Plaza Santo Cristo 10, Tel (952) 77 25 12.

Many of the smartest places, however, are not in Marbella itself, but in nearby **Puerto Banús**. It is a place to see and be seen in, and there is a voyeuristic pleasure in sipping coffee at one of the overpriced water-front bars.

Inland from the N-340, beyond Marbella's bullring and casino is an extensive *urbanización* of private villa developments, apartments, hotels and golf courses called **Nueva Andalucía**. Further west, **San Pedro de Alcantara** is the furthest-flung of the satellites to be marketed under the Marbella umbrella, and is the site of the famous Las Brisas championship golf course. The *pueblo* is situated on the inland side of the N-340, although many of the hotels are on the coastal side.

FROM ESTEPONA TO TARIFA

Estepona is a drab and mundane place that is, however, genuinely relaxing. Despite its marina, as a resort it's a low-key place, with a bank-lined commercial centre confirming that tourism is a secondary activity – you will still see fishermen mending their nets at the quayside, and unloading sardines and *boquerones* (anchovies) at the 6am fish market. The dark gold sand and pebble beaches are long, backed by an attractive palm-lined prom and a few smallish hotels. The large, facility-packed hotels that appear under the Estepona listing are in fact more than 10 kilometres east of the town. Behind the sea-front, the old quarter retains more than a vestige of Spanish character.

Further west, just beyond the quaintly named Buenas Noches, a 14-kilometre uphill detour from the N-340 on a minor road will bring you to the smashing little white town of **Casares**, which suddenly appears atop a rocky promontory as you round a bend, an explosion of white crowned by a steeple and a decaying castle, and because of its relative isolation, less visited than Mijas. Nearby **Manilva** is notable only for its allegedly restorative Roman sulphur baths.

The level of new development thins out along the coastal road beyond Estepona, although there is much evidence of British involvement in the huge luxury villa and sports facilities development at **Sotogrande**. The N-340 continues past **San Roque** with its turn-off for **Gibraltar**, heading towards **Algeciras**.

Algeciras is a poor place, despite its strategic and historical importance as the launch-pad for the Moorish occupation of Spain. Apartment blocks seem to be the trademarks of this town. Mainland Europe's North African migrant workers transit through Algeciras, adding a dash of exotic colour. There is an old colonial-style hotel, the Reina Cristina, situated in a park on the Paseo de la Conferencia, Tel (956) 60 26 22, should you decide to stay here.

Out of town, the sea disappears and lush green hills tumble right down to meet the road on the inland side. A good road twists and turns for a while before straightening out in a scenic stretch that leads to **Tarifa**, where the Mediterranean meets the Atlantic, and the **Costa de la Luz** begins.

EAST OF MALAGA

From Málaga to Nerja

The level of development east of Málaga bears little relation to the concrete sprawl that has engulfed almost everything to the west. The only major resort is **Nerja**, 52 kilometres from the city. The first resort to the east is **Rincón de la Victoria**, a low-key place with an old castle and an underground cave once rumoured to contain the treasure trove of the Moorish kings. There is one hotel and a few apartments, and unless you have a particularly compelling reason to visit, you would be well advised to forsake the coastal road, and instead head out of Málaga on the N-331, the major road which ultimately connects with Granada, Córdoba and Seville, along the path of the River Guadalmedina. After 25 kilometres you will reach **Casabermeja**, where you should turn left and follow a minor road for about 10 kilometres to **Colmenar**, and then on via the C-340 to **Perriana**, which is famous for its peaches. The road (now the N-335) winds down through the Sierra de Tejeda to **Vélez Málaga**, surrounded by vineyards, almond trees and olive groves, the capital of this little area known as Axarquia, or you can turn off to enter the Sierra Alcázar Natural at **Alcaucín**.

NERJA (H)

You perk up immediately at the first sight of **Nerja**, a sudden flash of stacked houses on a rocky outcrop that stretches into the sea. Unlike its neighbour, Nerja has a sense of a real town, and as you drive past, the streets seem neat and tidy. While not exactly unspoilt, it has escaped the worst excesses of the high-rise development found to the west, and, like many of the more recently established resorts, there is a heavy emphasis on self-catering accommodation, with the nearby smart El Capistrano complex. The local character has some-how managed to avoid being completely swamped by the foreign visitors.

The central focus of the town is the Balcón de Europa, the unusual promenade which occupies the rocky promontory jutting out into the sea, given its colourful name by the visit-ing King Alfonso XII in 1885, who enjoyed the splendid views. This is an agreeable spot, dotted with palm trees, and lined on one side by bars, restaurants and the eponymous hotel. To the west the coast is rugged, and grey-green spurs of mountain look like long limbs stretched into the sea.

As well as several small cove beaches tucked below the cliffs, Nerja has a large, popular beach at Burriana, crowded with sunloungers and umbrellas along its grey sand and peb-ble length. There is also a smaller, less crowded beach at Playa de la Torrecilla. The winding, narrow streets of the whitewashed old town are fun to explore, with all the typical resort shops selling ceramics, perfume, leather goods and jewellery, as well as art shops where paintings of local scenes draw admiring glances. Stalls are set up and illuminated, selling sweets, dates and coconut halves. Others sell leather items or costume jewellery, and caricature artists ply for trade. An atmospheric place to eat is the Rey Alfonso set into the cliff-side on the Balcón de Europa, Tel (952) 52 01 95. Otherwise try Pepe Rico, Almirante Ferrándiz 28, Tel (952) 52 02 47.

The main excursion is to the **Cuevas de Nerja**, five kilometres north-east of the village. There are paleolithic cave paintings, but the main focus of interest is the complex of grotto-like chambers with their stalactite formations, including what – at 61 metres – is reputedly the world's longest specimen.

From Nerja to the Costa de Almería

The landscape is craggy, with patches of terrace cultivation dug into the inland hillside, and cranes still at work on apartment blocks targeted at foreign buyers wherever the sea-front topography allows. A slight detour off the N-340 (at its most scenic at this point) brings you to the small resort of **La Herradura**, where a grey shingle beach runs between two headlands and slopes gently into the sea. The next *urbanización,* the smart development of **Marina del Este**, is a distinctly upmarket cluster of designer-ethnic villas with an integral country club, a small cove shingle beach and a marina for the local yacht club from which you can see the hideous towerblocks of **Almuñécar**. A tiled promenade skirts a rocky beach of dark grey pebble and shingles, on which upturned rowing boats rest, overlooked by a dreary jumble of '60s apartment blocks and hotels. There are Roman remains in the Parque del Majuelo, and a modest museum displays further finds and Moorish artefacts in the *Cueva de los Siete Palacios*, the Seven Palace Cave, which were possibly Roman stables. The town also provides the starting point for a spectacular 60-kilometre drive through the Sierra del Chaparral to **Puerto del Suspiro del Moro** where it meets the N-323 Motril road to Granada. It is from this viewpoint that Boabdil, the deposed Moorish ruler, wept after surrendering to the Catholic Monarchs in 1492. In recollection of this legend, the spot is known as 'The Moor's Sigh'.

Continuing eastwards from Almuñécar, the coast road reaches **Salobreña**, an impressive cluster of white houses slumping down a hill towards the sea, and crowned by the shell of a Moorish castle. The enchanting sleepy little town remains undeveloped, unlike its coastal strip where a jumble of villas and high-rise apartments fan out along a bare, shadeless promenade, fronted by a long, wide stretch of steeply shelving grey-brown pebbles and shingle, the Playa de Velilla. Salobreña's only sizeable hotel is set back on a headland from the N-340 and has wonderful views and simple but well-furnished rooms in its new extension. You would be better advised to eat at Mesón Dùran, about 500 metres east of the entrance to the hotel.

An alternative route into the Alpujarras would take you through the mildly industrial, workaday town of **Motril** where much of the sugar cane grown locally is refined, distilled and exported from its port, where there are some good *tapas* bars. It has a fine collegiate church that dates back to the sixteenth century and a Moorish castle that provides an atmospheric stage for some of the events in its lively August arts festival.

ALMERIA

The capital of Andalucía's dustbowl province is itself a dry, rather neglected place that has never regained its eleventh-century splendour, when for a short period it was Spain's most prosperous city, thanks to its silk and ceramic industries. Almería can trace its history back about 4,000 years, but it is the Moorish legacy, including its name (meaning Mirror of the Sea), which is the most striking. Its Alcazaba is believed to have been the most formidable fortress of Al-Andaluz, and its great palace on the hill of San Cristóbal was finally destroyed by a series of devastating earthquakes. During its golden age the enlightened ruler, Motacin, fostered an inventive court of musicians, poets and scientists. The city fell to the Christians in 1484, and a long period of decline was stalled only by the redevelopment of the local mining industry during the nineteenth century, and tourism in our own.

Everything of tourist interest is in the old sector of the city west of the wide central avenue, the Ramblas. The sole exception is the Archaeological Museum with its fine Bronze Age finds in Calle de Javier Sanz. There are a number of bars and restaurants along the Paseo de Almería, a boulevard of fading nineteenth-century elegance which runs diagonally off the Ramblas. Try El Alcázar for *tapas*. Of more formal restaurants, Anfora, González Garbín 25, Tel (951) 23 13 74 is highly regarded. Movie stars generally put up at the Gran Hotel Almería, Reina Regente 8, Tel (951) 23 80 11 when

Almería's arid plains are standing in for some Arabian desert or Wild West wilderness.

The main sights

● **The Alcazaba** was originally built in the tenth century by 'Abd Ar-Rahman III, and was enlarged a century later to make it a most formidable fortress. Hints of eastern promise are heavily dropped – camels sit outside waiting to be photographed, and gentlemen in Arab garb urge you to squat with them and drink mint tea. A long spur of wall reaches out to the neighbouring hill of San Cristóbal.

● **Cuevas de la Chanca**, the fishermen's quarter and home of Almería's small troglodyte community; most of the caves that surmount the low, flat-roofed whitewashed houses have been abandoned.

● **The Cathedral** occupies the site of a mosque destroyed in the earthquake of 1522, and was designed by Diego de Siloé. The splendid Renaissance façade is rather at variance with the enforced severity of the design. The eighteenth-century high altar and the marble and jasper pulpits are grand.

THE COSTA ALMERIA

The West: from Adra to Almería

As you cross the provincial boundary from Granada and the last outposts of the Costa del Sol, everything seems to become dusty. There is little to detain you at **Adra**, the first of the minor resorts, although two remaining Islamic towers might be of interest to specialists. Just beyond the village, the C-331 will take you north to **Berja**, where Moorish reservoirs hint at the complex engineering work devised by the Moors to irrigate these arid plains.

The importance of intense agricultural development to the modern economy of these parts can be seen in the area all around **El Ejido**, known as 'the sea of plastic' because of the vast areas given over to drip irrigation in improvised greenhouses.

Just beyond El Ejido, a spur from the main road of Roman straightness heads south for ten kilometres to the recently established and growing resort of **Almerimar**. The huge package hotels here compensate for their relative isolation by offering shopping arcades, lots of leisure facilities and a non-stop programme of activities, as well as a golf course designed by Gary Player. Building work continues to go on all around, but it all seems a little desolate, not to stay desperate, with curiously Moorish-looking stone windbreaks.

Back on the N-340, the turn-off at El Parador will bring you to **Roquetas de Mare**; the old whitewashed village has been totally swamped by a phalanx of undistinguished hotels, apartments and bars; more immediately noticeable is the wasteland that lies behind the coastal strip, with occasional building sites. The narrow beach of dark brown sand and shingle is a reasonable length but shelves very steeply. There is a golf course nearby but, all in all, this is a dismal place. **Aguadulce**, the largest and oldest-established of these resorts, is slightly better, with a palm-lined promenade and a more buoyant resort feel.

Beyond Almería

The salt flats at **Cabo de Gata** attract flamingos and other birdlife, and consequently birdwatchers. Apart from divers who haunt the clear waters around the coarse sand beach with its trademark lighthouse, few other people make it to Spain's remote south-eastern tip. The road climbs to the incipient cacti-backed resort of **San José** where a clutch of simple, small hotels have sprung up. Still fewer people venture to **Los Escollos**, or the fishing village of **La Isleta**, and only the dedicated will find true isolation by trekking from **San Pedro** where the road runs out, via **El Plomo** to **Agua Amarga**.

Those who want to explore Andalucía's eastern coast limit their attention to the northern area, and reach the target resort of **Mojácar** by heading north from Almería on the N-340. The road trails through parched, dusty terrain through **Bena-hadux** and **Rioja** close to *Mini-Hollywood*, south of **Tabernas**. Here, the frontier town set used in 'A Fistful of Dollars' and other spaghetti western epics has been preserved as a tourist attraction, where staged displays show the good guys sorting out the bad guys when visitor numbers warrant it. The area also masqueraded as the Sahara in 'Lawrence of Arabia'. Back on the N-340 a minor detour on the AL-102 will bring you to **Nijar**, a small palm-fringed town backed by the Sierra de Alhamilla which specialises in cheap, colourful ceramics and coarse-textured rugs in traditional Moorish designs. **Sorbas** is a tiered white town where a scattering of sugar-cube houses cling defiantly to a cliff, while modern suburbs spread out below. Return to the main road and at **Los Gallardos** take the turn-off for AL-150 to **Mojácar**.

MOJACAR (H)

The old Moorish town sits amid rugged hills about two kilometres above the modern beach resort. This is a picture-postcard place, where steep streets sweep up and down, and perfect, gleaming white houses sit next to semi-derelict ones with washing strung out on their balconies. The narrowness of the streets creates a wind tunnel effect, and a pleasant breeze filters through when the temperature is baking down on the beach. Several houses (and cars) bear the 5,000-year-old local symbol – the *indalo* showing a stick figure whose outstretched arms support an arc, believed to be a talisman against evil.

The new resort is very much a family-oriented place, and low-level building has begun to sprawl along the coast, the sole high-rise exception being the large Hotel Indalo. Among the available accommodation is a comfortable but slightly disappointing *parador* and good self-catering developments the Pueblo Indalo and Indamar Apartments.

The rough sand and shingle beach stretches on for about seven kilometres. To the south of the resort there are more remote and wilder beaches (accessible by car) for those who prefer their own company – try the unspoilt Playa de Macena.

North of Mojácar the busy (but not especially attractive) fishing village of **Garrucha** is being developed as a resort. For more cultural sightseeing return to the N-340 and proceed north through **Vera** and **Huércal Overa**, from where the C-321 brings you almost to **Vélez Rubio**. Important neolithic wall paintings are found in the Cuevos de los Letreros between this village and **Vélez Blanco**.

THE COSTA DE LA LUZ

Until very recently this area, which runs from **Tarifa** in the south to **Ayamonte** at the Portuguese border was popular with Spaniards only. Paradoxically, this coastline now marketed as the Costa de la Luz – 'the Coast of Light' – has by far the best beaches in Andalucía. Even now, when the world has found out about this previously unspoilt corner of Spain, they remain genuinely uncrowded, often empty. Planning laws have tightened up somewhat since Málaga's coast was ravaged in the '60s, but another factor helps to explain the tardy entry to tourism; fierce winds, the eastern *levantera* and western *poniente*, routinely gust in from the ocean.

None the less, the Costa de la Luz makes a good base. The resorts are on a human scale, and many are nothing more than a vast expanse of sand serviced by a couple of hotels, and few bars or restaurants. The traditional sherry exporting towns of **Sanlúcar de Barrameda** (H) and **El Puerto de Santa María** offer a more historic sort of tourist experience, and the ancient port of **Cádiz** has a special sort of roguish, down-at-heel charm. Visitors can also use the coastal resorts as a springboard to explore the *Ruta de los Pueblos Blancos* – 'the route of of the white towns' – or to visit Jerez, the sherry capital. Further north, in the province of Huelva, the Doñana National Park is a superb wildlife sanctuary, especially rewarding for birdwatchers.

From Tarifa to Cádiz

If you bypass **Tarifa** on the N-340 you will catch glimpses of aprons of white-gold sand, quite free of development, that immediately alert you to the fact that you have chanced upon something very different from the Costa del Sol. Head into town and you will find the entrance marked by a horseshoe arch, emphasising its Moorish roots. The restored tenth-century fortress known as **Castillo de Guzmán el Bueno** provided the stage for one of the most lovingly recounted of Spain's tales of heroically theatrical tragedy when Guzman 'The Good' allowed his son to be killed rather than capitulate to the Moors besieging the fortress.

Tarifa is now Europe's leading windsurfing resort, and a huge commercial industry has sprung up to service the demands of the sailboarders. There are a number of simple *hostales*. Of the beaches around the town, perhaps the most attractive is Punta Paloma, about ten kilometres away. Nearby are the Roman ruins of the first-century city of *Baelo Claudia*, alternatively known as Bolonia. The next resort, **Zahara de los Atunes**, is reached via a ten-kilometre stretch of minor road. It is a simple, but expanding place.

Proceeding north along the coast, **Barbate de Franco** is a rather dusty fishing village, with a small old quarter and a tiled promenade. Its beach, Playa Carmen, is of soft gold sand with a string of bars, restaurants and *hostales* further along, as it metamorphoses into **Los Caños de Meca** near Cape

Trafalgar (of Nelson fame). The next point of interest is the white town of **Vejer de la Frontera** (H) (see 'Los Pueblos Blancos' page 323).

Proceeding north, **Conil de la Frontera** is the most advanced of the newly established resorts, and its genuine fishing village feel may not last much longer. Even so, the number of hotels barely reaches double figures. Its long flat golden beaches are dotted with sandstone coves and backed by Algarve-like cliffs. This is an ideal spot for families, because the Atlantic is surprisingly calm here and the sea-bed shelves gently. Return to the main road at the white town of **Chiclana de la Frontera** (see page 323), and continue across the salt flats to **Cádiz** via the hideous industrial zone of San Fernando.

Cádiz (H)

This great maritime city is long past its hey-day, but a day exploring its sights is likely to be considered well spent. You can taste the corrosive salt in the air, and you can almost sense the buildings crumbling around you. On a stormy day the Atlantic sends waves crashing over the sea wall in great surges of white power, soaking anyone who gets in the way. Perhaps the best time to visit is during the Carnival, held in the second week of February.

The city lays claim to be being Europe's oldest continually inhabited town, tracing its history back 3,000 years to a Phoenician settlement in 1100 BC. It was the development of trade with the New World that was the basis of the city's prosperity, which reached its zenith during the eighteenth century, from which time most of the treasures of the old town – including the impressive sea walls – date.

The modern Parador Atlántico (H) provides the only really agreeable accommodation. It also has a very good restaurant. There are a number of cheap, rather grim *hostales* in the streets between the focal point Plaza de Juan de Díos (being ruthlessly dug up at the time of our inspection), Plaza de Candelaría and the Plaza Palillero. You should eat at El Faro, San Félix 15, Tel (956) 21 10 68, or in one of the many *tapas* bars (most of which specialise in fried fish) in Calle Zorilla, which runs between the tourist office and the sea.

The main sights

A view from the sea-wall of the golden dome of the cathedral soaring above the bulk of the church, with bell-towers to the rear and peeling stucco buildings to the fore makes a visit to Cádiz worthwhile. Inside, the **Cathedral** (still undergoing restoration) has wonderful proportions and ornate choir-stalls.

The **Museo de Bellas Artes y Arqueológico** on Plaza de Mina where it joins Calle Antonio López, has one of the best-known collections of works by Zurbarán – 21 in all – including the large *St Francis Receiving the Stigmata*. Unfortunately, a reorganisation of the gallery has kept these (and a collection of Murillos) out of the public view for a number of years, a cause of some controversy in the locale. The archaeology section displays well-preserved Roman sarcophagi and Phoenician tombs. There is also a marionette show called *Tía Norica* – a compelling but rather sinister display of puppets arranged in tableaux.

Jerez de la Frontera

This is a well-heeled place, and it seems that 'Andalucía's bottled sunshine' is still a multi-million-dollar earner. If you drive along the N-443 from Cádiz to Jerez you will be struck by the acres of vineyard that flank the road and the adverts that flash past you for Tio Pepe or the famous bull of the Osborne *bodegas*. The Alcázar is at the southern end of the central tourist zone; it dates back to the time of the Almohads, and sits on a mound west of the Plaza de Arenal, the main square. The Alcázar's most interesting feature is its small mosque, which became the chapel of Santa María Real. The town's cathedral, the former **Collegiate Church of San Salvador** is a bizarre building in hybrid Gothic-Renaissance style, currently undergoing extensive restoration.

But the main reason for coming to Jerez is to visit a *bodega*. All the big houses hold hourly tours between 10.30am and 1.30pm on weekdays. It is better to telephone ahead so that you can be sure that there will be an English-speaking guide. The tourist office on Alameda Cristina 7, Tel (956) 33 11 50 will give you a list of participating houses and times. One bonus in visiting González-Byass is that the site includes a grand circular ironwork pavilion, **La Concha**, designed and built by Eiffel. The visit ends with a visit to the tasting room, where you will be liberally served with as much fino, manzanilla, amontillado and oloroso as you can take at one sitting. There is an opportunity to buy at the end of the tasting, but no attempt is made to make you feel obliged to do so. The *bodegas* are closed in August.

The other 'unmissable' in Jerez is a visit to the **Real Escuela Andaluza de Arte Ecuestre** – the Royal Andalucian School of Equestrian Art – in Recreo de las Cadenas, Avenida Duque de Abrantes. This is in the north of the city centre, rather a long walk from the Alcázar. Formal displays, complete with music and costume, are held on Thursdays at noon, with special shows arranged from time to time. On other weekdays you can visit between 11am and 1pm, to see a 'training and practice session'. The city's connection with the equestrian world most visible during the April *Feria*, when the sherry barons don the traditional black broad-brimmed hats, short jackets and tight trousers, and parade on their prize animals. For the rest of Andalucía, Jerez is synonymous with 'toff', and when the patrician, self-assured members of the sherry dynasties mount their unflappable horses you can see why. It would be possible to link your visit to the school with a tour of the adjacent Garvey *bodega*.

Jerez is a short drive from Arcos de la Frontera, where you could stay at the exceptionally fine *parador* for not much more than half the price of Jerez's business-oriented hotels. It is, however worth staying in Jerez for lunch at El Bosque, Aveida Alcade Alvaro Domecq 26, Tel (956) 30 33 33, situated in a splendid park, or at Gaitán, Tel (956) 34 58 59

The coast north of Cádiz

A *vapor* steamer service plys across the bay from Cádiz to **El Puerto de Santa María**. The town is best known for the hulking Osborne and Terry sherry and brandy *bodegas*, which can be visited, near the water-front. The town has a very impressive bullring which ranks very high in the pecking order of the art, and holds up to 15,000 spectators. A palm-lined walkway leads to the **Castillo de San Marcos**, an eleventh-century fortress (with a later church) on the former site of a mosque. The area is becoming increasingly popular as a holiday destination, and has popular beaches at Fuentebravía, and Vista Hermosa. The town is well-known as a gourmet centre, and sophisticated fish dishes are a great draw at Alboronia, Santo Domingo 24, Tel (956) 85 16 09. There are a number of seafood restaurants in Calle Ribera del

Marisco, and *tapas* bars in the area known as Ribera del Río, where it is fashionable to promenade in the evening.

Rota hosts an American naval base, and so has a plethora of bars, discos and US-style fast-food joints, slightly at variance with its medieval walls, fourteenth-century castle, old fishing quarter and pine-fringed beaches. Proceeding north on the CA-604, you encounter **Chipiona**, a preferable, rather old-fashioned seaside resort with a smattering of small *pensiones* and a reputation as a spa town. It also has a fine long beach, the Playa de Regla.

Sanlúcar de Barrameda (H) stands on the left bank of the Guadalquivir, crowned with the castle of Santiago and dotted with towers and bell-gables. In the late fifteenth century Columbus, Magellan and their retinues used the port on their voyages of discovery, which helps to account for the number of venerable buildings.

The town is also famous for its special sherry known as manzanilla. There are *bodegas* on both sides of the Calle Luis de Eguilaz, which you can visit. Sanlúcar's *langostinos* are the most fitting accompaniment to manzanilla. The area has splendid beaches, and in August horse-racing is staged along the water's edge. A floral carpet is laid out to mark Corpus Christi, and at the end of May the jolly *Feria de la Manzanilla* is held. There are a few *pensiones* and this is a more agreeable place to stay than Jerez, 23 kilometres away and easily reached by the C-440.

HUELVA

This Andalucian province is little known to British tourists, except those scampering for the Algarve with car-loads of self-catering provisions. Extravagantly titled Costa de la Luz – Coast of Light – to lure foreign tourist trade, Huelva's seaside is still remarkably unspoilt compared with the Costa del Sol or the Algarve.

Huelva town must be the least appealing city for miles around. Yet unexpectedly, Huelva has a national park within its city boundaries. The **Marismas del Odiel**, made up of tidal marshes and saltpans, attract huge numbers of flamingos, spoonbills and many other winter migrants who seem quite unperturbed by the satanic smokestacks and bustling dockland activity along the estuary. Just outside Huelva is the Monasery of La Rábida, where Columbus spent six years studying with friendly monks who were convinced, like him, that the world was round. From here he planned and launched his first great voyage to the New World. The Monastery, under restoration recently, is normally visitable, and you can see the bleak cell where Columbus slept and worked, and models of the ships he sailed. There is a rather dull but serviceable hotel nearby, the Hostería de la Rábida, which is quietly set overlooking the Tinto estuary.

The coastline

Most visitors head for the huge beaches all along Huelva's coastline, where tracks lead from the well-surfaced coastal roads through pine groves and dunes to apparently endless vistas of firm, fine sand and crashing breakers. West of the Straits, the beaches of the Costa de la Luz are of course Atlantic, not Mediterranean. That means they are tidal and regularly washed. The sand is magnificent: shell-strewn and dazzling, as soft as icing sugar on bare toes.

The resorts of the Huelva are quiet and unexciting: mostly unplanned low-key clusters of villas and apartment blocks among the pines and eucalyptus trees. Punta Umbria and Matalascañas are the largest and most built-up centres, not as hideous as some Spanish Costa resorts, but as dull as ditch-water. The ambience is mostly Spanish: by far the largest group of holidaymakers here are locals. Hotel acccommodation is generally modest, both in facilities and price, and the season is short. By the end of September the beaches are almost deserted and many hotels closed.

The most comfortable place to stay is the modern *parador* a few miles south-east of Mazagón. An isolated beach location, but not cheap for three-star facilities. Budget options include Los Geránios, a simple friendly place at Isla Cristina, or the two-star El Cortijo, a recently renovated hotel in an old farmhouse on the back edge of Matalascañas, which caters well for prospective visitors to the Coto Doñana National Park (see over).

If you are heading west for the Algarve, there is another modern *parador* (under repair when inspected but reputedly comfortable) at the southern border town of Ayamonte, where a battered little shuttle ferry whizzes back and forth every half hour or so across the Guardiana estuary to Portugal. A new roadbridge is being built upstream.

Doñana National Park

South of Seville the River Guadalquivir makes it way to the sea through a vast and largely inaccessible wilderness of marshes, dunes and reedbeds. It is one of Europe's most important wildlife habitats. To visit the Park, contact the reception centre at Acebuche, a couple of miles north of Matalascañas, at least a day in advance (longer in high season; the tours get very full). Local tourist offices or hotels can help you book by telephone. At the centre you can visit bird hides, see films (showings available in English) and exhibitions about the Park, and buy guidebooks. Tours cost about £10. Convoys of rugged high-wheeled buses or Land Rovers set off twice a day in spring and summer (not Mondays) for a bumpy four-hour trek over beaches, sand-dunes and marshes, stopping at intervals to admire whatever species are in sight. What you see depends on the time of year. There are lots of deer, wild boar, and a few rare lynxes. But the biggest pull of the reserve is the migatory birds, and you will see more of these during the wet winter or spring months. The tours are of general interest, rather than for the serious the naturalist. If you want a more specialised tour with a smaller group, ask at any of the three Park information centres on the El Rocío road.

Around Huelva

North of Huelva the main road winds through the mountains towards **Jabugo**, famous for its home-cured hams and sausages. You may catch sight of a live ham in the shape of a genuine Iberian pig, a small grey-brown beast, snuffling among acorns in the local forests. You can taste the celebrated *jamón de Jabugo* in roadside cafés. In autumn bundles of fruit, walnuts and figs hang temptingly packaged for passers-by along the roadsides. East of the main road are the strange red hills of the copper-bearing **Río Tinto** mines, where the landscape, exploited since Phoenician times, is scarred and terraced by open-cast workings over a huge area. In the nineteenth century workers of the newly formed British Rio Tinto Company moved in to ravage the hillsides again, building a curious enclave of English suburbia in the village. **Aracena**, on the Seville road, lays claim to a very beautiful limestone cave, the Gruta de las Maravillas. Inside, limpid pools reflect an astonishing variety of formations. Aracena has a nice old town, and there is a good choice of simple bars and restaurants.

LOS PUEBLOS BLANCOS

One of the finest pleasures of Andalucía lies not in the undeniably great Moorish cities, but in simply wandering between the *pueblos blancos*, the little white hill towns that lie dotted around parts of the provinces of Málaga and Cádiz. You will not find a great deal to do, particularly in the smaller ones, other than to relax and enjoy great views and a less frenetic way of life. Some, like Ronda, have become tourist traps. Others are barely visited. All will enhance your understanding of life in Andalucía. You will find them set amidst rugged countryside, between the Atlantic and the Mediterranean, a frosting of gleaming white houses perched on clifftops, or lining the walls of spectacular gorges. There is no coherent route to follow between them that will not require you to double back on yourself.

Ronda (H)

Because of its proximity to the Costa del Sol, Ronda is the most visited of the white towns. It has a distinct day-trip-and-coach-parties feel, having become the *de rigueur* excursion, making it almost an outpost of Torremolinos. The best approach is to leave the N-340 at San Pedro de Alcantara. The road climbs steadily, and little villages appear dwarfed below you as the road twists and turns on its upward path. Ronda's most striking aspect is its deep gorge – **El Tajo** – which slashes the town in two, and which was a grisly scene of execution during the Civil War. Hemingway adapted the story as one of the core incidents in *For Whom the Bell Tolls*. You will see it at its most menacing in evening light, when the golden walls seeem to glow. The gorge is straddled by the imposing lantern-lined **Puente Nuevo** which leads into the old quarter. Most items of tourist interest lie here, with the exception of the **Bullring**, which is part of the **Mercadillo**, the New Town, although it dates back to 1785. It is the second oldest in Spain, and thanks to the local matador Pedro Romero has been traditionally considered to be the cradle of modern bullfighting. The attached museum has some fascinating exhibits, although labelled in Spanish only.

A constant stream of traffic makes its way across the bridge. On the other side in the **Ciudad** the Collegiate church is a former mosque, embellished with three Gothic naves and a baroque altar. It still retains its *mihrab*. If you go down the street called Marqués de Salvatiera, you will reach the seventeenth-century mansion of the same name. When the family are not in residence, groups of up to 12 are taken around its plateresque portal and marble stairs pillaged from Granada, Córdoba and Seville. There is a pretty patio with stunning views over the Sierra and down to the Arab Baths which are currently closed for renovation.

There are a number of hotels in Ronda including the grand but shabby Reina Victoria and the cheerful and comfortable Polo. The best place to eat is Don Miguel, Plaza de España 3, Tel (952) 87 10 90.

Around Ronda

Cueva de la Pileta is a series of caverns with remarkable Bronze Age paintings of bison and fish. Follow the roadsigns for **Benaoján** and continue for five kilometres following the signs.

North of Ronda

Much less commercialised than Ronda is **Zahara de la Sierra** (H), a dramatically located hill-fort town. It is a clutch of shining white-walled, red-tiled houses centred around a church and castle. Balancing on a rocky outcrop in a mountainous back-drop, this is an almost perfect example of a 'white town', its attraction enhanced by a lack of tourists. It is stark and relentlessly Spanish, and has a pretty *hostal* on a steep cobbled street. **Olvera** 25 kilometres north-east of Zahara on the N-342, seems from there to fan out horizontally along the side of a mountain, swamped by greenery and dominated by a Moorish castle. **Sentenil**, 15 kilometres south-east of Olvera, is one of the strangest of the *pueblos*. Some of the houses line the walls of a gorge, with roofs of overhanging rock above, making the streets cave-like.

West of Ronda

The village of **El Bosque** (H) has a municipal swimming-pool and an ancient bullring. It also has a charming hotel, **Las Truchas**. Driving into **Arcos de la Frontera** (H) is an experience. The town stands on a craggy hill high above the River Guadalete. An impregnable fortress, its strategic position made it one of the most important towns of Moorish Spain. It was certainly not designed for the motor car; narrow streets twist and turn upwards, like a helter skelter in reverse. You can stand on the observation post precariously overlooking the drop and enjoy the spectacular view. Despite the popular *parador* you can feel that this is a town that has refused to lose its soul to tourism.

Both the Parador Casa del Corregidor and El Convento have agreeable restaurants as well as comfortable and stylish accommodation.

South of Arcos de la Frontera

Medina-Sidonia sits 37 kilometres south of Arcos on the C-343. Having been both a Roman colony and a Visigothic bishopric, the Moors conferred city status upon it with the prefix 'Medina'. These days it is rather ramshackle but totally unspoilt, with its parish church erected on the former site of a mosque. From Medina-Sidonia, the C-346 will bring you the 21 kilometres to **Chiclana de la Frontera** one of the less memorable *pueblos* which connects with the little seaside hamlet of **Sanct Petri** on the Costa de la Luz. From Chiclana, it is a 23-kilometre journey along the N-340 to **Vejer de la Frontera** (H), one of the most exciting and unspoilt of the *pueblos*. This brilliantly white Moorish town occupies a cleft between disconcertingly sheer hills, high above the road to Cádiz. This is another testing ground for drivers. As soon as you find yourself in the town, 'No Entry' signs appear and you find yourself directed down narrow, one-way streets, following the signs for Cádiz. Hidden among these you will find ochre-stoned churches and a castle and a peeling, whitewashed convent. Vejer now has a splendid hotel, the Hospedería del Convento de San Francisco, a converted convent with an excellent restaurant.

SEVILLE (H)

Andalucía's capital, the nation's fourth city, is many people's favourite among the country's major cities. While it lacks a world-ranking sight to match Granada's Alhambra or Córdoba's Mezquita it is the most beguiling of places. The pleasures are simpler and more leisurely; sitting idly in pavement bars; walking in María Luisa Park; taking a horse and carriage ride. This is the city of Carmen, Don Juan and Figaro. But the origins of Seville's greatness lie not in epic operatic tales but in the River Guadalquivir which cuts the city in two, making it Spain's only river port. Christopher Columbus, having set out in search of the Indies from the nearby port of **Palos de la Frontera** in Huelva, made a spectacular entry to Seville on his return flaunting gold, exotic birds and natives. Both Amerigo Vespucci and Magellan launched expeditions from the city. The coffers of Seville were to be filled with New World riches for centuries to come, and the city remembers the first of the great explorers in many ways. Five hundred years on, the Genoese sailor continues to bring untold riches to the city – in the form of tourists – as it gears up to host Expo '92, the World Fair, marking the quincentennial.

Seville's history goes back much further. *Sevillanos* claim that the city was founded by Hercules. More prosaically, the Romans built walls and made it the chief city of their state of *Baetica*. (You can visit important Roman ruins just outside the city at *Itálica*.) After Rome fell Seville was for a while the capital of the Visigothic kingdom. The Moors arrived in 712 and named it *Izvilla*, from which the present name derives. After the fall of the Cordoban Caliphate the Almohades established a prosperous, though less tolerant, kingdom based in Seville, and Sultan Yacoub Al-Mansur ordered the construction of the Giralda and the Torre d'Oro, two of the city's remaining standards of its Moorish past. Seville fell to the Christians in 1248. The arrival of American riches, coinciding with the final fall of the Nasrid kingdom in 1492, kept the city in clover for almost two centuries. Just as decline was setting in, the city played host to the talents of Velázquez, Zurbarán and Murillo, but loss of empire brought economic lethargy which lingered for a long time. The city has recently re-established itself as a major industrial centre and port, but unemployment remains high in the surrounding agricultural area. This has one major consequence. The crime rate is high, and camera-touting, cash-rich tourists are a soft target. Both muggings and car break-ins are frequent.

Driving in Seville is a hot, stuffy and often bewildering. The city centre is small enough to negotiate on foot, and you can take a taxi reasonably cheaply to the María Luisa Park. The city has a fast ring-road, and a one-way system that is rather daunting on first acquaintance; you can often see where your hotel is but find it difficult to work out how to get there. Having dumped your baggage you should immediately take your car to an underground car park, if your hotel has none. Car parks within 15 minutes' walk of the cathedral which you might try include those at Calles Arenal, Genil and Albareda.

Excursions which would justify reclaiming the car would include a visit to the **Coto Donãna National Park** (see page 320), or – for those determined to get away from it all – leading north to **Constantina** to go hiking in the Sierra Morena. There are two railway stations: Estación Plaza de Armas (also known as Córdoba), Plaza de Armas 56 for connections with Madrid, Córdoba, Málaga and other directions; and Estación Calle San Bernando for Cádiz, Jerez and Huelva. The airport is 12 kilometres from the city centre on the road to Córdoba.

August and September are very hot. Hotel prices fall considerably during this period. Seville's great festival, *Semana Santa*, and the April *Feria*, put enormous pressure on hotel beds. Expo '92 will run from 20 April until 16 October 1992.

Eating out, accommodation and entertainment

There is plenty of accommodation in the picturesque Barrio de Santa Cruz. While there is a certain romantic glamour about the area, early-to-bedders should give it a miss. Our hotel recommendations are all within walking distance of the cathedral. You will find accommodation is generally more expensive than elsewhere in Andalucía. For reasonable food, especially fish, and a stunning location right next to the Giralda try **El Giraldillo**, Plaza Virgen de los Reyes 2, Tel (95) 421 45 25. Across from the cathedral try **Figon del Cabildo**, Plaza del Cabildo, Tel (95) 422 01 17 for good food in an attractive surrounding. In the Barrio Santa Cruz **La Albahaca**, Plaza de Santa Cruz Tel (95) 422 07 14, occupies a wonderful old mansion, and serves imaginative fare, such as swordfish in sherry vinegar. For a cheap option with friendly service, try **Punta del Diamante** on the corner of Avenida de la Constitución and Calle Alemanes. It is worthwhile crossing the river to **Río Grande**, Calle Betis for the splendid views of the Giralda and the Torre d'Oro and particularly good *fritura sevillana*, assorted fried fish. For *tapas* – called *aperitivos* in Seville – cross the river into the Triana district, where there are a number of *bodegas* along the river bank on Betis, and several in Calle San Jacinto, many of which specialise in seafood. Back on the east bank **Bar Alicantina** on Plaza del Salvador is another seafood specialist. For a trip into the surreal visit **Joven Castelero**, Calle Torneo 18. The bar, famous for its tacky décor, runs non-stop videos.

For organised flamenco shows try **El Patio Sevillano**, Paseo Cristóbal Colón 11, Tel. (95) 421 41 20, or **Los Gallos**,

Plaza de Santa Cruz 11, Tel (95) 421 69 81, which has a rather more serious reputation. For less traditional nightlife that lasts far into the night, try the Triana district after midnight. For guitar music and traditional singing try **Bar Anselma** at the corner of Calles Pages del Coro and Antillano Campos.

Exploring the city

Almost everything of tourist interest lies on the west bank of the river. The best reasons for venturing into the Triana district, the former gypsy quarter on the east bank, are to eat, hop between *tapas* bars, or to check out the nightlife. Another possibility is to pick up some real ceramic bargains, particularly tiles: try **Cerámica Santa Ana** or **Montalbán**, Calle Alfareria 23, Calle San Jorge 31.

The best way of getting your bearings in Seville is to climb

FLAMENCO

Whether you are a fan of the Gypsy Kings or can remember the heyday of the great Spanish dancer Antonio, you are likely to be familiar with flamenco in one form or other. Its great exponents – singers, dancers and guitarists – have created for flamenco a world-wide following, while inevitably encouraging imitation and emulation which fail to meet the highest standards.

Flamenco is the art of the individual. Performances are improvised to the accompaniment of clapping, stamping and shouts of *Olé!* from the percussion section represented by the rest of the troupe – support which creates its own excitement and spurs on the soloist (singer, dancer or instrumentalist) to ever greater heights. True flamenco happens spontaneously, in an intimate setting, which is somewhat at odds with the modern trend for packaged entertainment experience. It was chiefly the gypsies of modern Spain, themselves initially from the East, who originated the art of flamenco. Experts detect a resemblance in the melodies to the ragas of Hindustan, and an Arab influence in the performance styles. For a long time flamenco remained a folk art form, little known outside Andalucía, which was for a long time a melting-pot for all sorts of musical traditions from around the Mediterranean area. In particular, flamenco meant the songs and dances of the

---

to the top of the Giralda tower, next to the cathedral, from which you will see the whole of the city laid out before you. Five minutes' walk to the east will bring you to the Alcázar and the quaint, whitewashed Barrio Santa Cruz. North of here the city becomes progressively more run down, but if you bear east you will find the **Convent of San Leandro** where the nuns sell famous egg-yolk sweets known as *yemas*. Nearby is the Renaissance palace known as **Pilate's House**. You will find the main pedestrianised shopping is on **Calle Sierpes** just north of the cathedral. West of the cathedral, and by the river, are the **Torre d'Oro**, now a maritme museum, and the bullring. The magnificent former tobacco factory where Carmen strutted her stuff, now the university, lies further south, as does the **María Luisa Park** where there are a number of museums, as well as the dazzling Plaza d'España, erected for the 1929 Ibero-American exhibition.

Sevillian gypsy (in Seville the word *flamenco* means gypsy, while in Granada, Spain's other important gypsy centre the word used is *gitano*). But gypsies have had a chequered career in Spain, as in much of Europe; until the end of the eighteenth century they were outcasts. In the last century, however, flamenco was able to develop and to move, gradually, from the fields into the *cafés cantantes* (singing cabarets) as its entertainment value became more widely recognised. Professional singers, musicians and dancers latched on to it, creating more elaborate and stylised forms, and taking it ultimately into the theatres, where flamenco troupes became the established medium.

Passionate, dramatic, teasing, sorrowful, the songs of flamenco deal with the big topics of human emotion such as love and death. Vocal delivery is typically harsh and nasal, its tone as raw as the emotions exposed in the songs. A good guitarist will follow the singer's melodic line instinctively, anticipating each twist and turn with uncanny precision. A similar interaction can be seen between dancer and instrumentalist, or in the performance of a tango by a male/female couple. Regional styles too have their influence, but the temperament and mood of the performer is the element that will always guarantee excitement and unpredictability in true flamenco.

The main sights around the cathedral

● **The Giralda** Even the conquering Christians were so impressed by this glorious twelfth-century minaret that when they demolished the mosque of which it was a part, they decided to spare it and incorporate it as the bell-tower of their cathedral. Ironically, more than seven hundred years later the tower remains the symbol of the city, with its ornate, *sebka* rhomboid brick patterning intact. Not that the Giralda has survived entirely unscathed: in 1565 the architect Hernando Ruíz added a belfry, lantern and a thirteen-foot statue of *La Fe* – Faith – acting as a weather vane, hence *El Giralda*. It is well worth making the 98-metre climb up the sloping ramp that Fernando III used when he ascended on horseback, because there are superb views over the city and the ornate façade of the cathedral. The admission price includes entrance to the cathedral.

● **The cathedral** Having recognised the timeless artistic merit of the Giralda, the Christians resolved to build a mammoth edifice on an unprecedented scale. The result is the Cathedral of Santa María, the third largest Christian Church in the world (after St Peter's in Rome and London's Saint Paul's), and the largest in Gothic style. The true sweep of the bulk is difficult to appreciate because the Gothic choir, with 117 stalls, and the chancel (enclosed by an amazing three-sided gold *reja*) block the main aisle. The very grubby, though ornate, exterior gives little hint of the treasures which lie within, including the Gothic altarpiece – 20 metres high – begun by the Flemish sculptor Pieter Dancart in 1482.

At the south transept stands the enormous nineteenth-century tomb of Christopher Columbus, finally at rest, his remains having experienced almost as much transatlantic travel since his death as he did while alive. His coffin is shown borne by figures representing the kings of Aragón, Navarra, Castile and León. Look closely and you will see a pomegranate, the symbol of the Moors, pierced by a lance.

● **Los Reales Alcázares** The Royal Palaces were commissioned by King Pedro the Cruel in 1350 to occupy a site on the ruins of Al-Mutamid's palace. Of the twelfth-century Almohad Alcázar, only El Yeso courtyard, which is not open to the public, and the fortifications remain. For all his fratricidal tendencies (and he finally got his come-uppance, dispatched by another brother) Pedro deserves a pat on the back for bringing master Mudéjar craftsmen from Toledo, but most crucially from Granada, to work on a building that in places is remarkably similar to the Alhambra – right down to Moorish arches and ornamental stucco work that includes passages from the *Koran* in Kufic script.

The first courtyard, **Patio de la Montería**, was added by the Duke of Olivares in the seventeenth century and has fine arabesques with lions and castles, denoting the kingdoms of Castile and León. It is difficult to deduce any chronological pattern in the chambers and halls which follow, better simply to admire the beautiful tilework and ornate plaster decoration. The **Patio de las Doncellas** (Court of the Maidens) is the largest and has multi-lobed arches resting on twin columns and leads to the **Salón de Embajadores** (Ambassadors' Hall) where Carlos V married Isabella of Portugal. Here there are wrought-iron balconies, horseshoe arches, brilliant panels of *azulejo* tiles and walls completely covered with plant motifs. You can also enter the austere fifteenth-century additions including the **Casa de Contratación**, where the strategies for New World exploration and trade were plotted, overseen by a model of the *Santa María*. Carlos V added a palace, as he did at Granada. It is most notable for the splendid Flemish tapestries which detail his Tunisian campaign. The attached, rambling gardens with their goldfish ponds and waterlilies are a pleasant place to escape from the heat of the city, especially since they remain open over fiesta time.

● **Barrio de Santa Cruz** The most picturesque part of the old town cleaves to the walls of the Alcázar, its winding whitewashed streets a happy mixture of aristocratic houses with pretty patios and wrought-iron grilles and shops selling everything from antique furniture to ceramics.

● **Archivo General de los Indias** The fine sixteenth-century former Stock Exchange is now a repository for the vast volume of documents that tells the story of the discovery and colonisation of the New World.

● **Casa de Pilatos**, not far from the cathedral area, is another curiosity, a sixteenth-century mansion built for the Marqués de Tarifa and known as Pilate's House, allegedly based on the Praetor's (Roman Governor's) house in Jerusalem.

● **Museo de Bellas Artes (Fine Art Museum)** This collection – second only to the Prado in importance – has long been languishing in the old Convent of la Merced, a truly delightful seventeenth-century building which was beginning to show its age. Some rooms were re-opened in 1990, but the collection is unlikely to be completely accessible until 1992.

Visitors then will be able to see important works by members of the Sevillian school including Murillo, Zurbarán and Valdés Leal, as well as Velázquez and El Greco.

● **Torre del Oro** (Tower of Gold) This defensive tower dates back to 1220, and was one the most southern of 64 built along the city wall. Its function was to guard the city in times of trouble, and a chain could be stretched across the river to another tower to form a barrier. When it was built, the 12-sided building was adorned with long-vanished gold and *azulejo* tiles. These days it houses a small maritime museum.

● **Hospital de la Caridad** (Charity Hospital) In 1661 Don Miguel de Manara commissioned a church hospital in baroque style, allegedly as an act of expiation. His tomb, at the entrance to the Hospital says, with typical Sevillian overstatement, 'Here lie the bones and ashes of the worst man who ever lived'. The Hospital itself has a brilliantly colourful interior, twisting gold columns on either side of the altar – and two of Valdés Leal's most grotesque works, one of which shows a decomposing cardinal being eaten by maggots. Murillo found it so odious that 'You have to hold your nose to look at it'. His own works include massive canvasses on more conventionally religious themes, *Moses Striking Water from the Rock* and *Miracle of the Loaves and Fishes*. Above the altar is Pere Roldán's *Burial of Christ* with a painted background and a sculpted body being borne away. **Plaza de Toros de la Real Maestranza** Seville's bullring, one of the most beautiful, is also one of the most important; an appearance here will be one of the pinnacles of a matador's career. The season runs from Easter Sunday until October with *corridas* being held each Sunday, and daily during the April *Feria*.

Around María Luisa Park

This beautiful park was layed out for the 1929 Ibero-American exhibition, which came close to bankrupting the city when its staging coincided with the Wall Street crash. Some of the ornate pavilions from the exhibition are still used to house museums, and behind them you stumble across hidden bowers and exquisite flowers.

The **Museo de Artes y Costumbres Populares** (Popular Arts Museum) on the Plaza de América is housed in the quite fabulous Mudéjar Pavilion. This is a cheerful ensemble of traditional costumes, household effects and agricultural implements, as well as posters and other memorabilia connected with the April fair. The **Museo Arqueológico** sits across the Plaza in the Renaissance Pavilion. Exhibits range from Neolithic items through to Moorish ones, with a number of important Roman remains, including mosaics and busts excavated at *Itálica*.

Just beside María Luisa is the showpiece of the 1929 Exhibition, the **Plaza d'España**. This enormous folly sweeps in a grand semi-circle and is flanked by tall baroque towers filched from Santiago de Compostela, Busby Berkeley-type staircases and an enormous colonnade. The lower façade is decorated with *azulejo* tiles depicting maps and historical scenes from all of Spain's provinces, and a small, bridged moat has been dug, where rowing boats glide gently past.

Out of town

Itálica The main attraction at this Roman excavation, about eight kilometres north-west of the city on the N-630 near the town of Santiponce, is the enormous second-century amphitheatre, which is believed to have held crowds of 25,000 – making it the third largest in the Roman world.

Three emperors (Trajan, Hadrian and Theodosius) were born here in what was, in its day, an important outpost of the Empire, founded in the third century BC.

East of Seville

Carmona (H) This rather sleepy little town, perched on a high cliff overlooking the flat wheatfields of the Guadalquivir plain, has a long and distinguished history, and disputes with Cádiz the title of Europe's most venerable continuously inhabited town. The Romans knew it as Carmo, and sections of the wall remain. In 206 BC Scipio's Romans defeated Hasdrubal's Carthaginians nearby and two of the massive stone gateways from that time are still in use. The leaflet issued by the local tourist office claims that the **Puerta de Sevilla** was part of the most complicated defensive enclosure in Spain, and that the turret in the Alcázar – formerly the palace of Pedro the Cruel and now a wonderful *parador* – is the oldest artillery emplacement in Europe. If you wander down the steep streets from the *parador* into the little town you will stumble across one of Andalucía's best-preserved historic quarters. The cathedral-like **Church of Santa María**, which has Spain's oldest (sixth-century) calendar carved on an arch, is flanked by a collection of religious houses and palaces that seems quite out of proportion to the size of the place, including **San Pedro** whose baroque tower mimics the Giralda. The Plaza de San Fernando is lined by seventeenth- and eighteenth-century houses and wrought-iron lamp-posts.

The town also has an important necropolis a kilometre or so out of town where you can see circular family graves and stone caskets within the hollowed-out walls. Although many of the finds have been carted off to Seville, the small on-site museum displays various items of pottery and mosaic. The **Elephant Tomb**, named after the statue of an elephant found at its entrance, contains three dining-rooms and a kitchen, giving rise to a belief that the priests engaged in some form of banqueting ritual.

Ecija The notorious 'frying pan of Andalucía' – the region's hottest spot, 92 kilometres from Seville – has also had a chequered history, best seen in its Roman remains, including an amphitheatre, sections of the original wall and fragments of villas. As at Carmona, a number of churches and palaces sprang up in the seventeenth and eighteenth centuries, and the whole town is a canvas for examples of the baroque, plateresque and Mudéjar styles. The town is best known for its 11 *azulejo*-covered towers, which give it a distinctive skyline, visible from the main road.

Osuna, further south, and 92 kilometres from Seville, was an important Roman town, and at one time minted its own currency. Following the Reconquest the town was ceded to the Commander of the Knights of Calatrava, who became the first Duke of Osuna. The **Collegiate Church** displays a rich Churrigueresque altarpiece, while its **Museum** has a fine collection of paintings by Ribera. The **Encarnación Monastery**, now a museum, has gorgeous Sevillian tiles and a handsomely carved altarpiece. The town also has a number of baroque and Renaissance palaces. **Morón de la Frontera**, south-west of Osuna, has a ruined eleventh-century castle, below which the parish church of San Miguel has a west façade in a pseudo-Renaissance style, while San Ignacio has a baroque portal. Every July it holds a famous flamenco festival called *Gazpacho Andaluz*.

CORDOBA (H)

This compact city crammed full of sights is perhaps the least well-known of Andalucía's great Moorish cities. It is hard to believe, looking at it today, that it was once the centre of the western world. The Moors first arrived in Spain in 711 and quickly defeated King Roderick. By 756 the powerful leader Abd Ar-Rahman had overthrown the previous Emir of Córdoba and restored order where previously there had been anarchy, by promoting policies of religious tolerance. Once secure he embarked on an enormous building programme which established Córdoba as the power-house of Al-Andaluz for several centuries. At its zenith Córdoba was the biggest and most important city west of Constantinople, with Europe's first university, a library of over 4,000 volumes, and a reputation for pre-eminence in medicine and mathematics. After 1002, the glorious Caliphate dissolved in internecine conflict, its warring factions overseeing powerless kingdoms, *taifas*, and thus divided, it fell, never to retrieve its position.

The city divides fairly naturally into old and new sectors, and most of the places of interest to visitors lie north of the River Guadalquivir, and particularly in a boot-shaped area bounded by the river, the Alcázar to the west, Ronda de los Tejares to the north, and the roads that lead from the Capuchin convent back to the river, to the east. Parking is tricky, but there is a supervised car park in front of the Mezquita, to the left of the Roman bridge, or ask your hotel about long-term parking (many have underground carparks).

The province of Córdoba is at the physical centre of Andalucía, and its capital has good communication links with the rest of the region, with regular trains to Seville, Granada, Cádiz, Málaga, Jaén and Algeciras, as well as to Madrid and Barcelona. Buses visit Ubeda and Jerez, among other places.

Exploring the city

This is a city to explore on foot. The modern part, with its shops, banks and offices, focuses on the Plaza Antonio; the heart of the tourist area, the Judería, is a maze of tiny, cobbled alleys with whitewashed houses and splendid patios ablaze with delicate flowers or thick greenery, where tiny fountains send arcs of water into basins of *azulejo* tiles. In little workshops craftsmen work at delicate filigree jewellery, often sold in the Zoco, a modern rendition of an Arab souk.

To the east of the main new shopping area near Plaza Colón is a tiny square beside the Capuchin convent, the Plazuela de los Dolores, where a towering, stark, crucified Christ is surrounded by wrought-iron lanterns – Cristo de los Faroles. Further east there are more squares, churches and whitewashed houses in the Parish of Santa María, traditionally the home of Spain's greatest bullfighters. A flamboyant statue outside the church of Santa María de las Aguas Santas commemorates Manolete, Córdoba's most honoured matador of recent times, who died of injuries sustained in the ring in 1947. Here and there you can catch a glimpse of a palace, such as that of the Marqués de Vianda, a splendid sixteenth-century example with over a dozen wonderful interconnecting patios, opulent furniture and a number of tapestries by Goya. There are a number of venerable churches scattered througout the area north of the Mezquita, a legacy of the church-building programme instituted by the Catholic Kings following the Reconquest. South-east of the centre the **Plaza de la Corredera** is a pale-brick, arcaded square, built in 1690, where bullfights used to be held. A colourful market now sets up in the mornings.

Eating out, accommodation and entertainment

Córdoba excels on the *tapas* front and there are a number of *tascas*, especially in Calle Puerta de Almodóvar. Names to look out for include Taberna de Pepe, El de la Judería, Calle Romero 1, La Mezquita on Calle Cardenel Herrero (close to the mosque) where you can drink the local morilla wine straight from the barrel and, almost opposite the synagogue, Bodega Guzmán, Calle Judíos 9. The city also has a horde of places for more formal eating, including the much-praised El Caballo Rojo, Calle Cardenel Herrero 28, Tel (957) 47 53 75 one of the best places to try the local speciality *rabo de toro*, a bull's tail stew. A more recent off-shoot of the same enterprise, El Blasón, next to the Gran Teatro at Calle Zorrilla 11, Tel (957) 48 06 25, specialises in Cordoban *nouvelle cuisine*. Less expensive and more atmospheric is El Churrasco, Romero 16, Tel (957) 29 08 19, a lively patio-restaurant, covered by awnings by day, where you can dine under the stars at night. The *churrasco* dishes – kebab-like dishes prepared on a charcoal grill and covered in a peppery sauce – are highly recommended.

The most atmospheric places to stay are all in or around the old quarter of the Judería. The most agreeable exception is the *parador* which is situated in a residential area, some five kilometres away.

Nightlife is centred around Calle Reyes Católicos and Ronda de los Tejares. Flamenco shows are held regularly at the Zoco Municipal during the summer months. Serious lovers of the art should time their visit to coincide with the

Concurso Nacional de Arte Flamenco, a festival held in Córdoba every two years.

The main sights

● **La Mezquita** From the outside there is nothing to whet the appetite about Córdoba's Great Mosque. The thick, crenellated grimy walls have recently been shrouded in scaffolding and tarpaulin, like many of Andalucía's greatest treasures. Gypsy women haunt the entrance, the Puerto del Perda, the fine bronze-covered Mudéjar gateway, trying to force roses or carnations upon you, and a ghetto of tacky souvenir shops stretches from the mosque's immediate environs into the Judería. This opens into the Patio de los Naranjos, where orange trees have replaced the original laurel, cypress and olive trees, and fountains have been added. This was where the Moors carried out ritual ablutions prior to entering the holy place.

The mosque is entered by what is now known as the Doorway of the Blessings, where the standards of the Christian armies were blessed before being carried off on the campaign that led to the capture of Granada. Once inside, the Mezquita is a bewildering place, dark and gloomy thanks to the Christian insistence on sealing what had previously been open to the courtyard. They did this by lining the boundaries with a series of chapels, lessening the impact of one of the supreme design triumphs of the Moors – the symmetry between the trees of the courtyard and the columns of the mosque.

If you walk to the right and follow the dip of the floor you will reach the oldest part of the mosque which dates back to the late eighth century. There are eleven aisles separated by 110 orderly columns. Fifty years later the mosque had to be extended to accommodate an increasing population and 'Abd Ar-Rahman II added another five aisles to the south – 80 columns in all, the first of several extensions that took place over a 200-year period. In 961 Alhakem II added ten rows of alternating columns in blue and rose marble as well as the dazzling *mihrab*, the sacred prayer niche situated at the end of the main aisle, an octagonal chamber set into the wall whose doorway has a magnificent mosaic arch, with inscriptions from the *Koran*, and fabulously intricate patterns engraved in exquisite colours. The cupola takes the shape of a stone shell and rests on arches decorated with small interlaced ones.

But all is not as it was; following the Reconquest the Christians decided to set their seal on this Muslim holy place.

Alfonso X introduced a **Capilla Real** in 1258, using *azulejo* and lobed niches in a sympathetic Mudéjar style. Just in front of the great *mihrab* the **Capilla Villaviciosa** a Christian addition of 1377 with ornate stucco work occupies a former *mihrab*. Around 1520 the ecclesiastical authorities decided that the city needed a cathedral, and proposed to interpolate this within the mosque by removing 63 columns. The ostentatious superimposition runs the architectural gamut from Gothic to baroque and plateresque and, while over-florid, might be well regarded in another location. Set as it amid the gorgeous simplicity of the mosque, it is almost universally regarded as an act of artistic desecration.

Alcázar de los Reyes Cristianos (Palace of the Catholic Monarchs) One of the loveliest spots in the city is, unfortunately closed in the afternoons until 5pm. It was originally built as a fortress by Alfonso XI around a chapel built by Alfonso X. However, it was later turned into a glorious palace. Begin your visit by climbing the Tower of the Lions, for fine views over the gardens, the city and the Mezquita. The tower also contains the original chapel which is now a hall. Best of all are the exhibits in the **Salón de Mosaicos** including a large mosaic of geometric patterns, and a complete depiction of Polyphemus and Galatea, both from the first century, plus a substantial fragment of a third-century Venus and Psyche. For much of its life the fortress was a prison whose inmates included the captured King Boabdil of Granada.

From the Alcázar you should cross the Roman bridge to the **Calahorra Tower**. At the outset wax figures of the great and the good, including great Moorish thinkers, Alfonso the Wise and Maimónides, expound taped Utopian intellectual ideas with a portentous solemnity that makes you feel that you have stumbled upon an undergraduate philosophy tutorial, but that apart, you are whisked through Córdoba's importance in the history of western thought, scholarship and engineering in an entertaining way.

Museo Arqueológico Provincial. An important collection of finds from neolithic, Roman and Moorish times, situated in a splendidly attractive palace north-east of the Mezquita. If you pass through the El Portillo Arch you will come to the **Museo de Bellas Artes** (Fine Art Museum) in the former La Caridad hospital. This is a worthwhile collection with painters including Zurbarán, Murillo and Valdés Leal among those represented. The next-door museum is devoted to the local hack artist Julio Romero de Torres, of whom it might charitably be said that assessment of his work depends on matters of taste. You will see postcards of his best-known works, a dark-eyed, supposedly seductive woman cradling oranges to her ample breast, in every postcard rack in town. Both these museums stand on **El Potro** square named after the rearing horse which adorns its fountain, and which earned a mention in *Don Quixote*.

● **The Judería** A charming, haphazard quarter of whitewashed houses on narrow streets, the area around the mosque can be something of a bottleneck. On Calle Judíos you can visit the **Synagogue**, one of only three remaining in Spain. This is a small and simple place, but has fine fourteenth-century Mudéjar plasterwork and Hebrew inscriptions. **El Zoco** across the road is a collection of sixteenth-century buildings around a courtyard where local crafts – notably leather goods and silver filigree – are sold. It adjoins the **Museo Taurino y de Arte Cordobés**, a museum mainly devoted to bullfighting built around an attractive patio. Even if you have moral qualms about bullfighting you will find this collection – including the skin of the bull that dispatched the local superstar Manolete – fascinating.

Around Córdoba

Medina Azahara, six kilometres west of the city in the foothills of the Sierra Morena, was a palace retreat built by 'Abd Ar-Rahman III for his favourite wife Azahara in 936. It is believed that in its time it rivalled the Mezquita (4,000 columns decorated the palace, its own mosque and outbuildings) and that its attendant orchards, gardens and barracks occupied an incredible 275 acres, making it in effect a mini-city. Its splendour was short lived. Berber mercenaries called in to defend it treacherously razed it to the ground less than eighty years after it was built. Ironically, it then provided a sort of architectural 'scrap yard', and *spoglia* from it found its way into Seville's Alcázar in the same sort of recycling operation that had enhanced the Mezquita.

JAEN

East of Córdoba and north of Granada and sheltering beneath the mountains of the Sierra Morena lies Jaén province, the olive oil capital of Europe: almost everywhere you go the outlook is completely dominated by acres of olive trees.

While the provincial capital, the city of Jaén, is rather dull, the province boasts two wonderful Renaissance cities, **Baeza** and **Ubeda**, as well as an oustanding National Park in the Sierra de **Cazorla**, where anglers and huntsmen join walkers in exploring the undulating terrain.

Jaén has good road connections with Córdoba along the N-324, and a direct route to Granada, the N-323. The approach from the south to remote Cazorla via **Quesada** is one of the most spectacular but undiscovered drives in Andalucía, as valleys studded with olive groves unfold below you like a pointillist painting. Rail connections link Jaén with Córdoba and Madrid, but are otherwise sparse. The area has three splendid *paradores* at Jaén, Ubeda and Cazorla, as well as a rather functional one at Bailén. Otherwise both accommodation and food are likely to be simple.

The city of **Jaén** (H) is for the most part a charmless commercial centre. The cathedral, begun in 1548, was designed by the important architect Vandelvira, and construction continued until the eighteenth century. Most notable are the baroque west façade, and the cathedral's magisterial height. The choir-stall has memorable carvings of gruesome martyrdoms. The other important sight of the lower city is the Arab baths, the largest in Spain, which lies below street level on Plaza Luisa de Marillac. Jaén's dramatically located thirteenth-century castle has been sensitively restored and now houses a very fine *parador*.

Baeza, 48 kilometres north-east of Jaén, was a Renaissance university town with a thriving economy based on agriculture and textiles. Today's visitors will find three small palaces with impressive façades on the Calle San Pablo which leads to the arcaded and bar-lined main square. Just off it is the Plaza de Leones, where the lion fountain is surrounded by splendid Renaissance buildings. The fine cathedral, also designed by Valdevira, is currently undergoing extensive restoration, and is closed to visitors.

Splendid as Baeza is, it is but an appetiser for the larger town of **Ubeda** (H) nine kilometres further east, which seems to be bursting at the seams with Renaissance architecture. The tourist office produces a leaflet, which describes the amazing wealth of astonishingly fine buildings, many by Valdevira, which cluster around in a series of golden squares. Most of these are crowded together in a small area, the exception being St James' Hospital on the far side of the town.

The most sensible place to begin is in the Plaza Vázquez de Molino, where the *parador* is located in a lovely old palace.

Even if you are unable to stay, come and have a drink in its attractive patio. Immediately adjacent is the Church of El Salvador, with an ornate façade, and a sacristy by Valdevira, and a spectacular *reja* by Master Bartolomé. If it is closed – and restoration work is currently underway – knock on the door and the caretaker will show you around, enthusing in rapid Spanish over its considerable treasures, including a massive altarpiece. Also on the square is Valdevira's Casa de la Cadenas, now the town hall, its honey-coloured stone bright and dazzling under the sun, and the church of Santa María de los Reales Alcazares, which is also being renovated. Make sure your tour encompasses the central square where the bullet-holed statue of General Saro presides. His pock-marked face tells you more about modern Spanish politics than most books on the Civil War.

Seventy kilometres away, near the source of the River Guadalquivir, the Parador El Adalento, a former hunting lodge sits amid the spectacular scenery of a huge National Park, near the town of **Cazorla** (H). The little town, 26 kilometres from the *parador*, is an animated and busy little place. Above the ruins of the church of Santa María, the Sierra rises vertically, while a *balcón* gives good views of the white houses of the town. Near here is a photogenic little *hostale*, the Mesón de Cueva de Juan Pedro, its white-washed walls ablaze with strings of chillis and peppers which hang from its balconies. This is very much a place where you dine on *raciones* – *croquetas*, *calamares* and little open sandwiches. The bar Las Vegas, on the main square, is very popular with locals. Cazorla is very much a walking holiday centre, used by specialist tour operators, and there are a couple of good little *pensiones* in town, as well as the remote *parador* within the National Park.

GRANADA (H)

1492 and all that is a double-edged sword, for just as it com-memorates the achievement of Christopher Columbus in dis-covering the New World, and delivering the prospect of unimaginable riches to his patrons, Ferdinand and Isabella, it also marks the fall of the Nasrid dynasty of Granada, beget-ters of the Alhambra, the highest point of Moorish architec-ture, and so might be seen as tragedy, as well as triumph.

The complex of buildings that makes up the Alhambra is the best-known of Granada's – and indeed of Andalucía's –

sights. The city encompasses some significant art of the Reconquest, not least the Cathedral and Capilla Real, as well as Sacromonte – the gypsy quarter. The surrounding province is astonishing in its diversity, ranging from resorts such as Almuñécar on the Mediterranean coast, to Europe's highest village at Trevélez in the Sierra Nevada, the cave-dwellers of Guadix, and the villages of the Alpujarras.

Exploring the city

Framed by a backdrop of the snow-covered peaks of the Sierra Nevada, Granada lies on and around three low hills. The Alhambra hill, with its complex of palaces, gardens and fortifications is the most famous of these. The steep road which leads to it – Cuesta de Gomerez – is lined with tacky souvenir shops, in amongst which you will find some marquetry and antique shops, as well as guitar makers.

Much of the lower town is nineteenth-century or later, the best shopping areas are on the two main streets, Reyes Católicos and Gran Vía de Colón which meet at the Plaza de Isabel la Católica. Away from the main sights you can find some nice squares, where you can sit and watch the world go by.

In the centre behind the cathedral is a network of narrow streets the **Alcaicería**, which in Moorish times housed a raw-silk market. This has been restored as a tourist shopping area, where gaudy flamenco dresses and other items of colourful tourist tat are hung on display, spilling out into the street. Opposite is the **Corral del Carbón**, a fourteenth-century Arab caravanserai, now housing a branch of the quality government crafts chain Artespaña. Nearby is the Plaza de Bibarrambia, with flower stalls, small shops and pavement cafés, and just off it, in **Pescadería**, a morning market and more little shops.

The second hill is the **Albaicin**, the former Moorish quarter, on the right bank of the River Darro. Its steep and narrow cobbled alleys are lined with white houses, complete with wrought-iron balconies, window boxes, bird cages and washing hanging outside. The privately owned **Moorish Baths** (El Bañuelo), 33 Carrera del Daro are often closed, but are often considered the best preserved in Spain. Two of its four chambers have star-shaped holes in the vaulting, and some of the columns have Roman or Visigothic capitals. From the terrace in front of **San Nicolas** church you will find *the* view of the Alhambra, complete with snow-topped mountains in the background.

Beside the Albaicin, on the edge of town is the third hill, **Sacromonte**, the gypsy quarter. Gypsies try to exhort you to visit their whitewashed cave houses along the Camino del Sacromonte for flamenco sessions; often execrable, but occasionally what Jan Morris described as the best folk-dancing in Europe. If you want to explore this area at night, organise a group visit by taxi from your hotel. Do not wander around alone, as the streets are poorly lit.

Although the city has an airport 17 kilometres west of the town most vistors from the UK fly into Málaga. Daily rail services run from Granada to Madrid, Almería, Seville, Córdoba and Algeciras. Buses run to additional destinations including Barcelona, Valencia and Alicante. There is very little on-street parking in the lower city. Some hotels have car parks. Otherwise you will need to use an underground car park. In the central area try Calle de Recogidas, Carrera del Genil and Calle Espadero Pino.

Eating out, accommodation and nightlife

Although you can eat reasonably well, you are unlikely to hit upon anything truly memorable. Try Baroca, Pedro Antonio de Alarcón 34, Tel (958) 26 50 61 or near the Cathedral, Sevilla, Oficios 12, Tel (958) 22 12 23. It also has an excellent *tapas* bar. If you just want to eat with the locals head for Campo del Príncipe, (good for *tapas* snacks and full meals). Granada has a large number of hotels, both on the Alhambra hill and in the lower quarter. Alhambra hotels are generally quieter, but can be expensive. Don't be put off by the received wisdom about the need to book the *parador* six months in advance, it is always worth trying on spec. Attending the *zambras*, the gypsy flamenco shows, is often an expensive, disappointing, occasionally risky business. There are a couple of organised *tablao* shows, La Reina Mora, Mirador de San Cristóbal, Tel (958) 27 82 28 and Jardines Neptuno, Calle Arabial, Tel (958) 25 11 12. For discos, and youth-targeted bars try Calle Alarcón in the university area.

The main sights

● **The Alhambra** The historical circumstances that led to the initial flourishing of the Nasrid dynasty, and the quirks of fate that led to Boabdil's submission in 1492 are complex. By the thirteenth century, after the fragmentation that had led to the establishment of the *taifas*, Moorish Spain was consider-

341

ably weakened, particularly after the battle of Las Navas de Tolosa in 1212. Muhammad I emerged from the mayhem of the petty kingdoms to rule over the city or province of Granada in 1238 at a time when the Moorish world was shrinking. Córdoba fell to the Christians in 1236; Valencia, Jaén and Seville followed in rapid succession. The Moors retreated to Granada, their last bastion and there, against all odds, the Nasrid dynasty somehow engineered an intellectual and architectural Indian summer that produced the most triumphant statement of Moorish art ever seen, assisted by the *kismet* that had delivered all the greatest craftsmen to Granada, as they fled the rest of the peninsula.

The longevity of the Granada Sultanate can be ascribed to the continuing divisions within the Christian kingdom. These divisions effectively disappeared when Ferdinand and Isabella, having married in 1469, had succeeded to their respective thrones by 1479, thereby uniting the Kingdoms of Castile and Aragón. They determined to thwart their rivals by uniting the Christian world in a campaign to win Granada. It was internecine dispute that finally precipitated the fall of Granada. The Christians manipulated the situation to their advantage. After ten years of warfare Boabdil surrendered, and soon decamped to North Africa, together with many of his people. Those who remained and converted to Christianity were the craftsmen who brought the Mudéjar style, as Ferdinand and Isabella moved in and made the palace their own. Carlos V later interpolated a palace, but the royal court took to withdrawing for long periods, and the Alhambra developed a chequered history. Squatters moved in and used the palaces as stabling and a source of firewood. Napoleon's troops in retreat were ordered to blow it up, but the operation was sabotaged by a Spanish soldier who cut the fuse. Later on, in the nineteenth century, the Alhambra came to be noticed by travellers, not least the writer and diplomat Washington Irving, whose works led to international efforts and a campaign to restore the neglected masterpiece.

On approaching Granada you can see the Alhambra dominating the skyline, sitting impenetrably above the city. If you visit on a Saturday or Wednesday night take the chance to visit the floodlit Alhambra open between 10pm and midnight. There is a special magical atmosphere in the darkness, which leads everyone to speak in careful whispers which echo far into the night. The layout of the site can be confusing, so it is advisable to consider it as follows. Otherwise try to visit soon after 10am, before the coach parties descend.

The most venerable part of the site, the **Alc-azaba** is in fact the least exciting. The present structure, which dates from 1238 when Muhammad I won control, is a successor to the original Moorish fortress built in 889, probably on Roman foundations. Climb the watchtower for a fine view of the whole palace. The unpromising defensive walls of the **Casa Real** give way to a series of spectacular courtyards and reception halls where the imaginative use of light and space are almost overwhelming. In all of them are the carved wood cornices, delicate tracery, panels of ornate stucco work and dazzling glazed multi-coloured *azulejo* tiles which characterise the Alhambra. One of the more mystifying things is that although the design is made up of complex patterns and recurring Arabic inscriptions, it all seems incredibly simple. Throughout the palace you can hear the tinkling of water in pools and fountains. The Moorish love of water is seen at its best in the **Court of the Myrtles** where the central feature is the long ornamental pool, suurounded by an arcade of columns which flare into the ornate horseshoe arches which are the essence of Moorish architecture, and which are reflected in the pool. At one end is the **Tower of Comares** containing the **Hall of the Throne** and the **Room of the Blessings** where new rulers were invested. To one side are the **Court Hall**, the reception room and the **Mexuar**, – Hall of Audience – subsequently consecrated as a chapel.

At the centre of the palace is the famous **Court of the Lions**, named after the large low-lying fountain, resting on statues of grotesque lions which is its focal point. This courtyard is made to look quite different by the simple expedient of alternating single and paired slender columns throughout the arcade. The **Hall of the Kings** which has painted ceilings lies at one end and the **Hall of the Stalactites** because of the stalactite effect of its ceiling. Leading off the other sides, the **Hall of the Two sisters** (named after two identical marble slabs) has a magnificent sunburst dome, and the **Hall of the Abencerrajes** has a central fountain under a dome designed to look like hanging masonry. Legend has it that Boabdil's father ordered a mass beheading and threw the heads into the fountain.

The ticket also covers entry to the **Carlos V's Palace**. Following the Reconquest, the new rulers felt the need to stamp their mark on the place, and so Carlos V commissioned a grand traditional palace from Pedro Machuca, a pupil of Michaelangelo. Although begun in 1526 the controversial palace (felt by many to be an aesthetic desecration) was never finished. The palace also contains the Museo Hispano-Musulmán (Museum of Spanish-Muslim Art) which displays Greek, Roman and Moorish finds, and the famous blue *amphora* jar. The Museo de Bellas Artes houses Spanish art from the fifteenth century to the present.

● **Cathedral** After the splendours of the Alhambra, Granada's cathedral, begun in 1521 but unfinished until the eighteenth century, is disappointingly conventional, and hemmed in by the surrounding buildings. A succession of architects and builders had a hand in it, of whom Diego de Siloé is probably the best known. The visitors' entrance on Gran Vía de Colón leads to the ambulatory around the chancel where a 150-foot dome rises above a a double tier of stained-glass windows, and by scenes from the life of the Virgin by Alonso Cano. In accordance with contemporary practice, Ferdinand and Isabella, who commissioned the cathedral, appear as polychrome figures) at prayer on either side of the main arch. There is a spectacular side-chapel, Nuestra Señora de la Antigua, as well as an altar of St James. A small diocesan museum displays various cathedral treasures. **Capilla Real** The adjacent Royal Chapel is more memorable. This was built in the early sixteenth century as a flamboyant Gothic mausoleum for Ferdinand and Isabella. The plain lead coffins of Ferdinand and Isabella in the crypt are completely upstaged by the exuberant marble sculpted tomb showing the gruesome twosome in repose, complete with sleeping lions and fat cherubs. A similar memorial commemorates Philip the Fair and Juana the Mad. The transept screen, covered in heraldic devices and biblical scenes is regarded as one of the finest *rejas* in the world. The chapel's ground-plan takes the shape of a Latin cross, and chapels flank the spectacular high altar by Felipe de Bigarny, where bloody scenes of martyrdom are depicted in full Technicolor glory – look out for the decapitation of John the Baptist, or John the Apostle being doused with boiling oil before divine intervention secured his escape.

● **La Cartuja** There are more scenes of blood and gore at this Carthusian monastery in the northern outskirts of the town, where a friar painted hideously graphic scenes of martyrdom.

West of Granada

If you take the N-432 to Atarfe and turn off to the left you will come to **Fuente Vaqueros,** where the birthplace of the poet Federico García Lorca has been turned into a museum. It is a simple, white house, extensively altered since Lorca's day, but the exhibits – reflecting his interest in music as well as literature – are lovingly set out. Lorca buffs might also like to visit **Víznar**, eight kilometres north of the city, where a commemorative park has been opened.

Alhama de Granada The Moors showed good taste in developing this scenic little town, 53 kilometres from the city on the C-340, as a spa. The town clings to a rock ledge overlooking a steep gorge, and was the first part of the Kingdom of Granada to be lost to the Christians after Ferdinand and Isabella launched their campaign in 1482. You can visit the twelfth-century baths at the Hotel Balnearía, a fusion of horseshoe arches and Roman inscriptions. The town still has its decaying Moorish castle and a tiny medieval quarter. In the parish church you can admire vestments whose borders were allegedly Isabella's own handiwork, and a bell-tower designed by Diego de Siloé.

East of Granada

If you leave Granada on the N-342 you will skirt the foothills of the Sierra Nevada, gaining fabulous views over the city *en route*. After approximately 70 kilometres the hills subside and you come to the village of **Purullena**, where the highway is flanked on both sides by stalls selling ceramic ware. Strange rock formations squat at the roadside between here and the town of **Guadix**, where an incongruously large cathedral and a Moorish *alcazaba* combine in a striking combination. Guadix is best known for its 10,000-strong community of cave-dwellers.

South from Granada

This is an area of Spain where it is possible to drive for an hour without seeing another car, and to enjoy a landscape of wild beauty and dusty remoteness. The **Sierra Nevada** is best known for its ski resort, known as **Sol y Nieve**, or sometimes as **Prado Llano**. The skiing is on open slopes, vulnerable to bad weather and best suited to beginners or intermediate skiers. There is a modern *parador* about six kilometres south-east of **Monachil** (H) on the Pico de Veleta road, as well as a large hotel, the Melia Sol y Nieve, used by tour operators who offer combinations of a week's skiing with a week of winter sun on the Costa del Sol.

However, to get the best out of this area, venture south into the villages of the **Alpujarras**, immortalised in Gerald Brenan's book *South from Granada*. Beyond the *parador* a daunting track becomes the highest motorable road in Europe. It is negotiable only in summer, and then with care, and crawls past the mountains of Pico de Veleta and Mulhacén, finally winding down to the photogenic mountain village of **Capileira** which teeters on the edge of a gorge. Tourists do make it to this remote place, generally by the less demanding road that leads from the rather dull resort and mineral water bottling town of **Lanjarón** which is linked by the N-323 to Granada in the north, and to Motril and the coastal village of Salobreña to the south. A new *pueblo*-style development suggest that Capileira is not likely to remain unspoilt for much longer. The next village, slightly lower is **Bubión**, with a similar outlook over the Poqueira gorge and a smart but disconcertingly large new hotel, the Villa Turística de Poqueira, the most comfortable place to stay in these parts. The road winds down to the handsome village of **Pampaneira**, the lowest of this trio of mountain villages.

Beyond Pampaneira, the adventurous can head further east into the truly remote villages of the Alpujarras, such as **Pitres** and Pórtugos, dusty, sleepy places ignored by coach parties and visited by serious walkers. Specialist tour operators offer itineraries which let you explore this beautiful area on horse and mule safaris. The next village, at the end of a ravine is **Trevélez**, Europe's highest, and famous for its smoke-cured hams. The landscape remains captivating, but of the villages further east only **Yegen** is of more than passing interest. This was where Gerald Brenan based himself and was visited by various luminaries of the Bloomsbury Group, making it a minor place of pilgrimage for scholars of that eclectic band. Alternatively, take the western route to **Orgiva**, a timeless place, with a seventeenth-century church.

WHERE TO STAY

ANTEQUERA

Parador de Antequera   £££
Paseo García del Olmo s/n
29200 Antequera   Tel (952) 84 02 61; Fax (952) 84 13 12

A comfortable chalet-style modern *parador* in a quiet position, rather badly signposted on the western outskirts of Antequera. Interior decor is modern, somewhat minimalist and a little stiff, with split-level lounges. An attractive mezzanine level has lots of plants and is a more attractive place to linger. Bedrooms are simple though comfortable, and some have pleasant views of olive groves. The restaurant offers local dishes including an interesting cold garlic soup with moscatel grapes and salt crystals, and swordfish in orange sauce. Roast kid often appears on the menu.

Open: all year **Rooms**: 55 **Facilities**: swimming-pool
Credit/charge cards: Amex, Diners, Eurocard, Visa

ARCOS DE LA FRONTERA

Parador Casa del Corregidor £££
Plaza del Cabildo
11630 Arcos de la Frontera   *Tel (956) 70 05 00; Fax (956) 70 11 16*

A splendid *parador* on a precipitous cliff overlooking the Guadalete river. The journey through the busy, narrow streets of this interesting white town is alarming, but journey's end is worth it. There are doubts as to whether this ever was a magistrate's house as the name suggests, but the traditional furnishings are apposite. There's an attractive *patio andaluz* and the terrace is a fine setting for afternoon tea. Bedrooms have heavy, traditional furniture and religious paintings. Offerings in the restaurant include a fish-based soup, pork in a tomato and red wine sauce and the *tarta de la casa*, a sort of rough-textured Madeira cake.

Open: all year **Rooms**: 24 **Credit/charge cards**: Amex, Diners, Eurocard, Visa

El Convento ££
Maldonado 2
11630 Arcos de la Frontera   *Tel (956) 70 23 33*

A simple family-run hotel and restaurant in a converted convent overlooking the gorge, a runaway success since it opened in 1987. The small bedrooms are simply but stylishly furnished, and the Roldán family are charming, friendly hosts. Sr Roldań owns a vineyard which provides the house wine. Excellent food includes game, rabbit or partridge and some lovely home-made pastries.

Open: all year **Rooms**: 4 **Credit/charge cards**: Eurocard, Visa

BENALMADENA-COSTA

Hotel Triton £££
Av Antonio Machado 29
29630 Benalmadena-Costa   *Tel (952) 44 32 40; Fax (952) 44 26 49*

A ritzy,large package hotel with superior facilities and a lush pool area overlooking the beach and promenade along the front. Attractive grounds with palms and banana trees. Bedrooms are spacious and well furnished. Tennis courts and a sauna are welcome extras.

Open: all year **Rooms**: 196 **Facilities**: swimming-pool **Credit/charge cards**: Amex, Diners, Eurocard, Visa

CADIZ

Parador Atlántico   £££
Duque de Nájera 9
11002 Cadiz   Tel (956) 21 23 01; Fax (956) 21 45 82

A stark, white modern building in a good position on the Paseo de Maritimo overlooking the ocean, within walking distance of the old quarter, and with parking available – a bonus in this busy city. Public areas are bright and airy and bedrooms are modern, attractive and comfortable, with fine views. Restaurant service is efficient, and typical excellent dishes might include a salad of peppers with marinated pheasant, swordfish with garlic and a gateau of whisky and kiwifruit in a kiwi coulis.

Open: all year **Rooms**: 153 **Facilities**: swimming pool **Credit/charge cards**: Amex, Diners, Eurocard, Visa

CARMONA

Parador Alcázar del Rey Don Pedro   £££
41410 Carmona   Tel (95) 414 10 10; Fax (95) 414 17 12

A wonderful *parador* set in a fourteenth-century fortress of Pedro the Cruel with splendid views over the plains, and a very attractive (and very welcome in this hot region) swimming pool area, reached by some rathers steep steps. The nearest *parador* to Seville, it's a peaceful alternative to the hurly-burly. The conversion has been sensitive and the focal-point patio is particularly attractive. Bedrooms are furnished in traditional style with a religious triptych above the beds. There is a three-sided lift.

Open: all year **Rooms**:65 **Facilities**: swimming-pool **Credit/charge cards**: Amex, Diners, Eurocard, Visa

CAZORLA

Parador El Adelantado   ££
Sierra de Cazorla
23470 Cazorla   Tel (953) 72 10 75; Fax (953) 72 10 75

A modern mountain lodge situated in a wonderfully remote spot in the Sierra de Segura, about 28 kilometres from the town of Cazorla. Perfectly comfortable without being grand, the *parador* is popular with anglers and hunters. The restaurant is rustic in style and often offers game dishes such as rabbit, or trout with almonds.

Open: all year **Rooms**: 33 **Facilities**: swimming-pool **Credit/charge cards**: Amex, Diners, Eurocard, Visa

---

Hotel Andalucía £
Martínez Falero 42
23470 Cazorla   *Tel (953) 72 12 68*

Simple accommodation in a rather dull residential street about ten minutes' walk from the main square, but quieter than *hostales* in the noisy central area, where parking is difficult. Small bedrooms have good, solid furniture and a genuinely Spanish feel. It is good value but only serves breakfast.

Open: all year **Rooms**: 11 **Credit/charge cards**: Visa

Hotel Guadalquivir £
Nueva 6
23470 Cazorla   *Tel (953) 72 02 68*

Clean, simple facilities offered in modest, friendly hotel in the centre of this town which is popular with British walking parties. Good value.

Open: all year **Rooms**: 20 **Credit/charge cards**: Amex, Diners, Eurocard, Visa

---

CORDOBA

Parador La Arruzfa £££
Avda de la Arruzfa 33
14012 Córdoba   *Tel (957) 27 59 00; Fax (957) 28 04 09*

A modern *parador* in a very quiet residential area about five kilometres from the old quarter but clearly signposted. Rather formal public rooms, but bedrooms are extremely spacious in an elegant, simple style. A complete contrast to the hotels around the Mezquita.

Open: all year **Rooms**: 94 **Facilities**: swimming pool, tennis **Credit/charge cards**: Amex, Diners, Eurocard, Visa

Hotel Gonzalez   ££
Manriquez 3
14000 Cordoba   *Tel (957) 47 98 19*

A small family-run hotel in a restored sixteenth-century palace the heart of the Judería, with lots of Spanish character in the cheerful, crowded public rooms. Simple bedrooms have good quality furniture, attractive *en suite* facilities and a view over a pretty *patio andaluz*. The owners mind their splendidly tacky souvenir shop by day, but are efficient and friendly.

Open: all year **Rooms**: 17 **Credit/charge cards**: Eurocard, Visa

Hotel Albucasis   ££
Buen Pastor 11
14003 Córdoba   *Tel (957) 47 86 25*

An attractive small hotel with good facilities and stylishly simple modern decor, plus wall-mounted pistols, adding a touch of period charm. The cosy bedrooms are clean and comfortable.

Open: all year **Rooms**: 15 **Credit/charge cards**: Eurocard, Visa

Hotel El Triunfo   ££
Corregidor Luis de la Cerda 79
14000 Córdoba   *Tel (957) 47 55 00; Fax (957) 48 68 50*

A small friendly hotel in good position just behind the Mezquita. Excellent facilities for the price. Public rooms have a traditional feel (including a rather gloomy television area), but the small, spotlessly clean bedrooms are cheerful and well-furnished. The *menu del día* while hardly *cordon bleu* is tasty and excellent value – our inspector had *paella*, mixed salad, *merluza* and chips, ice-cream, bread and beer for less than a fiver. Efficient, service and very good value. Garage parking is available at extra charge.

Open: all year **Rooms**: 55 **Credit/charge cards**: Amex, Diners, Eurocard, Visa

EL BOSQUE

Las Truchas   ££
Avda Diputación 1
11610 El Bosque   *Tel (956) 71 60 61*

A simple, very Spanish, roadside hotel and restaurant with attractive traditional decor including antlers and colourful ceramics and cool, uncluttered public rooms. Bedrooms are clean and comfortable, with large modern bathrooms. Handy for the local outdoor swimming pool. The proprietors are friendly but do not speak English.

Open: all year **Rooms**: 24 **Credit/charge cards**: Amex, Visa

GRANADA

Parador San Francisco	£££

Alhambra
18009 Granada   *Tel (958) 22 14 40; Fax (958) 22 22 64*

One of the most famous *paradores* of all, it occupies a wonderful site within the Alhambra in an old convent built by Ferdinand and Isabella on 'liberating' the city. The received wisdom that you need book at least six months in advance is tosh, although the rooms with the best views are usually the first to go. The gardens are stunning, the patio glorious and the view from the terrace wonderful, but the bedrooms and some of the public rooms are less memorable than you might expect. The restaurant offers local and international food, perhaps tortellini with prawns ala creme, followed by goulash, and marmalade cheesecake.

Open: all year **Rooms**: 39 **Credit/charge cards**: Amex, Diners, Eurocard, Visa

Hotel America	££

Real de Alhambra 53
18009 Granada   *Tel (958) 22 74 71; Fax (958) 22 74 70*

A lovely old family house within the Alhambra walls. It is small and friendly with a delightful vine-covered patio and a dining-room crammed with knick-knacks. Bedrooms are very small, but clean and adequately comfortable. The hotel is very popular and you may be required to take the no-choice (but tasty and enjoyable) dinner.

Open: 1 Mar–8 Nov **Rooms**: 13 **Credit/charge cards**: none

Hotel Reina Cristina	££

Tablas 4
18002 Granada   *Tel (958) 25 32 11; Fax (958) 25 57 28*

City centre hotel with stylish reception and pretty patio. Bedrooms are furnished in a modern, stylish way and have excellent facilities for the price including television and mini-bar. Food is very good and excellent value.

Open: all year **Rooms**: 40 **Credit/charge cards**: Access, Amex, Diners, Eurocard, Visa

JAEN

Parador de Santa Catalina £££
Castillo de Santa Catalina
23001 Jaén *Tel (953) 26 44 11*

A dramatic fortress-like *parador* recently built in sensitive medieval style. It has a fine position above the city of Jáen, beside the castle of Santa Catalina. The public rooms are splendidly reminiscent of the Middle Ages, rather like a film set with vaulted ceilings, wall-hung tapestries and suits of armour. Bedrooms are bright, modern and simple but stylish, with excellent views. Dinner might offer scrambled eggs and ham, followed by duckling with figs and apple pudding with chocolate cream.

Open: all year **Rooms**: 45 **Facilities**: swimming-pool **Credit/charge cards**: Amex, Diners, Eurocard, Visa

MARBELLA

Hotel El Fuerte £££
Avda El Fuerta s/n
29600 Marbella *Tel (952) 77 15 00; Fax (953) 82 44 11*

A superior package hotel near the sea-front and within walking distance of Marbella's charming old quarter. This is an established hotel with a more recent extension and a rather schizophrenic feel, owing to the different ambiences prevailing in each. Gardens with terraces overlook the beaches. Bedrooms are spacious and comfortable, and pleasantly furnished.

Open: all year **Rooms**: 263 **Facilities**: swimming-pool, tennis **Credit/charge cards**: Access, Amex, Diners, Eurocard, Visa

Hotel Rincon Andaluz £££
Carratera Cadiz
29600 Marbella *Tel (952) 81 15 17; Fax (952) 81 41 80*

Just off the N340 about six kilometres from Puerto Banus, about five minutes' walk from a sandy beach, this large, modern pueblo-style complex consists of attractive low-rise buildings originally built as self-catering accommodation. It has well-kept grounds, and public rooms decorated in Andalucian style. Most bedrooms are spacious and simply decorated. Service is friendly and efficient.

Open: all year **Rooms**: 228 **Facilities**: swimming-pool **Credit/charge cards**: Amex, Diners, Eurocard, Visa

MIJAS

Hotel Mijas   £££
Urb Tamisa
29650 Mijas   *Tel (952) 48 58 00; Fax (952) 48 58 25*

A stylish hotel in a pretty if rather overwhelmed tourist village. The low-rise building is slightly weathered in places. Public areas are stylish and elegant, with a cool, modern feel although the dining-room is rather stiff. There are stunning views from the breakfasting terrace. Bedrooms are simple but stylishly furnished in a reproduction traditional style, and bathrooms are attractive. In many ways it is rather like a *parador* with glossy extras such as whirlpool baths and above average food. Quiet at night, there is some traffic noise during the day.

Open: all year **Rooms**: 100 **Facilities**: swimming-pool, tennis
Credit/charge cards: Access, Amex, Diners, Eurocard, Visa

MOJACAR

Parador Nacional Reyes Católicos   £££
Carretera de Carboneras
04638 Mojacar   *Tel (951) 47 82 50; Fax (952) 47 81 83*

A surprisingly quiet beach-front modern *parador*, with small well-kept garden areas. The fabric of the hotel is rather scruffy in parts. The attractive pool area has lots of loungers, but the decent-sized bedrooms are rather in need of refurbishment. Offerings on the *menu del parador* might include prawn and mushroom omelette, veal cooked in sherry with olives and chips, garnished with strips of bacon, and *creme catalana*.

Open: all year **Rooms**: 98 **Facilities**: swimming-pool, tennis
Credit/charge cards: Access, Amex, Diners, Eurocard, Visa

MONACHIL

Parador Nacional Sierra Nevada   £££
Ctra del Pico de Veleta
18196 Nr Monachil   *Tel (958) 48 02 00; Fax (958) 48 02 12*

A modern rustic-style stone building with pine furnishings, offering simple unpretentious accommodation aimed at skiers, with cosy fires burning in focal point grates. It is rather functional in character and rather scruffy in places, but the views are sensational. The restaurant often features local specialities such as Trévelez hams.

Open: 21 Nov to 14 Oct **Rooms**: 32 **Credit/charge cards**: Access, Amex, Diners, Eurocard, Visa

NERJA

Parador de Nerja £££
Playa de Burriana
29780 Nerja   *Tel (952) 52 00 50; Fax (952) 52 19 97*

A modern *parador* in a splendid position over Burriana beach, where you can listen to the sound of the crickets. It's about a fifteen minute walk from the *parador* to the town centre and Balcón de Europa. The swimming-pool and grounds are attractive, as is the *patio andaluz*. Bedrooms are simple but quietly stylish, with bamboo tables and basketweave chairs. Service is friendly and efficient and the food is good.

Open: all year **Rooms**: 73 **Facilities**: swimming-pool, tennis **Credit/charge cards**: Amex, Diners, Eurocard, Visa

Balcón de Europa £££
Paseo Balcon de Europa 1
29780 Nerja   *Tel (952) 52 08 00; Fax (952) 52 44 90*

A quiet and simple hotel built into a cliff with access directly from the famous Balcón de Europa. There's a small, pretty breakfast room with a terrace, and a traditional-style restaurant. Bedrooms are a good size and simply but adequately furnished. The hotel lacks a swimming-pool, but does have a pleasant, central location with peace and quiet.

Open: all year **Rooms**: 103 **Facilities**: swimming-pool, tennis **Credit/charge cards**: Access, Diners, Eurocard, Visa

RONDA

Reina Victoria £££
Avda Dr Fleming 25
Ronda 29400   *Tel (952) 87 12 40; Fax (952) 81 10 75*

A famous traditional and rather old-fashioned hotel in turn–of–the–century building with very pleasant gardens and terrace that over-look the Sierra. The breakfast room is preferable to the rather dreary restaurant, although a small formal dining-room used for private parties has some style, as does the drawing-room with its distinct sense of fading splendour. The poet Rilke once stayed here for a while and room 208 is maintained as a shrine. Bedrooms are a reasonable size and well furnished with modern reproduction furniture. Bathrooms are nicely decorated and a decent size. Food is rather disappointing.

Open: all year **Rooms**: 88 **Credit/charge cards**: Amex, Diners, Eurocard, Visa

Hotel Polo   ££
Mariano Soubiron 8
29400 Ronda   *Tel (952) 87 24 47; Fax (952) 87 43 78*

A plain, unpretentious and friendly hotel in the town centre. Public
rooms are functional, and the restaurant is busy and popular. Bedrooms are bright, cheerful and clean, and bathrooms are a good size
and well equipped. Guests should note that there is a three-sided lift
and an unenclosed staircase.

Open: all year **Rooms**: 33 **Credit/charge cards**: Access, Amex,
Diners, Eurocard, Visa

SANLUCAR DE BARRAMEDA

Posada de Palacio   ££
Caballeros 11
11540 Sanlucar de Barrameda   *Tel (956) 36 48 40*

A small, simple pension run by Swiss hosts in this atmospheric little
sherry town. Rooms are crammed with intersting objects which
create a real home-like atmosphere. Bedrooms are plain, simple and
shabby in places. Breakfasts are particularly good.

Open: all year **Rooms**: 11 **Credit/charge cards**: Amex, Diners,
Eurocard, Visa

SEVILLE

Hotel Doña María   £££
Don Remondo 19
41004 Seville   *Tel (95) 422 49 90*

A traditional hotel in a nineteenth-century town house very close to
the Giralda in the centre of the city. Unusually for Seville, there's a
pocket-sized pool on the roof. Bedrooms are individually furnished
with antiques, some with four-poster beds and gilt mirrors. Rather
functional breakfast room. Avoid bedroom four.

Open: all year **Rooms**: 61 **Facilities**: swimming-pool**Credit/
charge cards**: Amex, Diners, Eurocard, Visa

Hotel Becquer   ££
Reyes Católicos 4
41001 Seville   *Tel (95) 422 89 00; Fax (95) 421 44 00*

A pleasant business-type hotel with flair, in the city centre. Bright,
airy public rooms with pleasant atmosphere in the evenings and
comfortable, spacious bedrooms.

Open: all year **Rooms**: 120 **Credit/charge cards**: Access, Amex, Diners, Eurocard, Visa

---

Hotel Simon   ££
García de Vinuesa 19
41001 Seville   *Tel (95) 422 66 60; Fax (95) 456 22 41*

Be warned that the bedrooms here are now *very* shabby. That said, this old seventeenth-century town palace close to the Cathedral and Barrio Santa Cruz has marvellous public areas, including a pretty entrance patio, and a splendid dining-room with charming Andalucian decor. Bags of character, faded splendour, and very good value for those who value ambience above comfort.

Open: all year **Rooms**: 31 **Credit/charge cards**: Access, Amex, Diners, Eurocard, Visa

TORREMOLINOS

Parador de Málaga del Golf   £££
Apartado 324
29080 Torremolinos   *Tel (952) 38 12 55; Fax (952) 38 21 41*

Very close to Malaga airport (and consequently exposed to aircraft noise), this modern *parador* consists of two rather functional accommodation blocks. The simple dining-room is rather soul-less, but both food and service are good. Choices on the *menu del parador* might include garlic mushrooms, sole ala Romaine and coconut ice-cream. Other public rooms are decorated in club style. The principal attraction is the *parador's* on-site golf course. Bedrooms are simple but quietly stylish.

Open: all year **Rooms**: 60 **Facilities**: swimming-pool, tennis, golf **Credit/charge cards**: Amex, Diners, Eurocard, Visa

---

Aparthotel Aguamarina   £££
Camino del Bajondillo
29620 Torremolinos   *Tel (952) 37 41 42*

A superior, recently-opened aparthotel with stylish rooms and good facilities in a fairly quiet area a couple of streets behind Bajondillo beach. Bedrooms are a good size, with tasteful, modern furniture.

Open: all year **Rooms**: 130 **facilities** swimming-pool **Credit/charge cards**: Visa

UBEDA

Parador Condestable Dávalos	**£££**

Plaza Vásquez de Molina 1
23400 Ubeda   *Tel (953) 75 03 45; Fax (953) 75 12 59*

A lovely *parador* occupying a sixteenth-century palace and the best place to stay in the city. The central feature is the arcaded courtyard, with bedrooms leading from the gallery above, a very pleasant spot to linger with a pre- or post-dinner drink. Antique-lined corridors lead to comfortable bedrooms with ornate carved headboards, traditional-style furniture and incongruous modern furniture. The restaurant serves regional food, including scrambled eggs with mushrooms and prawns, kid cutlets in honey, and apple tart. The staff are efficient, but not particularly friendly.

Open: all year **Rooms**: 31 **Credit/charge cards**: Access, Amex, Diners, Eurocard, Visa

VEJER DE LA FRONTERA

Convento de San Francisco	**££**

La Plazuela 6
11150 Vejer de la Frontera   *Tel (956) 45 10 01*

An excellent hotel in a converted convent in one of the most memorable of the white towns. As part of the sensitive and atmospheric conversion, the restaurant El Refectorio has a choir-stall effect, and an adjacent longe with incongruous television. The food is excellent. You might be given quail as an appetiser! Excellent fish comes from Zahara de los Atunes. The fruity house wine is very good value. Bedrooms combine the austere look of convent cells with modern facilities, good quality furnishings and a complimentary half-bottle of sherry.

Open: all year (restaurant closed Mon) **Rooms**: 25 **Credit/charge cards**: Diners, Eurocard, Visa

ZAHARA DE LA SIERRA

Marqués de Zahara	**£**

San Juan 3
11688 Zahara de la Sierra   *Tel (956) 13 72 61*

A simple hotel with a pretty patio in a dramatic village of narrow cobbled streets. Bedrooms are clean, simple and comfortable and the public areas are decorated in local style.

Open: all year **Rooms**: 10 **Credit/charge cards**: Eurocard, Visa

CASTILLA-LA MANCHA

La MANCHA means the Dry Land, from the Arabic *manxa*. This is the south-east section of the great central table-land, which tilts downwards like a giant cartwheel resting on its hub. Since the last turn of historical fate, when Philip II relocated his capital in an upstart *pueblo* in 1561, that hub has been Madrid. Like Old Castile to the north, these later-consolidated provinces of Castilla-La Mancha (New Castile) still bear the marks of frontier land, dotted with castles and huddled, fortified settlements as the Moors were driven southwards during the Reconquest. The key date for La Mancha was 1085, when Alfonso VI recaptured Toledo for Christian Spain. Slowly the swords of the crusading military orders of Calatrava and Santiago turned into ploughshares, and La Mancha became the bread-basket of central Spain.

New Castile, though intensively cultivated by modern methods, still has a rural economy on ancient models. El Greco or Cervantes would recognise many of its towns. Present-day Toledo, for example, has barely regained the population of 55,000 it had at its peak in the fifteenth century.

For some people New Castile is Spain at its least welcoming: a place to be traversed rapidly in order to get somewhere else. To appreciate La Mancha's most typical landscapes you must abandon conventional ideas of 'pretty scenery'. At first, all you may be aware of is a desolate, baked flatness: *'Todo la espaciosa y triste España'* – 'all the space and sadness of Spain'. Cervantes set his doleful hero to roam these plains, and he lost his wits in the process.

Everything in La Mancha seems horizontal: power-lines, railway tracks, straight roads radiating like wheel-spokes from all the villages, and the monotony of countless rows of vines and olives. But in spring the red soils erupt in bright new leaves on vines and wheatfields, and wild flowers splash the unfenced roadsides. In autumn the most unpromising wastelands melt into soft purple pools as the saffron crocuses flower in millions to produce that precious, labour-intensive crop for the *paellas valencianas* of the world.

TOLEDO (H)

In any league, Toledo is one of Spain's major attractions. No guidebook omits it from the pages; no visitor to Castile leaves it off the itinerary. But this city of steel-makers, more than

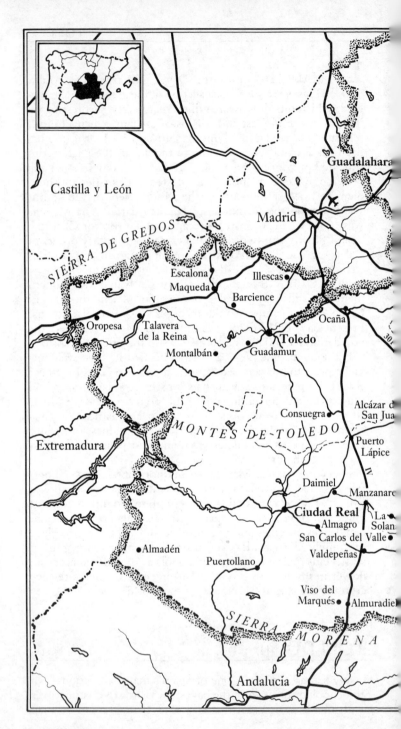

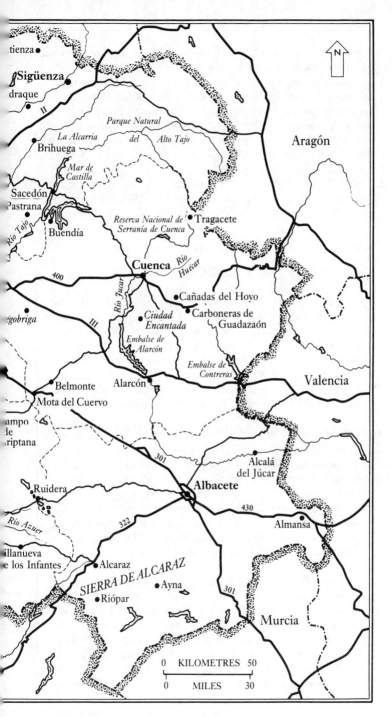

any other, knows what a double-edged sword tourism can be. Toledo's well-baited hook is its own snare.

Toledo's popularity is understandable; an accessible 70 kilometres from Madrid, it is many things the capital is not: ancient, compact, picturesque, and saturated in history. Few other Spanish cities are so whole-heartedly dedicated to the business of extracting revenue from visitors. So much so, that multilingual notices now warn tourists not to be duped by treacherous profiteering guides.

Toledo looks sublime. The houses, baked to the perfect golden biscuit of the surrounding terrain, climb from the ice-green Tagus to a huge horizon pierced by the solid bulwark of

---

Planning your holiday

There are people (British tourists, let it be documented) who choose to spend a long weekend in Albacete. These are exceptional folk. Not many people would choose to spend precious holiday time in the outlying parts of Castilla-La Mancha (i.e. those furthest from Madrid) on a first visit to Spain. But you could well find yourself travelling through them on the way from Madrid to the Costa Blanca or Andalucía. If so, the suggestions that we offer in this chapter should help you pick a memorable route.

La Mancha's greatest tourism asset is the city of Toledo. Everyone wants to see it, and in high season, you may get the impression everyone is doing just that. Next on the list is Cuenca, which has one of the most striking settings of any town in Spain. Then there are the smaller towns of Sigüenza, Alarcón and Almagro, all with much to recommend them – and lovely *paradores*. Make these your bases if you can. No visitor to La Mancha can fail to stumble across the trail of Don Quixote, laid by the regional tourist authorities in all the places mentioned in the novel.

To get the most out of rural touring and wildlife spotting, the most promising areas to head for are the high sierras and black slate villages of Guadalahara, or the Serrania de Cuenca and the mysterious Ciudad Encantada, a magical rock 'city' petrified by time and elements. Bird-watchers should make for two small wetland national parks (Las Tablas de Daimiel and Las Lagunas de Ruidera). Another choice would be to follow the course of the beautiful River Júcar as it swings south through its arid limestone

---

the fortress and the cathedral's Gothic spire. Castles, fortified bridges and ramparts guard the gorge, and seem to have held at bay the twentieth century too. A rich layer-cake of all Spain's historic and cultural influences, it has a huge amount to see: Visigothic, Moorish, Jewish, Christian architecture, and art treasures galore. Toledo comes from the Roman name, *Toletum*. Little remains now from that period except a scrap of Roman circus, just outside the walls. In AD554 the Visigoths made Toledo their capital, and King Reccared's conversion to Christianity in 587 established Toledo as a spiritual centre. Archbishops of Toledo are still the Catholic primates of Spain.

---

gorge past the hanging houses of Cuenca, the brown fortress town of Alarcón, and the cave-bored rock spur on which Alcalá del Júcar stands.

The region's main towns are all quite accessible by train, and you can get buses to the smaller places from the provincial capitals. As elsewhere, touring the remoter and more scenic areas is really only practical with a car. The Michelin map *Central Spain*, 1:400 000 sheet 444, covers the whole region on one sheet. Driving is mostly very easy, on good straight roads where your main danger is dozing off past those hypnotic vineyards. (Valdepeñas wine, incidentally, is usually fairly light, so an odd glass with a picnic should not do you much damage.) In winter, be cautious: a sudden frost can render the roads black glass in moments, and you will see car after car tumbling helplessly into the ditches. Snowfalls may block the sierra roads of Cuenca and Guadalahara for several days.

Many towns hold unusual Holy Week or Corpus Christi festivals (for instance Toledo's *Procesión del Silencio*). If you are touring the region in September, you may like to head for Cuenca's celebrated music festival, or Almagro's festival of drama (both are popular, so it may be difficult to get tickets on spec).

● **Regional Tourist Board:** Dirección General de Turismo, Plaza Santiago de los Caballeros 5, 45071 Toledo, Tel (925) 21 09 00. All the main centres have **tourist offices**, and at Toledo, used to its hordes of American and polyglot visitors, you will find that some English is spoken. If you are starting from Madrid, you can pick up maps and leaflets there and save yourself some time.

The Moors conquered Toledo in 712 and ruled until 1085, when Alfonso VI and El Cid recaptured the city for the Christians and made it the capital of Castile. Many converted Moors remained in the city and influenced its art and architecture (the Mudejar style).

The next few centuries saw Toledo's heyday, and the building of the cathedral which began in 1227 during the reign of Fernando III (the Saint). This was also a period of shameful pogroms of the Jewish community, at that time the largest and most flourishing in Spain. This persecution culminated in the massacre at the main town synagogue (now called Santa María la Blanca), instigated by Vicente Ferrer (later canonised for his pains). The Catholic Monarchs had a more peripatetic court, but spent much time in Toledo, building the Monastery of St John of the Kings (San Juan de los Reyes), as much a monument to themselves as to God. Charles V reestablished his capital here, and it enjoyed great prestige during his reign, since he was also Holy Roman Emperor. Philip II, however, took a dislike to the city and moved his court to Madrid. But if Toledo's political influence had waned, artistic talent was still burgeoning, for this was the time of El Greco's fruitful residence (1541–1614).

Since the Civil War Toledo has carefully rebuilt its damaged Alcázar, and led a quiet life as a small provincial capital. What the town lacks is genuine vitality. After the sightseeing is over, most tourists drift away.

There are some parking places on the main routes up to the cathedral and by the Hostal del Cardenal, just outside the city's main gate. The main tourist office is also here just opposite this gate, in a Mudejar-style cabin (there is a second branch in a kiosk on the main square, Plaza Zocodover). Toledo is an hour's drive from Madrid. Buses leave from Madrid's Estación Sur, Calle Canarias 17, take around one and a half hours, and drop you at Toledo's bus station, about ten minutes' walk from the main town gate. Trains are infrequent, and as the railway station is further out of the centre, are less convenient.

Eating out, accommodation and shopping

There are a number of reasonable places to eat just off Plaza Zocodover, notably on Calle Barrio Rey, but all are predictably touristy. Just outside the town, Venta Carranza, on the road up to the *parador*, is authentic and atmospheric, serving typical Toledan food such as partridge (*perdiz*). If you want a treat, the restaurant of the Hostal del Cardenal is highly recommended. Venta del Aires, on Circo Romano, a spacious airy place just outside the city walls, is popular with locals, especially for Sunday lunch. It also has shady gardens for *al fresco* dining. Casa Aurelio, Sinagoga 6, is near the cathedral; local specialities include a steak speared with a Toledan 'dagger' (which you can take home as a souvenir afterwards). Service is good and friendly.

Toledo has a good range of accommodation, but the city's popularity drives up the tariffs. If you have a car, you may choose to stay outside the walls on the corniche ring-road (look for '*Circunvalación*' or '*Ronda*' signs). The *parador* offers the best views on this road and there are one or two older-style and less expensive hotels in country villas (*cigarrales*). Business hotels in the newer sectors have few attractions and may be noisy, but there are plenty of small hotels and *hostales* within the walls, especially near the cathedral.

No visitor to Toledo leaves unaware of its souvenir specialities, forced on you by shop-keepers with a souk-like enthusiasm. Marzipan is sold all over the town; it is very sweet and the price is steep – try it before you buy. Shops on Plaza Zocodover specialise in the stuff. Elsewhere, especially towards the Jewish quarter, dozens of shops sell *damascene* ware, a Moorish craft of black steel inlaid with gold, silver and copper wire. The genuine article is expensive; quality varies widely, and finding authentic outlets is tricky. Artespaña, Calle Samuel Levi 2, is reliable. Less portable (illegal, in fact, to export) is Toledo's fake weaponry. Once the city's tempered steel was the envy of many a crusading knight; now murderous-looking hunting knives replace the Excaliburs of old.

Exploring the town

When Alfonso VI and El Cid captured Toledo from the Moors in 1085, they entered through what is now the town's only surviving Moorish gate, the horseshoe-arched **Puerta Vieja de Bisagra** (or Puerta de Alfonso VI). The more elaborate **Puerta Nueva de Bisagra** was built by Charles V after he had quashed the *Comuneros* revolt (see page 439), and has Charles's coat of arms on its façade and in the pattern of its roof tiles. Just inside the gate is the thirteenth-century Mudejar church of **Santiago de Arrabal**.

Beyond the Moorish gate known as the **Puerta del Sol** lies Toledo's only surviving mosque, **El Cristo de la Luz**, built in the tenth century on the site of a Visigothic chapel, and the scene of more religious conflict. The garden, which is laid out around a tiny pool, gives access to a belvedere alongside the turreted Puerta del Sol, with magnificent rooftop views of the town.

Wedge-shaped **Plaza Zocodover** is Toledo's main square, where tourists sit, sipping over-priced drinks in pavement cafés. Leading from Plaza Zocodover is Toledo's main street, the pedestrianised Calle Commercio, lined with cafés, jewellers, boutiques and souvenir shops, scene of the evening *paseo*, and congested throughout the day as it heads towards the immense Gothic **cathedral**. Before going inside, it is worth taking a walk around the cathedral walls to see its splendid portals. Best are the Puerta de Reloj at the foot of Calle Chapinería, with rows of biblical scenes and a sundial, and the triple portal of the west front, above which Christ and the disciples eat the Last Supper and gaze down at the camera-clickers.

After visiting the cathedral, most people head straight to the church of **Santo Tomé** to see El Greco's masterpiece, *The Burial of the Count of Orgaz*. You are likely to find a long queue here and another one down the hill outside the **Casa y Museo de El Greco**. This is the atmospheric old Jewish quarter (*Judería*), which has excellent views over the Tagus. Close by are Toledo's two surviving synagogues, and a little further on is the massive monastery church of **San Juan de los Reyes**. From the church you can walk down to the fourteenth-century fortified bridge, **Puente San Martín**, and then back to the Bisagra gates following a well-preserved stretch of Moorish wall.

However you travel to Toledo, do not miss a drive or taxi-ride around the **Carretera de Circunvalación**, which encircles the city on the opposite bank of the Tagus. The classic El Greco views of the city can be seen from the stretch near the *Parador*.

The main sights

● **Cathedral** Rising abruptly from a tortuous tangle of narrow streets, the colossal size of the cathedral is difficult to appreciate once you are close to it. Its dimensions are more impressive seen from a distance (the opposite side of the river). Toledo Cathedral is the seat of the Spanish Primate (the equivalent of the Archbishop of Canterbury). The cathedral took two hundred years to build. It is lit by kaleidoscopic rose windows and crammed with exuberantly carved marble, wood and alabaster.

You enter through the **Puerta de las Molletes** alongside the fancy doors of the west front, from which bread rolls (*molletes*) used to be distributed to the poor. It leads into the pretty pinkish-white cloister where guide books and tickets are sold. Inside, the magnificent screen that encases the choir is carved with angels, dragons and weird beasts.

The main altar, or **Capilla Mayor**, has a Gothic altarpiece stacked with three-dimensional tableaux of New Testament scenes. Behind the altar is the extraordinary **Transparente**, described with justification by Richard Ford in his *Handbook for Travellers in Spain* (1845) as a 'fricassee of marble'. Tumbling from a skylight is a baroque extravaganza of angel musicians, cute *putti*, bubble-gum clouds and frenzied frescoes, concocted in the eighteenth century to illuminate the back of the cathedral.

The **Sacristy** contains a collection of El Grecos (some ascetic apostles, and the powerful *Disrobing of Christ*), and works by Goya, Velázquez, Van Dyck, Raphael and Titian. Caravaggio's dark, broodily sensual *John the Baptist* is memorable in the Nuevas Salas, leading off the Sacristy. The **Chapterhouse** (Sala Capitular) has a splendid gilded ceiling, and frescoes of the Seven Deadly Sins above portraits of archbishops. The guarded **Treasury** holds a three-metre high silver reliquary by Juan de Arfe, weighing over 200 kilos.

● **The Alcázar** Standing at the highest point of Toledo, the Alcázar's severe bulk dominates the city. Virtually destroyed in the Civil War, it was rebuilt on the orders of Franco, as a monument to 1,201 brave Nationalists. Toledo fell to the Republicans in July 1936, and the Nationalists under General Moscardo barricaded themselves in the Alcázar, despite being shelled, mined and set on fire. Sanitation was virtually non-existent, and the corpses of victims were stacked in the lockers of the swimming-pool. The Nationalists' tenacity gave Franco a perfect symbol of Fascist heroism and martyrdom, which the displays inside the Alcázar still emphasise.

It is little surprise then, that even today the Alcázar is guarded by the military, for a tour round it can be a provocative experience. There are rooms devoted to the history of arms from palaeolithic flints to the submachine gun; photographs of the devastation wreaked by the Republicans and of Franco visiting on the day of liberation (the caption informs you that he is 'visibly emotional'). Tunnel-like cellars are studded with plaques honouring the 'heroes of anti-communism' from, among others, Bolivia, Argentina and Britain (the last outrageously appended with a quote from Byron's *Childe Harold*).

● **Hospital de Santa Cruz** Just below the Alcázar, this Renaissance orphanage and charitable hospital was ideally located for firing shots, slinging grenades and hurling bombs of scrap metal and dynamite at the Nationalists. Though the Republicans succeeded in virtually razing the Alcázar to the ground, the hospital sustained relatively little damage. Through the plateresque doorway, exotically carved with shells, saints, urns, masks and fruit, lies a series of spacious airy rooms where intricate stone arches support splendid coffered ceilings. The building houses a museum with a fine collection of Brussels tapestries, a colourful astrolabe crammed with mythological, zodiacal and courtly figures, and a patchy assortment of El Grecos, of which the *Assumption*, painted just a year before he died, is the best.

● **Santo Tomé** It is just about possible to concentrate on El Greco's masterpiece, *The Burial of the Count of Orgaz*, in an annexe of the cramped thirteenth-century church of Santo Tomé, if you can ignore the muggy garlic-scented air and stickily jostling bodies.

The Count of Orgaz, who founded the church and was buried here in 1323, was renowned for his charitable works, and the legend grew up that at his funeral St Augustine and St Stephen descended to carry his soul to heaven. Orgaz also made an annual bequest of money, rams, firewood and wine to the clergy and poor of the parish. Two centuries later, when the officials charged with carrying out his orders defaulted, the parish priest took out, and won, a law suit against them. To celebrate, he commissioned El Greco to paint the burial scene, paying him 1,200 ducats.

El Greco painted no sentimental period piece, but a work which embodies the attitude to death of sixteenth-century Spain. The faces of the ruffed, bearded gentlemen who attend the funeral betray no sadness at the death, nor a glimmer of surprise at the presence of the two saints.

● **Casa y Museo de El Greco** Hordes of people shuffle, squeeze and duck their way through the diminutive rooms of this sixteenth-century house, though historians say that El Greco almost certainly never lived here. The rooms were restored at the beginning of this century and say much about that era's concept of how the artist lived: a bedroom with lumpy bed, creased bedclothes, pile-less carpet and velvet chair buttock-worn to threads, a dining-room with the table laid for a solitary meal. A collection of El Greco canvasses hang on the walls or are propped up on easels. The twelve portraits of the Apostles are said to have been modelled by patients from a nearby lunatic asylum. In the *View of Toledo*, the Hospital of Tavera is plonked incongruously on a cloud (it lay beyond the city boundaries and would not fit on the canvas).

● **Hospital de Tavera** This late-Renaissance building now holds a small museum containing the art and book collection of its founder, Cardinal Tavera. The atmosphere is that of a collector-connoisseur's home, a refined private sanctum. Cases of vellum-bound volumes line the library walls, illuminated manuscripts lie casually open. Most appealing of the El Grecos is the *Holy Family*, with Joseph fondling Christ's toes as Mary breastfeeds him, but there are also a number of his mesmerising saints, and a gorgeously glowing *Nativity* by Tintoretto.

● **Santa María la Blanca** It was from here, in 1405, that San Vicente Ferrar and his mob ejected the Jews. The synagogue was renamed Santa María la Blanca, and has been used as a refuge for reformed prostitutes, an oratory and a barracks.

● **El Tránsito Synagogue** Recently renovated, this and Santa María la Blanca are the only two surviving examples of the eight original synagogues in Toledo's Jewish quarter. Dating from the fourteenth century, El Tránsito was converted into a church after the expulsion of the Jews, but its Mudejar features remained unaltered. A large single chamber is covered in delicate plaster work in shades of pale green, pink and white, decorated with a mix of strapwork foliage, Hebrew characters, scalloped ogees, pierced flower windows and stylised capitals.

● **San Juan de los Reyes** San Juan de los Reyes is an extravagant monument to the privileged relationship the Catholic Monarchs felt they enjoyed with God. Outside there are as many pages in heraldic dress as cassocked saints, and the rusty chains of Christian prisoners freed from the Moors at Granada droop from the walls. Inside Christian iconography comes a poor second to that devoted to the monarchs. It is, however, a fascinating church, one of the best examples of the so-called Isabeline Gothic style. The **cloisters** are particularly fine, with delicate tracery framing a lush garden, and centaurs, dragons, a vole and a dog among the supple foliage of the columns.

369

Other sights

Museum of the Councils and Visigothic Culture Housed in an eccentric building, half church and half mosque, the combination of horseshoe arches, Renaissance cupola and Christian frescoes (notably a Last Judgement with the dead popping up from their coffins), is more interesting than the rusty buckets, clumsy jewellery and gaudy reproduction regalia that make up the Visigothic collection (the best Visigothic finds from Toledo are now housed in the Museo Arqueológico in Madrid).

Museum of Contemporary Art Although only the two Mirós (*Homenaje a Joan Prats Nos 3 and 15*) and sculptures of women and bulls by Alberto Sánchez are worth more than a cursory glance, the labyrinthine raftered rooms that hold them are lovely.

Taller del Moro Yet another museum in which the contents are less interesting than the building. Architectural and decorative fragments from various churches, convents and palaces are laid out in the rooms of a Mudejar palace once used as a workshop by Moorish cathedral masons.

Around Toledo

Most of the scenery in Toledo province is unexceptional, and some of it, towards Madrid, is positively ugly. Apart from the city of Toledo itself, very little on the eastern side is worth much of a detour. **Illescas** is a dreary little industrial town bypassed by the N-401, but it has a surprising collection of five El Grecos in the convent church of La Virgen de la Caridad. Further east, **Ocaña** has a grand, curiously austere Plaza Mayor. In **Tembleque**'s much more appealing Plaza Mayor, the wooden balconies with their Maltese cross designs have a distinctly festive air. Southwards lies Don Quixote country (see page 372).

The countryside west of Toledo is the most worthwhile for touring, especially in spring when poppies and Spanish broom mingle with the terracotta and beige colours of the fallow earth. Several villages have castles in fine settings, particularly **Barcience, Maqueda** and **Escalona**. Along the C-401, **Guadamur** castle sprouts crenellated towers above a grassy moat. It is still inhabited and can be visited at limited times. The twelfth-century castle of **Montalbán** lies two Though a surprising number of people track it down on fine weekends, you may find it completely deserted, when it is an ideal spot for (cautious) scrambling and a picnic.

The main NV westwards takes you to **Talavera de la Reina**. Talavera is now an ugly and built-up industrial town, but its interest lies in a centuries-old and celebrated ceramics industry. Talavera jars bedeck many an apothecary's shelves, and the classic blue and yellow tile designs are instantly recognisable all around Spain. Sadly, the modern stuff produced for all the tourist shops is a crude and degenerate version of this once-great art: its irregularities the result of carelessness rather than individual craftsmanship. However, a brisk market exists for Talavera's colourful wares, and if it appeals to you, there are plenty of outlets to buy it. Artesanía Talaverana, at the west end of the main road through town, has a large quality-controlled selection.

Further west, **Oropesa**'s imposing castle (now an attractive *parador*, being renovated when inspected) seems completely out of proportion to the small town it guards. A local embroidery industry centres on the nearby village of Lagartera. The work can be seen in local shops: mats and runners with flower patterns in brilliant primary colours.

THE DON QUIXOTE TRAIL

The countryside of southern Toledo and Ciudad Real is Don Quixote's stamping ground: parched, flat, and virtually treeless, a landscape punctuated by castles and windmills, and millions of neatly spaced vines. Every *pueblo* on these Manchegan plains seeks some association with the demented knight. At **Consuegra**, a town little changed since Cervantes' times, signs for *Crestería Manchega* lead to a ridge of rock on which are poised a battered castle and half a dozen windmills in various stages of romantic dereliction. From below, the long black poles that trail behind the mills look (just a bit!) like the lances of medieval knights. From the top of the ridge, the only significant altitude in the area, the neat arable patchwork of La Mancha stretches far into the distance. Consuegra is an important centre for the local saffron industry, and in autumn piles of discarded purple petals build up in the neighbouring fields. At **Campo de Criptana** several decayed old mills have been neatly rebuilt. Close up they look very posed and artificial, but from a distance, marching along the ridgeway, they are photogenic enough to drag tourists out of their cars.

MAN OF LA MANCHA

As you explore New Castile (Castilla-La Mancha), two names loom inescapably on those wide horizons: Miguel de Cervantes and his inspired creation Don Quixote, the Knight of the Doleful Countenance. The pair are a boon to the tourist authorities. But pursuing Quixote's fictional footsteps too seriously across the dusty plains is as much of a delusion as our hero's windmill tilting. As visitors solemnly troop round 'Dulcinea's House' in El Toboso, take photographs of reconstructed windmills, and park themselves at ancient Quixotic inns, you can almost hear a shout of ironic laughter. Cervantes would have been mightily amused.

Miguel de Cervantes Saavedra occupies the same niche in Spanish literature as Shakespeare does in English. They were more or less contemporaries too; Cervantes was 15 years older, but by an odd coincidence both died on the same day, 23 April 1616. Cervantes was a prolific writer in several genres, and wrote many plays, poems, short stories and novels, many of which are lost or totally unreadable. His literary reputation today is based entirely on a single masterpiece, *The Adventures of Don Quixote*, which appeared in two parts towards the end of his life. This work is regarded as a prototype of the European novel, and it influenced many English writers from Fielding to Dickens. In fact, Cervantes' genius was acknowledged in France and England long before he was hailed as Spain's greatest writer. Although *Don Quixote* sold well during his lifetime, Cervantes never reaped much reward from it and died as he had lived, a relatively poor man.

He was born in Alcalá de Henares near Madrid in September 1547, the son of a surgeon. The family was bourgeois but impecunious, constantly moving house to make ends meet. At the age of 22, Cervantes enlisted as a soldier, and spent the next five years on active service in the Mediterranean. He took a heroic part in the naval battle against the Turks at Lepanto, but was wounded and lost the use of his left hand. He was all this time an avid reader of the epic chivalric romances of the day, which he later parodied so mercilessly in *Don Quixote*. On his voyage back to Spain he encountered a dramatic real-life adventure. His galley was attacked by a Turkish squadron, and Cervantes was captured and sold into slavery in Algiers. There he languished for five years, apparently organising unsuccessful Colditz-style escape attempts, until he was ransomed by his family in 1580.

Back in Spain, Cervantes found himself increasingly insolvent and on a social downslide. Determined to break into the literary scene, he wrote his first novel, *La Galatea*, published when he was nearly 40. Soon afterwards he married a much younger wife, but spent most of his time away from her, earning a living as a tax collector in Andalucía. Here his job involved drumming up provisions of grain, oil and other products to kit out the Armada. He wasn't much good at it, by all accounts, and spent some time in prison accused of embezzlement, though evidence suggests this was a result of incompetence and tactless handling of corrupt local officials rather than dishonesty. The idea of *Don Quixote* came to him during his imprisonment.

The first part of *Don Quixote* was published in 1604, when Cervantes was nearly 60. Unfortunately he surrendered the rights to his publisher, so never earned the money its unexpected popularity brought. In 1614, just before he completed the second part, someone pipped him at the post by publishing a spurious Part II under a pseudonym. Undaunted, Cervantes managed to turn this plagiary to comic advantage when he published his own version of *The Adventures of Don Quixote, Part II*. He died in Madrid soon afterwards, still unpraised by Spain's churlish literary establishment.

In simple terms, *Don Quixote* relates the story of a middle-aged impoverished gentleman (not unlike his creator) who embarks on a long series of ludicrous adventures on a broken-down old nag in pursuit of chivalry and the lady of his dreams, a village hoyden called Dulcinea. He is accompanied on these preposterous quests across La Mancha by his self-appointed 'squire', the worldly Sancho Panza, who gives a cynical commentary on his master's delusions. Don Quixote is completely absurd, a comic figure. Yet he has noble qualities, a generosity and dignity even in his worst humiliations that arouse not merely laughter or pity, but respect.

Cervantes' ambiguous attitudes towards chivalric ideals and the nature of sanity enmesh the novel in countless onion-skin layers of irony. The Romantic Age saw Quixote as much more of a tragic hero than Cervantes' more robust contemporaries would have done. Modern readers find the book's digressive, sometimes inconsistent narrative, and its sheer length difficult to tackle. Yet it is twentieth-century criticism that has done the most justice to Cervantes, and recognised the central theme: while a life based on delusions is impractical, a world devoid of ideals is intolerable.

The most accessible modern translation of *Don Quixote* in English is by J. M. Cohen (available in Penguin Classics).

The Venta del Quijote at **Puerto Lápice** (H), south-west of Alcázar de San Juan, trumpets itself as the authentic Quixotic inn. Coachloads pile in through the cartwheeled gates of this ancient hostelry to sit in a shady courtyard set with checkered tablecloths. At the shop here you can buy *queso manchego* (the famous regional cheese), local wines, saffron, and folk music tapes – and Quixote postcards, of course! Here, it is said, the rueful hero was dubbed knight by a drunken innkeeper. The Venta del Quijote has no rooms, but the Hotel Aprisco is a place of some character on the outskirts of the village, and the town also has several inexpensive *hostales*.

El Toboso claims one of the most famous Quixotic connections, as the alleged home of Dulcinea, Don Quixote's slatternly princess. This well-preserved village is surprisingly pleasant considering the contrived nature of its attractions. The village oil-mill has been restored in early seventeenth-century style as la Casa de Dulcinea (Dulcinea's House), and can be visited. A metallic statue of the besotted knight kneels to his lady-love in the square. In the town hall is an exhibition of rare Cervantes manuscripts and early editions of *Don Quixote* (including Mussolini's copy). On the main N-301 road near the village a light, airy restaurant called La Venta de Don Quixote makes a reasonable lunchtime pit-stop with Manchegan specialities and pleasant rustic décor.

CIUDAD REAL

Despite its dignified name (Royal City), Ciudad Real is one of the most forgettable towns in Spain. Built by Alfonso X in 1255 as a counterweight to the overweening power of the Knights Templar and other crusading military orders, Ciudad Real today has very little of interest except an old Moorish gateway. Don't worry if you miss it.

The main reasons for being in this province, besides following the Quixote trail, are to visit the charming town of Almagro, and a surprising palace in the village of Viso del Marqués. Quiet picnic routes through the green, hilly countryside west of Ciudad Real potter along the Guadiana valley towards the pine and eucalyptus woods of the Cijara reservoir, or south-east to the lonely mercury mines of Almadén. The dwindling wetland oasis of **Las Tablas de Daimiel** (H), systematically raped of its moisture by the thirsty vineyards of Valdepeñas, may take up an hour or two of your time. In winter, flocks of rare and exhausted migrant birds settle on the reedy lagoons. For the ornithologist, there are signed walks, hides and an information centre.

Almagro (H)

This little town 25 kilometres south-east of Ciudad Real is one of the most enjoyable places in the area, and the local *parador* makes an excellent base. Almagro was a stronghold of the military order of Calatrava, whose castles can be seen guarding hilltops to the south-west. To do the town justice, you have to walk through its cobbled grid-like streets and see the white houses, Renaissance palaces and brownstone churches at close quarters. Its most striking features are an unusual oblong Plaza Mayor with green glazed balconied houses in Flemish style, and in one of them, a perfectly preserved sixteenth-century theatre called the *Corral del Comedias*, which Cervantes must have known. Ask for the key at the tourist office, just off the main square. The *parador*, in an old Franciscan convent, is worth a look even if you are not staying there. Also peer into the Calatrava monastery on the edge of town, where you can see a fine two-storeyed patio decorated with the order's triple-key emblem, and connected by a plateresque staircase. Handily placed nearby is the Hotel Don Diego, Tel (926) 86 12 87 – useful if the *parador* is full.

Around Valdepeñas

The huge metal containers in Valdepeñas look at first sight like some giant petrochemical works. But no, these monstrous tanks hold wine – just a small fraction of the millions of litres this region produces from all those vines planted as far as the horizon. Both red and white wines are produced in La Mancha, and it is Spain's largest *denominación de origen*, with over a million acres of vines. Ordinary La Mancha wine used to have an unfortunate reputation as the sort of stuff people took to parties and hoped someone else would drink. Now, careful viticulture produces much more acceptable blends.

The countryside around Valdepeñas is very flat. Several of the towns and villages are worth a brief glance. Eastwards, **Villanueva de los Infantes** (H) is one of the prettiest and best preserved, with wide streets and squares of white houses, dignified mansions with carved eaves, and large churches. **La Solana**, northwards, is visible for miles across the plain, a populous village with a lovely Plaza Mayor by a large brown-red church, where pigeons flutter and old men in berets sit in the sun. You can see the spiky finials of **San Carlos del Valle**'s baroque church long before you arrive.

Manzanares (H) is a larger town, with strategic import-ance as a bridging point over the Azuer and a major road junction. Its *parador* makes a useful base. The old town has a southern-looking *plaza* with palm trees and topiary gardens, and a huge russet-coloured church.

Heading south, you will share the road with dozens of heavy trucks, for this is the main highway to Andalucía over the craggy Despenaperros Pass. A brief deviation from the main road takes you to the pretty village of **Las Virtudes**, where there is an ancient bullring (dating from 1641, and alleged to be the oldest in Spain), a square arena surrounded by terracotta-coloured wooden balconies oddly reminiscent of the theatre in Almagro (of roughly the same period). Beside it is an even older church, with a carved wooden ceiling and elaborate altarpiece.

A few miles further south, a short detour on the west side of the main road takes you to a most delightful and unexpec-ted village, **Viso del Marqués** (see Where to stay, Almuradiel). In the centre of this small place is an enormous Italianate palace. Cannons stand guarding the grand stairway to the front door. If you ring the bell someone will bob out and tell you when the next tour starts. Inside is a wonderland of Pompeian frescoes and *trompe-l'oeil* pilasters. Strange mythological scenes compete for your attention with naval battles and family portraits. The palace was built in the latter half of the sixteenth century for the celebrated naval comman-der Alvaro de Bazán, and appropriately enough, it now houses Spanish naval archives.

ALBACETE

Only the incurably inquisitive will find themselves in this quiet corner of Castilla-La Mancha. Much of the Albacete province is dull and flat, but three of its areas are worth touring, and there are several attractive small towns.

Albacete (H) is a knife-making town and a centre for the production of saffron and artichokes. During the Civil War it was the headquarters of the International Brigade, and paid for its temerity with almost total destruction. The town has since been rebuilt, and the modern version is a prosperous but

castrated conurbation of office blocks offering tourists little
except its excellent archaeological museum. The **Museo de
Albacete** is well laid out beside a municipal park. Inside are
some splendid Bronze Age and Roman finds, including
animal sculptures and ceramic articulated dolls amid the pre-
dictable assortment of arrowheads, flints, bones and oil-
lamps. A lion, looking something like a hedgehog, holds a
warrior's head triumphantly between its paws. The Hotel Los
Llanos, Tel (967) 22 37 50, is best placed as a base for the
museum, but pricier than the *parador*, five kilometres out of
town.

South-east of Albacete the small town of **Chinchilla de
Monte Aragón**, a former stronghold of the Marquess of
Villena, has a fine castle and a *plaza* with a collection of
golden stone monuments: a church, the Lonja (exchange
building), town hall, and several palatial mansions. It is only a
village now, but was once the capital of the Albacete province. A rough track leads up to the castle, from where there is
a spectacular breezy 360-degree view of the cereal plains
around. Caves are hewn out of the soft beige rock nearby.

Alcaraz, to the south-west of Albacete is a small, delightful town, well worth a lunch stop if not longer. The Plaza
Mayor is surrounded by fine buildings: a palace, church and
town hall in rosy-ochre stone. Stepped alleyways lead off it,
both up and down to the ruined castle and town gateway.
Plateresque decorations adorn the doorways on the Calle
Mayor. The eighteenth-century Lonja has an asymmetrical
tower, the fifteenth-century church next to it a Flamboyant
Gothic door. Alfonso VIII, Tel (967) 38 01 52, is an unpretentious, lively bar-café with rooms, on the top corner of the
Plaza Mayor.

Excursions through the hills of the **Sierra de Alcaraz**
nearby via Riópar and Fuente Higuera take you through
young pines, rocks, and almond trees. The little town of
Ayna surveys the most spectacular section of this route: brilliant grey and red cliffs and pinnacles of rock tower above the
Mundo Gorge. An unlovely but serviceable modern hotel,
the Felipe II, Tel (967) 29 50 83, hogs the best clifftop views.

North-west of Alcaraz is the small **Parque Natural de las
Lagunas de Ruidera**, a daisy-chain of a dozen or so clear,
turquoise lakes now used as a summer resort – a welcome
oasis in the dry Manchegan plains. An information centre in
Ruidera (H) village can point you to the park's minor
charms: waterfalls, a ruined castle, and the Cave of Montesinos, which makes an appearance in *Don Quixote*. Secluded

private villas and holiday homes have been built around some of the lakes, and there are several hotels. Lake Colgada is the most developed (offering watersports, etc.). The best hotel choice is undoubtedly the Albamanjón, by San Pedro Lake, but La Colgada (on Colgada Lake), Tel (926) 52 80 25, is less expensive, plainish but cheerful inside, with friendly owners and excellent lake views. Among several *pensiones* and *hostales* in Ruidera village, El León, Tel (926) 52 80 65, cheerfully decorated with gingham and *azulejos* ceramics, is one of the most promising. There are a couple of campsites round the lakes.

Alcalá del Júcar, north-east of Albacete, makes a brisk business from the accident of its extraordinary location. The River Júcar swirls sharply round a huge creamy cliff, and the little beige and white cubic houses are embedded in its sheer side, and seem almost piled on top of one another. There is a castle at the top of the village, but what makes this place most unusual are the houses hollowed out of the rock. You can see the backs of the cave houses from the Jorquera road, on the other side of the valley. This road follows the tree-fringed Júcar Gorge westwards through soft beige rocks eaten into caves and overhanging ledges – a lovely drive.

Right on the eastern boundaries of Albacete is the Moorish fortress town of **Almansa**, whose craggy castle on top of a jutting prong of limestone dominates the views along the well-trodden route (N-430) to Valencia and the Costa Blanca. You can visit the castle and walk along the fifteenth-century ramparts. The **Iglesia de la Asunción** (Church of the Assumption) and the **Casa Grande**, a fine mansion with a sixteenth-century doorway, both quite near the castle, are also worth seeing. The Hotel Los Rosales, Tel (967) 34 07 50, on the main road, is a popular lunchtime stop. It is rather charmless and noisy for an overnight stay, but the food is good, and the restaurant clean and efficient.

CUENCA

Of all Castilla-La Mancha's provinces, Cuenca is the most varied. Geological eccentricities (sink-holes, hot springs, precipitous gorges, curious rock formations) chequer this hilly limestone region. The disparate massifs of the Serranía de Cuenca, source of the River Tagus, break up plains of red earth and green wheat. Feathery poplars temper the harsh crags along the water-courses, and some of the northern slopes are newly planted with pine for timber; elsewhere nothing but aromatic scrubland relieves the dry karst landforms.

Clamped to a high rocky spine between two river-sculpted gorges, **Cuenca** (H) was for centuries New Castile's most isolated city. Not so long ago Hemingway complained of the bad roads, and even today, an unexpected snowfall can make many of the mountain routes impassable. But far from being a provincial backwater, Cuenca is now host to a daring contemporary cultural scene. It has museums devoted to abstract and photocopier art, a prestigious electro-acoustic workshop, and an avant-garde resident artistic community. In Holy Week the city holds a much-respected international festival of religious music.

Though undeniably romantic, Cuenca is not merely a picturesque playground for tourists. It is two towns in one: upper and lower. The lower town, which began to be developed in the nineteenth century, is a fume-ridden, chaotic place, sprawling towards light- industrial and housing estates. Most of the hotels, banks, shops and restaurants are here, along with the tourist office. The upper town is the place to make for. Ravines enclose the rocky bluff on which this old town is built. Far below on the north side flows the River Júcar (pronounced HOOcar); on the south side is the River Huecar (say WAYcar). Tortuous streets heave up between bulging, cracked façades and emerge on the lips of gorges with vantage-points of mellow churches and jumbled roofs. *Rascacielos* (skyscrapers) with four storeys at the front and twelve at the back, and the spectacularly sited *casas colgadas*, or hanging houses, are precariously cantilevered over sheer rock walls. Many artists (including some of those exhibited in the Museo de Arte Abstracto) have chosen to live or work here: the subtle, weathered beauty of old Cuenca provides a feast of colour, form, and texture.

Eating out and accommodation

It is worth booking well ahead to ensure a room in the upper town as there are only two places to stay. Otherwise there are plenty of adequate if uninspiring hotels at all prices in the lower town, and a quiet and much more appealing hotel some way out of town. But at last a gap is about to be filled. Planning permission to convert the San Pablo convent in the old town to a luxury *parador* was granted in December 1990.

The work is expected to take about two years. The location, and the building, are superb.

For budget eating there are several inexpensive *mesones* above the simple bars on Plaza Mayor, while the Fonda Tintes on Calle de los Tintes by the River Huecar serves local food in an ancient beamed inn. Equally atmospheric, and more convenient if you are staying in the upper town, is the Mesón el Caserio outside the castle gate. The picturesque San Nicolas just up from the Plaza Mayor keeps an eye firmly on the tourist trade with a multilingual menu, but it is conveniently placed, welcoming and reasonably priced. If you want something more sophisticated, head for the Mesón Casas Colgadas, a tastefully restored hanging house next to the Museo de Arte Abstracto.

Exploring the old town

After a lengthy and tortuous trek up steep cobbled streets from the lower town, the Plaza Mayor is a welcome flat space in which to pause and regain your bearings. If you are driving, there are limited parking spaces (metered) here but if you continue to the top of the old town you will find free parking near the castle. Apart from the Plaza Mayor and the main spinal street, Cuenca's old town is not suitable for vehicles and a car is an embarrassment.

The Plaza Mayor, entered through the baroque arches of the *ayuntamiento*, has a row of unassuming bars. The outlandish façade of the cathedral dominates the scene, a stark neo-Gothic veneer of bilious yellow-grey stone slapped on to the original thirteenth-century building in the seventeenth century, and rehashed yet again when the north tower collapsed in 1902.

Below the cathedral, the wooden balconies of carefully restored *casas colgadas* jut out above the Huecar Gorge; there are wonderful if vertiginous views of them from the narrow iron footbridge slung high above the green river. The massive ecclesiastical building visible on the opposite side of the Hoz (ravine) de Huecar is the San Pablo Convent, currently being converted into Cuenca's new *parador*. At the top of the town the road passes through a battered gateway, all that remains of Cuenca's castle. The northern exit from the Plaza Mayor takes you to San Miguel, a golden Gothic church on the lip of the Hoz de Júcar, where a religious music festival is held in Holy Week. Further along more stepped lanes is the ivy-smothered **Sanctuario de Nuestra Señora de las Angustias**.

The main sights

● **Cathedral** If this building seems vaguely familiar, that is because parts of it (the nave and transepts) are a rare Spanish version of the Anglo-Norman style found in many English and North European Gothic churches. Inside, its best features include a fifteenth-century triforium, a plateresque door decorated with skulls and helmets, and some intricate wrought-iron screens. In a side-chapel near the entrance is a crudely forceful wooden *paso* (a religious float carried through the streets in Holy Week) depicting the Last Supper.

● **Museo Diocesano de Arte Sacra** Many of the cathedral's treasures have been moved to this museum in the Bishop's palace, just round the corner. Superbly presented in the whitewashed rooms are tapestries, polychrome statues, peasanty Virgins, two El Grecos, gaudily opulent carpets and a lavish treasury – all the better for being skilfully lit.

● **Museo de Cuenca** Opposite the Museo Diocesano, this museum holds an archaeological collection which ranges from prehistoric jewellery to Mozarabic ceramics. Nothing is aesthetically outstanding, but among the better displays are the finds from the Romanised Celto-Iberian city of Segóbriga, some 75 kilometres south-west of Cuenca. Among the usual assortment of pins and coins are a portrait bust of Augustus and a headless woman in diaphanous robes. Best of all is the Roman kitchen with several huge *amphorae* and a detailed account of what the Romans ate for breakfast, lunch and tea.

● **Museo de Arte Abstracto** This museum alone would justify a visit to Cuenca. Hung in the beautifully restored whitewashed and dark-beamed rooms of a *casa colgada* is a stimulating collection of '50s and '60s abstract works by major Spanish artists. The best of the art is remarkably accessible, exploring the patterning of landscape, the textures and colours of decaying walls, weathered wood and rusted metal, or the aesthetic potential of mundane objects like sacking, wire mesh and gravel.

● **Museo Internacional de Electrografía** (Open Wed am only) Opened in May 1990, it is Europe's only museum devoted to photocopier art, and holds a dazzlingly diverse collection of works by artists from as far afield as Argentina.

Exploring the gorges

Roads follow the deep ravines around Cuenca, and drives (or walks) along them give superb views of the town, and of the fantastic, colourful rock formations that jut above the cliffs. Lay-bys and *miradores* give you a chance to stop and gaze at the best spots, or enjoy a picnic. The Hoz de Júcar is a deep cleft canopied by willows, poplars and plane trees.

The smaller River Huecar trickles through a wider, shallower gorge fringed with market gardens. Once beyond Cuenca's eye-catching houses, the phallic bulbous rocks assume many weird forms: hammers and anvils, camel's heads, hour-glasses. Some look like tawny fungi erupting suddenly from the grey wooded hills; and in places the overhanging rock faces are striped as though black paint has dripped down them. A side road leads through a wild landscape of pine and gorse to a mammoth statue of Christ, from which there are tremendous views of the city, the gorge and the patchworked plain beyond.

AROUND CUENCA

Serranía de Cuenca

Some twenty kilometres north of Cuenca are the bizarre rocks of **La Ciudad Encantada**, The Enchanted City: a chaos of great limestone boulders eroded into fantastic shapes by the elements. A spectacular circular drive takes you along the Hoz de Júcar, past the **Ventano del Diablo** (Devil's Window), two natural holes in the rocks which give dizzying views into the gorge below, and then off through a narrow gorge, where glimpses of totemic rocks emerging from the pines give a taste of what is to come.

Continuing northwards from the Ciudad Encantada you reach ever wilder and more mountainous countryside. The landscape is rich in wildlife, especially rare orchids and butterflies, deer, wild boar and birds of prey. Some areas have protected status and entry is restricted. Focal points of a touring route could include **La Toba**, where there is a beautiful reservoir often occupied by lots of birds; **Tragacete**, a mountain resort and trout fishing centre; **Beteta**, with castle ruins and a nearby spa; **Priego**, famous for osier-growing and wickerwork products; or the **Source** (*Nacimiento*) **of the River Cuervo**, where mineral springs form watery curtains as they pour over mossy rocks and caverns.

The sink-holes

Beyond the village of Cañada del Hoyo (off the N-420 Teruel road south-east of Cuenca) a group of circular sink-holes (*torcas*) has been formed where underground springs have dissolved the local limestone. The holes have filled with glassy green water which mirrors the cliff rims all around. It is not safe to swim here, but the pools make a lovely background for a picnic.

The main N-420 road leading beyond the sink-holes to the Aragón border is particularly beautiful, and becomes quite spectacular after Carboneras de Guadazaón, where a series of peculiar rock formations like piles of coppery dinner plates emerge from the cliffs to either side of the road. The River Cabriel potters along beside the road in a quiet valley of poplars and fruit trees. As you approach the Montes Universales the scenery takes on a lunar barrenness.

South and west of Cuenca

From the main N-111 road west of Motilla del Palancar you can just see the outlines of **Alarcón** (H) in the distance, like some becalmed minesweeper among the cereal fields. As you drive down the side road towards it the buildings steadily shift into focus on their pedestal of white rocks above the green ribbon of the Júcar. The great castellated fortress is now converted into one of Castile's most delectable *paradores*. It is worth booking ahead for this romantic hideaway.

Belmonte, (H) further west, is another town dominated by a remarkable castle, a hexagonal fortress with circular towers. It is currently being restored, but can be visited. Inside, several rooms have elaborate Mudejar-style ceilings. Best, though, are the views of this lovely town from the ramparts, through a light screen of trees. The Collegiate Church at the top of the town has polychrome wooden altarpieces and excellent castle views. The surrounding countryside and the 'Haro' villages nearby deserve a detour. **Villaescusa de Haro** has a church with a sixteenth-century chapel and a lacy top like a cake frill. At **Mota del Cuervo** the hilltop windmills announce you are in Quixote country. A number of grocery shops in town stay open through siesta time to serve Manchego cheese, wine, ham and bread to passing tourists.

About four kilometres south of Saelices, 75 kilometres south-west of Cuenca, lie the remains of **Roman Segóbriga**, still being excavated. Though not worth a long detour, it is well signed and easily reached from the main N-111 road.

Due south of Cuenca, near the turquoise Alarcón reservoir, a minor road leads through the depopulated village of **Valeria** in the Gritos valley. On the hillside nearby are the ruins of the Roman settlement of Valeria (finds also in Cuenca museum), and a lonely gorge of red and grey stripy rocks rising sheer above the roadside.

GUADALAJARA

The busy Madrid-Zaragoza N-11 road scythes a north-easterly swathe through the heart of the Guadalajara province. Sandwiched between fume-laden HGVs, you may find it hard to imagine this part of Spain offers much pleasurable touring. On both sides of the main road, however, lie areas of surprising remoteness and beauty. South-east is a region of reservoirs and olive groves known as the Mar de Castilla. North-west are several historic towns, the most interesting of which is Sigüenza, and beyond dozens of tiny villages built of dark slate amid picturesque hills.

The city of **Guadalajara** was very badly bombed during the Civil War and is now of little interest. However, the Palacio de los Duques del Infantado, at the top of Avenida del Ejercito is now being carefully restored (an ongoing process – even the scaffolding has acquired a venerable patina) to its former Isabeline glory. Built in the time of the Catholic Monarchs (1480, by Juan Guas, the Flemish master mason), it has a striking diamond-bossed façade with delicate corbelled windows. Inside (entrance round the corner, not through the main door where two wild men hold a large coat of arms) you find a lovely patio where lions and griffons snarl at each other between twisted columns.

If you need to stay near Guadalajara, the modern Hotel Pax, Tel (911) 22 18 00, set some distance back from the main Madrid road, is comfortable enough for a night (swimming-pool, tennis, restaurant), and makes a convenient and reasonably quiet base for Barajas Airport (the Madrid airport) if you have early or late flights.

Mar de Castilla

A massive engineering scheme along the course of the Tagus has altered the landscape and economy of this region: huge artificial lakes and hydro-electric power systems have now opened up both industrial and recreational potential east of Madrid. The best touring routes take in the steeply set town of **Brihuega**, and the old ducal town of **Pastrana**, where the palace on the main square, and the Collegiate Church and its museum contents (tapestries) are worth a look. Then follow the serpentine roads that hug the westerly lakeshores via Durón, Sacedón and Buendía (several excellent viewpoints and picnic spots).

Northern Guadalajara

North-west of the N-11 a number of minor roads trickle towards the wild sierras on the borders of Castilla y León. Depopulated villages, some little changed since medieval times, stud these mountainous routes. A number have interesting Romanesque churches (Villacadima, Campisábalos, Albediego). Many of the houses are built of thin black slates (a tourist office leaflet called *Arquitectura Negra* suggests a good touring route). These isolated villages, though very picturesque, are sadly decaying.

Closer to the main road, **Atienza**'s castle keep surveys the landscape from a dais of jutting rock, like a goat on a crag. The old centre of this medieval fortress town is completely unspoilt. **Jadraque** also has a splendid hilltop castle, visible from far across the colourful, rolling countryside.

SIGUENZA (H)

This ancient, serene town is built of deep golden, pink-tinged stone. Steep cobbled streets meander among rubble-walled, pantiled houses, arcaded squares and Romanesque churches. The cathedral holds one of Spain's most celebrated funerary statues, and if you want to stay, you can sleep in a medieval castle now converted into a *parador*. Despite these attractions, Sigüenza remains an intimate, quiet small town, compact enough to explore on foot, though it is a long climb to the top of the town.

Just below the cathedral, on Calle Cardinal Mendoza, the tourist office has a guide to the town in English, including a map. Throughout the town, monuments display helpful blue plaques announcing the main features of interest. Near the cathedral the arcaded main square narrows to Calle Mayor which climbs sharply past craft shops appealing enough to browse in while you catch your breath. At the top of the town is the huge castle *parador*, dominating the skyline. Whiffs of incense signal church doorways, and perspectives change at every step as the winding streets squeeze between yellowing houses with iron balconies and through ancient gateways.

Apart from the *parador*, hotels in Sigüenza are basic and no more than adequate. Possibilities include El Motor, Calle Calvo Sotelo 12, Tel (911) 39 03 43 or the more centrally placed El Doncel, at General Mola 3, Tel (911) 39 10 50. Food at the *parador* is somewhat overpriced, but there are several simple alternatives in the town, notably Laberinto, Calle General Mola 1, near the railway station.

The Cathedral

The dull clank of Santa María's cracked bell marks the hours and the times of Mass throughout Sigüenza's streets. Built of a mellow dark rose, coral and honey stone, the cathedral is all the more interesting for its eclectic mix of styles: Romanesque arches and windows, crenellated towers, a late-gothic sixteenth-century cloister, a neo-classical portico, plateresque and Mudéjar ornamentation. Inside clustered piers soar above a *coro*, where glossy rose and grey marble columns sensuously intertwine to form a palatial setting for a gawky Virgin and Child. The shallow north transept holds an elaborate confection of carved, gilded and painted altars and portals. Lovely old glass glows in the rose window, and two contrasting alabaster pulpits stand opposite each other in the nave, one with stylised Gothic carvings in pointed niches, the other bursting with lifelike muscular Renaissance figures.

Access to the rest of the cathedral is by ticket only at irritatingly limited hours, unless you can prevail on the good nature of the sacristan. The tour includes the extraordinary sixteenth-century Sacristy, where the barrel-vaulted ceiling is studded with hundreds of heads, rosettes and cherubs. Inside are an El Greco *Annunciation* and a porcelain Christ in a four-poster cot. Highlight of Sigüenza Cathedral, however, is the tomb of Martín Vásquez de Arce, who died in 1486 aged 25, fighting the Moors in the last great battle at Granada. The monument was commissioned by Queen Isabella herself for this favourite young knight. Little is known of its artist, Maestro Juan, but the sculpture of *El Doncel*, as he is known (the word means page, or squire) has become a sort of symbol for the whole town. He is shown propped up on one elbow reading a book, legs languidly crossed in a convincingly life-like pose. Relaxed, off-duty, El Doncel is Renaissance Man, with a contemplative as well as an active side to his nature. It is a remarkable departure from the stiff, formal conventions of medieval funerary sculpture.

WHERE TO STAY

ALARCON

Parador Marqués de Villena   **£££**
Avenida Amigos del Castillo
16213 Alarcón   *Tel (966) 33 13 50*

Apart from its impressive location and historic interest, this ancient castle has been most sympathetically converted to a cheerful, intimate, and stylish hotel, where modern facilities slot tactfully into the medieval setting. Staff are exceptionally helpful and friendly, and the food is highly recommendable; this *parador* is worth a detour.

Open: all year **Rooms**: 11 **Credit/charge cards**: Amex, Diners, Eurocard, Visa

ALBACETE

Parador de la Mancha   **££**
Crta Nacional 301
02000 Albacete   *Tel (967) 22 94 50; Fax (967) 22 60 92*

About five kilometres out of town, quietly set in open country (dead flat), this *parador* is a modern, purpose-built hotel, spaciously designed around a huge inner courtyard of lawns, trees and paved paths. Public rooms are white and raftered, tiles brighten the stairways, and a few unconvincing hayrakes combine decorative efforts with modern paintings on the walls. The facilities are 4-star, prices 3-star, so it makes a good-value base in this less than well-endowed area. Food is good too, partridge and game, biscuits with figs and raisins in strawberry sauce.

Open: all year **Rooms**: 70 **Facilities**: swimming-pool, tennis
Credit/charge cards: Amex, Diners, Eurocard, Visa

ALMAGRO

Parador de Almagro   ££
Ronda de San Francisco
13270 Almagro   *Tel (926) 86 01 00; Fax (926) 86 01 50*

The most interesting hotel in Ciudad Real. Set in a converted monastery, the rooms ramble via corridors and stairways round a confusing maze of tiny patios containing fountains and gardens. Bedrooms
are traditionally furnished – even the little cupboards disguising the
minibars are in keeping. Wine-presses and ancient vats stand in the
dark, barrel-vaulted *bodega*. The food is recommendable – don't miss
local pickled baby aubergines.

Open: all year **Rooms**: 55 **Facilities**: swimming-pool
Credit/charge cards: Amex, Diners, Eurocard, Visa

ALMURADIEL

Hotel Los Podencos   ££
Ctra Andalucía KM 232
13760 Almuradiel   *Tel (926) 33 90 00*

On the busy main road through this unexciting town, this hotel is
unprepossessing from outside but friendly and perfectly adequate
within, with solid wood furnishings and above-average food. It
makes a good base for Viso del Marqués and is used by businessmen
en route between Madrid and Andalucia. Rooms at the rear are
reasonably quiet. The restaurant serves an excellent house onion
soup and decent local wines.

Open: all year **Rooms**: 76 **Credit/charge cards**: Eurocard, Visa

BELMONTE

Hotel La Muralla   £
Isabell de Castilla
16640 Belmonte   *Tel (967) 17 07 79*

Quietly placed by the curtain walls on the street leading up to the
castle, this simple, white, low-rise hotel is popular with locals for
lunchtime *tapas*. An inexpensive base in a smashing little town.

Open: all year **Rooms**: 8 **Credit/charge cards**: none

CONTRERAS (EMBALSE DE)

Hotel Mirador de Contreras   £
Ctra Madrid-Valencia
Minglanilla Cuenca Contreras   *Tel (962) 18 61 71*

388

Where Cuenca's most south-easterly road meets the Valencia border, a large dam bars the River Cabriel. This small hotel monopolises the most scenic viewpoint on the main road, overlooking the winding river behind and the reservoir ahead. The dining-room has views. The rear bedrooms are quieter. It makes a useful and inexpensive lunchtime or overnight stop in this isolated area.

Open: all year **Rooms**: 12 **Credit/charge cards**: Amex, Diners, Visa

CUENCA

Posada de San Jose   **££**
Julián Romero 4
16001 Cuenca   *Tel (966) 21 13 00*

A delightful and memorable hotel in an ancient restored convent overhanging the edge of the Hoz de Huecar, where you sleep in quirkily shaped rooms with white plaster walls and low beamed ceilings. Not all rooms have bathrooms or views; it is worth booking in plenty of time to secure a room with both. Tricky car access and parking.

Open: all year **Rooms**: 25 **Facilities**: no restaurant **Credit/charge cards**: Diners, Eurocard, Visa

Pensión Real,   **£**
Barrio del Castillo 37
16001 Cuenca   *Tel (966) 22 99 77*

A recently opened family-run *pensión* in the last house in Cuenca, beyond the castle gate. It has six spotless rooms with white walls, pine fittings and flowery bedspreads, though none has a bathroom or washbasin.

Open: all year **Rooms**: 10 **Credit/charge cards**: none

Pensión San Julian   **£**
18 de Julio 1
16001 Cuenca   *Tel (966) 21 17 04*

Simple whitewashed and beamed rooms (five with bath) above a popular local restaurant in a picturesque corner of the lower town, close to the diminutive River Huecar.

Open: all year **Rooms**: 20 **Credit/charge cards**: Amex, Visa

389

Hostal Mora £
San Francisco 1
16001 Cuenca *Tel (966) 21 41 38*

Quietly, rather than attractively located in a side street close to the centre of the lower town, this *hostal* has white rooms with bright woven bedspreads and clean communal bathrooms.

Open: all year **Rooms**: 18 **Credit/charge cards**: none

Hotel Arévalo ££
Ramón y Cajal 29
16001 Cuenca *Tel (966) 22 39 79*

Good value and comfortable rooms with matching wooden furniture and spotless bathrooms, in a fairly quiet position close to the city centre.

Open: all year **Rooms**: 35 **Credit/charge cards**: Amex, Visa

Hotel Alfonso VIII ££
Parque de San Julián 3
16002 Cuenca *Tel (966) 21 43 25*

A modern hotel overlooking a park. Rooms are comfortable if characterless, but the restaurant has superb views up to the old town, and pretty upholstery and paintwork. Breakfast is eaten in bed or a noisy public café.

Open: all year **Rooms**: 48 **Credit/charge cards**: Amex, Visa

Hotel Cueva del Fraile ££
Ctra-Cuenca a Buenache Km 7
16001 Cuenca *Tel (966) 21 15 71; Fax (966) 21 15 73*

A quietly located country hotel in a restored sixteenth-century hospice with comfortable, tasteful rooms, a restaurant, barbeque, tennis court and pool. Coach parties sometimes descend for lunch.

Open: all year **Rooms**: 63 **Facilities**: swimming-pool, tennis
Credit/charge cards: Amex, Diners, Eurocard, Visa

DAIMIEL

Hotel Las Tablas £
Virgen de las Cruces 3
13250 Daimiel *Tel (926) 85 21 07*

In the town centre, this lively, modern building blends well into its surroundings and makes a convenient base from which to explore the Daimiel National Park. The café-bar is a good place for snack lunches or *tapas*. For a 2-star hotel, facilities are good.

Open: all year **Rooms**: 28 **Credit/charge cards**: Amex, Diners, Eurocard, Visa

MANZANARES

Parador de Manzanares ££
13200 Manzanares   *Tel (926) 61 36 00; Fax (926) 61 09 35*

This stands just outside the town on an island between busy main roads. No more than functional in style, it is friendly and reasonably quiet despite its location. One plus point is its excellent value buffet meals – you can munch away at 30 or 40 different dishes, hot and cold, with local specialities – for an all-in price (less for children).

Open: all year **Rooms**: 50 **Facilities**: swimming-pool
Credit/charge cards: Amex, Diners, Eurocard, Visa

PUERTO LAPICE

Hotel Aprisco £
Crta N14
13650 Puerto Lápice   *Tel (926) 57 61 50*

Just out of town on the Madrid road, this aged rambling farmhouse has bright blue windows and wooden balconies. Don Quixote coach parties may possibly engulf the bar briefly, but once they have gone the place reverts to a pleasantly simple and genuine hostelry of wooden furniture, stripy loose-weave curtains, beams, and big wine jars. There is a garden and pool at the rear. Rooms are quite basic but have character, and are very cheap.

Open: all year **Rooms**: 17 **Facilities**: swimming-pool
Credit/charge cards: none

RUIDERA

Aparthotel Albamanjón ££
Laguna de San Pedro
Camino de Montesinos
13326 Ossa de Montiel   *Tel (926) 584 15 58; (926) 52 80 88*

This hotel wins hands down among its lakeshore rivals for location, décor and family-run friendliness. It is a most imaginative hotel, very peacefully disguised among the trees by San Pedro lake. Built into a rocky cliff overlooking the lake, extraordinary decorative effects have been created with coloured tiles, windmill features, handpainted plates, and swathes of creeping plants. Bedrooms are tiered in the steep, pretty gardens behind the hotel entrance. Some are apartments carved into the living rock, with open fireplaces. Simple, wholesome country cooking.

Open: all year **Rooms**: 10 **Credit/charge cards**: Visa

SIGUENZA

Parador Castillo de Sigüenza   ££
Plaza del Castillo s/n
19250 Sigüenza   *Tel (911) 39 01 00; Fax (911) 39 13 64*

A restored medieval castle, magnificently sited at the top of the town. Public rooms are furnished in period style, some attractively with wooden chests and woven rugs, others cavernous and gloomily cluttered with suits of armour and stern, studded chairs. Bedrooms are well-equipped, large and comfortable; the bathrooms have beautiful sea-green tiles. Satellite TV does not entirely compensate for erratic hot water and no extra pillows or blankets. Some splendid views. There are pretty courtyards and a Romanesque chapel.

Open: all year **Rooms**: 77 **Credit/charge cards**: Amex, Diners, Eurocard, Visa

TOLEDO

Hotel Maravilla   £
Barrio Rey 7
45001 Toledo   *Tel (925) 22 33 00*

An adequate and convenient hotel if you are on a budget. Clean, plain rooms with bathrooms above a restaurant just off Plaza Zocodover.

Open: all year except 15 Dec-Jan **Rooms**: 18 **Facilities**: restaurant closed Sun eve and Monday **Credit/charge cards**: Amex, Diners, Eurocard, Visa

Parador Conde de Orgaz   £££
Paseo de los Cigarrales
45000 Toledo   *Tel (925) 22 18 50; Fax (925) 22 51 66*

An expensive modern hotel built in a traditional style of brick and stone, wonderfully sited on a hill two kilometres outside the old town. The views of Toledo are splendid, public rooms are scattered with intriguing antiques, and there is an outdoor swimming-pool. Rooms have whitewashed walls and beamed ceilings, ample marble bathrooms and many have balconies. This *parador* is extremely popular, so book well in advance.

Open: all year **Rooms**: 77 **Facilities**: swimming-pool **Credit/ charge cards**: Amex, Diners, Eurocard, Visa

---

Hostal del Cardenal   **££**
Paseo Recaredo 24
45004 Toledo   *Tel (925) 22 49 00; Fax (925) 22 29 91*

An eighteenth-century mansion built into the turreted town walls, very close to the Bisagra gates. Through a fortified gate lies a secluded shady garden, and corridors and public rooms are elegantly furnished with antiques. Rooms are simple but tasteful and some overlook intimate paved courtyards. The restaurant is excellent.

Open: all year **Rooms**: 27 **Credit/charge cards:** Amex, Diners, Eurocard, Visa

---

Hotel Los Cigarrales   **££**
Carretera de Circunvalación 32
45004 Toledo   *Tel (925) 22 00 53; Fax (925) 21 55 46*

A hotel and restaurant in a restored farmhouse five minutes' drive or fifteen minutes' walk from the town. The reception area and lounge are whitewashed with a dado of blue, yellow and white ceramic tiles, and rooms have wooden floors, whitewashed walls and simple furniture. All rooms have bathrooms, eight have balconies and sixteen have views of Toledo.

Open: all year **Rooms**: 36 **Credit/charge cards**: Eurocard, Visa

---

Pintor El Greco   **££**
Alamillos del Tránsito 13
45002 Toledo   *Tel (925) 21 42 50*

A newly opened hotel set in an old Toledan house, once a bakery. Original features are carefully conserved (façade, patio, etc.) and tastefully kitted out with *azulejos* tiles, light wood and pleasing country furniture. Modern bedrooms have excellent facilities. It offers good value in an overpriced town and is attractively located at the edge of the Jewish quarter, with good views across the Tagus.

Open: all year **Rooms**: 33 **Credit/charge cards**: Amex, Diners, Eurocard, Visa

VILLANUEVA DE LOS INFANTES

Hostal Imperio   £
Monjas Franciscas 2
13320 Villanueva de los Infantes   Tel (926) 36 00 77

An imposing and well-preserved house on the Villahermosa exit road, shuttered, with window grilles. Inside is a patio courtyard set with plants in urns and pots, a dining-room bright with stuffed and model birds, and a simple bar. No bedrooms were seen, but it seems full of character and a great find for a simple base in a lovely out-of-the-way town.

Open: all year **Rooms**: 27 **Credit/charge cards**: Amex, Visa

MADRID AND AROUND

MADRID is a city where you can largely forget about traditional sightseeing and concentrate on having a good time. It is an ugly place with few historic buildings but the exuberant streetlife makes it one of the most exciting cities to explore. Madrileños have celebrated the post-Franco thaw by perfecting the art of enjoying themselves and as a result the nightlife here is amongst the best in Europe. Madrid was never a solemn city. Casanova came solely to sample its decadent delights and Hemingway reported that nobody went to bed until they had killed the night. Today the city's trendier clubs stay open till dawn, and even the staider inhabitants do not eat dinner until well after 10pm. Far into the night in summer in Plaza de Santa Ana, for example, children play, dealers hustle, while respectable burghers and beautiful young things drink in pavement cafés.

Madrid is an artificial capital, selected by Philip II in 1561 because it lay virtually in the centre of the country. He considered this would symbolise and emphasise the (comparatively recent) unity of the state. The city has no natural advantages – it lies on a plateau 480 kilometres from the sea and 646 metres above sea level, and has freezing winters and scorching summers. Few of the kings did much to improve it. Philip II had the Plaza Mayor built, but spent most of his energy and money on the monastery of El Escorial 30 kilometres away, and subsequent monarchs neglected it, so that by the time the crown passed to the Bourbon dynasty in 1700, it was one of the filthiest cities in Europe.

The first Bourbon king, Felipe V, was forced to build a new royal palace when the old one burned down, but otherwise, like most of his successors, he concentrated on surrounding the city with extravagant country retreats. The only king to do much for the city was Carlos III, who laid out parks, paved streets and embellished the city with elaborate fountains and triumphal arches. He also initiated the construction of the building that was to become the Prado, home of the vast and priceless collection of royal paintings that is Madrid's one true claim to cultural fame.

Madrid's central location came into its own with the industrial revolution, the development of transport and the rise of capitalism. Indeed, its most magnificent buildings are monuments to this age – sumptuous hotels like the Ritz and the Palace, an extraordinarily ornate post office, and any number of elaborate banks. Yet Madrid has no outstanding churches, the cathedral is still not finished and the seat of the

Spanish parliament is so insignificant that you could walk past without noticing it. Its main cultural attractions, the Prado and Palacio Real, lie in easy walking distance of the centre, Puerta de Sol. Visits to both are quite tiring, but there are parks nearby in which to unwind. You can do most of your drinking and eating in the centre, along the main street, Gran Via (still called Avenida José Antonio on many maps) and around Plaza Mayor, Plaza de Santa Ana and Plaza de Oriente.

Puerta del Sol

Puerta del Sol was long believed to be the central point of Spain, and is very much the heart of the city. A major Metro station and bus terminus here ensure that virtually everybody crosses Sol (as it is known) at some point in the day, and as it lies close to the main shopping streets and drinking areas it is the place where most Madrileños choose to meet their friends. Buskers, black marketeers and blind lottery-ticket sellers hustle for custom; businessmen sit shoulder-to-shoulder with bag-ladies on the rims of the fountains and tourists frown over their Metro plans.

Puerta del Sol is surrounded by uniform neo–classical façades, among them that of a pedimented eighteenth-century palace. Embedded in the pavement in front of it is the **Zero Kilometre** stone, from which all distances in Spain are measured. Across the square, at the foot of Calle del Carmen, is another Madrid landmark – a statue of a bear pawing an arbutus tree – part of the city's coat of arms.

From Sol you could shop along Calles del Carmen and Preciados to the Gran Vía; go to the bars around Plaza Santa Ana, head down the Carrera San Jerónimo to the Prado or stroll along Calle Mayor to Madrid's grandest square, Plaza Mayor, and the Palacio Real.

Carrera de San Jerónimo takes you down towards the Prado, passing the elaborate *fin-de-siècle* **Palace Hotel** and the unimpressive neo–classical **Cortes**, seat of the Spanish parliament. This was the scene of the 1981 coup when an officer of the Guardia Civil, Colonel Tejero, and his right-wing flunkies stormed in during a session, fired their pistols at the ceiling, and held the MPs hostage for 24 hours. Tejero followers expected the backing of the King and the rest of the army, but when Juan Carlos ordered them to stand down, they surrendered, and the next day saw massive demonstrations in support of democracy led by the leaders of the four main political parties.

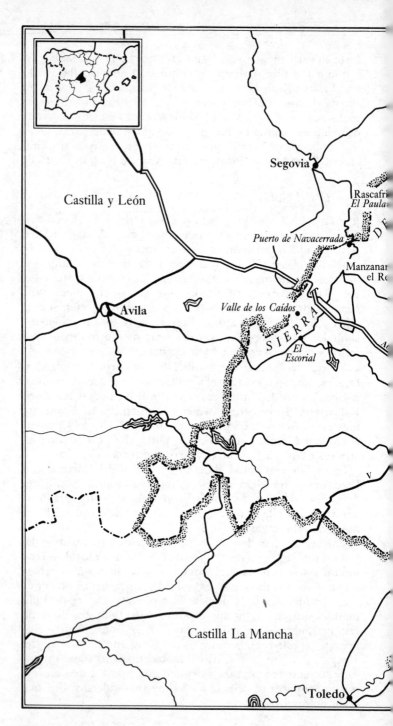

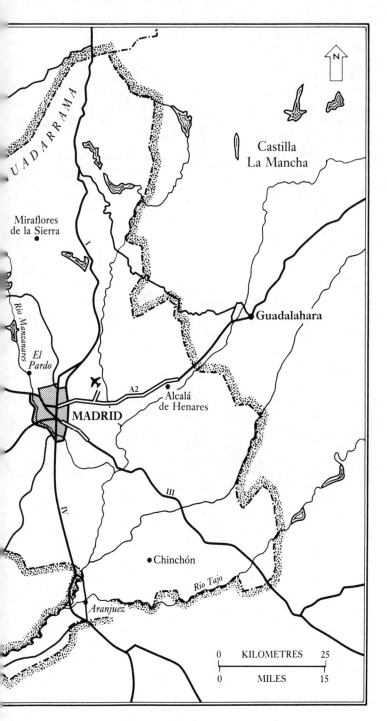

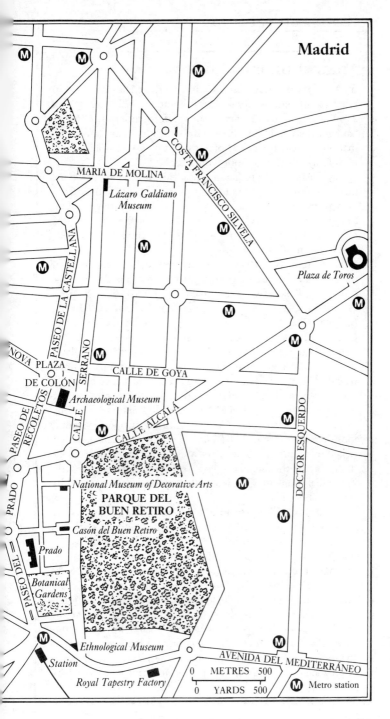

Madrid

MARIA DE MOLINA

COSTA FRANCISCO SILVELA

Lázaro Galdiano Museum

Plaza de Toros

PASEO DE LA CASTELLANA

NOVA

PLAZA DE COLÓN

SERRANO

CALLE DE GOYA

PASEO DE RECOLETOS

Archaeological Museum

CALLE

CALLE ALCALÁ

DOCTOR ESQUERDO

PRADO

PASEO DEL

National Museum of Decorative Arts

PARQUE DEL BUEN RETIRO

Casón del Buen Retiro

Prado

Botanical Gardens

Ethnological Museum

Station

Royal Tapestry Factory

AVENIDA DEL MEDITERRÁNEO

| 0 | METRES | 500 |
| 0 | YARDS | 500 |

Ⓜ Metro station

401

Madrid practicalities

● **Arrival and departure** Madrid's airport is at **Barajas**, 16 kilometres from the city centre. It is a functional place, with a 24-hour bureau de change; a tourist information office (Mon-Sat 8am–8pm and Sun 12.30–5pm) which has maps and information on the city, and a hotel reservation service (daily 8am-midnight) which will book you a room.

The cheapest way to get into Madrid from Barajas is on the bus. These leave approximately every fifteen minutes from outside the Arrivals hall. They drop you in an underground car park on Plaza de Colón, from where you could take a taxi or metro (from Serrano or Colón) to the centre. The bus ride costs a sixth of the price of a taxi.

The two major **railway stations** are Atocha (in the south of the city) and Chamartín (in the north). Atocha is closer to the centre, and the two are linked by Metro (line 8 from Chamartín to Plaza de Castilla, then line 1 to Atocha RENFE (not Atocha). Many trains stop at both Atocha and Chamartín, and call at a number of stations in between, so if you are heading north from Madrid at weekends and holidays, it is advisable to get on at Atocha, because by the time the train reaches Chamartín there may be no seats left. Leave plenty of time to buy your ticket, and be sure to join the correct queue – there's one for local trains (*cercanías*) and another for long distance (*largo recorrido*). Chamartín has a queuing system – look out for the sign '*salida hoy*' (today's departures), take a ticket from the machine, and wait for your number to be flashed up on the digital display. As departure times approach, individual trains may be assigned to specific booths, listed by their final destination.

A number of **bus stations** for long-distance journeys are inconveniently scattered around the city. The main station is the Estación Sur de Autobuses, Calle de Canarias 17 (Metro line 3: Palos de la Frontera) but buses run by Auto Res (to, amongst other places, Cuenca, Valencia, Seville and Salamanca) leave from the Auto Res station, Calle Fernandez Shaw (Metro line 6: Conde de Casal). The Auto Res station is up-to-date, and the ticket system computerised, but at the seedier Estación Sur, you have to walk up and down the ranks of *taquillas* (ticket offices) until you find the company that runs the service you want, during which time you can expect to be approached by beggars, and if you are female, pestered by unsavoury youths.

● **Getting around** As Madrid's streets are horribly congested, the quickest and easiest way to get around the city is by **Metro**. There are free, colour-coded plans available from most stations. Tickets for individual journeys are inexpensive and you can get a ten-ride ticket. It is a good idea to write down both the names of the stations where you have to change and the number of the lines you need to take. The direction of a train and line is indicated by its terminus. (e.g. to travel from Sol to Atocha RENFE, you need line 1 direction Portazgo). Routes and timetables are listed on station platforms. Few trains have automatic doors, so you have to open them yourself. There are few escalators, and changing lines can involve a long walk, often through dingy, unkempt tunnels, so solo women should think twice before travelling late at night.

Buses and **trams** are also quite straightforward to use, as the routes are listed on bus-stops. You can buy tickets from the driver or a *Bonobus* pass (valid for ten journeys) from kiosks around the city (the most convenient are on Puerta del Sol, Plaza de la Cibeles and Plaza del Callao). Underground and overland transport both run from around 6am to 2am.

Taxis are metered and reasonably cheap – but in the rush hour you can easily spend a lot of money sitting in a traffic jam.

When walking, hang on to bags and cameras. Women should avoid walking alone at night in inner city areas like Lavapiés, Latina and Malesana. Even those walking in pairs would do well to memorise the route before setting out.

● **Sightseeing tours and excursions** Sightseeing tours and excursions can be booked in most hotels. If you do not want to tackle the Prado alone, you might consider taking a half-day tour, which also includes the Palacio Real, but the night-time excursions to flamenco shows and night-clubs with floor-shows are overpriced. It is easy to get to the royal palace at Aranjuez and the monastery at El Escorial on public transport, and it is only worth taking an excursion if you are keen to have a commentary in English.

There are also day trips further afield to Toledo, Cuenca, Avila, Segovia and La Granja. You will not have time to see everything, but if you are pressed for time a few hours in one of the towns will probably make you determined to return at leisure. You could easily do your own day trip to Toledo (one and a half hours by bus) or Segovia (two hours by train).

● **Booking accommodation** Whatever time of year you go to Madrid, it is worth booking in advance. The most atmospheric locations for hotels are in the old town between Puerta del Sol and the Prado, though there is one tiny *pensión* wonderfully sited on Plaza de Oriente, opposite the Palacio Real. The convenience of staying on the Gran Vía compensates for the brassiness of the surroundings, and the facilities in hotels on Paseo de la Castellana for the inconvenience of being outside the centre.

● **Information** In the city centre there are tourist information offices at Plaza Mayor 3 (Mon-Fri 10am-2pm and 4-8pm; Sat and Sun 10am-5pm) and on the ground floor of the Torre de Madrid on Plaza de España (Mon-Fri 9am-7pm and Sat 9.30am-1.30pm) – the latter tends to be less crowded and the staff more helpful. Both offer free maps, which indicate the main sights and museums and include a plan of the Metro, but if you are intending to explore the city in detail, it is advisable to buy *Madrid y sus Aldrededores* (published by Firestone and available in Britain) as it includes a street directory. The tourist office also produces a booklet on museums, which, usefully, also gives public transport details, but is unreliable on opening times. The free *What's On* weekly (or so) magazine lists festivals, flamenco, bullfights and so on.

Parque del Buen Retiro

This park once formed the grounds of a seventeenth-century complex which included gardens, lakes, a theatre and a palace built for Felipe IV as 'a place for pleasure and laziness'. It came in useful when the old Palacio Real burned down in 1737, and the Bourbons moved here until the new palace was ready. After Carlos III had moved out, he opened the grounds to the public, but they were badly damaged during the Napoleonic war. Of the old buildings only the Casón del Buen Retiro, an ex-ballroom (now housing *Guernica*), and a hall (now holding an Army museum, Museo del Ejército) survived and stand beyond the borders of the park.

The park is well worth a stroll, especially on Sundays. Formal gardens opposite the Casón de Buen Retiro give way to shady clumps of trees popular with napping backpackers, and an artificial lake, the Estanque Grande, overlooked by a grandiose colonnade and equestrian statue of King Alfonso XII. Art exhibitions are frequently held in one of the two pavilions: the lovely brick and *azulejos*-decorated Palacio de Velázquez and the Palacio de Cristal, based on the Crystal Palace and standing on the shores of a small pond.

West of Puerta del Sol

Once the scene of bullfights, Inquisition trials and *autos-da-fé*, **Plaza Mayor** is now the heart of tourists' Madrid. The severe liverish-red façades shelter expensive *tapas* bars and restaurants. During the festival of San Isidro, 11–20 May, the square becomes an open air theatre for dance, flamenco, comedy, folk and pop.

Continuing along Calle Mayor, you reach Plaza de la Villa, a stark pedestrianised alcove headed by the sixteenth-century Casa de Cisneros, and flanked by the baroque town hall and the Torre de Los Lujánes. In 1525, after losing a battle against the Spanish in northern Italy, Francisco I of France was held prisoner in the tower, and he was forced to hand over Milan and Naples to Spain: possessions which were to become not only politically significant, but fundamental to the artistic heritage and architectural development of Madrid.

Calle Mayor emerges opposite Nuestra Señora de la Almudera which will eventually become Madrid's cathedral, an aesthetic disaster set to become an ecclesiastical white elephant. Financial problems and damage during the Civil War have left it incomplete after over a century, and for some time to come you can expect to see it surrounded by scaffolding and cranes. Next door to it is the infinitely more graceful Palacio Real, a neo-classical building of silver-grey Guadarrama granite commissioned by Spain's first Bourbon King, Felipe V. Its elegance is echoed by the Plaza de Oriente facing it, with a geometrical array of statues and topiary.

Parque del Oueste

Many Madrileños prefer the Parque del Oueste to the more famous Retiro. The park begins north-west of the Palacio Real and Plaza de España, with shadeless, formal gardens around the most bizarre building in the city: an ancient Egyptian temple given by Egypt to the Spanish engineers who worked on the Aswan dam, which led to the flooding of the temple's original site. Just beyond it you can catch a cablecar to the Casa del Campo, the city's largest park, the best of which lies to the north of Paseo de Moret.

Plaza de España and the Gran Vía

Madrid's main street, the Gran Vía, begins a short walk from the Palacio Real, and stretches from Plaza de España down towards Plaza de Cibeles. Jammed with elbowing crowds and lanes of traffic, it is a fumy, sweaty thoroughfare laid out between 1910 and 1929 to give the city an east–west axis. Behind flashing advertisements and gaudy cinema hoardings, its buildings reveal half a century's changes in taste and fortune. Most famous are the Manhattan-style Edificio de España and 31-storey Torre de Madrid on Plaza de España, both built in the '50s. At the time, the Torre de Madrid was the world's highest concrete structure and a symbol of Spain's post-war economic recovery. It is still the city's highest building.

On the Gran Vía, look out for the Capitol cinema on the corner of Plaza del Callao with its curved '30s façade; the '20s Telefónica, which was the city's first skyscraper, and became the Republicans' chief observation post during the Civil War; and the golden phoenix perched on the dome of the fancy Fenix y Unión building just above Plaza de Cibeles. For more corporate flamboyance, look across the road at the Banco de España building like a giant wedding cake, and walk a little way up Calle de Alcalá to see the Banco Español de Crédito, with its balustrade supported on elephants' heads, and the Banco de Bilbao, crowned by sculptures of chariots.

THE SIGHTS

The Prado

In 1785 Carlos III commissioned Juan de Villanueva, architect of many neo-classical Bourbon palaces, to build a natural history museum. The building was completed in the early nineteenth century, but before the exhibits could be installed, the Napoleonic army invaded and occupied it. When the Spanish monarchy returned, the Prado was turned into a public gallery for the vast collection of royal paintings.

The Prado opened to the public in 1819, and for many people since has been the sole reason for visiting Madrid, for whatever their failings as monarchs, the Spanish royal family were discerning patrons and collectors of art. Titian, Velázquez and Goya all worked as court artists and over three centuries the Habsburgs and Bourbons amassed collections of choice Italian and Flemish works. It is to their credit that although the Spanish ruled the Low Countries and parts of Italy, they actually bought rather than looted these works of art.

Though only around 1,000 of the gallery's hoard of paintings are on show, the collection can still be overwhelming and it is essential to decide on your priorities in advance.

Catalogue/guides in English are available at the first-floor shop (though their plans may be out of date). There are also excellent leaflets in English about the works by the most important and popular artists (Velázquez, Goya, Bosch etc.) on display in the relevant galleries.

● **Goya (1746–1828)** *Cartoons: rooms 19–23; paintings: rooms 34–39; Black Paintings: room 67.*

Bucolic scenes of peasants at work and play, including *The Injured Mason (796)*, *Poor Children at the Well (797)* and *The Snowstorm (Winter) (798)*, show an empathy with the poor and implicit criticism of the system which oppressed them. As court artist, Goya produced scathing portraits of Carlos IV *(719* and *727)*, María Luisa *(720* and *728)* and their family *(726)*. Yet there were no repercussions; María Luisa even admitted to her lover, Prime Minister Godoy, that she found herself 'very much herself' in the portrait *Queen María Luisa with a mantilla (728)* which reveals her as vain, defiant, and very ugly.

The Nude Maja (742) and *The Clothed Maja (741)* were believed to have been modelled by Goya's alleged mistress, the Duchess of Alba.

In 1808, during the struggle against Napoleon's army, Goya was commissioned by Fernando VII to paint two works 'to perpetuate … the memorable and heroic feats … of our glorious rebellion against the tyrant of Europe'. Goya responded with *The 2nd of May (748)* and *The 3rd of May (748* and *749)*, works in which there is neither heroism nor glory, but simply raw violence and debilitating fear.

In the so-called *Black Paintings (754–768)*, painted between 1819 and 1823 straight on to the walls of Goya's home (and removed to the Prado in 1873), were horrifying visions realised with an extraordinary expressionistic technique.

● **Velázquez (1599–1660)** *Rooms 12, 13, 15, 16,*

The portraits of *Felipe IV (1182–1185)*, who engaged Velázquez as court painter, his younger brothers *Infante Don Carlos (1188)* and *Cardinal-Infante Don Fernando (1186)* and Felipe's six-year-old son *Infante Baltasar Carlos in Hunting Dress (1189)* bear witness to the artist's long career at court.

Baltasar Carlos is also shown (sumptuously clad in pink silk and gold lace) on the back of his favourite pony *(1180)*. If the horse looks slightly odd, it's not surprising, for it died before the portrait was painted, and the prince is posing on its stuffed corpse. The unfinished, almost impressionist, portrait of Felipe IV's nine-year-old daughter, *Infanta Margarita in Pink (1192)*, was possibly his last work.

In Velázquez's greatest and most famous work, *Las Meninas* or *The Ladies in Waiting (1174)*, light, colour and space work perfectly together to create the illusion of looking into a real room, so much so that you can stand on the same spot as the king and queen who are shown reflected in a mirror.

Make sure you also see *The Topers* or *The Triumph of Bacchus (1170)*, and *Las Hilanderas (1173)*, which shows women at work in the royal tapestry factory.

● **El Greco (1540/1–1614)** *Rooms 10B and 9B*

Having given up hope of royal patronage, El Greco, originally from Crete, spent his life in Toledo painting religious canvasses and portraits of Castillian nobles. He treats subjects like *The Adoration of the Shepherds (2988)* in as mystical and cerebral a manner as abstract concepts like *The Resurrection (825)* and *Trinity (824)*, taking no notice of the Counter-Reformation dictum that biblical subjects should be presented in familiar settings and that subjects should display recognisable emotions.

● **The Golden Age of Spanish painting** *Rooms 16A, 16B, 17A*

Among the artists represented are José de Ribera, born in 1591, who worked in the Caravaggio-inspired Tenebrist style, which makes dramatic use of light and shadow. There is an unpleasantly violent streak in many of his paintings, notably *The Martyrdom of St Philip (1101)*, but the mood later softened. The tender *Mary Magdalene (1103)* is thought to be a portrait of his daughter.

Ribera's contemporary Francisco de Zurbarán (1598–1664) was influenced by the polychrome religious statues for which the town was famous. He executed many paintings of solemn, almost sculptural saints for austere religious orders. Bartolomé Esteban Murillo (1618-1682) is best known for his dreamy virgins and curly-headed cherubs, which were perfectly in tune with the Counter-Reformation's demand for religious art that would move the hearts of everyday folk, but some may prefer the fine seriousness of works like *The Adoration of the Shepherds (961)* and *St Jerome (987)*.

● **Titian (c1487/90–1576) and the Italians** *Titian: rooms 8, 8B, 9; Tintoretto: room 9A; other Italians: rooms 4 and 5*
Among many portraits of Titian's employer and friend are the superb *Emperor Charles V at Mühlberg (410)*, rescued from the 1734 fire in the Palacio Real. Charles's son Philip II commissioned three works on mythological subjects, the eroticism of which suggests that the king was not quite the ascetic he is made out to be: one of them is *Danaë Receiving the Shower of Gold (425)*, but there are many other alluring mythological scenes, notably *Bacchanal (418)*, an evocation of sexual abandonment, with Titian's auburn-haired lover, Violante, pictured in a red dress with her name written on her breast. The Prado also holds some of Titian's last works, notably the *Self Portrait (407)* painted when the artist was in his late eighties.

Works by Titian's fellow Venetians include Tintoretto's intriguing *Lady Revealing her Bosom* (also known as *The Young Venetian*) *(382)*. Those by earlier Italian artists include Fra Angelico's formal, limpid *Annunciation (15)*, a portrait by Antonio del Sarto of his wife *Lucrezia di Baccio del Fede (332)*, and paintings by Raphael, the most arresting of which is the *Portrait of a Cardinal (299)*.

● **Bosch and the Flemish Collection** *Rooms 57A (Bosch) 56, 56A, 54, 58, 61 & 61B (Rubens)*
Hieronymus Bosch (1450–1516) is represented by *The Garden of Delights (2823)* a psychedelic triptych of heaven, earth and hell. *The Hay Wain (2052)*, probably an illustration of a Flemish proverb, likewise features human greed and an appalling hell; *The Adoration of the Magi (2048)* is disrupted by paparazzi-like peasants, a semi-naked Antichrist, and a distant figure about to be devoured by a boar. Finally, don't miss the (unmarked) *Seven Deadly Sins (2822)* table top in the centre of the room.

Pieter Brueghel the Elder, best known for his socially satirical religious and peasant scenes, is here represented by the horrifying *Triumph of Death* (1393). The familiar snowy scenes are copies of his works by his son, Pieter the Younger. Other famous works in the Flemish collection include Roger Van de Weyden's *Deposition* (2825); Quentin Matsys' gripping *Ecce Homo* (2801); and works by Memling, van Orley and the Master of Flemalle. Also worth a look is the *Portrait of Mary Tudor* (2108) by Philip II's court artist Antonio Moro.

Velázquez' patron, Felipe IV, bought many of the works in Rubens' private collection after the artist's death and these are now on view at the Prado.

Palacio Real

Facing the Plaza de Oriente over the Calle de Bailén, the Palacio Real replaced a Habsburg palace burnt down in 1734. Felipe V hired architects from Italy accustomed to designing opulent palaces for the kings of Savoy, who created an elegant Italianate building containing some of Europe's most excessively ornate rooms.

King Juan Carlos and Queen Sofía live elsewhere in more modest surroundings, but they still use the palace for state occasions, so security is almost airport tight, and tour groups are trailed by armed guards. There are some 2,800 rooms in the palace, but thankfully the obligatory guided tours (in English) only take you through a fraction of them.

Such a room is the stunning Salón de Gasparini, one of a suite created for King Carlos III by Matteo Gasparini, a designer from Naples. Gasparini designed everything from the ceiling, stuccoed with fruit, foliage and Chinamen, to the silk-embroidered upholstery and inlaid marble floor. This shrine to Bourbon extravagance was the King's dressing room. Carlos brought the entire staff of the Neapolitan porcelain factory at Capodimonte to form the core of the new Buen Retiro porcelain factory. Their work is to be seen in a tiny parlour, the Sala de Porcelana, its walls plated with revolting porcelain panels of putti, urns and grapes, which formed the entrance to his bathroom.

Look out for Goya's notoriously unflattering portraits of Queen María Luisa and her eccentric husband Carlos IV (in the Gasparini Antechamber); a circular divan incorporating a candelabra (in the Gasparini Lobby); and chandeliers in the form of a temple (Yellow Room) and crown (Carlos III's Apartment).

The entrance ticket admits you to other sections of the palace, although these are of limited appeal. A separate guided tour is necessary to see the Biblioteca, which, despite some beautifully bound books and a couple of inlaid Stradivari violins, will excite only experts. In the Armoury suits of armour pose on steel-plated steeds, and in the Farmacía are pots, phials and drawers of medicinal herbs and a replica of an alchemist's den. Ornate state coaches in the Museo de Carruajes (not far from the Palacio Real, just off the Paseo del Virgen del Puerto) add to the picture of the Bourbon lifestyle, while the topiaried symmetry and statues of the Jardines Sabatini, at the far end of the palace, are ideal for a stroll.

Guernica and the Botanical Gardens

South of the Prado and facing the Paseo del Prado are the Botanic Gardens laid out by Carlos III in the late eighteenth century. He gave citizens the right to take cuttings from any of the many medicinal plants. The edict has never been revoked, so in theory Madrileños could still help themselves.

A short walk from the gardens, suspended behind a bullet-proof screen in the Casón del Buen Ritiro, is Picasso's *Guernica*, one of the most devastating and politically con-troversial paintings of the century, commemorating the world's first mass bombing of civilians. The raid happened on 26 April 1937, market day in the small Basque town of Gernika; the bombers were German Nazis, supporting Franco by attempting to intimidate Basque nationalists; and in three hours over 2,000 people died. The painting only came to Spain in 1981, for Picasso stipulated that it should remain outside the country until the restoration of democracy. The work is still loathed by Spain's ultra-right – hence the bullet-proof glass and bag-searches.

Picasso began work five days after the raid, and his sketches provide a sombre, yet fascinating insight into his exploration of themes and development of images.

Museo Arqueológico

The museum is just north of the city centre, on the west side of Calle Serrano, next to the bleak concrete monoliths of the Jardines del Descubrimento which are inscribed with extracts from Columbus' journal. The museum's collection is mag-nificent and eclectic, ranging from Ancient Egyptian mummy cases to Greek pottery, and from inlaid Visigothic jewellery to Ibizan idols. The most famous artefact is the *Dama de Elche*, a Celtiberian cult figure discovered near Alicante. Finally, beneath the courtyard is a reproduction of the Altamira caves with their prehistoric frescoes of bison.

Museo Lázaro Galdiano

Situated on Calle Serrano 122, this is towards the north end of Calle Serrano, this museum is one in which to linger and savour detail. There are some of Goya's *Black Paintings*, a portrait by Velázquez of his wife, and works by Gainsborough and Reynolds; Limoges enamels, Byzantine cloisonné, exquisite bronze Renaissance statuettes and a

411

superb collection of jewellery ranging from Hellenistic and Phoenician work to a pair of ear-rings by Cellini.

Monasterio de las Descalzas (Descalzas reales convent)

The convent, dwarfed by an immense department store, is in the heart of Madrid, on the Plaza San Martín. It was founded in the sixteenth century by Philip II's sister Juana who, widowed at 19, decided she wanted a retreat from the duties of state. Although Juana died before it was completed, many aristocratic women joined the order – the reason that the monastery is today packed with treasures and works of art. Some are in dubious taste: notably the blood-spattered Christs, and altars featuring 3D tableaux, artificial flowers and Madonnas with glittering tiaras.

Museo Nacional de las Artes Decorativas

Laid out in an elegant old mansion on Calle de Montalbán 12 by the Buen Retiro park is a collection of ornamental artefacts ranging from Chinese figurines to Lalique glassware. There is a gorgeous collection of fans, dolls' houses and toys (including a miniature Singer sewing machine) and on the top-floor is a room laid out as a kitchen. The walls are tiled with *azulejos* work featuring tray-bearing footmen, hanging game, bunches of onions and baskets of fruit. The museum is not labelled in English.

Real Fábrica de Tapices

Here on weekday mornings you can watch tapestries and carpets being woven on hand-looms to designs by Goya as they were in the eighteenth century.

Centro de Arte Reina Sofia

This stylishly converted and extended eighteenth-century convent in Calle de Santa Isabel 52 is Madrid's main venue for temporary exhibitions, and attracts shows of world-class standard. There is also a reasonably-priced café, a grassy courtyard and a well stocked shop. The city's (rather dull) contemporary collection is due to move here from the **Museo Español del Arte Contemporáneo**, inconveniently located at Avenida Juan de Herrera 2 on the university campus. The grounds of this museum, with sculpture laid out among fountains and trees, are lovely, and there is also a café and excellent shop. The permanent exhibition, however, in no way represents the achievement of Spanish artists this century, and a three-piece Picasso, a Miró design for a mural and Diego Rivera's *Flower Seller* hardly compensate for the poverty of the rest.

Museo de América

This is closed at present, but has a reputedly excellent pre-Columbian section, along with Hispano-American crafts and Inca and Aztec artefacts.

Museo Etnlógico

Costumes, crafts, tools, weapons, ceramics, and musical instruments from all over the world are beautifully displayed, with information boards in Spanish.

SHOPPING

Shopping in Madrid takes you into parts of the city you might not otherwise visit: from the Rastro, a colourful and chaotic flea market held on the Plaza de Rastro in the working-class quarter around the Latino metro station, to Chueca, where recently restored art nouveau houses hold the modernist boutiques of up-and-coming designers.

The Rastro is held on Sundays, between 10am and 3pm. Stalls selling grubby and crumpled jumble and junk have now been joined by a host of crafts, jewellery, and ethnic and alternative clothes stands. A recently opened and extremely upmarket shopping mall, specialising in antiques and design, is just by the Puerta de Toledo Metro station.

If you are looking for exclusive and expensive crafts, branches of *Artespana* on Plaza de las Cortes and at Calle Hermosilla 14 off Calle Serrano sell textiles, ceramics and furniture from all over Spain. Even more upmarket, *Najera* on Plaza de la Independencia is a fascinating place to browse.

For real bargains try Cava Baja, in the Latina quarter between Plaza Mayor and the Rastro. *Antonio Sanchez* at No. 19 has glazed earthenware and a painted plates; and for unusual presents, *Luis Goya* at Cava Baja 42 sells guitars, *Munoz* at Cava Baja 12 hide water-carriers and wooden barrels of all sizes. Among the mousetraps and wooden spoons in the nameless shop next door there are some lovely polished salad bowls. Finally, there are tasteful and incredibly cheap painted ceramics at *Cerámica Sanz* at Segovia 5 (closed Saturdays).

For mainstream shopping, you can stay in the city centre. Calle del Carmen and Calle de Preciados, just off Puerta del Sol, are packed with shoe shops, but most of their many clothes shops are unexciting. At the foot of Calle de Preciados are two immense department stores, *Corte Inglés* and *Gallería Preciados*, selling everything from cosmetics to kitchenware.

There are more inspiring (and expensive) clothes shops in the wealthy Salamanca quarter to the north of town. Calle Serrano, the parallel Calle Claudio Coello to the north and the streets in between hold most big-name designer boutiques, while young Spanish designers are based in and around Calle de Almirante and Calle de Argensola in Chueca.

EATING AND DRINKING

Breakfast, cakes and pastries

Unless you can stomach a breakfast of heavy Danish pastries, toast grilled on an oily hot plate or thick chocolate and *churros* (strips of deep fried dough) first thing in the morning, eat in a hotel. The classic hotel breakfast is bread rolls and jam, sponge cake and coffee, but many of the larger hotels lay on generous buffets.

La Menorquina Puerta del Sol. Wonderful croissants and pastries in a pretty *pastelería*. Eat them at the bar.

Café Concierto Calle de Prado 4. A comfortable and civilised wood-panelled bar and coffee house. It is also a lovely place for pre-dinner drinks, and on Thursday evenings there is live music.

Embassy Paseo de la Castellana 12 (entrance on Paseo de Serrano, on the corner with Calle de Ayala). A genteel tea room founded by an English governess which attracts members of the aristocracy, and is perfect for morning coffee, light lunch or afternoon tea. There is also a restaurant above.

Restaurants and tapas bars

At lunchtime and early evening, most tourists head straight for the *tapas* bars of Plaza Mayor. These are expensive and impersonal, and *tasca* hopping is better done in the streets below the Plaza (notably Cava de San Miguel and Calle Cuchilleros).

Bar Roldan Calle de Postas 12. Good selection of fresh *tapas* in a clean, neighbourly bar.

Los Galayos Plaza Mayor. Overpriced, like the rest on the Plaza, but the *tapas* are good.

Mesón de Champignon Cava de San Miguel. Specialises in mushroom *tapas*.

La Chata Cava Baja 24. Tiled façade, bull's head on the wall, and full of elderly people drinking sherry.

Bar Gallego Plaza de Puerta Cerrada. Galician delicacies and wines.

La Trucha Manuel Fernández y González 3. Imaginative and sophisticated *tapas*.

Cervecería Alemana Seafood *tapas* (and see bar listing over).

L'Hardy Carrera de San Jerónimo 8. Meals in the *belle époque* dining-rooms upstairs are expensive, but it is worth popping in to the marvellously ritzy delicatessen below to participate in an ancient Madrid ritual. In the late morning it is full of over-'50s serving themselves with consommé from a silver samovar. There are also delicate sandwiches and *tapas*.

Museo de Jamónes Carrera de San Jerónimo. Hams suspended from the ceiling and counters packed with hundreds of salamis and cheeses make this a great place to buy provisions for a picnic. In the centre is a large bar where you can stand having a beer and sandwich until around midnight.

Among the restaurants worth seeking out are:

Taberna Toscana Calle Ventura de la Vega. Despite the name, a traditional Spanish place with gourds, dried peppers, and bunches of bay leaves hanging from the beamed ceiling. The mock-medieval décor attracts quite a few tourists, but it is popular with locals too and serves good *tapas* and *raciones*.

El Botín Calle Cuchilleros 17. According to the *Guinness Book of Records*, this is the world's oldest restaurant. Hemingway raved about its roast baby pig and lamb.

Casa Ciriaco Calle Mayor 84. Traditional place which is popular with the arts and media crowd, but remains surprisingly unpretentious. The big draw is the *gallina en pepitoria*.

Posada de la Villa Cava Baja 9. Suckling pig and baby lamb roast in a beehive oven in a smartly restored seventeenth-century inn. Good *tapas* too.

Lerranz Calle de Echegaray 26. Minimalist décor, relaxed atmosphere and superb food based on traditional *tapas*. Specialities include sardine pâté and *bogaza* (bread toasted with tomato) served with a variety of side-dishes.

Spaghetti & Bollicine Calle de Prim 15. Imaginative Italian restaurant with a stylish clientele.

Cervantes Calle León corner Calle Infante. A comfortable place near Plaza Santa Ana which serves inventive salads and pizza, and a potent sangría.

Biblos Calle de San Vincente Ferrer 32. One for the adventurous. A Lebanese café in an old pharmacy at the heart of the seedy Malesana district. Tacky décor, but good *tabouleh* and *falafel*, and unforgettable cardamom-scented coffee.

La Biótika Calle Amor de Dios 3 (off Calle Huertas). One of Spain's few vegetarian restaurants.

Bars and nightlife

Madrid has an extraordinary variety of bars: antique *cervecerías* with nicotine-stained panelling and paintwork or sumptuously tiled walls; smoky jazz venues and civilised classical music cafés; touristy *tascas* and '30s cocktail bars; trendy clubs for hip young things, and venerable cafés where august old men meet to discuss politics.

Most bars do not close till very late, and some clubs only really liven up after 4am (and close at breakfast time). Clubs go in and out of fashion rapidly. Current darlings of the club scene include **Archy**, Marqués de Riscal 11, **El Cielo** (housed in the Pacha theatre on Barceló 11) and **Voltereta**, Calle de Princesa 3. Less trendy, but usually good fun, is **Joy Eslava**, Calle del Arenal 11, housed in an ornate old theatre.

Bars and clubs on and around Calles San Vicente Ferrer and San Andrés in the Malesana quarter play more alternative music, which ranges from thrash metal and punk to salsa and reggae. The area itself can be quite dangerous, as it is also the territory of prostitutes, skinheads and bikers.

Santa Ana and Huertas districts

This is the most traditional of Madrid's drinking areas, home to the most extravagant of the tiled bars and some of the oldest *cervecerías*. There are also numerous ultra-violet-lit youth bars on Calle Huertas.

Café Central, Plaza Matute. Famous jazz venue where the details of stained glass, mirrors and carved wood are just discernible through the smoke. There is live jazz most nights between 10pm and midnight, when you will have to pay to get in. At other times, it is a scruffy and amicable café favoured by students, arty types and intellectuals.

Cervecería Alemana Plaza Santa Ana. A traditional old panelled *cervecería* with carved beams, graced by white marble-topped tables and yellowing photos of matadors. It is quiet at noon except for a few regulars popping in for a chat and the famous seafood *tapas*, but is inevitably heaving by 9pm.

Viva Madrid! Calle de Manuel Fernández González 7. A lively young *cervecería* with a gorgeous tiled façade, and beams supported on winged caryatids. It gets packed at night.

Los Gabrieles Calle de Echegaray 17. The most extravagantly tiled bar in Madrid. It is animated at night, but you should also pop in during the day to take a look at the colourful ceramic sherry and anis advertisements.

La Fidula Calle de Huertas 57. Classical music in a subdued, civilised salon, ideal for a quiet evening.

Alcalá, Chueca and Salamanca districts

Some of the most sophisticated bars and cafés are around and along the Gran Vía and Alcalá. The outdoor cafés of Paseo de la Castellana, beloved of Madrid's wealthy young things, are rather less appealing.

Circulo de Bellas Artes Calle de Alcalá 42 corner Marques de Casa Riera. The austere bar of the Museo de Bellas Artes attracts a Bohemian crowd. In winter you sit on leather sofas in a vast hall with a dingily frescoed ceiling; in summer outside on the terrace.

Museo de Chicote Calle de Alcalá 12. A cocktail bar favoured by Hemingway: '30s décor, sophisticated people, genteel service and unforgettable gin fizzes.

Cock Calle Reina 16. Sumptuous '20s cocktail bar. The drinks are better at Chicote, but it is worth coming here to see the spiralling columns, gilded curlicues, and gleaming wood.

Bodega Angel Sierra Plaza Chueca. Stand-up neighbourhood place where the vermouth is on tap from a barrel.

Hanoi Calle Hortaleza 81. Minimalist décor and a seriously trendy young clientele. Open till very late, and ideal for people-watching.

Café Gijón Paseo de Recoletos 21. The most famous of Madrid's old cafés is an august place with wooden pillars and marble tables, and has long been a venue for *tertulias*, regular discussions on politics and current affairs by like-minded men. The atmosphere lightens at lunchtime, when the café

417

fills with business people and office workers. *Tapas* and light meals are availability.

Café Comercial Glorieta de Bilbao 1. This is similar in style to the Gijón, but it was once a Republican meeting place, and still attracts a more radical, intellectual crowd. In the afternoons there are as many people reading, writing and studying as chatting.

The Castellana Terrazzas In summer the central spine of Paseo de la Castellana is lined with outdoor cafés or *terrazzas* and flanked by multiple lanes of traffic. It is here that Madrid's beautiful young things kill the hours before going to a club (around 3am).

Mayor and Opera districts

Plaza Mayor's bars are overpriced tourist traps, but Opera holds two of Madrid's most civilised cafés.

Chocolatería San Ginés Calle de Coloreros. A gleaming cream marble and mirrored café behind the Joy Eslava disco. Boppers wind up a night on the dance floor with a chocolate and *churros*, but at other times it attracts an older (sometimes very old) crowd.

La Carbonería Calle de Coloreros. Classical, folk and medieval music provides an unusual soundtrack for this gently alternative bar. The notice-board, with adverts for dance and music lessons, Greenpeace and gamelan concerts, gives an idea of the clientele.

Las Revas off Plaza Mayor. Stone-vaulted cellar in one of the alleyways that leads off the Plaza Mayor, which attracts locals as well as tourists.

Café de Oriente Plaza de Oriente 2. An elegant, if touristy, café and restaurant on Madrid's loveliest square.

Solesmes Calle Amnestía 5. Madrid needs more bars like this. It is cultured yet unpretentious, plays classical music and has the look of an eighteenth-century salon.

FESTIVALS AND ENTERTAINMENT

The liveliest time to visit Madrid is May. From 29 April to 6 May the city council holds the Fiestas de Dos de Mayo in memory of the city's resistance to the Napoleonic invasion in 1808, and from 11 to 20 May there is the more famous Fiesta de San Isidoro. There are masses of cultural events at both festivals – flamenco, *zarzuela*, ballet, rock, jazz, folk and classical concerts – held at various venues, indoor and out-door, around the city. The selection of artists for the Dos de Mayo tends to be more adventurous.

Madrid's classical music and opera scene is not particularly dynamic, though it gets its quota of international performers. You might be interested to sample *zarzuela*, something like a cross between operetta and vaudeville. The tourist offices have two free listings magazines, *Guía de Ocio* and *En Madrid*.

Flamenco is not native to Madrid, but as well as the tourist traps there are a few authentic venues frequented by aficio-nados: **El Portón** Calle López de Hoyos 25 (Tel 262 49 56) and **Candela** Calle Olmo 2 (Tel 467 33 82). Friday and Saturday appear to be the big flamenco nights, but it is worth phoning in advance to check on opening times and current prices (which can be steep).

Bullfighting remains a Madrid institution, though it is now less popular than football. Fights are held from Spring until early October on Sunday afternoons at the 26,000-capacity Las Ventas bullring at Plaza de Toros, Calle del Alcalá 237. Tickets are available at major hotels and at the booking office on Plaza del Carmen, just off Calle Carmen. There is also a bullfighting museum at the ring.

NORTH OF MADRID

The royal monastery of El Escorial is an hour's train ride (from Atocha or Chamartín) or a 45-minute drive from the capital. If you are touring, you could take a trip around the monastery (or the two diminutive palaces) on your way to Segovia or the Sierra de Guadarrama. In between El Escorial and Segovia the Valle de los Caídos (Valley of the Fallen) is monument to the Civil War. The whole valley is dominated by a cross of prodigious size, alleged to be the largest in the world.

Manzanares El Real and Miraflores de la Sierra are the main resorts in the Guadarrama foothills, less than an hour's drive from Madrid. They are now popular weekend retreats for Madrileños. The classiest hotel in the area is in El Paular, a more isolated mountain monastery village (a good base if you are touring the Sierra de Guadarrama). Do not miss the most spectacular part, the Sierra de la Pedriza, reached from Manzanares.

The Bourbon palace of El Pardo is just on the fringes of the city, but it is the least rewarding of the northern sights.

El Pardo

El Pardo is a fifteen-minute drive from Madrid, and you can also get there by regular bus (601) from Paseo de Moret. El Pardo was the residence of Franco from 1940 to 1975 and the palace is now used as a residence for visiting heads of state. Designer telephones sit on rococo tables, a TV, video and contemporary sofa stand awkwardly among the gilt and chandeliers, and you may even glimpse the fitted kitchen with microwave where illustrious guests presumably fix themselves TV dinners. All this is in bizarre contrast to the rooms of tapestries (many designed by Goya) and paintings.

A short walk along a plane-lined avenue takes you to the far more enjoyable **Casita del Príncipe**. Like the similarly named *casitas* at Aranjuez and El Escorial, it was built for Carlos IV, and is, if anything, even more excessive. Walls and upholstery are gorgeously embroidered, and stucco and gilt are used to opulent effect especially in the vestibule and in the Salón Amarillos, which has *trompe-l'oeil* decoration.

El Escorial

Monastery, palace and royal mausoleum, was built by Philip II, and from here he ruled his immense empire, holed up in a spartan study within its prison-like walls, poring over state documents and files of secret information gleaned by his vast network of spies. Time has done nothing to mellow the place. The stark granite walls and blank windows of the façades are unnerving, the bleak basilica intimidating, and the main mausoleum, with its shelves of royal bodies in marble tombs, chilling.

Philip had El Escorial built to fulfil the dying wish of his father for a church with a royal mausoleum, as well as a vow he himself had made after the Spanish won a victory in 1557 over the French at San Quentin, on the feast day of St Lawrence. Not only had the Spanish destroyed a church dedicated to St Lawrence in the process, but the victory was supposedly secured through the saint's intercession, and Philip swore to build a new church to St Lawrence in recompense and gratitude. St Lawrence was a Roman Christian who had been grilled to death; criss-cross layout of El Escorial could be said to resemble a grid iron.

Guided tours are at breakneck speed and in Spanish only, so you might consider it worthwhile taking an excursion from

Madrid – although if you find yourself the only English speaker, you may still have to insist that the guide translates for you. Excursions include a trip to the Valle de Caidos (see p.422) but not the two miniature palaces, the Casita del Príncipe and the Casita Arriba, built by the Bourbons as a riposte to Habsburg sobriety. These are within walking distance of the main complex, and you could abandon the excursion and make your own way back to Madrid by train after visiting them.

If you arrive by train, the Casita del Príncipe is a few minutes' walk from the station, after which you can walk up to the monastery along the avenue of horse-chestnuts and conifers that form the spine of the rather neglected Jardín del Principe. The town of El Escorial is dull, but there are plenty of places to eat and drink near the palace.

● **Basilica** The basilica is approached through the west entrance, via the Patio de los Reyes, named after the six statues of Biblical kings perched high up on the façade of the church.

● **The Royal Apartments** Access to the royal apartments is by guided tour only. The two frescoes in the Hall of the Battles catalogue the battle of La Higuerela against the Moors in 1431, and the battle of St Quentin against the French in 1557. The red-tiled floors, threadbare chairs and sagging beds of the Habsburg apartments are shockingly stark. They have scarcely changed since the days of Philip II. Philip would give audiences to visiting dignitaries from a simple wooden seat, his gouty left leg propped up on a folding stool. The austere suites of Philip and his daughter, Isabel Clara Eugenia, flank the high altar of the basilica, with doors leading directly from their bedrooms into the church. When Philip was dying, his gangrenous body stinking so intensely that his aides could hardly bear to be near him, he would join in services, or simply gaze at the altar, from his bed.

● **The Royal Mausoleums** A flight of steps leads down to the Panteón de los Reyes, passing the grille of the *pudridero*, in which royal corpses were left to rot. After decomposing for ten years they were placed in the marble and gilt coffins that are shelved on the walls of the octagonal mausoleum.

● **The El Escorial paintings** There are fine works by Titian, Ribera and Tintoretto, but the highlight is Bosch's circular *Ecce Homo* in which Christ is insulted by characters whose crazed reality makes them all the more disturbing.

● **Library** The splendid barrel-vaulted library with Tibaldi's vibrantly coloured frescoes of the seven liberal arts is the most cheerful of El Escorial's rooms. Books were one of Philip II's few indulgences, but he was more interested in the sumptuous bindings than the contents. Since the library was founded, the books have been placed with their spines to the walls, prettily (but uselessly) revealing their gilt-edged pages.

● **Casita del Príncipe** Carlos IV, a king so stupid that he was virtually the only person in Europe not to know that his wife was having an affair with his Prime Minister, had miniature palaces built all over Castile where he could escape the responsibilities of court. The Casita del Príncipe at El Escorial was one of the first, built while he was still Prince of Asturias, but it bears all the Carlos IV hallmarks – exquisite stuccoed ceilings, brocaded walls, glittering chandeliers and fancy furniture.

● **Casita Arriba** A short drive or ten-minute walk, beyond the monastery, the Casita Arriba is a tinier version of the Casita del Príncipe, built for Charles's younger brother Gabriel as a hunting lodge. More recently, it was used by the then student King-in-waiting Juan Carlos.

Valle de Los Caidos

A short drive north from El Escorial, and usually included in half-day excursions, is a vast, dank underground basilica that was hollowed out of a rocky hill on Franco's orders by political prisoners (many of whom died in the process) as a monument to the dead of the Civil War. The claim that it is dedicated to the dead on both sides is hard to swallow, for there are statues representing the Army, Navy and Air Force, and the only named tombs are to Franco and José Antonio (Primo de Rivera), founder of the Falangists. This hideous monument is Spain's most awesome tribute to forty years of Fascism.

Sierra de Guadarrama

These hills north of Madrid provide a welcome breath of cool unpolluted air for harassed city-dwellers, and in winter, the first flurry of snow sends a posse of skiing enthusiasts heading for the Navacerrada Pass on the Segovia border.

Manzanares El Real is a burgeoning playground village in the Guadarrama foothills, easily accessible at only half an hour's drive from Madrid. Its focal point is a large castle whose perfect battlements make it hard to believe that it is the genuine fifteenth-century article. Beyond it lies a dreary-looking artificial lake, used for various watery leisure activities. More interesting is the excursion up a side-road to the **Circo de la Pedriza**, an extraordinary wilderness of rocks, ravines and pinewoods now given natural park status. Entrance is free, but at the gate a firm hint in the shape of a large plastic bag for your rubbish is thrust into your hand. A five-kilometre circular drive takes you round the park to commune with nature – or your fellow-men at weekends. The ancient granite rocks have been weathered into disturbing fungoid forms which seem to crouch, toad-like, on precarious ledges, ready to leap on to unwary passers-by. The views of the mountains and the lake (which looks better from up here) are excellent. There is a nice picnic spot by the River Manzanares.

Further north, the mountain and woodland scenery becomes more dramatic as you pick a route through the resort villages of Soto del Real and Miraflores de la Sierra to the Morcuera Pass. **El Paular** (H) has a Carthusian monastery, now occupied by Benedictine monks. A luxury hotel has been built in part of its buildings. The little church of San Bruno is worth a look for its fifteenth-century Gothic altarpiece and baroque chapel.

From El Paular the C-604 heads along to the Puerto de Navacerrada, an 1,860-metre-high pass giving access to Segovia province in Castilla y León. It now holds a grim, dilapidated ski resort and is a starting point for undemanding walks through pine woods to the village of Cercedilla, or a more challenging hike up to the seven granite serrations known as the Siete Picos.

SOUTH AND EAST OF MADRID

Aranjuez is the perfect place to which to escape from the capital, and its palaces and gardens are only a forty-minute train ride (around thirty minutes by road) from Madrid.

Chinchón is another appealing day-trip from Madrid, and, if you have your own transport, could be combined with Aranjuez. The pleasantest way to do this would be to see Aranjuez first, and then drive up to Chinchón, which has one of the nicest *paradores* in Castile. You could then indulge in Chinchón's famous and alarmingly fiery aniseed spirit without worrying about getting home.

Aranjuez

As lush and lavish as the guitar concerto it inspired, Aranjuez burgeons without warning on the bare Castilian plain, a leafy enclave which was for centuries the spring and autumn retreat of Spanish monarchs. It serves the same function today for smog-weary Madrileños, and at weekends you may find the whispering trees that inspired the composer Rodrigo are drowned by squealing children and teenagers with ghetto-blasters. But even they cannot wholly detract from the sheer romanticism of the place, which was laid out by the Habsburgs and improved by the Bourbons, and which was the understandable choice of Isabel II for many of the illicit liaisons that led to her abdication.

The two disparate royal palaces are monuments to Bourbon extravagance – the stately, symmetrical **Palacio Real**, and the diminutive **Casa del Labrador**. In the Palacio Real, guided tours hustle you through a bewildering series of rooms decorated with damask, silk and brocade, where crystal chandeliers cascade from ceilings inspired by the excavations at Pompeii and Herculaneum. In the Porcelain Room panels latticed with foliage, monkeys clamber, exotic birds pose and elaborately dressed Chinese figures enact scenes from oriental life. Next door is the bedroom of Isabel II, its furniture a wedding gift from the city of Barcelona. As her husband was gay, it was doubtless more often appreciated by her numerous lovers. The Room of the Two Sisters in the Alhambra has a gaudy honeycombed cupola and low divans creating an ambience more appropriate for hookah pipes than post-prandial cigars. There are more exotica beyond, in the Chinese Room, whose walls are studded with over two hundred miniature paintings presented to Isabel II by the Emperor of China.

Behind the palace is the formal **Jardín del Parterre**, dominated by an immense fountain of Hercules. To the east a bridge leads across to the Jardín de la Isla. On an artificial island created by diverting the Tagus, planes and horse-chestnuts form a leafy canopy above elaborate but dry fountains. There is a grossly overweight Bacchus at the far end and an intriguing fountain of children playing with a syringe.

The main entrance of the **Jardín del Príncipe**, laid out by Carlos IV in 1780, lies on the opposite bank of the Tagus. A lovely twenty-minute walk along its poplar-vaulted avenues brings you to the **Casa del Labrador** or the Labourer's House. This is no peasant's hovel, but a miniature pleasure dome in whose silk-embroidered rooms the Bourbons could shrug off the cares of state by partying, gambling or playing billiards with an ivory-tipped cue inlaid with gold, silver and platinum. It was built in 1803 for Carlos IV.

If you have not yet had your fill of Bourbon profligacy, head down to the Casa de Marinos, a modern-looking building also in the Jardín de Príncipe. It holds some of the barges used for royal river parties, the most excessive of which belonged to the first Bourbon, Felipe V.

Aranjuez is famed for its asparagus and strawberries, both of which make the menus of most restaurants as well as being sold on street stalls. There is no shortage of places to eat: **El Jardín de Isabel II** has one of the nicest settings, on a shady formal garden across the road from the Palacio Real.

Chinchón (H)

This picturesque little town has two alcoholic associations. The first is obvious. They distil a ferocious aniseed spirit here, one brand of it in the gap-toothed fortress at the top of the hill. It comes in two varieties: *anis dulce* (for the ladies) and *anis fuerte* (*extraseco*), which sorts out the men from the boys. Drinking it feels a bit like lighting the fuse to a bomb which you happen to have swallowed. If you get round to analysing the taste, it is pleasant enough if you like aniseed balls. Be warned at 55 per cent proof the spirit is stronger than neat Scotch or brandy.

The second alcoholic association concerns the Countess of Chinchón, wife of the viceroy of Peru, who was cured of malaria by a mysterious potion brewed from the bark of a tree. The tree was brought back to Europe, where Linnaeus named it 'chinchona' after the countess. The drug extracted from the chinchona tree is quinine, which the British in India began to add to tonic water to protect them from malaria, and to give them an excuse for another gin.

Chinchón's Plaza Mayor has the air of a circular theatre. Surrounded by frail, green-balconied houses that seem as rickety as a stage set, the rest of the town rises in tiers above it, the handsome parish church dominating the whole scene like the royal box. Theatrical performances are held in Chinchón as well as bullfights, and Saturday markets. The church has some alarming cracks in its walls, and a Goya over the altar. From just outside the church there is a wide view of the town's mottled grey and red pantiles, wood-smoke wafting from chimneys on winter evenings.

425

Alcalá de Henares (H)

Alcalá suffered terribly during the Civil War, battered first by one side, then the other. Many of its buildings were destroyed, but now a belated programme of restoration is patching the Herreran churches and neglected palaces together. The sleek silhouettes of storks crowning the shabby buildings contrast oddly with their untidy nests, apparently oblivious of the most biting Castilian skies. Besides being a stork nursery, Alcalá functions as a dormitory for Madrid and the densely built-up suburbs and traffic congestion take some braving. It is heavily industrialised, and has one of Spain's largest and most prestigious military academies.

The old quarter is a lively and youthful place; soldiers doing 'mili' (military service) search out the bars; students lark in groups round the university doorways, and skateboarders display ankle-breaking prowess on and off the benches of the Plaza de Cervantes.

Alcalá is something of a literary shrine. Cervantes, creator of Don Quixote, was born here, and a small house furnished in seventeenth-century style is set up as a museum celebrating his birthplace on the basis of decidedly thin evidence. But Alcalá's main interest for present-day visitors is its academic associations. In 1498 Cardinal Jiménez de Cisneros established a university (one of Spain's Big Three, along with Salamanca and Valencia), progressive enough to arouse the suspicious attention of the authorities. It was swallowed up by Madrid University in 1836, but the university has undergone a post-war renaissance, and Alcalá is once again a seat of learning. It is the old university buildings and the restored area around the Plaza de Cervantes that make Alcalá worth a brief visit – but do not choose a Monday, when the university is closed to visitors.

If you can find a parking place in **San Diego Square** or the **Plaza de Cervantes**, all the buildings of interest lie within a ten-minute walk. Make sure you are in time for the 11am guided tour of the **university** (check with the tourist office nearby).

The rest of the old town is surprisingly charming, a sharp contrast to its ghastly outskirts. The arcaded **Calle Mayor** is a seemly array of balconied houses, old-fashioned shop fronts and good *tapas* bars. The famous **Hostería del Estudiante**, a *parador*-restaurant (no rooms), which backs on to the Three-Languages Patio of San Ildefonso College. A fine collection of Spanish ceramics decorates the highly traditional Castilian interior, and the food is good (chestnut and celery soup, braised lamb knuckles, and exotically named puddings.

WHERE TO STAY

MADRID

Gran Hotel Tryp Victoria £££
Plaza del Angel 7
28012 Madrid   Tel (91) 531 60 00; Fax: (91) 22 03 07

A striking cream metal-framed building, dating from 1925, which overlooks lively Plaza Santa Ana, the Victoria has just been completely refurbished. The spacious reception area is paved with ivory marble, the restaurant pretty and spring-like and the bar is restful, with traditional rugs and marble-topped tables. Rooms are smart, colour-co-ordinated and air-conditioned, and though some of the bathrooms are small, they are new and well-designed.

Open: all year **Rooms:** 201 **Credit/charge cards:** Amex, Diners, Eurocard, Visa

---

Hotel Residencia Santander ££
Echegeray 1
28014 Madrid   Tel (91) 429 95 51

A rambling '30s mansion with a fading frescoed façade on the corner of Carrera San Jerónimo and Calle Echegeray. Rooms are large and old-fashioned with parquet floors and original furniture, and all have bathrooms. Rooms facing the Carrera can be noisy and there is no air-conditioning. At present the public rooms are closed for refurbishment and breakfast is served in bedrooms. Smoking is not allowed in rooms. There is a café.

Open: all year **Rooms:** 38 **Credit/charge cards:** None

Villa Real £££
Plaza de las Cortes 10
28014 Madrid   Tel (91) 420 37 67; Fax (91) 420 25 47

A short walk from the Prado and the bars and restaurants of the Santa Ana area, the Villa Real is only a couple of years old, but is built in a style redolent of the turn of the century. The reception area is furnished with repro antiques, with embroideries of pastoral scenes on the walls, and the large lounge also has a traditional air, with scrunchy leather sofas. Rooms are on two levels, with a small sitting area below the bedroom, and are tastefully decorated and furnished in co-ordinating pastels. The marble bathrooms come with bathrobes and hair-dryers, and all rooms have air-conditioning, mini-bars and safes. There is a café.

Open: all year **Rooms:** 115 **Facilities:** swimming-pool, golf simulator **Credit/charge cards:** Amex, Diners, Eurocard, Visa

---

Villa Magna   ££
Paseo de la Castellana 22
28046 Madrid   *Tel (91) 578 20 00; Fax (91) 575 31 58*

An extremely luxurious contemporary hotel. The lobby is paved in gleaming ivory marble, lit by chandeliers, and opens on to a small courtyard with shrubs and a fountain. The piano bar is paved in white and grey veined marble, with eighteenth-century-style chairs and black granite-topped tables. The basement restaurant is smart and stylish. Rooms are spacious, with the television concealed in eighteenth-century-style cabinets. Dressing rooms lead into marble bathrooms, all with hair-dryer, bathrobe and a generous selection of toiletries. All rooms are air-conditioned.

Open: all year **Rooms:** 182 **Credit/charge cards:** Amex, Diners, Eurocard, Visa

---

Fenix   £££
Hermosilla 2
28001 Madrid   *Tel (91) 431 67 00; Fax (276 06 21*

A little out of the centre, on Plaza Colón at the beginning of the Paseo de las Castellana, the Fenix was completely refurbished three years ago. The marble-paved reception area is dominated by the gilded balustrade of a curving staircase, and the lounge is furnished with a happy combination of repro and contemporary sofas and chairs. Rooms are elegant, restful, and air-conditioned, with eighteenth-century-style furniture, and pastel décor and furnishings. The marble bathrooms come with a liberal supply of toiletries.

Open: all year **Rooms:** 226 **Facilities:** swimming-pool
Credit/charge cards: Amex, Diners, Eurocard, Visa

Arosa   £££
Salud 21
28013 Madrid   *Tel (91) 532 16 00; Fax (91) 531 31 27*

A grand old hotel on the corner of Salud and the Gran Vía, the Arosa has many gorgeous, individually decorated and furnished rooms, though some are still awaiting refurbishment. Rooms are varied in size and style, but all are air-conditioned: the just-opened rooms on the fourth floor are contemporary, slick and stylish, with co-ordinating décor and furnishings, and gleaming new bathrooms. Other rooms are furnished and decorated in a period style. Bathrooms vary in size and design. Rooms facing Gran Vía are double-glazed.

Open: all year **Rooms:** 139 **Facilities:** swimming-pool
Credit/charge cards: Amex, Diners, Visa, Eurocard

Emperador   £££
Gran Vía 53
28013 Madrid   *Tel (91) 247 28 00; Fax (91) 247 28 17*

A '40s hotel towards the Plaza de España end of Gran Vía, the Emperador is comfortable, and has the attraction of a rooftop swimming-pool and restaurant in summer. The pleasantest of the public rooms is the wood-panelled lounge, with tapestry and velvet upholstery, and an almost stately atmosphere. The adjoining bar is dimly lit, and the breakfast and wood-panelled breakfast and lunch room cheered up with dried-flower arrangements. Rooms are simple, but tasteful, with cream walls, brass light fittings and good-quality furniture. All are air-conditioned. Bathrooms vary in size, but all have hair-dryers. Those facing the Gran Vía are double-glazed. The corridors have parquet floors.

Open: all year **Rooms:** 232 **Facilities:** swimming-pool
Credit/charge cards: Amex, Diners, Eurocard, Visa

Opera   ££
Cuesta Santo Domingo 2
28013 Madrid   *Tel (91) 541 28 00*

Though the exterior is prison-like and the atmosphere sterile, this '60s hotel is worth considering as it is clean, reasonably priced, and one of the few hotels in the area around the Teatro Real and Palacio Real. Some of Madrid's most civilised cafés and restaurants are close by. The reception area, bar and cafeteria (where breakfast is eaten) are merely functional, but the lounge is pleasant. Rooms are likewise plain and institutional, and the tiled bathrooms are small, but adequate.

Open: all year **Rooms:** 81 **Credit/charge cards:** Amex, Diners, Eurocard, Visa

---

Hostal Valencia   £
Plaza de Oriente 2
28013 Madrid   *Tel (91) 248 75 58*

The tiny Valencia looks over the topiary and statues of Plaza de Oriente to the façade of the Palacio Real. It is on the third floor of a grand nineteenth-century terrace, and has just seven rooms, furnished with antiques and the occasional kitsch picture. If you want a quirky family-run hotel, with loads of atmosphere, you will love it – but be prepared to put up with traffic noise in the front-facing rooms; using the family telephone; a few damp patches on the walls in winter, and the limited supply of hot water. There are no keys for guests – when you arrive home (at whatever time) you ring the bell and the keys are thrown down to you. No meals or drinks are served, but the elegant Café de Oriente is directly below.

Open: all year **Rooms:** 7 **Credit/charge cards:** None

Ritz   ££
Plaza de la Lealtad 5
28014 Madrid   *Tel (91) 521 28 57; Fax (91) 532 87 76*

The Ritz is a sumptuous *belle époque* hotel right next to the Prado, and was built on the orders of King Alfonso XIII for his guests. Much frequented by royalty, politicians and the rich and famous, for many years it was so exclusive that its doors were closed to actors – Olivier was accepted only because he was titled. Nowadays you can take a package to the Ritz. The hotel is exquisitely decorated and rooms individually furnished with repro antiques. Service is personal – when you arrive there will be fresh flowers, a bottle of vintage sherry, chocolates and fruit awaiting in your room – and the strict dress code only adds to the atmosphere. The sumptuous dining room serves some of the best food in Madrid.

Open: all year **Rooms:** 56 **Credit/charge cards:** Amex, Diners, Eurocard, Visa

---

Palace   ££
Plaza de las Cortes 7
28014 Madrid   *Tel (91) 429 75 51; Fax (91) 420 00 56*

Directly across from the Ritz, the Palace is the Ritz's younger sister, also built on the orders of Alfonso XIII. Past guests include Mata Hari, Hemingway, Rubinstein, Joan Baez and Placido Domingo. The restaurants and bar open off a summery lounge, whose hand-made carpet reflects the colours of the vast stained-glass dome above. Approximately half the rooms have now been refurbished, but even those which have not are elegant and comfortable with repro antique furniture. All rooms are air-conditioned. The atmosphere is slightly more relaxed than the Ritz.

Open: all year **Rooms:** 480 **Credit/charge cards:** Amex, Diners, Eurocard, Visa

CHINCHON

Parador de Chinchón	£££
28370 Chinchón	Tel (918) 94 08 36

One of the nicest *paradores* in Castile, skilfully shoe-horned into an old creeper-draped convent of tiny rosy bricks. Glazed cloisters enclose a courtyard of fountains and flowers. Modern tapestries deck the plain walls; frescoed ceilings liven up the stairs to the upper floor. Public area furnishings are a mix of stilted French boudoir style and country furniture (mostly soft greens) charmingly painted with floral motifs. The beautifully kept gardens are an oasis of bird-song, pomegranates and shady arbours.

Open: all year **Rooms:** 38 **Facilities:** swimming-pool
Credit/charge cards: Amex, Diners, Eurocard, Visa

ALCALA DE HENARES

El Bedel	££
Plaza San Diego 6	
28801 Alcalá de Henares	Tel (918) 89 37 00

Right by the old university, this well-kept building overlooks the neat square where Cardinal Cisneros presides. The low-rise, shuttered, creamy exterior is in keeping with its old-town surroundings; inside furnishings are darkish and masculine, and facilities match its status as Alcalá's premier business hotel. There's a café.

Open: all year **Rooms:** 51 **Credit/charge cards:** Amex, Diners, Eurocard, Visa

EL PAULAR

Hostal Santa María del Paular	£££
28741 El Paular	Tel (918) 69 10 11; Fax (918) 69 10 06

A modern luxury hotel built in the peaceful confines of a fourteenth-century Carthusian monastery set high in the Guadarrama pine-woods near Navacerrada. Extensive grounds, lots of facilities, including a pool, and tasteful, traditional décor help to justify its steep tariff. Both the main restaurant and and the Mesón Trasta María in the grounds are recommendable (solid Castilian specialities, and local trout from the monks' pond).

Open: all year **Rooms:** 58 **Facilities:** swimming-pool, tennis
Credit/charge cards: Amex, Diners, Eurocard, Visa

CASTILLA Y LEON

NOWHERE in Spain has a simpler or more graphic name. Castile derives from the word for castle, and that is what this sparsely populated plateau is all about. As the Moors were driven back from Asturias during the Reconquest, lines of castles sprang up to guard the regained territory.

The boundaries of Castile have ebbed and flowed many times since the Dark Ages. The latest redrawing of the map took place in 1977, when the territories north and mostly west of Madrid that used to be known as Old Castile became the Autonomous Community of Castilla y León. The region incorporates nine provinces (Avila, Segovia, Burgos, Soria, León, Salamanca, Palencia, Zamora, Valladolid), and covers about one-fifth of mainland Spain. Since the Reconquest, when Spain pushed out its last wave of invaders and became a nation, Old Castile has been the centrifugal unifying force of Spain. During the late Middle Ages it grew enormously rich from the proceeds of the wool trade. Sheep-farmers formed a powerful self-interested guild known as the Mesta, which held grazing rights throughout central Spain.

Spain's nerve centre is now the Johnny-come-lately city of Madrid, and its biggest economic power-houses elsewhere, in the Basque Country and Catalunya. But the language of Castile (*castellano*) is still the official language of Spain. Spanish laws, political institutions and religion all bear the unmistakable stamp of Castile. In short, Castilla y León is Real Spain, not the Spain of the tourist brochures, clutching a carnation between its teeth. This is the Spain of the '*hidalgos*' (*hijos de algo* – men of substance): those austere, dignified people who welded Spain together through centuries of strife. The women of Castile were even more extraordinary. Isabella the Catholic was the indomitable force who presided over Spain's unification, the discovery of the New World, and the Inquisition. St Teresa the mystic crusaded round Spain, levitating, experiencing ecstatic visions, founding convents, and setting an example of austerity and self-denial.

Castile forms the *Meseta*, the great high plain that fills the whole of central Iberia, reaching a height of around 1,000 metres above sea level. Mountains ring the plateau: the Cordillera Cantábrica to the north; the Sierras of Gredos and Guadarrama in the south; Urbión and Ayllón to the east; and the Salamancan mountains and Portuguese hills to the west. Inevitably such a vast area is full of scenic variety. The greenery of upland districts contrasts sharply with the browns and ochres of the dry, intervening plains. The archetypal

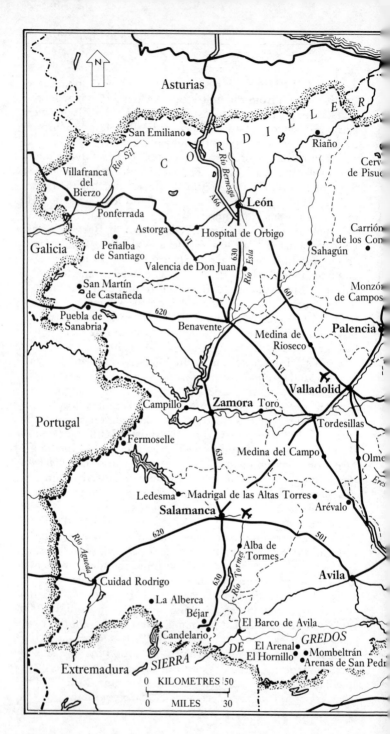

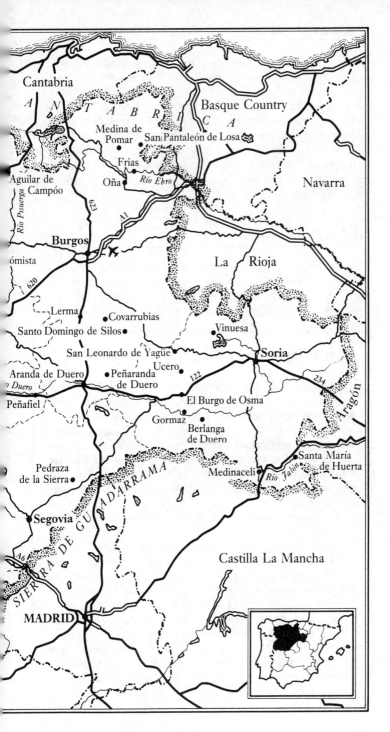

435

Castilian scene is a sun-bleached cereal plain, stretching towards a distant, flat-topped sierra. Thin lines of poplars and birches chart the watercourses, and a rugged castle crowns an earth-coloured town somewhere on the horizon.

Some of the scenery is truly extraordinary, accentuated by brilliant light and space on a scale that you will never experience in Britain. Long after memories of a Costa holiday have faded with the suntan, the bleak expanses of the Castilian *Meseta* stay in the mind's eye, as vivid as the mark of a branding-iron.

SEGOVIA (H)

Segovia stands on a rocky spur encircled by the Eresma and Clamores rivers. Its dramatic profile is often compared to a ship, but the cliché is accurate: from a distance that is exactly what the city's golden skyline looks like. The town has two

Planning your holiday

Any list of Castilla y León's highlights would include its great cathedral towns: Salamanca, Burgos, León and Segovia, all of which make excellent places to stay. Less well-known, and less overcrowded, are the smaller historic towns of Zamora, Ciudad Rodrigo, Toro, Tordesillas and El Burgo de Osma. Picturesque villages are quite thin on the ground, but among the best are Candelario, La Alberca, Peñeranda de Duero, Pedraza, Frías and Covarrubias. Castle-spotters, head for Coca, Peñafiel, Berlanga de Duero and Gormaz. Many of the best castles lie along the strategic bridging-points of the River Duero. Valladolid, Castilla y León's largest city, is remarkable for its art and architecture, and Avila has the best-preserved city walls in Europe.

Without a car, it is difficult to visit any but the major centres conveniently, though parts of the region can be explored by public transport if time is not a priority. The Michelin map *Northern Spain* (1:400,000, sheet 442) covers most of Castilla y León; for the western areas you also need *North-West Spain*, 1:400,000, sheet 441. Many routes (road and rail) converge like a spider's web on Madrid. The main cities are reasonably well linked with each other, too. For instance, about seven trains a day connect Salamanca and Valladolid; five link León and Burgos. The best bus connections centre on Burgos and Salamanca:

parts: the lower modern section is mostly dull and shabby, the upper town a hilly tangle of ochre-, cream- and peach-coloured houses. Many of the façades are decorated with *esgrafiado*, a technique of scraping plaster into patterns, revealing a different coloured layer beneath, and sometimes dotted with dark stones or pieces of coal like raisins in a pudding. The old town makes an atmospheric place to wander, its steep narrow streets suddenly opening out to reveal a mellow church, or a hawk's-eye-view of the surrounding countryside. Segovia lies just 88 kilometres from Madrid, following a steep climb over the Navacerrada Pass. Road connections are excellent (mostly motorway) so it takes only just over an hour to drive. It is also easily accessible by train from the capital. The town also makes a convenient springboard for explorations of the nearby Guadarrama mountains where in winter you could even be tempted to put in a day's skiing.

Segovia absorbs visitors and caters for them sensibly (even

---

many interesting smaller places can be reached from these cities.

Some package holidays adopt historic themes: the specialist operators link *paradores* or luxury hotels in tours like 'Gothic Journey', or the 'Parador Road to Santiago de Compostela'. Plenty for wildlife enthusiasts lies in the remote sierras, and all over Castile you will see many birds of prey.

Northern Castile is scorching in summer and bitter in winter, so prepare for extremes. Spring and autumn are more comfortable for touring holidays and the landscape is more attractive.

Religious festivals are marked with fervour in Castilla y León. The Holy Week celebrations of Zamora and Valladolid are particularly remarkable, with processions of *pasos* (religious floats) through the streets. Many more secular fiestas are accompanied by bullfights or bull-running ceremonies, while in San Pedro Manrique, the local men run barefoot over smouldering coals in the Paso del Fuego, the Feast of St John, on Midsummer's Eve.

● **Regional Tourist Board**: Dirección General de Turismo, Pº de Zorrilla 48–1°, 47006 Valladolid, Tel (983) 33 00 99. All the provincial capitals and many smaller towns have **tourist offices**. Those in Segovia, León, Salamanca and Soria are particularly helpful for large areas, while at a more local level, Aguilar de Campóo has good information on Palencia's Romanesque churches, Benavente is useful for touring routes in Zamora, and El Burgo de Osma for the castles of the Duero.

---

forgoing its siesta in summer) without exploiting or being overwhelmed by them. In that sense it scores over Toledo, its rival excursion city on the other side of Madrid. Its rhythms remain the slow-paced ones of a small town with a resident population of only 50,000.

Eating out and accommodation

Segovia is famous for its cuisine, specialising in *cochinillo asado* (roast suckling pig). The most famous (and expensive) restaurant is Mesón de Cándido at the foot of the aqueduct, (Tel (911) 42 59 11 – expect to queue if you do not have a reservation). More reasonably priced is El Hidalgo, which serves a set meal that includes *cochinillo asado*.

In high season and at holiday weekends it can be very difficult to find a room in Segovia. The most appealing and best-value hotels are in old buildings in the upper town, but for views of Segovia's stately skyline, the best choice is the modern, purpose-built *parador*, Tel (911) 43 73 62, two kilometres out along the Valladolid road. It is worth the trek up to its enormous picture windows just for lunch or a drink.

Exploring the town

If you are not perturbed by steep hills it is best to park outside the walls, perhaps near the aqueduct. You can drive into the centre, but the narrow streets are congested and confusing. Before heading up to the old town on the hill, have a look at Segovia's oldest church, twelfth-century **San Millán**, now stranded somewhat forlornly on a dusty, littered square in the heart of the shabby modern sector. A good example of Segovia's distinctive Romanesque style, the church is flanked by arcades, and the eaves shelter carvings of birds, entwined snakes, monsters, human figures and foliage.

The old town's high street leads off Plaza Azoguegoi various sections along its length are named Calle de Cervantes, Calle Juan Bravo and Calle Isabel la Católica. Narrow, cobbled and pedestrianised, with iron-balconied, ochre-washed houses containing diminutive shops, restaurants and trendy boutiques, it is the route of the evening *paseo*, but lively all day long. One of the most distinctive buildings is the diamond-pointed **Casa de los Picos**, a fortified mansion thought to have been built by Juan Guas, architect of the cathedral cloister and San Juan de los Reyes in Toledo.

Beyond the Casa de los Picos, the street opens out to form a

harmonious stepped *plaza* around the Romanesque church of
San Martín. This has an exterior arcade which served as a
meeting place for guilds and councillors, and capitals carved
with bizarre bird-women. Across the square is the **Torre de
Lozoya**, a fortified town house with *esgrafiado* walls, now
used as an exhibition hall. Outside are two weird granite pig-
like beasts (*verracos*) and a statue of Juan Bravo, the local
leader of the Comuneros revolt. Riots against new taxes
levied by Charles V took place in many Castilian towns. The
uprising was crushed in 1521, the leaders rounded up and
beheaded in this square.

In the centre of the upper town is the arcaded **Plaza Mayor**
(still called Plaza Franco on some maps), where the great
golden dome and bristling spires of the cathedral dominate
the view. The tourist office is here, a helpful one with
English-speaking staff. There are several other attractive
Romanesque churches to spot as you wander through the old
town; particularly worth finding is **San Estéban** with its
distinctive five-storey tower. At the far end of the town is the
Alcázar, a Mad King Ludwig fantasy of witch-hat turrets
and crenellated towers.

The main sights

● **The Aqueduct** This single surviving structure from
ancient Segóbriga ranks among the finest Roman monuments
anywhere in Europe. Built of Guadarrama granite to carry
water from Riofrío, 12 kilometres south-west, to the upper
city, the section now visible in Segovia is only a small fraction
of the total massive span. Considering it is such a formidable
piece of engineering, solid facts about its construction are
scanty. No one seems to know exactly when it was built, for
instance, though the Emperor Trajan is strongly tipped to
have commissioned it in the first century AD. Authorities
quarrel over its exact vital statistics. It is something like 800
metres long; with about 165 (mostly double) arches; and
attains a height of 28 metres above the Plaza del Azoguego.
Today's conservationists survey the traffic that hurtles
through the archways with concern.
● **The Cathedral** Built of peach-tinged golden stone, the
Gothic cathedral is splendid outside, disappointing within.
Grooved columns soar up to form the ribs of the vaults, but
the nave is blocked by a hideous *coro* of garish fake orange,
yellow and brown marble. The cathedral houses some extraordinary examples of popular church art. The most sac-

439

charine of the chapels is Sant Anton, with gilded baroque columns, rose-cheeked cherubs and a diminutive Virgin in a grubby lace dress.

The oldest part of the building is the cloister, all that was left after the previous cathedral, near the Alcázar, had been destroyed in the Comuneros revolts. The cloister was dismantled and rebuilt on its present site, and now stands around a scruffy garden. Beneath its arcades are scale models of the Alcázar and Segovia's main churches, and a tiny museum with a collection of reliquaries full of the labelled bones of sundry saints. Here too, is the tomb of twelve-year-old Don Pedro, son of King Enrique II of Trastamara, who fell to his death while playing in the Alcázar. Local legend prefers to lop ten years from his age, and have him dropped by a nurse, who swiftly leapt from the window after him to avoid worse punishment. Don Pedro's death hastened Isabella the Catholic's progress to the throne of Castile, which casts even more doubt on the manner of his demise.

● **The Alcázar** Palace, fortress, state prison, and latterly a school for cadets, the Alcázar featured in the film *Camelot*, and is credited as the inspiration for Walt Disney's castle in *Snow White*, but its history is colourful enough without resorting to fiction. Alfonso X (the Wise) earned himself a reputation as a necromancer by converting one of the towers into an astronomical observatory, and was said to have attracted a punishing bolt of lightning for declaring that he could have organised the universe better than God. Isabella the Catholic was living here when she learnt her faction had won the struggle against La Beltraneja for the Castilian throne, and Philip II came here in disguise for a glimpse of Anne of Austria before making her an offer she couldn't refuse. On his fourth leap through the matrimonial hoop, he presumably wanted a good look first. Most of what exists today is a reconstruction, for the Alcázar was virtually destroyed in a fire in 1862.

● **Vera Cruz** This is the most interesting of several ecclesiastical buildings outside the city walls by the River Eresma. Founded in 1208 by the military Christian Order of the Knights Templar, this twelve-sided church has an unusual circular interior, with a two-storey cylindrical chapel in the centre. On the upper level is a stone table on which the fragment of the True Cross (*Vera Cruz*) was placed, guarded in an all-night vigil by would-be knights as part of their initiation ceremony.

La Granja and Riofrío

Eleven kilometres from Segovia, with the Sierra de Guadar-rama as a splendid backdrop, are the royal palace and gardens of La Granja, an audacious riposte to Habsburg austerity by Spain's first Bourbon king, Félipe V. Indeed, seeing elements of the El Escorial palace creeping into the work of the first architect, Theodore Ardemens, Félipe called in the Italian architects Sacchetti and Juvara, to remodel the garden façade. Félipe's *pièces de resistance*, however, are the fountains, flam-boyant fripperies that well and truly pronounce the Habsburg era dead. The interior of the palace was gutted by fire in 1918 and the restored rooms have an institutional feel.

Much better is the **Tapestry Museum** (Museo de Tapices), with a series of Honours and Virtues designed by the six-teenth-century Flemish master Bernard Van Orley, filled with confusing scenes of carnage and heroism. Try to time your visit so that you can see the gardens at 5.30pm when the fountains are switched on. Water spouts from the mouths of geese, reindeer, dogs and frogs, cascades over scallop shells, forms liquid stairways, and erupts in geysers nearly 50 metres high.

If you need a simple base in La Granja, the Hostal Roma, Tel (911) 47 07 52, easily spotted in a green-shuttered house near the palace gates, is just off the main road. It has tables set on the cobbled square outside a pleasant café-bar.

Riofrío is the same distance from Segovia as La Granja, but in a south-westerly direction. A long trek through oak parkland full of roaming deer rewards you with an enormous pink and green palace. Inside, a guided tour is obligatory to visit numerous ornately furnished apartments and a museum of hunting.

TOURING SEGOVIA PROVINCE

North-east of Segovia is **Pedraza de la Sierra (H)** (not to be confused with the natural park of La Sierra de la Pedriza), a self-consciously pretty medieval hill town. Located within easy day-trip distance from Madrid, Pedraza is immensely popular for those long family lunches that Spaniards love at weekends. Several canny restaurants satisfy this market, offering classic Castilian roasts of pork and lamb. Parking is difficult on the narrow twisting lanes of the town centre, but as the town is so tiny it is no hardship to leave your car outside, perhaps near the castle. From there you can contemplate the surrounding hilly scenery, then wander back towards the circular Plaza Mayor, surrounded by arcaded timbered houses of aristocratic demeanour.

For lunch, you have a choice of a *parador* restaurant, the Hostería Pintor Zuloaga, in the former Casa de la Inquisición (cosy medieval interior and a cool terraced restaurant with lovely views of the countryside), or perhaps El Yantar de Pedraza, where you can look on to the Plaza Mayor.

North of Pedraza, pick a route along minor roads via the towns of **Turégano** (fine castle); **Sepúlveda** (beautiful setting above a terraced valley); **Riaza** (H) (large sandy-coloured *plaza* surrounded by porticoed houses) and **Ayllón** (palace, fountains and pit-prop arcades in an old square). This takes you through some of Segovia's most attractive scenery, wild and remote in places. You may see vultures and eagles hovering above the Sierra de Ayllón on the Guadalajara border.

North-west of Segovia, an easy journey along straight but fairly quiet roads takes you through Santa María la Real de Nieva (pause to see the church if it is open) and then through groves of umbrella pines and cereal plains to **Coca Castle**, a marvellously frivolous Mudejar castle of pale rose thin bricks. Dating from about 1400, it was owned by the powerful Fonseca family, whose influence spanned temporal and spiritual empires. It is now peacefully occupied by a School of Forestry.

AVILA (H)

Europe's most perfectly preserved *enceinte* of medieval walls, its most celebrated citizen, St Teresa, and a handful of diverting churches may tempt you to visit, though Ávila, the most lethargic of Castilian capitals, is not a place worth much of your time. Perhaps the listlessness is due to altitude, for at 1,131 metres, Avila is the highest city in Spain, its climate correspondingly harsh. Ávila's heyday was in the fifteenth century; since then it has gently slid into decline and depopulation. See it in a day-trip from Segovia, or *en route* to the Sierra de Gredos.

During the Civil War Avila surrendered without protest to the Nationalists. The ghost of Fascism lingers. On Calle Generalisimo Franco *El Caudillo's* paunchy portrait still stares from a carved medallion, and on Plazuela del Rastro no one has bothered to remove the plaque informing you in the name of Franco that 'offences against Christian morality are not tolerated'. Isabella the Catholic, instigator of the Inquisition, was born in the north-west of the province, at Madrigal de las Altas Torres.

Exploring the town

Plaza de Santa Teresa, the modern town's main square lying just outside the eastern walls, is as good a starting point as any for a detailed exploration. A soulless arena for a statue of a rapt St Teresa, chill granite arcades covered with peeling posters look on to a wind-swept oval of sand. At one end the apricot-coloured walls of the Romanesque church of San Pedro set off its striking, cartwheel-shaped rose window, and at the other the imperious Puerta de Alcázar gives access to the old town within the walls.

On three sides the land falls away below the walls, giving extra protection, but the eastern wall, stretching from Puerta de Alcázar to Puerta de San Vicente, was vulnerable, as it rose directly from the plain. It was therefore heavily defended, not only by the town's mightiest gates, but by the formidable battlemented apse of the cathedral. As you follow the walls along to the cathedral, look out for *verracos* (bull- or boar-shaped Celtiberian statues hollowed out to hold funeral ashes), and the fragments of Roman inscriptions, which Count Raimondo's workers found lying around the site and built into the walls.

Just beyond the cathedral's apse, Puerta del Peso de la Harina leads on to Plaza de la Catedral. The cathedral itself is a grim, granite early-Gothic structure, its stern façade unadorned save for some serpent-bodied caryatids and two scaly wild men added in the eighteenth century. At the far end of the eastern wall is Romanesque San Vicente, a splendid church shrouded in Christian myths standing on the supposed site of a martyrdom.

Avila is not a particularly exciting place to stay, but if you need to you can do so comfortably either at the *parador*, or at the Palacio de Valderrabaños near the cathedral; both hotels have good restaurants. The most appealing *hostales* are within the walls, or around Plaza Santa Teresa.

The main sights

● **The Walls** Stretching for over two and a half kilometres, pierced by eight gates, and studded by 88 defensive towers, it is estimated that 1,900 men worked for nine years building the circuit of medieval walls. When work started in 1090, Avila was a small village on the site of a neglected Roman fort, selected by Alfonso VI to form part of a line of defence that stretched from Salamanca to Segovia. Raimundo of Burgundy, Alfonso's son-in-law, had the task of overseeing the building and repopulation of the town.

● **The Cathedral** The date of the cathedral's foundation is uncertain but it seems likely that the apse was constructed at

THE ST TERESA TRAIL

Avila's most famous daughter draws the crowds. St Teresa (1515–1582), one of the Catholic Church's great mystics, was born Teresa de Cepeda y Ahumada, to a wealthy family of Jewish origin. She first made her mark while still a child by setting off to Morocco believing that martyrdom at the hands of the Moors would guarantee her a place in heaven. Her family caught up with her just outside the city walls: the spot is now marked by four columns (Cuatro Postes) across the road from a petrol station. She took Carmelite vows at 18, and led an uneventful convent existence until an angelic visitation in her forties transformed her life. In middle age she travelled all over Spain founding convents in empty buildings, where nuns could live the simple, poverty-stricken life recommended by the original founders of the Carmelite order, rather than the feather-bedded existence that had become the norm in sixteenth-century Carmelite establishments. Best known for her ecstatic relationship with God, which involved cataleptic seizures, levitation and piercings of the heart, she was also accustomed to sleeping in flea-ridden inns, and once compared life to a night in a bad hotel! Sadly, this spirited woman is now the centre of a sentimental pilgrimage industry, in which she is remembered by schmaltzy chapels, tasteless souvenirs, and squidgy crystallised egg yolks known as *yemas de Santa Teresa*. The other Castilian town most closely associated with her life (or rather her death) is **Alba de Tormes**, near Salamanca, another place of pilgrimage.

Walking around the three convents in Avila associated with St Teresa, you learn less about the saint than about the way in which the Church has marketed her. Her reforms met fierce opposition from mainstream Carmelites, unwilling to swap their comfortable

the same time as the walls, while the rest was built during the thirteenth and fourteenth centuries.

The best feature is the sumptuous Renaissance altarpiece, glowing in the light that filters through the church's few surviving stained-glass windows, most of which were shattered in an earthquake in 1755. Also worth seeing are a series of martyrdoms carved on the choir-stalls, the carvings of the Adoration and the Flight into Egypt in the retrochoir, and the tomb of the fifteenth-century bishop, Alfonso de Madrigal,

---

lives for the stringency and abstinence of her reformed *Descalzadas* (Shoeless Carmelites). After her death the Church found it more expedient to concentrate on Teresa's mysticism, and present her as an object of popular devotion and role model for little girls, than to heed her reforms. In the **Convento de Santa Teresa**, a baroque convent built on the site of the saint's birthplace, the tough intelligent woman who trekked around Spain founding and reforming convents is represented as a homely nun encased in gaudy altars. Her bedroom has been transformed into a baroque chapel, her body was chopped up for relics and packaged off around Europe (a revered finger rests here), and the garden where she and her brother played at being hermits is now a dingy courtyard with two statues of the pious children.

North of the city walls lies the **Monasterio de la Encarnación** where St Teresa first took her vows at the age of 21, and where she lived for 27 years. You see the Capilla de la Transverberación built on the site of the cell where she was twice overwhelmed by an angel piercing her heart and entrails with a burning arrow. The subject of Bernini's famously orgasmic sculpture in Rome, she vividly describes the experience in her *Life*: 'The pain was so severe that it made me utter several moans. The sweetness caused by this intense pain is so extreme that one cannot possibly wish it to cease.' You can also visit the room in which Teresa and St John of the Cross fell into ecstasies and began to levitate while discussing the Holy Spirit. There is a small museum of memorabilia.

The **Convento de San Joséo de las Madres** was the first convent the saint founded. Next door to the undistinguished Renaissance church is the **Museo Teresiano**, with Teresa's saddle, a collection of the musical instruments she would play to cheer up her travel-weary nuns, and a reproduction of her cell.

author of some 54 books, who is represented as virtually blind, straining to write at his desk. Known as 'El Tostado', the Toasted One, because of his dark complexion, he was so small that when he met Pope Eugenius IV, the pontiff thought he was kneeling and asked him to rise. El Tostado irritably replied that he was already standing and, pointing from his eyebrows to his hairline, added 'A man's stature is measured from here to here'. The museum gives access to the sacristry with a gilded vaulted roof, and a treasury stacked with glittering crucifixes, and a silver monstrance by Juan de Arfe. An ivory cross is doubtfully attributed to Cellini.

● **Museo Provincial** Outside the walls, just off Plaza Italia, the sixteenth-century residence of the cathedral deans now houses the museum. Laid out in rooms opening off a pretty arcaded courtyard, exhibits range from granite boar-shaped *verracos* to Castilian china and nineteenth-century furniture. Best are the displays of folk life. The collection of paintings is patchy, but there is a splendid Flemish triptych from the school of Hans Memling: the pensive Mary in the Burial scene is probably by Memling himself.

● **San Vicente** A welcome touch of exuberance in restrained Avila, San Vicente is a remarkable and highly original building lying just outside the north-east corner of the city walls. Built in the shape of a Latin cross somewhere between the twelfth and fourteenth centuries, the style veers from distinguished Romanesque to Gothic. Its most striking external feature is an ornate bell-tower.

● **El Real Monasterio de Santo Tomás** Financed by the Catholic Monarchs Isabella and Ferdinand, and by goods confiscated from the victims of their Inquisition, the monastery is an elegantly restrained Gothic structure founded in 1482. Ferdinand and Isabella used it as a summer residence and selected it as the burial place for their only son Juan, and for the Grand Inquisitor, Tomás de Torquemada, under whose regime some 2,000 heretics were burned alive and a further 17,000 mutilated. Gleaming eerily in the dim church is the marble effigy of Juan, whose death at the age of 19 changed the course of Spanish history by leaving the throne vacant for his mother's Habsburg relatives.

THE SIERRA DE GREDOS

The route from Avila into the Sierra de Gredos along the N-502 is initially dull, crossing a plain bordered by grey, bare foothills. Once you get into the mountains, however, the drive is wonderful, through boulder-strewn fields and deep wooded valleys. The highlight is **El Pico Pass**, where a 1,352-metre-high *mirador* gives spectacular views of five villages nestling in a fertile valley of olives and tobacco, linked to the heights by a serpentine Roman road which is still used as a track for animals.

Beyond is the sleepy village of **Mombeltrán**, dominated by an overgrown fourteenth-century castle. Beyond, **Arenas de San Pedro** is a dull and largely modern town in a beautiful mountain setting with a cluster of old beamed houses, and a castle (now used as a theatre).

A lovely drive from Arenas leads along the valley of the diminutive River Arenal to the village of **El Hornillo** six kilometres to the north. A well-kept village of old and new whitewashed and red-roofed houses in the crook of the valley, it is the starting point for the challenging trek across the mountain range to Hoyos del Espino. There is nowhere to stay in El Hornillo, but the little modern village of El Arenal, three kilometres beyond, has the small, clean family-run Hostal-Residencia Pierre, Tel (918) 37 05 28, on the main street.

Six kilometres south-east of Arenas, is the scruffy wayside village of Ramacastañas, close to which are the **Cuevas del Aguila**, a series of caves with magnificent limestone formations. To reach them turn right at a bar marked Mesón de Chuletas, on to an unmetalled road which runs four kilometres along the broad valley bottom.

The Bulls of Guisando and the northern Gredos

On Avila's southern boundary, just before you get to San Martín, a signed minor road leads to an isolated spot where four well-preserved Celtiberian granite statues (*verracos*) known as the Bulls of Guisando stand in a field behind a broken wall. No one knows quite how old these strange, primitive creatures are, or what they were for, but similar ones have been found in many places in western Castile. A plaque on the nearby wall declares this is the place where Isabella the Catholic was first proclaimed legitimate heir to the throne of Castile.

South of Avila several scenic minor roads lead across the Sierra de Gredos. The C-500 takes a northerly route from San Juan de la Nava past some excellent walking country, finishing up at the splendid castle of **El Barco de Avila**. The winding road passes little stone-walled fields and conical haystacks, and probably a good many farmers riding or leading donkeys and mules with panniers. From **Hoyos del Espino** (H) hiking and riding expeditions can be taken to the deep blue glacial lake called **Laguna Grande de Gredós** and the highest peak of the range, **Almanzor** (2,592m). This remote location is the haunt of ibex. Spain's first *parador*, opened in 1928 in a location selected by King Alfonso XIII, is situated just east of Hoyos del Espino. There are inexpensive alternatives in the area, including campsites and a mountain refuge.

SALAMANCA (H)

The city of Salamanca is a Spanish Oxford. The skies are sunnier, the architecture more florid, but the spirit of the place is the same: academic, mercantile, religious.

Hannibal conquered the city in 220BC, ushering in a period of peace and stability for Salamanca, which became an important staging-post on the Silver Way. Later, the Romans, Vandals, Visigoths and the dreaded Moorish leader Al-Mansur took the city in turn. In 1218 Alfonso the Wise founded a university to rival Oxford and the Sorbonne, and Salamanca's Golden Age began. Napoleonic pillaging after the Battle of Salamanca in 1812 (in which the Duke of Wellington played a victorious but less than glorious role) left many of the city's colleges and medieval buildings in ruins. The university influence means the city is always culturally lively with concerts, plays and exhibitions. In the evenings taverns and inexpensive eating houses in the old quarters around the Plaza Mayor hum, full of customers. Sometimes the atmosphere even verges on the rowdy, reviving a latent antagonism between town and gown. Prepare to be serenaded by *tunas* (bands of student minstrels in black Renaissance garb of doublet and hose) – a genuine tradition, not simply a way of embarrassing tourists into submissive donations.

The surrounding province is underpopulated and remote, with more varied, less arid countryside than central Castile. Muscular black cattle with curved horns placidly graze over huge ranches. These are fighting bulls destined for a painful twenty minutes of fame in some future *corrida*.

Exploring the city

Bus and train stations are both about fifteen minutes' walk from the city centre. If you arrive by car, arrange to park somewhere convenient. The only way to see central Salamanca effectively is on foot. The streets by the provincial tourist office on **Gran Vía** are a good starting point (pop in there for up-to-date advice), but spaces anywhere near the central area are vigilantly metered for two-hour periods (not long enough for a proper visit), and a ten-minute overstay will leave a reproachful parking ticket fluttering on your windscreen (fines are very modest). If you are staying at the *parador*, leave your car there, and walk over the Roman bridge into the city.

Eating out and accommodation

In the Plaza Mayor, the Café Altamira gives you a pleasant choice of *sol y sombra* (sun and shade) at lunchtimes, and good views of the square. Novelty is a long-established bar frequented by the intelligentsia, where you can try to imagine Miguel de Unamuno (see below) ordering a cold beer. The *tapas* bars of the student quarter around the University and by the Plaza del Mercado are the best haunts to look for inexpensive evening eating places, but the city has its share of prestigious restaurants too. Chez Victor at Espoz y Mina Plaza 26, and Candil Nuevo on Plaza de la Reina, are two of the most reputable. *Chanfaina*, a spicy rice and sausage dish, is a local speciality. Salamanca has many hotels and *hostales*, but bear in mind that it has to find room for 16,000 students in termtime, so the cheaper end of the market may be difficult then. Conversely, you can get a very good deal during holidays, when touts may accost you to offer rooms.

The main sights

● **The Cathedrals** Salamanca has two cathedrals, the Old (Vieja) and the New (Nueva). But they are entwined as closely as mating snails, and it is difficult to work out where one finishes and the other begins. From outside, the new one hogs the limelight, Flamboyant Gothic spires and baroque domes soaring triumphantly above the skyline. Its west front is a virtuoso example of stonework statuary and embroidery. Inside the **Catedral Nueva** is light and spacious, and gracefully vaulted. The surprisingly restrained interior (money ran a bit short after the extravagant shell was completed) is a fine setting for some lovely side-chapels and a frieze of animals chasing each other's tails. Begun in 1513, the New Cathedral took about 220 years to complete, and it is quite a hotchpotch of styles. Among many artists and craftsmen associated with its construction, the Churriguera family were the most famous, and Salamanca is the city to see their high-baroque style at its most brilliant. Altarpieces were their speciality, but in the New Cathedral the choir-stalls, lantern paintings, and *trascoro* are also Churrigueresque.

The most striking exterior feature of the **Catedral Vieja**, which dates from the twelfth century, is an unusual tiled conical tower of Byzantine influence, the Torre del Gallo (Cock Tower). You enter the older building from inside the New Cathedral – steps lead from the south transept. The *pièce de resistance* here is Nicolas Florentini's 53-panelled altarpiece of dark lustrous colours, where risen souls pop out of their tombs like jacks-in-the-box. The dome under the Cock Tower, shaped like half an orange, the cloister and the museum are also worth seeing (works by Fernando Gallego), and there is a stimulating view of the roofline from the Patio Chico.

● **The University buildings** In its heyday, Salamanca was Spain's greatest seat of learning. An avant-garde one too: Columbus came here to discuss his transatlantic project with the Faculty of Astronomy, which was the first to teach Copernican theory. It even had the novelty of a female classics professor in the fifteenth century, Beatriz de Galindo, who taught Queen Isabella Latin. Later, the university declined under the repressive onslaughts of the Catholic Church and Fascism. The Hebrew scholar Fray Luis de León was dragged off by the Inquisition in the middle of a lecture, and imprisoned for five years. An oft-quoted anecdote relates how on his return he continued his lecture where he left off with the immortal insouciance 'As I was saying yesterday...' Today Salamanca University still has social cachet, but not the academic standing of Madrid or Barcelona.

The **Patio de las Escuelas** (Schools Square), contains the most impressive of Salamanca's many sumptuous façades. Plateresque in style, it is a *tour de force* of masonry, a flourish of embellishment more suited to filigree jewellery than resilient stone. If you can take in any of the details, you will see the Catholic Monarchs in there somewhere, among the swirls and curlicues, hobnobbing promiscuously with the Pope, the Virtues, and classical worthies. The statue in the square is of Fray Luis, the persecuted Hebrew theologian, and in the cloister beyond you can find his lecture theatre, left as it was in the sixteenth century with its inhospitable wooden benches notched and scarred by generations of uncomfortable scholars. The Renaissance staircase in the cloister is exceptionally fine. Climb it to see the elaborate gallery ceiling and carved frieze on the first floor. Among other rooms to visit is the Paranfino Hall (baroque tapestries and a Goya portrait of Carlos IV).

Nearby, the **Escuelas Minores** (minorite Schools) have another lovely patio and Plateresque doorway. Track down Fernando Gallego's zodiac painting known as the Salamanca Ceiling, where constellation signs whirl in a snowstorm of gold stars.

● **Plaza Mayor** Built during the eighteenth century by those versatile Churriguera brothers, the money came from Philip V – a thank-you present to the city for its support during the War of Succession.

Other city sights

● **Convento de San Estéban** (St Stephen's Convent) The church is remarkable for yet another of those amazing Salamancan façades. Inside the Dominican monastery see the Cloister of the Kings and the altarpiece in the church by José Churriguera, entwined with vine tendrils and luscious bunches of grapes like some orgiastic Bacchanalian scene. Modern tastes find it hard to enthuse over those cumbersome barley-sugar pillars and over-egged gilding, but there is an undeniable panache about the best work of the Churrigueresque school.

● **Las Dueñas Convent** Beyond another notable plateresque doorway is a serene Renaissance courtyard of pretty gardens and dribbling fountains. Upstairs on the first floor of the cloister the capitals seem plucked from some Hammer House of Horror: frightful demons, skulls and screaming faces.

● **Casa de las Conchas** (House of Shells) A mansion dating from the time of the Catholic Monarchs, simple and fortress-like, apart from dozens of scallop shells, symbol of the Santiago pilgrimage (see page 60), that seem to have attached themselves like limpets all over the walls.

Buen Amor and Alba de Tormes

Close to Salamanca, a brief excursion northwards takes you to the privately owned castle of **Buen Amor** just off the road to Zamora, now a family home and a moated oasis of bird-song in a park of holm-oaks. A few interesting original features remain (patios, ceilings and a dungeon cellar). Once a stronghold of the Catholic Monarchs in the struggle against La Beltranaje, it later functioned as a love-nest for the Arch-bishop of Toledo, one of the powerful Fonseca family.

On a more respectable note, **Alba de Tormes**, 21 kilometres south-east of Salamanca, is the last resting place of St Teresa of Avila (see page 444). Today coachloads of ardent pilgrims beat a path to the shrine, a glum enough memorial to this great and indomitable woman. You can pay homage to St Teresa's arm, or her heart, transplanted into separate reliquaries in the Carmelite convent, or see the cell where she died, saying simply 'Have you no place here for me?' when asked if she would like to die in Avila. The tower guarding the Tormes is all that is left of the medieval castle of the Dukes of Alba, but the 22-arched bridge still stands.

TOURING AROUND SALAMANCA

The heights of the Duero

An odd contrast between barren-looking scenery and a sheltered microclimate which produces prolific early crops of grapes, figs and almonds characterises this isolated region of lakes and canyons on the borders with Portugal, known as the Heights of the Duero (Los Arribes del Duero). In places the river systems are harnessed for hydro-electric power. **La Saucelle** is one of the prettiest villages, in a setting of three divergent valleys. Between Salamanca and this western extremity, the old walled town of **Ledesma** is worth a brief look. This important bridging-point over the Tormes river has a balcony view over landscapes dotted with holm-oaks and gnarled olives where fighting bulls graze.

Ciudad Rodrigo (H)

The Duke of Wellington picked up another handle to his name here. After a long siege and battle against the French in 1812, he was honoured with the title of Duke of Ciudad

Rodrigo. Though strategically brilliant, it was something of a pyrrhic victory. Allied Spanish and English losses were about twice those of Napoleon's troops, and in the course of the battle this beautiful old town suffered much unnecessary damage. The cathedral bell-tower still bears the marks of British guns. Now carefully restored, Ciudad Rodrigo is a most enjoyable place, well worth a night's stay. The medieval fortress has been converted into an attractive *parador* with a hawk's-eye vantage-point of the Portuguese borderlands over the old walls and the River Agueda.

In the **Plaza Mayor**, Renaissance palaces (one now functions as the Town Hall) stand cheek by jowl with old-fashioned shops. The best building in town is the **Cathedral**: racy choir-stalls by the master Rodrigo Alemán (whose *risqué* work can also be seen in Zamora, Avila, Toledo and Plasencia); marvellous carving on portals, cloister capitals and the alabaster altar; and unusual windows and vaulting are just a few of its more impressive features.

Sierra de Peña de Francia

Twin attractions of wooded *schist* scenery (shale pinnacles and crags) and lovely villages in sunny orchards make this area one of Salamanca province's prize touring routes. The highest peak is the *Peña* (comb) itself, with a Dominican monastery and a TV tower perched on its windy summit at 1,732 metres. A steep winding road leads through woods to the top, from where the views stretch to Avila and Extremadura. The grotto-like church hides a blackened Virgin and Child in a Byzantine setting of lustrous blue and gold tiles.

La Alberca (H) is the most popular of several mountain villages. Now declared an inviolable national monument, La Alberca is experiencing the double-edged sword of tourist prosperity and exploitation. On highdays and holidays (especially the Feast of the Assumption, on 15 August) the local people dress in traditional costumes.

A less well-known but similarly pretty village is **Miranda del Castañar** (castle, ancient wooden houses and grandstand sierra views). Mogarraz, Monforte and San Martín nestle in flourishing almond and cherry orchards, vineyards and olive groves. A scenic drive swoops down grand wooded spurs past the hidden monastery of **Las Batuecas**, where Luis Buñuel retreated during the '30s to make a controversial film of the region, *Tierra sin Pan* (Land without Bread).

Béjar and Candelario (H)

Béjar's eponymous sierra is the westerly extremity of the Sierra de Gredos. This textile town has a fine site, spread out on a long ridge. You get a good idea of Béjar's houses, all facing the same way, from the main road leading to Plasencia. It has a fairly well-preserved old quarter of porticoed *plazas*, and a few ramparts, but no great sights. Smaller, but more picturesque, is the mountain village of **Candelario** to the south-east, another village that tourists have discovered, carefully preserved but still fortunately alive and kicking. At one end of the main street is a tiny bar, where the few seats are firmly occupied by locals: tourists hover round the counter for *tapas* and swiftly served beers.

ZAMORA (H)

Butted up against Portugal's top right-hand corner, the province of Zamora has often been a strategic prize. The capital town, cloaked in thick medieval walls (Fernando I referred to it as 'La bien cercada' - the well fortified city), played a significant role in several eventful chunks of Spanish history. Its castles face west, to repel the threat of Portuguese invasion across the Duero. Today the misty grey-green hills and vineyards by the Portuguese frontier are anything but belligerent, and if you are exploring western Zamora, a trip through northern Portugal via Bragança and the lovely old town of Miranda do Douro makes an interesting diversion and may save you having to retrace your steps from the area around Puebla de Sanabria.

Zamora town itself is often unfairly missed off the itinerary between the blockbusting neighbouring cities of León and Salamanca. As a result, it is usually quiet, even in high summer. Franco spotted potential in Zamora's remoteness; it was a useful place to keep his more embarrassing prisoners of conscience. Zamora prison at one point is alleged to have held more 'turbulent priests' (segregated from other prisoners) than all the Warsaw Pact countries put together. Scenically the area around Zamora is varied: hilly and green near the Galician border, flat and hot further east. Huge river and reservoir systems cut through the province, which can make touring routes tricky. North of the Duero Zamora is known as Tierra del Pan (Land of Bread); south of the river it is

Tierra del Vino (Land of Wine), and the crops you see reflect this difference.

Zamora and Toro are on the main bus and train routes between Madrid and Galicia, but if you are heading this far west it is worth having a car. Accommodation is not exactly thick on the ground, but the province has three pleasant *paradores*, two in historic buildings, and these rarely become too busy.

Exploring Zamora town

The gaunt, Stalinist apartment blocks on Zamora's eastern outskirts will not impress much, but the old town encased in its walls is a real gem. Besides its architectural interest, Zamora's old quarter has a particularly tranquil atmosphere and it has a surprisingly prosperous air. Stylish fashion and shoe shops line the pedestrianised sectors; others sell attractive handicrafts and local produce. Though peaceful and unthreatening at night even for lone walkers, Zamora has plenty of bars and cafés, and a disco or two, filled with a mix of out-of-town or foreign visitors and locals. Zamora boasts two attractive hotels (one *parador*), both of which have good food. If you do not want to eat in hotels, there are several reputable restaurants, Serafín and París are among the best. Budget accommodation is scattered throughout the old quarter. Calle Benavente has three *hostales* close together.

The cobbled streets around the Plaza Mayor lend themselves to casual wandering, and look especially attractive at night when many of the mellow stone buildings are softly spotlit. Look out for the Isabeline windows of the **Casa de los Momos** and the **Casa del Cordón**. A maze of tiny streets trickles past Romanesque churches and ancient houses to the old bridge over the Duero.

Zamora's churches are individually quite simple, but most have one or two noteworthy features. The local style is distinctive: multi-lobed arches and light-filled domes are common features. One church, **San Ildefonso**, supports its mighty weight on flying buttresses slung across the street to the houses opposite, as though propping itself up on its elbows. Up by the old walls, El Cid was knighted at the altar of **Santiago de los Caballeros**.

Just outside the cathedral you can see the remains of Zamora's **castle** and bits of wall in a little park, and can get a good vantage-point of the city, looking west over the Duero. If you follow the walls round you soon come to the **Postigo**

de la Traición (Traitor's Gate). This is where King Sancho II was treacherously done to death in El Cid's time.

Housed near the church of Santa María la Nueva is the **Museo de la Semaña Santa** or Holy Week Museum. This contains a collection of life-size religious scenes on carnival floats, or *pasos*. During Holy Week celebrations the *pasos* are paraded through the streets amid spectacular festivities.

The Cathedral

Zamoran architecture quivers on the cusp between Romanesque and Gothic styles, and in the cathedral you can see the rounded archways just starting to elongate towards a point. Outside and in, the cathedral is a most unusual building. Its most remarkable feature, making it instantly recognisable among Spanish churches, is the exotic, Byzantine-looking dome.

Inside, the cathedral is light and spacious. If you are lucky enough to get close enough to them, the carved choir-stalls display a lively range of saints and sinners, including monks and nuns in mind-boggling postures. They so offended sixteenth-century sensibilities that the misericords were nailed down. Even today, the prim verger is reluctant to let curious idlers inspect: 'I have my orders', he says pompously. If you are disappointed in this, make sure to wait for a cathedral tour (in slow, clear Spanish) and visit the museum, which contains a truly spectacular collection of Flemish tapestries.

TORO (H)

This historic walled town stands magnificently on a scarred yellow-pink cliff by a bend in the Duero, and the approach from the south is dramatic. The state of some of its buildings and dusty old streets is initially disappointing once you get into the town, but it has a pleasant Plaza Mayor, and several notable churches, including the brick-built **San Lorenzo**, with Mudejar features. Best is the **Collegiate Church of Santa María la Mayor**, a splendid Romanesque building with an unusual many-sided two-tier lantern tower. The seven arches of the west portal are one of Spain's finest examples of Romanesque carving, though it is quite difficult to see it as it is now closed off from the main church – ask church staff about access. Inside the church is a famous painting known as *The Virgin and the Fly*, attributed to Fernando Gallego, where an incongruous bluebottle loiters on the sacred knee. Isabella the Catholic is alleged to have been the model for Mary, and the painting is supposed to be one of the best likenesses of her.

Toro, as its location and fortifications suggest, was an important strategic town during the Middle Ages, and it crops up several times in Castile's checkered history. Pedro the Cruel incarcerated his wife María of Portugal here, presumably the better to enjoy the favours of his mistress in Tordesillas further upstream. A century earlier Fernando III, the saintly conqueror of Córdoba and Seville, was crowned king of León in 1230, so uniting the two rival kingdoms of León and Castile. Most significant of all, Toro was the site of a decisive battle in 1476 between Isabella the Catholic and the supporters of her niece, Juana, known as La Beltraneja.

PUEBLA DE SANABRIA (H)

The old market town of **Benavente** (H) in the fertile Esla valley has an exceptionally well-stocked tourist office where you can pick up information about the region. **Puebla de Sanabria** is a large village of stone-roofed grey and white houses in mountain and lake scenery close to the boundaries with Galicia and north Portugal. To reach it from Benavente you have to cross the Sierra de la Culebra, a range of gentle hills with a light covering of oak woodland and broom, now a hunting reserve. The region is a popular spot with tourists and locals alike for its sports and recreational facilities. Puebla de Sanabria has a modern *parador*, and less expensive accommodation is scattered around the lakeshore to the north. The most attractive part of Puebla de Sanabria is the older quarter by the twelfth-century church and castle, reached by a steep hill. Quaint houses with huge overhanging eaves and wooden balconies, some carved with family crests, line the streets. The views from the *plaza* at the top of the village are excellent. The church doorway is decorated with naïve figures and a simple but effective pattern of large beads.

Roads leading from the village are signposted 'Portugal' or 'Lago de Sanabria'. The latter route is a pretty drive through stream-filled woodland. The road round the southern lakeshore leads to the resort of **Ribadelago**, a not-particularly-exciting collection of bars, small *hostales*, picnic spots and watersports centres. If you persist right to the end of the road you reach what remains of the ancient village (most was drowned when the lake was dammed), and that really is a time-warp. If you take the road along the north shore, it rises to a marvellous vantage-point over the lake near the picturesque village of **San Martín de Castañeda** – a great place for a picnic.

PALENCIA

Once Palencia was an important place. The eleventh-century warrior El Cid married Doña Jimena in the church of San Miguel. In the twelfth century it was a royal residence, and Spain's first university was founded here in the thirteenth century. Since then its fortunes have wavered; it fell from grace after the Comuneros revolt and suffered Charles V's displeasure, but then grew prosperous from its coalmines in the north and the fertile wheatlands of the nearby Tierra de Campos.

The city of Palencia is dull, and scarcely worth using as a base, but it is by no means as unpleasant as some of Spain's northern cities. Many gardens and parks soften the buildings, watered by the River Carrión and the Castilian Canal. Nor is it difficult to drive in, though parking near the cathedral can be a problem. Bus and train stations are both near Plaza Calvo Sotelo, just outside the city centre ring road, and a long walk from the tourist office.

Compared with the glamorous neighbouring provinces of Burgos and León, Palencia province has a tough time in the tourist stakes. There *are* many good things in Palencia, some would say the best Romanesque architecture in Spain. But many sights are on a minor scale, most are churches, and sometimes much is made of little.

Palencia Cathedral

Palencia has just one sight worth a detour, and that is its Gothic **Cathedral**, a patchwork of accretions built over many centuries, from an original Visigothic chapel dating back to the seventh century and a Romanesque chapel built by Sancho the Great in 1034. Vestiges of these earlier structures can be seen in the crypt.

Inside, the interior is lavish. To see its treasures it is advisable to buy a ticket for a guided tour and suffer a lengthy and enthusiastic discourse in rapid Spanish on every aspect of the building. Only then will you get to see the lovely altarpiece by Juan de Flandes and Felipe Vigarni fully illuminated, the cloister museum with an El Greco version of San Sebastían and Flemish tapestries, and the fascinating crypt.

AROUND PALENCIA

Just west of the city, at the village of **Autilla del Pino**, is a hilltop vantage-point called the Mirador de Tierra de Campos. It is one of the best places to view the huge extent of the Palencian plains, and the huddled, earth-coloured villages almost indistinguishable from the rest of the terrain.

Again close to the city, on the south side, the little seventh-century church of **Baños de Cerrato** is worth a visit. Purists consider it one of the most important Visigothic buildings in Spain, and it is certainly one of the oldest churches still standing. The horseshoe arches on marble columns even predate the Moorish style. Ask for the key in the village if the church is locked.

North of Palencia there is another viewpoint from the ramparts of the castle of **Monzón de Campos**, now a hotel. If you strike west from there you reach the little town of **Paredes de Nava**, home of the painter Pedro Berruguete and his sculptor son Alonso. You can see good examples of their work in the parish church of Santa Eulalia, a striking building with a square Romanesque belfry of brightly coloured tiles, patterned in Burgundian style.

Frómista, on the way to Santiago, north of Palencia, has a famous Romanesque church. The date of its foundation is easy to remember – 1066. If today San Martín's gold-stone capitals and corbels seem a little too neat and tidy, that is because it has had a brisk twentieth-century restoration, and any nasty latter-day impurities have been whisked away. Unfortunately much of its atmosphere has also vanished because it has been deconsecrated, and is now only used as a postcard backdrop for local wedding ceremonies. Inside it is rather bare apart from a crucifix. The slight sterility, though, does not detract from its beautifully proportioned exterior: a mellow assembly of rounded apses and low towers. It is the only remaining building in what was the sizeable complex of a Benedictine abbey. Frómista was once an important stopping point on the Way of St James, with several pilgrim hostels as well as the San Martín monastery, but now it has only a village atmosphere, and that somewhat spoiled by

459

passing traffic. The town's hotels no longer cater so well for travellers as in medieval times, but the ancient Hostería de los Palmeros, Tel: (988) 81 00 67 at least soothes hunger pangs.

Carrión de los Condes, the next main centre on the pilgrim route, is the setting for a tall tale. The last story in *El Cantar del Mio Cid* (The Song of My Cid), the epic poem of the romantic warlord's deeds, relates how the caddish Counts (Condes) of Carrión married El Cid's daughters for their dowries. After their weddings in Valencia the counts stripped and beat their new wives and dumped them in a forest, making off with all their possessions. El Cid was not a man to overlook such loutish behaviour. As the poem relates, 'He stood a long hour in thought, and then he grasped his beard and swore'. Needless to say, the wicked Counts got their just deserts, and the daughters Doña Sol and Doña Elvira were remarried to kinder husbands with whom they lived happily ever after.

THE ROAD TO CANTABRIA

As soon as you arrive in **Aguilar de Campóo** (H), on the main N-611 near the Cantabrian border, you notice the smell of baking, for this is a great biscuit-making town. Several large old-fashioned factories are scattered around the town. Aguilar de Campóo, now a popular resort, is the main town of the Campóo region. Poised on a knife-edge between the dairy country of Green Spain and the cereal plains of Dry Spain; the countryside perceptibly changes colour as you leave the town. A small, squat castle stands above the town, and below it, a twelfth-century chapel to St Cecilia. The most interesting building in the town is the **Monasterio de Santa María la Real**.

The hills of northern Palencia rise to about 2,500 metres, nearly as high as any in the Picos de Europa. For some reason they don't give the impression of crowding in on you, but seem to recede into the distance in soft, gentle layers, like chiffon scarves. One of the best ways to see them is to take the minor road P-210 that skirts the southern edge of the Fuentes Carrionas Park (otherwise virtually inaccessible by car) between Velilla del Río Carrión and Cervera de Pisuerga. It is a slow narrow winding route past several reservoirs, and takes a good hour.

Cervera de Pisuerga is a junction for one of the main passes into the Picos (see page 116), and now an expanding holiday resort and walking base. Some of the old buildings have been allowed to decay, and stand uncomfortably alongside brash new holiday flats. The town has a pleasant Plaza Mayor, where there are several cheap *hostales*. The road down to the old village and dam of Ruesga is a good picnic spot. From here you can see the modern *parador* which commands the best vantage-point for miles. North of the town a scenic drive leads to the Puerto de Piedrasluengas and the road to Potes in the Picos.

VALLADOLID

Valladolid is the largest and most industrialised city in northern Castile. Dense suburbs packed with food-processing firms and car-manufacturing plants spread far beyond the original city core. However, it has an impressive historic pedigree. The Catholic Monarchs Ferdinand and Isabella were married here, in the Vivero Palace. Philip II was born and baptized in the city, and it was twice the capital of Spain before the court was uprooted to Madrid. Cervantes lived in Valladolid for a while, and Columbus died here, alone and forgotten. Always a conservative city, Valladolid was a thriving Falangist centre in Franco's time.

Apart from the great River Duero slicing through the Valladolid province from east to west, there is little natural beauty about this flattish, heavily cultivated region of wheatfields and vineyards. Visitors come here for man-made treasures: art and architecture, castles, and Spain's most expensive wines.

Exploring the city

The monarchs, scholars, clerics, artists and writers who patronised Valladolid left behind several genuinely three-star sights. But these jewels are stuck in a tarnished setting of second-rate decaying buildings. Apart from its sights, Valladolid has little appeal, and no particular charms as a touring base. It is a dull and ugly place, but it does have several excellent restaurants. A day's sightseeing, interspersed with a hearty Castilian lunch at, say, Mesón La Fragua at Paseo Zorrilla 10, Mesón Panero at Marina Escobar 1, or Mesón Cervantes at Calle del Rastro 6, should leave you with some pleasant memories of the city.

For the new arrival, Vallodolid is one of the worst sign-

461

posted cities in the whole of Spain (even worse when you attempt to escape from its stranglehold). If you come by public transport you will arrive at the south end of town, near the well-kept triangular municipal park called Campo Grande, a good place for a rest while sightseeing (something you may be glad of in Valladolid's hot bustling streets). If you arrive by car, there are parking places near the Plaza del Poniente, the Plaza Mayor, and the University, a few blocks east of the river. From any of these a walking route curving northwards will lead you past most of the city's more interesting buildings.

The main sights

● **Colegio de San Gregório** If you have time for only one thing in Valladolid, make sure this is it: a fifteenth-century college, founded by Queen Isabella's confessor, containing one of the finest collections of religious art in Spain. The entrance façade is wonderful. Technically, the style is known as Isabeline Gothic, but experts argue over how much was influenced by the slightly later plateresque style. For the non-specialist, the subtle differences between these two types of riotous stone confectionery are immaterial – both result in a dazzling fantasy of detailed carving in shallow relief. The stonework is alive with monsters, thorny trees, cherubs playing in fountains, snarling lions and heraldic crests. It looks as crisp and sharp as though the mason has just gone for a tea-break. No one seems to know exactly who was responsible for this marvel, but it is believed to be mostly by Gil de Siloé. Inside, the two-storey arcaded patio is even more striking.

● **Museo Nacional de Escultura** (National Museum of Polychrome Sculpture) This museum housed inside San Gregório is a good place to get Spain's great Renaissance masters into perspective: Berruguete, Pedro de Mena, Diego de Siloé (Gil's son), Gregório Fernandez and Juan de Juni are all well represented here.

Look out particularly for Berruguete's altarpiece (dismantled and at eye level, so you can study each magnificent section in detail), Diego de Siloé's carved choir-stalls from San Benito, and Juan de Juni's *Entombment*. During Holy Week the expressive processional floats (*pasos*) of heart-rending religious scenes (in rooms 4–8) parade through the streets, turning Valladolid into an unwontedly lively spectacle.

● **San Pablo** Next to San Gregório is the Gothic church of San Pablo, where Philip II was baptized, and in whose restoration the infamous Torquemada, the Grand Inquisitor, had a hand. Inside, the church is fairly plain as a result of a thorough smash-and-grab raid by Napoleon's troops during the Peninsular War. But the outside is even more exotic than San Gregório's, and possibly by the same artists, Gil de Siloé and Simón of Cologne.

● **Cathedral** Its plainness, and unfinished state, are a disappointment after the richness of other buildings in the city, but Valladolid's cathedral has some good points. Philip II commissioned his favourite architect, Juan de Herrera, to build it, but he never completed it. Churriguera the baroque artist added some contrasting flourishes to Herrera's austere work. Inside, the cathedral is pure Herrera. The characteristic giant square pillars and gloomy recesses are impressive, but cheerless. The florid gilt altarpiece is attributed to Juan de Juni.

Other sights

● **Santa Cruz Palace** Yet another startling fifteenth-century façade, profusely decorated with a mixture of winged lions, dolphins, and foliage.

● **University** Students mill informally around the buildings, diluting some of the baroque pomposity of columns, balustrades, and statuary.

● **Santa María la Antigua** One of Valladolid's more elegant smaller churches, with a fine Romanesque pyramid-topped tower crowning its Gothic base.

● **Las Angustias** This church is mainly notable for the extraordinary statue known as the Virgin of the Knives, one of Juan de Juni's more extreme productions. Seven silver daggers symbolising the seven sorrows pierce Our Lady's heart, and her expression is understandably pained.

● **Oriental Museum** The most fascinating of several small historical museums in the city, pleasantly placed beyond the gardens of the Campo Grande in an Augustinian seminary.

TORDESILLAS (H)

Passing the grey hulk of Simancas Castle (now Spain's state archive) as you leave the city by the south-west (N-620), you can reach the historic town of **Tordesillas** in about twenty minutes. This convenient location makes the town a good base from which to explore Valladolid. It is a pleasant pinky-brown town on the River Duero with an arcaded Plaza Mayor, a fine medieval bridge and several interesting churches. In the mid-fourteenth century, Pedro the Cruel renovated a royal palace in Moorish style for his Andalucian mistress, María de Padilla. After his reign, the palace reverted again to respectability; it is now the **Convento de Santa Clara** still occupied by cloistered nuns. But its splendid Mudejar interior is intact, including a patio of horseshoe arches and coloured tiles. There are Moorish baths, and an *artesonado* coffered ceiling carved into glittering star shapes in the church (the former throne room).

In a neighbouring set of apartments (since destroyed by fire), Juana the Mad, the unfortunate daughter of the Catholic Monarchs, was locked away in a tiny windowless room. This is ironic, for Santa Clara faced one of the best views in Castile, on a natural balcony overlooking the Duero. Already mentally unbalanced, Juana was finally unhinged by the early and unexpected death of her beloved husband, Philip the Fair.

History took another interesting turn in Tordesillas when in 1494 Spain and Portugal signed a treaty, under the benevolent gaze of the Borgia Pope Alexander VI, to divide up the spoils of the New World. Drawing an imaginary line 370 leagues west of the Cape Verde Islands, Spain declared herself entitled to anything west of the line, and Portugal helped herself to anything east of it. This neatly left the huge territorial prize of Brazil (officially discovered six years later) in Portuguese hands, which must have irritated the Spaniards beyond measure.

South of Tordesillas, the Rueda wine region is a group of little villages scattered on dry hills where wheat rather than vines seem to be the dominant crop. **Rueda** and the neighbouring village of **La Seca** are good places to buy white wine and cheese for a picnic.

WINING BY THE DUERO

If you head upstream from Valladolid, striking due east on the N-122 towards Soria, you hit wine country again. Valladolid province has the little-known honour of making Spain's rarest and most expensive wine, produced in a few chalky fields along the banks of the River Duero. Most people think the best wine in Spain comes from La Rioja, but the priciest comes from the village of **Valbuena de Duero**, and is called Vega de Sicilia; Winston Churchill lent the weight of his personal recommendation to this heady stuff. The Cistercian monks from the abbey near Valbuena may well have spurred on the production of this excellent wine. The Vega de Sicilia winery is easily spotted along the main road, at Quintanilla de Onésimo, but this may not help much, for it is no common-or-garden *bodega* for passing trade. They take themselves and their product extremely seriously here, and casual callers may neither buy, nor look around. You must make an appointment in advance, Tel (983) 68 01 47, to arrange a visit. You can see the precious Vega de Sicilia vineyards, carefully cordoned off with ferocious warnings to trespassers, as you drive along the main road. The sales office of Bodegas Mauro nearby, which also sells excellent local wines (at more affordable prices), may give you a better welcome.

If you are curious about Vega de Sicilia wine, you couldn't do better than splash out on a bottle to accompany the food at an unostentatious but excellent restaurant called Mesón 2,39, at Calle Antonio Machado 39 in **Tudela de Duero**, just off the N-122, 16 kilometres east of Valladolid. The knowledge-able and civilised proprietor really cares about food, and wines too: take his suggestions seriously.

The *denominación* of Ribera de Duero is becoming steadily more famous for the quality of its wines. Many of the best wine villages are in neighbouring Burgos province a few miles east off the N-122 beyond Peñafiel. **La Horra, Roa de Duero** and **Pedrosa de Duero** are good bets for buying and tasting wine, though they are not especially pretty villages. The *bodegas* here are not touristy, and few have organised visiting hours or retail outlets. But if you speak a little Spanish the owners are very willing to show you round their vineyards and wineries, and sell you a few bottles of reds.

LEON (H)

León means 'lion' in Spanish, which explains the shaggy rampant lions that adorn the tourist literature. But it was a legion (Rome's seventh, the *Legio Septima*), not a lion, that gave its name to the province. The modern boundaries enclose a formidable chunk of land. Medieval León was even bigger, and no mere province. It was a kingdom, encompassing the neighbouring territory of Zamora, Salamanca, Palencia and Valladolid, with temporary footholds in

Asturias, Galicia and Portugal. For administrative purposes wing–clipped León now forms the top left-hand corner of Castilla y León. Judging by the graffiti on the road signs, many of its inhabitants wish it were not so. León, like every part of Spain, has its dissidents.

Historically, though, León's destiny has been linked with Castile's for centuries. Despite internecine struggles, the kings and warlords of Castile and León united in their mutual battle against the Moors. The city took its turn at being the Christian capital during the Reconquest, and a torrent of medieval pilgrims used it as a thoroughfare from Castile on the Way to Santiago (see page 61).

Exploring the city

León flourished in the late Middle Ages. Its great monuments date from the eleventh to the fourteenth centuries. After Pedro the Cruel removed his court to the sunnier climes of Seville, León's importance diminished, reviving in the twentieth century with a second renaissance of art and architecture. Today the modern city centre, more successfully planned than most, adjoins the ancient quarters in a well-kept expanse of green spaces, wide streets and fountain-filled *plazas*. The main sights are fairly spread out, but walking round León is a pleasurable experience. Both bus and train stations are within easy walking distance of the main tourist zone, and **Plaza San Isidoro** makes a convenient parking point for exploring the old city. Or leave your car near the riverside **Hostal de San Marcos**, León's spectacular monastery *parador*, and tackle the whole place on foot. Avenida de José Antonio makes a beeline for the busy central circus called **Plaza Santo Domingo**, which stands between the old and new parts of the city.

Pedestrianised Calle de la Rua is the place to head for shopping. For a rest, make for the peaceful gardens on Calle del Cid where venerable citizens in black berets contemplate the putti on a trickling fountain.

Eating out and accommodation

The city of León deserves at least one night of anyone's time. If you can, push out the boat and stay at the Hostal de San Marcos. It is one of the most fascinating places to stay in Spain, a costly but unforgettable treat for a night.

The nearby Hotel-Residencia Quindos is a pleasant and

convenient alternative at a much lower price. For budget accommodation, evening atmosphere and a good choice of restaurants and *tapas* bars, head for the area around Plaza San Martín. For lunch, try the old-fashioned Café Victoria on Generalisimo where you can have your shoes cleaned as you eat your *plato combinado*, or the cheerful Casa Pozo on Plaza San Marcelo (good lamb, *gazpacho*, or an imaginative salad served with *élan* and courtesy).

The main sights

● **The Cathedral** It is Gothic, it dates from mid-thirteenth to late fourteenth century, and it was strongly influenced by the French style of cathedral-building, as in Reims and Chartres. These dull facts give no inkling of León's glories. Outside the main entrance, two graceful but asymmetrical towers flank a superb west portal, with three deeply shadowed arches surmounted by a vast rose window. The archways are splendidly carved, those to the right and left depicting the childhood of Christ and the Coronation of the Virgin, the central one a Last Judgement, where the saved look on with a smug, 'There but for the grace of God!' as the damned discover their horrific destiny amid flames and demons. Inside, it feels almost like walking into the ever-lasting bonfire; huge windows of red and gold flash sparks through the gloom of the high, slender-vaulted nave, settling in soft pools of rainbow light on the floor. The cloister and museum are also worth seeing. The guided tour is a bit rushed and muddled, but good things to look out for include a marvellous crucifixion sculpture by Juan de Juni – Christ's sinews tensed in agony; Juan de Badajoz's pale staircase carved in plateresque style, and a collection of charming large-headed Romanesque Virgins like ancient dolls on the top floor.

● **San Isidoro** This complex of church, treasury museum and royal pantheon is no anti-climax after the cathedral. A mix of different styles – Romanesque, Gothic, Renaissance, and baroque – it still manages to look all of a piece on its seemly cobbled square. The twelfth-century basilica of narrow brick and gold stone adjoins the bulbous old city walls. St Isidore, the battling Archbishop of Seville to whom the church is dedicated, waves a hasty Lone Ranger benediction from the elaborate pediment over the main door before galloping off to slay a few Moors. The treasury lives up to its name, stuffed with beautiful enamelled caskets, tapestries and early manuscripts in gold wire cases. Look out for St Isidore's reliquary and Doña Urraca's lopsided chalice of onyx, tortoiseshell and gold. More memorable is the trip downstairs to the pantheon, a barrel-vaulted crypt of splendidly carved columns and twelfth-century frescoes.

● **Monasterio de San Marcos** León's third great building is now a luxury hotel, recently incorporated into the state *parador* chain. It always was a hotel, or rather a hostel and hospital, for the pilgrims on their way to Santiago de Compostela. Founded in the twelfth century, the present building is a steady process of construction right up to the present day, when modern hotel wings have been discreetly added at the rear. Despite the name, it has more to do with Santiago (St James) than St Mark. The Military Order of Santiago began the present lavish building in 1513, and no expense was spared. The enormously broad Renaissance façade is carved with a plateresque extravaganza of scallop shells, coats of arms, swags and medallions. St Mark's bookish figure quietly records his gospel at one end, but it is the swashbuckling Santiago who catches the eye above the main entrance, as usual crushing startled Muslims beneath the heels of his rearing steed.

WESTWARD HO! THE PILGRIM WAY

Astorga (H)

After León, Astorga was the next destination on the medieval beaten track to Santiago de Compostela, normally a single day's march for the pilgrims. It is unlikely you will be hindered now, but if you had travelled this way in July 1434 you would have encountered a quixotic knight, Don Suero de Quiñones, guarding the long bridge at **Hospital de Orbigo** (bypassed by the modern road). Don Suero and his nine companions challenged all passers-by to confess that his lady was the fairest of them all. Apparently 727 knights contested the challenge, and the jousting continued for a month. Only one knight was killed, but Don Suero's demented chivalry became quite a legend. We are not told whether it impressed the lady. The fine Paso de Honor bridge is still there.

Astorga seems poised on a dais above its sturdy ramparts. As you approach it, a whimsical silhouette of towers, turrets and pinnacles emerges from the city walls. The **cathedral** is massive, with enormously tall twin towers, one pink, one grey, as though they ran out of stone halfway through. The main doorway shows some fine carving. Inside, a lovely marble altarpiece by one of Michelangelo's pupils is noteworthy.

The Maragatos people live in and around Astorga. Their origins are uncertain, but they have preserved their unique customs and costumes, and still live within their own communities in the villages nearby. If you follow the minor road westwards from Astorga (LE-142), you will pass through some of them. **Castrillo de los Polvazares** is one of the best and most interesting.

El Bierzo

Ponferrada, further west, is the capital of the Bierzo region. The twelfth-century castle built by the Knights Templar in the old town is well preserved and you can go inside it, although there is not much to see. Apart from the castle and the moderately quaint old quarter around the Plaza Mayor, Ponferrada is of little interest, and though its location makes it an obvious base for exploring the Bierzo region, there is not much recommendable accommodation. The tourist office near the castle (if you can find it open) can produce some good leaflets about touring routes. It is worth stocking up with a picnic and plenty of petrol for these: you may find few provisions *en route*.

South of Ponferrada, a minor road (LE-161) meanders through vineyards and orchards to the beautiful dappled Valley of Silence (Valle de Silencio). **Peñalba de Santiago**, at the far end of the valley, is the most appealing village of all.

Las Medulas: Realms of gold

South-west of Ponferrada is the route (N-536) to Las Medulas, an extraordinary region of open-cast goldmines exploited during Roman times. Using thousands of slaves, the Romans dug a phenomenal system of canals to wash out the gold-bearing ore. It is believed they extracted hundreds of tons of gold. The hills, now eroded by wind and sun, are still honeycombed by tunnels. Giant red termite heaps rear up from a landscape of brilliant pink soil and stunted chestnut trees. You can enter some of the ancient workings, but the best view of Las Medulas is from the Orellan *mirador* (clearly signed, but a very rough steep track).

Villafranca del Bierzo (H) and the Ancares hills

Continuing west of Ponferrada along the pilgrim's way to Santiago the village of **Corullón** is worth a visit: a sunny and prosperous village of grey-roofed houses and unusual churches. Figs, vines, walnuts and fruit-trees flourish on its sheltered amphitheatre of hills, and just above the village is a magnificent viewpoint of the surrounding countryside. A little further on is **Villafranca del Bierzo**, one of the most atmospheric towns of western León. Its aristocratic history shows through in many crested palaces and huge churches, and a proud, military-looking castle on its outskirts, but some of the houses of the old town seem perilously dilapidated: balconies cling on by a whisker. In the old quarter you may run across a knife-grinder plying his trade. Jars of fruit, preserved in local brandy, are stacked up in the windows of local shops. Calle del Agua is one of the best-kept streets, with one or two quaint *hostales* and La Charola, an ancient *mesón* where countless pilgrims have enjoyed a cheap hearty meal. A more comfortable base is Villafranca's *parador*, a modern building on the edge of town.

The Ancares hills lie on the remote borders of Galicia. It is beautiful and very quiet once you leave the main road over the Cebreiro Pass. Minor roads leading across the Galician border to Becerreá take you through fat cushions of green coombed hills, sometimes castle-crowned.

THE ROUTES TO ASTURIAS

The **Pajares Pass** (Puerto de Pajares) is on the old Oviedo road from León, not the new motorway which tunnels through the highest section of the pass. The road is good, tackling the fierce gradient with wide smooth bends. Near the top, the village of **Arbás** has a Romanesque church with exotic carved capitals. From the summit of the pass, crowned with an undistinguished hotel, extensive views pan westwards over the wild and jagged Somiedo mountains, one of the last remaining haunts of Spain's rare brown bear. Once over the pass, you leave Castile and enter Asturias. The road signs change.

The excursion west of the motorway along the Luna reservoirs is an attractive drive, and if you need an overnight base for exploring this area or the Reserva Nacional de Somiedo to the north, head for a simple hotel in the unspoilt village of **San Emiliano** (H). East of the Puerto de Pajares you can divert to the limestone **Caves of Valporqueras**, a popular coach-party outing.

The road continues through Boñar to **Riaño**, where the recent creation of an enormous reservoir caused great local resentment from people whose homes were destroyed without adequate compensation. Protesters were clubbed by riot police, and one person died. The incident seriously embarrassed the socialist government in 1988. Spaniards had hoped those undemocratic tactics had disappeared for ever. Hideously inappropriate hotels and apartments have sprung up in a new lakeside resort safely above the waterline, but so far it seems few people want to live in modern Riaño. Out of sight of the town, the roads around the reservoir lead through fertile valley scenery towards the Picos de Europa (see page 116).

South and east of León towards Palencia is Dry Spain, mostly flat and of limited interest, though rapidly traversible on fast straight roads. If you are driving through this area an isolated Mozarabic church, **San Miguel de Estéban**, and a couple of towns are worth a stop. **Valencia de Don Juan** (H) has the remains of a large castle. There is little to attract visitors to this town, but it has two exceptionally pleasant small hotels.

BURGOS (H)

The fine city of Burgos stands midway between Madrid and the north coast of Spain, a strategic link on the fast road and rail routes to the Pyrenees and the cities of Bilbao, Pamplona and Santander. Once capital of Castile, Burgos has now been demoted to provincial capital, but has lost little of its old civic pride and conservatism.

Burgos played an important part in the lengthy process by which Castile unyoked itself from Moorish domination and gradually asserted its own power over the whole of Spain. It became rich, first from Moorish tributes, then from merino wool: Burgos was the headquarters of the powerful Mesta sheep-farmers. Gothic monuments sprang up; artists and artisans flocked to the city to embellish the buildings.

Burgos's most famous son is El Cid (see page 478) and the city has always had a militaristic bent. In recent times it was closely associated with the *Movimiento Nacionale*, which hoisted Franco to power. It is said of Burgos that even the

stones are Nationalist. It still has its Avenida del Generalísimo, when most Spanish towns have changed the names
that remind them of the dictatorship. Crime rates are
relatively low, and walking about the city, even at night,
seems unthreatening. It makes an excellent base, and has a
good range of accommodation and eating places, though its
prosperity and importance as a business centre mean that
prices are sharp.

A wise choice for eating in the old town is Casa Ojeda on
Plaza Calvo Sotelo, which combines the pleasures of *al fresco*
eating and drinking in one of Burgos's pleasantest squares,
with a lively young-set bar, and a smart traditional
dining-room.

Exploring the city

Once inside the grim belts of industrial and residential buildings that surround the old city, make for the cathedral. The
lacy Gothic spires can easily be seen from any raised part of
the city, but in any case, Burgos is obliging with its signposts.
Finding a conveniently close parking space in high season,
though, can be a problem. It may be easier to park across the
river (in Plaza de Vega, say), then walk across the bridge and
through the triumphal **Arco de Santa María** (Santa María
arch), decorated with portentous statues and carvings.

The original gateway through the old walls would have
welcomed El Cid, hotfoot from his battles, but the present
structure dates from the 1530s, and is said to have been erected to appease Charles V for Burgos' part in the Comuneros
revolt. Charles is flatteringly depicted consorting with the
great Castilian heroes El Cid, Fernán González and Diego
Porcelos, the founders of Burgos. By the gateway is the
Paseo del Espolón, a walkway beside the River Arlanzón.
Always lively with strollers, especially in the evenings, it is an
attractive paved precinct of shady cafés, statues, fountains,
and gardens.

Heading east from the cathedral you find the most interesting and atmospheric streets of Old Burgos, full of *tapas* bars,
quaint shops, fountains, and disembodied archways. Pick a
route leading through **Plaza José Antonio**, a roughly oval
'square' surrounded by pleasant old houses. If you climb
through the backstreets behind the cathedral you reach sections of the old city walls, and the ruined castle on a wooded
mound, now used mostly as a city park. You can drive up to

the castle for quite good views; otherwise it is of no great appeal.

Leaving the walled city via another bridge, **Puente de San Pablo**, you pass a huge equestrian statue of local hero El Cid, galloping into battle on his trusty steed Babieca, sword outstretched, cloak flying round his shoulders like angels' wings. A slightly ambiguously worded tribute to El Cid is carved on the monument, declaring him a man of prudence, steadfastness and heroic valour. The bridge itself is studded with statues, some connected with El Cid's life.

The Cathedral

One of Spain's most magnificent Gothic cathedrals, it is best to tackle it in several visits if you have the time. It is built on a sloping site, so as you walk around it the shape becomes more complex than it appears at first, with little stairways and connecting passages linking the levels. The building took many years to complete, from the foundation stone in 1221 to the central lantern in the mid-sixteenth century, and many different artists from all over Europe were involved.

Johan of Cologne and his son were the main architects in the mid-fifteenth century, and the influences of Franco–Germanic styles are clear. The **Puerta Santa María** on the west front is the main entrance. Both Jewish and Mudejar motifs are incorporated into the carvings, a reminder that artists of other than Christian faiths worked on the building.

Aim to be standing somewhere near the west entrance on the hour. If you look upwards and left to the top of the nave you will see a sixteenth-century clock known as the **Papamoscas** or Flycatcher Clock. As the hour strikes, the bizarre red-costumed jack opens and closes his mouth like a goldfish. On the south side is the **Puerta del Sarmental**, the cathedral's most beautiful doorway.

The cathedral is broken up by the central *coro*, so there is no single sweeping view of the interior. Instead, look up to the glorious vaulting under the lanterns, and concentrate on the rich detailing of its separate parts. All of its dozen or so chapels have some features of interest, and fine works of art. The ones most visitors like to see are the **Santo Cristo Chapel** (first on the right), which contains a curious and disturbing image of Christ made of buffalo hide. The torso gleams in the dull light, and a long hank of dark hair, allegedly human, straggles over the lolling head. Christ wears a sort of white skirt, and (it is claimed) the fingernails and beard need cutting every so often. It is a grotesque, but tragic figure.

Best of all the chapels is the one at the far end, Simón de Colonia's so-called **Constable's Chapel** (Capilla del Condestable), founded by Hernández de Velasco, Constable of Castile in the time of the Catholic Monarchs. He and his wife lie peacefully side by side on a great waxy tomb of Carrara marble, like a respectable middle-aged couple in bed. Overhead, light floods from a star-shaped lantern tower, which hangs over the tomb like a giant drooping flower.

Other things among the panoply of art inside the cathedral are Diego de Siloé's diamond-shaped Golden Staircase leading to the locked Coronaria Door on the north wall, the walnut choir-stalls by Felipe Vigarni, the black carved transept door leading through to the cloister, the bubbly crowded ceiling in the sacristy where figures erupt from the plaster dome, and El Cid's plain red marble tomb directly under the central lantern.

Other sights in town

● **San Nicolás** Just behind the cathedral, this church contains a dazzling altarpiece carved by Simon of Cologne in 1505.

● **Casa del Cordón** This Renaissance mansion (named because of the thick Franciscan cord motif carved on the façade) now houses a bank. It once belonged to the Constable whose chapel is in the cathedral. In this house Isabella and Ferdinand, the Catholic Monarchs, welcomed Christopher Columbus back from his second voyage to the New World on St George's Day 1497, and publicly thanked him for his efforts. A few years later Philip the Fair, the handsome husband of Juana the Mad, daughter of Isabella and Ferdinand, died here. It is said he caught a sudden chill after a *pelota* game, though rumours of poison circulated, as after most unexpected royal deaths.

● **Burgos Museum** Housed in the sixteenth-century Casa de Miranda across the River Arlanzón this elegant Renaissance palace is worth a visit. Inside, the museum is in two sections. The archaeological museum contains Moorish and Visigothic items and some interesting finds from the Roman site of Clunia. The Fine Arts section (undergoing restoration when visited) has a prized tomb of Juan de Padilla sculpted by Gil de Siloé.

Four Great Monasteries

Three of these are within short driving distance of the city centre. The fourth, **Santo Domingo de Silos** (H), is more of an excursion, some 40 kilometres south-east, though it is the best of the four.

Las Huelgas

The twelfth-century nunnery is less than a mile from the city centre. It was founded by Alfonso VIII and his queen Eleanor of Aquitaine, sister of Richard the Lion-Heart. A Cistercian convent for nuns of high birth, the abbess here held great sway. Guided tours (none in English) take you round the Romanesque cloister, the chapter house, the gracefully vaulted church, and a textile museum containing costumes and bits of medieval fabric. The building has many fascinating features, some beautiful, some merely curious: banners captured from the Moors, a revolving pulpit, and a statue of Santiago with a moveable arm holding a sword, used to dub Castilian princes Knights of St James.

La Cartuja de Miraflores

This monastery stands in a pleasant wooded park about three kilometres east of Burgos. Two things besides its splendid contents make it well worth a visit. First, entrance is free. Second, you do not have to put up with an interminable Spanish tour, so you can explore on your own. The Carthusian order took over the monastery in 1442, and it became a royal pantheon for Isabella the Catholic's parents. The treasures of Miraflores lie in the church. Best of all is an **altarpiece** by Gil de Siloé. In front is the lovely marble **mausoleum** by Gil de Siloé to King Juan II and Queen Isabella of Portugal, in the shape of an eight-pointed star. This tomb, though damaged, still rates as one of the finest in Spain.

San Pedro de Cardeña

This is about 10 kilometres south-east of Burgos in a peaceful setting of oakwoods. El Cid fans should note that this was where their hero parted from his beloved Doña Jimena before he rode into exile. And here she brought his body after the siege of Valencia, where it remained until the French removed it during the Peninsular War. During building works the ancient bones of a horse were discovered, and conveniently assigned to El Cid's legendary charger Babieca, whose monument can be seen in the grounds.

Santo Domingo de Silos (guided tours)

If you have limited time or energy for monasteries, this is the one you should choose, on the old Way of St James. Founded by St Dominic in the eleventh century, as a hostelry and place of worship for pilgrims, it is now inhabited by monks of a Benedictine order who keep bees and sing the most beautiful Gregorian chant. The church is a neo-classical building of no great interest, but its Romanesque cloister, is a magnificent example, with an extraordinarily tranquil atmosphere. The stone capitals are carved with mythical beasts and foliage; some are crisply restored, others gently blurred by time and elements. Even better than the capitals are the corner piers, where larger scenes are carved. A splendid one at the northwest corner depicts Doubting Thomas probing Christ's wounds. The disciples incline their haloed heads in the same direction, like sheep in a storm. Look out as well for the fine Mudejar ceilings in painted panels, the tomb of Santo Domingo on its pedestal of strange beasts, and many ancient items in the museum. Best of all is the pharmacy, where mysterious potions were once brewed in stills, retorts, and pestles to the recipes in ancient tomes of pharmacology and botanical lore. **The village** of Santo Domingo itself makes a pleasant base, and there are several places to stay, but you may have to share it with coach-trippers. You can stay inexpensively at the monastery (by prior arrangement) if you happen to be male. Otherwise the Hostal Residencia Cruces is one of the best budget bases. Just a mile or two away is a local beauty spot known as the **Yecla Gorges** (Desfiladero de la Yecla), where a limestone cleft hems in a mountain stream.

SOUTH OF BURGOS

Sierra de la Demanda

Over towards the borders of La Rioja is the mountainous wildlife reserve of the Sierra de la Demanda. Here the land rises to around 2,000 metres in an ancient range of rounded peaks. Vegetation consists of mixed woodland, scrub and many rare plants. It is good and varied country for walking. In the foothills of the sierra is the **Laguna Negra** (black lake) **de Neila**, actually a group of glacial lakes linked by rough forest tracks. The scenery around the upper lake, where there is a bar, is rather bleak but views are extensive. A lower lake by a mountain hut makes a sheltered picnic spot.

Lerma and Covarrubias

There are several towns and villages of passing interest in southern Burgos. **Quintanillas de las Viñas** has a very early Visigothic church with mysterious (possibly pagan) carvings. It is quite a trek from the village, and you need to ask for directions in the village. **Lerma** is a haughty, distinctive town poised proudly over the River Arlanza. The town's remarkable collection of palaces is the virtually single-handed creation of Philip III's corrupt first minister, the Duke of Lerma, who schemed and bribed his way through vast quantities of Spain's new-found wealth in the early seventeeth century. He was finally elbowed aside by his own son, who was presumably a chip off the old block. Today Lerma is a rare example of Classical town-planning in Spain.

Much more seductive is the beautifully preserved medieval town of **Covarrubias**, one of the best bases in Burgos, surrounded by excellent touring routes. The road along the green banks of the Arlanza, towards the evocative ruins of the Monastery of San Pedro, is one of the most scenic. The monastery of Santo Domingo de Silos (see page 476) is about 18 kilometres down the road. Covarrubias is closely associated with one of Burgos's epic heroes, Fernán González, who created the County of Castile in the tenth century and played a great role in the Reconquest by consolidating separate, often warring factions. He is buried in the Gothic collegiate church here, where there is a fine museum. Berruguete, Gil de Siloé, Van Eyck and the Flemish School are represented – look out for the triptych with the Adoration of the Magi, and the gold processional cross. A focus for tourists is the medieval Plaza Mayor, where there is a hotel, the beamed restaurant El Galín and several attractive souvenir shops selling baskets, honey and local pottery.

NORTH OF BURGOS

Castles in the hills

Striking north-west of Burgos, the old pilgrim way to Santiago (N-120) leads to the small towns of Sasamón, Olmillos and Castrojeriz with their oversized churches and battered castles. This is Dry Spain, where raised concrete irrigation channels ferry water across the thirsty plains and poplar-fringed river courses make a sudden, limited splash of lushness. In spring the countryside is a blaze of poppies and other wild flowers.

Northwards, **Medina de Pomar's** (H) sturdy fortress once belonged to the Velasco family, the hereditary Constables of

EL CID CAMPEADOR (H)

The exploits of Rodrigo Díaz de Vivar (Cid to his friends) are now so confused with the romantic myths of medieval epic poetry and Hollywood that it is difficult to sort out the facts from the fiction. Like King Arthur, El Cid undoubtedly existed, but many of the stories associated with him are obviously mere legends. El Cid was a brilliant soldier, a courageous leader, and a charismatic personality. He was also a ruthless opportunist, unscrupulous and devious, ultimately loyal only to his own interests. In most of his military adventures he acted simply as a mercenary, at different times fighting for and against the Moors, and for and against his King.

The word Cid comes from the Arabic *Sidi*, meaning 'Lord' or 'Master'. Born in the first half of the eleventh century, El Cid at first served King and Country (i.e. Castile) loyally and successfully in the struggle against the Moors, first under Fernando I, then Sancho II. When Sancho died in mysterious circumstances and his brother Alfonso VI succeeded, El Cid had suspicions, and made them uncomfortably public. He made Alfonso swear three times in the church of Santa Agueda, Burgos, that he was innocent of any part in Sancho's death. This episode clearly shows El Cid's influence and force of character. The popular hero was getting too big for his boots. On some trumped-up charge of corruption, Alfonso sent El Cid into exile. Sadly he left his wife (the king's own

Castile, whose tomb is in Burgos Cathedral. From shady café terraces in the old town you can look down over neat vegetable plots in the valley below. There is a useful hotel on the main square. **San Pantaleón de Losa**'s Romanesque church stands precariously on a rocky spur. At **Frías** a castle is similarly poised on a bulging crag, high above the surrounding countryside. This village is making its mark as an excursion destination, but as yet is not widely popularised. Just outside Frías, the road south to Ranera leads through some striking rock formations. The historic town of **Oña** stands on a bend of the Oca in a verdant gorge setting, its monuments set round a split-level square. There is more gorge scenery at the Desfiladero de Pancorbo near **Miranda de Ebro**, a fair-sized town of *solanas* (glass-fronted houses) reminiscent of the north coast.

---

cousin Doña Jimena) and family, and rode off to seek his fortune – and his revenge. Joining up with the Moorish king of Zaragoza, El Cid fought many battles, often against Christian forces.

The climax of his career came in 1094, when, leading 7,000 Moorish troops, he captured Valencia after a long siege. Switching sides again, he routed the Moors and ruled Valencia himself until his death in 1099. His widow Doña Jimena, obviously no shrinking violet either, held the city alone until 1102, when she set fire to it and returned to Castile with El Cid's body, which she buried at the Monastery of San Pedro de Carmeña, just outside Burgos. During the Peninsular War the French sacked the tombs and El Cid's remains ended up in the cathedral, where they were solemnly re-interred in 1921. Many of El Cid's exploits, real or imagined, were recorded in an epic poem, *El Cantar del Mío Cid*, which appeared in 1180 and transformed the warrior forever into a heroic romance figure of great valour.

It seems El Cid was not above some dubious tricks, however. One story relates how he duped some Jewish moneylenders into funding his wars by giving them as collateral a locked chest, which he said was full of treasure. In fact it was filled with sand. Modern legend, sensing that public opinion might baulk at this behaviour, says that El Cid repaid his debt. You can see the alleged coffer today, hanging on a wall in Burgos Cathedral.

SORIA (H)

In the daytime the strange red hills of the Soria province shimmer and crumble under the onslaught of sun and wind. On clear nights the temperature plummets with almost Saharan suddenness. Soria is a Castilian backwater bounded by La Rioja, La Mancha and Aragón. Its isolated location keeps it comparatively little known and nearly always quiet. The local economy is still based on agriculture, as it was in the thirteenth century when the wealthy Mesta sheep-owners commanded great influence and Soria town was a most important place. Today it is the smallest provincial capital in Castile and a friendly place, more like a big village than a city. It keeps late hours, and on summer evenings you can still find the tourist office open and in a good humour, or visit its excellent museum, until 9pm.

Exploring the town

The sights are rather spread out, and you certainly need a car (or lots of energy) to make it to the top of the castle hill where the *parador* is located (worth doing for the excellent views). Besides the *parador*, there are several cheap but possibly noisy *pensións* in older buildings in the town centre, and a few dull business hotels. The Maroto near the museum is widely considered Soria's best restaurant.

The picturesque old quarter lies around Calle Aguirre, where the carved coats of arms and heraldic figures of the **Gomara Palace**, rosy orange at night, are cast into shadow by old-fashioned street-lamps. The best churches in the town centre are **San Juan de Rabanera** and **Santo Domingo**, both of which have fine portals. The **Co-Cathedral of San Pedro** has a good plateresque façade, but is disappointing and very dark inside. Bumbling about in the gloom, you may spot a couple of frothy monuments, but the best thing to make for, if it is open, is the Romanesque cloister. Further down the road, just over the Duero, is the Templar monastery of **San Juan de Duero**, now a small museum. It has a lovely and very unusual cloister of interlaced Mudejar arches. Both San Juan, and the little frescoed hermitage of **San Saturio** further downstream, have river views.

Museo Numantino

Newly opened after renovation, this provincial museum is an excellent one of its kind, containing mostly archaeological finds from the nearby Celtiberian and Roman site of Numancia. These evocative ruins lie about seven kilometres north-east of the town. There is not a great deal to see at this desolate, windswept site, but its history is stirring. The Numantines, an Iberian tribe, bravely resisted an eight-month siege by the Romans in AD133–134. It was a hopeless struggle: the Romans outnumbered the Numantines by six to one, and Scipio eventually marched into Numancia to find that the 10,000 Numantines had fired the city and killed themselves rather than surrender.

AROUND SORIA

Sierra de Urbión and the Río Lobos Nature Park

North and east of Soria are two exceptional touring areas, both ideal for picnic excursions. The Sierra de Urbión, on the borders of La Rioja, is the mountain range where the River Duero rises. To reach it, drive west from Soria, then north (SO-821 or SO-840) past the dammed tentacles of the Cuerda del Pozo reservoir to **Vinuesa**, a pretty old village which once had an important cart-building industry. You can stock up here with provisions for lunch, and head off north through a fragrant pine forest, passing sawmills and piles of logs. Signs indicate a popular destination: the **Laguna Negra de Urbión** (Black Lagoon). At the end of the road, park under the trees, and scramble for five minutes up a rocky path. At the top a startling sight greets your eyes: a dark lake (actually a glacial tarn), lies still and mirror-like beneath tall cliffs.

South of the main N-234, between San Leonardo de Yagüe and Ucero, is a newly designated Nature Park, the **Parque Natural del Canyón del Río Lobos**. Approached from the south end, from El Burgo de Osma, the scenery is gentle at first, a potter through a valley of poplars and market gardens. At the stone village of **Ucero** the landscape changes abruptly. Turn off the metalled road at the sign to the Nature Park and drive through a spectacular canyon of orange and grey cliffs, where hawks and vultures wheel in the thermals.

El Burgo de Osma (H) and South

The huge baroque tower of a splendid cathedral dominates the historic walled town of El Burgo de Osma. The bishopric was founded by the Visigoths in the sixth century, and it is still an important religious centre. The body of the cathedral is Gothic, and mostly thirteenth century. Once past an unpleasantly morbid rendering of Christ displaying his wounds on the south door, you will find that the interior amply justifies a visit. Beneath the lofty nave are chapels of dark jasper, a pulpit of white marble, a Juan de Juni altarpiece and exquisite wrought-iron screens. Unseen treasures, for which you need to join a tour, include San Pedro de Osma's tomb and various rare illuminated manuscripts.

Outside the cathedral the beautifully preserved cobbled streets are lined with noble palaces and eighteenth-century houses. The porticoed street by the Plaza Mayor is particularly attractive; see the **San Agustín Hospital** decorated with baroque motifs and, less neatly, a sagging stork's nest. The town makes a pleasant base, with inexpensive *hostales* in the old town, and a newly opened 3-star hotel on the main road, under the same ownership as the long-established restaurant Virrey Palafox, with one of the highest reputations for food in the area. Pork dishes are a speciality (the spring pig-slaughtering festival, or *matanza*, is based here).

South-east of El Burgo is **Gormaz**, where the shell of one of Spain's largest fortresses, originally a Moorish building, stands guarding a massive hilltop. It completely dwarfs the village crouched below its ramparts, and the views are amazing. It is being restored now, and has something of the air of a Hollywood film set. Further east lanes potter through cereal plains and pinewoods where the resin is tapped in little bowls to make turpentine. **Berlanga de Duero** has another magnificent castle, where the restored curtain walls form a grand medieval backdrop to the town. The Plaza Mayor, old town and Gothic collegiate church are also of some interest, and there is a well-kept *hostal* called La Hoz on the main road just west of town, Tel (975) 34 31 36. About eight kilometres south-east is a tiny but most unusual Mozarabic chapel, the **Ermita de San Baudelio**. Many of the best frescoes from the chapel were sold to the United States by an unscrupulous art dealer in the '20s, but they are now housed in the Prado Museum, Madrid. Still further east is **Almazán**, where the church in the main square contains a carving depicting the assassination of Thomas à Becket.

Beyond the great looping bends of the River Jalón stands the mysterious, aristocratic little town of **Medinaceli**, stranded on a high ridge at the end of a road. The first thing you notice, outlined on the skyline, is a monument that may seem oddly familiar. It is a Roman triple archway, used in stylised form as the road sign pointing to classical antiquities. From the top of the town the views are tremendous. Now greatly depopulated except for a colony of artists who are enthusiastically restoring the old mansions on the dilapidated Plaza Mayor, Medinaceli seems almost a ghost town. Beyond the Jalón gorges, on the main road where heavy lorries trundle between Zaragoza and Madrid, is the vast crumbling monastery of **Santa María de Huerta** (fine cloister and rose window). A newly renovated, motel–style *parador*, Tel (975) 32 70 11, stands on the outskirts of the town, a useful base in an area less than overrun with hotels.

WHERE TO STAY

AGUILAR DE CAMPOO

Hotel Valentín   ££
Av Generalísimo 21
34800   *Tel (968) 12 21 25; Fax (968) 12 24 42*

A vaguely alpine-looking structure on the edge of the old quarter where the scent of biscuits wafts. It is well run, with friendly staff and comfortably furnished to a good standard throughout. Pleasant coffee–shop and restaurant.
Open: all year **Rooms**: 50 **Credit/charge cards**: Amex, Diners, Eurocard, Visa

ALBERCA (LA)

Hotel París   £
La Chanca s/n
37624 La Alberca   *Tel (923) 43 70 56*

A simple, country-style hotel, restaurant, and bar (popular with locals). It has well-above-average bedrooms with good modern bathrooms.

Open: all year **Rooms**: 10 **Credit/charge cards**: none

Hostal Castillo £
Ctra Mogarraz s/n
37624 La Alberca *Tel (923) 41 50 01*

Near the entrance to the village, in a sunny position, this hotel has glorious mountain views from balconies. The lively, popular restaurant and bar serve local specialities, but otherwise facilities are limited. The modern wing is light and attractively decorated.

Open: all year **Rooms**: 9 **Credit/charge cards**: Visa, Eurocard

ARANDA DE DUERO

Hotel Los Bronces ££
Crta Madrid-Irún km 160
09400 Aranda de Duero *Tel (947) 50 08 50; Fax (947) 50 24 04*

A soundly run business hotel on a main exit road, traditionally furnished with stag's heads, wood panelling, and elaborate metal-work screens and light-fittings. It contains one of Aranda's best traditional *asador* restaurants, specialising in hearty Castilian roasts and excellent wines.

Open: all year **Rooms**: 29 **Credit/charge cards**: Amex, Diners, Eurocard, Visa

ASTORGA

Hotel Gaudí ££
Eduardo de Castro 6
24700 Astorga *Tel (987) 61 56 54*

Opposite the palace and cathedral, this solid hotel is a safe bet, with comfortable well-furnished rooms and friendly staff.

Open: all year **Rooms**: 35 **Credit/charge cards**: Amex, Diners, Eurocard, Visa

---

La Peseta £
Plaza de San Bartolomé 3
24700 Astorga *Tel (987) 61 72 75*

Within earshot of those clanking Maragatos figures on the town hall clock, this simple hotel and restaurant offers adequate rooms and more than adequate food, at very reasonable prices. A good base for exploring the old town and enjoying the views from the city ramparts.

Open: all year (restaurant closed Sun except in Aug and 15 Oct to 5 Nov) **Rooms**: 22 **Credit/charge cards**: Eurocard, Visa

AVILA

Parador Nacional Raimundo de Borgoña   ££
Marqués de Canales y Chozas 16
05001 Avila   *Tel (918) 21 13 40; Fax (918) 22 61 66*

Housed in a restored fifteenth-century palace by the city walls, the medieval interior is fairly contrived (as in many 'historic' *paradores*). The restaurant has a modern beamed ceiling and heavy iron candelabra. Some rooms are furnished with single four-poster beds. A relaxing retreat, though some reception staff suffer from Avila's all-embracing lethargy. The city walls rise right at the edge of the gardens (grandstand views from the battlement walkway), and there is a pretty courtyard with a *verraco* where you can have drinks.

Open: all year **Rooms**: 62 **Credit/charge cards**: Amex, Diners, Eurocard, Visa

Grand Hotel Palacio de Valderrabanos   £££
Plaza Catedral 9
05001 Avila   *Tel (918) 21 10 23; Fax (918) 25 16 91*

A smart, highly traditional hotel in a palace (a city 'sight' with a fine fifteenth-century doorway), right by the cathedral. It has a rather staid atmosphere, but is well-run, and furnished in grand style with many antiques. There is a good restaurant downstairs.

Open: all year **Rooms**: 73 **Credit/charge cards**: Amex, Diners, Eurocard, Visa

Mesón del Rastro   £
Plaza del Rastro 1
05001 Avila   *Tel (918) 21 12 18; Fax (918) 25 00 00*

Simple, clean and recently refurbished rooms above a popular beamed restaurant and bar, on a tiny square just inside the Puerta del Rastro.

Open: all year **Rooms**: 14 **Credit/charge cards**: Amex, Diners, Eurocard, Visa

BENAVENTE

Parador Rey Fernando II de León   ££
49600 Benavente   *Tel (988) 63 03 00; Fax (988) 63 03 03*

The best choice in town, though quite expensive for what it offers.

The site is historical, and the unusual snail-shell tower is a photo-genic feature, but basically the building (and fortunately its facilities) are modern. It is comfortable if rather heavily furnished, but staff are friendly and the views from here are excellent. Don't miss the quaint dungeon-like tower bar downstairs.

Open: all year **Rooms**: 30 **Credit/charge cards**: Amex, Diners, Eurocard, Visa

BURGO DE OSMA (EL)

Virrey II   ££
Calle Mayor 4
42300 El Burgo de Osma   *Tel (975) 34 13 11; Fax (975) 34 08 55*

This hotel is newly opened and ambitiously furnished in a slightly overblown style of chandeliers and marble, but is very comfortable and has luxurious bedrooms. Its location on the main road, is rather uninspiring. Run by the same owners as a well-known and long-established restaurant further up the road, the Virrey Palafox, which has one of the highest reputations for food in the area, it is good value for the facilities offered.

Open: all year **Rooms**: 52 **Credit/charge cards**: Amex, Diners, Eurocard, Visa

BURGOS

Landa Palace   £££
Carretera Madrid-Irun km 236
09000 Burgos   *Tel (947) 20 63 43; Fax (947) 26 46 76*

Poshest stop-over in Burgos is this privately owned 5-star, con-verted grandly from a medieval castle. It lacks much of a setting, being a mile or two out of the centre on a dull and busy exit road, and is inconvenient without a car. At weekends it is extensively used for wedding receptions and private parties. Rooms are spacious and sumptuous, with terrace access to quiet gardens. The facilities are suitably lavish and the restaurant is spoken of in hushed tones (milk-fed lamb is a speciality). Bar fare could be a little more imaginative at lunchtimes.

Open: all year **Rooms**: 42 **Facilities**: 2 swimming-pools
Credit/charge cards: Eurocard, Visa

Mesón del Cid   ££
Plaza Santa María 10
09003 Burgos   *Tel (947) 20 87 15; Fax (947) 26 94 60*

A less extravagant and excellent choice in Burgos, this hotel commands the very best of all locations, right in front of the west front of the cathedral. From some of the bedrooms you can see what time the doors open, and at night keep curtains and shutters open for spectacular floodlit views. The stylish interior successfully combines medieval and modern charms. A popular and lively restaurant with costumed staff is attached. Staff speak English, and there is even a private garage – a real bonus around the cathedral.

Open: all year **Rooms**: 29 **Credit/charge cards**: Amex, Diners, Eurocard, Visa

---

Cordon   £
Calle La Puebla 6
09004 Burgos   *Tel (947) 26 50 00; Fax (947) 20 02 69*

Tucked down a narrow old street in the most atmospheric part of town, this hotel is surprisingly modern inside, all chrome and black leatherette. Staff are friendly, rooms are quite adequate and for such a central location the price is low. Access and parking can be tricky.

Open: all year (no restaurant) **Rooms**: 35 **Credit/charge cards**: Amex, Diners, Eurocard, Visa

---

Norte y Londres   £
Plaza de Alonso Martínez 10
09003 Burgos   *Tel (947) 26 41 25*

A quiet, traditional, inexpensive hotel ideally placed at the back of the old town. Furnishings in the large foyer lounge are genteel, if a little faded.

Open: all year (no restaurant) **Rooms**: 50 **Credit/charge cards**: Amex, Diners, Eurocard, Visa

---

CANDELARIO

Hostal Cristi   £
Plaza Béjar 1
37710 Candelario   *Tel (923) 41 32 12*

A charming old house in a quiet but central part of the village. Characterful, family-run, welcoming and extremely good value. Don't expect luxury, but you will get a well-cooked supper, and peaceful rooms in a newer wing overlooking the garden.

Open: June-end Oct **Rooms**: 40 **Credit/charge cards**: Visa

CERVERA DE PISUERGA

Parador Fuentes Carriones   £target£
Crta de Ruesga
34840 Cervera de Pisuerga   *Tel (988) 87 00 75; Fax (988) 87 01 05*

Palencia's only national *parador* is a modern and rather stark grey-roofed building of no great architectural or decorative interest, but splendidly designed to take advantage of a magnificent lake-and-mountain location. All the rooms are spacious, with large box-like balconies and excellent views. The one serious drawback is that, as in so many Spanish hotels, no attention has been paid to interior sound-proofing. The beds creak!

Open: all year **Rooms**: 80 **Credit/charge cards**: Amex, Diners, Eurocard, Visa

CIUDAD RODRIGO

Parador Enrique II   ££
Plaza del Castillo 1
37500 Ciudad Rodrigo   *Tel (923) 46 01 50; Fax (923) 46 04 04*

Set in the old fortress overlooking the walls, reception and restaurant areas are predictably furnished in lumber-room baronial style, but the cosy bar downstairs has a more appealing intimate atmosphere, and the views, small gardens and bedrooms are certainly attractive.

Open: all year **Rooms**: 27 **Credit/charge cards**: Amex, Diners, Eurocard, Visa

Conde Rodrigo   ££
Plaza de San Salvador 9
37500 Ciudad Rodrigo   *Tel (923) 46 14 04; Fax (923) 46 14 08*

A clubby, traditional hotel in a lovely sixteenth-century palace near the cathedral. A darkish mode of repro and leatherette furnishings prevails within. Bedrooms are comfortable, but disappointingly unimaginative after the promising façade.

Open: all year **Rooms**: 35 **Credit/charge cards**: Amex, Diners, Visa, Eurocard

Conde Rodrigo II   ££
Huerta de las Viñas s/n
37500 Ciudad Rodrigo   *Tel (923) 48 04 48; Fax (923) 46 14 08*

The annexe, in fields just outside the town, is a modern unobtrusive building with the advantages of peace, good distant views (of the city walls and the back of the *parador!*), and country house facilities such as riding, a pool and tennis courts. It is much used for functions and wedding receptions at weekends.

Open: all year **Rooms**: 27 **Facilities**: swimming-pool, tennis courts, riding **Credit/charge cards**: Amex, Diners, Eurocard, Visa

COVARRUBIAS

Hotel Arlanza   ££
Plaza Mayor 11
09346 Covarrubias
Burgos   *Tel (947) 40 30 25; Fax (947) 40 63 59*

This charming hotel is a renovated mansion of character, with tiled stairways and brick arches. Tables and chairs are set under the shady porticos by the entrance, where you can sit and enjoy the action in the cobbled main square. Tour coaches use the hotel, and there is the occasional medieval banquet, but generally it seems extremely quiet. Bedrooms are quite simple, even plain.

Open: mid Mar-mid Dec **Rooms**: 40 **Credit/charge cards**: Amex, Diners, Eurocard, Visa

HOYOS DEL ESPINO

Mira de Gredos   £
05634 Hoyos del Espino
Avila   *Tel (918) 34 81 24*

Just a mile or two further along the road from the Parador de Gredos (see Navarredonda), in a sunny spot, this charming simple hotel is a much cheaper alternative. Newly decorated rooms, furnished in green fabrics and pine, have excellent modern bathrooms. Terraces with balcony views from the lounge and restaurant overlook the mountains.

Open: all year, except Oct **Rooms**: 16 **Credit/charge cards**: none

LEON

Hostal de San Marcos   £££
Pl San Marcos 7
24001 León   *Tel (987) 23 73 00; Fax (987) 23 34 58*

This magnificent building houses one of Spain's finest hotels. It is a former pilgrim hostel and hospital, now a luxurious *parador*, and one of the city's major sights. Public areas are vast and sumptuous, with ancient carpets, tapestries, and *artesonado* ceilings. The older bedrooms with their three-foot thick stone walls and antique furnishings

489

are the most interesting, but the modern ones are very spacious and comfortable too. Rear rooms have quiet river and garden views. The Rey Sancho restaurant serves excellent classic Castilian specialities, including trout.

Open: all year **Rooms**: 253 **Credit/charge cards**: Amex, Diners, Eurocard, Visa

---

Hotel-Residencia Quindos   ££
Avenida José Antonio 24
24002 León   *Tel (987) 23 62 00; Fax (987) 24 22 01*

A smart modern building just five minutes towards town from San Marcos, offering pleasant and well-equipped accommodation. It is on a fairly busy corner, but the atmosphere is quiet inside. Stylish décor is a mix of traditional and modern. The restaurant (under separate management) is next door.

Open: all year **Rooms**: 96 **Credit/charge cards**: Amex, Diners, Eurocard, Visa

---

Hotel-Residencia París   £
Generalísimo 20
24002 León   *Tel (987) 23 86 00; Fax (987) 27 15 72*

In the heart of the city just off Plaza Santo Domingo, the hotel is well placed for sightseeing, but in a busy location. Parking is difficult. A quaint and creaking place with wrought-iron balconies, not smart, but it has character and a certain faded charm. A café-bar and small sitting-room are downstairs. Try to get a quietish room at the side.

Open: all year **Rooms**: 81 **Credit/charge cards**: Amex, Diners, Eurocard, Visa

---

MEDINA DE POMAR

Hotel Las Merindades   ££
Plaza Somovilla s/n
09500 Medina de Pomar   *Tel (947) 11 08 22*

Efforts have been made to personalise this well-kept old house on the main square with plants, ceramics and rustic furnishings. It is only a minute or two from the old quarter. Staff are friendly, and the restaurant is the best in town.

Open: all year **Rooms**: 23 **Credit/charge cards**: Amex, Diners, Eurocard, Visa

MONZON DE CAMPOS

Castillo de Monzón ££
34410 Monzón de Campos *Tel (988) 80 80 75*

This hilltop castle a few miles north of Palencia has been converted into a provincial *parador*, though it is not in the national chain. Inside, it is quite grand in a Spanish medieval style, though it conspicuously lacks the personal touch, and service is somewhat offhand.

Open: all year (restaurant closed Mon) **Rooms**: 10 **Credit/charge cards**: none

NAVARREDONDA

Parador de Gredos ££
05132 Navarredonda *Tel (918) 34 80 48; Fax (918) 34 82 05*

This has the distinction of being the very first *parador*, opened in 1928, allegedly a brilliant wheeze dreamt up by King Alfonso XIII while out hunting. It is a stern building of grey slate and stone, screened from traffic noise by pinewoods, but easily accessible on the C-500. Many rooms have magnificent views. Inside, a mountain look of leather and hunting trophies prevails. There is a notable lack of frills, but it is comfortable and well-run, if faintly austere and old-fashioned.

Open: all year **Rooms**: 77 **Credit/charge cards**: Amex, Diners, Eurocard, Visa

PEDRAZA DE LA SIERRA

La Posada Don Mariano ££
Mayor 14
40172 Pedraza de la Sierra
Segovia *Tel (911) 50 98 86*

Recently opened, this deceptively simple two-star hotel is on the castle road. Charmingly furnished in an unusually lavish *Homes and Gardens* style, some rooms have painted furniture and all are different, if quite small. It does not undercharge for its wares, but Pedraza is that sort of place. Some noise transmission from bar on ground floor.

Open: all year **Rooms**: 18 **Credit/charge cards**: Diners, Eurocard, Visa

491

PUEBLA DE SANABRIA

Parador Puebla de Sanabria   **££**
Crta del Lago
49300 Zamora   *Tel (988) 62 00 01; Fax (988) 62 03 51*

A modern *parador* has been built to service the needs of this resort area. Located in a quiet area towards the lower town, it has views of, though not the atmosphere of, the old village. Furnishings inside are plain, and parts could do with a facelift, but it is adequate and comfortable, in rustic mountain style.

Open: all year **Rooms**: 44 **Credit/charge cards**: Amex, Diners, Eurocard, Visa

RIAZA

La Trucha   **££**
Avenida Dr Tapia 17
40500 Riaza   *Tel (911) 55 00 61*

A simple, good value but very civilised and friendly hotel with rooms built ranch-style around a garden and pools. Bedrooms are peaceful and attractively decorated with green fabrics. As the name suggests, local trout are a speciality.

Open: all year **Rooms**: 30 **Facilities**: swimming-pools **Credit/ charge cards**: Eurocard, Visa

SALAMANCA

Parador de Salamanca   **£££**
Teso de la Feria 2 al 48
37008 Salamanca   *Tel (923) 26 87 00; Fax (923) 21 54 38*

The building takes no architectural prizes, being a characterless modern block, but it scores highly on location (best views of the city), facilities (spacious well-equipped rooms and a pool), and friendliness. The tariff is steepish (it is a 4-star *parador*), but compared with the top city centre hotels it represents good value, and has plenty of convenient parking space.

Open: all year **Rooms**: 108 **Facilities**: swimming-pool **Credit/ charge cards**: Amex, Diners, Eurocard, Visa

Hotel Emperatriz   **££**
Compañía 4/Doctrinos 7
37000 Salamanca   *Tel (923) 21 92 00*

A less expensive alternative in the old quarter, a quaint building in a 'studenty' location of *tapas* bars and narrow streets. Access and parking are tricky, and the area is quite noisy. Simply furnished; the dining-room is quite dark and cramped.

Open: all year **Rooms**: 37 **Credit/charge cards**: None

Hostal Tormes   £
Rua Mayor 20
37000 Salamanca   *Tel (923) 21 96 83*

A friendly little *hostal* with clean, basic rooms overlooking a pedestrianised street with lots of outdoor cafés.

Open: all year **Rooms**: 12 **Credit/charge cards**: none

SAN EMILIANO

Asturias   £
24144 San Emiliano   *Tel (987) 59 60 50*

A peaceful, remote village handily poised for exploring the Somiedo wildlife reserve near the Puerto de Pajares, or the Luna valley to the south. Here you will find a simple family-run small hotel, where most of the male population of the village congregates to watch football in the bar. The back rooms, quite spartan but clean and light, overlook pastoral scenes of grazing livestock and rocky crags. It is a truly Spanish experience (no English spoken).

Open: all year **Rooms**: 24 **Credit/charge cards**: none

SANTO DOMINGO DE SILOS

Tres Coronas   ££
Plaza Mayor 6
09610 Santo Domingo de Silos   *Tel (947) 38 07 27*

Close to the monastery and full of eighteenth-century charm, this grandly portalled stone building and its coat of arms dominate the village centre. Well-kept, with darkish period furnishings and small but pretty bedrooms. There is an attractive bar and restaurant area.

Open: all year **Rooms**: 16 **Credit/charge cards**: Amex, Eurocard, Visa

SEGOVIA

El Hidalgo   £
José Canalejas 5
Plaza Iglesia de San Martín
Segovia   *Tel (911) 42 81 90*

Tasteful rooms with whitewashed walls and parquet floors above a restaurant in a thirteenth-century mansion with sixteenth-century additions and *esgrafiado* walls. The hotel is tucked away behind the Romanesque church of San Martín. All rooms have bathrooms, and there is a good restaurant downstairs. In good weather you can eat in the intimate courtyard.

Open: all year; restaurant closed 15 Jan–15 Feb **Rooms**: 12 **Credit/charge cards**: Amex, Mastercard, Visa

---

Las Sirenas   ££
Juan Bravo
40001 Segovia   *Tel (911) 43 40 11*

This hotel is across the square from El Hidalgo, on the main *paseo* route. The interior, though pretty, does not quite live up to the expectations of the *esgrafiado* façade with its coat of arms, but the accommodation is both convenient and comfortable. The black and white corridors are painted pistacchio and white. Bedrooms have wooden floors, simple candelabra and pale green bedspreads.

Open: all year **Rooms**: 39 **Credit/charge cards**: Amex, Diners, Mastercard, Visa

---

Los Lingjes   ££
Doctor Velazco 9
40003 Segovia   *Tel (911) 43 12 01*

An eleventh-century mansion on a steep, quiet street below Plaza Mayor, with views of the surrounding countryside from some rooms. The reception area has varnished earthenware tiles, monastic benches, and a copper cauldron in an ancient fireplace. In contrast, the cafeteria is disappointingly modern. Rooms are simple but comfortable and all have bathrooms. The hotel is currently being extended.

Open: all year **Rooms**: 55 **Credit/charge cards**: Amex, Diners, Eurocard, Mastercard, Visa

---

SORIA

Parador Antonio Machado   £££
Parque del Castillo
42005 Soria   *Tel (975) 21 34 45; Fax (975) 21 28 49*

This hotel commands the best views, though you need transport to get to it up the tortuous roads. It is a modern building which has eschewed the standard *parador* furnishings of dark wood in favour of lighter, more modern fittings. The interior is spacious, airy, and quite stylish. Huge picture-windows make the most of the views, but keep them shut at night: it's chilly up here. Sorian specialities like *trucha escabecha* (marinaded trout) are served in the restaurant, as well as a good line in fresh fruit at breakfast.

Open: all year **Rooms**: 34 **Credit/charge cards**: Amex, Diners, Eurocard, Visa

---

Mesón Leonor   **££**
Paseo del Mirón
42005 Soria   *Tel (975) 22 02 50; Fax (975) 22 99 53*

A fine raised location just outside the town on the Numancia road. It is a pleasant building, not particularly old, but in traditional Spanish style, and the location is quiet, though internal noise includes a disco. Comfortable, well-managed and friendly – you may get a peach liqueur after dinner.

Open: all year **Rooms**: 32 **Credit/charge cards**: Amex, Diners, Eurocard, Visa

TORDESILLAS

Parador de Tordesillas   **££**
47100 Tordesillas   *Tel (983) 77 00 51; Fax (983) 77 10 13*

There is a vaguely Italianate colonnaded villa look to this unobtrusive pantiled modern building in a secluded pine-grove setting about one kilometre south-west of town. Leather and wall-hangings, and stern oil-paintings deck the public areas, but though perfectly comfortable, it has a slightly institutional feel to it. There is a significant business trade and a good restaurant.

Open all year **Rooms**: 73 **Credit/charge cards**: Amex, Diners, Eurocard, Visa

---

El Montico   **££**
Apartado 12
47100 Tordesillas   *Tel (983) 77 06 51; Fax (983) 77 07 51*

A business hotel with spacious rooms and good facilities set in a new development amid pine trees, three kilometres towards Valladolid. It has a good restaurant and wine-list.

Open: all year **Rooms**: 55 **Facilities**: swimming-pool, tennis **Credit/charge cards**: Amex, Diners, Eurocard, Visa

TORO

Juan II   **££**
Paseo del Espolón 1
49800 Zamora   *Tel (988) 69 03 00; Fax (988) 69 23 76*

This hotel by the collegiate church commands wonderful views over the Duero valley. It is of no great interest inside, and public areas are institutionally furnished, but bedrooms are quite adequate. The pretty public rose gardens outside are a plus point for warm evenings.

Open: all year **Rooms**: 41 **Facilities**: swimming-pool **Credit/charge cards**: Amex, Diners, Eurocard, Visa

VALENCIA DE DON JUAN

Villegas II   **£**
Palacio 10
24200 Valencia de Don Juan   *Tel (987) 75 01 61*

This small hotel has the air of a private villa. It is set in tranquil gardens with a pool. The reception is tiled with blue Andalucian *azulejos*, and everywhere is personally furnished with plants and pictures. Bedrooms are unusually stylish and light with big, blue-tiled bathrooms. (Villegas I, incidentally, is a far less attractive modern block further along the road.)

Open: Mar-mid Jan **Rooms**: 6 **Facilities**: swimming-pool **Credit/charge cards**: none

VILLAFRANCA DEL BIERZO

Parador del Bierzo   **££**
Avenida de Calvo Sotelo
24500 Villafranca del Bierzo   Tel (987) 54 01 75; Fax (987) 54 00 10

A good base from which to explore the Bierzo region, this small modern *parador* on the outskirts of town is modest in style, but very pleasant inside, though unfortunately it lacks the ambience and views of the distinguished old quarter (within walking distance).

Open: all year **Rooms**: 40 **Credit/charge cards**: Amex, Diners, Eurocard, Visa

ZAMORA

Parador Condes de Alba y Aliste   **£££**
Plaza Viriato 5
49001 Zamora   *Tel (988) 51 44 97; Fax (988) 53 00 63*

A justly famous member of the national hotel chain, in a fine fifteenth-century palace in the centre of the old quarter. Its surroundings, though urban, are appropriately grand. Inside the *parador* the
most notable feature is a large, dignified patio cloister, whose symmetry can seem severe at first. Public rooms are on the ground floor,
bedrooms above. Furnishings adopt a suitably baronial mode of
stone, wood, and leather, with many antiques. Even if you do not
stay here, it is worth peering in, at least for a drink.

Open: all year **Rooms**: 27 **Facilities**: swimming-pool **Credit/
charge cards**: Amex, Diners, Eurocard, Visa

Hostería Real de Zamora　　　　　　　　　　　　　　　　**££**
Cuesta de Pizarro 7
49001 Zamora　　　　　　　　　　　　　　*Tel (988) 53 45 45*

Recently opened, this charming historic mansion with Jewish and
Conquistador connections has stylish bedrooms and excellent facilities. Its great plus is a colonnaded patio of Andalucían style with
tiles, pools and potted plants, where there is a well-established
restaurant called Pizarro (recommendable). The setting is quiet, but
noise from the restaurant may affect some bedrooms on the upper
gallery.

Open: all year **Rooms**: 15 **Credit/charge cards**: Eurocard, Visa

EXTREMADURA

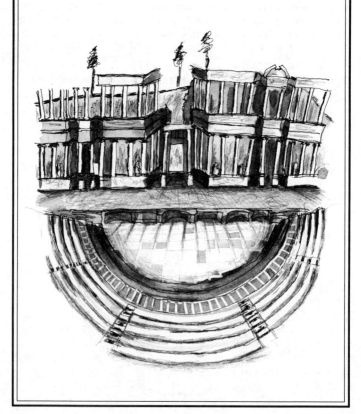

THE name means 'beyond the Duero'; for many Spaniards it is the back of beyond. These underpopulated tracts of land spread over a vast area about half the size of neighbouring Portugal. It is definitely not on Spain's main tourist beat, but adventurous travellers who explore this strange terrain find their curiosity rewarded: Extremadura has a distinctive and fascinating flavour.

It is a transitional province as far as inhabitants are concerned. In the north the people have Castilian traits: reserve, hauteur, dignity. They like their space and do not chatter to strangers. Further west and south, Extremadurans are more relaxed – the mix of garrulous Andalucian charm and a Portuguese friendliness to newcomers may be a welcome change if you have spent time in Castile. Very few people speak any English, even in tourist offices.

There are no large cities today. Even the capitals of the two Extremadura provinces, Badajoz and Cáceres, have an almost village-like quality within their carapace of modern suburbs. But in Roman times Extremadura was an important place: in 25 BC Augusta Emerita (now Mérida), capital of the Iberian province of Lusitania, was founded here on the Silver Way (Via de la Plata). It was said to be the ninth most important city in the Roman empire, and many of its monuments can still be seen scattered among the undistinguished rubble of the twentieth century. For those who like classical antiquities, it is a must.

More generally appealing are the smaller towns, whose ancient quarters are well preserved and unspoilt by tourism. The best are Trujillo, Guadalupe, Plasencia and Old Cáceres. Other places to look out for are Alcántara, Coria and Olivenza in the west; Zafra and Jerez de los Caballeros in the south; and Hervás, Garganta la Olla and Jarandilla de la Vera in the eastern mountains. While touring you will pass through wild mountains, lush valleys, rocky moorland, and sparsely wooded, almost African-looking plains.

The economy is mostly based on agriculture, especially stock-rearing. Sheep, fighting bulls, horses, and the pigs used to make the prized local hams and sausages, roam over huge open spaces which, parched to barren savanna in late summer, are a mass of wild flowers in spring. Cork-and holm-oak forests, vineyards, sunflower fields, olive groves, cereal fields and tobacco plantations dapple the landscape, watered by the vast river systems of the Tagus (Río Tajo) and the Guadiana. But it is not and never has been easy to make a

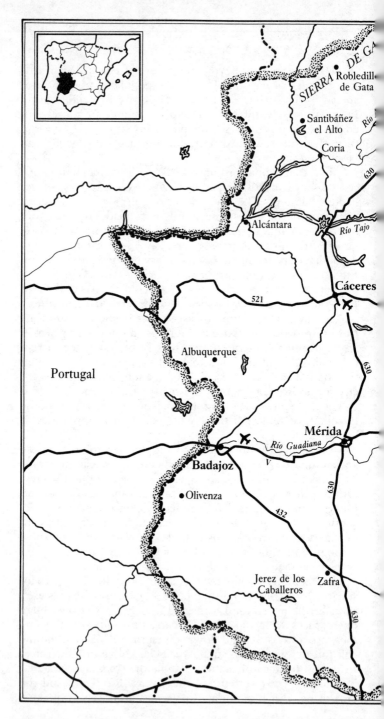

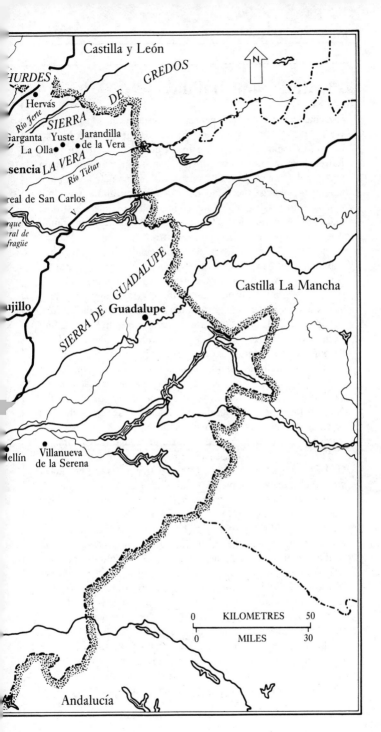

Planning your holiday

Extremadura is still comparatively obscure to most foreign visitors, as it is indeed to most Spaniards. Few British holiday brochures mention the region by name, and if you can place Extremadura accurately on a map, chances are you know Spain pretty well. For all that, the tourist authorities now go to great lengths to publicise the attractions of the region, and interest in it is steadily increasing. The Latin connection is particularly strong; many of Extremadura's foreign visitors come from South America to find their roots and relatives.

Most people visit Extremadura independently, by car, often combining an exploratory foray with a tour of Portugal, Andalucía, or Castile. The quickest way to reach Extremadura is to fly to Madrid, then drive down the NV main highway which steers a fume-laden course towards Portugal through Trujillo, Mérida and Badajoz. Alternative fly-drive routes to Extremadura lead across the less well-maintained roads of Portugal from Lisbon, or northwards from Seville. The area is difficult to explore by public transport, though you can reach the larger towns (Cáceres and Mérida, for example) on rail or coach excursions from Madrid. The railway runs more or less parallel to the NV, linking Cáceres, Mérida and Badajoz. Generally the bus services are more convenient than the trains. An express bus service connects Cáceres with Madrid in around four hours.

The main trunk roads, such as that from Madrid to Portugal via Badajoz, are heavily used, but the minor roads can be almost worryingly lonely. In some areas rural roads are being upgraded.

Extremadura's main attractions are half a dozen or so fairly small historic towns, and if many people converge on the same place at once, the pressure on sights and limited accommodation may build up. You could see all the main centres, and get a taste of Extremadura's scenery and minor towns, in eight or ten days.

The best bases for charm and choice of accommodation are **Trujillo, Guadalupe** and **Zafra**. Those who love classical antiquities may want to linger at least one or probably two days in Mérida. Wilderness seekers could spend several days exploring the remote and little-known hilly districts on the Extremaduran borders: the Sierra de Gata, Las Hurdes, or the Sierra de Guadalupe. The Monfragüe Nature Park is particularly good for spotting wildlife. Some of the region's most beautiful scenery is in the northern valleys of La Vera and the Jerte.

Lower priced accommodation is limited: almost non-existent outside the main towns. But the region does have half a dozen good *paradores*, and several excellent independent hotels. Given that they are so widely scattered, it is as well to book ahead in high season.

Fly-drive holidays are the most convenient way to see Extremadura. Several specialist operators offer touring holidays based on Extremaduran *paradores*, usually combined with Portuguese, Andalucian or Castilian destinations. Ramblers Holidays offer a walking tour based in Trujillo and the Jerte Valley.

The countryside looks at its best in spring and early summer, before the sun bakes it to a crisp. Winters can be chilly on this exposed tableland, but in general the climate is not as extreme as the higher central parts of Castile. Extremadura holds some unusual annual events you may want to link with a trip. During the summer a classical drama festival takes place in Mérida, in the appropriate setting of the Roman amphitheatre. On 12 October (Columbus Day) Guadalupe renews its links with the New World with a procession. The quiet villages of La Vera have some startling customs. Valverde de la Vera still conducts a watered-down version of a masochistic flagellation ceremony on Maundy Thursday, in which hooded penitents are each strapped to a cross in a ghastly parody of the Crucifixion. Villanueva de la Vera has a strange Shrovetide festival called Pero Palo, associated with casting out devils. The festival recently attracted some adverse publicity when a British tourist took up tabloid cudgels against a brutal ritual in which a donkey is trampled to death.

Extremaduran cuisine is hearty rather than refined, but the local ingredients are certainly good, particularly pork products from the pigs that forage for acorns – they are also apocryphally reputed to enjoy the odd snake! As a wine-producing region Extremadura is a bit of a let-down. An exception to look out for is a potent pale red or white brew called Pitarra which is readily available in the Plasencia area.

● **Regional tourist board**: Director General de Turismo, Cárdenas II, 06800 Mérida, Tel (924) 31 30 11. **Tourist information offices** Trujillo has an especially helpful and well-stocked office conveniently located in the Plaza Mayor. Tourist information offices can be found in Guadalupe, Cáceres, Badajoz, Plasencia and Zafra. All of Extremadura's towns of interest, and touring regions are described and illustrated in a series of handy separate leaflets which include a map on which major sights are plotted; some are available in English.

living here. Land ownership remained largely feudal long after the Middle Ages. The aristocracy stripped Extremadura's wealth to finance crusades against the Moors, then the powerful Mesta shepherds (see Castilla y León) drove their Merino flocks into the province from Castile to graze the land bare.

When rumours of new-found land across the ocean reached Extremadura in the closing years of the fifteenth century, local youths leapt at the chance of a fresh start and wealth beyond their wildest dreams. Many of the Conquistadors who claimed Central and South America for Spain came from these landlocked western marches. Those who survived brought back enough treasure to rock the Spanish economy and transformed their home towns with grand palaces and churches.

Ardent religiosity was almost as much of a spur as fame and avarice to these adventurers. They embarked on their ruthless and desperate voyages with an almost missionary zeal. And when they succeeded, they thanked God for it. The great Marian shrine at Guadalupe is a classic example of the extreme nature of Extremaduran Catholic fervour. Local piety, sometimes taken to maudlin excess, shows also in Extremadura's accomplished religious painters, Luis de Morales ('the Divine') and the less sickly Zurbarán.

NORTHERN EXTREMADURA

Plasencia (H)

The main routes to Extremadura from the north and east (Salamanca or Avila) converge on the old town of Plasencia, which makes a useful touring base for a day or two. As in many Spanish towns, the outskirts are off-putting, but a wander round the old quarter will soon reveal unexpected charms. First follow the main Avila-Cáceres road and park in a sidestreet as close as you can to the cathedral, an easy landmark looming above the turreted town walls. From there you can walk up steps to the old quarter of town.

The old town stands on a fortified knoll partly encircled by the River Jerte, at the western tip of the Sierra de Gredos. Obligatory sightseeing here is limited, but it is a relaxing place to explore. A great number of tiny bars are tucked down quaint alleyways, where little snacks (*pinchos*) are served (free) with a glass of the deceptively powerful Pitarra.

On Tuesdays you will find it livelier than usual, when the market takes place and locals flock into town. It is the centre of an important agricultural area.

The **cathedral**, is actually two cathedrals – old and new – joined together. Bits of it are thirteenth-century Romanesque, other parts Gothic, and it culminates in a Renaissance plateresque façade like a lacy dinner shirt. Inside, look for the splendid inlaid choir-stalls by Rodrigo Alemán. From the fine cloisters you can see the chapterhouse capped by a pyramidal tower of crocketed, fish-scale tiles.

Outside the cathedral you find yourself in a quiet square surrounded by lovely buildings. Opposite is the sixteenth-century **Dean's House**, with orange trees in front and a strange balconied corner window that appears to be scooped from the walls. A few steps away you find the Renaissance **Mirabel Palace** with a beautiful patio surrounded by arches, and the church of **San Vicente**, where storks have colonised all but one of its towers. Steep cobbled streets of humbler white houses lead to the walls, which are now an integral part of the town buildings.

Eating out and accommodation

When you are ready for a rest make for the lively Plaza Mayor, where the tables outside the Goya Bar make a good vantage point or thread your way through to the backstreets and search for some of the dark *tapas* bars (Calle Pantalón makes a good start). If you want to stay here you will be made comfortable at the traditional Hotel Alfonso XIII near the cathedral or, in the old town, at the friendly Hostal Rincón Extremeño.

La Vera (H)

North-east of Plasencia, the minor C-501 signed Jarandilla skirts the southern shoulder of the Sierra de Gredos, and trickles towards Avila through a fertile suntrap of maize, olives, vines, fruit-trees and the spinach-like leaves of tobacco plants. The whaleback mass of the Bejar hills shelters the villages of La Vera from cold north winds, and dozens of mountain streams (*gargantas*) obligingly irrigate the valley side on their way to join the broad River Tiétar on its sunny plains. Several minor detours are worth taking. At Jaraiz de la Vera a short drive northwards brings you to **Garganta la Olla**, a showcase village of picturesque old houses with jutting wooden balconies. The next turning off the main road, at Cuacos, leads to the **Monasterio de Yuste** where the Emperor Charles (Carlos) V spent his last years pottering about on gouty limbs, mending watches and morbidly contemplating the next world.

You can visit the unassuming monastery-palace of Yuste on its sunny hillside, and wander through the small spartan rooms, see the special chair where Charles propped up his aching legs, peer through the windows, each pane with its own beautifully made little shutter, and visit the bedroom where he died, still shrouded in the same black drapes.

Jarandilla de la Vera (H), a few kilometres further east, is a pleasant little agricultural town where you may see bunches of tobacco leaves, curled and brown, or red peppers hanging to dry in the sun. The local castle has been turned into a *parador*.

Two other roads north-east of Plasencia pick their way through valleys in the westerly spurs of the Sierra de Gredos. The N-110 is the better road for touring, giving a charming drive along the **Jerte Valley** through cherry orchards (best at blossom time in March but also attractive in autumn) and terraced olive groves. Just before Jerte a side-route curls through the wooded hills towards the unusual village of **Hervás** which still has a well-preserved Jewish quarter. The community was expelled in the late fifteenth century when the Catholic Monarchs, flushed with intolerance after their final conquest of the Moors, banished all Jews from Spain.

Coria and the Sierra de Gata

North-west Extremadura is remote, peaceful and beautiful, though again it has suffered badly from lack of investment and many of the farmers are very poor. You rarely see tractors or expensive machinery here; panniered mules and donkeys are still the norm.

Tortuous little lanes make for slow progress through the green hills, terraced with olives and vines and orange-trees. Some of the villages such as **Robledillo de Gata** are built of mud-brick and shale, with red pantiled roofs. Others are stone – such as **Santibáñez el Alto** which gives you a marvellous panorama of the surrounding countryside – or whitewashed, like **Gata**. Nearly all the roads are marked with green ('scenic route') stripes on the Michelin map, and when you get there, you will see why.

Coria, further south on the River Alagón, is in dustier, more intensively farmed countryside. It is not worth a long detour, but if you find yourself nearby, the Roman walls (rebuilt in the Middle Ages), castle, white-painted old town and unusual cathedral make a pleasant diversion for an hour or so. The walls are alleged to be the best extant examples of Roman construction, but the cathedral will impress more. A frivolous plateresque façade leads into a vast single aisle, the largest in Spain. An enormous and hideous gilt altarpiece glitters sombrely behind fine iron screens.

Monfragüe Nature Park

The Tagus flows through this lonely region, joined by the Tiétar from the north-east. It is the only nature park in Extremadura, and is a former bandit stronghold, that has been wrenched from a powerful local paper industry with vested interests that did not include wildlife or environmental concerns. It is a marvellous preserve of many different species, particularly birds of prey and some scarce reptiles and amphibians.

It is quite difficult to visit the interior of the park because effectively only two roads traverse it, but if you follow the minor road CC-911 along the grand bends of the River Tiétar to the junction with the C-524, you get some idea of the terrain. There is an information kiosk at the nearby village of **Villareal de San Carlos**, where you can find out about nature trails and camping. Heading south for Trujillo, past the Sanctuario de Monfragüe (there is a castle viewpoint and chapel here), you may well catch sight of vultures or eagles soaring high over the southern plains.

The road to Trujillo leads through a strange, monotonous landscape of sparsely planted cork-and holm-oaks and weirdly twisted thorn-trees that look as though they have stepped from the pages of some illustrated fairy-tale.

CONQUISTADOR TOWNS

Trujillo (H), cradle of the Conquistadors

In the Plaza Major stands a statue of Francisco Pizarro, conqueror of Peru (see the Conquistadors, page 512). With his ludicrous plumed helmet he looks more like a court jester than a conquering hero, and his horse carries equally strange headgear. In the mid-sixteenth century about six hundred of

Trujillo's citizens were carving out personal kingdoms in the Americas. When the survivors swaggered home with their Inca brides and chests of treasure, they built splendid palaces all over town. The Plaza Mayor is lined with them, façades laden with elaborate coats of arms.

Today, Trujillo is as classy and as proud of itself as it ever was. Deservedly so, for it is the most attractive town in Extremadura. No hideous high-rise suburbs mar its perfect castle-crowned outline seen from the approach-roads. And inside the old walls, sensitive restoration has revitalised its ancient buildings without turning it into an architectural zoo solely for tourists.

Start at the irregularly shaped **Plaza Major** (where you can park – an attendant may ask you for a few pesetas as you leave). The Marquess de la Conquista's Palace, built by Francisco Pizarro's brother, has an unusual Renaissance corner window and carvings illustrating the conquest of the New World, including many sad, chained slaves. The House of Chains has real shackles on its walls, allegedly brought by grateful Christians freed from Moorish yokes. Nuns will take you round the Dukes of San Carlos Palace, now a convent, to see the arcaded inner patio. Do not miss the Orellana Pizarro Palace, just off the main square, with its plateresque gallery.

Up steep cobbled streets past plainer houses, and more escutcheoned mansions, is the church of **Santa María**, where the colourful 24-panelled retable over the altar is attributed to Fernando Gallego. To see it properly you need to stump up a few pesetas for some illumination (look for the light-box near the altar). The colours will sparkle as though you have just looked into a kaleidoscope. Beyond the church is the solid Moorish castle. It has good views from its ramparts.

The main square is a split-level affair, linked by flights of steps. There is a very good well-stocked tourist office on the lower level, with plenty of leaflets and maps covering the whole of Extremadura. If Trujillo is your first stop in central Extremadura, it is a convenient place to plan the rest of your explorations. Up the steps, under arcades, several small restaurants and *hostales* with tables outside suggest an excellent spot for a rest and a meal, with a dais-like vantage point over the square.

Eating out and accommodation

A good bet for an inexpensive meal is the Mesón La Troya, a well-established and popular place serving regional dishes (*tapas* and extra helpings may appear free of charge). You can also eat well at Pilete, on the lower level of the square. There are two small *hostales* near Mesón La Troya: Pizarro, Tel (927) 32 13 64, which also has an attractive restaurant overlooking the square and La Cadena, Tel (927) 32 14 63. But the smartest place to stay is the converted convent *parador*, Santa Clara, a few minutes' walk through the cobbled streets. The restaurant has a good reputation for local dishes.

Guadalupe – Our Lady of the New World (H)

The Guadalupe legend is typical of many Spanish shrines. A thirteenth-century herdsman wandered through the forest in search of his lost cow, saw a vision, and stumbled on a buried image of the Virgin Mary, allegedly carved by St Luke. The Virgin assisted Alfonso XI in a battle against the Moors, and he built a great monastery in gratitude.

Subsequent monarchs enriched the building, but much of its present-day lavishness is due to the Conquistadors, who adopted Guadalupe as their chosen shrine and toiled over the mountain passes laden with New World treasure to pile at the feet of the Virgin. Columbus brought a batch of American Indian converts for baptism here, and Cortés took the cult of Nuestra Señora de Guadalupe (Our Lady of Guadalupe) to Mexico, where she is still the patron saint. In the Spanish-speaking world, Guadalupe attracts the faithful from far and wide, especially from Latin America.

The monastery's remote hilltop setting adds to its romance. It really does feel like a pilgrimage to get there along those winding mountain roads, even by modern transport. A good vantage point is the little chapel where pilgrims knelt to pray, the **Ermita del Humilladero**, about four kilometres north on the road to Navalmoral.

The town itself is still no more than a village; you can still enjoy strolling through balconied backstreets and leave the tourist coaches behind in the central square.

Visiting the monastery

The monastery is a rich brownstone building adorned with spires and battlements and a swirling tracery of unusual Moorish Gothic carving. Fortified with ramparts and bristling with towers, it covers several acres and encompasses many separate parts added over the centuries. Franciscan monks now occupy the monastery, and one section of it is a

509

fine hotel. Have a look inside the church if it is open – it is not included in your tour. El Greco's son Jorge Theotocopuli did some of the work on the carved altarpiece.

The ticket office is stacked with multi-lingual guidebooks, postcards and mementos; if you turn up on a Friday morning you will get a pleasant surprise – entrance is free! The tours are highly professional and very well organised, with guides who are both knowledgable and enthusiastic about their subject (but alas most tours are in Spanish). The route is carefully stage-managed to keep your eyes popping right to the dramatic finale.

First the tour groups file obediently towards the frescoed Charter Salon, used as a museum for illuminated manuscripts, then through a Mudejar cloister of horseshoe arches. Then follows a room full of magnificent embroidered robes and copes, on which flowers, birds and religious scenes are interspersed with grim skulls and reminders of mortality. The painting and sculpture museum comes next – depictions of nailings and scourgings in the best Christian tradition. The next stop is the barrel-vaulted sacristy, where every inch is smothered with baroque frescoes and some of Zurbarán's best religious art. The great Turkish lamp swinging from the cupola of Sant Jerónimo's shrine at the far end was captured during the Battle of Lepanto.

Finally, with suitable melodrama, the guide relinquishes his charges to a brown-robed monk, and the visitors troop solemnly upstairs for the grand denouement. In an anteroom they admire Our Lady's treasure: jewelled reliquaries and gorgeous ceremonial crowns. Then they process into the locked last room, the Camarín, the sacred shrine itself. This is an ornate, baroque semicircular chamber only a few feet across, but crammed with rich wood inlay, gilt and jasper. Our Lady of Guadalupe is a small, simple figure of blackened wood with a serious expression, like some Byzantine icon.

The monk invites everyone in the group to kneel and kiss a shiny round plaque dangling from the Virgin's robes which he mops between visitors. Nearly everyone does so, with apparent reverence. If you do not want to take part in this disconcerting ritual, stand somewhere near the back.

Eating out and accommodation

There are plenty of bars and cafés, handily placed to catch the tourist trade by the monastery entrance. A few steps take you away from the crowds. For a well-prepared meal, try the Mesón El Cordero (not Mon or Feb) in Calle Convento.

There are plenty of cheap *hostales* around the main square too, but for a more interesting stay, choose the nearby *parador*, or stay in the monastery itself, at the Hospedería Real Monasterio. You will have to book ahead to stay at either of these; neither has many rooms and they are very popular.

Cáceres – monumental capital (H)

The approach to Extremadura's northern capital is disappointing; the surrounding countryside is flattish and the modern town full of dreary high-rise blocks. You have to battle through a confusing belt of new development and one-way systems before you get into old Cáceres, the part all visitors want to see. It is best to leave cars outside the walls, perhaps near the tourist office on the main square.

Shrouded in its ancient walls, the old town is a solid core of golden stone, escutcheoned palaces and churches. The grand mansions were the homes of rich nobles. Some won their spurs in battles against the Moors; the Military Order of Santiago was founded in Cáceres in 1170. Others gained wealth later in the New World. Each aristocratic palace was a tangible symbol of its builder's power and success, and was a way of cocking a snook at a neighbour. The families of Cáceres became such quarrelsome, vainglorious rivals that Isabel the Catholic ordered the high towers of their houses to be chopped off to take them down a peg or two.

Not many of the houses are open, though you may be lucky enough to glimpse a Moorish patio or two if the gates are ajar. A couple of palaces contain small museums. You can see round the old city quite easily within an hour or so, admiring this doorway or that window, and peering over the new town from the pierced walls. The main buildings are the two **Golfines palaces** (lower and upper: Palacio de los Golfines de Abajo, and Palacio de los Golfines de Arriba); the **House of the Storks** (Casa de las Cigüeñas), still with its tower intact; and the **House of the Weather Vane** (Casa de las Veletas), built over an Arabic cistern on horseshoe arches (it has a provincial museum inside). The two churches of note are Gothic **Santa María** (the closest Cáceres comes to a cathedral), and **San Mateo**, plain inside and out apart from its decorated tombs.

THE CONQUISTADORS

Spain honours the young men who left Extremadura in the fifteenth and sixteenth centuries to seek their fortunes in the New World, though many historians now condemn them for their ruthlessness, and their indifferent destruction of the cultures they subdued. Some of their actions were disgracefully brutal, treacherous, even genocidal, though the customs of the peoples they conquered were often bloodthirsty too. It was not a kindly age. Everyone else was cashing in on the empire-building bonanza: the Portuguese, the English, the Dutch. For the Conquistadors, the world was one big oyster and they believed (whenever they bothered to think about it) that the Catholicism they took with them was a pearl of greater price than any they plundered on arrival.

The Conquistadors were not all illiterate yokels (though they sometimes behaved like hooligans). Often they were the second or illegitimate sons of high-born families searching for destiny or adventure. Some were certainly poor, driven to desperate measures by the sheer hardship of life and lack of prospects in Extremadura.

Francisco Pizarro (1475–1571) Peruvian hero, or a bit of a bastard? Pizarro, illegitimate son of a gentleman soldier, began life as a pig-keeper. By good fortune he discovered what later became Spain's richest colony. Fellow-conquerors eventually murdered him amid his stolen treasures in a Borgian fit of betrayal and jealousy.

Francisco's father, Gonzalo Pizarro, was a doughty old general, a hero of the Granada campaign when Spain was finally recaptured from the Moors. Though respectably married, Gonzalo had a weakness for the maids who worked in the convent where his aunt lodged, and under the pretext of visiting his relation, managed to sire no fewer than seven children. Though prospects for the illegitimate sons seemed less than glowing, they all apparently got on well with each other, and with their half-brothers born on the right side of the sheets. When Francisco led his tiny expeditionary force to Peru, four of his half-brothers were with him.

This handful of men managed to cross the Andes, overthrow the Incas, murder their king and take Peru in 1533. Francisco married Princess Inés Yupanqui, and they had a daughter. But it was his wily brother Hernando who eventually ended up with Francisco's plundered treasure, and the spoils of the silver mines. He married Francisco's daughter (incestuously), and brought her home to

Trujillo. There he built a magnificent palace on the Plaza Mayor, and took the title Marques de la Conquista.

Hernan Cortés (1485–1547) Founder of Mexico. Medellín, Cortés' dusty and unremarkable home-town, has a great bronze statue to its local hero. Opinions of Cortés differ sharply, some praising his great courage and determination, others declaring him 'devoid alike of mercy, justice or good faith'.

In 1519 he landed in Mexico and set about demolishing the Aztecs. He it was who murdered Montezuma, installing himself as ruler in Mexico City. But Cortes was not simply a smash-and-grab raider; he had the vision to realise that only colonisation would give Spain permanent control of the Americas. Eventually he returned to Spain, and after the initial excitement about his discovery had ebbed, Cortes died in comparative obscurity. Mexico, the land he conquered, refuses to honour him with a monument.

Vasco Nunez de Balboa (1475–1517) Discoverer of the Pacific. He left his home-town of Jerez de los Caballeros to seek his fortune, but was so badly in debt after some disastrous early adventures that he had to stow away in a barrel to reach Panama. There he first heard of the vast ocean beyond the mountains and also of the fabled Inca gold in Peru. Spurred on by these rumours, Balboa bravely hacked through the perilous jungle until he reached a crest of mountains, and there below him lay the Pacific. Close behind him in the same small crew of pioneers was Francisco Pizarro, who first learnt of Peru from Balboa.

In his sonnet 'On first looking into Chapman's Homer' (the 'realms of gold' one) Keats got it wrong, and put 'Stout Cortez' in the role of Pacific discoverer. Poor old Balboa never seemed to have much luck. Betrayed by jealous superiors – and by his fair-weather friend Pizarro who did nothing to help him – Balboa was unjustly charged with treason, convicted by a kangaroo court, and publicly beheaded.

Several other Conquistadors stand out among the hundreds of Extremaduran emigrés who left for the New World. **Francisco de Orellana**, a cousin of Pizarro, also from Trujillo, set off in 1542 and became the first European to navigate the Amazon, on which he finally died. **Hernando de Soto**, from Balboa's home-town, confined his attention to North rather than South America, exploring what is now Florida and Tennessee, via the Mississippi. **Pedro de Valvidia** from Villanueva de la Serena conquered Chile and founded Santiago in 1541.

Eating out and accommodation

Recently the *hostería* in the Palacio del Comendador has been converted from a restaurant into a 27-room *parador*, but it is the only place to stay in the old town and if you cannot stay here your choices are limited to the new town: uninteresting modern business hotels or cheaper places around the Plaza Mayor. Choose quieter back rooms if possible. Both the *parador* and our recommended Hotel Alcantara have good restaurants.

SOUTHERN EXTREMADURA

Mérida – a Roman retirement home (H)

When Caesar Augustus pensioned off his elderly legionnaires from service in the Iberian province of Lusitania, he sent them here. Looking at it now, you may think it a bit of a short straw as a place to spend your twilight years. But in 25 BC Mérida was the cynosure of Roman Spain, a great centre of culture and wealth, and an important point on a hub of routes, one of which was the Silver Way to the mines of Galicia. If archaeology bores you, there is no other reason to come here: the modern town is ugly, the surrounding farmland dull.

The main sights

To explore properly, you need to spend at least a full day here. The most impressive complex of remains lies on the east side of town, in the **Parque Arqueológico**. If you make your way to it first you can collect plans, maps and inclusive tickets from the information centre by the entrance and get your bearings. This is advisable because Mérida is a confusing town to drive in, and the sights are rather spread out.

Inside the park is the old **Roman Theatre**, marble lined and acoustically perfect. It is still in use; every summer a festival of classical drama is held here. Nearby are the **amphitheatre** and a **Roman villa**. Just outside the Parque Arqueológico is the **Museo Nacional de Arte Romano**, a well-designed modern brick building. Its excellent contents, displayed in small bays on three floors, include many items from pagan religious shrines: look out for the statue of Chronos ensnared by a serpent. A huge mosaic of a boar-hunt covers an entire wall.

This is merely a start to a full exploration of Roman Mérida. Among many other antiquities perhaps the most interesting are the 60-arched bridge across the Guadiana, still one of the longest in Spain, and the **Mithraeum** where mysterious rites connected with bull sacrifices were held.

The Portuguese Marches and Zafra (H)

The far west and south of Extremadura has no remarkable sights or places of interest, but the hilly borderland with Portugal is beautiful, fertile and very peaceful (apart from the main roads near Badajoz). A few small towns are worth a brief stop. As you head southwards the Andalucían influence -neat white houses, green shutters, mosaic tiles – becomes more pronounced, and the vegetation gets more Mediterranean. North-west of Cáceres, a lonely drive across rocky moorland scattered with strange grey boulders takes you to the white-painted town of **Alcántara** (an Arabic name meaning 'The Bridge'), where a fortified Roman bridge spans the Tagus. Southwards, en route for Badajoz, is the hilltop town of **Alburquerque**, with 360-degree views from the castle.

Badajoz's attractions are limited and it is not a particularly good base. Close to the border, it acts as one of the main gateways to Portugal: escudos are easily changed here. Pause briefly to look at the ruined Moorish **Alcazaba** citadel and walls, and the **Torre de Espantaperros** (Dog Scarer Tower), which houses an archaeological museum (being restored at present). From here you get a good view of the fine bridge, the **Puente de Palmas** by Juan de Herrera, architect of El Escorial near Madrid. The yellowish cathedral in the centre of the town is thirteenth-century Gothic.

Three little towns further south are more cheering destinations. First comes **Olivenza**, a sort of hybrid Spanish-Portuguese town so close to the frontier that it sometimes changed sides, notably during the War of the Oranges in 1801. It has a very southern-looking main square with date-palms and blue and yellow patterned tiles. The church of **Santa María Magdalena** is built in the Manueline style – a sixteenth-century form of Gothic usually peculiar to Portugal.

Jerez de los Caballeros is visible for miles around. From a distance, pinnacles and spires erupt triumphantly from a hill-top cluster of whitewashed, grey-roofed houses. Jerez's *caballeros* were knights: first the Templars, then the military Order of Santiago, who built palaces and churches in the town. But the church towers were built later, in the mid-eighteenth century: San Miguel, Santa Catalina, and the amazing San Bartolomé, encrusted with glass paste and painted stucco like a jewellery box.

Zafra is the best of Extremadura's little southern towns, an agricultural centre famous for lively cattle markets where several main routes converge. It makes a good base for exploring southern Extremadura, and a convenient spring-board for travellers heading to or from Andalucía. There is life and style in Zafra's Andalucian palm-filled squares. The main sight is a fine church, the sixteenth-century **Colegiata de la Candelaria**, which contains nine panels painted by Zurbarán.

WHERE TO STAY

CACERES

Parador de Turismo	£££
Ancha 6	
10003 Cáceres	*Tel (927) 21 17 59*

A newly established *parador* (formerly a restaurant only) in the heart of the picturesque old quarter, the fourteenth-century stone-towered Palacio del Comendador was founded by Diego de Ulloa, a former governor of the city, and a Commander of the military crusading Order of Santiago. Coats of arms and old tapestries set the tone inside. The restaurant is good; regional specialities include roast partridge and lamb stew. Car access and parking is tricky.

Open: all year **Rooms**: 27 **Credit/charge cards**: Amex, Diners, Eurocard, Visa

Hotel Alcántara	££
Av Virgen de Guadalupe 14	
10001 Cáceres	*Tel (927) 22 89 00*

This modern business-oriented hotel is on a busy boulevard, hence the somewhat noisy front rooms. The furnishings are unexciting but the hotel is well-kept and efficient, with an above-average, though not cheap, restaurant. It has reasonably easy access and parking.

Open: all year **Rooms:** 67 **Credit/charge cards:** Amex, Diners, Eurocard, Visa

GUADALUPE

Parador Zurbarán ££
Marqués de la Romana 10
10140 Guadalupe Tel (927) 36 70 75; Fax (927) 36 70 76

A sensitively converted sixteenth-century building arranged around a patio of citrus trees. The public rooms are rather dark, but the bedrooms above have charming views of the garden and monastery.

Open: all year **Rooms**: 40 **Facilities**: swimming-pool, tennis
Credit/charge cards: Access, Eurocard, Visa

Hospedería Real Monasterio ££
Plaza Juan Carlos I
10140 Guadalupe Tel (927) 36 70 00

A serious and perhaps more interesting rival to the *parador* is the monastery's own hotel, approached from the opposite side of the complex from the main façade where the tour groups assemble. You can stay here just as, or even more grandly than, at the *parador*, for rather less money. It has a delightful Gothic patio cloister full of plants in huge pots and jars. Bedrooms vary, some handsomely furnished in traditional styles with their own sitting-rooms, and many have excellent views.

Open: all year except 15 Jan-15 Feb **Rooms**: 40
Credit/charge cards: Eurocard, Visa

JARANDILLA DE LA VERA

Parador Carlos V £££
Carretera de Plasencia
10450 Jarandilla Tel (927) 56 01 17

The local *parador* in the castle follows a long-standing tradition of hospitality. Charles V lodged here for several months while his rooms at Yuste were being completed. As you enter the solid original walls of this stoutly fortified building you find an elegant Moorish patio with fountains.

Open: all year **Rooms**: 53 **Facilities**: swimming-pool, tennis
Credit/charge cards: Amex, Diners, Visa

MERIDA

Parador Vía de la Plata £££
Plaza de la Constitución 3
06800 Mérida Tel (924) 31 38 00; Fax (924) 31 92 08

A peaceful and convenient base for exploring the Roman city, in a baroque building that once served as a jail and a convent, and which is believed to stand on the site of the palace of the Pretorian Guard. Public areas have a slightly echoey, institutional feel, but the furnishings are an interesting mix of ancient and modern. Bedrooms overlook convent gardens and a Moorish-style patio. It has a recommendable restaurant.

Open: all year **Rooms**: 82 **Credit/charge cards**: Amex, Diners, Eurocard, Visa

---

Hotel Emperatriz   ££
Plaza de España 19
06800 Mérida   *Tel (924) 31 31 11*

On the main square, this is a sixteenth-century palace with a Moorish tiled foyer and a garden. Many illustrious royal visitors are alleged to have stayed here. A terrace at the front makes a good vantage point for watching street life.

Open: all year **Rooms**: 41 **Credit/charge cards**: Visa

PLASENCIA

Hotel Alfonso VIII   £
Alfonso VIII 34
10600 Plasencia   *Tel (927) 41 02 50*

This is a highly traditional town hotel, solidly and rather darkly furnished with stern wooden panelling, stained glass windows, and gilt candelabra. Efficiently run by courteous staff, and well placed for exploring the old town. Good road access.

Open: all year **Rooms**: 57 **Credit/charge cards**: Amex, Diners, Eurocard, Visa

---

Hostal Rincón Extremeño   £
Vidirieras 6
10600 Plasencia   *Tel (927) 41 11 50*

A cheerful, simple, friendly *hostal* with a rustic bar restaurant in the heart of the old town. From the balconied windows of its adequate little rooms you can look down over bustling narrow streets, or peer into the Spanish living rooms opposite if you are nosy enough.

Open: all year **Rooms**: 22 **Credit/charge cards**: Amex, Diners, Eurocard, Visa

TRUJILLO

Parador de Trujillo   £££
Plaza de Santa Clara
10200 Trujillo   *Tel (927) 32 13 50*

One of Spain's nicest *paradores*, set in an old convent. Rooms are arranged in a cloister-like square around a courtyard and swimming-pool. Azulejos tiles, oak chests, sampler wall-hangings and Ali Baba-style pots are incorporated into the décor. The bedrooms are spacious and well-equipped (hair-dryers and so forth; it is a four-star *parador*), and the barrel-vaulted restaurant has a good reputation for local dishes.

Open: all year **Rooms**: 46 **Facilities**: swimming-pool
Credit/charge cards: Amex, Diners, Eurocard, Visa

ZAFRA

Parador Hernan Cortés   £££
Plaza Corazón de María 7
06300 Zafra   *Tel (924) 55 45 40*

Recently reopened after extensive renovation, this *parador* in Zafra's castle combines solid medievalism in its round towers and battlements with the austere symmetrical work of Juan de Herrera, architect of El Escorial, in its Renaissance courtyard. The interior has not been inspected since refurbishment.

Open: all year **Rooms**: 45 **Facilities**: swimming-pool
Credit/charge cards: Amex, Diners, Eurocard, Visa

Huerta Honda Hotel   £££
Av López Azme 30
06300 Zafra   *Tel (924) 55 08 00*

Close to the *parador*, this is one of Extremadura's most delightful hotels. A low-slung building around a central patio and pool, it is stylishly furnished inside, making great use of plants, painted furniture, antiques and tiles. A wicker pig lurks jauntily under the legs of a grand piano. Bedrooms are prettily decorated, and the bars are very much a focus of local life without being in the least rowdy. The plant-filled restaurant has a fine reputation.

Open: all year **Rooms**: 46 **Facilities**: swimming-pool
Credit/charge cards: Amex, Diners, Eurocard, Visa

THE BALEARIC ISLANDS

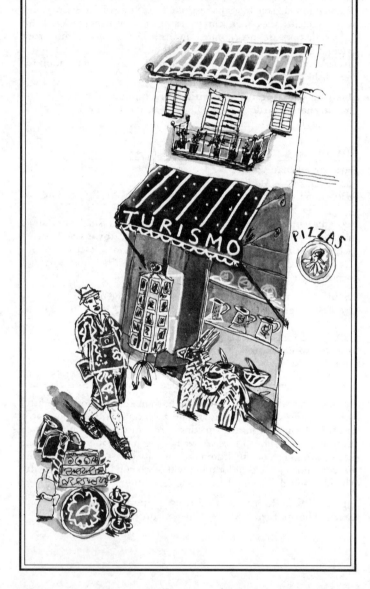

THE BALEARIC islands of Mallorca, Menorca, Ibiza and Formentera straggle out into the Mediterranean about half-way down the east coast of Spain. Their potential as holiday islands was spotted early by tour operators, and since the package holiday boom of the early '70s the coastline has been remorselessly developed to provide accommodation for the plane-loads of visitors arriving from Northern Europe. But, contrary to popular opinion, there is more to the Balearic Islands than high-rise concrete, packed beaches and fish and chips. It is true that you're not going to discover an unspoilt village or unknown beach, only Mallorca has any real 'sights' (and even these are architecturally mediocre), and if you're in search of the 'real Spain' you will be disappointed. That said, the islands should not be dismissed as packaged playgrounds for the undiscerning holiday-maker. There are some sensitively developed resorts and each island has its own attractions and distinct character.

Mallorca has the noisiest resorts and the most crowded beaches and wherever and whenever you go, you are not going to escape the sounds of English and German voices for long – in summer at least, most people bump into someone they know from home. But Mallorca also has tremendous mountains, pretty stone villages and some of the best walking in Spain. Indeed, the most appealing aspect of the island is that you can combine a seaside and a country holiday. Palma is the most cosmopolitan town in the Balearics – a good base for an off-season holiday.

Low-lying, with coastal hills cloaked in maquis, and thicketed hillocks poking up from meadows blazed with wild flowers, **Menorca** is much gentler and a subtly beautiful island. It is the least exploited of the three main Balearics, and development is mostly low-rise, well cared-for and limited to relatively small areas of its coast. The people are reserved and rather old fashioned, and the two towns, Mahón and Ciutadella, are snug, neighbourly places, where life revolves around the family. This is not somewhere to come for thrilling nightlife or spectacular countryside; rather, it is an island for a quiet family holiday.

By contrast, **Ibiza** is a magnet for fashion victims and all-night clubbers. The main town doesn't wake up until after 11pm, but by then the boutiques, cafés and restaurants and the bars, catering for people of every sexual preference, come alive. The old hill-top town rises above the night-time noise. Its steep streets, lined with cracked and faded stone façades,

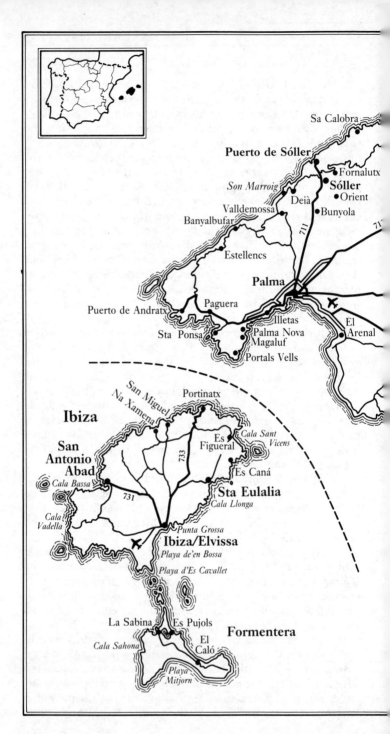

523

have a distinctive, melancholy charm. The rest of the island fails to live up to the promise of its capital. Santa Eulalia del Río is a neat resort and Portinatx is a possible choice for a family beach holiday, but most of the best beaches have been badly or over-developed.

Tiny **Formentera**, a few miles off the Ibizan coast, has only recently begun to exploit its potential as a holiday island and it is still possible to find some peace on its long dune-backed beaches. But don't expect a very lively atmosphere.

Planning your holiday

The weather in the Balearics is slightly cooler than mainland Spain, and many hotels open only from April to October. In the island capitals, and in major resorts on Mallorca and Ibiza, there are a few hotels open all year. Sunbathing and swimming are not really possible until May or June, and the rainfall in Mallorca's mountains is pretty high until July. Menorca can also be cool and windy, and it is not really advisable to go there until June or July. All the islands are particularly busy during the British Spring Bank and summer school holidays. Easter is a great time to visit, as there are tremendous processions on Good Friday in all the island capitals, and in the Mallorquin village of Pollença.

For a beach holiday, choosing the right resort is more important than choosing the right island. They vary widely – from quiet, low-key developments on beaches, to mega-package resorts which throb with deafening Euro-Pop all night long. The most attractive resorts on each island are Puerto de Pollença on Mallorca, Cala Santa Galdana on Menorca, and Santa Eulalia del Río on Ibiza. All three are large enough to offer some variety and liveliness in the evenings, but are quiet enough to allow you to get some sleep at night. Ibiza town is a wonderful place to stay for the young and trendy, and villages like Deià and Bañyalbufar (both on Mallorca) are good bases for walkers.

Watersports fanatics will find windsurfers for hire at most resorts but only the bigger developments have ski-boats. Cala'n Bosc on Menorca has particularly good facilities while Magaluf and Palma Nova in Mallorca specialise in parascending and high-speed tows on the inflatable 'banana'. Most of larger hotels on all the islands can arrange equipment and boat hire.

Independent or package holiday? About two million British people visit the Balearics on holiday each year and numerous tour

A little history

Though today's islanders depend on tourism for their income, their ancestors fiercely resisted foreign interference and were notoriously skilled sling-throwers. Indeed, it is thought that the name, Baleares, comes from the Greek verb *ballein*, to throw. The first island to be conquered was Ibiza, which was settled by the Carthaginians in the middle of the sixth century BC. They were attracted by the island's salt

operators offer beach holiday packages. Some operators sell more specialised packages such as walking tours. If you want to stay in a mid- or upper-range beach hotel, packages often work out cheaper than making your own arrangements, because tour operators negotiate discounts on the standard prices. If you can find a cheap charter flight, the very cheapest way to visit the islands is to travel independently. Because of the high numbers of charter flights (see below) you stand a good chance of getting a last-minute deal. Once you are there a simple double room with bathroom can cost as little as £16 a night.

During the summer there are charter flights to Mallorca from 22 UK airports (15 during the winter months) and scheduled flights all year round from Heathrow (British Midland and Viva Air) and from Gatwick (Viva Air). Both Menorca and Ibiza are served by charter flights from 15 UK airports in summer and three during the winter. Dan Air operate year-round scheduled services to both islands from Gatwick, and Monarch Airlines have scheduled flights to Mahón from Luton. Aviaco fly several times a day between the islands (although you cannot fly directly between Ibiza and Menorca). Formentera is reached by ferry or hydrofoil from Ibiza port – in season there are sailings every hour or so. You can also get to the Balearics direct by air from major Spanish cities or by car ferry from Valencia or Barcelona.

You can hire cars with local and international firms at all the airports and all but the smallest of the resorts. The best maps are the *Firestone* series, widely available on the islands. They include useful town plans as well as the main maps.

● **Regional tourist offices**: Mallorca: Jaime III 10, 07001 Palma de Mallorca, Mallorca, Baleares; Tel (71) 71 22 16. Menorca: Plaza de la Explanada 40, 07701 Mahón, Menorca, Baleares; Tel (71) 36 37 90. Ibiza: Paseo Vara del Rey 13, 07800 Ibiza, Baleares; Tel (71) 30 19 00.

deposits (used to preserve fish for export), lead mines (used for pellets) and the availability of a type of snail, from which they extracted a purple fabric dye. They also grew olives, figs and onions – locals will still point out olive trees they claim were planted by the Carthaginians – and made ceramics, which were exported to various Greek colonies. Sling-throwers from Menorca and Mallorca resisted invasion, and were eventually enlisted as mercenaries by the Greeks, Phoenicians and Carthaginians.

In 143BC Carthage fell to the Romans and Ibiza became an ally of Rome. In 123BC, Quintus Cecilius Metellus seized Mallorca and Menorca, after covering the sides of his ships with animal skins and giving his troops shields to protect them from the islanders' stones. The Romans built towns and roads, cultivated vines and olives and introduced Christianity. After the decline of the Roman Empire the Balearics fell to a succession of powers, and were eventually taken by the Moors in the ninth century. The Moors remained for around 500 years, and their influence can still be seen in place names (such as those beginning with 'Ben'). The best-preserved Moorish buildings are in Palma.

The next invader was Jaime I of Aragón in the early thirteenth century, who immediately built a church on the site of the main mosque on each island. Once the crowns of Aragón and Castile were united, and the monarchs set their sights on colonising the world, the Balearics were neglected, and began to fall prey to pirate attacks. Many pirates holed up in Menorca's coastal caves, and the island became a notorious hot-bed of banditry. The Ibizans, on the other hand, formed their own fleet of pirates to counter- attack.

In the eighteenth century, during the War of the Spanish Succession, Mallorca and Menorca supported the Habsburg nominee of the Austrians and British. Menorca became a British naval base and, under the Treaty of Utrecht, a British possession. By the early nineteenth century Menorca became once again a part of Spain.

MALLORCA

Mallorca is by far the most popular of the Balearics, attracting over five million foreign visitors each year. As a result, almost all the good sandy beaches (and many of the bad ones) have resorts or *urbanizaciones* developed around them. But it is possible to escape from the crowded coastline for days in the mountains. The most striking of Mallorca's scenery lies along the western shore, where the Sierra de Tramuntana erupts from the sea, its crevassed ridges and gnarled peaks forming a spectacular contrast with the coastal developments. In the foothills and valleys are golden limestone villages like Deià and Fornalutx surrounded by citrus, almond and olive groves.

The landscape along the east coast is gentler, with undulating pine-clad hills and small sandy coves or long stretches of sand. Most of the beaches have been swamped by characterless resorts, although a few are still undeveloped. There are also some superb caves, with magnificent stalactites and stalagmites. The north coast has two enormous bays fringed with beaches. The Bahía de Alcudia's resorts are charmless, but Puerto de Pollença is very pleasant, and close to a beautiful beach on the spindly Formentor peninsula.

The coast on either side of the capital, Palma, has been intensively developed – there are over 200,000 tourist beds in this area alone. The resorts to the east are very downmarket, and best left to boozy British lads. Palma Nova and Magaluf, to the west of Palma, are marginally pleasanter and have reasonable beaches, but they too, are pretty raucous at night. The quieter and classier developments, like Illetas, have tiny beaches.

Palma is an elegant town, and a good base for an out-of-season holiday. In high summer, however, it is overwhelmed with foreigners on excursions. So too are most of the island's 'sights' – the caves of Drac and Artà, the monastery of Valldemossa, and Son Marroig, a house built by an Austrian archduke.

Inland Mallorca is fertile, flattish and fairly dull, though the windmill waterpumps along the road to Manacor are quite striking. Towns such as Manacor and Inca are dreary, and the much-hyped excursions to their artificial pearl and leather factories are a waste of money – you can buy the goods for the same price in normal shops.

Palma (H)

Palma is civilised, relaxed, and immediately likeable, and its water-front, with the pinnacles and buttresses of the Gothic cathedral soaring above the sweeping bay, is one of the most remarkable in Spain.

On Sundays the city relaxes, and people stroll along the boulevards, outdo the tourists in the time spent over a coffee, then disappear into restaurants for a three-hour lunch. The town is heaven for anyone with a sweet tooth, even if you're not a fan of hot chocolate as thick as custard, or the soft coiled *ensaimada* pastries.

Around the town

Overlooked by the crenellated Almudaina and adjacent cathedral, Paseo del Born is a lively tree-lined boulevard – the heart of the town – running from the water-front to the main shopping street, Calle Rey Jaime III. It was once a narrow sea-inlet, but was filled in during the seventeenth century and was used for festivals (and even jousting). The best café for people-watching is the Antonio, a popular place which is used by as many locals as tourists. It serves light meals (and gargantuan portions of lemon meringue sponge) as well as drinks, but the food prices are outrageous.

The oldest streets are directly behind the cathedral, in a shady quarter of sturdy stone houses and seigneurial mansions. Calle Almudaina is spanned by the Almudaina arch, the old entrance into the Moorish fortress. There is now a house sitting astride it. Close by (and clearly signposted) are the Arab baths and a couple of churches, Santa Eulalia with a bobbled spire and doily rose window, and San Franciso with a peaceful Gothic cloister.

Just north of the seventeenth-century *ayuntamiento* with its mighty carved wooden eaves is the tangled nineteenth-century shopping and residential district. Calle Colón and Calle Jaime II are particularly striking as most of the houses have wrought-iron balconies or *solanas*. There are also some fancy art nouveau buildings in the neighbourhood: notably the **Can Rey** at the top of Calle Colón, faced with gorgeous pastel mosaics, and the extraordinary pair of houses on Plaza Santa Catalina Tomás, which at first glance appear to have no straight lines at all.

Above the Can Rey is arcaded Plaza Mayor, traffic-free, surrounded by uniform pink and grey façades, and almost entirely given over to touristy cafés. Just north of here La Rambla Roma is a heavily trafficked avenue whose tree-shaded pedestrianised spine is lined with flower stalls. Like the Paseo del Born, it was once a waterway. The grimy neo-classical theatre and the famous **Forn del Teatre**, which specialises in *ensaimada*, are near the beginning of La Rambla, on Plaza Weyler.

Walking along Paseo de Maritimo which runs along the

harbour is a must, especially at night when the cathedral is floodlit, and the lights from the yachts are reflected on the oscillating inky waters. You will also pass the Gothic Lonja, a fifteenth-century commercial exchange with swirling tracery and stepped turrets, now opened only for exhibitions.

Eating out and drinking

Unless you are on a tight budget, avoid the cheap eateries along Calle Apuntadores (behind the Lonja) where basic Spanish *tapas* bars and restaurants compete with downmarket establishments advertising steak and kidney pudding. Utterly incongruous in this setting, but none the less magnificent, is Abaco (on the corner with Calle Joan), an astonishingly opulent bar housed in a fifteenth-century mansion. Fruit cascades on to a stone-flagged floor, exotic flowers burgeon from elaborate vases, candles drip wax on ornate candelabra, and the hall is suffused with clouds of incense. All this comes at a price (1300 pesetas for a cocktail, 800 for a beer) but it is money well spent.

Fortunately you can get very reasonable and delicious Italian food next door at Vecchio Giovanni. It is extremely popular, so you may have to wait for a table, but it is worth the wait for the warm, unpretentious atmosphere. Starters include an immense and filling cauliflower cheese and a salad of lettuce, orange, Roquefort and nuts. The home-made almond ice-cream (*helado de almendra*) is outstanding, and comes with a slice of cinnamon sponge cake.

More typically Mallorquin places to eat include La Lubina, Muelle Viejo, which specialises in fish and seafood, and Ca'n Juanito, Calle Aragón 11. For international cuisine, you could splash out at either Koldo Royo, Paseo de Maritimo 3 or Porto Pi, Joan Miró 174. Those with a sweet tooth will enjoy a couple of rather more hedonistic Palmaian institutions: the Xocolatería Xicara, Carrer Morey, just off Plaza Santa Eulalia, and the Ca'n Joan de S'Aigo, Calle Sans 10, a couple of blocks from San Francisco, both specialising in thick hot chocolate. The Xicara is the livelier, with marble tables in a cosy beamed room cooled by helicopter fans and lit by unusual ceramic lamps. The Ca'n Joan was founded in 1700.

The main sights

● **The Cathedral** Work began on Palma's cathedral in 1230, just a few months after the Christians had recaptured Mallorca from the Moors. As usual, the Christians demolished the Moorish mosque and built their cathedral in its place, on a low hill overlooking the harbour. Probably designed by the King of Aragón's military architect and built of a local sandstone, which looks golden in some lights and pinkish-beige in others, its most fearsome feature is the buttressing: parallel walls like the wings of a stage set are anchored to the Gothic nave by a double row of arches.

Inside the cathedral, the most striking feature is the height, a sensation enhanced by columns soaring uninterrupted to the vaults – the nave is 43.95 metres high, the world's second-highest Gothic cathedral (Milan beats it by 5cm). The sun streams through the rose windows and dapples the golden limestone columns with a translucent patina of amethyst, jade and amber. Every fifteen minutes the lights on the peculiar crown, designed by Gaudí to hang above the chancel, flash on.

● **Arab Baths** Overlooked by a pale church tower, in the tangled heart of the old quarter, the Moorish baths are one of the most evocative corners of the town. The tiny garden is especially lovely with its palms, cacti and lemon trees. The baths themselves were built in the tenth century, based on Roman designs.

● **Bellver Castle** Crowning a pine-clad hill which rises behind the touristy Terreno quarter, Bellver was built by Pere Salver for Jaime II, during Mallorca's brief period of independence (1262–1349) as a royal summer residence. Shortly after it was built, Mallorca was recaptured by the kingdom of Aragón and from then, until 1915, the castle was used as a prison. Its most remarkable feature is the arcaded circular courtyard.

● **The Almudaina** Dwarfed by its neighbour the cathedral, the Almudaina was a Moorish fortress, converted into a royal palace by Pere Salva, the architect of Bellver. The austerity of its turreted towers is tempered by a pleasant garden and delicate Gothic loggia, which looks out to sea. You can visit only on a guided tour – it's worth popping in when it opens at 10.30am to find out the time of the English-language version.

The coast around Palma

The worst of Mallorca lies to the east of Palma, where high-rise hotels and apartments stretch for five kilometres along a sandy beach. There is little to choose between the two main resorts – ageing, high-density, high-rise, concrete developments of the worst kind. **Ca'n Pastilla** suffers from aircraft noise and the beach at **El Arenal** is backed by a busy road. El Arenal is particularly popular with raucous British lads, and its nightlife is brash and boozy. Immediately west of Palma the beaches are poor.

The coast to Andratx

The first base worth considering west of Palma is **Illetas**. It is a chic resort, with smart restaurants, an exclusive residential complex, The Anchorage (Tel (71) 40 52 12) and several classy hotels standing on the low cliffs above scraps of sand. Stay somewhere like the Gran Hotel Albatros, where you can lie by the pool listening to the sea crashing below the terrace. The Anchorage's bar and restaurant is the most sophisticated place to spend evenings. It's a fair walk to The Anchorage from the resort centre (and you have to pass an armed security guard) so you might prefer to go by car or taxi.

Palma Nova (H) and **Magaluf**, merging almost imperceptibly into one resort, form the biggest package holiday centre on the island. They are neither stylish nor even very Spanish, but if you want fun, sun and to party till you drop, you'll have a good time. Palma Nova is slightly quieter, though its beach is smaller. Life in Magaluf, a high-rise Legoland, is more extrovert, where entertainment is provided by the likes of Benny Hill's British Bar. At night the competing stereo systems from English 'pubs' and German 'Bierkeller' (with a bit of flamenco thrown in for good measure) provide a crazy, deafening soundtrack, especially around Terrenova, where the two resorts meet. However, the end of the Terrenova peninsula, away from the bars and discos, is a much quieter place to stay.

Paguera is a well-established and predominantly German resort, in which pils, sauerkraut and bratwurst are more readily available than beans on toast or Spanish omelettes. The beaches are of a reasonable size, but soon get grimy and crowded, and the busy road which slices through the resort means that parents of young children are unlikely to relax. There are a couple of smaller developments nearby. **Cala Fornells**, has two hotels and a rather cute villa complex (they look like illustrations from a fairytale) close to a microscopic beach. **Camp de Mar** has a pretty, gently sloping sandy beach backed by pines, and two rather listless hotels.

Not long ago **Puerto de Andratx**, about five kilometers from Camp de Mar, was a pretty fishing port on a sheltered bay. Today staircases of holiday villas mount the hills flanking the bay, the port has become a marina, and the village has been transformed into a small resort popular with the boating set. Socialising centres on the yacht club and Tim's Bar, while the best places to eat are reckoned to be Layn and Miramar. Unless you have the use of a yacht (or even windsurfer) however, there is little to do as there is no beach.

Just inland from Puerto de Andratx, **Andratx** is a modest town of ochre and white houses built on to the flank of a hill. From here there's a popular walk down to the small village of **San Telmo**, standing on a rocky bay with the craggy Dragonera islet offshore. If you don't want to walk, you could go by car down a narrow lane which winds through almond trees and terraced fields. In low season San Telmo's two waterside fish restaurants are good for a long, lazy lunch. Sadly, however, the narrow streets and small shingly beach cannot cope with the midsummer crowds.

The north-west

North of Andratx the C-710 climbs up into the mountains, eventually becoming a corniche road with views through pine trees to the sea. There are also a couple of *miradores* with superb views of the serrated coast. The first really interesting place along the coast is **Banyalbufar** (H). Terraces descend like staircases to the jabbing rocky shore below the village, which has some of the best views on the island. Today the terraces are under-used, holding wind-lashed olives and lemon trees, but until the vines were destroyed by phylloxera, the village's herb-scented Malvasia was in demand all over Europe.

Banyalbufar is a pleasant touring base for western Mallorca, with lots of gentle walks around the village. There are a considerable number of British visitors, but it is still popular with former inhabitants, most of whom now live in Palma. There are three hotels, a handful of bars and restaurants, and a couple of shops selling ceramics, and although there are no beaches nearby, the Hotel Mar i Vent has an outdoor swimming-pool.

The mountains

A wooded hill with a rocky crest forms the backdrop for **Valldemossa**, a pretty stone village with a Carthusian monastery where Chopin and George Sand spent a melancholy winter in 1838–9. The couple's brief presence (and Chopin's near death) have furnished the village with a profitable tourist industry, though their misery is conveniently forgotten, and Chopin's profile appears on jaunty tea towels, plastic grand pianos and ash trays. George Sand's damning account of the Mallorquin people is available in four languages (usually with an indignant preface by a local historian) and she has even given her name to an *urbanización* nearby. Cassettes of the music Chopin wrote on the island are also on sale.

George Sand was basically correct when she wrote that the monastery had 'no particular architectural beauty'. Built in the seventeenth and eighteenth centuries, it is institutional and the barrel-vaulted church dull, apart from an altar featuring a blood-dripping Christ. The gardens, however, with their shaggy box trees and obelisk-like cypresses are lovely, and glimpses of their rich, dark greens temper the austerity of the cool, white vaulted corridor.

The monks' cells open off the corridor, each of them consisting of three rooms opening on to a garden. Only a few are open, but each of these has its own souvenir stand. One of the more interesting rooms is the pharmacy, its walls lined with shelves of matching ceramic pots for drugs, chemicals and herbs. The last of the dispossessed monks worked as an apothecary here, charging Chopin and Sand outrageous prices for his sedatives. According to Sand he would secretly dress up in his old robes to pray, but hurriedly change into black breeches, stockings and a short jacket whenever anyone called.

The three rooms in which Sand, Chopin and Sand's two children lived contain the composer's upright Pleyel piano (which didn't arrive in Mallorca until 20 days before they left for Paris), various manuscripts (most of them copies), Chopin's death mask, and a cast of his narrow hand.

As for the rest of the village, you could do the round of the souvenir shops, imbibing free samples of lurid coloured liqueurs, drink rather less arcane liquids in one of the many pavement cafés, or try *cocas de patatas*, a sweet bread speciality of Valldemossa, sold in the bakery on the main street.

Son Marroig was the Italianate mansion of Luis (or Ludwig) Salvador, an Austrian archduke who lived for 53 years on Mallorca studying and writing about the geography, history, language and traditions of the Balearics. Visit if you can out of season.

Salvador chose a magnificent site for his house, on a west-facing cliff-top among holm oaks and pines. It is directly above the Foradada islet, a crumpled crag pierced by a jagged hole. Though the house looks rather severe from the outside, the interior still feels like a home, smelling of woodsmoke and polish, and is especially lovely on a sunny afternoon, flooded with light and heat. Much of Salvador's traditional Mallorquin furniture is still here – notably a four-poster bed with an abacus-style head-rail, and a rocking chair where the caretaker's dog likes to sleep. The intimate garden, planted with palms and cacti, has a circular Ionic temple. There is also a bar and restaurant.

A short drive along the coast from Son Marroig, **Deià** (H) is the most famously picturesque village on the island. Over-looked by a crag whose rumpled crest soars above a pine forest, meticulously renovated cottages cling to a hump high above a startlingly blue sea, and farmhouses and mansions stand on terraced slopes among citrus, and olive groves.

Deià was made famous by the poet Robert Graves, who lived here from 1929 until his death in 1985, and became a favourite with the arty set. Stylish country house hotels, chic restaurants and contemporary art galleries have now been established, and the local grocery sells Tiptree jam, Bovril and HP sauce to inhabitants yearning for a taste of home. Such humble fare does not, however, make the menus of Deià's restaurants, and you can eat extremely well at any number of places, notably the C'an Quet, housed in a tradi-tional Mallorquin mansion, and the Cau Xelini, which specialises in fresh pasta.

Deià makes a very comfortable touring base, though as the local beach is little more than a few sharp rocks in a small craggy bay, it is not ideal for families with children.

Sóller

A bustling little town of green-shuttered rubblestone houses at the foot of a rearing cliff, **Sóller** lies inland about 11 kilometres from Deià. The traffic-choked Plaça de la Con-stitució is the centre of activity, with lots of cafés and two Modernist buildings – an extravagant bank and a frivolous church. The side-streets are pleasanter for shopping and wandering. Directly off the square Calle Sa Lluna is crammed with colourful groceries, dour gents' outfitters, ironmongers selling hand-painted ceramics (for half the price of a souvenir shop) and a winery where a hundred pesetas buys a litre of wine poured direct from the barrel.

Try to do the trip from Sóller to **Puerto de Sóller** on the old open, wooden bone-shaking tram. They leave roughly every half hour from the railway station. The port stands on a bay shaped like a slice of mushroom and backed by an amphitheatre of hills. The setting and harbour are magnificent, but the beach is gritty, and fishing and pleasure boats make the bay's water murky. Along the water-front trams rattle along tracks sticky with dates fallen from the palm trees; shuttered stone façades rise above cheery café, fast-food and souvenir shop signs and fishermen sort through nets or prepare their boats. At the far end of the bay is a submarine base. Its outer gate is not very conscientiously guarded, so be careful not to drive in by mistake – reversing out is not easy.

Puerto de Sóller is a possible base for touring the north-west (although the hotels are pretty dull and basic) but is also worth a visit in order to take a boat trip along the coast. These leave from Mondays to Saturdays at 11am, and call at Sa Calobra, Cala Tuent, San Telmo and the Dragonera islet, among other places.

Mountain villages

A tortuous hairpinned road leads from Sóller to Orient via **Bunyola**, a modest village of green-shuttered houses painted white, ochre and buttermilk. On Saturday mornings a makeshift market takes over its tiny square.

No more than a hamlet, **Orient** (H) has just 14 houses, built of honey-coloured stone with pale roofs and behatted chimneys, and a simple church with a square façade. The only permanent residents are the owners of the hotel and two restaurants. The Mandela restaurant/bar is the best place to eat or drink, its menu ranging from *osso buco* to artichoke and mushroom *torte*. The French owners' taste in music is equally eclectic, and you may be greeted by the strains of North African blues or Andean panpipes.

Fornalutx and **Biniaraix** are gorgeous little villages, reached by back roads from Sóller. The cluster of prettily restored rubblestone houses at Fornalutx are surrounded by gentle hills planted with citrus, almond and olive groves and sprinkled with renovated farms. There are no hotels, but a large number of the farms and cottages are British-owned, so there is always a chance of finding one advertised for rent in a UK newspaper. Though it now has a couple of smartish restaurants, Fornalutx is nowhere near as precious as Deià.

A tiny lane, just one car wide, connects Fornalutx with Biniaraix, a cobbled hamlet of peach-coloured stone houses with flowers spilling over garden walls.

North to Sa Calobra

Climbing out of Fornalutx's sunny, fertile valley you join the C-710 and press on into the heart of the mountains. The road climbs up to a tunnel (from outside which there's a good view of the Sóller valley) and then winds through a lonely defile which edges past the island's highest peak, Puig Mayor (1445m). A military base at its foot and antennae on the summit create a sinister mood which is only broken when the valley broadens at the Gorg Blau reservoir. Just beyond here the Sa Calobra road begins its extraordinary descent to the coast, hairpinning, and at one point tying itself in a knot.

The road ends above a small rocky cove with a tiny grey beach and congested car park. **Sa Calobra** is also accessible by boat from Puerto de Sóller, so the place gets pretty busy. A path leads through two tunnels to **Torrent de Paréis**, a beach of pastel pebbles flanked by scrunched crags and crossed by the River Paréis. It is extremely popular, and one of the most photographed beaches on the island.

An even more dramatic way to approach the beach is by foot from Escorca, along the wild gorge of the River Pareis. Unless you are prepared to walk through waist-high water, tackle the walk between May and September when the river is dry. Though it is quite challenging in any season, it is one of the most trodden trails on the island, and appears in most of the Mallorquin walking guides. It is also meticulously detailed in Marc Dubin's *Trekking in Spain*.

If the Torrent de Paréis beach is too busy for comfort, you could try **Cala Tuent**, the next cove to the south. Drive back up the Sa Calobra road, and turn off after about two kilometres (the road is not very clearly marked). The road passes a miniature thirteenth-century hermitage.

Eight and a half kilometres from the Sa Calobra turn-off, just off the C-710, is the **Monasterio de Lluc**. It is a dull complex strikingly sited below forested slopes and an amphitheatre of rock. Because it holds a fourteenth-century wooden statue which has become the island's patron, it is the most important place of pilgrimage on Mallorca. If you fancy an ascetic night, there are 95 cells to rent. For a not-so-ascetic night, ensure you get one of the 48 which have a bathroom.

If you do go, pop into the basilica, which has peculiar gilded reliefs curling over its walls, a tortured metal altarpiece and candlestick designed by Gaudí in the side chapel. There is also a small archaeological museum.

Pollença is a far more rewarding place to visit. Cars seem out of place in its narrow streets, and each time one passes, cats scurry away and chatting neighbours are forced to pause. It is a pleasantly unhurried town of ochre-washed and rubblestone houses, many with ancient arched doorways opening directly on to living-rooms lit only by the flickering screen of a TV. Pollença lies between two hills, one crowned by a convent, the other by a Calvary chapel reached by 365 steps from the primary school.

There are a couple of restaurants (Le Font del Gali has an English-language menu and vegetarian options) and lots of old-fashioned bakery and grocery shops. The most distinctive bar is the El Gallito at the bottom of the Calvary steps. Just outside town, by the turn-off for Lluc and Sóller, is a rambling antique shop, Paco Mobles Artesan, which is more interesting than many folk museums.

The north coast

The island's north coast consists of just two bays, the huge Bahía de Alcudia, and smaller Bahía de Pollença, a serene stretch of water sheltered by hilly headlands. Tucked into the western corner of the bay, **Puerto de Pollença** is an extremely pleasant place to stay.

The nicest and quietest part of the resort is the northern end, where a pine-shaded pedestrian-only promenade runs between the hotels and the sea. There is virtually no beach here, but if you stay somewhere like the Illa d'Or you can sunbathe on the hotel terrace and swim from a pontoon.

The best restaurants are the waterside Becfi, where King Juan Carlos has been known to eat, and the Ivy Tree, Calle Llevant 14, run by a friendly English couple. Try blinis with smoked salmon; sour cream and caviare; avocado and goat's cheese soufflé; tagliatelle with avocado; mushroom and tomato or chicken *burritos*.

A corniche road hairpins through the harsh mountains of the Formentor peninsula to the **Playa de Formentor**, its soft, white duny sands backed by pines and fringing the brilliant blue (if occasionally wind-stirred) waters of the Bahía de Pollença. There's a terrace bar on the beach, and a secluded hotel, the Formentor (Tel (71) 53 13 00), in its own grounds a short distance away. The road continues gently through a pine and eucalyptus wood, then runs along the lip of a sheer cliff before a rollercoastering series of acute bends, and vertigo-inducing drops carved out of towering walls of scored rock. Eventually you reach the tip of the peninsula, with a lighthouse clamped to the pale, splintered rock, and views of jagged cliffs erupting from the sea.

Cala de Sant Vicenç (H) is a modest resort backed by grey scrub-speckled mountains with a couple of small sandy beaches in rocky coves and a handful of simple hotels and apartments. It has most appeal early or late in the season when the beaches are quiet.

Puerto de Alcudia, with its three-mile strip of hotels and apartments built along a fine sandy beach, would be a reasonable choice as a beach resort if it were not for the main road which slices the development in two. English food is widely available. The nicest places to stay are away from the resort centre, where the fine pale sands are screened by trees. If you are interested in ornithology, make sure you visit **S'Albufera** marshes, a nature reserve behind the resort which attracts over 200 different species of bird.

The little town of **Alcudia**, which lies just inland of the port, is worth a brief stop. Houses the colour of wet sand, all with green shutters, are surrounded by crenellated walls dating from the fourteenth century, while an imperious gate which once gave access to the port now stands on a traffic island. There is a recently opened archaeological museum.

If you have transport, take your picnic on to the Cabo de Pinar peninsula, following the signs to the Ermita de la Victoria. The road winds through pines to a small, but pretty shingle beach, **S'Illot**, with a small islet offshore. A youth hostel is just behind, so it can get packed with children.

The road twists up steeply to the Ermita de Victoria, once a rather drab hermitage, but now a popular spot for country lunches. The views from the terrace of the restaurant/bar are superb, and there are picnic tables in the woods. The restaurant is closed in the evenings and on Monday lunchtimes between December and March.

The east coast

The east coast of Mallorca is wooded and planted with almonds. Undulating hills form an indented coastline of beaches and small sandy coves. Unfortunately most resorts and *urbaniziciones* are far too big for the beaches. In high season the sands are uncomfortably crowded and the resorts cheerful. Out of season, you may have a beach to yourself, but most of the resorts are desolate – unreal towns of clinical apartments and Identikit villas where the only people are construction workers, and the only sounds are of cement mixers and pneumatic drills. The most northerly resort is **Cala Ratjada**, just beyond **Capdepera**, a little town shabbily huddled below a castle ringed by a circuit of impressively crenellated walls. The resort on the other hand is well cared-for, its low-rise hotels and apartments attractively set among pines. There are bars and restaurants along the sea-front and overlooking the small harbour and more places to eat, drink and shop along a lively main street. The resort is more popular with Germans than the English, so don't be surprised to be welcomed with 'Guten Abend' when you enter a restaurant. Most places, however, do have English-language menus. The resort beach, **Son Moll**, is quite small, and the sea bed deeply shelving, but **Cala Aguila**, a couple of kilometres north, is splendid, its pale duny sands lying at the head of a long, deep, limpid inlet. **Cala de la Font**, about five kilometres from Cala Ratjada, is a pretty cove with large hotels.

Cuevas de Artà and Cuevas del Drac

The great arch of rock which forms the entrance to the **Cuevas de Artà** was hollowed out by the sea in the rugged cape that encloses the bay of Canyamel. The caves have been open to the public since the nineteenth century, and early visitors included Jules Verne, Alexander Dumas and Victor Hugo. The stone staircase that gives access to the caves was created for another illustrious visitor, Queen Isabel II. The multilingual guides are good, and the caverns are deftly lit, with bizarre formations resembling strings of melting mozzarella, sheets of salt-cod and a satellite dish. But the fun really starts, when, with the help of coloured lights and the Ride of the Valkyries, you are plunged into Hell and put through your paces in Purgatory before arriving in Paradise.

A short drive south brings you to **Porto Cristo**, a slightly dog-eared resort with souvenir shops and restaurants cram-med around a small harbour. It is packed throughout the summer with coach parties that come to visit the nearby **Cuevas del Drac**, in which the main attraction is a concert of classical music given by a quartet floating on one of the world's largest underground lakes.

On the coast between the caves are **Cala Bona** and **Cala Millor** – two large resorts which roll into one along a long sweep of sand. Dozens of uncompromisingly functional hotels line the sea-front, which is well cared-for but soulless.

South to Cala Figuera

The first place worth stopping south of the Cuevas del Drac is **Porto Colom**, a small, working fishing village. Its sheltered harbour lies in a bottlenecked bay and is overlooked by terraces of white houses with green shutters. Just over the headland, a resort with a large hotel and villas and apartments has been built above the beach of **Cala Marsal**. The beach, a tongue of sand at the head of a long, narrow rock-flanked inlet, is quite attractive, though, as ever, too small for the size of the resort.

The problem is similar at **Cala d'Or**, a well-designed resort of villas and hotels along a series of sandy coves. The development includes a marina and there are eight tiny sand beaches, of which Cala Sanau, the most northerly (and most difficult to find), is quietest.

The development continues without a break to **Porto Petro**, once a quiet fishing port, but now an unappealing, unfinished resort with no beach, built around a rectangular harbour. Give it a miss, and head instead to **Cala Mondragó**, reached along a narrow lane through wild olives and juniper bushes. There are two white sand beaches in the bay, Mondragó and S'Amarador, flanked by woods and linked by a path over a rocky promontory. There is a *hostal* here, the Playa Mondragó, Tel (71) 65 77 52, which was closed when we inspected, but looked a promising, if simple, base for a beach holiday. If you want to stay somewhere where there's a bit more to see and do, continue south to **Cala Figuera**, a small village where you can watch the fishermen at work.

Inland Mallorca

Inland Mallorca is pretty dull, and travelling across the island is something you do from necessity rather than desire. Between the Sierra de Tramuntana and the low hills of the east coast is a plain, once intensively cultivated, but now largely neglected as the people have given up their farms to work in the resorts. On the east of the island prickly pears flop by the roadside, weeds rampage across the fields, and the metal vanes and arrow tails of the hundreds of windmills have rusted. Originally designed to suck the water from the marshy land, they were more recently used to irrigate the fields.

There are a number of factories along the road, aimed at tourists. Gordiola, housed in a turreted mansion, is a glass-works where you can watch the craftsmen at work in a vaulted hall with a blazing furnace. The dreary town of Manacor is dedicated to the production of artificial pearls.

The road north is even less interesting, with a good deal of light industry on the fringes of Palma and around the town of Inca. Almond groves growing in the gaps between workaday villages, and vineyards around the wine-producing village of Binissalem, are slightly more engaging, but the first place worth stopping is Santa María, which has a couple of at ceramics shops and leather stores.

MENORCA

In the eighteenth century Menorca was occupied by the British, whose legacy is most immediately apparent in the capital Mahón's Georgian houses and gin distilleries. But there is also something very British about the pleasantest of its twentieth-century holiday *urbanizaciones*, which, with their neat and often privet-hedged gardens, would not look out of place in the suburbs of south-east England.

Menorca is the most northerly of the Balearics, and as it is windier and rainier than Mallorca and Ibiza, the season is slightly shorter – from about May to September. Hotels and apartment complexes are newish, low-rise and built in traditional style – which means that the breeze-blocks are either whitewashed or covered in bits of local stone.

There are some lovely beaches, and not all of them have been developed – access to most of these is along rough tracks or by sea. Cala Santa Galdana, set on a pine-fringed bay with a golden sandy beach is one of the best all-round family resorts in the whole of the Balearics. There are boat-trips to undeveloped beaches nearby, and it is well placed for trips to Mahón and Ciutadella. However, many of the newest complexes have little or no beach. Complexes close to good beaches include Son Parc, in the north-west and San Jaime on the south coast.

On the whole, Menorca is not a good island for sightseeing, and some people find its landscape and towns dull. The most striking man-made features are the T-shaped *talayotes* and boat-shaped *navatas*, built by the island's Bronze Age inhabitants. If you are looking for water-skiing or windsurfing, head for the main resort beaches. Opportunities for other activities are limited – although there is a nine-hole golf course at Son Parc.

Mahón/Maó (H)

The diminutive capital of a tiny island, Mahón is a homely, old-fashioned place. It stands on plant-tufted cliffs above the longest and deepest natural harbour in the Mediterranean, and looks most impressive from the sea. If you don't arrive by ferry, be sure to take a boat trip around the harbour.

Much of Mahón was built during the British occupation of the island. There is a distillery on the port-side, which still bottles its gin in replicas of the flagon with a handle (for easy swigging) favoured by eighteenth-century sailors.

Plaza Explanada, a large square overlooked by a red and white army barracks and surrounded by cafés and ice-cream parlours, is the centre of the town. The tourist office at number 40 has free maps and information about the island.

Calle Dr Orfila leads to the old city. Off to the left, **Plaza Bastio** is dominated by a towered medieval gate which belonged to the old city walls. There are some small pavement cafés here, and a couple of modest restaurants just off it along a tiny cul-de-sac, Calle d'Alaior. Another nice place is the unnamed café on the corner of Calle Isabel II and Calle Rosario, an amicable place where old men play dominoes and 'thirtysomethings' gather for early evening drinks.

Down the hill from the medieval gate is Plaza de la Constitució, overlooked by the neo-classical town hall and stark ochre walls of the main church, Santa María. Inside there is a magnificent organ, with 3,006 pipes, 51 stops, 30 pedals and four keyboards. It was built in 1810 by a Swiss craftsman in Barcelona, on the orders of a British admiral, Collingwood. Tucked behind the church is Mahón's Georgian showpiece, Plaza de la Conquista, where the British colonials built themselves comfortable town houses.

On the other side of the church, Carrer Nou and Calle S'Arravaleta are pretty pedestrianised streets lined with shops selling conventional clothes and sensible shoes. Rather more frivolous is La Turronera, a café and shop which sells home-made ice-cream, *horchata*, *granizado* and delicious cakes. Calle S'Arravaleta emerges on heavily trafficked Plaza Carme, which stands on the fringes of a neat grid of cosy whitewashed terraced houses. These date from the early nineteenth century, when the population was swelled by Catalans seeking refuge from the Napoleonic wars.

The *plaza* is named after the Carme church, a sturdy neo-classical building whose cloister houses a small archaeological museum. Behind the cloister there are fine views of the harbour from Plaza Miranda, and excellent *tapas* at the Miranda bar. Plaza Carme is linked to Plaza de España. It slopes between some fine sash-windowed houses, and without the crazy traffic would be one of the town's most picturesque squares. The primrose and white market building at its foot is worth a visit in the mornings. A snaking road, the Abundance Ramp, and a short-cut flight of steps, leads down to the water-front.

To the left of the Abundance Ramp a long terrace of scuffed white cottages leads up to the Xoriguer gin distillery, past the Estación Maritima, where ferries from Palma and the Spanish mainland dock. There are a number of bars along here, the most striking of which is the Baixamar, with mirrored walls, a chequerboard floor and iron columns, and frequented mostly by the local youth. One place to book boat trips around the harbour is the Mad Hatter's Tea Bar, also sought out by those in search of a real cuppa.

Immediately to the right of the Ramp, the houses are scruffier, and used as equipment stores by the fishermen. Eventually fishing boats give way to yachts, and you reach a spruce terrace of boutiques, smart cafés and classy fish restaurants. One of the best restaurants is *Gregal*.

A couple of kilometres along the coast from Mahón, **Villacarlos** is an orderly village built by the British in the eighteenth century as a garrison town. The old British parade ground is now the central square, overlooked by a toytown *ayuntamiento* with a balustraded clock tower and a walled barracks which is now used by the Spanish army. Villacarlos is liveliest at night, when guitarists play in the bars and restaurants, some of which are gouged out of the cliffs, around the coves. There is also a hippy craft market in season.

The south coast

The nearest purpose-built resort to Mahón is S'Algar (H), a well-established *urbanización* which stands on a rocky corner above a craggy inlet. Most of the villas have their own gardens, sometimes bordered with a privet hedge and, were it not for the stubby palm trees and surrounding thickets of wild olive, you could almost be in British suburbia. There is no beach, but watersports are popular, and the Hotel S'Algar has a swimming-pool on the sea-front. If you want a resort with a beach **Cala Alcaufar**, just beyond, is a better choice.

A little further south on the extreme south-east corner of the island is **Punta Prima**, a styleless and disorderly resort with a fairly large, and very popular, pale sandy beach. Beyond, new villa complexes straggle along the rocky coast without a break. The Pueblo de Pescadores at **Binibeca Vell** is strikingly different. Above a craggy cove, tiny cobbled streets squeeze between dazzling white houses with curvy walls, arched doorways and fake chimneys, in what is supposed to resemble a typical fishing village. There are restaurants, shops, and pubs in a discreetly designed commercial centre. The main disadvantage is the lack of a beach, though you can swim off the rocks.

Cala'n Porter to Cala Santa Galdana

Cala'n Porter has a lovely sandy beach in a broad, tongue-shaped inlet bounded by high cliffs. Unfortunately, ugly apartments and bars are welded to the cliffs, and the resort dribbles back over the bleak scrubby hinterland. The cliffs are riddled with caves, once used by the island's prehistoric inhabitants.

To get to the best of Menorca's beaches, you have to head inland to Alaior, and then cut back to the coast. **Son Bou** is the longest beach on the island, a sweep of duny sands, unfortunately marred by two towering hotels. One compensation is that the hotels' facilities, including windsurfer hire, are open to non-residents. You should, however, beware of strong undercurrents. A nicer place to stay is **San Jaime**, at the other end of the beach. There are also secluded villas on the pine-wooded slopes of the hill behind the main part of the sand dunes, and a neat, if rather dull, complex of apartment blocks closer to the sea.

The next resort, **Santo Tomás**, has to be approached from Es Mercadal on the main cross-island road. The resort lacks focus and the dull, concrete hotels do little to improve the atmosphere. The long beach is not as good as that of Son Bou.

Cala Santa Galdana, approached from the village of Ferreries, is without doubt the island's pleasantest resort. Flanked by wooded hills, scattered with expensive villas, and bisected by a creek where small boats are moored, it sits on a sheltered scallop-shaped bay embraced by rugged cliffs. A pale golden crescent of fine sand is backed by pines and looks out to a tiny islet. There are three large hotels and a number of apartments, as well as villas, cafés, shops, and restaurants.

The road to Ciudadela

The drive across the island is not particularly interesting – gently undulating fields, drystone walls concealed under tangled hedgerows, and hillocks thicketed with wild olives and holm-oak. You pass through three workaday, whitewashed towns – **Alaior**, untidily stacked around two churches, **Mercadal**, a sleepy market town overlooked by El Toro, the highest point on the island, and **Ferreries**, tucked in a valley below terraced market gardens. Alaior is the base of the island's cheese factories, and the Menorquina ice-cream factory, whose elaborate confections are sold all over Spain.

It's worth making a short diversion at Mercadal to wind up the windswept, wooded slopes of **Monte El Toro** for a view of the island. You are greeted by a giant statue of Christ, a convent, satellite dishes and a forest of aerials and antennae. This is not because the nuns belong to a hi-tech order with a direct line to God, but because the hill, as the highest point on the island, is the obvious place for Menorca's communications links. The views are more memorable than the whitewashed chapel.

Ciudadela/Ciutadella

Ciudadela was Menorca's capital until the British arrived and decided that Mahón, with its strategically important harbour, was a more logical place for a headquarters. Its cathedral remains the seat of the Menorcan bishopric. Despite a thorough sacking by the Turks in the sixteenth century, and considerable damage during the Civil War it still retains flamboyant palaces, streets lined with Moorish-style arcades, and narrow cobbled alleys which tangle among cream and white houses. The skimpy local beaches and overdeveloped coast mean that it is not a good place to stay, but it is worth a visit. Aim to arrive mid-morning or late afternoon when there should be people out shopping, strolling or sitting in cafés.

Ciudadela sits on cliffs above a narrow inlet, which is much smaller than Mahón's, but cheerfully lined with bars and restaurants, some of which are hollowed into the high mossy, creeper-covered walls. Overlooking the harbour, Plaza d'es Born is the best place to begin a tour. In the centre is an obelisk, dedicated to those who died attempting to defend the city from the Turks. Fused to the harbour walls is the mock-Gothic town hall – which occupies the the site of the Moorish *Alcázar* – and opposite is the Saura palace, an elaborate nineteenth-century structure. There are a number of simple cafés each with a few tables on the pavement outside – the nicest is the Bar Círculo Artístico which stands next to a neo-classical theatre now used as a cinema.

Carrer Antig d'es Born leads off the square to the cathedral, a tremendous ship-like Gothic edifice, built of a creamy butterscotch stone. The whitewashed arcades which run along Calle Quadrado shelter boutiques, souvenir shops, restaurants, cake shops and ice-cream parlours. There are more arcades and cafés on Plaça Nova (Plaza de España on old maps) – the only really lively part of town. Carrer de Mao (Carme on old maps) leads out of the old quarter to Plaza Alfonso III, a small square with a couple of pavement cafés where the town's older generation gather to chat under a ring of palm trees.

The west coast

The west coast has been heavily exploited, and the toytownish resorts continue to spread along a barren rocky coastline with skimpy beaches tucked into its sharp serrations. **Cala'n Blanes**, to the north of Ciudadela, has a fairly pretty beach at the head of a long inlet flanked by low wooded cliffs, but the surrounding developments, Cala Forcat and Los Delfines look like space-age council estates. The only remotely attractive place to stay at this side of the island is **Cala Morell** on the north coast, a small villa development above a tiny rocky bay with a minute beach.

To the south, **La Caleta** is a new development with a tiny beach and **Cala Santandria**'s sheltered cove gets murky as soon as the crowds arrive. As well as a large hotel, **Cala Blanca** has some reasonable-looking villas and a soft white sand beach in a long inlet with a pleasant terrace restaurant. It gets extremely crowded, but might be worth considering in the low season. **Cala'n Bosc** (aka Tamarinda) is a large and rapidly developing complex of beach-club aparments, with two small sandy beaches and good watersports.

The north-east coast

Menorca's most appealing scenery lies along the rock-fretted north-east coast. Directly north of Mahón waves of deep green maquis undulate towards the coast, splashed with brilliant yellow gorse. Further north you enter a restful landscape of meadows, apple orchards and pine woods, a striking contrast to the savagery of the island's eastern headland, Cabo de Favaritx, where rubbery green and red plants with yellow flowers cling to flaky wafer layers of slate. There are some good beaches along here, notably Cala Mesquida, Arenal d'en Castell and Son Parc. **Son Parc** has a very pleasant *urbanización*, but the more intimate resorts of **Na Macaret** and **Puerto Addaya** are nicer places to stay than Arenal.

Along the northern coast, the almost enclosed bay of Fornells looks splendid, but has no beach – though the fishing village of **Fornells** is rightly famed for its lobster dishes. Beyond Fornells the beaches get increasingly remote.

The east coast

Cala Mesquida lies just six kilometres north-east of Mahón, a fine sandy beach in an irregular hilly bay guarded by a watch-tower, which is popular with picnicking Mahonese. There are walks along the cliffs, and a bar in the small village which serves egg, sausage and chips as well as more conventional Spanish fare. To the north, **El Grao** is worth considering if you have very young children, for it has a safe and shallow bay, although the greyish and rather muddy beach, backed by a marsh, is not particularly alluring.

The marsh-fringed lake, or **S'Albufera**, behind El Grao is a resting place for migratory birds, and has been designated a nature reserve. In spite of this, **Shangri-La**, a villa complex and nine-hole golf course (now disused), was built directly behind it. The first really nice place to stay is **Puerto Addaya**, a small resort popular with the sailing crowd. Its villas and low-rise apartments stand on either side of a deep, sheltered, fjord-like anchorage, and there are lovely views of the craggy, serrated coast, and across to a rocky islet offshore. **Na Macaret** is an alternative base, an intimate village with little houses and apartments built along the water-front and ranged around a square with a row of restaurants and bars.

Arenal d'en Castell has a fine beach, a crescent of rich golden sand in a calm bay. The resort is less attractive, and the cliff-tops are crammed with cramped villas and apartments and dominated by two large, ugly hotels. There are, however, plenty of cafés and restaurants, and one fairly pleasant apartment complex, White Sands, which has its own small beach. If you want a fairly lively holiday, and don't want to have to drive to beaches, it is worth considering.

A more exclusive option for a beach holiday is **Son Parc**, set among pine woods above a gorgeous pale sand beach in a rock-fringed bay. The complex is spacious and well-planned with whitewashed villas, apartments and a hotel. There are tennis courts and a golf course, as well as horse-riding.

Fornells and around

A fishing village of red-roofed and green-shuttered cottages on a calm lake-like bay, Menorcan families come to Fornells for a delicious though outrageously expensive stew called *caldereta* which is made of locally caught lobster. It is served in restaurants on the water's edge, the most famous of which is Es Pla, where, every local will tell you, King Juan Carlos has eaten.

There is also an upmarket country club and villa development, **Playas de Fornells**, on the headland above the village. The villas stand in gardens of cacti and tropical plants. Most have sea views. The club has a pool, tennis court, restaurant and supermarket, and activities like skin-diving. In the bay below **Cala Tirant** is a pleasant beach of red-gold sand backed by dunes with a small villa development in one corner. To get there you need to take a narrow lane marked Urbanización Cala Tirant, which turns off the Fornells road about three kilometres south of the village. After a couple of kilometres the road forks – one branch leads to Cala Tirant, and the other to Binimel'la, a remote beach popular with (mostly Menorcan) campers.

IBIZA

Whatever else can be said of Ibiza, it certainly isn't dull. In Ibiza town cobbled streets throb to the latest dance beats, shop assistants drink wine and share cigarettes with customers, and hippy stall-holders light joints as they haggle over prices. Meanwhile, in San Antonio Abad, the other main town, British lads stagger from bar to bar, and on the beaches across the island designer people and beautiful gays concentrate on getting the perfect all-over tan. But the traditional ways of life persist. In Ibiza town old ladies in local costumes rub shoulders with outrageously dressed foreigners. Inland, among the hills farmers maintain their olive, fig or almond groves while their offspring work in the resorts in season.

The capital is definitely the most interesting place to stay, an old whitewashed town packed with fashion boutiques, designer bars and classy restaurants. The legendary night clubs are all on the outskirts, and though the beaches closest to the town are unappealing, the duny nudist beach, Es Cabellet, and the chic Ses Salines, are nearby.

Outside Ibiza town there's not a lot of sightseeing – indeed, most people who stay in the capital venture no further than Ses Salines beach. Of the main resorts around the coast, San Antonio Abad is a charmless packaged hell. The best of a poor selection of other resorts is Santa Eulalia, a good base for families with an injection of Ibizan style. Portinatx is not a bad place to stay, but its beaches are rather small. Of the many apartment and villa complexes, the nicest are around the pretty bay of Cala Llenya and the upmarket complex at Na Xamena. The tiny island of Formentera has long, undeveloped beaches.

Ibiza town (H)

Ibiza town rises white from the sea on a hill crowned by a sturdy cathedral. Headless Romans in eroded togas guard a gate in citadel walls tufted with weeds; on house fronts, the whitewash has cracked and crumbled to reveal the grainy golden limestone beneath; and car tyres squeak as they slither down steep streets of time-polished cobbles. Lichen forms a lacy patina on rose, grey and biscuit roof tiles, and the sun-silvered wind-ruffled sea resembles crushed velvet. Cats sidle in the shadows or bask in the sun; gypsy children approach you with outstretched palms; and old women hang out their washing on narrow iron balconies.

Ibiza is the loveliest town in the Balearics, with a superb beach, Ses Salinas, nearby, and there are stylish restaurants and bars which attract an older and more sedate clientele. Wandering the streets, browsing in shops and watching people are obviously major attractions, but there are also more conventional sights – a museum with a rare Carthaginian collection, exhibitions of contemporary art, and a cathedral whose display of ecclesiastical garb rivals the excesses of the boutiques.   The old upper town, Dalt Vila, is best entered through the Portal de las Tablas, one of three gates in the hefty sixteenth-century walls, built to protect the town from North African pirates. The gate is L-shaped, and flanked by headless and armless statues of a Roman senator and the goddess Juno, in decaying toga and chiton, which were discovered while the walls were being built. In the arcaded quadrangle inside the gate soldiers used to store their arms. Nowadays, in summer, there are stalls selling jewellery, clothes and trinkets manned by ageing flower children. The Contemporary Art Museum stands above in the old, golden-stone city hall.

Most of the Dalt Vila's restaurants and shops lie just inside the gate, on Plaza de Vila, Plaza Desamperados, and Avenida General Franco. El Olivo is a lovely restaurant, where you can eat outside, below scuffed whitewashed façades and balconies hung with washing, or inside in an intimate beamed and whitewashed interior. The chicken with honey and thyme is magnificent, served with rice, spinach and a cheese and vegetable pastry. Ca'n den Parra, set on various levels in another ancient beamed house, is equally good.

There are also some good shops around here – notably Cha Cha, which sells ethnic jewellery along with Buddhas and Indonesian shadow puppets, The Sandal Shop, which makes sandals to measure, and S'Espardenya, which has embroidered, crocheted, patterned and baby-sized espadrilles. Above Avenida General Franco is the Baluarte de Santa Lucía, an arrowhead-shaped bulwark fused to buckled cliffs. A path leads from the bastion along the cliffs at the foot of the walls. Just before the path meets a road, a long, dark tunnel smelling of stale urine ducks under the walls, and emerges on the Baluarte Santa Tecla at the foot of the cathedral. Only the severe keep-like belfry remains from the original church, built on the site of a Roman temple and mosque shortly after the island had been seized from the Moors by Christians in 1235. The rest of the cathedral dates from the seventeenth century, and is unusually plain.

Sa Penya and the new town

Sa Penya is Ibiza's old fishing quarter, a maze of narrow cobbled streets and flat-roofed whitewashed houses, which stands between the citadel walls and the sea. Although this is the trendiest part of town, it is still very much lived in, mostly by old people and gypsies. Just below the Portal de Tablas, on Plaza de la Constitución, is the market, with colourful stalls of fruit and vegetables, and nuts and pulses. The Croissant Stop is a great place for breakfast.

Calle Mayan's shoe shops, notably Lucky Lizard, are a good introduction to Ibiza's consumer delights. Most of the boutiques are on Calle Barcelona, Calle de la Virgen, Calle D'Emmig and Calle Sa Creu (Cruz on old maps). On Plaza Sa Tertulia, just off the sea-front, there is a hippy market.

There are lots of bars along the water-front, notably Mar y

Sol, a stylish café on the corner with Avenida Ramón y Tur, which serves scrumptious toasted sandwiches and fresh fruit juices and milk shakes as well as more conventional drinks; and Zurito, a state-of-the-art *tapas* bar, where the delicacies include stuffed artichokes and canapés of smoked salmon and caviare. At the far end, on Calle Garigjo, by the sea wall, Coqueiro is a pretty cocktail bar, where the drinks come with nibbles of roasted almond and fresh pineapple. The best of the reasonably priced places to eat are Italian.

Avenida Ramón y Tur, and its continuation, Calle Conde de Rosellón run from the water-front to the old walls, forming the border between Sa Penya and the new town. There are some good shops along here, and the bar of the Teatro Pereyra is one of Ibiza's best, a stylish place which attracts an eclectic crowd for its nightly jazz, soul or funk gigs. The music starts at 10pm, after which the price of drinks doubles.

The main avenue of the new town is Paseo Vara del Rey, along whose tree-lined spine there is a craft market at Easter.

Main sights

● **The Museo Arqueológico** is housed at different levels inside the fortifications. The finds here come from all over Ibiza and Formentera and range from a pre-Carthaginian grinder found in a megalithic tomb at Ca na Costa on Formentera to eighteenth-century ceramics. The comical (and X-rated) terracotta figures of men and women of 400–600 BC were found in a well on the Illa Plana, the islet in Ibiza bay which is now joined to the mainland by a causeway, and it is assumed that they were thrown there as part of some ritual. Also worth seeing are the images of the Carthaginian goddess Tanit.

● The **Puig des Molins** museum stands at the foot of a hillside honeycombed with tombs, and the entrance ticket includes a visit to one of the tomb chambers. The necropolis was used from pre-Carthaginian to Roman times, and despite having been looted on numerous occasions, yielded a fantastic range of objects buried with the dead. Visits to the necropolis leave at quarter past the hour, and take you inside one of the burial chambers, with their large stone tombs *in situ*.

Ibiza's town beaches

The beaches to the immediate west of Ibiza town are uncomfortably close to the airport and suffer from aircraft noise.

They are also pretty unappealing – **Figueretas**, is a small wedge of hard-packed sand backed by apartments, and **Playa d'en Bossa**, a two-kilometre ribbon of fine pale sand overlooked by a styleless resort. **Talamanca**, to the west, is unalluring, a coarse sand beach with bars, and hotels.

Further east, and reached along a road by the salt pans, **d'Es Cavallet** is the island's official nudist beach. On the other side of the headland, **Ses Salinas** (Platja de Mitjorn on some maps) is one of the best beaches on the island. There is a cheap beachside *hostal* here, the Mar y Sal (Tel (971) 30 74 42) which has nine basic rooms with tiny bathrooms.

The coast to San Antonio Abad

There is no road along the south-west coast apart from a short stretch north of Cala Vadella. Instead you drive inland through groves of olives, figs and almonds, with views of thickly wooded hills sprinkled with white villas and refurbished farms. The best place to stop for a drink inland is **San José**, a spruce village of cubic whitewashed houses.

Cala Jondal has a coarse sand beach uncomfortably strewn with large round pebbles in a sheltered bay overlooked by private cliff-top villas. Much sandier, but very small, are **Cala d'Hort** and nearby **Cala Carbo**. They look out to the rocky Es Vedrá islet, which played the part of Bali Hai in the film of 'South Pacific'. All these beaches are reached along rough tracks.

Cala Vadella has a pleasant soft, pale sandy beach in a calm bay flanked by rocks and pines and some villa developments and apartments. The cliff-top road beyond is lovely, with views over to the craggy serrated coast. Further on **Cala Tarida** is a secluded, if crowded beach between two rocky headlands and backed by beach club development. **Cala Comte** (Cala Conda on road signs) is a calm, limpid bay with a small sandy beach fringing the foot of a cliff, a wedge of sand backed by dunes and pines, and an islet offshore. There is a bar open in season. It is accessible by road, or by bus or ferry from San Antonio, so gets pretty packed. **Cala Bassa**, beyond, is even more popular, as it is also served by regular boats from San Antonio.

San Antonio Abad

If you know anyone who has been to Ibiza and loathed it, it's more than likely they stayed in San Antonio Abad. The once-beautiful bay is hemmed in by towers of white concrete, the skimpy man-made beaches are dirty, the resort spills back over a dreary plain and bars have names like The Geordie Lad and Don Juan. During the day holidaymakers head off to nearby beaches by boat-trip or moped. At night the 'West End' starts shaking with the beat pumping out of the bars and discotheques.

Just north of San Antonio Abad, **Cala Salada** is a small sand and shingle beach backed by pines at the mouth of a sheer ravine.

The north coast: Puerto de San Miguel to Portinatx

From **San Miguel**, a village of low-rise apartments dominated by a cubic church on a mound, a road winds down a neatly terraced hillside to **Puerto de San Miguel**. Embraced by creamy-gold cliffs tufted with scrub is a calm, turquoise bay with a sandy beach, unfortunately marred by the two giant butterscotch-coloured hotels clamped to the rocks.

A short drive away, however, isolated high up on the wooded cliff tops, above a narrow valley is an exclusive hotel, the Hacienda and a discreet *urbanización*, **Na Xamena** (H). The only sounds are the wind in the trees and the waves stirring the shingle and breaking on boulders at the foot of the tumbling cliffs. The villas come with and without swimming-pools, and some pools are shared. For details write to 344 Aparteda de Correos, Ibiza, Tel (71) 33 30 31.

Hillsides terraced like an amphitheatre and planted with olives and almonds rise behind a tremendous bay, Cala Xaracca. There are only rocks to swim off, but the water is fantastically clear, and it is understandably popular with snorkellers. Over the headland, is **Portinatx**, a peaceful family resort on a rock- and pine-fringed bay. There are ample places to eat and drink, plenty of accommodation in low-rise apartments and simple hotels, but little nightlife.

The bay is warm and shallow, and good for young children, but the beaches are small and get very busy with coach-loads of trippers from elsewhere on the island. The resort is quietest at the far end, where there is a hotel, Cas Mallorquin, and block of apartments, Holitel, by a tiny beach used by fishermen. The main beach is sandy and backed by pines, and there's another, minute beach, just outside the resort which belongs to the Club Portinatx hotel.

Cala Sant Vicens to Cala Llonga

Pine-cloaked hills fringe the serrated, foam-frilled coast, and inland olives, almonds and figs grow in fields and terraces of red-gold earth. There are a number of pretty (and busy) coves, and larger beaches at Cala Sant Vicens and Santa Eulalia. Only stay at **Cala Sant Vicens**, a small and rather bland resort at the foot of the craggy Punta Grossa headland, if all you want is a hotel, a beach and the sea. There are a couple of large hotels, and the beach is narrow, but the water in the rock- and pine-flanked bay is wonderfully deep.

South of Sant Vicens the road runs along the cliffs above the scalloped coast to **Agua Blanca**, a shingle beach with patches of sand which is mostly used by nudists. To reach the next beach, Es Figueral, you have to cut inland across a plain where wind-blown figs and almonds grow in the rich red soil. The village of San Carlos, south-west of Es Figueral, used to be popular with local hippies. **Cala Mastella**, a tiny pale sand beach in a pretty bay fringed by low rocks and overhanging pines, boasts a bar (in season), a restaurant, Sa Seni, in the shallow valley behind, and a handful of secluded villas.

Cala Llenya has a sandy beach at the head of a long, deep inlet enclosed by red-gold cliffs. The neat white villa clubs among the pines are mostly used by Germans. The nicest are in the La Joya area. Signs for 'Home do it' pizzas and 'all well done' *sangría* might endear you to **Es Caná**, but the resort is too big for its strip of sand, and the apartment blocks look like British comprehensive schools. There are boat-trips to Santa Eulalia, the Tagomago islet and Formentera.

Within walking distance of Es Caná is **Punta Arabi**, a large apartment complex where a hippy market is held every Wednesday.

Santa Eulalia del Río (H)

Santa Eulalia is a well-established (though still-growing) resort, and one of the first places on the island to be settled by foreign hippies and artists. Many of them are now buried in the graveyard of Santa Eulalia's little hill-top church. Today it is a relaxed, lively and unmistakably Ibizan resort, with stalls selling hippy and ethnic crafts along its tree-lined avenue. It also opens out of season, and is a good choice for an Easter holiday.

The resort is currently being extended to the south, along a roadside beach of fine sand. The central beach is far pleasanter, a crescent of pale sand overlooked by palm trees and cafés – The Owl and the Pussycat is one of the more stylish. There are plenty of places to eat, drink and shop, and a reasonable selection of nightlife. The beaches can get rather scruffy in high summer but there are ferries to local coves.

Cala Llonga, to the south, is a characterless and rapidly expanding resort in a lovely wooded, hilly setting around a long, indented bay. The sand is greyish at the best of times and rain can reduce the beach to a mud bed.

Formentera

Once a primitive paradise for beach bums, Formentera now appears in package brochures, although a shortage of water has kept development in check. There are regular ferries and hydrofoils from Ibiza, which lies just three nautical miles away – an hour by ferry and half an hour by hydrofoil.

That said, the beaches are far larger and considerably quieter than Ibiza's, though frequent choppy seas, and a number of strong undercurrents, mean that swimming can sometimes be risky. The few villages are extremely dull places, worth visiting only to stock up on food, and there is little else to do apart from splashing in the sea and sunbathing. Most people get around by cycle or moped – but though the going is easy, the landscape is hardly inspiring. Frankly, you'd be better off staying on Ibiza and coming to Formentera on a day-trip.

The island is only about 25 kilometres long, and apart from a hill at the far end, it is flat and almost barren. Under the Romans it was a major producer of wheat (its name was originally frumentaria, or granary) but nowadays the fields are over-run with wild herbs and little grows except fig trees. Virtually all the island's provisions come from Ibiza.

Formentera is really two islets joined by a sand-fringed causeway, which is only about two kilometres wide. Platja de Mitjorn is the island's longest beach, but there are more sheltered beaches at the resort of Es Pujols and on the spindly Trucadors peninsula. Nudism is common.

Ferries dock at La Sabina, a little port with a handful of *hostales* and bars set between two lagoons: the Estang de Peix, used for watersports and the Estang Pudent, fringed by salt pans. Taxis and a bus meet the ferries, and there are plenty of places to hire bicycles, mopeds and cars.

If you're on Formentera only for the day, hire a bike or moped, and head up to the Trucadors peninsula, a couple of kilometres away. It form a long spit of pale dunes, sprouting shrubs, pines and sea grasses, and is traversed by a track sparkling with salt crystals. There are beaches on either side, and a number of bars. Illetas, on the left, is quite exposed and breezy, but Llevante is fairly sheltered.

The two nicest places to stay on the island are Cala Sahona and Es Caló, though you'll need transport to reach beaches where you can swim. **Cala Sahona** has a hotel above a white powdery sand beach backed by pines in a rocky cove, but there are dangerously strong undercurrents. **Es Caló**, has a pleasant *fonda*, Rafalet, adjoining a restaurant on a rocky stretch of the causeway's north shore.

Platja Mitjorn, forms the south side of the causeway, a seemingly endless fine sandy beach. There are apartments at the east end but the west end is quite wild, backed by apricot-coloured rocks and pine trees. The sea can get quite choppy.

The one real resort, **Es Pujols**, is not particularly attractive, but its talcum powdery crescent of sand is pretty and the sea is fairly sheltered. There are lots of hotels, apartments, cafés, restaurants and souvenir shops – so avoid it if you are coming to Formentera for peace.

Finally, you could drive up La Mola, the highest point on the island. The ascent through pine woods, with glimpses down the the sea, is lovely, and there are great views from the *mirador* restaurant-bar.

WHERE TO STAY

Mallorca

BANALBUFAR

Hotel Mar i Vent   ££
Mayor 49
07191 Bañalbufar   *Tel (971) 61 80 00*

A thoughtfully managed hotel sitting on terraced slopes stepping down to the sea, with a pleasant garden, swimming-pool and tennis court. Most of the public rooms have shiny chequerboard floors.

Open: Feb–Nov **Rooms**: 25 **Facilities**: swimming-pool, tennis **Credit/charge cards**: none

CALA RATJADA

Hotel Cala Gat ££
Ctra Del Faro s/n
07590 Cala Ratjada Tel (971) 56 31 66

Large, functional public rooms, and plain, rather dated bedrooms, in an unfussy but comfortable hotel a little way out to the north of the resort. Some balconies overlook gardens and a pool amongst pine trees.

Open: Apr–Oct **Rooms**: 44 **Facilities**: swimming-pool, table-tennis **Credit/charge cards**: none

Ses Rotges ££
Rafael Blanes 21
07590 Cala Ratjada Tel (971) 56 31 08

Not easy to find, Ses Rotges is better known locally as a restaurant with rooms rather than a hotel. But there is no compromise on comfort or style in the bedrooms, which have solid wooden furniture, cool cotton upholstery and plenty of space. Public rooms have lots of interesting nooks and crannies with Spanish ceramics, exposed beams and huge urns with gigantic plants which spill out on to a lovely courtyard restaurant.

Open: Apr–Oct **Rooms**: 24 **Credit/charge cards**: Amex, Diners, Eurocard, Visa

CALA DE SANT VICENC

Hostal Los Pinos £
Cala de Sant Vicenç
07460 Pollença Tel (971) 53 12 10

A white villa with Moorish arches, cut into the hillside 150 metres from the rocky beach. Bedrooms are old-fashioned with high old beds, and views a bit marred by nearby hotel development. Basic furnishings make this *hostal* comfortable rather than luxurious, but the atmosphere is informal and friendly, and the grounds are lovely, with landscaped shrubs and trees.

Open: Apr–Oct **Rooms**: 19 **Facilities**: swimming-pool **Credit/charge cards**: Eurocard

DEIA

Pensión Miramar £
07179 Deià Tel (971) 63 90 84

This is a small family-run hotel in an old stone villa which stands by a small stream above the village's vegetable gardens and orchards. There are paintings by local artists in the reception hall, and furnishings throughout are rustic, complementing shrubs in terracotta pots and cool marble floors. Rooms vary in size and the larger ones have *en suite* bathrooms.

Open: Mar–Nov **Rooms**: 9 (2 with bathroom) **Credit/charge cards**: none

LLUCH ALCARI

Costa d'Or	**£**
Lluch Alcari	
07179 Nr Deià	*Tel (971) 63 90 25*

Lovely views from this cool villa on the hillside, but a long walk down to the rocky beach. Accommodation is good value in simple rooms with hard tiled floors and small, clean bathrooms. Elsewhere furnishings are solid and plain with heavy print wallpaper – an unusual feature in a Mallorcan villa. The terraced gardens include a bar, pool, mini-golf and tennis – diversions you'll appreciate as you are some distance from the nearest town.

Open: Apr–Oct **Rooms**: 42 **Facilities**: swimming-pool, tennis, mini-golf **Credit/charge cards**: Eurocard, Mastercard, Visa

ORIENT

L'Hermitage	**£££**
Carretera de Sollerich	
07349 Orient	*Tel (971) 61 33 00; Fax (971) 61 33 00*

A seventeenth-century convent which has been converted into a comfortable country hotel. The chapel remains, with a plain stone altar, the restaurant is dominated by an olive press and in the entrance hall plants stand on chunks of twisted columns. Most of the rooms are in a terrace of bungalows, which look more authentic inside than out – beamed ceilings, abacus-legged Mallorquin furniture, and some four-poster beds – but are kitted out with mini-bars and TVs. Rooms in the newer annexe are modern and smart. There is an outdoor swimming-pool.

Open: 16 Dec–31 Oct **Rooms**: 20 **Facilities**: swimming-pool, tennis **Credit/charge cards**: Amex, Diners, Eurocard, Visa

PALMA

Hotel Mirador	**££**
Paseo Maritimo 10	
07014 Palma	*Tel (971) 23 20 46; Fax (971) 23 39 15*

There are large rooms, many of which have magnificent views of Palma and its bay, in this medium-sized water-front hotel. The furniture is a bit worn, and there is some street noise.

Open: all year **Rooms**: 78 **Credit/charge cards**: Amex, Diners, Eurocard, Visa

---

Hostal Pinar   £
Camillo José Cela
6 Son Armadans
07014 Palma   *Tel (971) 23 65 05*

Simple rooms with whitewashed walls and shuttered windows just below the castle Bellver on the fringes of the lively tourist area of Palma.

Open: all year **Rooms**: 30 **Facilities**: swimming-pool
Credit/charge cards: none

PALMA NOVA

Hotel Punta Negra   £££
Carretera de Palma
07011 Portals Nous   *Tel (971) 68 07 62; Fax (971) 68 39 19*

A wonderful, luxury hotel with excellent food and a prime position on Mallorca's south coast. The hotel has two tiny private beaches, immature but shady gardens and a pool outside, and cool, spacious public rooms inside. The receptionist doubles as a water-ski instructor on request.

Open: all year **Rooms**: 61 **Facilities**: swimming-pool; tennis and golf nearby **Credit/charge cards**: Amex, Diners, Eurocard, Visa

PUERTO DE POLLENCA

Hotel Formentor   £££
Playa de Formentor
07470 Puerto de Pollença   *Tel (971) 53 13 00; Fax (971) 53 11 55*

You should not let the hair-raising drive along twisty mountain roads from Puerto Pollença put you off this hotel. Its isolated position amongst woodland and fragrant gardens overlooking the sea is its main attraction. Rooms are simple with plain furnishings which are characteristic of the hotel throughout. The huge dining-room expands on to an elegant terrrace.

Open: Apr–Nov **Rooms**: 127 **Facilities**: swimming-pool, tennis, mini-golf **Credit/charge cards**: Access, Amex, Diners, Eurocard, Visa

Hotel Illa d'Oro   £££
Paseo Colón
07470 Puerta de Pollença   *Tel (971) 53 11 00; Fax (971) 53 32 13*

A splendid 1929 hotel, right on the water-front, at the quiet end of
the resort. The rooms are dazzlingly white, with rich blue soft
furnishings, and all have balconies. The first-floor rooms have enormous terraces which virtually overhang the water. There is no beach
at this end of the resort, but you can swim from pontoons.

Open: all year **Rooms**: 119 **Facilities**: tennis **Credit/charge cards**:
Amex, Diners, Eurocard, Visa

Miramar   ££
Paseo Anglada Camarasa 39
07470 Puerto de Pollença   *Tel (971) 53 14 00*

Close to the Hotel Illa d'Oro, and ideally situated on the water-front
at the better end of the resort, Hotel Miramar is half Spanish villa –
with heavy wooden antiques, copper plant pots and cane chairs – and
half anonymous tower block which provides an ugly six-storey
extension. Rooms in the older half are nicer, especially on the first
floor where balconies constitute terraces. Those in the modern block
are plain with '70s décor and good-sized bathrooms.

Open: Apr–Oct **Rooms**: 69 **Credit/charge cards**: Amex, Diners,
Eurocard, Visa

Sis Pins   ££
Anglada Camarasa 77
07470 Puerto de Pollença   *Tel (971) 53 10 50; Fax (971) 53 40 13*

The best of the hotels along this pedestrianised water-front. Sis Pins
is comfortable and stylish, with rugs on its hard tiled floors, fresh
flowers at every table in the dining-room and original paintings on
the walls. Rooms are not large and can be rather noisy on the roadside; ask for one with a sea view.

Open: Apr–Oct **Rooms**: 50 **Credit/charge cards**: Diners, Visa

Menorca

MAHON

Hotel La Isla   £
Santa Catalina 4
071701 Mahón   *Tel (971) 36 64 92*

Incredible value for money is this newly refurbished family-run *hostal* in a quiet quarter of orderly whitewashed terraced houses. Rooms are simple, with tiled floors, pastel-coloured curtains and woolly bedspreads, but not all have bathrooms. The communal bathrooms, like the whole hotel, are, however, gleamingly clean. There is a bar and basic restaurant downstairs.

Open: all year **Rooms**: 15 **Credit/charge cards**: Mastercard, Visa

---

Port Mahón   £££
Avenida Fort de L'Eau 12
07701 Mahón   *Tel (971) 36 26 00; Fax (971) 36 43 62*

A modern, henna-coloured hotel in a built-up area overlooking the port. Rooms on the port-side can be noisy, but they have the better view. Rooms are neither stylish nor luxurious, but are comfortable and well maintained. There is a small amoeba-shaped pool.

Open: all year **Rooms**: 74 **Facilities**: swimming-pool
Credit/charge cards: none

Hotel del Almirante   £££
Fonduco Puerto de Mahón
PO Box 246 Carretera de Villacarlos   *Tel (971) 36 27 00*

This hotel is a real treat. Once the home of Lord Collingwood, friend and colleague of Nelson, the house is full of naval memorabilia, and the present owner greets his guests with a live parrot on his arm. Most of the interior is genuinely antique with dark oil paintings and a marble backgammon table. Bedrooms are simple with views over surrounding countryside.

Open: May–Oct **Rooms**: 38 **Facilities**: swimming-pool, tennis, pool table **Credit/charge cards**: none

---

SAN LUIS

Hotel S'Algar   ££
Urb S'Algar s/n
07710 San Luis   *Tel (971) 15 17 00; Fax (971) 35 04 65*

Serene rooms with tasteful modern furniture and terraces in a comfortable whitewashed hotel with restaurant, café and swimming-pool. There is no beach, but tennis, windsurfing, sailing and mini-golf are available in the purpose-built resort.

Open: May–Oct **Rooms**: 228 **Facilities**: swimming-pool, tennis, mini-golf **Credit/charge cards**: Amex, Eurocard, Mastercard, Visa

Ibiza

IBIZA

El Corsario ££
Poniente 5
07800 Ibiza   *Tel (971) 30 12 48*

A hotel with a Bohemian atmosphere and good views from an ancient and rambling whitewashed house in Ibiza old town. The rooms are all different, but if you're lucky it will be enormous, with a heavy moulded fireplace, a rosary, a stopped clock and pictures ranging from Napoleon at Elbe to an Andrea del Sarto Virgin on the wall, and a large terrace. The water supply can be temperamental.

Open: all year **Rooms**: 14 **Credit/charge cards**: Amex, Eurocard, Mastercard, Visa

Hostal Marina £
Olozaga 7
07800 Ibiza   *Tel (971) 31 01 72*

The new rooms (all with bathroom) are right in the heart of the trendy Sa Penya quarter, above a bar where the DJ stands in the window playing deafening club tracks. The rooms have whitewashed walls and pine furniture and the bathrooms are rather small. Surprisingly, the window and shutters block out most of the racket. The older rooms without bathrooms across the road above the owner's restaurant are less comfortable.

Open: all year **Rooms**: 25 **Credit/charge cards**: none

SAN MIGUEL

Hacienda £££
en Na Xamena nr San Miguel
07800 apartado 423 Ibiza   *Tel (971) 33 30 46; Fax (971) 33 31 75*

Probably the best hotel in Ibiza, and luxury of course doesn't come cheap. Surrounded by trees, high above the sea, the Hacienda is peaceful and has wonderful views. Decorated in archetypal Spanish style, with plain white walls and, in some rooms, highly patterned ceramic tiles, bedrooms are grand. Some have massive Jacuzzi baths and dramatic views of the gorge below. There are three pools.

Open: May–Oct **Rooms**: 63 **Facilities**: swimming-pool, tennis, hairdresser **Credit/charge cards**: Amex, Diners, Eurocard, Visa

SANTA EULALIA DEL RIO

Hostal Yesibah   £
Avenida Generalísimo s/n
07840 Santa Eulalia del Río   Tel (971) 33 01 60

A small and very simple *hostal* in a pretty square near the beach.
Much less frenetic than the large hotels nearby, the Yesibah is family
run and its bar is popular with locals. Rooms are plain with just
enough comfort and have small but spotless bathrooms.

Open: Apr–Oct **Rooms**: 26 **Credit/charge cards**: none

Hostal Jerez   £
Del Mar s/n
07840 Santa Eulalia del Río   Tel (971) 33 02 32

A very reasonably priced hotel close to the beach and above a bar run
by friendly British people. The rooms have whitewashed walls,
prettily scalloped bedheads and peachy satin soft furnishings. Bathrooms are small, but adequate.

Open: Apr–Oct **Rooms**: 24 **Credit/charge cards**: none

THE CANARY ISLANDS

THE seven major Canary Islands, and six little islets, lie scattered in a roughly horizontal line across about 500 kilometres of sea just a shade north of the Tropic of Cancer. The nearest mainland is the bulge of Africa, over 100 kilometres east of Fuerteventura.

The Canaries form an autonomous region of Spain. Since the last administrative shake-up, they have been split into two separate provinces. The western group, centred on Tenerife, includes Gomera, La Palma and Hierro. The eastern islands are Lanzarote, Fuerteventura and Gran Canaria, with the capital in Las Palmas.

The total population of the islands is about one and a half million, including many different nationalities. Several thousand British expatriates live on the islands permanently, and many more own second homes. Each year the population is greatly distorted by an influx of about five million tourists, most of whom are British or German. Many of the workers in the tourist industry are 'godos' (peninsular Spaniards – literally, 'Goths'), not native Canarians. In fact, the indigenous pure-bred *Canario* is nearly as elusive as that little yellowish finch which you may be lucky enough to hear singing uncaged on these islands.

Outside the characterless mediocrity of the tourist resorts, the range of landscapes in the Canary Islands is astonishing. You can drive from semi-desert to a snow-line in under an hour; from ancient forests to treeless lava badlands, through luxuriant banana plantations or carnation farms to sand dunes, Arizona-like gorges and arid plains. The Canaries owe their most spectacular scenery to their volcanic origins, yet here again, the islands are dissimilar. Fuerteventura has seen no volcanic activity for many thousands, perhaps millions of years; La Palma last erupted as recently as 1971. Fortunately for the tourist industry, no human fatalities have been recorded, though economic damage to the islands has been enormous.

Cultural interest on the Canaries is limited. There are still a few places where you can see something like a pre-tourism existence, particularly in Lanzarote and the tiny islands to the west, where traditional ways of life and agriculture continue. The older towns, notably cosmopolitan Las Palmas and Santa Cruz, have a more genuine local feel than any of the new resorts. You will encounter vestiges of folklore – jolly, lilting dances and songs – and island sports like *lucha Canaria* (Canarian wrestling), but these seem mostly put on for the

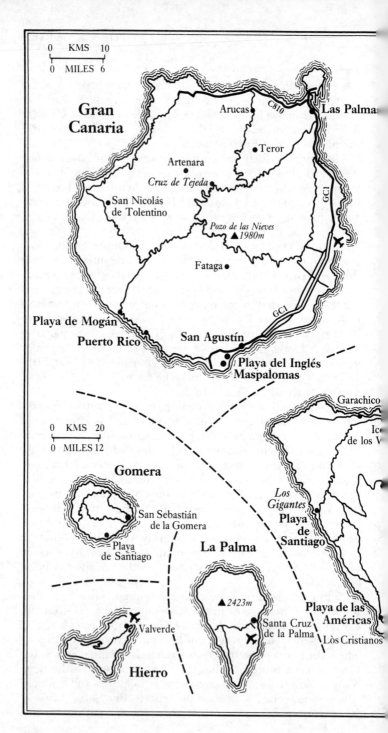

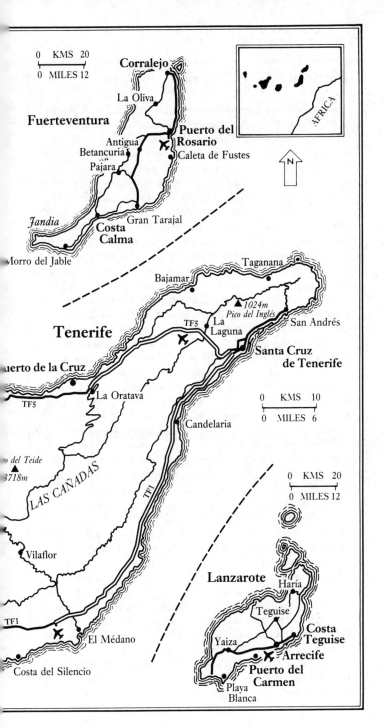

0 KMS 20
0 MILES 12

Corralejo

La Oliva

AFRICA

N

Fuerteventura

**Puerto del
Rosario**

Antigua
Betancuria
Pajara

Caleta de Fustes

Jandia

Gran Tarajal

**Costa
Calma**

Morro del Jable

Taganana

Bajamar

▲ *1024m*
Pico del Inglés

TF5
La
Laguna

San Andrés

Tenerife

**Santa Cruz
de Tenerife**

uerto de la Cruz

0 KMS 10
0 MILES 6

TF5

La Oratava

Candelaria

o del Teide
▲
3718m

LAS CAÑADAS

TF1

0 KMS 20
0 MILES 12

Vilaflor

Lanzarote

Haría

Teguise

TF1

El Médano

Yaiza

**Costa
Teguise**

Arrecife

Costa del Silencio

**Puerto del
Carmen**

Playa
Blanca

Planning your holiday

The tourist areas are mostly brash and ugly, full of high-rise hotels or sprawling villa complexes. Car hire agencies, exchange offices, shopping malls (*centros commerciales*), nightspots and tourist offices fill the spaces between accommodation blocks. Not every example of recent architecture is unpleasant however, and at least the kind Canarian climate means that plenty of luxuriant vegetation rapidly disguises the rawness of the concrete slabs.

The tempering influences of trade-winds and ocean currents produce an equable climate, but individually the islands vary enormously: the easterly islands of Fuerteventura and Lanzarote have a great deal in common with the nearby Sahara desert; the tiny westerly ones are much wetter, lusher and cooler; and the mountainous central islands of Tenerife and Gran Canaria have mixed climates: sunny and arid in the south, much cloudier and greener in the north. High season in the Canaries is Christmas to Easter which is when most North Europeans go for winter sun. You can virtually guarantee that the weather will be milder than it is at home, but it may not be hot and sunny. Rain can really bucket down in the western islands and it is quite often cloudy, even chilly enough to require an extra blanket at night. You will certainly need an extra layer or two for exploring the mountain areas. For a better chance of sunshine, head for the southern beaches of Tenerife or Gran Canaria, or the eastern islands of Lanzarote or Fuerteventura.

Plenty of organised excursions are available from the resorts on Gran Canaria and Tenerife. There is also a reasonably efficient bus network on the larger islands. (The local word for bus, incidentally, is *guagua* (pronounced wahwah), not *autobus* as in the rest of Spain.) If you plan to do much exploring on any of the islands, it is a good idea to hire a car. Car-hire is on the cheap side, and compares favourably with the cost of whole-day excursions, or with using island taxis for long distances. An hour's taxi ride between Tenerife's two airports (there is no direct bus) costs far more than hiring a small car for a day. Be warned that roads can be very variable – good or excellent between big resorts; but often bumpy, narrow and winding in mountain regions. Fuerteventura and Gomera currently have the poorest roads, but these are steadily being improved.

It is easy to hop between islands. The most popular 'excursion' trips are ferry journeys from Tenerife to Gomera, or between Lanzarote and Fuerteventura. Two rival ferry companies operate regularly from Los Cristianos in south Tenerife to San Sebastián de la Gomera, one providing a conventional car-ferry, the other a jetfoil service (although this is cancelled in choppy conditions). A ferry links Playa Blanca in Lanzarote with Corralejo in Fuerteventura, a 45-minute journey. All the islands except Gomera are accessible by air; the fares are not too expensive, and you waste very little time travelling as direct flights take half an hour or less from the major islands. The eastern island services are routed via Gran Canaria; western ones via Tenerife (mostly from the small northern airport of Los Rodeos).

You do not have to stay in big resorts, though it is difficult to avoid being automatically 'ghettoised' in unimaginative surroundings on a conventional package holiday. All but one of the islands have a *parador* in some scenic location (though that on Gran Canaria is only a restaurant). The exception, rather surprisingly, is Lanzarote, though in most other respects it scores highly for tourist facilities. Charming little *pensiones* in out-of-the-way places are, sadly, rare or non-existent.

Canarian food scarcely constitutes a distinctive cuisine, but there are a few specialities to look out for among the mass of international-style dishes. The most common are *papas arrugadas* (wrinkled little potatoes cooked in brine), and peppery sauces called *mojo*. Local fish is excellent. The best Canary wines come from Lanzarote, La Palma, and Tenerife, but the quantities produced are very small, so they tend to be expensive. Sticky liqueurs made from bananas and other fruits can be very sweet indeed, but are worth trying.

'Duty-free' is used to sell a range of items to tourists, but is a misnomer: goods sold in the Canaries are now subject to duties and taxes. But there are still bargains to be picked up if you know what to look for, and what you should expect to pay. Tobacco (especially local cigars) and alcohol are reliably inexpensive, but check UK prices of electronics or luxury goods (perfume, jewellery, leather or silk) before you leave home.

● **Regional Tourist Board**: Director General de Promoción del Turismo (planta 6º), Plaza de los Derechos Humanos, Edificio Usos Múltiples, plantas 6º y 7º, 35003 Las Palmas de Gran Canaria, Tel (928) 36 16 00. Each of the Canary Islands has a main **tourist office** in its capital, and additional offices in all the main resorts. You can also obtain information and leaflets about local attractions, events, festivals and so on from hotels, car-hire offices and travel agencies. All the larger tourist offices have English-speaking staff.

sake of visitors. Island crafts, too, are the sort designed to catch the tourist's eye and wallet. The most memorable surviving examples of Canarian culture are festivals such as the great Lenten carnival in Santa Cruz, the Corpus Christi celebrations in La Oratava, or the village pilgrimages to local shrines.

A little history

The Canary Islands have been variously identified as Homer's Elysian Fields, Herodotus's Hesperides, and Pliny's Fortunate Islands, and are yet another candidate on that long list of Atlantis suspects. Many medieval travellers passed close to the Canaries, some unintentionally, blown there by storms. But no one took much notice of the islands until the Frenchman Jean de Bethencourt seized control of Lanzarote in 1402, and handed over his conquests to his liege and paymaster, Henry III of Castile. Later, the Catholic Monarchs scooped the Canary Islands into their rapidly growing pile of Spanish acquisitions.

When the first Europeans arrived to conquer and settle the Canaries, they found aboriginal inhabitants on all the islands. These Guanche people had a neolithic lifestyle, living in caves and wearing skins. Where they came from is a mystery, for they seem to have known nothing of navigation or boat-building, and apparently feared the sea. The Spaniards subdued them with the usual *conquistador* blend of perfidy and brutality, and within a few generations the Guanches were more or less extinct. No doubt a few Guanche genes linger on in present-day Canarians, but they have left little of their culture behind.

TENERIFE

Tenerife's massive appeal as a classic sun-and-sand destination is hard to understand. It is not always sunny, especially in the north. And the beaches are not natural blondes, though some are bleached with tons of imported Saharan sand. The choice for holidays lies between green scenery, black beaches and possibly damp, cloudy weather in the north, or sunny resorts in a parched setting in the south. On the grounds of charm and local atmosphere, the the northern resort of Puerto de la Cruz scores over its main rival Playa de las Américas. A two-centred package, with a hired car for at least part of the time, probably gets the best out of the island.

Puerto de la Cruz (H)

Tourism has completely taken over from fishing as the main business in this 400-year-old port. The picturesque old quarter around Plaza de la Iglesia, all wooden balconies and flower-filled squares, is carefully preserved as a place for thousands of cosmopolitan visitors to stroll and shop, but first impressions of the resort are of dozens of high-rise hotels dating from the '60s and '70s. The main clusters of these detergent packet-like blocks are in the new quarter behind the Lido, and in the La Paz and Botánico districts above the cliffs to the east. In the older central quarter are many small, budget hotels, including two charming old mansions. Behind the resort is a hilly green park where the Taoro casino is located, and several more scattered and secluded hotels. There is a huge range of restaurants of many ethnic types in the resort, some with terraces and gardens for dining outside. One of the most attractive in the old quarter is La Papaya.

The town has a long pedigree as a resort. The British began coming here over a century ago to convalesce or escape northern winters in the genteel grandeur of the Taoro Hotel (now the casino). Puerto (as it is generally abbreviated) has tried to maintain its image as a place for the more discerning tourist. Your first impressions may not entirely support this view, as touts accost you on the sea-front.

Puerto is not a beach resort. There is a small black-sand beach, but water babies head for the huge Lido designed by the imaginative Lanzarote artist and architect César Manrique. This beautiful complex of open-air seawater pools, islands, restaurants and sun-terraces covers eight acres on a rocky promontory. Along the landscaped traffic-free promenade, Calle de San Telmo is the prettiest stretch.

Sights worth visiting

Jardín Botánico (Botanic Gardens) Over 1,500 species are on show in these gardens, founded in 1788 by Carlos III. The centrepiece is a colossal 200-year-old specimen tree from South America labelled *Coussapoa dealbata*, with a mass of strangely fused trunks and aerial roots.

Bananera El Guanche A pricier, but well-organised tourist attraction in a commercial banana plantation.

571

Loro Parque Your entrance ticket includes a show involving parrots performing circus tricks such as flag-pulling and bicycle riding. Dolphins, flamingos and a large aviary are among other attractions.

Santa Cruz de Tenerife (H)

Most tourists limit time spent in the island's capital to a couple of hours' shopping. It is not an especially beautiful town, nor are its sights remarkable, but it is relaxing, a world away from the cosmopolitan razzmatazz of the big resorts. The shops near the Plaza de la Candelaria are good places to look for electronics, leather and Canarian crafts, and their prices are lower than in the main resorts. The African-style market, like an apricot-coloured souk, offers a daily cornucopia of fruit, spices, herbs and salted fish.

Santa Cruz's limited sightseeing includes an archaeological museum containing Guanche artefacts, and the fortress of Paso Alto, where the cannon that knocked Nelson's arm off during a raid on the city takes pride of place among its museum exhibits. The Municipal Park of García Sanabria is an attractive oasis of tropical trees and modern sculpture just off the Ramblas, a shady boulevard curving through the city centre.

At the Estación de Guaguas (bus station) or Plaza de España on the sea-front you can catch a bus to take you up towards the white fishing village of **San Andrés** (you can find excellent, untouristy fish restaurants here – choose Don Antonio, on the sea-front road), and the best beach on the island, **Las Teresitas**, constructed in 1975 from four million sacks of golden sand shipped from the Spanish Sahara. There are no hotels nearby.

CHASING THE DRAGON

DRAGON trees are a curiosity of the Canary Islands (particularly Tenerife) and much is made of them. These strange, primitive plants date back to the age of the dinosaurs and are scarcely graceful: bulbous, dropsical branches sprout tufts of stiff, spiky leaves at all angles. When the trunk is cut, the dragon tree oozes a reddish resinous sap, like blood. This peculiarity led to many weird legends, and magical properties were attributed to the resin, such

Northern Tenerife

The north-east peninsula

From San Andrés a lonely road climbs inland through wild mountain scenery of spurge, cacti and goats to the picturesque white fishing village of **Taganana**, a wrecker's paradise amid a scatter of sharp rocks on the north coast. Back inland, the mountain route across the Monte de las Mercedes ridge leads through a dense forest of primeval laurel trees, and past several panoramic *miradores*, the most dramatic of which is Pico del Inglés.

The resort of **Bajamar** on the north-east coast is run-down, with poor accommodation. For a treat, park yourself in the civilised, German-owned Café Melita near Bajamar to watch the sun sink over the waves from a glazed clifftop terrace, while sampling a tempting range of cakes. Back near the northern motorway, **Tacoronte** is the centre of a wine-producing area and the Bodegas Alfaro are worth a visit for tasting and buying (and also for a wine museum).

The town of **La Laguna** (H) is home to the University of the Canaries, and was Tenerife's capital until 1822. The old quarter has a fine main square and many palatial buildings, including a florid pink cathedral guarded by a row of slender palm trees.

La Orotava is popular with excursionists from the big resorts who want to remind themselves what a real town looks like. The main buildings to see are the Iglesia de la Concepción, a baroque flourish built in the eighteenth century, and the Casas de los Balcones, seventeenth-century mansions with ornate carved balconies of red pine. One contains a shop and showroom of Canarian crafts.

---

as the power to cure leprosy. Unlike other trees, they do not make annual rings, so like fading actresses their age is a mystery. Tourist literature exaggerates and declares the trees live for thousands of years. One huge specimen that blew down in a hurricane was alleged to be 6,000 years old. The tree in Icod is claimed variously to be somewhere between 500 and 3,000 years old. One thing is sure: if you buy Dragon tree seeds as souvenirs, you will have to wait a long time for them to grow up.

Playa de Santiago

This resort is also known as Los Gigantes (The Giants) from the black cliffs that lour claustrophobically over this part of the west coast. Developers have swarmed in the past decade to take advantage of the natural setting, the high sunshine record and its potential for sport fishing and scuba diving. The resort has a raw and chaotic look, as though the builders have only just left (and in some cases they are still there). A small marina has been constructed on the sea-front, with an unconvincing 'Canarian village' complex of shops, restaurants and apartments behind. Most of the resort consists of expensive villas and apartments; hotel accommodation is disappointing.

Teide and the National Park

A visit to Mount Teide counts as Tenerife's top excursion in more ways than one. The volcano stands in **Las Cañadas National Park** (H), a spectacular crater region of mineral-tinted, strangely shaped rocks and unusual vegetation. Lava streams from periodic volcanic activity lie all over the ancient beds of basalt. The Parador de Cañadas del Teide bags the best views of this dramatic scenery, a good place to base yourself (there is little choice!) either for lunch, or for a longer stay if you want to do some walking in the park. Apart from the peak itself, which most people ascend by cable car, the terrain is surprisingly flat. The cable car station is a mile or two from the *parador*, and the journey to the top takes eight minutes. Lengthy queues form in summer. Once disgorged, the fitter passengers scramble the last 160 metres past sulphurous blow-holes to the final crater at 3,718 metres. You can walk to Teide's summit along a footpath which begins at the edge of the Park near El Portillo, where there is a visitor centre.

Twisty roads from the southern resorts pass through semi-desert, flowery villages, and almond groves to converge at **Vilaflor**, the highest village on Tenerife and a fertile spa famous for the purity of its air and water. Lace and pottery and local produce (wine and cheese) are on sale at a craft centre. The scenery around the village is exceptional, and if you want to stop here, there are several pensions, bars and restaurants. An excellent place to stop for a meal, or a simple room, is the Belgian-run inn called Tajinaste, Tel (922) 70 90 49, standing on a hillside at the edge of the village.

Southern Tenerife

Los Cristianos/Playa de las Américas (H)

These two resorts in flattish, arid terrain have all but merged. Los Cristianos is the original fishing port; Playa de las Américas the purpose-built resort. (All road signs from other parts of the island show only Los Cristianos.) A certain amount of fishing still goes on at Los Cristianos and it is also a ferry port, so its harbour has a business-like air. The large hotels and new apartment complexes on the surrounding bare hills have placed rather too much strain on this little place: it is just about impossible to drive or park in the centre, and the small beach areas are insufficient for the number of tourists using them.

Playa de las Américas is unashamedly dedicated to the fun-shine cause. The resort appears at first sight to be a homo-geneous slab of modern hotels and shopping malls, but is quite a curate's egg. The main beach is a long, dreary, greyish stretch of sand and rounded pebbles cast up in mounds against the palm-lined promenade. But at either side, some hotels have scooped their sections of sand into sheltered coves which they have had protected by walls and reefs. Torviscas, towards the north, is one of the best beaches. Hotels and apartments are, for the most part, boring boxes, interspersed here and there with an occasional individual and imaginative design. The better complexes have large garden and pool areas which act as secluded oases for their inmates.

Local attractions include a mundane assortment of go-karts, aquaparks, fun cruises, cactus gardens and medieval banquets. One less run-of-the-mill sight is the **Barranco del Infierno**, near Adeje, a brown volcanic ravine of spiky crags.

Costa del Silencio

The southern tip of the island is dry and scrubby, but the charmless coastline is now peppered with low-rise self-cater-ing developments, some of which form huge self-contained estates. Ten Bel is one of the largest of these. Perhaps because of its flatness, this area is popular with disabled visitors, and some of the complexes have made efforts to accommodate people with special needs. Despite its nearness to Tenerife's Reina Sofia Airport, the name 'Silent Coast' is not completely inappropriate. But there is very little to do. The nearby fish-ing village of **Los Abrigos** is a promising lunch-stop: it has

575

seductive fish restaurants lining the narrow street by the harbour. La Langostera is one of the best, with excellent *tapas* and very fresh fish which you choose raw from the counter. **El Médano**, right next to the airport, has a couple of passable sandy beaches and good facilities for windsurfing, but the scruffy little town takes the biscuit as Tenerife's worst example of ugly jerry-building.

GOMERA

An easy ferry-hop from Tenerife, Gomera makes a popular excursion. For most people, a day of Gomera's luxuriant scenery and mountainous terrain is enough. Some Europeans have even colonised parts of the island permanently, choosing alternative lifestyles on sternly 'green' lines. Gomera is only about 25 kilometres across at its widest, and not particularly high (1,487 metres), but the central plateau of dead volcanoes is corrugated by deep ravines, making access very difficult.

The capital, **San Sebastián de la Gomera** (H), is a cluster of white, boxy buildings scattered around a grey beach. Its attractions are confined to a handful of minor Columbus associations. On the main square, you can see the Casa de la Aduana, where Columbus took water from the well for his ships. The inscription reads 'With this water, America was baptized'. In the Casa de Colón, where Columbus stayed, is a small museum containing models of his ships. The best view of the town and harbour is from the balcony gardens of the *parador*, which you reach by a steep and tortuous road leading up beside the church. This lovely house is well worth a look, even if you do not stay there.

The southern part of the island is much drier and more barren than the north. On the coast, down a long, time-consuming road of hairpin bends with fine coastal views, is the island's best beach, the grey, pebbly **Playa de Santiago** (H). Behind it is the Hotel Tecina, which functions as a self-contained mini-resort. In the centre of the island you reach the highest point, where, weather permitting, *miradores* on either side of the road give panoramic views of the island. All around is the **National Park of Garajonay**, important enough to rate as a UNESCO natural world heritage site. A rare example of well-preserved *laurisilva* (ancient native woodland of myrtle, ferns, laurel and giant heather trees), it covers about ten per cent of the island. Marked paths and picnic tables can be found among the trees.

On the west coast, the sheltered valley of **Gran Rey** has the mysterious hidden peace of Shangri-La. It grows a great variety of tropical crops like avocados and pineapples, on steeply terraced hillsides. Date palms give it a most exotic look and produce the local speciality, palm honey. Northwards you find Gomera's best scenery, where the villages of **Vallehermoso**, **Hermigua** and **Agulo** glow with flowers and shining banana leaves, and tiny tracks plunge down steep ravines to the coast. One leads to **Los Organos**, a minor curiosity of basalt rocks that look like organ pipes, though you need to take a boat trip to see them. **Las Rosas** is a popular spot for coach-trippers. A visitor centre has a tasteful display of local handicrafts and natural history.

LA PALMA

Without sandy beaches, flashy hotels or contrived amusements, La Palma offers visitors other attractions: peace, dramatic scenery, wildlife. It is probably the most ecologically aware of all the Canaries. The national park in the crater is carefully managed, and even the amount of lighting at night is controlled to keep the astronomers happy.

Two roads cross the central mountains offering a choice of plunging viewpoints of the big crater. The other roads all meander around the fertile coastal zones, where you are rarely out of sight of the sea. If you want to hire a car to explore, book before you arrive, and buy petrol in Santa Cruz; you can use an unexpected amount of fuel on low-gear mountain driving. The weather can make a great difference to your enjoyment of La Palma, so check a forecast before you go: it is a pity to trek up those steep mountains to a wall of mist.

Agriculture and home-grown industries of cigar-making and silk-weaving keep La Palma fairly prosperous, and it shows. The islanders seem to take an aesthetic pride in their surroundings. Their villages may be simple, but generally avoid the careless, even wilful ugliness of some Canarian architecture.

Santa Cruz de la Palma is the most elegant and best kept of any of the smaller Canarian capitals. In former centuries its wealth, based on sugar-cane growing and the timber trade, attracted unwelcome attention. The French pirate François le Clerc, known as Pie de Palo (Peg Leg), looted and fired Santa Cruz in 1553. The town you see today was subsequently rebuilt by royal grant. The historic centre lies around Plaza de

España and Plaza de Santo Domingo, a block behind the sea-front road. Many of the seventeenth- and eighteenth-century houses have large ornate balconies of red pine. One of the most interesting streets has the unexpected name of Calle O'Daly – after a successful Irish banana trader who settled here. The church of El Salvador, which survived Peg Leg's fire, contains a coffered ceiling in Mudejar style. The town hall dates from Philip II's reign.

If skies look clear, head without delay for one of the viewpoints of the Caldera de Taburiente. The southern route leads to viewpoints at the **Cumbrecita** and **Lomo de las Chozas** Passes. The north road climbs through pine and laurel woods to the **Roque de los Muchachos**, the highest point on the island. It is a tiring drive: steep, winding, and sometimes dangerous with loose rocks littered on the road. The final *mirador* gives a glimpse right over the lip of the volcano into the lost world of the huge wooded 900-metre-deep crater, sometimes a cauldron of boiling mist. But it may be completely clear on the other side, with plunging views across the north of the island to the sea beyond. Right at the top of the mountain is a cluster of little domed buildings like a space station. This is the International Astrophysics Observatory, opened in 1985 and it houses the William Herschel Telescope, the largest in Europe.

Lush banana palms wave around **Los Llanos**, La Palma's second town, and in early spring the stony volcanic terraces blush pink with almond blossom. Lava flows from past eruptions scar the landscape on this side of the island, completely dividing the village of San Nicolás, where Bodegón Tamanca, a roadside cave-bar where huge hams hang over wooden casks, makes a good stop for lunch. Here you can try La Palma's local wines by the glass, tapped straight from the cask. Service is cheerful and fast, food is simple but well-prepared, and the helpings are enormous.

At the southern tip of the island, vines struggle for survival among fields of recently cooled volcanic ash. Heading northwards towards Santa Cruz again is a lovely sea-view drive, past villages vivid with flowers and the winking mirrors of dozens of water cisterns. Gums and pines of prodigious size line the roadside. The coastal route north of Santa Cruz leads to the myrtle forests of Los Tilos, and several pretty fishing villages on a scenic stretch of coast around Barlovento.

HIERRO (H)

Hierro has virtually no sand, and no entertainment. What it does offer is a wild natural beauty, unusual trees and lizards, excellent walking, and peace and quiet. What little tourist development has taken place is small-scale and in harmony with its surroundings. The island's white wine is definitely worth sampling.

Very close to the airport is **Tamaduste**, the nearest thing Hierro has to a seaside resort. This little hamlet stands by a calm inlet protected by a sandbank. The dark pebbly scraps of beach have been augmented by artificial sun-terraces.

Hierro's main town, **Valverde**, the only Canary capital that is not a port, is placed some way inland from the little east-coast harbour where ferries land, Puerto de la Estaca. Nearly half of Hierro's population of 7,000 souls live in Valverde. The tourist office and couple of tiny museums are here; otherwise little will detain you. The large church of Nuestra Señora de la Concepción has patchy powder-blue columns and an air of having just called in the decorators. Bazar El Placer at Dr Quintero 23 is a worthwhile stop for the island's subtly flavoured speciality cheese-cakes (*quesadillas*). The best place to stay in Valverde is the Boomerang Hotel, Tel 55 02 00, a simple but well-kept house with green shutters.

From Valverde roads diverge to encircle Hierro, and you do not have to drive far in either direction to realise how varied this tiny island is. In some places the scenery is green and lush, bright with poppies, asphodels and almonds at various times of year. The northern part of Hierro is occupied by a large coastal plain called **El Golfo**, hemmed in by steep sheltering hills like the sides of a bowl. This is what remains of an ancient volcanic crater, half of which now lies under the sea. The plain is plotted and pieced with many crops, some growing under plastic. One of Hierro's spectacular view-points, the **Mirador de la Peña**, overlooks El Golfo. At the north-east end of El Golfo, a little building called the **Club Punta Grande**, Frontera, has managed to earn a *Guinness Book of Records* entry as the smallest hotel in the world. Precariously ledged just above the waves on a promontory around which cobalt water lathers into detergent suds, this tiny place has only four rooms, and is really a sort of simple pub which has achieved a certain cult status.

In contrast to the carefully farmed plots of bananas and

pineapples on El Golfo, the mountains behind are cloaked in a wild covering of ancient woodland, including a type of juniper known as the Sabine tree, which develops an extra-ordinary gnarled and twisted trunk when bowed by gales. Northern Hierro is also home to a large lizard (*lacerta simonyi*) found nowhere else in the world, a latter-day version of some primitive dinosaur now scaled down to about two or three feet long.

The southern peninsula is a region of volcanic badlands. In places the black and red lava has formed strange whorls as if it is still molten, and sometimes it is worn into holes like Swiss cheese. Beyond the badlands is a vivid turquoise sea boiling into lacy froth as it meets the black rocks and stacks at the foot of the cliffs. The best route to see this scenery is the road to the southern tip of Hierro, where a few bars, a café-restaurant or two and a couple of simple *pensiones* have turned the little white fishing port of **Restinga** into a simple resort for a few adventurous visitors.

GRAN CANARIA

In profile Grand Canary, to use its English name, is a classic volcanic cone, with its highest point, Pozo de las Nieves, slap in the centre of the island. Inland the roads follow the steep ravines (*barrancos*) that plunge through the mountains, weav-ing a tortuous path through beautiful but often intensely buc-kled terrain. Gran Canaria is the third-largest Canary, but the most densely populated. Over half its 600,000 inhabitants live in Las Palmas, the seat of the archipelago's autonomous government, and though much faded, still one of the most important ports in the world.

Las Palmas (H)

The area of Las Palmas most visitors are interested in stretches southwards down the east coast. This includes the smart residential district of parks and villas called **Ciudad Jardín** (Garden City), and the old quarters of **Vegueta** and **Triana**, where most of the sights and many 'duty-free' bazaars can be found.

Las Palmas looks beautiful from a distance, and in the sun. Close up, in grey weather, the charm fades. Columbus could probably still chart his way round the carefully restored mansions of Vegueta but the newer sections of the city have withered most gracelessly. For a good overview of the city, head for the **Paseo Cornisa** in Ciudad Jardín. From this height you can see dozens of ships at anchor and the marina bristling with the masts of smart ocean-going yachts. The leafy parks and gardens of expensive colonial-looking houses merge into the jostling high-rises of Las Canteras.

Not far below Paseo Cornisa is **Doramas Park**, a haven of palms and flowering shrubs away from the city's impatient traffic. The centrepiece is the traditional Canary-style Santa Catalina Hotel, a minor 'sight' in itself, and incidentally, the home of Las Palmas's casino. Nearby is the tourist attraction of **Pueblo Canario**, a little 'village' complex of a small museum, and Canarian-style shops selling local handicrafts. On Thursday afternoons and Sunday mornings a troupe of folk musicians gather here to perform local songs and dances.

The **Museo Canario** in the Vegueta district is a Canary-style house of wooden balconies and patios. Guanche exhibits are housed on two floors, including some gruesomely trepanned skulls and mummified corpses.

Columbus's House, the Casa de Colón, is an elegant mansion with a plant-filled patio, the residence of the island's first governor, Pedro de Vera, where Columbus is alleged to have stayed before and after his momentous first voyage. The most interesting exhibits are the maps showing the exact routes, timings and crews of each of Columbus's four voyages, and which of the Canary Islands he visited. In another room you can see parts of his diary.

The Cathedral is built in a variety of styles with three wide naves separated by a forest of palm-like columns. A small entrance charge includes admission to a museum. The well-kept square of Santa Ana in front of the Cathedral is surrounded by bronze statues of the Canary Islands' famous indigenous dogs, now extinct, which gave them their name (from the Latin *canis*; the birds were named after the islands).

South-west of the city is **Tafira Alta**, where a British colony of genteel invalids, tea-drinkers and tennis-players (advised by their doctors to avoid harsh northern winters) built fine villas in the nineteenth century. Here garden-lovers will find the **Jardín Canario**, containing groves of dragon trees and many native Canarian plants.

Eating out and shopping

Shopping is a traditional attraction of Las Palmas. Most of the shops advertising duty-free goods are behind Las Canteras, or in the Triana district near San Telmo Square. As in other great world bazaars, there are many counterfeit products and dubious guarantees to catch the unwary. Haggling is possible in many shops, especially those run by African or Asian traders.

Las Palmas has a huge range of restaurants of all ethnic types. Tenderete, Calle León y Castillo 91 does good classic Canary dishes, especially fish. On the sea-front, El Espagnol Típico is an unassuming, cheerful pizzeria serving competent versions of many Spanish dishes. At the north end of the beach, Casa Carmelo does a good range of well-prepared meat dishes in a civilised ambience, with good sea views.

The big resorts

Maspalomas (H) is built on a long series of sandy beaches, and now consists of a massive and more or less continuous 15-kilometre stretch of boom-town sprawl. It is actually three quite separate resorts: San Agustín, Playa del Inglés, and (confusingly) Maspalomas itself, sometimes referred to as Playa de Maspalomas, or El Oasis. There are further complications, with resorts within resorts, and straggling mini-developments further up the coast. These places offer beach-based activities, sunshine, a raucous round of nightlife and contrived entertainments such as camel rides, parrot shows, and Wild West theme parks.

Many confusing access roads trail to each resort from the main coastal highway. The first thing to do is try to establish some landmarks which will enable you to relocate your own accommodation. As a museum of package hotel architecture from the '60s onwards, Maspalomas is some collection.

San Agustín (H) has a pleasant mix of nationalities, and a more sedate atmosphere than the other two resorts. A narrowish strip of development extends over several beaches of varying quality. Playa de Tarajadillo to the east is quiet and attractive, monopolised by the isolated resort complex of Bahía Feliz. Playa de las Burras, westwards, is much more urban. The main beach, Playa de San Agustín, is darkish, but fine and soft, backed by cliffs and a winding narrow walkway that leads southwards through landscaped shore gardens past rocks and low-rise villas.

For a meal, try the San Agustín Beach Club, an expensive and smart restaurant with a luxurious swimming-pool, African décor (and waiters), and classy fish dishes.

As the name suggests, **Playa del Inglés** (H) has strong

British connections. A triangular development, solid with hotel and apartment blocks, extends towards a huge sandy beach. Many of the hotels have no seaside feel or views at all, and there is little relief from the concrete. Complexes vary in style from tastefully discreet to award-winningly horrific, but most are somewhere in the middle – just very boring. At night the resort twinkles with the neon of discos and nightclubs.

At **Playa de Maspalomas**, three luxury compounds now vie for exclusive rights to a romantic stretch of sand-dunes and palm-groves near the lighthouse. Notices telling you not to do this or that add an irksome note to the unquestionably good facilities. The dunes are officially a protected nature reserve, but naturists are more in evidence than flora and fauna. Further inland lie countless complexes of ritzy little bungalows around a golf course.

Best local attractions

Sioux City The rugged cactus scenery of the Cañon de Aguila is a perfect setting for this *paella* Western filmset. Shows are held twice a day, including cattle driving, stunt 'Indian' riding, lassooing tricks, and of course a bank holdup, followed by a mock lynching. It makes quite an expensive outing for a family, but it can be fun.

Palmitos Park This well-laid out park, again in a spectacular canyon setting, offers parrot shows every hour: obliging birds perform circus tricks like bicycle riding, roller skating, and bullfighting. The birds are kept in pleasant conditions (many flying freely), and the gardens are lovely.

Puerto Rico and Puerto de Mogán (H)

West of Maspalomas the recently developed resort of Puerto Rico concentrates more on low-rise self-catering and time-share complexes rather than large hotels, but the amount of building is ludicrous for the capacity of local beach space. Sports facilities and boat trips are advertised; otherwise there is very little to do within the resort, and the arid scenery and greyish beaches are not inviting.

Much better is **Puerto de Mogán**, a bright spark in Gran Canaria's diminished tourist scene. This new marina 'village' of low-rise apartments and a single hotel is a Scandinavian project, and exceptionally pretty. The houses are built in a stylish reinterpretation of local architecture and climbing plants romp all over the rooftops. Houses are arranged in little traffic-free 'streets' overlooking the luxury yacht marina and its associated restaurants, bars and shops. A sheltered crescent of artificial beach provides limited space for sunbathing.

Touring the island

Most excursion programmes include a trip to one of the island's most scenic spots, **Cruz de Tejeda**, where several roads meet at a spectacular viewpoint with a *parador* restaurant (a popular lunch-spot). Nearby is the highest peak of the island, **Pozo de las Nieves** (1,980 metres), topped by a meteorological station. From the southern resorts coaches grind in low gear up a scenic ravine road of candelabra cacti and shattered brown rock, past the white villages of **Fataga** and **San Bartolomé**, and the awesome crags of the **Roque Nublo**, a reddish spike of basalt sacred to the old Guanche kings. From a gap in the hills, the snow-capped peak of Mount Teide on neighbouring Tenerife can be seen, floating serenely on its dais of clouds and sea.

Teror is a fine old town with a famous shrine church, buttressed and belfried in tawny blocks of stone. Inside the silvery Virgin of the Pine Tree is kept busy with the prayers of distressed parishioners, whose votive images indicate the cause of their sufferings. Heading westwards from Cruz de Tejeda towards the village of **Artenara**, shaggy moss and lichen hang from the pine trees, and the rocks are riddled with caves. The best reason to stop in this high village is to track down the Mesón la Silla, a cave restaurant reached through a tunnel. The cave opens on to a sunny, rock-ledge belvedere with a magnificent view. Beyond Artenara is the pine forest of **Tamadaba** and here a scenic circular drive gives glimpses of reservoirs glinting far below. If you turn off west at the sign marked Acusa, the lonely minor road down to the market town of **San Nicolás de Tolentino** is one of the most spectacular on the island. It is not for the faint-hearted, being very steep and winding (going down is easier than coming up). Red rock pinnacles, cascades and jade reservoirs line this picturesque ravine.

Routes along the north coast are a total contrast to those in the arid south. Here luxuriant banana plantations cloak the slopes towards the sea. The best views are not from the low coastal road, but from the winding roads inland, which make for a grandstand journey most of the way. **Arucas** is a pros-

perous town with an enormous Gothic church of grey stone.
Firgas is a spa, where the island's mineral water is bottled.
Moya's church peers over the edge of a ravine. Near Guia,
the Guanche antiquity known as **Cenobio de Valerón** is a
mass of caves cut into a vertical cliff-face, variously thought
to have been used for religious purposes, as a refuge, or a
food-store.

More caves can be seen on the east side of the island. Those
in the red rocks lining the **Barranco de Guayadeque** have
been colonised by latter-day troglodites. Curious coach
parties find their way up here to have lunch in cave
restaurants.

The west coast of the island is isolated and difficult to reach
without your own transport, but the drive there is remarkably scenic, through the fertile Mogán valley planted with
pawpaws, aubergines and flowering shrubs. Further inland
the winding road passes through steadily more austere and
dramatic scenery of red-grey rocks, cliffs and quiet shingle
beaches. The fish restaurants of **La Aldea** and **Puerto de las
Nieves** make good lunch-stops.

LANZAROTE

Many people would cast a vote for Lanzarote if asked to say
which of the Canaries is their favourite. It is the most startling
of all the islands, a place of crisp shapes and vivid colours,
predominantly white (houses), black (fields) and green (windows). Most of the volcanic terrain is arid and treeless, yet the
emerald shoots of many different crops miraculously force
their way through the ashes and give the island a productive,
well-tended air. Several beaches of soft sand, dropped like
manna for the tourist industry by obliging Saharan siroccos,
line its coast. New development has been carried out with far
more respect for the environment than on the other Canaries,
and Lanzarote has managed to retain its reputation as a
'quality destination' in the travel trade.

Arrecife

The modern capital, where the airport stands, is a dullish
fishing port with dusty, pot-holed streets and mostly modern
buildings. The best things to see in Arrecife are two little sea-
front forts, both of which house museums. The more interesting is **Castillo de San José**, which contains a collection of

modern Spanish art on its upper floors. Downstairs is an imaginatively designed airy modern restaurant with panoramic views over the port. Day or night, it is a fine place for a meal. The other little castle, across a causeway bridge topped by cannonballs, is the sixteenth-century fortress of **San Gabriel**, where there is a small archaeological museum containing Guanche pots and primitive figures.

The main resorts

Millions have been poured into the dream playground of **Costa Teguise** (H) by one of Spain's largest mining conglomerates, the overt aim being to attract the jet-set. New roads complete with lamp standards and designer vegetation extend surreally between ready-staked but as yet unmolested building plots on an unpromising stretch of flattish and desolate coastal land. A few kilometres away, a golf course lies among the ash-strewn wasteland, as unnatural-looking as if it were made of astroturf. Upmarket time-share developments, several large hotels and countless neat little villas surround the limited facilities of half a dozen small sandy beaches.

Puerto del Carmen (H) is Lanzarote's largest resort. New development here has swamped two large, older hotels, and extends several kilometres along the coast and inland in dozens of accommodation complexes, all trimmed in blue, green or brown. The brand-new buildings still look very raw; more established ones luxuriate in a cladding of brilliant bougainvillea, hibiscus and mimosa. At the west end of the resort is the original village, which now functions mostly as staff quarters for local people who work in the resort.

The reason for all this building is a large stretch of excellent sandy beach, in several separately named sections. The best part is the secluded area by the Hotel Los Fariones. Other sections are more exposed to traffic noise and overlooked by developments behind, and the busy sea-front road presents a hazard for children or elderly people. The eastern section called Playa de los Pocillos is as wide as a football pitch. At night the bustling atmosphere continues with several discos and late-opening restaurants. Watersports facilities, including a windsurfing school, are available.

At the southern tip of the island is up-and-coming **Playa Blanca** (H), which takes advantage of several small but very beautiful sandy beaches, some hidden away in secluded coves on the rocky peninsula of Papagayo. Development here has generally been low-key but genuinely stylish – more casually chic than the other main resorts. The centre of the resort is in a state of upheaval as roads, drainage systems and telephone lines are put in place.

People who come here are the type who are happy with quiet beach pursuits and limited nightlife, and who do not mind the comparative isolation of the resort from the rest of the island. It is best to have your own transport – buses are infrequent and taxis expensive. The peaceful Papagayo beaches are very popular with naturists, but access to them, across a maze of unmarked dirt-tracks behind the resort, is less than obvious.

A promenade of cafés and apartments now replace Playa Blanca's original fishing cottages, but the fleet still offloads its daily catch by the harbour, and you can get excellent fresh fish in local restaurants. From Playa Blanca's little harbour it is an easy ferry hop to the neighbouring island of Fuerteventura, and a further choice of soft, white-sand beaches.

The Timanfaya National Park

From 1730 Lanzarote suffered a catastrophic series of volcanic eruptions that lasted six years. About eleven villages are buried under Timanfaya's lava. The volcano craters, though not very high (510 metres), form a fascinating landscape of what look like dying embers: smoothish red-black cones emerging from the corrugated rubble of the *malpaís* (badlands), a wilderness of lava where scarcely a leaf survives. Near the entrance to the park is the **Islote de Hilario**, a visitor centre where you board one of the buses that leaves every hour or so for a circular tour (included in the price of your entrance ticket). Commentaries relay fascinating facts and figures in several languages, accompanied by eerie 'volcano' music. At the visitor centre you will be entertained by little experiments which show the Fire Mountains are not yet dead. Sausages and steaks steadily barbecue over a natural geothermal grill, and are later served in the panoramic restaurant of El Diablo.

Touring the island

A good main road traverses Lanzarote like a spinal cord. Along it lie several of the island's prettiest villages. One of the largest is **Yaiza**, a well-kept place with a Moorish look to its white cube-shaped houses scattered in a fertile landscape of palm-trees and bright flowers. The Fire Mountains loom in

587

the background, and crops of onions, potatoes, melons and vines sprout from carefully tended beds of black ash. A roadside bar/restaurant complex makes a popular coach tour pitstop, but a classier and more memorable experience is the typical Canarian restaurant of La Era, in an old shuttered house at the back of the village.

Further inland lies an agricultural region called **La Geria**, where each plant (mostly ancient, gnarled vines) is carefully protected from wind and sun in its own little pit with a lava wall around it. The product is an unusual white wine made from Malvasia grapes. **Mozaga** is the centre of the wine industry.

Teguise, the island's capital until 1852, is a lovely old-fashioned small town with wide cobbled streets and white aristocratic-looking houses. On the main square is a fine church with a bell-tower of brownstone, and the Spinola Palace, which can be visited. Every Sunday there is a market, a good place to buy local handicrafts – a speciality is the *timple*, a stringed instrument. The views from the nearby castle on the Guanapay volcano top are excellent.

Towards Lanzarote's northern tip, you enter the Valley of Ten Thousand Palms (an exaggeration), like some desert oasis. White, African-looking houses scatter the fertile valley sides, and the largest settlement is **Haría**, one of Lanzarote's most beautiful villages. Several appealing *miradores* with restaurants make good stopping-places on this route. The most well-known and spectacular is the Manrique-designed Mirador del Río at the north tip of the island, where a dramatic cliffside belvedere overlooks the peaceful islet of **Graciosa**. Boats leave daily for the beaches of Graciosa from **Orzola**, but this little port is well worth a visit in any case for a fish lunch by the quayside, stationed over turquoise seas and black rocks.

On the east coast the villages of **Mala** and **Guatiza** are famous for prickly pears, the foodplant of the cochineal bug, once a significant Canarian industry.

The Main sights

● **Cueva de los Verdes** This lava cave was formed by a great tube of molten material solidifying into an underground tunnel. Hourly tours take you through the passages, where lava drips form rooftop 'icicles' and metallic ores colour the rocks. The best part of the tour is an astonishing lake (actually a shallow puddle) which perfectly mirrors the roof.

● **Jameos del Agua** Another section of the Cueva de los Verdes system, now imaginatively transformed by César Manrique into a spectacular restaurant and nightclub, in several landscaped caves with pools, gardens and a natural underground lake inhabited by a unique species of blind white crab which glow like stars in the water.

● **Las Salinas** At Janubio the sea is trapped in progressively smaller and shallower grid-like walled pits, and the white crystalline piles of gathered salt glint in the sun.

● **Los Hervideros** The sea rushes in and out of underground caves in the rocky lava coast, spouting out of blow-holes.

● **El Golfo** A mysterious green pool below a much sculpted cliff. From a distance, it looks like a large puddle of anti-freeze, a weird contrast with the bright cobalt of the sea on the other side of the grey beach.

FUERTEVENTURA

The second largest of the Canary Islands lies less than 100 kilometres from the Saharan coast of Africa. Barren, sandy, windswept, poor, its human population of 30,000 is outnumbered by over 60,000 roaming goats who reduce what little vegetation exists to stunted scrubland. What people come to Fuerteventura for, and find, is a beach-bum's paradise: white sand secluded enough for naturism; a hot, dry climate; and a brilliant, unpolluted sea ideal for scuba diving, windsurfing and snorkelling. The tourist culture of the island is predominantly Germanic. Car hire is expensive because of the bad condition of the roads. If you plan to head for beaches down dirt tracks, you will be better off with a four-wheel-drive jeep.

The north and the centre

The island's capital, **Puerto del Rosario** (H), lacks conspicuous charm: half-built houses and piles of rubble litter the outskirts, and a perfectly decent road suddenly disintegrates into unsigned chaos to herald your arrival. You are unlikely to want to linger long here but the *parador* behind the beach makes an adequate base for a night.

Corralejo (H) is a fairly drab fishing village, its limited charm now being further eroded by crass and ugly buildings. Good points include the little offshore islet of Los Lobos (boat trips and fishing are available), and the sandy beach which is still lovely, despite the two graceless hotels plonked on it.

South of Puerto del Rosario, just past the airport, is a small resort of low-rise apartments and villas called **Caleta de Fustes**, around a pleasant sheltered bay of white sand. Castillo de Fustes, Tel (928) 16 31 00, is one of the self-catering villages here, set around a carefully reconstructed eighteenth-century watchtower and a neat marina of pleasure boats. This is one of Fuerteventura's more tasteful developments, with a pleasant mix of nationalities and good, family-oriented facilities.

The old capital of **Betancuria** is no more than a village now, but one of the few genuinely attractive places on the island. Small white houses cluster round a fertile valley of palms, a secret oasis amid bare mountain crests. The large cathedral is one of the most visually appealing buildings on the island. Frustratingly, Betancuria seems to lack not only accommodation, but even a decent bar or restaurant.

A good lunch-spot is the nearby village of **La Antigua** on the so-called 'windmill route'. The journey from Betancuria is quite beautiful, a steep descent through a startling landscape of ancient russet volcanoes, worn into smooth, soft undulations like quilted eiderdowns. La Antigua stands in a gentle valley of dusty palms. One of its aged windmills, at the north end of the town, has been restored and converted into an attractive restaurant, La Molina, serving Fuerteventuran specialities – the local cheese is worth trying.

South of **Pájara**, where the church has unusual carvings of allegedly Aztec origin, the minor road leading over the mountains to La Pared is one of the most scenic on the island; a fine route to reach the southern peninsula. Towards sunset the antique sleeping volcanoes burst into a vivid mosaic of pinks, mauves and terracottas, and as the road twists, you glimpse first northern, then southern vistas of turquoise sea, and views of the serpentine hills of Jandía stretching into the distance.

Jandía

Gran Tarajal, in the south of the island, merits little time, but close by to the east is the hilly fishing village of **Las Playitas**, where white houses splashed with vivid creepers surround a small bay of dark rocks and grey sand. Here there is a delightful simple restaurant called Brisamar, where a glazed terrace festooned with plants overlooks the waves a few feet away.

The **Playas de Jandía** proper start around the burgeoning artificial *urbanización* of Costa Calma on the southern side of the peninsula. Although the word '*playas*' is plural, the beach is actually a single more or less uninterrupted, though variable, 22-kilometre stretch of sand – sometimes scooped into attractive shallow bays, sometimes stretching out of sight with the dismal sterility of a desert.

Costa Calma (H) is a new and rapidly mushrooming resort, with perhaps twenty or thirty modern complexes of hotels, villas and apartments so far, spaced along the low cliffs behind the best section of the Jandía Playa, a beautiful crescent of pale golden sand given visual interest by low headlands at either end. Accommodation is generally of a high standard and the resort rises, and retires, early. A welcome exception to the curfew is the cheerful Posada San Borondón in the Centro Comercial, which keeps good beer and food flowing until after midnight, in a rustic ambience. Further down the coast the main road becomes more tortuous, climbing steeply round the hills, as far as **Morro del Jable**, a disfiguring rash of building works.

WHERE TO STAY

Fuerteventura

CORRALEJO

Hotel Tres Islas	**£££**
35660 Corralejo	*Tel (928) 86 60 00; Fax (928) 86 61 50*

Of the two large high-rise blocks that grace, or disgrace, the beach, the Tres Islas is infinitely nicer in atmosphere, furnishings and facilities than its neighbour. The tariff reflects this in no uncertain terms.

Open: all year **Rooms**: 365 **Facilities**: swimming-pool, tennis **Credit/charge cards**: Amex, Diners, Eurocard, Visa

COSTA CALMA

Hotel Fuerteventura Playa	**£££**
35627 Costa Calma	*Tel (928) 54 73 44; Fax (928) 87 00 97*

Well-designed shallow curved bedroom blocks form an open-ended oval of gardens and pools, and all rooms have balcony views of the sea. There is easy access through gardens to an excellent stretch of the Jandía Beach. Public areas are a little echoey in evenings, but bedrooms are unusually spacious, stylish and peaceful, fitted with practical modern furnishings. Good value.

Open: all year **Rooms**: 300 **Facilities**: swimming-pool, tennis **Credit/charge cards**: Amex, Eurocard, Visa

---

Sotavento Beach Club   £££
35627 Costa Calma   *Tel (928) 54 70 41; Fax (928) 87 10 41*

It has mainly German clientele and public areas can feel noisy and crowded when in full swing, but the apartments by the beach score for architectural imagination (Moorish arches, textured rendering, complex roofscapes) and seem very luxuriously fitted.

Open: all year **Rooms**: 294 **Facilities**: swimming-pool, minigolf **Credit/charge cards**: Amex, Diners, Eurocard, Visa

---

Bahía Calma   ££
35626 Costa Calma   *Tel (928) 54 70 31; Fax (928) 85 00 32*

An unobtrusive pleasant white bungalow complex towards the southern end of the resort. Several slightly different types of villa give it a village-like appeal. Lots of established vegetation and direct access to the sea.

Open: all year **Rooms**: 111 **Facilities**: swimming-pool, children's playground **Credit/charge cards**: Amex, Visa

---

Hotel Risco del Gato   £££
35627 Costa Calma   *Tel (928) 54 71 75*

The poshest and most expensive development in Costa Calma, exclusively sited on its own stretch of clifftop and beach. Futuristic architecture of space-age 'bubbles', virtually concealed in the hillside. Each forms a separate luxury unit with its own little garden and sitting-room. Still very new, so it feels rather raw.

Open: all year **Rooms**: 51 **Facilities**: swimming-pool, tennis **Credit/charge cards**: Eurocard, Visa

---

PUERTO DEL ROSARIO

Parador de Fuerteventura   £££
Playa Blanca
35610 Puerto del Rosario   *Tel (928) 85 11 50; Fax (928) 85 11 58*

A vaguely colonial, green and white building; not an especially luxurious or high-profile *parador*, but pleasantly furnished in an eclectic mix of traditional styles. Convenient and comfortable enough as an overnight base.

Open: all year **Rooms**: 50 **Facilities**: swimming-pool, tennis
Credit/charge cards: Amex, Diners, Eurocard, Visa

Gomera

PLAYA DE SANTIAGO

Hotel Tecina   ££
Lomada de Tecina
38811 Playa de Santiago   *Tel (922) 89 50 50*

This modern low-rise complex forms the largest hotel on Gomera, and functions as a self-contained resort with many sports and entertainment facilities. Tastefully designed in traditional style (white walls, wooden balconies, pantiles), it is owned by the Olsen family, of Norwegian ferry fame.

Open: all year **Rooms**: 258 **Credit/charge cards**: Amex, Diners, Eurocard, Visa

SAN SEBASTIAN

Parador Conde de la Gomera   £££
Balcón de la Villa y Puerto Apartado 21
38800 San Sebastián   *Tel (922) 87 11 00; Fax (922) 87 11 16*

A peaceful hotel with friendly staff but an exclusive air. It successfully evokes a local manorial style, and is attractively furnished with dark wood and plants. The shallow pantiled roofs and mottled walls ramble round sheltered patios and beautiful tropical gardens. The views are spectacular from this clifftop site; Teide is visible on a clear day. Many German guests: it is very popular and you are advised to book in advance.

Open: all year **Rooms**: 42 **Facilities**: swimming-pool
Credit/charge cards: Amex, Diners, Eurocard, Visa

Gran Canaria

LAS PALMAS

Hotel Santa Catalina   £££
León y Castillo 227
35005 Las Palmas   *Tel (928) 24 30 40; Fax (928) 24 27 64*

Not, as might be expected, in Santa Catalina Park, but in Doramas

Park, near the Pueblo Canario. This famous secluded hotel displays remarkable architecture, in traditional Canarian style, with wooden balconies and baroque turrets. Inside, its old-fashioned character does not quite excuse the dowdiness, and the facilities are not quite up to the mark for the prices charged.

Open: all year **Rooms**: 208 **Facilities**: swimming-pool
Credit/charge cards: Amex, Diners, Eurocard, Visa

Hotel Reina Isabel   £££
Alfredo L Jones 40
35008 Las Palmas   *Tel (928) 26 01 00; Fax (928) 27 45 58*

Las Palmas's most comfortable and best-equipped hotel, slap in the centre of the Las Canteras promenade with a panoramic (recommendable) restaurant on the eighth floor, called La Parilla.

Open: all year **Rooms**: 233 **Facilities**: swimming-pool
Credit/charge cards: Amex, Diners, Eurocard, Visa

Hotel Imperial Playa   £££
Ferreras 1
35008 Las Palmas   *Tel (928) 26 48 54*

An unlovely block from outside, but recently renovated with smart, practical modern facilities, and new fire safety systems. Excellent views and a good position at the quiet end of the beach, with fishing boats below. Access and parking are tricky, but it is good value.

Open: all year **Rooms**: 142 **Credit/charge cards**: Amex, Diners, Eurocard, Visa

---

MASPALOMAS

Hotel Maspalomas Oasis   £££
35100 Maspalomas   *Tel (928) 76 01 70; Fax (928) 76 25 01*

Of all the luxury compounds near the lighthouse, this well-established hotel has the most exclusive and secluded air, with stylish modern paintings, excellent facilities, and peacocks strutting among the palms. Some bedrooms have less than interesting car park views, and staff can be offhand.

Open: all year **Rooms**: 335 **Facilities**: swimming-pool, tennis
Credit/charge cards: Amex, Diners, Eurocard, Visa

PLAYA DEL INGLES

Hotel Sandy Beach   ££££
Menceyes s/n
35100 Maspalomas   *Tel (928) 76 33 78; Fax (928) 76 72 52*

Above-average and pleasantly designed on a hilly central site, this place scores for its exceptionally attractive gardens and Andalucian-style public areas. Bedrooms are spacious. The accent is on the young, and there is some noise from surrounding nightspots.

Open: all year **Rooms**: 256 **Facilities**: swimming-pool, tennis **Credit/charge cards**: Access, Amex, Diners, Eurocard, Visa

Hotel Parque Tropical   ££££
Avenida Italia 2
35100 Maspalomas   *Tel (928) 76 07 12*

One of the most pleasing of all Playa del Inglés hotels, secluded but easily spotted because of its distinctive pagoda-like entrance tower. Inside it is a charming Canary-style complex, built round central tropical gardens with running water. Views to open sea and direct access to beach make it popular – and it is often fully booked.

Open: all year **Rooms**: 235 **Facilities**: swimming-pool, tennis, playground **Credit/charge cards**: Amex, Diners, Eurocard, Visa

PUERTO DE MOGAN

Club de Mar
Puerto de Mogán
35140 Playa de Mogán   *Tel (928) 56 50 66; Fax (928) 74 02 23*

A sophisticated hotel/apartment complex in Scandinavian style, casual but chic, and representing remarkable value. Low-rise, it is distinguised by blue and white features, and has charming painted wooden furniture. There are lovely views from its dining-room and sun terrace. Apartments in this marina village are also very pretty, but some may suffer from late-night noise.

Open: all year **Rooms**: 160 **Facilities**: swimming-pool **Credit/charge cards**: Amex, Eurocard, Visa

SAN AGUSTIN

Hotel Melia Tamarindos   ££££
Las Retamas 3
35100 Maspalomas   *Tel (928) 76 26 00; Fax (928) 76 21 56*

This civilised, peaceful five-star, one of Gran Canaria's best hotels, occupies an amphitheatre-like setting in beautifully landscaped gardens behind the sea-front. A casino and large popular nightclub, La Scala (cabaret shows) are attached to it.

Open: all year **Rooms**: 332 **Facilities**: swimming-pool, tennis
Credit/charge cards: Amex, Diners, Eurocard, Visa

Bahía Feliz £££
Playa de Tarajillo
35100 Maspalomas *Tel (928) 76 46 00*

This large but pleasantly designed Scandinavian complex of apartments, shops, restaurants and a hotel is effectively a self-contained mini-resort. It has a friendly feel and small but pretty beach areas and is particularly good for windsurfers and families with children.

Open: all year **Rooms**: 255 **Facilities**: swimming-pool, private beach
Credit/charge cards: Amex, Diners, Visa

Hierro

Parador Isla de El Hierro £££
38900 Valverde *Tel (922) 55 80 86*

This low-rise, modern pantiled building lies south of the airstrip, at the end of a long, lonely coastal drive sheltered by a dramatic black volcanic cliff (beware rockfalls on road). The hotel is pleasantly informal and intimate inside with attractive local décor – weavings and pottery. There is a pebbly beach and the sea is right next to the hotel, which is very peaceful.

Open: all year **Rooms**: 47 **Facilities**: swimming-pool
Credit/charge cards: Amex, Diners, Eurocard, Visa

Lanzarote

COSTA TEGUISE

Meliá Salinas £££
Playa de las Cucharas
35500 Costa Teguise *Tel (928) 81 30 40; Fax (928) 81 33 90*

An award-winning design by César Manrique, this is one of Lanzarote's most luxurious and expensive hotels. A central atrium drips with plants and water-gardens. Its excellent facilities, well-tended grounds and fine sea-front position on the best beach insulate it from oppressive surrounding development.

Open: all year **Rooms**: 310 **Facilities**: swimming-pool, tennis, golf
Credit/charge cards: Amex, Diners, Eurocard, Visa

PLAYA BLANCA

Hotel Lanzarote Princess
Costa Papagayo
35570 Yaiza   *Tel (928) 51 71 08; Fax (928) 51 70 11*

An airy green and white tent-like building, pleasantly and stylishly furnished inside, though it is already showing a few signs of wear.

Open: all year **Rooms**: 407 **Facilities**: swimming-pool, tennis
Credit/charge cards: Access, Amex, Diners, Eurocard, Visa

Playa Flamingo Apartments   **££**
Playa Blanca
35570 Yaiza   *Tel (928) 51 73 00*

These score highly for their excellent location on a sunny slope, with direct access to twin sandy beaches. Facilities are fairly basic but pleasant enough with pine and light striped fabrics. Noise from the pool and bar area affects some apartments. Many of the guests are Swedish.

Open: all year **Rooms**: 300 **Facilities**: swimming-pool
Credit/charge cards: Eurocard, Visa

PUERTO DEL CARMEN

Hotel Los Fariones   **£££**
Acatife 2 Urbanización Playa Blanca
35510 Puerto del Carmen   *Tel (928) 51 01 75; Fax (928) 51 02 02*

An older and more established hotel than most on Lanzarote, occupying the best and most secluded section of beach at the west end of the resort, including a pretty and virtually private cove. Good facilities, lovely gardens, peaceful atmosphere, and large, comfortable bedrooms. Well-furnished apartments (separately managed) are available in an adjacent complex.

Open: all year **Rooms**: 231 **Facilities**: swimming-pool
Credit/charge cards: Amex, Diners, Eurocard, Visa

Tenerife

CANADAS DEL TEIDE

Parador de Cañadas del Teide ££
38300 La Orotava *Tel (922) 23 25 03; Fax (922) 23 25 03*

A fairly spartan version of the *parador* experience, with a rustic mountain-chalet look and wooden furnishings. Picture windows take advantage of the splendid views of Los Roques and Teide.

Open: all year **Rooms**: 18 **Facilities**: swimming-pool, tennis **Credit/charge cards**: Amex, Diners, Eurocard, Visa

LA LAGUNA

Hotel Aguere £
Obsispo Rey Redondo 57
38200 La Laguna *Tel (922) 25 94 90*

A distinctive hotel of great character, though not luxury, in a palatial mansion near the old quarter. It has a colonnaded plant-filled foyer, and simple, old-fashioned bedrooms with solid furnishings.

Open: all year **Rooms**: 20 **Credit/charge cards**: none

LOS CRISTIANOS

Hotel Oasis Moreque ££
Avenida Penetración s/n
38650 Los Cristianos *Tel (922) 79 03 66*

A small hotel with a secluded, personal feel even though it is surrounded by large hotels. The gardens are attractive and the pool palm-fringed.

Open: all year **Rooms**: 105 **Facilities**: swimming-pool, tennis **Credit/charge cards**: Amex, Eurocard, Visa

Tenerife Sur Hotel Apartments ££
Avenida en Proyecto s/n
38650 Los Cristianos *Tel (922) 79 14 74; Fax (922) 79 27 74*

One of the most appealing and well-kept complexes in the resort, though it is some way from the sea, with colourful gardens around irregular pools.

Open: all year **Rooms**: 189 **Facilities**: swimming-pool, squash **Credit/charge cards**: Access, Amex, Diners, Eurocard, Visa

PLAYA DE LAS AMERICAS

Hotel La Siesta   ££
Avenida Litoral
38660 Playa de las Américas   Tel (922) 79 23 00; Fax (922) 79 22 20

There is nothing remarkable about this low-rise beige block from outside, but it scores highly for its gardens and pool with oriental pavilion and palms. It has spacious, stylish bedrooms with sitting and dining areas; pleasant service, and good facilities.

Open: all year **Rooms**: 280 **Facilities**: swimming-pool, tennis
Credit/charge cards: Amex, Diners, Eurocard, Visa

Hotel Gala   £££
Avenida Litoral s/n
38660 Playa de las Américas   Tel (922) 79 45 13; Fax (922) 79 64 65

Large, box-like tiered balconies dripping with foliage overlook the sea and gardens on rising land at the north end of the resort. Though there is no shortage of action a short distance away, the hotel feels pleasantly peaceful. Stylish bamboo-and-cane look and light modern fabrics predominate.

Open: all year **Rooms**: 315 **Facilities**: swimming-pool
Credit/charge cards: Amex, Diners, Eurocard, Visa

Hotel Jardín Tropical   £££
Urbanización San Eugenio
38660 Playa de las Américas   Tel (922) 79 41 11; Fax (922) 79 44 51

One of the most beautifully designed of all Tenerife's hotels: a Disneyish fantasy of arches, turrets and galleries in an irregular complex. Lovely gardens, stylish Moorish décor and an excellent position make it highly recommendable, despite the price.

Open: all year **Rooms**: 380 **Credit/charge cards**: Diners, Eurocard, Visa

PUERTO DE LA CRUZ

Hotel Meliá Botánico   £££
Richard J Yeoward s/n
38400 Puerto de la Cruz   Tel (922) 38 14 00; Fax (922) 38 15 04

This is a traditional, well-established five-star hotel near the Botanic Gardens with a loyal band of adherents. Its main attraction is a secluded garden full of fountains and twittering birds and makes up in courteous service and magnificent breakfasts for what it lacks in fashionable furnishings.

Open: all year **Rooms**: 282 **Facilities**: swimming-pool, tennis
Credit/charge cards: Amex, Diners, Eurocard, Visa

Hotel San Telmo   ££
San Telmo 18
38400 Puerto de la Cruz   *Tel (922) 38 58 53*

San Telmo overlooks the pretty pedestrianised promenade by San Telmo beach in the resort centre. As it is situated above various commercial enterprises, expect some evening noise. Parking and access are tricky, and facilities are limited, but this hotel is good value if you like a sea view and nightlife close at hand. There is a terrace restaurant and lounge on the top floor.

Open: all year **Rooms**: 91 **Facilities**: swimming-pool
Credit/charge cards: Visa

Hotel Monopol   ££
Quintana 15
38400 Puerto de la Cruz   *Tel (922) 38 46 11; Fax (922) 37 03 10*

One of the quaint hotels in the old quarter skilfully converted from a traditional Canarian-style mansion. There is a tall plant-filled patio-foyer and public areas (some rather dark) include a quiet reading room. Bedrooms are simple.

Open: all year **Rooms**: 94 **Facilities**: swimming-pool
Credit/charge cards: Amex, Diners, Eurocard, Visa

Hotel Marquesa   ££
Quintana 11
38400 Puerto de la Cruz   *Tel (922) 38 31 51*

A very similar, slightly creakier version of the Monopol, with even simpler facilities and a lower tariff.

Open: all year **Rooms**: 88 **Facilities**: swimming-pool
Credit/charge cards: Diners, Eurocard, Visa

SANTA CRUZ DE TENERIFE

Hotel Mencey   £££
Avenida Dr José Naveiras 38
38001 Santa Cruz de Tenerife Tel (922) 27 67 00; Fax (922) 28 00 17

One of Tenerife's most superior hotels, recently renovated and firmly in the deluxe bracket. Staff are helpful and pleasant. It has an urban setting on the tree-lined Ramblas, but is near a park, and has its own gardens.

Open: all year **Rooms**: 298 **Facilities**: swimming-pool, tennis **Credit/charge cards**: Amex, Diners, Visa

---

Hotel Atlántico   ££
Castillo 12
38001 Santa Cruz de Tenerife   *Tel (922) 24 63 75*

A bright, clean, town-centre hotel which overlooks a pedestrianised shopping street near Plaza de España. There is a terrace bar-café on the first floor.

Open: all year **Rooms**: 30 **Credit/charge cards**: Diners, Eurocard, Visa

---

Hotel Náutico   £££
Profesor Peraza de Ayala 13
38001 Santa Cruz de Tenerife Tel (922) 24 70 66; Fax (922) 24 72 76

A newly opened, convenient business hotel in a quiet street near the port. Ultra-modern, antiseptic décor, but facilities are very good for the price. An easy walk will take you to port or town centre, and the hotel is near bus routes to Las Teresitas beach.

Open: all year **Rooms**: 40 **Credit/charge cards**: Amex, Diners, Eurocard, Visa

PRACTICAL
INFORMATION

USEFUL ADDRESSES

Spanish National Tourist Office, 57–58 St James's Street, London SW1A 1LD, Tel 071–499 0901

The Royal Automobile Club, RAC House, South Croydon, Surrey CR2 6XW, Tel 081–686 0088

The Automobile Association, Fanum House, Basing View, Basingstoke, Hants RG21 2EA, Tel (0256) 20123

Iberia International Airlines, 130 Regent Street, London W1R 5FE, Tel 071–437 5622

RENFE, Spanish National Railways, European Office, 1–3 Avenue Marceau, 75116 Paris, Tel (010 33 1) 47 23 52 00

British Rail, International Rail Centre, Victoria Station, London SW1V 1JY, Tel 071–834 2345

TRAVEL

Prices quoted below are intended as a guide only, to help you make comparisons. They are for the high season 1991, and rounded up to the nearest £5. Information and advice that applies specifically to each region is given under the 'Planning your holiday' sections of each chapter.

Air

There is a vast choice of cheap **charter flights** from the UK to destinations all over Spain; the bulk of the flights land in Majorca, Málaga and Alicante – where, even in mid-summer you can pick up a bargain for around £100 or even less. As well as from London (Gatwick and Stansted), you can fly direct from Birmingham, Bristol, Cardiff, East Midlands, Edinburgh, Glasgow, Leeds/ Bradford, Luton, Manchester, Newcastle and Teesside. You can book these flights through travel agents (who often advertise last minute deals with worthwhile savings), but it is worth shopping

603

around: look at the small adds in daily and Sunday newspapers, or magazines like *Time Out*. Several tour operators publish flight-only brochures: they are listed in the Spanish Tourist Office fact sheet *Holidays of Special Interest* (under Cheap Flights).

The Spanish state-owned airline, Iberia, operates the biggest number of regular direct scheduled flights from Heathrow, Gatwick, Birmingham and Manchester. Information and bookings can be made through their London office, 130 Regent Street, W1R 5FE (Tel 071-437 5622), or through any travel agent. In high season, return fares to Madrid start at around £240; prices are similar for Málaga, Seville and Costa del Sol, slightly less for Barcelona. Special early summer saver fares cut the prices drastically, making them very competitive with the charter flights.

Very useful for those touring a large area are Iberia's special tickets, which allow you to fly into one Spanish airport and home from another. The cheapest fare is called the Moneysaver – it costs from around £225 on the London Seville-Barcelona-London route, for example.

British Airways operate scheduled flights from London to twelve Spanish cities including Madrid, Málaga, Bilbao and Barcelona from London and also fly from Birmingham to Málaga three times a week and Barcelona four times a week. They also have a scheduled service to Madrid from Manchester daily, except Saturday. Other, smaller airlines also operate scheduled flights to the most popular tourist destinations, from London, Luton and Manchester.

Internal flights in Spain are operated by Iberia or its smaller subsidiary Aviaco. Most internal flights radiate from Madrid or Barcelona. A shuttle links these two cities – you just turn up and pay at the airport.

Rail

Getting there

The best rail route from the UK to Spain is via Paris, where you change stations (from Gare du Nord to Gare d'Austerlitz). From Gare d'Austerlitz, direct fast trains – called Talgos – run daily to Madrid and Barcelona via Portbou and Irun on the French/Spanish border. Journey time is 24 hours. The Talgos are modern, air-conditioned and have both seats and sleeping accommodation, which you should reserve before you travel. Most other types of trains from Paris to Spain involve a change, and they are slower and cheaper than the Talgos; for those going at any kind of pace a 'speed supplement' is charged. A new fast alternative to the Talgo is the new TGV Atlantique train Paris (Gare Montparnasse) to Irun, from where you can catch a Spanish (RENFE) train to Madrid. There is also a direct train from Calais to Portbou (daily in high summer, twice weekly the rest of the year) with connection to Barcelona.

Information and tickets Rail buffs can get hold of the Thomas

Cook Continental Timetable (available from Thomas Cook shops or by mail order from Thomas Cook Publishing, PO Box 227, Thorpe Wood, Peterborough PE3 6SB) to plan their own routes. Otherwise an information leaflet on services from London to Spain is available from the main British Rail stations, or phone 071–834 2345. A second-class return fare to Madrid costs £175, Barcelona £155, valid for two months. Tickets from British Rail worth looking into include the Inter-Rail 26-plus Pass (for those over 26) which gives unlimited one-month travel in 24 countries and is valid on all the Spanish national rail network (£235); the similar but cheaper Inter-Rail under 26 Pass; and the Rail Europe Senior Card for over 60s. You will still have to pay supplements for the very fast trains. Tickets are available from most major British Rail stations, British Rail appointed travel agents and from the International Rail Centre, Victoria Station, London SW1V 1JY. Credit card bookings can be made by telephoning 071–828 0892.

Getting around

A Tourist Card for the Spanish national railway network (RENFE) is available in the UK. This used to be good value, but has recently doubled in price which makes it quite an expensive option unless you are going to use the RENFE network almost constantly. Its one big advantage is that it saves you buying lots of individual tickets. The card allows unrestricted travel on all lines and by all scheduled trains (not the Paris-Madrid Talgo) in both first and second class for 8, 15 or 22 days. With the Tourist Card there are no speed supplements, but you still pay for other extras, like seat reservations. The card costs £120 second class for 8 days and £190 for 15 days. It can be used at any time without restriction. You can purchase it at British Rail's Victoria Station in London or from Wasteels Travel Ltd, 121 Wilton Road, London SW1V 1JZ, Tel 071-834 7066.

There is a perplexing variety of fares and surcharges on RENFE. Make sure you get the best value ticket for your journey: big savings can be made on Blue Days – *Dias Azules* – when you can get between 20 and 80 per cent discount for round trip, depending on the number of people travelling together. Blue Days are most days of the year except the main public holidays. Information is available from the RENFE offices (in the centre of nearly all big towns) or from the local Tourist Information Office. Buy your tickets well in advance, as ticket offices are almost constantly crowded. You can also buy tickets from Spanish travel agents displaying the RENFE sign: they may well be less crowded and the staff may be able to help out in English.

The RENFE network covers Spain pretty comprehensively. From Madrid, the distance to any city on the coast is around 400 kilometres, with a journey time of at least four and a half hours – slower trains take nine hours. Fast Talgo trains connect Madrid daily with all the major cities. The Estrella and Electren are also fast.

605

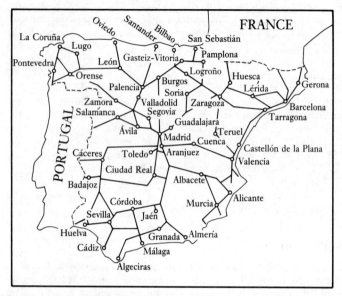

Rail routes in Spain

Rapido and Expreso are standard journey time trains and the Correo calls at every little village.

You can buy a timetable guide – *Guia RENFE* – at major stations in Spain or in the UK by mail order from BAS Overseas Publications Limited, Unit 1c, 159 Mortlake Road, Kew Surrey PW9 4AW, Tel 081–876 2131. Current cost is £9.50 including postage and packing. RENFE can also be contacted direct at Spanish National Railways RENFE, General Agency for Europe, 1 Avenue Marceau 75116 Paris, France, Tel 47 23 52 01.

There are a small number of narrow-gauge lines in Spain run by the privately-owned FEVE company. The main service runs from Bilbao to El Ferrol, and there is another between Alicante and Denia. The fares are more expensive than the buses, and the trains infrequent and slow.

Excursion trains

There are two major excursion trains in Spain – one of which runs on the narrow guage FEVE line in the north. Called the Transcantabrico, the train travels between Santiago de Compostela and San Sebastián. Sleeping accommodation is on board (the train stops at night), with meals in *paradores* and inns. The second excursion train is the Al Andalus Express – vintage carriages which run two regular itineraries around the Andalusian capitals (Seville, Córdoba,

Granada) and from Seville to Málaga and Marbella. The third itinerary is from Barcelona to Santiago. For information and booking details contact Marsans Travel, 65 Wigmore Street, London W1H 9LG, Tel 071–224 0504.

Coach and Bus

Getting there

You can catch a bus from London's Victoria Coach station to over 50 destinations in Spain. The main operator is Eurolines (UK) Ltd, 52 Grosvenor Gardens, Victoria, London SW1W 0AU, Tel 071–730 8235. You can also get booking details from any National Express office or from Victoria Coach Station, Tel 071–730 0202.

The five main services are London-Barcelona-Alicante, London-Madrid-Costa del Sol-Algericas; London-Vitoria-Zaragoza; London-Bilbao-Santiago; and London-Santander. Frequencies range from three times a week to Alicante to daily in peak summer to the Costa Brava and Barcelona. Fares are cheaper than travelling by rail, but not necessarily cheaper than bargain basement charter flights.

Another company, SSSI International Ltd, 314–316 Vauxhall Bridge Road, London SW1V 1AA, Tel 071-233 5727, run services from London to La Coruña and to Gijón, in Galicia, twice weekly through the year.

Getting around

Travelling round Spain by bus is the one way of getting off the beaten track. Prices are much the same as for the train and the whole country is covered by individual companies. For the main journeys from Madrid to the coastal resorts the coaches are large, fast and air-conditioned. You may also be able to leave luggage at bus stations – this facility having been withdrawn at most railway stations due to the threat of terrorism.

There may be two, three or more bus stations (*Estación de autobuses*) in any one of the big towns, and the best way of finding which one to aim for is through the local tourist information office. When consulting timetables posted up at stations, *diario* means daily, *laborales* means workdays including Saturdays and *domingos y festivos* means Sundays and holidays.

Ferries to the Balearics and Canaries

It is best to book the ferry before you leave the UK. Melia Travel, 273 Regent Street, London W1R 7PB (Tel: 071-409 1884) are agents for Transmediterranea who operate the main car ferry sailings to the Spanish islands. A small booking fee is payable. Ferries for Palma and Ibiza and on to the Spanish mainland at Valencia leave Sete, near

Marseille in southern France, once a week. Single adult fares start at around £130 for the car. The crossing takes 24 hours. Transmediterranea also operate ferries from Barcelona to Palma (8 hours), Mahón (9 hours) and Ibiza (9.5 hours) and from Valencia to Palma and Ibiza (both 9 hours), six days weekly in high season. Weekly ferries for the Canary Islands leave from Cadiz and call at Tenerife, Las Palmas and Arrecife. The journey time is around 18 hours.

Motoring Information

Driving licence

Holders of the old green UK driving licence are required to have an International Driving Permit, but an IDP is recommended even if you hold a pink EC licence (which is now issued automatically), to avoid local difficulties. An IDP is available by applying in person to AA or RAC offices for immediate purchase. A current full driving licence and a passport photograph are required. An IDP is valid for one year and can also be applied for by post – allow 28 days.

Insurance and Green Cards

British insurance policies now provide cover for accidents that occur in EC and other selected countries. However, the cover normally extends only as far as is necessary to comply with the legal minimum in the particular country through which you are motoring. So even if you have comprehensive insurance in the UK, you may not automatically get the same standard of cover abroad. If you give your insurance company notice (allow at least two weeks), it will extend your comprehensive insurance to include Europe. Some companies will do this free, others will make a charge.

When cover is extended insurance companies should also issue a Green Card. This is an internationally recognised certificate which proves that the holder is insured to the required minimum level for all the countries of Europe. The card is no longer compulsory within the EC (so Spain, too); an ordinary UK insurance certificate offers the same proof, but it is a moot point how many traffic policemen know that. Therefore, for the time being at least, it is worth carrying a Green Card. You can also purchase a Green Card at major Spanish border posts.

If you are involved in an accident in Spain, you may be imprisoned and your car impounded unless you produce a 'bail bond'. Most insurance companies issue these if you state you are heading for Spain, but it is best to check. Bail bonds can also be bought from the AA or RAC.

Breakdown cover is available through schemes like the AA's '5 Star', the RAC's 'European Service' and Europ Assistance's 'Premier

Service'. You can also buy medical and personal insurance combined with the breakdown cover – a convenient way of obtaining all your cover with one transaction.

Petrol

Fuel for your car costs roughly the same throughout Europe. There are two basic grades of petrol (*gasolina*) – Super and Regular. Most cars use Super. Diesel is also available at all stations (called *gas-oil or petroleo*) but lead-free petrol is still not commonly found away from large towns and tourist areas. Look for the sign *gasolina sin plomo*. The petroleum company CAMPSA produces a map of Spain showing all stations which sell unleaded (available in local tourist information offices) and there is a special consumer telephone number for this information in Spain – freephone 900 15 25 35. Credit cards are accepted at some stations, but cash is a safer bet in rural areas. You can import 10 litres of petrol in a can duty-free to carry as spare.

Route planning

Detailed information on route planning is available (to non- members, too, but more expensively) from either of the two big motoring organisations. The RAC will tailor a route for you, with their European Route and Touring Information Pack. They also provide a pack with European Routes and Town Plans. Both are available from RAC House, PO Box 100, South Croydon, Surrey CR2 6XW. If time is short you can ring and request a route (if it is available) on 081–686 0088. The AA produce tailor-made motoring routes and direct driving routes with no detours. Both are available from the Automobile Association, Fanum House, Basing View, Basingstoke RG21 2EA. The AA also produce a free brochure, *Guide to Motoring Abroad* and operate a telephone line with updates on traffic, weather and other road information for Spain, Tel (0836) 401 879. The RAC produce a booklet, *European Motoring Guide*, available from all RAC offices.

Crossing the Channel

Brittany Ferries operates the only ferry crossing from the UK to the Spanish mainland. There is a crossing twice a week from Plymouth to Santander in Northern Spain. The crossing takes 24 hours and the ferries are heavily booked at peak holiday times. Information and reservations from Brittany Ferries at The Brittany Centre, Wharf Road, Portsmouth PO2 8RU. Tel (0705) 827701 or Millbay Docks, Plymouth PL1 3EW, Tel (0752) 221321. The office in Santander is at Estación Maritima, Tel (942) 21 45 00. Fares start at around £90 to £105 per adult, £85 to £169 per car for an 8-day special return.

Calais and Boulogne are the best landing ports if you are going to

Barcelona and the coastal resorts. For Madrid and western Spain, it may be better to take one of the slightly longer channel crossings – to Caen, Cherbourg or St Malo. It can still work out cheaper than the Plymouth to Santander crossing, depending on the season and the number of people you travel with.

Motorail

French Motorail will take your car from Paris to Madrid (two trains leave daily all year round). Information and bookings are through French Railways Ltd (SNCF), 179 Piccadilly, London W1V 0BA, Tel 071–409 3518. Or you can book through the Royal Automobile Club. Return second class journeys cost £450 for the car and driver, £75 for each additional adult passenger. You can also book sleepers or couchettes and there are additional fast-train supplements.

Car hire

A fly-drive holiday is a good alternative to taking your own car to Spain, and can prove less expensive, particularly if you use low-cost flights and the cheapest hire-cars. The major car rental companies (including Avis, Europcar and Hertz) have offices throughout the mainland and on the islands. It is best to book in the UK before you leave. Two companies specialising in car hire in Spain from the UK are Atesa, through Marsans Travel, 65 Wigmore Street, London W1H 9LG, Tel 071–224 0504 (or through Iberia airlines); and Trans Hire, Unit 16, 88 Clapham Park Road, London SW4 7BX, Tel 071–978 1922. Fully inclusive rates for a week start from around £135 for a B group car (eg Peugot 205) on the Spanish mainland and on the Balearic islands. Prices are lower – from just under £100 – on the Canary Islands. Car hire is also readily available through tour operators in conjunction with a flight, a villa or hotel package holiday.

Motorway tolls

On the majority of toll motorways a travel ticket is issued on entry and the toll is paid on leaving the motorway. Examples of tolls are – A1 Burgos to San Sebastian, 2,625 ptas; A7 Salou to Valencia, 2,165 ptas and A9 Pontevedra to Vigo, 280 ptas.

Car parking

As well as the usual restrictions on parking, Spain has some rather odd practices. In a one-way street cars should be parked on the side of the road where houses have uneven numbers on uneven dates, and even numbers on even dates. Park facing the traffic flow. In Madrid and Barcelona meters and wardens are in operation. Parking zones signposted in blue – *zona azul* – are clearly marked. The maximum period of parking between 8am and 9pm is one and a half hours. Parking discs are available from hotels, the town hall and travel agencies. In the centre of some large towns there are signs marked 'Zona ORA' where parking is allowed only if you display a ticket bought from a tobacconist. If you have to park in a city overnight and there are no parking facilities at your hotel, then pay to put your car in a supervised car park. Theft from cars in Spain is notoriously prevalent.

Common road signs

Carretera cortada – road closed
Ceda el paso – give way
Cuidado – take care
Desvío – detour
Encender las luces – lights on
Apagar las luces – lights off

Obras – road works
Peligro – danger
A – *autopista* (toll road/motorway)
N – *nacional* (main road)
C – minor country road

Driving regulations

The minimum age for driving a car in Spain is 18. A GB nationality plate is compulsory throughout Europe. A spare set of light bulbs for every light on your car must be carried by law. A red warning triangle is advisable, but not compulsory except for vehicles with 9 seats or more, when 2 triangles must be carried. Seat belts must be worn once outside built up areas and worn on the ring roads round major Spanish towns; children under 12 should travel in rear seats. Dipped lights are compulsory on motorways and fast major roads at night. You should carry your driving licence and car registration documents at all times.

You drive on the right and give priority to traffic coming from the right. When entering a major road, where there is normally a stop or give way sign, traffic from both directions on the major road has priority. Traffic lights mean the same as in the UK, but two red lights mean no entry. You must use your indicators when overtaking and you may signal your intention to do so outside built up areas by sounding your horn in the day or flashing your lights at night. The driver of a heavy vehicle will switch on his near-side flashing indicator when he thinks it is safe for you to overtake. If there is danger ahead he will switch off and flash his offside light until the road is clear again.

Spanish police can impose an on-the-spot fine of up to 20,000 pesetas for traffic offences. In certain cases there will be a 20 per cent reduction for immediate payment. A Boletin de Denuncia is issued giving details of the offence and the fine. There are instructions on the back in English for an appeal. This must be made within 10 days and you can write it in English. If the level of alcohol in your bloodstream is 0.08 per cent or more, severe penalties will be imposed – a hefty fine or the withdrawal of your driving licence.

The speed limit in built-up areas is 60kph (37mph); outside built-up areas it varies: 90/100kph (56/62 mph); on motorways it is 120 kph (74mph).

Emergency help

The Traffic Control Department operates an assistance service for road accidents – this includes a telephone network on motorways and some major roads. When you ring for assistance ask the operator for *auxilio en carretera*. Ring 091 if you need emergency help in Madrid or Barcelona, 092 for medical assistance. The national motoring organisation in Spain is Real Autómovil Club de España (RACE), Jose Abascal 10, Madrid 3, Tel (91) 447 32 00 from 9am to 2pm.

Maps

We recommend detailed maps for each region in the 'Planning your holiday sections' of each chapter. For general route planning you might also need a smaller-scale whole-country map (1:800,000 or 1:1,000 000) – several are easily available in this country, published by Michelin, Hildebrand, Robertson McCarta, Bartholomew and Hallwag, which also include Portugal. Their design and place-name spellings vary, but most are adequate for the purpose. Spain is currently undergoing a vast road improvement and building programme and sections of maps can become quickly out-of-date.

PACKAGE HOLIDAYS

Up to 200 tour operators offer package holidays to Spain. The majority operate classic stay-put sun and sea holidays to one of the costas or the islands, but the choice of holiday is vast and covers all tastes and pockets – from independent car touring and staying in *paradores* to golfing, wildlife, rambling and card-game holidays.

If you are looking for a good value stay-put package, shop around. Several tour operators may offer packages to the same resort and the same hotels, with big price differences. Look out, too, for last-minute cheap deals or out-of season offers, advertised in travel-agents' shop windows, but bear in mind that you often have no choice of accommodation on such deals. Make sure that the operator you book with is a member of ABTA or AITO and therefore properly bonded, so that your money is protected and so that you are not stranded if the company goes bust. Other bonding schemes include ATOL (holidays using charter flights), Bus and Coach Council (coach holidays), Passenger Shipping Association (cruises and ferries), IATA (most scheduled airlines).

The Spanish Tourist Office publish two very useful leaflets which list all the tour operators: *Companies Operating to Spain* and *Holidays of Special Interest*. Here are the main Spanish specialists that offer a variety of packages for independently minded travellers to all parts of Spain: **Hartland Holidays**, Tel 081–368 0148; **Magic of Spain**, Tel 081–743 9900; **Mundi Color**, Tel 071–828 6021; **Unicorn Holidays**, Tel (0462) 422223

PRACTICAL DIRECTORY

Children and babies Most toiletries like disposable nappies and food can be bought when you arrive in main towns, although items like a first-aid kit, sunscreen and mosquito repellent are worth having with you all the time. Children under 3 can travel free and those between 4–12 are entitled to a 50% reduction on train journeys. However, there are no reductions on buses or coaches. Before you go, check with your tour operator or travel agent whether items like cots can be provided in hotels and how much they will cost, also whether babysitters can be arranged by the hotel. If you rent a hire-car make sure (especially the smaller companies) that they have sufficient notice to fit a child seat.

Health and insurance The Department of Health leaflet SA30 lists the countries where UK citizens can receive local NHS-style treatment free, or at reduced cost. This is available in Spain, but the Department of Health recommends private holiday insurance for this country, and we agree. This is because of the bureaucracy involved and the inadequacy of state health provision.

Most holidaymakers buy an inclusive, ready-made policy, which you should arrange at the time of booking your holiday. Here, briefly, are some tips on choosing your policy: the insurance offered by the tour operators may not be the best for you – it is worth shopping around if you have particular needs; you need to be insured against cancellation or curtailment of your holiday, medical expenses, baggage and valuables loss/damage, and accidents causing death or disability. Always check the exclusion clauses in the small print. The limit of cover on medical expenses should be at least £500,000 and make sure you are covered for repatriation to the UK by air-ambulance. If you hire a car, make sure you take out collision damage waiver and personal accident cover, if you have not arranged this through your general holiday insurance.

Information Spanish Tourist Office, 57–58 St James's Street, London SW1A 1LD, Tel 071–499 0901. It is best to write well in advance with particular queries. Phone numbers of regional tourist boards are given in the 'Planning your holiday' sections of each chapter. Again, you should write to them well in advance – and do not rely on a hundred per cent response rate.

Money You may take as much money as you want into Spain but you are only allowed to take 100,000 pesetas out, unless you can prove that you brought more with you originally. Sterling traveller's cheques and Eurocheques are the safest, and can be exchanged in banks, most building societies *(cajas de ahorro)*, hotels and even big stores, but remember to take your passport with you and beware of hefty commissions. Most Eurocheque cards (and credit cards too) can be used for withdrawing cash in main towns and resorts from machines on which the appropriate card sign is displayed. Credit and charge cards, (Visa being the more widely accepted) are also useful in main tourist resorts, although not often accepted at petrol stations. Banks are open Monday to Friday from 9am-2pm, Saturday 9am-1pm (except June-August/September when all banks are closed on Saturday), although you may find some banks staying open until around 5pm.

Museum opening times State owned museums offer free admission to teachers and groups of students, although permission must be obtained at least a fortnight in advance from Ministerio de Cultura, Museums Department, Plaza del Rey no.1, Madrid. Tel 341-280 7171. Holders of International Student Cards may also be granted free admission in certain cases.

See About This Guide at the start of the book for rule-of-thumb opening times. Here are the opening times for some of the major museums:

The National Archaeological Museum (Madrid) 9.15 am-8.30 pm. Sundays 9.30am-2.30pm. Closed Monday. **The Catalan Art Museum** (Barcelona) is closed until the Olympics. **The National Sculpture Museum** (Valladolid) 10am-2pm; 4pm-6pm. Closed Monday. **The Prado Museum** (Madrid) 9am-7pm. Closed Monday. **The Museum and Home of El Greco** (Toledo) 10am-2pm; 4pm-6pm. Closed Monday and Sunday afternoons. **The Picasso Museum** (Barcelona) 10am-8pm. Closed Monday. **The Museum of Santa Cruz** (Toledo) 10.30am-6pm, Monday 10am-2pm; 4pm-6.30pm, Sunday 10am-2pm. **The National Museum of Roman Art of Mérida** Tuesday to Saturday 10am-2pm; 4pm-6pm, 5pm-7pm in summer. Closed Monday. **The Dalí Museum** (Figueres), winter 11.30am-5pm, summer 9am-6.30pm.

Public holidays 1 January (Año Nuevo), 6 January (Día de los Reyes, Epiphany), 1 May (Día del Trabajo, Labour Day), (late May early June) Corpus Christi, 24 June (San Juan, St. John's Day), 25 July (Santiago St James' Day), 15 August (Asunción, Assumption), 12 October (Día de la Hispanidad, Discovery of America – Columbus Day and in 1992 Expo '92 will be held in Seville in commemoration of this founding). 1 November (Todos los Santos, All Saints' Day), 6 December (Día de la Constitución Española, Constitution Day), 8 December (Immaculada Concepción, Immaculate Conception), 25 December (Navidad, Christmas Day), 26 December (San Esteban, St Stephen's Day).

Good Friday, Easter Monday, and Pentecost are moveable dates. In addition to these national holidays most villages and towns have their own fiestas and festivals. August is the holiday month for most Spaniards, so do not be surprised to find towns and cities semi-deserted and many shops and restaurants closed.

Shopping hours Most shops are open from 9.30am-1.30pm, close for lunch and the traditional 'siesta' and re-open around 4.30pm-8pm, although in most capital towns the larger general stores stay open all day. You will find that some shops may stay open later in high season and close earlier in winter.

Telephones You can telephone direct to the UK from any public pay phone or from Telefonica offices (found in most capital towns and resorts), where you are allocated a cabin to phone from and pay after your call. Card-operated telephones are now being introduced in major centres. You can also call from most hotels. Cheap rate is usually between 10pm and 8am with no cheap weekend rate. To call the UK from Spain, dial 07 (international tone) followed by 44 (code for Britain), then the area code, omitting the initial 0, followed by the telephone number. Area codes within Spain work by provinces, each with its own dialling code beginning with a 9. For emergency services dial 091.

Tipping It is customary to leave a tip for waiters (if service is not included in the bill) of 10% of the amount. Porters and cinema usherettes also expect small tips (50–200 ptas) while taxi drivers expect about 5%.

WEATHER

The Spanish peninsula, with its differing altitudes in the interior and varying influences from the Atlantic and Mediterranean on the coasts, presents a range of weather conditions throughout Spain.

The area from Galicia along the coast to Catalunya is generally the wettest part of Spain. The summer months are cooler than in the rest of Spain, but there is still a considerable amount of warm sunny weather, making it ideal for walking or touring in late spring and summer.

The plateau area of Central Spain has long, cold winters and hot dry summers. Spring and early summer tend to be the wettest with short, heavy showers.

Sheltered by the mountain ranges of the Sierra Nevada and the central plateau, the Mediterranean coast enjoys long, hot, humid summers and mild winters. The best time to go is between May and September, although you may find good weather in March and April. In spite of sea breezes temperatures can soar when the *leveche* (a hot dry wind from North Africa) blows inland. The town of Ecija in Andalucía is known as the 'frying pan of Spain' because of its intense heat and is typical of the hotter temperatures that can be found in southern Spain. Rain is rare during the summer months, although north of Valencia there may be occasional thundery showers.

MAINLAND

	Jan °C R	Feb °C R	Mar °C R	Apr °C R	May °C R	June °C R
Alicante	16 5	17 4	19 6	21 6	24 6	28 3
Barcelona	13 5	14 5	16 8	18 9	21 8	25 6
La Coruña	13 19	13 15	15 16	16 12	18 12	20 9
Madrid	9 8	11 7	15 10	18 9	21 10	27 5
Santander	12 16	12 14	14 13	15 13	17 14	20 13
Seville	15 8	17 6	20 9	24 7	27 6	32 1
London	6 15	7 13	10 11	13 12	17 12	20 11

	Jul °C R	Aug °C R	Sept °C R	Oct °C R	Nov °C R	Dec °C R
Alicante	31 1	32 2	29 5	25 7	20 6	17 6
Barcelona	28 4	28 6	25 7	21 9	16 6	13 6
La Coruña	22 8	23 9	22 11	19 14	15 17	13 19
Madrid	31 2	30 3	25 6	19 8	13 9	9 10
Santander	22 11	22 14	21 14	18 14	15 15	13 18
Seville	36 <1	36 <1	32 2	26 6	20 7	16 8
London	22 22	21 11	19 13	14 13	10 15	7 15

°C=Average daily maximum temperature in °C
R=Average number of rainy days per month

BALEARICS

	Jan °C R	Feb °C R	Mar °C R	Apr °C R	May °C R	June °C R
Ibiza	15 6	15 6	16 6	19 5	22 3	26 3
Palma	14 8	15 6	17 8	19 6	22 5	26 3
Mahón	14 9	14 8	16 8	18 7	21 5	25 3
London	6 15	7 13	10 11	13 12	17 12	20 11

	Jul °C R	Aug °C R	Sept °C R	Oct °C R	Nov °C R	Dec °C R
Ibiza	28 1	29 1	27 4	23 8	19 10	16 8
Palma	29 1	29 3	27 5	23 9	18 8	15 9
Mahón	28 1	28 3	26 6	22 11	18 9	14 12
London	22 22	21 11	19 13	14 13	10 15	7 15

°C=Average daily maximum temperature in °C
R=Average number of rainy days per month

CANARIES

	Jan °C R	Feb °C R	Mar °C R	Apr °C R	May °C R	June °C R
Gran Canaria	21 8	22 5	22 5	22 3	23 1	24 <1
Tenerife	21 7	21 6	22 5	23 4	24 2	26 <1
London	6 15	7 13	10 11	13 12	17 12	20 11

	Jul °C R	Aug °C R	Sept °C R	Oct °C R	Nov °C R	Dec °C R
Gran Canaria	25 <1	26 <1	26 1	26 5	24 7	22 8
Tenerife	28 0	29 <1	28 2	26 6	23 9	22 9
London	22 22	21 11	19 13	14 13	10 15	7 15

°C=Average daily maximum temperature in °C
R=Average number of rainy days per month

The Balearics

Mallorca, Menorca and Ibiza have a climate similar to that of south-eastern Spain, with hot, dry summers, and are warm even in October and November. Menorca is wetter and windier than Mallorca because of the *tramontana* wind which blows over it, while Ibiza is the driest of the islands because of the hot winds it receives from the Sahara.

The Canaries

The seven Canary islands experience a temperate climate, although extreme contrasts between islands occur. Some, like the islands of Fuerteventura and Lanzarote, have a hot, desert-like climate because of the nearby Sahara, while the smaller, volcanic islands of Gran Canaria and Tenerife are sunny in the south and cooler and greener in the north; it is not uncommon to find blistering heat in May.

GOOD BOOKS

Guidebooks

Blue Guide, *Spain: The Mainland* (A & C Black) Dense, detailed rubric on virtually every place of note in Spain. For those particularly interested in culture and history, but not a good read.
Marc Dubin, *Trekking in Spain* (Lonely Planet).
Michelin Tourist Guide, (New edition due in 1992).
The green one, an invaluable potted summary of Spain's major sights and useful general information.
Michelin España Portugal The red one, annually updated. A very useful list of recommended and graded restaurants and hotels throughout the peninsula.

Background and fiction

Gerald Brenan, *The Face of Spain* (Penguin)
J.H. Elliot, *Imperial Spain 1469–1716* (Penguin)
Richard Ford, *Handbook for Travellers in Spain*, (Centaur Press)
Ian Gibson, *The Assassination of Frederico Garcia Lorca* (Penguin)
Graham Greene, *Monsignor Quixote* (Penguin)
Ernest Hemingway, *For Whom the Bell Tolls* (Panther) *Death in the Afternoon* (Panther) *The Dangerous Summer* (Grafton)
John Hooper, *The Spaniards* (Penguin)
Washington Irving, *Tales of the Alhambra* (Darf Publishers)

Julian Jeffs, *Sherry* (Faber)
Simon J. Keay, *Roman Spain* (British Museum Publications)
Juan Lalaguna, *A Traveller's History of Spain* (Windrush)
Laurie Lee, *As I Walked Out One Midsummer Morning* (Penguin)
Norman Lewis, *Voices of the Old Sea* (Penguin)
Frederico Garcia Lorca, *The House of Bernarda Alba* (Grant & Cutler)
Garrett Mattingly, *The Defeat of the Spanish Armada* (Penguin)
Jan Morris, *Spain* (Penguin)
George Orwell, *Homage to Catalonia* (Penguin)
V.S. Pritchett, *The Spanish Temper* (Hogarth)
Jan Read, Maite Manjon, Hugh Johnson, *The Wine and Food of Spain* (Weidenfeld & Nicholson)
A.W. Taylor, *Wild Flowers in Spain and Portugal* (A. Clarke Books)
Hugh Thomas, *The Spanish Civil War* (Penguin)

GLOSSARY

Art, architecture, geography

Alcázar Moorish fortress
Artesonado wooden coffered ceiling of Moorish origin
Azulejo glazed ceramic tile
Barranco ravine
Barrio district or quarter of town
Bodega wine cellar, warehouse, bar
Calle street
Camino road
Capilla Mayor high altar chapel
Capilla Real royal chapel
Castillo castle
Churrigueresque extremely flamboyant form of baroque art, named after José Churriguera (1650 -1723) and his family
Circunvalación bypass
Claustro cloister
Coro choir
Corrida de Toros bullfight
Cueva cave
Desfiladero pass, gorge
Embalse reservoir
Ermita hermitage or chapel
Fonda inn
Garganta gorge
Herreran pre-baroque architectural style, named after Juan de Herrera (1530 – 97)
Hórreo (raised) granary, common in Galicia and Asturias

Iglesia church
Isabelline ornate late Gothic architectural style, developed during the reign of Ferdinand and Isabella
Lago lake
Lonja stock exchange building
Mercado market
Meseta plateau
Mesón inn
Mirador viewing point
Morisco Muslim convert to Christianity
Mozárabe Christian under Moorish rule; their style of church architecture is called Mozarabic
Mudéjar Muslim under Christian rule; term extended to their style of architecture
Palacio palace
Paseo promenade
Pico mountain peak
Plateresque literally 'silversmith-like', a very lavish form of architecture popular during the sixteenth century, using Gothic, Renaissance and even Moorish ornamental motifs.
Posada inn
Pueblo village
Puente bridge
Puerta gate, doorway
Puerto mountain pass, harbour
Rambla avenue, watercourse
Retablo altarpiece, reredos
Ría Galician estuary
Río river
Seo cathedral
Sierra mountain or hill range
Solana sun gallery, sun lounge
Torre tower

Food and Drink

Aceite oil
Aceitunas olives
Agua minerale mineral water
Aguacate avocado
Ajo garlic
Almejas baby clams
Arroz rice
Atún tuna
Azúcar sugar
Bacalao cod
Berejenas aubergines
Bocadillo sandwich

Bonito tuna fish
Boquerones fresh anchovies
Cabrito kid (goat)
Café coffee
Calamares squid
Caldo broth
Callos tripe
Cangrejo crab
Carne meat
Cerdo pork
Cerveza beer
Champiñones mushrooms
Chorizo spicy pork sausage
Cochinillo suckling pig
Cordero lamb
Empañada meat pie
Ensalada salad
Entremeses starters
Espinaca spinach
Fiambres cold meats
Fresas strawberries
Fruta fruit
Gambas prawns
Gazpacho cold soup
Habas broad beans
Helado ice-cream
Higado liver
Huevos eggs
Jamón ham
Judías beans
Langostinos large prawns
Leche milk
Lechuga lettuce
Limón lemon
Limonada lemonade
Mantequilla butter
Manzana apple
Mariscos shell fish
Mejillones mussels
Melocotón peach
Merluza hake
Miel honey
Naranjada orange juice
Ostras oysters
Pan bread
Pastel cake
Pato duck
Patatas potatoes
Pimienta pepper

Pimiento red pepper
Piña pineapple
Pollo chicken
Pulpo octopus
Queso cheese
Sal salt
Salchichón salami
Salsa sauce
Setas mushrooms
Sopa soup
Té tea
Ternera veal
Tortilla omelette
Tostada toast
Trucha trout
Uvas grapes
Vinagre vinegar
Vino blanco white wine
Vino tinto red wine
Zumo de fruta fruit juice

INDEX

Note: places on Balearic Islands are indicated by (BI), those on Canary Islands by (CI).

Hotel reports

The report forms on the following pages may be used to endorse or criticise an existing entry or to nominate a hotel that you feel deserves inclusion in the next edition of the *Guide*, or in an issue of *Holiday Which?* magazine. There is no need to restrict yourself to the space available. All nominations should include your name and address, the name and location of the hotel, when you stayed there and for how long.

There is no need to give details of prices or number of rooms and facilities, as all nominated hotels will be inspected by the *Holiday Which?* team. We are anxious to find out from readers details of food, service and atmosphere, and should also be grateful for any brochures and menus.

To: *The Which? Guide to Spain*

FREEPOST, 2 Marylebone Road, London NW1 4DX

NOTE No stamps needed in UK, but letters posted outside the UK should be address to 2 Marylebone Road, London NW1 4DX and stamped normally. It is not our policy to publish names of readers who recommend a new hotel or criticise an existing entry. Unless asked not to, we shall assume that we may publish extracts from any report either in the *Guide* or in the magazine *Holiday Which?*.

Name of hotel ....

Address ....

....

Date of most recent visit ....

Duration of visit ....

Report:

(Continue overleaf if you wish or use separate sheet)

Signed ....

Name and address (CAPITALS PLEASE) ....

....

To: *The Which? Guide to Spain*

FREEPOST, 2 Marylebone Road, London NW1 4DX

NOTE No stamps needed in UK, but letters posted outside the UK should be address to 2 Marylebone Road, London NW1 4DX and stamped normally. It is not our policy to publish names of readers who recommend a new hotel or criticise an existing entry. Unless asked not to, we shall assume that we may publish extracts from any report either in the *Guide* or in the magazine *Holiday Which?*.

Name of hotel ....

Address ....

....

Date of most recent visit ....

Duration of visit ....

Report:

(Continue overleaf if you wish or use separate sheet)

Signed ....

Name and address (CAPITALS PLEASE) ....

....

Which? and Holiday Which?

Published once a month, *Which?* gives you comparative reports on the merits and value for money of many products and services that you buy for yourself, your family and your home.

Because Consumers' Association is an independent organisation our product testing is completely unbiased, so you can be sure you are getting the facts.

As a *Which?* subscriber, you can also get *Holiday Which?,* published 4 times a year in January, March, May and September. It reports on a wide range of holiday destinations in the UK and abroad, with details on food, excursions and sight-seeing as well as background information on climate, scenery and culture.

To claim your free trial subscription to *Which?* and *Holiday Which?* just complete and return the form opposite. No action is necessary if you wish to continue after your free trial: your subscription will bring you *Which?* and *Holiday Which?* for £16.75 a quarter until you cancel by writing to us (and to your bank to cancel your Direct Debiting Mandate), or until we advise you of a change in price. Your subscription becomes due on the first of the month, three months after the date on the mandate. If you do not wish to continue beyond the trial period, simply write and let us know before your first payment is due.

Gardening from Which?

Published 10 times a year with bumper issues in spring and autumn, this magazine aims to help you in your gardening by sharing the results of our thorough research and the experience of our gardening experts.

Every issue of *Gardening* contains something for everyone; from beginner to expert. The magazine's 80 or so comparative reports a year look at a wide variety of subjects from shrubs, flowers and cacti, fruit and vegetables to tools, techniques and equipment. So whether you've got a few window boxes, a lawn, well-established ornamental borders or a greenhouse, *Gardening* will help you to find ways of improving what you have and save you time and money.

To claim your free trial subscription to *Gardening from Which?* just complete and return the form opposite. No action is necessary if you wish to continue after your free trial: your subscription will bring you *Gardening from Which?* for £11.75 a quarter until you cancel by writing to us (and to your bank to cancel your Direct Debiting Mandate), or until we advise you of a change in price. Your subscription becomes due on the first of the month, three months after the date on the mandate. If you do not wish to continue beyond the trial period, simply write and let us know before your first payment is due.

Which? way to Health

This lively and authoritative magazine will help you and your family stay healthy. You'll find articles on staying fit, eating the right foods, early detection of any health problems, health products and how to get the best from the NHS.

This magazine is published every two months and, like *Which?*, is completely independent – bringing you unbiased facts about health in Britain today. The magazine takes a close look behind the scenes exposing bad practice and harmful products to help prevent you, the consumer, being deceived. We also report on any medical breakthroughs which could bring relief or cure for victims.

To claim your free trial subscription to *Which? way to Health* just complete and return the form opposite. No action is necessary if you wish to continue after your free trial: your subscription will bring you *Which? way to Health* for £5.75 a quarter until you cancel by writing to us (and to your bank to cancel your Direct Debiting Mandate), or until we advise you of a change in price. Your subscription becomes due on the first of the month, three months after the date on the mandate. If you do not wish to continue beyond the trial period, simply write and let us know before your first payment is due.

Consumers' Association, Castlemead, Gascoyne Way, Hertford X, SG14 1LH

FREE TRIAL ACCEPTANCE

Please send me free the next 3 issues of *Which?* and a free issue of *Holiday Which?* as they appear. I understand that I am under no obligation. If I do not wish to continue with *Which?* and *Holiday Which?* after the free trial, I can cancel this order at any time before payment is due on the 1st of the month three months after the date shown. But if I decide to continue I need do nothing – my subscription will bring me *Which?* and *Holiday Which?* for the current price of £16.75 a quarter.

☐ Tick here if you do not wish your name and address to be added to a mailing list to be used by ourselves or third parties for sending you further offers.

KC _

DIRECT DEBITING MANDATE

I/We authorise you until further notice in writing to charge to my/our account with you unspecified amounts which may be debited thereto at the instance of Consumers' Association by Direct Debit.   Originator's Ref. No. 992338

Signed	Today's date
Bank account in the name of	
Bank account number	
Name and address of your bank	
	Postcode

Banks may decline to accept instructions to charge direct debits to certain types of account other than current accounts.

YOUR NAME AND ADDRESS

Name	
Address	
	Postcode

FREE TRIAL ACCEPTANCE

Please send me free the next 3 issues of *Gardening* as they appear. I understand that I am under no obligation. If I do not wish to continue with *Gardening* after the free trial, I can cancel this order at any time before payment is due on the 1st of the month three months after the date shown. But if I decide to continue I need do nothing – my subscription will bring me *Gardening* for the current price of £11.75 a quarter.

☐ Tick here if you do not wish your name and address to be added to a mailing list to be used by ourselves or third parties for sending you further offers.

L _ F

DIRECT DEBITING MANDATE

I/We authorise you until further notice in writing to charge to my/our account with you unspecified amounts which may be debited thereto at the instance of Consumers' Association by Direct Debit.   Originator's Ref. No. 992338

Signed	Today's date
Bank account in the name of	
Bank account number	
Name and address of your bank	
	Postcode

Banks may decline to accept instructions to charge direct debits to certain types of account other than current accounts.

YOUR NAME AND ADDRESS

Name	
Address	
	Postcode

FREE TRIAL ACCEPTANCE

Please send me free the next 2 issues of *Which? way to Health* as they appear. I understand that I am under no obligation. If I do not wish to continue with *Which? way to Health* after the free trial, I can cancel this order at any time before payment is due on the 1st of the month three months after the date shown. But if I decide to continue I need do nothing – my subscription will bring me *Which? way to Health* for the current price of £5.75 a quarter.

☐ Tick here if you do not wish your name and address to be added to a mailing list to be used by ourselves or third parties for sending you further offers.

E _ XN

DIRECT DEBITING MANDATE

I/We authorise you until further notice in writing to charge to my/our account with you unspecified amounts which may be debited thereto at the instance of Consumers' Association by Direct Debit.   Originator's Ref. No. 992338

Signed	Today's date
Bank account in the name of	
Bank account number	
Name and address of your bank	
	Postcode

Banks may decline to accept instructions to charge direct debits to certain types of account other than current accounts.

YOUR NAME AND ADDRESS

Name	
Address	
	Postcode

*Which? and
Holiday Which? –
details overleaf*

Consumers' Association, Castlemead,
Gascoyne Way, Hertford X, SG14 1LH.

✂ -

*Gardening from
Which? –
details overleaf*

Consumers' Association, Castlemead,
Gascoyne Way, Hertford X, SG14 1LH.

✂ -

*Which? way to
Health –
details overleaf*

Consumers' Association, Castlemead,
Gascoyne Way, Hertford X, SG14 1LH.